TYNDALE'S
NEW TESTAMENT

The 'Ploughboy' Edition

The fyrste Chapter.

Mat. iij.
a Lu.iij.a

Mal. iij.a

Esa.xl.a
John.j.c

The begynnynge of the Gospell of Jesu Christ the sonne of God/as yt is wrytten in the Prophetes: Beholde I sende my messenger before thy face/which shall prepared thy waye before ye. The voyce of a cryer in the wildernes: prepare ye the waye of the lorde/make his pathes streyght.

John baptised.
Mat.iij.a

John dyd baptise in the wyldernes / & preche the baptyme of repentaunce/ for the remission of synnes. And all the londe of Jurie & they of Jerusalem/went out vnto him/& were all baptised of him in the ryver Jordan/ confessynge their synnes.

Mat.iij.c
Luk.iij.c
John.j.d

John was clothed with cammylles heer/ & with a gerdyll of a skyn a bout hys loynes. And he dyd eate locustes & wylde hony / and preached sayinge: a stronger then I commeth after me/whose shue latchet I am not worthy to stoupe doune and vnlose. I have baptised you with water: but he shall baptise you with the holy goost.

Jesus is baptised.
Mat.iij.d
Luk.iij.d

And yt came to passe in those dayes / that Jesus cam from Nazareth/ a cyte of Galile: & was baptised of John in Jordan. And assone as he was come out of the water / John sawe heaven open/ and the holy goost descendinge vpon hym/lyke a dove. And ther came a voyce

The opening of St Mark's gospel in Tyndale's New Testament of 1534 (The British Library).

TYNDALE'S
NEW TESTAMENT

Translated from the Greek by

WILLIAM TYNDALE

in 1534

*In a modern-spelling edition
and with an introduction by*

DAVID DANIELL

YALE UNIVERSITY PRESS · NEW HAVEN AND LONDON

For Christopher Daniell, with love

Designed by Gillian Malpass

Set in Linotron Bembo by
Best-set Typesetter Ltd, Hong Kong
Printed and bound at
The Bath Press, Avon

Library of Congress Cataloging-in-Publication Data

Bible, N.T. English. Tyndale, 1989.
  The New Testament / translated from the Greek by William Tyndale in 1534; in a modern spelling edition and with an introduction by David Daniell.

ISBN 0-300-04419-4 (hbk)
    0-300-06580-9 (pbk)
    1. Tyndale, William, d. 1536.   II. Daniell, David.   III. Title.
BS140 1989
226.6'201—do19   88-37938
                                                            CIP

CONTENTS

CONTENTS

INTRODUCTION

William Tyndale's Bible translations have been the best-kept secrets in English Bible history. Many people have heard of Tyndale: very few have read him. Yet no other Englishman – not even Shakespeare – has reached so many.

Tyndale translated the New Testament twice, and continually revised. His 1534 New Testament was his greatest work. With modernised spelling, and no other changes at all, that translation is here uncovered to show it as the modern book it once was. It is thus offered as a contribution to the work of understanding the history of the New Testament in English, the most influential text the world has known, and of assessing other translations. Professional historians of the English Bible with access to Bagster's *Hexapla* (1841) or Weigle's *Octapla* (1962) may feel this enterprise unnecessary. A stronger objection could come from experts in late Middle English who also have access to a text, which would probably be a copy of Hardy Wallis's limited-edition transliteration (1938): a modern-spelling edition of Chaucer is regarded as something unsound. There is, however, a powerful case for a modern-spelling Tyndale. In the clangour of the market-place of modern popular translations, Tyndale's ravishing solo should be heard across the world. Astonishment is still voiced that the dignitaries who prepared the 1611 Authorised Version for King James spoke so often with one voice – apparently miraculously. Of course they did: the voice (never acknowledged by them) was Tyndale's. Much of the New Testament in the 1611 Authorised Version (King James Version) came directly from Tyndale, as a glance at Luke 2 or most of Colossians or Revelation 21 will show. Some was subtly changed. What those facts mean has not until now been easily open to view.

In 1611, there were six million English speakers; there are today at least six hundred million. The Bible, or parts of it, is now published in over one thousand seven hundred vernaculars. It follows that the dozen or so modern English translations in commonest use today should be of great interest. The American Revised Standard Version (1952); the Jerusalem Bible (1966); the New English Bible (1970); Today's English Version of the New Testament (1966), now usually known as part of the Good News Bible (1976); the New International Version (1979); the New Authorised Version (1985) – these (and there are many others) have large numbers of devoted followers. Yet even some of those admirers might concede that some parts of some modern versions might be felt to be lacking. Tyndale's opening of John 14, 'Let not your hearts be troubled', renders the Greek exactly. The popular Good News Bible has 'Do not be worried and upset', wrong both in sense and tone. Not everyone agrees that the alternation of the pompous and the bland is appropriate for the word of God. In their new allegiance to 'relevance', publishers and the public have been allowed to forget the man who laid the foundation of the Bible in English, who so astonishingly gave the Bible to the people. Traces of his marvellous work are still just discernible in most of the modern competitors. In some special ways, this earliest translation, made over four hundred and fifty years ago, is still the best.

There are no changes to Tyndale's text here: the wayward spelling of the 1530s has simply been brought into the conventions of twentieth-century England, so that, for example, the 'quaint' word 'lyttel' now appears as 'little'. Prescriptions in living languages are always on the move (witness the differences between English English and American English). Tyndale is absolutely not 'quaint': the word implies condescension. Perhaps now, having suffered some modern versions concocted by committees of people with no ears, we may approach Tyndale's solitary music with a little humility.

The Life of Tyndale

Tyndale wrote very little about himself. For most details we are dependent on that enormous and popular tome, *The Arts and Monuments* of John Foxe ('Foxe's Book of Martyrs'). William Tyndale was born about 1494 in Gloucestershire, took his B.A. at Oxford in 1512 and his M.A. in 1515, and apparently spent time in Cambridge. Even his enemy More said of him that he was 'well known, before he went over the seas, for a man of right good living, studious and well learned in scripture, and in divers places in England was very well liked, and did great good with preaching.' He was for some time tutor to a Gloucestershire family. He disturbed local divines by routing them at the dinner table with chapter and place of scripture, and by translating Erasmus's *Enchiridion militis Christiani*. He was accused of heresy, but nothing could be proved. 'Soon after', Foxe records,

> Master Tyndall happened to be in the company of a learned man, and in communing and disputing with him drove him to that issue, that the learned man said: 'We were better be without God's law than the Pope's.' Master Tyndall, hearing that, answered him: 'I defy the Pope and all his laws'; and said: 'If God spare my life, ere many years I will cause a boy that driveth the plough shall know more of the Scripture than thou dost'.

To pursue his intention of translating the Bible, he offered himself to the Bishop of London, Tunstall, with an example of his skill as a translator from Greek in his hand – a speech of Isocrates. Tunstall, though a friend of Erasmus's, rebuffed him. Realising he could not translate the Bible in England,

Tyndale accepted the financial help of a London cloth-merchant and sailed for Hamburg in 1524. He never returned to England. He lived a hand-to-mouth existence, dodging the Roman Catholic authorities. In the autumn of 1525, he and his amanuensis moved to Cologne and began printing the New Testament. He was betrayed and fled up the Rhine to Worms. Here he started printing again, and the first complete printed New Testament in English appeared towards the end of February 1526. Copies began to arrive in England about a month later. In October, Tunstall began to have all the copies he could trace gathered and burned at St Paul's Cross. Still they circulated. Tunstall arranged to buy them before they left the continent, so that they could be burned in bulk. Tyndale used the money for further translation and revision. He began the Old Testament, apparently in Antwerp: Foxe tells how, sailing to Hamburg to print Deuteronomy, he was shipwrecked and lost everything, 'both money, his copies, and time', and (Foxe says, with Coverdale) started all over again, completing the Pentateuch between Easter and December. Back in Antwerp, Tyndale printed it in early January 1530. Copies were in England by the summer. In 1531 he translated Jonah; in 1531 a revised Genesis; in 1534 his completely revised New Testament – very slightly revised again in 1535. The same year, the fanatical Englishman Henry Phillips betrayed him to the Antwerp authorities and had him kidnapped. He was imprisoned at Vilvorde, near Brussels, for sixteen months. A letter from him, in Latin, has survived:

> I suffer greatly from cold in the head, and am afflicted by a perpetual catarrh, which is much increased in this cell. . . . My overcoat is worn out; my shirts are also worn out. . . . And I ask to be allowed to have a lamp in the evening: it is indeed wearisome sitting alone in the dark. But most of all I beg and beseech your clemency to be urgent with the commissary, that he will kindly permit me to have my Hebrew Bible, Hebrew Grammar, and Hebrew Dictionary, that I may pass the time in that study.

Even Thomas Cromwell, the most powerful man next to King Henry VIII, moved to get him released: but Phillips in Belgium, acting for the papal authorities, blocked all the moves. On the morning of 6 October 1536, now in the hands of the secular forces, he was taken to the place of execution, tied to the stake, strangled and burned.

The Authorised Version

Though now less commonly read than it was by our elders, the Authorised Version has been loved throughout the English-speaking world, and considered a particular glory of English letters. Right through the sixty-six books of the Bible, from 'And God said, Let there be light, and there was light' (Genesis 1) to 'And God shall wipe away all tears from their eyes' (Revelation 7), phrases of lapidary beauty have been admired: 'Ask, and it shall be given you; seek, and ye shall find; knock, and it shall be opened unto you' (Matthew 7); 'With God all things are possible' (Matthew 19); 'In him we live and move and have our being' (Acts 17); 'Be not weary in well doing' (2 Thessalonians 3); 'Fight the good fight of faith; lay hold on eternal life' (1 Timothy 6); 'Looking unto Jesus, the author and finisher of our faith' (Hebrews 12); 'Behold, I stand at the door and knock' (Revelation 3). Indeed, phrases from the Authorised Version are so familiar that they are often thought to be proverbial: 'Am I my brother's keeper ?' (Genesis 4); 'The salt of the earth' (Matthew 5); 'The signs of the times' (Matthew 16); 'Where two or three are gathered together' (Matthew 18); 'The burden and heat of the day' (Matthew 20); 'They made light of it' (Matthew 22); 'The spirit is willing, but the flesh is weak' (Matthew 26); 'Eat, drink, and be merry' (Luke 12); 'Clothed and in his right mind' (Luke 18); 'Scales fell from his eyes' (Acts 9); 'Full of good works' (Acts 9); 'A law unto themselves' (Romans 2); 'The powers that be' (Romans 13); 'Filthy lucre' (1 Timothy 3); 'Let brotherly love continue' (Hebrews 13); 'The patience of Job' (James 5). If such are not proverbs, then they must surely be Shakespeare.

All these phrases, and many, many more, were taken by the Authorised Version translators directly from Tyndale. Throughout the New Testament, where the Authorised Version is direct, simple and strong, what it prints is pure Tyndale. Yet Tyndale's name is never mentioned. The long preface of 1611, 'The Translators to the Reader', usually now omitted from editions of the Authorised Version and difficult to find, acknowledges only in passing the existence of earlier English translations, without naming them, though it mentions many foreign-language versions.

For two hundred years, from the middle of the eighteenth century until after the Second World War, the Authorised Version had an increasingly bright halo, which it did not altogether deserve. It became glorified in a process that at the same time exalted the nation (God had chosen English for the supreme expression of his word) and turned the Bible into literature. The Authorised Version became the acme of achievable literary perfection, with the works of Shakespeare – another Englishman, of course. Now that such extravagance is waning, we can begin to see the history of Bible translation a little more clearly.

The Bible in English

The Bible was written in two languages. The Jewish scriptures, the Old Testament, were written in Hebrew, with a little Greek. The Christian books, the New Testament (by Christian belief, recording the fulfilling of the Old Testament), were written in Greek. (The language of Palestine in New Testament times was Aramaic). Both Testaments circulated widely in Greek in the first centuries AD. It was the translations into Latin, however, particularly that made by Jerome and others in the fourth century and known as the Vulgate or common version, that the Church regarded as its own for a thousand years. Parts of this Latin Bible were translated into Anglo-Saxon and Middle English with some brilliance. In the lifetime of Chaucer, just before 1400, followers of Wyclif translated the whole Bible into English, from the Vulgate, twice. This was before printing, of course; yet, in spite of official prohibition, copies of these bulky, hand-written, expensive volumes circulated widely.

Tyndale's pioneer work was to start afresh; to translate the New Testament from the original Greek, at least twice, and a good deal of the Old Testament from the original Hebrew. He was caught and killed as a heretic before his work was finished. Though he apparently did not know of it, just before he died his translations were being incorporated into the first complete Bible printed in English, the work of Miles Coverdale in Cologne. Only months after Tyndale's murder King Henry VIII licensed the first official English translation, known as 'Matthew's Bible' as a cover for Tyndale's colleague John Rogers, who put together the published and unpublished work of Tyndale and edited the rest from Coverdale. This, printed probably in Antwerp, is the real foundation of the English Bible. It reprints Tyndale's final revision of his 1534 New Testament, his 1530 Pentateuch, and the rest of his Old Testament work as far as Chronicles. (Eighteen years later, Rogers was himself martyred, the first of the three hundred or so burned during the five-year reign of Catholic Mary.) In 'Matthew's Bible', at the end of Malachi and thus between the Testaments, are large ornamental intials, 'W. T.', a silent acknowledgement of William Tyndale's presence.

In 1539 the Greek scholar Richard Taverner issued a revision of 'Matthew's', The same year Thomas Cromwell, as King Henry's vice-regent, ordered a magnificent lectern Bible, known as the 'Great' Bible, to be set up in churches. This was a further revision of 'Matthew's' by Coverdale, in a more Latinate direction, to appease bishops who were alarmed by the moves away from the Latin Bible. So almost exactly three years after Tyndale's martyrdom, his work was officially, even lavishly, established – his work, note; not Tyndale himself. The title-page of the 'Great' Bible runs: 'The Bible in English, that is to say the content of all the holy scripture, both of the old and new testament, truly translated after the verity of the Hebrew and Greek texts, by the diligent study of diverse excellent learned men, expert in the foresaid tongues...'. Many printings of these Bibles followed until the accession of Queen Mary on 6 July 1553, when all such work stopped instantly.

In 1560 the most international of all English Bibles appeared, a remarkable result of humanist and Reformation scholarship. English Protestants escaping from Mary had arrived in Geneva, which was then a power-house of textual research and translation into European vernaculars, of secular classics as well as of Scripture. The English exiles worked on a new translation of the Bible: a New Testament was printed in 1557, and the whole Bible in 1560. This Bible was divided into verses, had copious explanatory notes on every page, detailed cross-references, concordances, maps and elucidatory pictures – illumination, as a preface frankly said, of 'all the hard places'. This, the Geneva Bible, was made for readers at all levels, and it was for nearly a century the Bible of the English people, used by all wings of the English church. It was designed to be studied, alone or round the table. It influenced Shakespeare, Milton and very many others. It set a new standard in Greek and Hebrew scholarship, particularly important in the Old Testament books that Tyndale had not reached. Its English phrases kept close to Tyndale. It was beautifully produced: the printers in Geneva were setting new standards in book-design. It was usually in clear Roman type, not the heavy Gothic black letter. It is surprisingly modern in design, type, page-layout, clarity of text and uncluttered white spaces. In 1576 the New Testament was re-done, with slight changes in the text but complete reworking of the notes – now full and often unexpectedly engaging – by Laurence Tomson of Magdalen College, Oxford. Just under a half of the known editions of the Geneva Bible contain Tomson New Testaments. In 1599 the Book of Revelation was given vast new notes by the European theologian 'Junius'. In its long life the Geneva Bible came in all sizes. It ran through one hundred and fifty editions before it was suppressed in the seventeenth century.

All this can be hard for modern readers to grasp, for the Geneva Bible has either disappeared from view, or remained in sight only as the target of abuse. What was a *locus* of Renaissance and Reformation scholarship, a triumph of textual, theological, and linguistic excellencies, universally admired, has been subject to curious mythologising. Many people who pass on or extend vilification of it cannot have seen a copy. Least damaging is calling it a Puritan Bible, which mistakes both it and Puritanism. Somewhat worse is its modern representation, usually intemperately expressed, as an extreme Calvinist tract: in fact, there is nothing in it that is in conflict with the Thirty-Nine Articles of the Church of England, and nothing from which Elizabethan or Jacobean divines would have dissented (King James's neurosis is a different matter). A modern legend that it was disliked before 1604 is difficult to relate to the known facts. Worst of all has been its reduction to a snigger because, like other translations, it gave Adam and Eve in Paradise 'breeches' – the foolish nickname 'The Breeches Bible' kills any other significance. Possibly particularly unhelpful has been the survival of many of the quarto Geneva Bibles, all falsely dated '1599', imported from the Low Countries early in the seventeenth century – unattractive, squat, packed black volumes, many miles from the beauty of the first Geneva New Testament.

In the 1560s, the Archbishop of Canterbury, Matthew Parker, called together about a dozen bishops, scholars and dignitaries to revise King Henry VIII's 'Great' Bible. Published in 1568 as a black-letter folio even more lavish and expensive – and even bigger – than its original, sumptuously printed as a lectern Bible with few marginal notes, it was absolutely not intended for the private reader. Known since as the Bishops' Bible it was, and is, not loved. Where it reprints Geneva it is acceptable, but much of the original work is incompetent, both in its scholarship and its verbosity. It was a turning-back by the Establishment in the direction of those clergy who still believed that the true Bible was the Latin version.

In January 1604, King James called a two-day conference at his palace at Hampton Court, ostensibly to try to resolve sharp religious conflicts. In the closing moments a suggestion for a new translation of the Bible came from the Puritan side. The proposal was a thoughtful one. Since the last successful translation from those languages, the Geneva Bible of half a century before, there had been advances in understanding Hebrew and Greek; better texts were available and the English language was changing rapidly. After the conference, nothing very much happened about the matter for some years. Eventually panels were set up in Oxford, Cambridge and London, under firm instructions from King James. The work was to be a revision, not a fresh translation. There were to be no marginal notes. The panels were to base their work on the Bishops' Bible, of which multiple copies were issued. For King James to lay down as the foundation of his new version the most Latinate of recent indigenous Bibles was unfortunate indeed, and destroyed the chance of the new version being in the best modern English. Another, more serious, push towards Latinity came from the influence on the panels of the extremely Latinate Roman Catholic translation from Rheims (1582). King James had decided, for his own reasons, not only to announce suddenly that the Geneva Bible was to be despised, but also to pretend that he would have been quite ignorant of its existence if he had not been shown a copy by 'a lady'. This outrageous royal posturing cannot be reconciled with the Geneva Bible's near-universal use, particularly in pulpits (of all persuasions), not to mention the dedication of the Scottish printing of the Geneva Bible (the first Bible printed in Scotland, in 1579) to James when he was a book-loving student prince.

The title-page of the Authorised Version announces that it is 'appointed to be read in churches', which is precisely right. It is first of all another lectern Bible, its Latinity very suitable for declamation in stone buildings. The aim of this version, stated in the 1611 preface, 'The Translators to the Reader', was 'to make a good one better'. That this refers to the Geneva Bible – though for political reasons it could not be stated – is clear from the fact that whenever in that long preface the Bible is quoted (fourteen times) the authors do not do so from their own translation, nor from the Bishops', but from Geneva. Moreover, though nowhere do they acknowledge it, they took over a great deal of Geneva's text verbatim; in doing so they were taking over much of Tyndale, though they clearly went directly to him as well.

Illustration of the extent of the borrowing from Tyndale may be seen by comparing Luke 15 (pp. 116–17) with the Authorised Version. There are minor differences of wording, but there is an absolute dependence on Tyndale's rhythms. As we shall see below, the Authorised Version's scholars tended to remove the Bible safely away from daily life; but that, for whatever reason, they chose in so much to follow a translator of genius rather than royal whim, must make us generally thankful. The new version was never authorised: it had no royal seal upon it at all. The designation 'Authorised Version' is the first of many myths about it. Why King James did not give his name to the work he had enthusiastically fathered is unknown; but he cannot have failed to notice its dependence on Geneva, and thus Tyndale.

The full idolatry of this 'Authorised' version did not begin until the 1760s, but then grew steadily: the official revisers in 1881 declared in their Preface that the Authorised Version had been venerated as a classic since 1611, which is untrue. With that, there grew the worship of the Authorised Version as Sublime English Literature, a movement which reached its height in the first half of the twentieth century. This notion would have been incomprehensible, and indeed alarming, to earlier ages. Sir Philip Sidney, for example, in the 1580s, certainly recognised the value of the Psalms as models of poetic range in themselves; but they were the Word of God. Something called 'literature', detached from the truths of Scripture, would be impossible for him to grasp. God's Word was vitally important: one's soul's life depended on it. There could be no other reason for receiving it.

Tyndale's 1534 New Testament

Tyndale's 1534 New Testament is a small thick book of four hundred pages which sits comfortably in the hand. It is six inches tall, four inches wide and one and a half inches thick, the exact size, for example, of Langenscheidt's modern Pocket German Dictionary. A first impression must be of its compactness: there is a lot of material between those strong covers. A second could be of its attractiveness: the old black letter printing can make a pleasing page. There is a good deal of white space. The outside margins are an inch wide, and top and bottom margins are generous. Those outside margins contain the notes, that is, Tyndale's occasional comments and the cross-references. The inside margins have only capital letters, a method that had for a long time been used to locate passages within chapters. (The Old and New Testaments had been divided into chapters since the thirteenth century. Numbered verses were not used in English Bibles until the Geneva New Testament of 1557 and the Geneva Bible of 1560.) There are running titles across the page tops, and on the upper-right corner the folio number in lower-case roman numerals. Most of the books and prologues have small decorations at the head. The Book of Revelation has twenty-two woodcuts, two thirds page size; not great art, but full of energy. Chapter numbers, spelled out in small roman letters, are inserted without line-spaces. The paragraphing follows the Greek. The effect of these blocks of uninterrupted type is that the books of the New Testament appear as continuous discourse, which is of course correct – the later habit of separating them out into numbered clauses for ease of reference makes them a little more like legal documents. The Prologues to the Epistles are in slightly smaller black letter type. The comments in the margins are sometimes in roman, sometimes in black letter. The more doctrinal ones are keyed into the text with a star. Passages used in services are indicated by crosses.

The total effect is of a compact page of type in which a great deal is going on, in what is not at all a specifically 'religious' format. Black letter was the standard, indeed the only, printing type from Gutenberg and Caxton until the later sixteenth century. Antiquarian, Gothic religiosity came in a later age and from the opposite, that is, from the Roman Catholic, camp. Tyndale's New Testament is, for 1534, a well-produced, attractive, commercial, modern book. It does not look like that to us for several reasons. Black letter is not easily read: the strange characters, the abbreviations and the lack of spaces between the words all look alien. Even when the black letter is transliterated into roman type, the spelling still looks peculiar. This is a matter only of convention; not only have many spellings changed, but twentieth-century spellings are fixed, whereas sixteenth-century spellings were not. Tyndale, the learned humanist scholar, spells 'righteousness' five different ways on the same page. Later in the century the surname of the poet's father, John Shakespeare, is spelled twenty different ways. Students of textual problems in Shakespeare's works are familiar with the orthographic waywardness of the printers of the time. Convention has simply hardened; there is not necessarily improvement.

In the 1534 New Testament, William Tyndale's name appears on the title page for the first time in his Bible translating. The prefaces, 'W. T. unto the reader' and 'William Tyndale, yet once more to the Christian reader', are wholly Tyndale's own. The first preface is completely new, with no relation to the 1525 prologue and 1526 epilogue: in fact, though it begins with a ringing sentence, it is not quite like his usual explanation of the law and the gospel, being more concerned with declaring that the key to understanding the New Testament is the 'convenant' made between God and man. It seems to a modern eye not quite the expected Reformers' liberation: 'All the promises of the mercy and grace that Christ hath purchased for us are made upon that condition that we keep the law.' Later he swings to the classic Protestant emphasis on faith: 'Faith unfeigned in Christ's blood causeth to love for Christ's sake.' The second preface, after the brief prologues to the Gospels, defends his work with some passion against the unauthorized and unattributed tinkering by a fellow-exile, George Joye. Joye was a scholar and fellow of Peterhouse, Cambridge, who lived in Antwerp. There in August 1534 he published a version of Tyndale's 1526 New Testament – clearly without Tyndale's authority – with no names on the title-page and with some considerable changes to Tyndale's text. Tyndale felt strongly. Joye was not only putting out his own work as Tyndale's, he was making silent, and vital, alterations, changing 'resurrection' to 'life after this life', a theological issue that still, today, raises heat. It struck to the heart of Tyndale's method and belief – his whole life, in fact. 'If the text be left incorrupt,' he says, 'it will purge herself of all manner false glosses, how subtle soever they be feigned, as a seething pot casteth up her scum'.

Further inside the volume, Tyndale's prologues to the epistles are different again, and might be described as reconstructed Luther, from his 1534 German *Biblia*. The prologue to Galatians fills out Luther's; even in that to 1 Corinthians, though beginning with his own paragraph, Tyndale follows Luther. Romans was the book of the New Testament of greatest importance to the sixteenth, as to other, centuries. Tyndale's long prologue is taken almost entirely from Luther, making a treatise almost as long as Paul's epistle. It is a densely written statement of the centrality of the 'most pure Evangelion, that is to say glad tidings and that we call gospel, and also a light and a way into the whole scriptures'. That emphasis is pure Luther – and pure Tyndale. In matters of scholarship, however, Tyndale made up his own mind. Unlike Luther, he avoided condemning any Scripture as it was in the Greek. Over the matter of the Epistle to the Hebrews, where the ascription to Paul has been disputed from earliest times, Tyndale is more charitable than Luther. Tyndale's consistent argument is that he works to promote 'right understanding' of the Scriptures – and the Scriptures had been formerly 'locked up' by false glosses.

Tyndale did not invent marginal notes: such glossing has a long history. A frequently repeated legend has it that Tyndale's marginal notes are inflammatory, fanatical or simply intemperate. Let the reader judge.

Tyndale's Greek and Hebrew

The story of Tyndale is part of that of the revival of learning. His exceptional strengths were twofold. First was his good Greek and Hebrew, when such knowledge was not at all common. Indeed, he was a pioneer in the great movement of the translation of texts of all kinds into English throughout the century. In the 1480s, scholars from Oxford – John Colet, Thomas Linacre, William Grocyn, William Lyly and others (they were all acquainted, and all took senior posts as humanist teachers) – had learned Greek, some travelling to Italy to do so and to bring the knowledge back with them to England. In Oxford from 1496–1504 John Colet lectured on Paul's epistles. What was quite new in these lectures was the theology of Paul from the original Greek, shorn of any other interpretation than what Paul said he meant. Colet said of the New Testament: 'Except of the parables, all the rest has the sense that appears on the surface, nor is one thing said and another meant, but the very thing is meant which is said, and the sense is wholly literal.' Since Origen in the third century, it had been automatic in the Church, much influenced by Augustine, to treat every sentence, and often every word, of the Latin scripture as allegorical. On top of the first meaning, the literal, were piled the allegorical (animals, for example, suggesting virtues); the tropological or moral, involving tropes (figures) of morality; and the anagogical (from the Greek word meaning to rise), that is, elevatory, especially to future glory. Thus in the famous example Jerusalem means literally the city of the Jews; allegorically the church of Christ; tropologically the human soul; and anagogically the heavenly city. That method is what, in Germany two decades later, the Oxford man Tyndale attacked while engaged in translating Paul's Greek into English:

> The greatest cause of which captivity and the decay of the faith, and this blindness wherein we now are, sprang first of allegories. For Origen and the doctors of his time drew all the scripture unto allegories; whose example that came after followed so long, till they at last forgot the order and process of the text, supposing that the Scripture served but to feign allegories upon; insomuch that twenty doctors expound one text twenty ways, as children make descant upon plain song. Then came our sophisters with their anagogical and chopological sense, and with an antitheme of half an inch, out of which some of them drew a thread nine days long.

The all-important theology of Paul, to take the most powerful example, had vanished, smothered under tomes of what amounted to free association, and was absolutely not available to the common man.

In 1499 the greatest of the humanist scholars, Erasmus of Rotterdam, went to Oxford and heard Colet lecture. That meeting settled the direction of the rest of his life, and to some extent the direction of the Renaissance New Learning in northern Europe, and the Reformation in England. Erasmus saw that the recovery of the Bible and of its authentic interpretation meant first of all the editing, printing and circulation of as good a text as possible of the Greek New Testament. Without it, Colet's recovery of Paul would not have any great impact outside Oxford. In the autumn of 1515 a Swiss printer, Froben of Basle, approached Erasmus to commission from him a Greek New Testament. Erasmus had been preparing to make an edition for a decade and a half, but now he had to work quickly to Froben's deadline and could use only what manuscripts there were at Basle, with some reference to what he had been assembling from manuscripts in England. His printed Greek New Testament, the first ever, appeared in March 1516. It was epoch-making. With his own parallel Latin version of the Greek in a column alongside, and its prefatory notes and 'Exhortation', it challenged the infallibility of the Vulgate. As he wrote in his preface, it gave to men the *philosophia Christi*, and 'the living image of that holy mind', that is, Paul. This challenge was all the more powerful in coming not from some obscure fanatic, but from the most brilliant man of letters of the century, already known and admired all over Europe for *Adages*, *The Praise of Folly*, *Enchiridion Militis Christiani* and much else. Luther and Tyndale were the first to translate into the vernacular from it.

We do not know where Tyndale learned Greek: probably at Oxford, and possibly at Cambridge as well, which he attended, it seems, soon after Erasmus's stay there. In Germany, he translated from the second and third editions of Erasmus's Greek Testament, of 1519 and 1522. Like any good translator, he took additional help from where he could find it: from Luther's 1522 translation into German, occasionally from the Vulgate. But he was a better Greek scholar than Luther, and his understanding was more than just competent. He saw, for example, the Aramaic behind the Greek of the Gospels, and tried to capture it in English, as he points out in his preface (see below p. 3). Anyone today who knows the Greek New Testament, including the most difficult passages of Paul, will find Tyndale wholly familiar.

His knowledge of Hebrew was altogether more remarkable for his time. Germany was the centre of what slender knowledge of Hebrew there was in Europe in the 1520s, and Tyndale clearly learned it there – no-one in England at that time knew it. His work of Englishing the Greek New Testament, with repeated revisions, has always to be put into the context of his parallel work on the Hebrew Old Testament, which, as recent studies maintain, is still superior in tone to many late-twentieth-century translations.

Any translator of the Bible has to come to terms with two problems. One is the sheer bulk, which modern paper-making and printing techniques tend to conceal. Even without the Apocrypha, the Bible contains sixty-six books, many of them long. The other, greater, difficulty is the variety within the Hebrew and Greek. Hebrew poetry has a small vocabulary, but can vary from epic and primitive ballad-of-victory to poems for congregational worship, private religious meditation, eroticism, or proverbial declaration: in the vivid, powerful, desert-wind intensity of much of Hebrew prophecy the poetry, once more, is continually various. Hebrew prose, within one book, can range from the surreal bare narrative of Genesis 22 to the rich *Novelle* of Genesis 37–50. Similarly, though the Greek of the New Testament is the *koiné* (κοινή), the ordinary language of transaction throughout the Eastern Mediterranean at the time (only Luke 1:1–4 is classical Greek), there is a great difference between the Greek of the four gospels, and between them and the Hebrew mind of Paul writing in philosophical, theological Greek, to say nothing of the special effects of the Epistle to the Hebrews or of Revelation. A good Bible translation gives some sense of all these differences. Tyndale, for example, in his account of the Fall of Man in his translation of Genesis 2 and 3 makes an English as raw as the Hebrew. His English in each of the four gospels is noticeably different, with his John's gospel particularly, and appropriately, fluent. Interestingly, Luke's narrative in Acts has needed the least work in modernising spelling.

Tyndale published his translation of the Pentateuch, the first five books of the Old Testament, in 1530, probably in Antwerp. It was the first English translation of any text written in Hebrew and was the basis for all following English versions. His ability to catch the Hebrew spirit, and his boldness with English, are remarkable and are now at last becoming more appreciated. As in all his Biblical translations, he coined words where he needed them: he gave us *Jehovah, passover, scapegoat*. He did not understand all the technicalities of Hebrew poetry – no one did, until Bishop Robert Lowth expounded them in 1753 – but he grasped that Old Testament poetry needed dignity, simple vocabulary, a special rhythm and stress on open vowels. We must grieve that he was killed before he could translate the whole of the Old Testament, the Psalms and the great prophets in particular. What we have is the Pentateuch of 1530 and the revision of Genesis in 1534, the prophet Jonah in 1531, and, not printed until 'Matthew's' complete Bible in 1537, Joshua to Chronicles. His touch outside those books was sure. At the back of his 1534 New Testament are fifteen pages containing forty Old Testament passages (see below pp. 391–408) translated so that all Scripture readings in services could be in English. These were the extracts read on certain days in Salisbury Cathedral; that whole 'Sarum use' became the basis of the first Book of Common Prayer of 1549, and all that followed. Tyndale translates not from the Latin of the service-book, but from the Hebrew (Greek in the Apocrypha). The passages are from the Pentateuch, Kings, Esther, Isaiah, Jeremiah, Ezekiel, Proverbs and the Song of Solomon, and a few from the Apocrypha. He recognised that he was dealing mostly with poetry. Though the Hebrew is printed as prose, as are his translations, it is clear that he has understood the first structural principle of Hebrew poetry, that of parallelism – 'He was wounded for our transgression, and bruised for our iniquities.' In most of the passages Tyndale translates Hebrew into English for the first time. It is perhaps hard for us to grasp that this was happening for the first time ever, and at a time when Hebrew was not known in England. There are other evidences of what we have lost by his early death. Embedded in his New Testaments are fragments of translation of the Hebrew of the Psalms and great prophets. For example, in the first chapter of the Epistle to the Hebrews (see below p. 348, at D), Tyndale has gone behind the Greek to translate the quotation from Psalm 102 directly from the original Hebrew. The result, from 'And thou Lord in the beginning...' to '...shall not fail', was used by Coverdale in his version of the Psalms, the version which was used daily in the Church of England from 1549 until the Book of Common Prayer was abandoned in the 1960s.

Comparison of Tyndale's work with that of other translators needs to include the fact that different materials are in use. Before Tyndale – for the two Wycliffite versions, for example – the basis was the Vulgate. Tyndale for the first time used the best Hebrew and Greek texts then available. After Tyndale, translators, particularly in the twentieth century, face at every point a mass of textual information not dreamed of before. Even so, it is striking how it is Tyndale who gets to the heart of the matter in English. Consider the difference between Tyndale and a modern reading at one of the most powerful moments in the Joseph story (Genesis 37 to 50), Genesis 45:3. Joseph, betrayed by his brothers many years before, reveals his identity to them. Tyndale has 'And he said unto his brethren, I am Joseph, doth my father yet live? But his brethren could not answer him, for they were abashed at his presence.' The Authorised Version follows this, except for changing 'abashed', with its idea of open shame, to 'troubled', which is internal unease, and wrong for the Hebrew. The New English Bible has 'Joseph said to his brothers, "I am Joseph; can my father be still alive?" His brothers were so dumbfounded at finding themselves face to face with Joseph that they could not answer.' This not only goes even further from the Hebrew, but in modernising does not achieve a modern direct expression of the Hebrew's five simple words, 'Is my father still alive?': not even, as Gerald Hammond points out, 'Can my father still be alive?' but 'can my father be still alive?' – which, as Hammond notes, 'has all the unnecessary precision of an Oxford don speaking' (The Making of the English Bible, p. 41).

Here is one further example of Tyndale as a translator of Hebrew, from the prophets: in the Epistle for the first Friday in Advent and thus at the beginning of the Christian year (see below, p. 391), at Isaiah 51/4a, Tyndale has 'Hearken unto me my people, and turn your ears to me my folk.' The Authorised Version quite often gets the Hebrew into better sense, as Hebrew scholarship had improved over eighty years; here it has 'Hearken unto me, my people; and give ear to me, O my nation', clearly following Tyndale, but unhappy with turning ears and folk, and elevating with an 'O'. The Revised Standard Version (1952) gives 'Listen to me, my people,/and give ear to me my nation', which has lost the sharpness of 'Hearken' altogether for the rather petulant 'Listen to me'. (It is hard to believe that 'hearken' would not be understood.) The New English Bible (1970) has 'Pay heed to me, my people,/and hear me, o my nation'. Petulance has now given way to the schoolmasterly pedantry of a language spoken nowhere on this earth; when both are equally archaic, one would surely rather 'hearken' than 'pay heed'. These are Protestant readings. The Roman Catholic Jerusalem Bible (1966) follows a different tack: 'Pay attention to me, you peoples,/Listen to me, you nations'. This is chillingly distant, peremptory and dictatorial. The perspective of the people has vanished: no more turning ears or 'my folk'. Now it is a Latin abstract, 'attention', that 'you peoples' are to 'pay'. If we are being invited in English to God and salvation, give us Tyndale any day.

Illustration of the accuracy of Tyndale's Greek translations will be easily found in the next 390 pages, from his translation of *metanoeo* (μετανοέω) as 'repent' and not 'do penance', to *agapé* (ἀγάπη) as 'love' and not 'charity'. Here is a small example of his honesty as a translator of Greek. In 2 Thessalonians 2 (see below p. 306, at B) is the phrase, 'And now ye know what withholdeth: even that he might be uttered at his time. For the mystery of that iniquity doth he already work which only locketh, until it be taken out of the way.' The Greek is mysterious: we do not know to what Paul is alluding. The principal verb and noun are from *katecho* (κατέχω), to hold, keep back, retain; in the second part, the earlier neuter construction has become masculine and personal. 'Which only locketh' is as good a shot as Geneva's two decades later: 'only he which now letteth, *shall let*' (followed by Authorised in substance) – in fact, better to modern view because of the semantic change in 'let'. Modern translations sometimes admit difficulty, and they all paraphrase the problem away, variously; but if the Greek is mysterious, we should know.

Understanding the original Greek has become a more formidable task than Tyndale could have imagined, as modern translators are faced with so many families of textual variants and vast accumulations of knowledge of vocabulary, idiom and social and religious contexts. By modern standards, Tyndale got things wrong. He followed Erasmus's Greek New Testament. Though he pursued true Greek manuscript readings like a modern scholar, Erasmus had occasional second thoughts between his first (1516) edition, and the four more he published (1519, 1522, 1527, 1535). Tyndale used the second and third editions, where Erasmus sometimes went astray, as in including (albeit in parentheses) the sentences in 1 John 5 that have no proper Greek authority. Tyndale misunderstood the Greek word ἆσσον (*asson*, 'nearer') in Acts 27, and also the Greek word for serving as a soldier in James 4, which he translates as 'rain' (i.e., reign). Also in James 4 Tyndale has 'ye envy', following a conjecture of Erasmus, instead of 'ye kill'. Tyndale was, as any translator must be, an incessant reviser, and he restored in 1534 the doxology at the end of the Lord's Prayer (omitted by the Vulgate) in Matthew 6; and so on. Exploring the manuscript authority of Erasmus's texts, and Tyndale's use of them, belongs to a separate essay. More seriously, Tyndale can be accused, on occasion, of not properly appreciating the importance of Greek particles, the little words which give the language its characteristic suppleness. Most seriously of all, he never satisfactorily solved the problem of what to do consistently with proper names – whether to transliterate or translate them. Thus in the gospels he can give 'Sabot' (Sabbath) and then, anachronistically, 'Sunday', leading to 'Good Friday', 'Easter', and in Acts, 'Whitsunday', leaving him wide open to all those attacks on him as 'homely' and rather comic. Today it seems an unfortunate decision to have followed Luther's German and given 'sweet bread' for *azumos* (ἄζυμος) – what, since the Geneva Bible, we know as 'unleavened bread'.

Of the words to which Sir Thomas More took exception so bitterly, the most objectionable was 'congregation' instead of 'church' for *ekklesia* (ἐϰϰλησία). It is a word most common in Acts and the Epistles, referring to the communities of Christians around the Mediterranean early in the second half of the first century. These were, of course, literally 'congregations' of people, and that Greek sense cannot be avoided. What More found heretical in the word 'congregation' was the implication that there is not one hierarchical body, The Church, of which all churches are members, but rather, self-governing communities of Christians, led by the Spirit, with allegiance only to God through their experience of Christ: precisely the New Testament sense. The same point is made by Tyndale's correct translation of the last words of John 10:16 as 'one flock and one shepherd', which became in the Latin-based versions, including the Authorised Version, 'one fold and one shepherd'.

Tyndale's English

The second of Tyndale's strengths is his power with the English language. He has an extraordinary ability to reach off the page and seize the reader's interest, both in his own theological writing and in his Biblcal translations. This alertness comes from a conscious use of everyday words without inversions, a neutral word-order, and a wonderful ear. Rhythm depends on the pattern, and to some extent the weight, of stresses. Tyndale understood how to get variety of secondary stresses to make an even flow that pulls the reader along. The opening line of Psalm 115 (possibly Coverdale rather than Tyndale, in fact), is a sentence famously right for public declaration: 'Not unto us, O Lord, not unto us...'. At that point both the Revised Standard Version and the New English Bible have 'Not to us, O Lord, not to us...'. This hurts the ear both in the clash of 't' sounds and in the change from the double light stress in the middle, 'unto' (which allows the fullest, and proper, weight on 'Not' and 'us'), to three thudding heavy stresses, 'Not to us'. Tyndale's own variation of 'to' and 'unto' would make a rich study. His occasional use of 'be' rather than 'are' as a present-tense plural, quite acceptable at the time, is as much a matter of stress as of variation, as in 'The powers that be are ordained of God' (Romans 13). (The New English Bible and Good News Bible duck out of the Greek word-play and turn it into Latin – not the Vulgate – to produce: 'the existing authorities'.) Tyndale's skill with cadences, when to let the voice fall and when not to, would also make a useful study. Compare, for example, the firm endings of sentences in the famous Greek *bravura* passage in Romans 8, beginning

'For we are saved by hope...', to the end of the chapter (see below p. 233, from E). To take the first four sentences only: the first three end in a mono-syllabic stress, 'hope', 'hope', 'seeth'; the next, longer sentence, ends with a dactyl, (/ ʋ ʋ) '...bide for it'. The following paragraph again alternates final monosyllabic, and powerful, stresses – 'ought', 'tongue', 'God', 'called' – with trochees (/ ʋ) – 'spirit', 'purpose', 'brethren' – and the ends of the first and last sentences are dactyls again – '... firmities', 'glorified'.

Tyndale felt passionately about the value of English. He made his unpopular point, which was heretical according to some bishops, strongly. In the 'Preface to the Reader' to *Obedience of a Christian Man* (1528), a book that Ann Boleyn admired and gave her royal husband-to-be to read, he wrote:

> They will say it [the Bible] cannot be translated into our tongue, it is so rude. It is not so rude as they are false liars. For the Greek tongue agreeth more with the English than with the Latin. And the properties of the Hebrew tongue agreeth a thousand times more with the English than with the Latin. The manner of speaking is both one, so that in a thousand places thou needest not but to translate it in to the English word for word when thou must seek a compass in the Latin & yet shalt have much work to translate it well-favouredly, so that it have the same grace and sweetness, sense and pure understanding with it in the Latin as it hath in the Hebrew. A thousand parts better may it be translated into the English than into the Latin.

The originality of Tyndale is clear. It is unlikely that the Wyclif Bibles of 150 years before influenced him. These 'Lollard' Bibles, hand-written versions in English of the Latin Vulgate, were unquestionably important in their own time, and later; particularly the second, probably by John Purvey, which dates from 1389. There is some overlap with Tyndale, no doubt because of common ground. Thus in Luke 2, Purvey has 'And the shepherds turned again, glorify-ing and heriyng God in all things that they had heard and seen, as it is said to them'. But for the last sentence of Matthew 6, so striking in Tyndale, Purvey's 'Sothly it sufficeth to the day his malice' follows the Vulgate's 'Sufficit diei malitia sua'. Taking a characteristic phrase of Tyndale's shows the difference clearly. In 1 Corinthians 14, Purvey has 'Therefore if all the church come together into one, and all men speak in tongues, sothly if idiots enter, or men out of the faith, where they say not, What been ye wood?'. Even reproducing the Middle English original in modern spelling does not entirely produce recognisable modern English; by contrast, Tyndale has 'If therefore when all the congregation is come together, and all speak with tongues, there come in they that are unlearned, or they which believe not: will they not say that ye are out of your wits?'

One part of the older prejudice against Tyndale maintained that he knew little Greek and simply translated Luther's German and fiddled with Erasmus's Latin version. This idea collapses instantly under the weight of the evidence. It is overwhelmingly clear that his authority comes directly from the Greek.

(Significantly, his English is noticeably less agile when he is translating Luther directly, as in all but the last five paragraphs of the Prologue to Romans.) The fact that the specialist international Greek scholars in Geneva in the late 1550s, not to mention King James's New Testament panel, were happy to take over so much of his work can speak for itself. This is now becoming understood. Taking longer to establish is the significance of Tyndale as a highly conscious craftsman. Shakespeare was for three centuries considered by many to be an untutored genius: only now is he allowed to have been a well-educated, deeply read, working dramatist who knew a great deal about the business of using language and making plays. Tyndale is still too often considered the 'homely' genius, devoid of conscious effects.

The scholar Buschius is reported to have said that Tyndale's 1526 New Testament had been translated by a man 'who is so skilled in seven tongues, Hebrew, Greek, Latin, Italian, Spanish, English, French, that whichever he speaks you might think it is his native tongue' (German is taken for granted). As a humanist scholar brought up on Latin, and being exceptionally well versed in Greek and Hebrew, Tyndale had the makings of an exotic stylist. Indeed, we should expect Latinised periods, with a leaning to 'inkhorn' terms, embellished vocabulary in the fashionable 'augmented' style – the schoolmaster Holofernes in *Love's Labour's Lost* shows Shakespeare affectionately mocking that fashion – or to winding sentences that lose themselves in wordiness. But instead, Tyndale chose increasingly to write within the simple, pellucid structures of medieval devotional prose (Cranmer's 'Collects' in the Book of Common Prayer belong in the same line), and to translate Scripture for the ordinary man and woman, the 'boy that driveth the plough', the tenant farmer, the servant and dishwasher, for all of whom he says he is writing. New Testament Greek is written for that readership. Until comparatively recently there was an idea abroad that the language of New Testament was a special Greek, divinely given to carry the sacred freight. We know now that the *koiné* (κοινή) was the language of ordinary transaction throughout much of the Roman Empire. Tyndale understood that fact himself, and, especially in the Gospels, he used short sentences paratactically linked, that is, short main statements linked by 'and' or 'but' with little or no subordination. This is the style of many of the narratives of the Gospels (see, for example, Mark 3). Structures like this are characteristic of spoken language, and therefore strike the reader as informal. When Tyndale came to exhortation, or to theological exegesis, either in the Gospels or the Epistles, he could bring into play other devices of rhetoric. That, in which sixteenth-century education was rooted, was a Greek and Latin skill, after all, and again faithful to the New Testament. In other words, it could not be more wrong to patronise Tyndale by suggesting that he knew no better, or was 'primitive' on some evolutionary scale. His clear, short sentences and trenchant reasoning came from knowing very well how to do it. Tyndale was a student in humanist Oxford, and possibly Cambridge: rhetorical training was a far more conscious craft than we, still the children of Romantic self-expression, allow.

When James I gave his Bible revisers the huge Bishops' Bible as their founda-tion, which meant that the Vulgate-based Rheims version would be attractive to them, he ensured that a wash of Latinity would be spread over Tyndale's English. The result, and, we must assume, the intention, was to create a safer distance between the Scriptures and the people. Though in the general working vocabulary there were more Latinate terms in use by 1611, Latin words and constructions have, as they had then, the ring of Establishment authority, which is not the same as the *koiné* (κοινή) Greek that Tyndale was translating for the first time. Thus, at pro-Establishment moments, as we might call them, as in Titus 3, where Tyndale has 'Warn them that they submit themselves to rule and power, to obey the officers...', the Authorised Version has (and the capitals appear in 1611 and many following editions) 'Put them in mind to be subject to Principalities and Powers, to obey magistrates...'. One of the reasons for fearing Tyndale lies just there: a safe distance had disappeared. The Greek Testament, Englished, was in the hands of the people. The objection was not narrowly political. Powerful ecclesiastical voices throughout Europe maintained that the Latin Bible was the true word of God and that the moves of humanist scholars to press for the originality of Hebrew and Greek was a blasphemous and seditious conspiracy born of hatred; indeed, the Jewish scholars who were publishing the Hebrew Bible (the Old Testament, to Christians) were, it was suggested, deliberately poisoning the wells of God's word (the Latin Bible) as revenge for fourteen hundred years of persecution. The prejudice that maintained that the Latin Bible was the original was deep and bitter enough to cost lives: it is not quite unknown even today, even though we know that Jerome's translation into Latin was made several hundred years after the original Greek texts of the New Testament.

Latinising Tyndale distances him. It also flattens him, making everything nearer to one sonorous tone. So the kaleidoscope of the Hebrew Pentateuch can appear in one sombre colour, and Paul, a brilliant mind exploring in Greek new frontiers of experience, can sound musty and old-fashioned – and thus safer.

Tyndale's Directness

Tyndale's everyday immediacy can be startling. In Hebrews 12, instead of the Authorised Version's 'as Esau, who for one morsel of meat sold his birth-right', Tyndale has the birthright sold 'for one breakfast'. Tyndale in 1 Peter 3 has 'be not afraid of every shadow', where the Authorised Version has 'be not afraid with any amazement' (the Greek suggests terror). In 2 Thessalonians 1, where the Authorised Version has 'and the charity of every one of you all towards each other aboundeth', Tyndale gets much closer to both the Greek and the English metaphor with 'and every one of you swimmeth in love toward another between yourselves' (the Greek verb *pleonazei* [πλεονάζει] means 'is more than enough'; the Authorised Version has substituted for this the Vulgate's 'abundat', and 'caritas' for the Greek *agapé* [ἀγάπη]). In Matthew

19, at the conclusion of a paragraph about chastity, the Authorised Version has 'He that is able to receive it, let him receive it': Tyndale has 'He that can take it, let him take it'. This is closer to the Greek *ho dunamenos chorein choreito* [ὁ δυνάμενος χωρεῖν χωρείτω], with its verb of power and its pun on the idea of giving way, and is more splendidly modern than that 1966 Jerusalem Bible's 'Let anyone accept this who can', or the 1976 Good News Bible's 'Let him who can accept this teaching do so'.

This direct, everyday manner suits well the 'pastoral' epistles, with their more personal style of Greek. In 2 Timothy 4, Tyndale reads: 'For the time will come when they will not suffer wholesome doctrine: but after their own lusts shall they (whose ears itch) get them an heap of teachers, and shall turn their ears from the truth, and shall be given unto fables.' In 1 Timothy 3, Paul is giving advice about office-holders in the young Church and about whom to avoid appointing. Tyndale has 'He may not be a young scholar, lest he swell and fall into the judgement of the evil speaker'. The Authorized Version is quite different in feeling: 'not a novice, lest being lifted up with pride, he fall into the condemnation of the devil'. Not only does Tyndale hit more sharply home, but 'novice' is too monkish a word for the Greek *neophutos* (νεόφυτος), which means 'newly planted'. ('Neophyte' did not arrive in general English use until the nineteeth century, though it appears in the Roman Catholic Rheims New Testament as one of an amazing string of coinages such as 'be docible of God', 'new paste as you are Azymes', 'conquinations and spots', 'concorporat and comparticipant', and many more.) Tyndale's 'the evil speaker', though odd to us, is more precise than the Authorised Version's 'the devil'. Tyndale distinguishes two Greek words, *daimonion* (δαιμόνιον), which he gives as 'devils', for example, in the following chapter, and *diabolos* (διάβολος) (not quite so common in the New Testament as is the other), which means a slanderer, someone who falsely accuses.

In Titus 2, Paul, on the behaviour of servants, says in Tyndale: 'neither be pickers, but they that show all good faithfulness'. 'Pickers', for pilferers, is in the Catechism in 'picking and stealing', and in Hamlet's metaphor for his fingers as 'pickers and stealers'. It is a word which has rightly lived on for a sort of petty theft, the appropriation of small things whose absence wouldn't perhaps be noticed. The Authorised Version has 'Not purloining, but showing all good fidelity'. Not only is Tyndale's 'pickers' better (Geneva kept it), but the Authorised Versions Latinizing 'faithfulness' into 'fidelity' has a touch of formality that is wrong for the passage. Tyndale scores directly in Philemon: 'For by thee (brother) the saints' hearts are comforted', against the Authorised Version's 'because the bowels of the saints are refreshed by thee, brother'. For the Greek *splanchna* (σπλάγχνα), inward parts, a metaphor for 'heart', the Vulgate gives 'viscera', and the Authorised Version sadly follows Rheims back to that. (Tyndale gives σπλάγχνα as 'bowels' himself, twice, in the following paragraphs: there is some sort of bowel infection here.) In 1 Timothy 6, Tyndale translates, 'For we brought nothing into the world, and it is a plain case that we can carry nothing out': and in the margin of 1 John 1 he says of

Christ's mercy, that it is from Christ 'without all other respect and then-what'.

This everyday directness suits large parts of the Gospels, too, as in the 'comers and goers' of Mark 6, 'grudged' as intransitive in Mark 14 and Luke 22, 'said grace' in Matthew 26 – these are random illustrations of hundreds that could be given, such as 'ye shall have poor folk always with you' (Matthew 26); 'both hearing them and posing them' (Luke 2); 'the people kept him that he should not depart from them' (Luke 4); 'the very sinners love their lovers' (Luke 6). 'Here a row and there a row' in Mark 6 is interesting: the Authorised Version has 'in ranks'; the Revised Standard Version, 'in groups'; the Jerusalem Bible, 'in squares'; the New English Bible, 'in rows, a hundred rows...'; the Good News Bible, the 'groups and...groups of'. Tyndale catches the Greek *prasiai prasiai* (πρασιαὶ πρασιαὶ) into English very well: both the repetition, and the sense of a garden, are precise; the Greek refers to garden beds. In Matthew 10, in Tyndale, Jesus sends out the twelve on their first mission 'to the lost sheep of the house of Israel', indicating the size of their task with the words, 'I tell you for a truth, ye shall not finish all the cities of Israel, till the Son of man be come'. The Greek verb is *telesete* (τελέσητε), that is, finish. The Authorised Version has, oddly, 'have gone over the cities of Israel', and the Jerusalem Bible is peculiar with 'gone the round of'. Direct brevity enlivens the margins in Tyndale: towards the end of Matthew 11 he has 'The wise knew not. Babes knew.'

In narrative passages, Tyndale's very English (as opposed to Latin) prose is most effective – as in Luke 17: 'They ate, they drank, they married wives and were married, even unto the same day that Noah went into the ark: and the flood came and destroyed them all.' This has a forward movement slightly spoiled in the Authorised Version's 'They did eat, they drank, they married wives, they were given in marriage, until the day that Noe entered into the ark, and the flood came and destroyed them all.' It is also characteristic of the Authorised Version to elevate 'went into the ark' to 'entered into...', as if Noah's direct action has to be a little more formal. The last paragraph of Mark 6 (see below p. 71) is a good example of the way Tyndale can drive a narrative on. The Authorised Version took Tyndale over almost unchanged, but the tiny alterations are significant, having the effect of restraint, which the more head-long, even rather excited, Greek, does not have: the Authorised Version panel made the rhythms a little more solemn, moving a tense back in time, changing 'as soon as' to 'when', regularising 'went...and drew' to the slightly more correct 'came...and drew', changing 'all that were sick' to 'those that were sick', 'entered into' to 'entered, into', elevating 'prayed' to 'besought' and 'edge' to 'border' – and, curiously, lowering Tyndale's Latin 'vesture' to 'garment': perhaps Tyndale preferred 'vesture' with 'edge'.

Similarly, the words of the father of the epileptic boy in Luke 9 (see below, p. 106, at E) make a good illustration of Tyndale's rendering of painful immediacy, and the Authorised Version's determination to smooth away the (surely necessary) roughness. The father's 'behold my son' becomes 'look upon', which loses some force of the Greek *epiblepsai* (ἐπιβλέψαι), which implies 'look at with favour'; and Tyndale's 'for he is all that I have', though less technically correct than the Authorised Version's 'for he is mine only child' for *monogenes* (μονογενής), is perhaps closer to the situation. Tyndale's succession of coordinated clauses, concluding with a single, mournful, subordinate clause – 'and see, a spirit taketh him, and suddenly he crieth, and he teareth him that he foameth again, and with much pain departeth from him, when he hath rent him' – is surely spoiled when, in the Authorised Version, among other changes, the 'when' clause is turned into a Latinate participle in a Latin position: 'and lo, a spirit taketh him, and he suddenly crieth out, and it teareth him that he foameth again, and bruising him, hardly departeth from him.' Sometimes, the simplicity of Tyndale's narrative prose inspires the Authorised Version to match the beauty, as in Mark 10: 'And they brought children to him, that he should touch them...Suffer the children to come unto me...', where the additions of 'young' and 'little' are hauntingly right.

Tyndale's Craftsmanship

Yet Tyndale can do equally well what Sir Walter Scott, in another context, called 'the Big Bow-Wow Strain', as the Pauline Epistles and Hebrews show. The Greek of those books is often difficult, with the arguments falling over themselves; but Tyndale, it must be agreed, does more than merely manage. A study of the openings of Romans 2 or 5 (below, pp. 226 and 229) will show this. Supreme examples are the opening of Revelation 21 and the whole of 1 Corinthians 13. The bad press that Tyndale has had in the past has sometimes grudgingly acknowledged his simplicity but accused him of ineptness in the grander passages. If a reader's taste is for Latin decoration, then Tyndale will not do. If 'the former things are passed away' is preferred to 'the old things are gone', then Tyndale will be disliked and there is no way to mend it. Tyndale was writing for ordinary men and women reading the Greek New Testament in English to themselves and to each other, round the table, in the parlour, under the hedges, in the fields; not for those obediently sitting in rows in stone churches being done good to by the squire at the lectern – it was the Authorised Version that was 'Appointed to be read in churches'.

King James's New Testament panel, however, when not over-influenced by their Latinate prejudices – their own or their monarch's – could tune Tyndale's effects finely: one of the reasons for producing an accessible Tyndale is to enable us to judge these moments (which could be even better judged if we had accessible Geneva versions). Not only is it to their credit, to take a random example, that in Hebrews 13 they kept Tyndale's 'Let brotherly love continue', and rejected Rheims's 'let the charity of the fraternity abide in you', it is also in their favour that they made a large number of small adjustments to the rhythm, as in Mark 10, noticed above, where Tyndale's 'Suffer the children' and Geneva's 'Suffer young children' became 'Suffer the little children...'. Nevertheless, as a general rule, when they depart from Tyndale, they do so towards a greater formality.

Tyndale's humanist training made him at home with the vigorous conduct of argument. The preface to this 1534 New Testament shows him composing with that rhetorical craftsmanship that is right when he is translating Paul in high flight. The thought is coming from one mind; Tyndale was not a committee. There have been 'one-man' New Testaments, and even Bibles, in the last hundred years, and some of them, like those of Farrar Fenton, James Moffat or J. B. Phillips, have been unusually effective. The modern double arguments that the textual complexities, to say nothing of pitfalls in the changing English language, are beyond one person working alone, and that, thus, there is every justification for launching new and profitable versions made by syndicates of supreme scholars – these seem to be punctured by the fact of Tyndale working alone and in danger. The sense of the driving mind of Paul, in Romans particularly, is gripping in Tyndale. His humanist training also actively encouraged his boldness with words. This can be seen in his coining (another advantage of working alone: as well as *Jehovah, passover, scapegoat,* as we saw above, we owe to him *shewbread, peacemaker, mercy seat* and many more), and in his use of 'low' words (like 'wenches' in the Passion story). The world is divided into those who think that sacred Scripture should always be elevated above the common run – is not, indeed, sacred without an air of religiosity, remote from real life, preferably both charming and antiquarian; and those who say that the point of the incarnation was that God became man, low experiences and all, and if the Greek is ordinary Greek, then ordinary English words are essential. Paul's Greek can rise to sustained heights; so can Tyndale's English to match it. Both can also descend, and know what it is to be human. The classic example of the latter is at the end of Matthew 6: the Authorised Version panel, Latin-inspired, spoke for the mandarin classes in the unforgettable 'Sufficient unto the day is the evil thereof'. But Tyndale spoke for all humanity in his, even more memorable 'For the day present hath ever enough of his own trouble'.

Tyndale as Enemy

Why, then, the silence? If so much of the later translation work is taken from Tyndale, why couldn't his name be mentioned? The short answer is that he was thought to be a Lutheran, and thus a heretic. Indeed, all his writings (and his translations and other major works are all of a piece in this) press his joyous discovery that the Bible, and especially the New Testament, and particularly the Gospels and the Epistle to the Romans, tell of God's responding to an individual's faith, without the paraphernalia, and repression, of the Church. In this he was true to the New Testament, which finds justification in faith, not in buying indulgences. True Christianity always releases. The New Testament is full of verbs expressing this, from the cures in the Gospels – and very early on in the synoptic Gospels we meet a paralytic released – to the raising of Lazarus from the dead in the fourth Gospel, to the scales falling from Saul's eyes, to that galaxy of 'release' verbs in the Epistles. True Christianity thus threatens those, that is, the political and religious powers, who see in release only sedition. After the Diet of Worms, the fear of Lutheranism across Europe suggested that it would bring anarchy, schism and the dislocation of authority.

The longer answer is more complicated. The Bishop of London hunted down and burned many thousands of Tyndale's successive New Testaments and Pentateuchs with fanatical thoroughness, a ruthlessness that seems close to hysteria – only a dozen in all survive. King Henry VIII's Chancellor, Sir Thomas More, showed himself less than gentle, reasoned, saintly and urbane in his long, and indeed violent. polemics against Tyndale. He calls him, in his *Confutation*, 'a beast', as one of the 'hell-hounds that the devil hath in his kennel', discharging a 'filthy foam of blasphemies out of his brutish beastly mouth'. Elsewhere, More calls him a deceiver, a hypocrite, 'puffed up with the poison of pride, malice and envy'. And so on. Yet the best that More, in all the great length of his tirades, can summon against Tyndale, when all is boiled down, is that he translated the Greek word for 'elder' as 'elder' (not 'priest') and the Greek word for 'repentance' as 'repentance' (not 'do penance'), the Greek work for 'congregation' as 'congregation' (not 'church'); 'charity' became 'love', 'confess' became 'acknowledge'. More was on very weak ground. Even Erasmus, More's friend, had translated the Greek *ekklesia* (ἐκκλησία) as *congregatio*, not 'church'. Every change that Tyndale makes is more than defensible: it is correct. More was wrong. Tyndale patiently explained that he used 'elder' for *presbuteros* (πρεσβύτερος) (*presbyter*) and reserved 'priest' for *hiereus* (ἱερεύς) (*sacerdos*), and so on. More was not listening. He abandoned his attempts to answer Tyndale. He was objecting to the translation, but even more to the translator – a Lutheran, a heretic, incapable of right. Translation of the Bible could not come from unauthorised amateurs. More's persecution of reformers is a blot on his reputation. His logical base, that the church *could not* be wrong, was flawed. He can be dry, and witty, and appeal to logic, but all he writes against Tyndale is flawed by that terrible absolutism, and his outpourings reveal not only inhuman bigotry but viciousness: in hard reality, More flogged heretics, and while he was Chancellor he, with the new Bishop of London, burned John Tewkesbury, Richard Bayfield and James Bainham at the stake for the heresy of not renouncing what Tyndale had written.

Moreover, Tyndale contravened the Church's prohibition known as the 'Constitutions of Oxford', made by a synod of clergy in 1408, which forbade anyone to translate, or even to read, any parts of vernacular versions of the Bible, without express episcopal permission. (Tunstall, Bishop of London, in inviting More to attack Tyndale, gave him permission to read the offending books.) Many copies of the second Wycliffite version of the Bible were in people's homes in the early 1400s; but the prohibition still stood, and now printed versions from the Greek and Hebrew threatened to flood the country. A royal injunction of 1530 forbade buying or owning an English Bible.

We can now buy English Bibles freely. Our persecution of Tyndale is subtler. Incorporated into the Geneva Bible, Tyndale's notes and text are still attacked, by people who haven't read them, for their extreme Calvinism. So if he isn't Lutheran, he's Calvinist. Any stick will do, it seems. He has been denied his place in the sixteeth-century revival of learning; and the history of that century has been written entirely in terms of economics, political events or sociology, not mentioning religion or giving the Bible even a footnote. Such ancient, or modern, arrogance is rebuked by the fact of Tyndale's work, the translation of the Greek and Hebrew Bible into his own, beloved vernacular language. It is commonly said that Luther's 1522 New Testament gave Germany a language: it ought to be said more clearly that Tyndale's 1534 New Testament gave to English its first classic prose. Such flexibility, directness, nobility and rhythmic beauty showed what the language could do. There is a direct line from Tyndale to the lucidity, suppleness and expressive range of the greatest English prose that followed: English, that is, rather than Latinised, prose. The sixteenth century began with debate about the worthiness of English. The later poets under Elizabeth and James – Shakespeare above all – showed that English was a language which could far out-reach Latin in stature: but Tyndale and his successors made an English prose which was a more than worthy vehicle for the most serious matter of all.

Editor's Note

I stress that no word, or word-order, has been changed: only spelling, including such regularising as, for example, 'a farre' to 'afar', 'be cause' to 'because', 'for as much' to 'forasmuch'. There are, of necessity, grey areas. I have left 'mary', and glossed it, but silently changed 'other' to 'or' where appropriate, and 'ensample' to 'example'. Modernising means, perforce, regularising, and Tyndale's time allowed much greater freedom. The considerable problem that instantly presents itself is the period's waywardness with proper names. Here I have had to be decisive. I have given 'God' and 'Jesus Christ' and 'Lord' their upper-case initial letters throughout; in all other cases I have regularised the proper name to its Authorised Version form. My experiments with regularising to very modern versions produced bizarre results, and further, implied my approval of one, rather than another, modern translation. I accepted the Greek form 'Elias' for Elijah, 'Esaias' for Isaiah, as the Authorised Verison does, and then spent some time thinking about leaving Tyndale's 'Iesus', 'Iesu', 'Iames', 'Iohn', 'Ierusalem' and so on, to demonstrate the very proper Greek-ness of his terminology. Happily, common sense intervened: in a text dedicated to showing the accessibility of Tyndale's New Testament even after 450 years, that seemed eccentric. In any case, Tyndale's spelling was, as usual, not consistent: he sometimes printed 'Hierusalem' and sometimes 'Ierusalem', and quite often, 'Ihon'. I wanted, too, to avoid an appearance of Tyndale being charming and quaint. I have kept Tyndale's familiar 'Zachary' in Luke 1, and his vocative in Luke 19 to Zaccheus, where Jesus looked up 'and saw him, and said unto him: Zache, at once come down...'. Tyndale is faithful to the Greek there, which has *Zakchaie* (Ζακχαίε). Tyndale's running page-heads are not consistent, alternating, for example, between 'unto the Romans' and 'to the Romans'. I have regularised them to the use at the beginning of the epistle concerned; so I give 'to the Romans' but 'unto the Galatians' as running heads, following his first use.

It is striking how modern Tyndale feels. A few minutes spent with other writings of the 1520s and 1530s, even when transliterated into modern spelling, shows this vividly. Instead of the long, wandering sentences, half in English, half in Latin (and another half in Latinised English) which were the general manner of communication found even in writings of higher style, such as Lord Berners's translation of Froissart, Tyndale's usually short sentences and English words hit home. It is uncomfortable, therefore, when a late Middle-English word, long ago defunct, suddenly jars the reader and needs glossing. 'Advoutry' (adultery), 'harbourous' (given to hospitality), 'pyght' (pitched) and nearly a hundred others present a special problem, including particularly Tyndale's odd choice of 'debite' (deputy) for 'governor'. (They belong to a separate category from the many strange apparitions like 'ayght' and 'yerre', which are period spellings for 'eight' and 'ere' [before].) There are three classes of words that need to be glossed. First, those late Middle-English words not now in common use, such as 'advoutry', 'partlet', 'noosell', 'byss' and 'debite'. Next, those that are familiar, but clearly mean something different, such as 'haunt', or 'hag him'. Finally, those that contain a concealed trap, where the shift in meaning is not immediately apparent, such as 'prevent', 'anon' or 'by and by'.

The cross-references in the margins I have generally left alone, apart from naming, or abbreviating, the books of the Bible according to modern usage, instead of Tyndale's Vulgate or Septuagint (Greek Bible) usage. (It takes a moment to recall that Tyndale had nothing else to use.) Thus, his 'l and ll Parali' are l and ll Chronicles; his 'Thre.' is Lamentations; and of course his 'l, ll, lll, and IV Reg' are the two books of Samuel and the two books of Kings. Some silent correcting I have done where it seemed necessary, however: not only obvious errors such as 'Luke 32', 'Matt 31', 'Mark 28': or 'Mark 13' for Mark 14, or Hosea '13' for 14, but also in the special problem of the Psalms. Because the Vulgate did not divide Psalm 10 into two, all Tyndale's Psalm-numbers after 11 have to have 1 added, so that his 'Psalm 23' I have silently corrected to Psalm 24, and so on. The marginal capitals are frequently wrong: I have let them stand.

Punctuation is generally much lighter than we are used to. As Tyndale's rhythms are distinctive, I have tried to leave it alone, apart from supplying an obviously missing full point or adding a clarifying comma or a hyphen where an epithet is multiple.

I have supplied modern verse numbers at the top of each page, for ease of reference. I have silently corrected Tyndale's placing of crosses and half crosses, with reference to the Sarum Missal. It should be noted that Tyndale's order of the later books is different, Hebrews and James being unfamiliarly placed, following Luther.

Further Reading

For the history of the Bible in English, B. F. Westcott's *A General View of the History of the English Bible* (1905, 3rd edition revised) is still hardly superseded.

The volume edited by H. Wheeler Robinson, *The Bible in its Ancient and English Versions* (1940) is useful, as is F. F. Bruce, *The English Bible: a History of Translations* (1961). J. F. Mozley, *William Tyndale* (1937) and S. L. Greenslade, *The Work of William Tindale* (1938) have been influential. Fuller altogether is the volume *The Work of William Tyndale* edited by G. E. Duffield (1964), with many texts and a useful introduction. Outstanding is Gerald Hammond's *The Making of the English Bible* (1982), a pioneer study of the earliest translations: though it is confined to Old Testament work, almost ignoring Tyndale as a translator of Greek, the book is a particularly valuable study of Tyndale and others as the earliest, remarkable, translators of Hebrew. Further study of this can be found in *Tyndale's Old Testament: A Modern-Spelling Edition with an Introduction by David Daniell* (1992). The most recent Life is David Daniell, *William Tyndale: A Biography* (1994), where there is further commentary on Tyndale as a translator of the Greek New Testament.

Note to the Second Edition

There are many occasions when apparent errors in Tyndale's 1534 New Testament are simply older English usage. Six readings, however, must be put down to faulty setting up and proof correction in Martin de Keyser's Antwerp printing house. These are marked in the text with[††].

(1) At Mark 5 D (v.41) de Keyser prints the Aramaic words of Jesus, clear in the Greek as *Talitha koum*, as 'Tabitha, cumi'.

(2) At John 14 B (v.11) de Keyser omits an essential 'in' after 'I am' and prints 'Believe me, that I am the father and the father in me.'

(3) At Acts 17 B (v.7) de Keyser prints 'the elders of Cesar', where the Greek, *dogmaton*, can mean only 'decrees'.

(4) At Hebrews 9 C (v.12) de Keyser prints 'by his awne bloud we entred once for all into the holy place', where the Greek *eiselthen* and the sense both insist on 'he entered'.

(5) At Revelation 2 D (v.14) de Keyser prints 'that mayntayne the doctryne of Balam which taught in Balak', where the Greek *edidasken* and the sense deny the 'in'.

(6) At Revelation 17 D (v.16) de Keyser prints 'shall make her desolate and naked, and shall eate their flesshe, and burne her with fyre', where the Greek *autes* and the sense demand 'eat her flesh'.

GLOSSARY

This glossary gives words and phrases that are likely to give difficulty. A number are specific to this New Testament translation, some being Tyndale's coinages for the occasion.

advoutry	adultery
anon	at once
arede	make known, guess
assoil	answer (an argument)
bidden (Luke 22)	remained
botch (n.)	boil
broided	plaited
by and by	at once
byss	fine linen
Candy (Acts 27)	Crete
cavillations	legal quibbles to defraud
charger	platter
clave	split
cods	husks or pods
compass	circle
complexion	temperament
conclude	convince
cruses	smaller earthen pots
debite	deputy
degree	respect, standing (1 Tim. 3)
despitions	outrages (n.)
disease (v.) (Mark 5, Luke 8)	trouble
divers (n.)	various people
do cost on them	support their expenses
do you to wit	cause you to know, call to your mind
duetie	what is due

earable	capable of being ploughed, arable
earer	ploughman
eareth	ploughs
egalness	equality
Elias	the Greek form of Elijah
Eliseus	the Greek form of Elisha
envieth against	vies with, seeks to rival
ere than	before
erewhile	some time ago
Esaias	the Greek form of Isaiah
evidently	clearly
the evil speaker	the devil
forthwithal	immediately
favour (v.)	deal gently with, spare
finding	keep, provision (n.)
flaw	sudden gust or blast
ghostly	spiritual
groundly	profoundly
gray (n.)	badger
grece	flight of steps
habergeon	a sleeveless coat of mail
hag (v.)	torment as a hag or witch
harbour (v.) (Roman 12)	to be given to hospitality
harbourless	homeless, destitute of shelter
harbourous	given to hospitality (Tyndale's coinage ?)
harness	armament
haunted	remained
heads	leaders, rulers
hoised	hoisted, raised by means of tackle
information (Ephesians 6)	instruction, admonition
kind (Prologue to Romans)	natural
labour (Leviticus 19)	wages
lay	religion, sect
leasings	lies (n.)
let	hinder
liefer	rather
livelihood	property, income, means of living
longed	belonged

lordship	estate
lust	wish
mary	marrow
meeked	tamed
mete (v.)	measure
nay, without	without denial
naughty	valueless
noosell	train, nurture
nurse-fellow	foster-brother (Tyndale's coinage ?)
Osee	the Greek form of Hosea
ought	owed
parlous	perilous
partlet	neckerchief
peased	pacified
perceivance	discernment, perception
pickers	petty pilferers
pill	rob
pillers	those who pillage, despoilers
prevent	go before
prevented	anticipated
pyght	pitched
quick	living, alive
raynes (Revelation 19)	an obscure and rare word: the Greek means 'made of fine linen'
shapen (Prologue to Romans)	fashioned
shore (Acts 18)	shaved
sickles	the Greek form of shekels
silverlings	shekels
sound (v.)	signify
steps (Esther 13)	soles
stert	started
strait	narrow: strict, severe
straitly	strictly
sweet bread	unleavened bread
Syrtes (Acts 27)	the Syrtis sands
thyne (Rev. 18)	an obscure and rare word; probably a gum-bearing tree

tuns	casks
trying-fire	fire for testing, purifying or extracting a substance
wealth	well-being, health
weet	know
weenest	supposes
wreak (n.)	revenge
wit (n.)	mental capacity
wit (v.)	to know
witesafe	vouchsafe
without forth	everywhere outside
wot	know

THE NEW TESTAMENT

diligently corrected and compared with the Greek

By

WILLIAM TYNDALE

and finished in the year of our Lord God

A. 1534

in the month of November

W. T. UNTO THE READER

Here thou hast (most dear reader) the new testament or covenant made with us of God in Christ's blood. Which I have looked over again (now at the last) with all diligence, and compared it unto the Greek, and have weeded out of it many faults, which lack of help at the beginning, and oversight, did sow therein. If ought seem changed, or not altogether agreeing with the Greek, let the finder of the fault consider the Hebrew phrase or manner of speech left in the Greek words. Whose preterperfect tense and present tense is oft both one, and the future tense is the optative mode also, and the future tense is oft the imperative mode in the active voice, and in the passive ever. Likewise person for person, number for number, and an interrogation for a conditional, and such like is with the Hebrews a common usage.

I have also in many places set light in the margin to understand the text by. If any man find faults either with the translation or ought beside (which is easier for many to do, than so well to have translated it themselves of their own pregnant wits, at the beginning without fore-example) to the same it shall be lawful to translate it themselves and to put what they lust thereto. If I shall perceive either by myself or by the information of other, that ought be escaped me, or might be more plainly translated, I will shortly after, cause it to be mended. Howbeit in many places, me thinketh it better to put a declaration in the margin, than to run too far from the text. And in many places, where the text seemeth at the first chop hard to be understood, yet the circumstances before and after, and often reading together, maketh it plain enough etc.

Moreover, because the kingdom of heaven, which is the scripture and word of God, may be so locked up, that he which readeth or heareth it, cannot understand it: as Christ testifieth how that the scribes and Pharisees had so shut it up (Matt. 23) and had taken away the key of knowledge (Luke 11) that their Jews which thought themselves within, were yet so locked out, and are to this day that they can understand no sentence of the scripture unto their salvation, though they can rehearse the texts everywhere and dispute thereof as subtly as the popish doctors of dunce's dark learning, which with their sophistry, served us, as the Pharisees did the Jews. Therefore (that I might be found faithful to my father and Lord in distributing unto my brethren and fellows of one faith, their due and necessary food: so dressing it and seasoning it, that the weak

3

stomachs may receive it also, and be the better for it) I thought it my duty (most dear reader) to warn thee before, and to shew thee the right way in, and to give thee the true key to open it withal, and to arm thee against false prophets and malicious hypocrites, whose perpetual study is to leaven the scripture with glosses, and there to lock it up where it should save thy soul, and to make us shoot at a wrong mark, to put our trust in those things that profit their bellies only and slay our souls.

The right way into the scripture.

The right way: yea and the only way to understand the scripture unto our salvation, is, that we earnestly and above all thing, search for the profession of our baptism or covenants made between God and us. As for an example: Christ saith (Matt. 5) Happy are the merciful, for they shall obtain mercy. Lo, here God hath made a covenant with us, to be merciful unto us, if we will be merciful one to another: so that the man which sheweth mercy unto his neighbour, may be bold to trust in God for mercy at all needs. And contrary-wise, judgement without mercy, shall be to him that sheweth not mercy (Jas. 2). So now, if he that showeth no mercy, trust in God for mercy, his faith is carnal and worldly, and but vain presumption. For God hath promised mercy only to the merciful. And therefore the merciless have not God's word that they shall have mercy: but contrary-wise, that they shall have judgement without mercy. And (Matt. 6) If ye shall forgive men their faults, your heavenly father shall forgive you: but and if ye shall not forgive men their faults, no more shall your father forgive you your faults. Here also by the virtue and strength of this covenant wherewith God of his mercy hath bound himself to us unworthy, may he that forgiveth his neighbour, be bold when he returneth and amendeth to believe and trust in God for remission of whatsoever he hath done amiss. And contrary-wise, he that will not forgive, cannot but despair of forgiveness in the end, and fear judgement without mercy.

The general covenant wherein all other are comprehended and included, is this. If we meek ourselves to God, to keep all his laws, after the example of Christ: then God hath bound himself unto us to keep and make good all the mercies promised in Christ, throughout all the scripture.

Law.

All the whole law which was given to utter our corrupt nature, is comprehended in the ten commandments. And the ten commandments are comprehended in these two: love God and thy neighbour. And he that loveth his neighbour in God and Christ, fulfilleth these two, and consequently the ten, and finally all the other. Now if we love our neighbours in God and Christ: that is to weet, if we be loving, kind and merciful to them, because God hath created them unto his likeness, and Christ hath redeemed them and bought them with his blood, then may we be bold to trust in God through Christ and his deserving, for all mercy. For God hath promised and bound himself to us: to show us all mercy, and to be a father almighty to us, so that we shall not need to fear the power of all our adversaries.

Now if any man that submitteth not himself to keep the commandments, do think that he hath any faith in God: the same man's faith is vain, worldly, damnable, devilish and plain presumption, as it is above said, and is no faith that can justify or be accepted before God. And that is it that James meaneth in

4

his Epistle. For how can a man believe saith Paul, without a preacher (Rom. 10). Now read all the scripture and see where God sent any to preach mercy to any, save unto them only that repent and turn to God with all their hearts, to keep his commandments. Unto the disobedient that will not turn, is threatened wrath, vengeance and damnation, according to all the terrible curses and fearful examples of the Bible.

Faith now in God the father through our Lord Jesus Christ, according to the covenants and appointment made between God and us, is our salvation. Wherefore I have ever noted the covenants in the margins, and also the promises. Moreover where thou findest a promise and no covenant expressed therewith, there must thou understand a covenant. For all the promises of the mercy and grace that Christ hath purchased for us, are made upon the condition that we keep the law. As for an example: when the scripture saith (Matt. 7) Ask and it shall be given you: seek and ye shall find: knock and it shall be opened unto you. It is to be understood, if that when thy neighbour asketh, seeketh or knocketh to thee, thou then shew him the same mercy which thou desirest of God, then hath God bound himself to help thee again, and else not.

Also ye see that two things are required to begin a Christian man. The first is a steadfast faith and trust in almighty God, to obtain all the mercy that he hath promised us, through the deserving and merits of Christ's blood only, without all respect to our own works. And the other is, that we forsake evil and turn to God, to keep his laws and to fight against ourselves and our corrupt nature perpetually, that we may do the will of God every day better and better.

This have I said (most dear reader) to warn thee, lest thou shouldest be deceived, and shouldest not only read the scriptures in vain and to no profit, but also unto thy greater damnation. For the nature of God's word is, that whosoever read it or hear it reasoned and disputed before him, it will begin immediately to make him every day better and better, till he be grown into a perfect man in the knowledge of Christ and love of the law of God: or else make him worse and worse, till he be hardened that he openly resist the spirit of God, and then blaspheme, after the example of Pharaoh, Coza,[†] Abiram, Balaam, Judas, Simon Magus and such other. *What the nature of God's word is.*

This to be even so, the words of Christ (John 3) do well confirm. This is condemnation saith he, the light is come into the world, but the men loved darkness more than light for their deeds were evil. Behold, when the light of God's word cometh to a man, whether he read it or hear it preached and testified, and he yet have no love thereto, to fashion his life thereafter, but consenteth still unto his old deeds of ignorance: then beginneth his just damnation immediately, and he is henceforth without excuse: in that he refused mercy offered him. For God offereth him mercy upon the condition that he will mend his living: but he will not come under the covenant. And from that hour forward he waxeth worse and worse, God taking his spirit of mercy and grace from him for his unthankfulness' sake.

[†] Cora, Numbers 16.

And Paul writeth (Rom. 1) that the heathen because when they knew God, they had no lust to honour him with godly living, therefore God poured his wrath upon them, and took his spirit from them and gave them up unto their hearts' lusts to serve sin, from iniquity to iniquity till they were thoroughly hardened and past repentance.

And Pharaoh, because when the word of God was in his country and God's people scattered throughout all his land, and yet neither loved them or it: therefore God gave him up, and in taking his spirit of grace from him so hardened his heart with covetousness, that afterward no miracle could convert him.

Hereto pertaineth the parable of the talents (Matt. 25). The Lord commandeth the talent to be taken away from the evil and slothful servant and to bind him hand and foot and to cast him into utter darkness, and to give the talent unto him that had ten, saying: to all that have, more shall be given. But from him that hath not, that he hath shall be taken from him. That is to say, he that hath a good heart toward the word of God, and a set purpose to fashion his deeds thereafter and to garnish it with godly living and to testify it to other, the same shall increase more and more daily in the grace of Christ. But he that loveth it not, to live thereafter and to edify other, the same shall lose the grace of true knowledge and be blinded again and every day wax worse and worse and blinder and blinder, till he be an utter enemy of the word of God, and his heart so hardened, that it shall be impossible to convert him.

And (Luke 12) The servant that knoweth his master's will and prepareth not himself, shall be beaten with many stripes: that is, shall have greater damnation. And (Matt. 7) all that hear the word of God and do not, thereafter build on sand: that is, as the foundation laid on sand cannot resist violence of water, but is undermined and overthrown, even so the faith of them that have no lust nor love to the law of God built upon the sand of their own imaginations, and not on the rock of God's word according to his covenants, turneth to desperation in time of tribulation and when God cometh to judge.

And the vineyard (Matt. 21) planted and hired out to the husbandmen that would not render to the Lord, of the fruit in due time, and therefore was taken from them and hired out to other, doth confirm the same. For Christ saith to the Jews, the kingdom of heaven shall be taken from you and given to a nation that will bring forth the fruits thereof, as it is come to pass. For the Jews have lost the spiritual knowledge of God and of his commandments and also of all the scripture, so that they can understand nothing godly. And the door is so locked up that all their knocking is an vain, though many of them take great pain for God's sake. And (Luke 13) the fig tree that beareth no fruit is commanded to be plucked up.

And finally, hereto pertaineth with infinite other, the terrible parable of the unclean spirit (Luke 11) which after he is cast out, when he cometh and findeth his house swept and garnished, taketh to him seven worse than himself, and cometh and entereth in and dwelleth there, and so is the end of the man worse than the beginning. The Jews, they had cleansed themselves with God's word, from all outward idolatry and worshipping of idols. But their hearts remained still faithless to Godward and toward his mercy and truth and therefore without love also and lust to his law, and to their neighbours for his sake, and through false trust in their own works (to which heresy, the child of perdition, the wicked bishop of Rome with his lawyers hath brought us christians) were more abominable idolaters than before, and become ten times worse in the end than at the beginning. For the first idolatry was soon spied and easy to be rebuked of the prophets by the scripture. But the later is more subtle to beguile withal, and an hundred times of more difficulty to be weeded out of men's hearts.

This also is a conclusion, nothing more certain, or more proved by the testimony and examples of the scripture: that if any that favoureth the word of God, be so weak that he cannot chasten his flesh, him will the Lord chastise and scourge every day sharper and sharper, with tribulation and misfortune, that nothing shall prosper with him but all shall go against him, whatsoever he taketh in hand, and shall visit him with poverty, with sicknesses and diseases, and shall plague him with plague upon plague, each more loathsome, terrible and fearful than other, till he be at utter defiance with his flesh.

Let us therefore that have now at this time our eyes opened again through the tender mercy of God, keep a mean. Let us so put our trust in the mercy of God through Christ, that we know it our duty to keep the law of God and to love our neighbours for their father's sake which created them and for their Lord's sake which redeemed them, and bought them so dearly with his blood. Let us walk in the fear of God, and have our eyes open unto both parts of God's covenants, certified that none shall be partaker of the mercy, save he that will fight against the flesh, to keep the law. And let us arm ourselves with this remembrance, that as Christ's works justify from sin and set us in the favour of God, so our own deeds through working of the spirit of God, help us to continue in the favour and the grace, into which Christ hath brought us; and that we can no longer continue in favour and grace than our hearts are to keep the law.

Furthermore concerning the law of God, this is a general conclusion, that the whole law, whether they be ceremonies, sacrifices, yea or sacraments either, or precepts of equity between man and man throughout all degrees of the world, all were given for our profit and necessity only, and not for any need that God hath of our keeping them, or that his joy is increased thereby or that the deed, for the deed itself, doth please him. That is, all that God requireth of us when we be at one with him and do put our trust in him and love him, is that we love every man his neighbour to pity him and to have compassion on him in all his needs and to be merciful unto him. This to be even so, Christ testifieth (Matt. 7) saying: this is the law and the prophets. That is, to do as thou wouldest be done to (according I mean to the doctrine of the scripture) and not to do that thou wouldest not have done to thee, is all that the law requireth and the prophets. And Paul (to the Romans 13) affirmeth also the love is the fulfilling of the law, and that he which loveth, doth of his own accord all that the law

Love is the fulfilling of the law

7

requireth. And (1 Tim. 1) Paul saith that the love of a pure heart and good conscience and faith unfeigned is the end and fulfilling of the law. For faith unfeigned in Christ's blood causeth to love for Christ's sake. Which love is the pure love only and the only cause of a good conscience. For then is the conscience pure, when the eye looketh to Christ in all her deeds, to do them for his sake and not for her own singular advantage or any other wicked purpose. And John both in his gospel and also epistles, speaketh never of any other law than to love one another purely, affirming that we have God himself dwelling in us and all that God desireth, if we love one the other.

Seeing then that faith to God and love and mercifulness to our neighbours, is all that the law requireth, therefore of necessity the law must be understood and interpreted by them. So that all inferior laws are to be kept and observed as long as they be servants to faith and love: and then to be broken immediately, if through any occasion, they hurt either the faith which we should have to Godward in the confidence of Christ's blood or the love which we owe to our neighbours for Christ's sake.

And therefore when the blind Pharisees murmured and grudged at him and his disciples, that they brake the sabbath day and traditions of the elders, and that he himself did eat with publicans and sinners, he answereth (Matt. 9) alleging Esaias the prophet: go rather and learn what this meaneth, I require mercy and not sacrifice. And (Matt. 12) Oh that ye wist what this meaneth, I require mercy and not sacrifice. For only love and mercifulness understandeth the law, and else nothing. And he that hath not that written in his heart, shall never understand the law, no: though all the angels of heaven went about to teach him. And he that hath that graven in his heart, shall not only understand the law but also shall do of his own inclination all that is required of the law, though never law had been given: as all mothers do of themselves without law unto their children, all that can be required by any law, love overcoming all pain, grief, tediousness or loathsomeness: and even so no doubt if we had continued in our first state of innocency, we should ever have fulfilled the law, without compulsion of the law.

Love only understandeth the law.

And because the law (which is a doctrine through teaching every man his duty, doth utter our corrupt nature) is sufficiently described by Moses, therefore is little mention made thereof in the new testament, save of love only wherein all the law is included, as seldom mention is made of the new testament in the old law, save here and there are promises made unto them, that Christ should come and bless them and deliver them, and that the gospel and new testament should be preached and published unto all nations.

Gospel.

The gospel is glad tidings of mercy and grace and that our corrupt nature shall be healed again for Christ's sake and for the merits of his deservings only: Yet on the condition that we will turn to God, to learn to keep his laws spiritually, that is to say, of love for his sake, and will also suffer the curing of our infirmities.

New testament.

The new testament is as much to say as a new covenant. The old testament is an old temporal covenant made between God and the carnal children of

8

Abraham, Isaac and Jacob otherwise called Israel, upon the deeds and the observing of a temporal law. Where the reward of the keeping is temporal life and prosperity in the land of Canaan, and the breaking is rewarded with temporal death and punishment. But the new testament is an everlasting covenant made unto the children of God through faith in Christ, upon the deservings of Christ. Where eternal life is promised to all that believe, and death to all that are unbelieving. My deeds if I keep the law are rewarded with the temporal promises of this life. But if I believe in Christ, Christ's deeds have purchased for me the eternal promise of the everlasting life. If I commit nothing worthy of death, I deserve to my reward that no man kill me: if I hurt no man I am worthy that no man hurt me. If I help my neighbour, I am worthy that he help me again etc. So that with outward deeds with which I serve other men, I deserve that other men do like to me in this world: and they extend no further. But Christ's deeds extend to life everlasting unto all that believe etc. This be sufficient in this place concerning the law and the gospel, new testament and old: so that as there is but one God, one Christ, one faith and one baptism, even so thou understand that there is but one gospel, though many write it and many preach it. For all preach the same Christ and bring the same glad tidings. And thereto Paul's epistles with the gospel of John and his first epistle and the first epistle of saint Peter, are most pure gospel and most plainly and richly described the glory of the grace of Christ: If ye require more of the law, seek in the prologue to the Romans and in other places where it is sufficiently intreated of.

Repentance

Concerning this word repentance or (as they used) penance, the Hebrew hath in the Old Testament generally *Sob* [*shub*] turn or be converted. For which the translation that we take for saint Jerome's hath most part *converti* to turn or be converted, and sometime yet *agere penitenciam*. And the Greek in the New Testament hath perpetually *metanoeo* to turn in the heart and mind, and to come to the right knowledge, and to a man's right wit again. For which *metanoeo* S. Jerome's translation hath: sometime *ago penetenciam* I do repent: sometime *peniteo* I repent: sometime *peniteor* I am repentant: sometime *habeo penitenciam* I have repentance: sometime *penitet me* it repenteth me. And Erasmus useth much this word *resipisco* I come to myself or to my right mind again. And the very sense and signification both of the Hebrew and also of the Greek word, is, to be converted and to turn to God with all the heart, to know his will and to live according to his laws, and to be cured of our corrupt nature with the oil of his spirit and wine of obedience to his doctrine. Which conversion or turning if it be unfeigned, these four do accompany it and are included therein: Confession, not in the priest's ear, for that is but man's invention, but to God in the heart and before all the congregation of God, how that we be sinners and sinful, and that our whole nature is corrupt and inclined to sin and all unrighteousness, and therefore evil, wicked and damnable, and

9

his law holy and just, by which our sinful nature is rebuked: and also to our neighbours, if we have offended any person particularly. Then contrition, sorowfulness that we be such, damnable sinners, and not only have sinned but are wholly inclined to sin still. Thirdly faith (of which our old doctors have made no mention at all in the description of their penance) yet God for Christ's sake doth forgive us and receive us to mercy, and is at one with us and will heal our corrupt nature. And fourthly satisfaction or amends-making, not to God with holy works, but to my neighbour whom I have hurt, and the congregation of God whom I have offended, (if any open crime be found in me) and submitting of a man's self unto the congregation or church of Christ, and to the officers of the same, to have his life corrected and governed henceforth of them, according to the true doctrine of the church of Christ. And note this: that as satisfaction or amends-making is counted righteousness before the world and a purging of the sin, so that the world when I have made a full amends, hath no further to complain. Even so faith in Christ's blood is counted righteousness and a purging of all sin before God.

Moreover, he that sinneth against his brother sinneth also against his father almighty God. And as the sin committed against his brother, is purged before the world with making amends or asking forgiveness, even so is the sin committed against God, purged through faith in Christ's blood only. For Christ saith (John 8) except ye believe that I am he, ye shall die in your sins. That is to say, if ye think that there is any other sacrifice or satisfaction to Godward, than me, ye remain ever in sin before God, howsoever righteous ye appear before the world. Wherefore now, whether ye call this *metanoia*, repentance, conversion or turning again to God, either amending and etc. or whether ye say repent, be converted, turn to God, amend your living or what ye lust, I am content so ye understand what is meant thereby, as I have now declared.

Elders

In the Old Testament the temporal heads and rulers of the Jews which had the governance over the lay or common people are called elders, as ye may see in the four evangelists. Out of which custom Paul in his epistle and also Peter, call the prelates and spiritual governors which are bishops and priests, elders. Now whether ye call them elders or priests, it is to me all one: so that ye understand that they be officers and servants of the word of God, unto the which all men both high and low that will not rebel against Christ, must obey as long as they preach and rule truly and no longer.

A prologue into the four Evangelists showing what they were and their authority. And first of

St Matthew

As touching the evangelists: ye see in the New Testament clearly what they were. First Matthew (as ye read Matt. 9, Mark 2, Luke 5) was one of Christ's apostles, and was with Christ all the time of his preaching, and saw and heard his own self almost all that he wrote.

Mark

Of Mark read (Acts 12) how Peter (after he was loosed out of prison by the angel) came to Mark's mother's house, where many of the disciples were praying for his deliverance. And Paul and Barnabas took him with them from Jerusalem and brought him to Antioch, (Acts 12). And (Acts 13) Paul and Barnabas took Mark with them when they were sent out to preach: from whom he also departed, as it appeareth in the said chapter, and returned to Jerusalem again. And (Acts 15) Paul and Barnabas were at variance about him, Paul not willing to take him with them, because he forsook them in their first journey. Notwithstanding yet, when Paul wrote the epistle to the Colossians, Mark was with him, as he saith in the fourth chapter: of whom Paul also testifieth, both that he was Barnabas' sister's son and also his fellow worker in the kingdom of God.

And (2 Tim. 4) Paul commandeth Timothy to bring Mark with him, affirming that he was needful to him, to minister to him. Finally, he was also with Peter when he wrote his first epistle, and so familiar that Peter calleth him his son. Whereof ye see, of whom he learned his gospel, even of the very apostles, with whom he had his continual conversation, and also of what authority his writing is, and how worthy of credence.

Luke

Luke was Paul's companion, at the least way from the 16th chapter of Acts forth and with him in all his tribulation. And he went with Paul at his last going up to Jerusalem. And from thence he followed Paul to Cæsarea, where he lay two years in prison. And from Cæsarea he went with Paul to Rome where he lay two other years in prison. And he was with Paul when he wrote to the Colossians, as he testifieth in the fourth chapter saying: the beloved Luke the physician saluteth you. And he was with Paul when he wrote the second epistle to Timothy, as he saith in the fourth chapter saying: Only Luke is with me. Whereby ye see the authority of the man and of what credence and reverence his writing is worthy of, and thereto of whom he learned the story of his gospel, as he himself saith, how that he learned it and searched it out with all diligence of them that saw it and were also partakers at the doing. And as for the Acts of the Apostles, he himself was at the doing of them (at the least) of the most part, and had his part therein, and therefore wrote of his own experience.

John

John, what he was, is manifest by the three first evangelists. First Christ's apostle, and that one of the chief. Then Christ's nigh kinsman, and for his singular innocency and softness, singularly beloved and of singular familiarity with Christ, and ever one of the three witnesses of most secret things. The cause of his writing was certain heresies that arose in his time, and namely two, of which one denied Christ to be very man and to be come in the very flesh and nature of man. Against which two heresies he wrote both his gospel and also his first epistle, and in the beginning of his gospel saith that the word or thing was at the beginning, and was with God, and was also very God and that all things was created and made by it, and that it was also made flesh: that is to say, became very man. And he dwelt among us (saith he) and we saw his glory.

And in the beginning of his epistle, he saith we shew you of the thing that was from the beginning, which also we heard, saw with our eyes and our hands handled. And again we shew you everlasting life, that was with the father and appeared to us, and we heard and saw, and etc.

In that he saith that it was from the beginning, and that it was eternal life, and that it was with God, he affirmeth him to be very God. And that he saith, we heard, saw and felt, he witnesseth that he was very man also. John also wrote last, and therefore touched not the story that the other had compiled. But writeth most of the faith and promises, and of the sermons of Christ.

This be sufficient concerning the four Evangelists and their authority and worthiness to be believed.

A warning to the reader if ought be escaped through negligence of the printer, as this text is that followeth, which if thou find any more such: compare the English to the other books that are already printed, and so shalt thou perceive the truth of the English.

In the 23rd chapter of Matthew and in the 33rd leaf on the second side and last line [page 52], read the sentence thus: Thou blind Pharisee, cleanse first the inside of the cup and platter, that the outside of them may be clean also.

WILLIAM TYNDALE, YET ONCE
MORE TO THE CHRISTIAN READER

Thou shalt understand most dear reader, when I had taken in hand to look over the New Testament again and to compare it with the Greek, and to mend whatsoever I could find amiss and had almost finished the labour: George Joye secretly took in hand to correct it also by what occasion his conscience knoweth: and prevented me, insomuch, that his correction was printed in great number, ere mine began. When it was spied and word brought me, though it seemed to divers other that George Joye had not used the office of an honest man, seeing he knew that I was in correcting it myself: neither did walk after the rules of the love and softness which Christ, and his disciples teach us, how that we should do nothing of strife to move debate, or of vainglory or of covetousness: Yet I took the thing in worth as I have done divers other in time past, as one that have more experience of the nature and disposition of the man's complexion, and supposed that a little spice of covetousness and vainglory (two blind guides) had been the only cause that moved him so to do, about which things I strive with no man: and so followed after and corrected forth and caused this to be printed, without surmise or looking on his correction.

But when the printing of mine was almost finished, one brought me a copy and shewed me so many places, in such wise altered that I was astonied and wondered not a little what fury had driven him to make such change and to call it a diligent correction. For throughout Matthew, Mark and Luke perpetually: and oft in the Acts, and sometime in John and also in the Hebrews, where he findeth this word resurrection, he changeth it into the life after this life, or very life, and such like, as one that abhorred the name of the resurrection.

If that change, to turn resurrection into life after this life, be a diligent correction, then must my translation be faulty in those places, and saint Jerome's, and all the translators that ever I heard of in what tongue soever it be, from the apostles unto this his diligent correction (as he calleth it) which whether it be so or no, I permit it to other men's judgements.

But of this I challenge George Joye, that he did not put his own name thereto and call it rather his own translation: and that he playeth boo peep, and in some of his books putteth in his name and title, and in some keepeth it out. It is lawful for who will to translate and show his mind, though a thousand had

13

translated before him. But it is not lawful (thinketh me) nor yet expedient for the edifying of the unity of the faith of Christ, that whosoever will, shall by his own authority, take another man's translation and put out and in and change at pleasure, and call it a correction.

Moreover, ye shall understand that George Joye hath had of a long time marvellous imaginations about this word resurrection, that it should be taken for the state of the souls after their departing from their bodies, and hath also (though he hath been reasoned with thereof and desired to cease) yet sown his doctrine by secret letters on that side the sea, and caused great division among the brethren. Insomuch that John Frith being in prison in the tower of London, a little before his death, wrote that we should warn him and desire him to cease, and would have then written against him, had I not withstood him. Thereto I have been since informed that no small number through his curiosity, utterly deny the resurrection of the flesh and body, affirming that the soul when she is departed, is the spiritual body of the resurrection, and other resurrection shall there none be. And I have talked with some of them myself, so doted in that folly, that it were as good persuade a post, as to pluck that madness out of their brains. And of this all is George Joye's unquiet curiosity the whole occasion, whether he be of the said faction also, or not, to that let him answer himself.

If George Joye will say (as I wot well he will) that his change, is the sense and meaning of those scriptures: I answer it is sooner said than proved: howbeit let other men judge. But though it were the very meaning of the scripture: yet if it were lawful after his example to every man to play boo peep with the translations that are before him, and to put out the words of the text at his pleasure and to put in everywhere his meaning: or what he thought the meaning were, that were the next way to stablish all heresies and to destroy the ground wherewith we should improve them. As for an example, when Christ sayeth (John 5) The time shall come in the which all that are in the graves shall hear his voice and shall come forth: they that have done good unto resurrection of life, or with the resurrection of life, and they have done evil, unto the resurrection or with the resurrection of damnation. George Joye's correction is, they that have done good shall come forth into the very life, and they that have done evil into the life of damnation, thrusting clean out this word resurrection. Now by the same authority, and with as good reason shall another come and say of the rest of the text, they that are in the sepulchres, shall hear his voice, that the sense is, the souls of them that are in the sepulchres shall hear his voice, and so put in his diligent correction and mock out the text, that it shall not make for the resurrection of the flesh, which thing also George Joye's correction doth manifestly affirm. If the text be left uncorrupt, it will purge herself of all manner false glosses, how subtle soever they be feigned, as a seething pot casteth up her scum. But if the false gloss be made the text, diligently overseen and correct, wherewith then shall we correct false doctrine and defend Christ's flock from false opinions, and from the wicked heresies of ravening of wolves? In my mind therefore a little unfeigned love after the rules of Christ, is worth much high learning, and single and slight understanding that edifieth in unity, is much better than subtle curiosity, and meekness better than bold arrogance and standing overmuch in a man's own conceit.

Wherefore, concerning the resurrection, I protest before God and our saviour Jesus Christ, and before the universal congregation that believeth in him, that I believe according to the open and manifest scriptures and catholic faith, that Christ is risen again in the flesh which he received of his mother the blessed virgin Mary, and body wherein he died. And that we shall all both good and bad rise both flesh and body, and appear together before the judgement seat of Christ, to receive every man according to his deeds. And that the bodies of all that believe and continue in the true faith of Christ, shall be endued with like immortality and glory as is the body of Christ.

And I protest before God and our saviour Christ and all that believe in him, that I hold of the souls that are departed as much as may be proved by manifest and open scripture, and think the souls departed in the faith of Christ and love of the law of God, to be in no worse case than the soul of Christ was from the time that he delivered his spirit into the hands of his father, until the resurrection of his body in glory and immortality. Neverthelater, I confess openly, that I am not persuaded that they be already in the full glory that Christ is in, or the elect angels of God are in. Neither is it any article of my faith: for if it so were, I see not but then the preaching of the resurrection of the flesh were a thing in vain. Notwithstanding yet I am ready to believe it, if it may be proved with open scripture. And I have desired George Joye to take open texts that seem to make for that purpose, as this is: Today thou shalt be with me in Paradise, to make thereof what he could, and to let his dreams about this word resurrection, go. For I receive not in the scripture the private interpretation of any man's brain, without open testimony of any scriptures agreeing thereto.

Moreover I take God (which alone seeth the heart) to record to my conscience, beseeching him that my part be not in the blood of Christ, if I wrote of all that I have written throughout all my book, ought of an evil purpose, of envy or malice to any man, or to stir up any false doctrine or opinion in the church of Christ, or to be author of any sect, or to draw disciples after me, or that I would be esteemed or had in price above the least child that is born, save only of pity and compassion I had and yet have on the blindness of my brethren, and to bring them unto the knowledge of Christ and to make every one of them if it were possible as perfect as an angel of heaven, and to weed out all that is not planted of our heavenly father, and to bring down all that lifteth up itself against the knowledge of the salvation that is in the blood of Christ. Also, my part be not in Christ, if mine heart be not to follow and live according as I teach, and also if mine heart weep not night and day for mine own sin and other men's indifferently, beseeching God to convert us all, and to take his wrath from us, and to be merciful as well to all other men, as to mine own soul, caring for the wealth of the realm I was born in, for the king and all that are thereof, as a tender-hearted mother would do for her only son.

As concerning all I have translated or otherwise written, I beseech all men to read it for that purpose I wrote it: even to bring them to the knowledge of the scripture. And as far as the scripture approveth it, so far to allow it, and if in any place the word of God disallow it, there to refuse it, as I do before our saviour Christ and his congregation. And where they find faults, let them show it me, if they be nigh, or write to me, if they be far off: or write openly against it and improve it, and I promise them, if I shall perceive that their reasons conclude I will confess mine ignorance openly.

Wherefore I beseech George Joye, yea and all other too, for to translate the scripture for themselves, whether out of Greek, Latin or Hebrew. Or (if they will needs) as the fox when he hath pissed in the gray's hole challengeth it for his own, so let them take my translations and labours, and change and alter, and correct and corrupt at their pleasures, and call it their own translations, and put to their own names, and not to play boo peep after George Joye's manner. Which whether he have done faithfully and truly, with such reverence and fear as becometh the word of God, and with such love and meekness and affection to unite and circumspection that the ungodly have none occasion to rail on the verity, as becometh the servants of Christ, I refer it to the judgements of them that know and love the truth. For this I protest, that I provoke not Joye nor any other man (but am provoked and that after the spitefullest manner of provoking) to do sore against my will and with sorrow of heart that I now do. But I neither can nor will suffer of any man, that he shall go take my translation and correct it without name, and make such changing as I myself durst not do, as I hope to have my part in Christ, though the whole world should be given me for my labour.

Finally that New Testament thus diligently corrected, beside this so oft putting out this word resurrection, and I wot not what other change, for I have not yet read it over, hath in the end before the Table of the Epistles and Gospels this title:
(Here endeth the New Testament diligently overseen and correct and printed now again at Antwerp, by me widow of Christopher of Endhoven. In the year of our Lord 1534 in August.)

Which title (reader) I have here put in because by this thou shalt know the book the better.

Vale

THE NEW TESTAMENT

Imprinted at Antwerp

by

Martin Emperor

Anno. 1534

THE BOOKS CONTAINED IN
THE NEW TESTAMENT

1 The Gospel of St Matthew
2 The Gospel of St Mark
3 The Gospel of St Luke
4 The Gospel of St John
5 The Acts of the Apostles, written by St Luke
6 The Epistle of St Paul to the Romans
7 The first epistle of St Paul to the Corinthians
8 The second epistle of St Paul to the Corinthians
9 The epistle of St Paul to the Galatians
10 The epistle of St Paul to the Ephesians
11 The epistle of St Paul to the Philippians
12 The epistle of St Paul to the Colossians
13 The first epistle of St Paul to the Thessalonians
14 The second epistle of St Paul to the Thessalonians
15 The first epistle of St Paul to Timothy
16 The second epistle of St Paul to Timothy
17 The epistle of St Paul to Titus
18 The epistle of St Paul to Philemon
19 The first epistle of St Peter
20 The second epistle of St Peter
21 The first epistle of St John
22 The second epistle of St John
23 The third epistle of St John
   The epistle unto the Hebrews
   The epistle of St James
   The epistle of St Jude
   The revelation of St John

THE GOSPEL OF ST MATTHEW

A This is the book of the generation of Jesus Christ the son of David, the son also of Abraham.

Abraham begat Isaac:

Isaac begat Jacob:

Jacob begat Judas and his brethren:

Judas begat Phares and Zara of Thamar:

Phares begat Esrom:

Esrom begat Aram:

Aram begat Aminadab:

Aminadab begat Naasson:

Naasson begat Salmon:

Salmon begat Booz of Rachab:

Booz begat Obed of Ruth:

Obed begat Jesse:

Jesse begat David the king:

David the king begat Solomon, of her that was the wife of Urias:

Solomon begat Roboam:

Roboam begat Abia:

B Abia begat Asa:

Asa begat Josaphat:

Josaphat begat Joram:

Joram begat Ozias:

Ozias begat Joatham:

Joatham begat Achaz:

Achaz begat Ezekias:

Ezekias begat Manasses:

Manasses begat Amon:

Amon begat Josias:

Josias begat Jechonias and his brethren about the time they were carried away to Babylon.

And after they were brought to Babylon,

Jechonias begat Salathiel:

Salathiel begat Zorobabel:

David and Abraham are first rehearsed: because that Christ was specially promised unto them to be of their seed.

Gen. 28. g.

1 Chr. 2. a.
Ruth 4. d.

2 Sam. 12. f.
1 Chr. 3. b.

2 Chr. 36.

1 Chr. 3. c.

Zorobabel begat Abiud:
Abiud begat Eliakim:
Eliakim begat Azor:
Azor begat Sadoc:
Sadoc begat Achim:
Achim begat Eliud:
Eliud begat Eleazar:
Eleazar begat Matthan:
Matthan begat Jacob:
Jacob begat Joseph the husband of Mary, of which was born that Jesus, that
is called Christ. ⊦

All the generations from Abraham to David are fourteen generations. And C
from David unto the captivity of Babylon are fourteen generations. And from
the captivity of Babylon unto Christ, are also fourteen generations.

+ The birth of Jesus Christ was on this wise. When his mother Mary was
betrothed to Joseph, before they came to dwell together, she was found with
child by the holy ghost. Then Joseph her husband being a perfect man and loth
Example: that is to say, to bring her out to punishment for the example of other. to make an example of her, was minded to put her away secretly. + While he
thus thought, behold the angel of the Lord appeared unto him in a dream,
saying: Joseph the son of David, fear not to take unto thee, Mary thy wife. For
that which is conceived in her is of the holy ghost. She shall bring forth a son,
A promise. and thou shalt call his name Jesus. For he shall save his people from their sins. ⊦
Isa. 7. c. All this was done to fulfil that which was spoken of the Lord by the prophet, D
saying: Behold a maid shall be with child, and shall bring forth a son, and they
Emmanuel. shall call his name Emmanuel, which is by interpretation, God with us. ⊦

And Joseph, as soon as he awoke out of sleep, did as the angel of the Lord
bade him, and took his wife unto him, and knew her not till she had brought
Jesus, that is a saviour. forth her first son, and called his name Jesus.

CHAPTER TWO

+ When Jesus was born at Bethlehem in Jewry, in the time of Herod the king, A
behold, there came wise men from the east to Jerusalem saying: Where is he
that is born king of the Jews? We have seen his star in the east, and are come to
worship him.

When Herod the king had heard this, he was troubled, and all Jerusalem with
him, and he gathered all the chief priests and scribes of the people, and asked of
them where Christ should be born. And they said unto him: at Bethlehem in
Jewry. For thus it is written by the prophet. And thou Bethlehem in the land of
Jewry, art not the least concerning the princes of Juda. For out of thee shall
Mic. 5. John 7. f. come the captain, that shall govern my people Israel.

Then Herod privily called the wise men, and diligently enquired of them, the B
time of the star that appeared, and sent them to Bethlehem saying: Go and
search diligently for the child. And when ye have found him, bring me word,
that I may come and worship him also.

When they had heard the king, they departed: and lo the star which they saw in the east, went before them, till it came and stood over the place where the child was. When they saw the star, they were marvellously glad: and went into the house, and found the child with Mary his mother, and kneeled down and worshipped him, and opened their treasures, and offered unto him gifts, gold, frankincense and myrrh. And after they were warned of God in a dream, that they should not go again to Herod, they returned into their own country another way. ⊦

C When they were departed: + behold the angel of the Lord appeared to Joseph in dream saying: arise, and take the child and his mother, and fly into Egypt, and abide there till I bring thee word. For Herod will seek the child to destroy him. Then he arose, and took the child and his mother by night, and departed into Egypt, and was there unto the death of Herod, to fulfil that which was spoken of the Lord, by the prophet which saith, out of Egypt have I called my son. *Hos. 12. a.*

Then Herod perceiving that he was mocked of the wise men, was exceeding wroth, and sent forth and slew all the children that were in Bethlehem, and in all the coasts thereof, as many as were two year old and under, according to the time which he had diligently searched out of the wise men.

D Then was fulfilled that which was spoken by the prophet Jeremy saying: On the hills was a voice heard, mourning, weeping, and great lamentation: Rachel weeping for her children, and would not be comforted, because they were not. ⊦ *Jer. 31. c.* *Were not: that is, because they appeared nowhere.*

+ When Herod was dead: behold, an angel of the Lord appeared in a dream to Joseph in Egypt saying: arise and take the child and his mother, and go into the land of Israel. For they are dead which sought the child's life. Then he arose up, and took the child and his mother, and came into the land of Israel. But when he heard that Archelaus did reign in Jewry, in the room of his father Herod, he was afraid to go thither. Notwithstanding after he was warned of God in a dream, he turned aside into the parts of Galilee, and went and dwelt in a city called Nazareth, to fulfil that which was spoken by the prophets: he shall be called a Nazarite. ⊦ *Judg. 13. Isa. 11.*

CHAPTER THREE

A + In those days John the Baptist came and preached in the wilderness of Jewry, saying: Repent, the kingdom of heaven is at hand. This is he of whom it is spoken by the prophet Esaias, which saith: The voice of a crier in wilderness, prepare the Lord's way, and make his paths straight. *Mark 1. a.* *Luke 3. a.* *Isa. 21. c.* *and 45. c.* *Zech. 1. a.* *Isa. 40. a.* *John 1. c.* *Mark 1. a.*

This John had his garment of camel's hair, and a girdle of a skin about his
B loins. His meat was locusts and wild honey. Then went out to him Jerusalem, and all Jewry, and all the region round about Jordan, and were baptised of him in Jordan, confessing their sins. ⊦

When he saw many of the Pharisees and of the Sadducees come to his baptism, he said unto them: O generation of vipers, who hath taught you to *Luke 3. b.*

23

flee from the vengeance to come? Bring forth therefore the fruits belonging to repentance. And see that ye once think not to say in yourselves, we have Abraham to our father. For I say unto you, that God is able of these stones to raise up children unto Abraham. Even now is the axe put unto the root of the trees: so that every tree which bringeth not forth good fruit, is hewn down and cast into the fire.

Mark 1. b.
Luke 3. c.
John 1. d.

I baptise you in water in token of repentance: but he that cometh after me, is mightier than I, whose shoes I am not worthy to bear. He shall baptise you with the holy ghost and with fire: which hath also his fan in his hand, and will purge his floor, and gather the wheat into his garner, and will burn the chaff *Luke 3.d.* with unquenchable fire. ⊦

Mark 1. b.
Luke 3. d.

⊦ Then came Jesus from Galilee to Jordan, unto John, to be baptised of him. But John forbade him, saying: I ought to be baptised of thee: and comest thou to me? Jesus answered and said to him: Let it be so now. For thus it becometh *All righteousness: that is to do all the ordinances of God for such purpose as God ordained them for.* us to fulfil all righteousness. Then he suffered him. And Jesus as soon as he was baptised, came straight out of the water. And lo heaven was open over him: and John saw the spirit of God descend like a dove, and light upon him. And lo there came a voice from heaven saying: This is that my beloved son in whom is my delight. ⊦

CHAPTER FOUR

Mark 1. b.
Luke 4. a.

⊦ Then was Jesus led away of the spirit into wilderness, to be tempted of the devil. And when he had fasted forty days and forty nights, he was afterward an-hungered. Then came to him the tempter, and said: if thou be the son of God, command that these stones be made bread. He answered and said: it is written, man shall not live by bread only, but by every word that proceedeth *Deut. 8. a.* out of the mouth of God.

Then the devil took him up into the holy city, and set him on a pinnacle of the temple, and said unto him: if thou be the son of God, cast thyself down. For *Psa. 91. c.* it is written, he shall give his angels charge over thee, and with their hands they shall hold thee up, that thou dash not thy foot against a stone. And Jesus said to *Deut. 6. c.* him, it is written also: Thou shalt not tempt thy Lord God.

The devil took him up again and led him in to an exceeding high mountain, and shewed him all the kingdoms of the world, and all the glory of them, and said to him: all these will I give thee, if thou wilt fall down and worship me. *Deut. 6. c. and 10. d.* Then said Jesus unto him. Avoid, Satan. For it is written, thou shalt worship the Lord thy God, and him only shalt thou serve.

Then the devil left him, and behold, the angels came and ministered unto him. ⊦

Mark 1. b.
Luke 4. c.
John 4. f.
Mark 1. c.

⊦ When Jesus had heard that John was taken, he departed into Galilee and left Nazareth, and went and dwelt in Capernaum, which is a city upon the sea, in the coasts of Zabulon and Nephthalim, to fulfil that which was spoken by Esaias the prophet, saying: The land of Zabulon and Nephthalim, the way of *Luke 4. c.* *Isa. 9. a.* the sea beyond Jordan, Galilee of the Gentiles, the people which sat in darkness, saw great light, and to them which sat in the region and shadow of death, light is begun to shine.

From that time Jesus began to preach, and to say: repent, for the kingdom of heaven is at hand. ⊦

⊦ As Jesus walked by the sea of Galilee, he saw two brethren: Simon which was called Peter, and Andrew his brother, casting a net into the sea, for they were fishers, and he said unto them, follow me, and I will make you fishers of men. And they straightway left their nets, and followed him.

D   And he went forth from thence, and saw other two brethren, James the son of Zebedee, and John his brother, in the ship with Zebedee their father, mending their nets, and called them. And they without tarrying left the ship and their father and followed him. ⊦

⊦ And Jesus went about all Galilee, teaching in their synagogues, and preaching the gospel of the kingdom, and healed all manner of sickness, and all manner diseases among the people. And his fame spread abroad throughout all Syria. And they brought unto him all sick people that were taken with divers diseases and gripings, and them that were possessed with devils, and those which were lunatic, and those that had the palsy: and he healed them. And there followed him a great number of people, from Galilee, and from the ten cities, and from Jerusalem, and from Jewry, and from the regions that lie beyond Jordan. ⊦

Marginal notes:
Mark 1. a.
Luke 5. a.
Peter and Andrew.
James and John.

CHAPTER FIVE

A   ⊦ When he saw the people, he went up into a mountain, and when he was set, his disciples came to him, and he opened his mouth, and taught them saying: Blessed are the poor in spirit: for theirs is the kingdom of heaven. Blessed are they that mourn: for they shall be comforted. Blessed are the meek: for they shall inherit the earth. Blessed are they which hunger and thirst for righteousness: for they shall be filled. Blessed are the merciful: for they shall obtain mercy. Blessed are the pure in heart: for they shall see God. Blessed are the peacemakers: for they shall be called the children of God. Blessed are they which suffer persecution for righteousness' sake: for theirs is the kingdom of heaven. Blessed are ye when men revile you, and persecute you, and shall falsely say all manner of evil sayings against you for my sake. Rejoice, and be glad, for great is your reward in heaven. ⊦ For so persecuted they the prophets which were before your days.

B   ⊦ Ye are the salt of the earth: but and if the salt have lost her saltness, what can be salted therewith? It is thenceforth good for nothing, but to be cast out, and to be trodden under foot of men. Ye are the light of the world. A city that is set on an hill, cannot be hid, neither do men light a candle and put it under a bushel, but on a candlestick, and it lighteth all that are in the house. Let your light so shine before men, that they may see your good works, and glorify your father which is in heaven.

C   ⊦ Think not that I am come to destroy the law, or the prophets: no I am not

Marginal notes:
Luke 6. d.
Covenants.
1 Pet. 3. c.
Salt.
Mark 9. a.
Luke 14. a.
Light.
Mark 4. c.
Luke 8. c.
and 11. c.

come to destroy them, but to fulfil them. For truly I say unto you, till heaven and earth perish, one jot or one tittle of the law shall not scape, till all be fulfilled.

Luke 16. d.
Jas. 2. b.

Whosoever breaketh one of these least commandments, and teacheth men so, he shall be called the least in the kingdom of heaven. But whosoever observeth and teacheth, the same shall be called great in the kingdom of heaven. ⊦

+ For I say unto you, except your righteousness exceed the righteousness of the scribes and Pharisees, ye cannot enter into the kingdom of heaven. ⊦

Exod. 20. c.
and Deut. 5. b.

Ye have heard how it was said unto them of the old time: Thou shalt not kill. For whosoever killeth, shall be in danger of judgement. But I say unto you, whosoever is angry with his brother, shall be in danger of judgement. Whosoever sayeth unto his brother Raca, shall be in danger of a council. But **D** whosoever sayeth thou fool, shall be in danger of hell fire.

Raca.
Hell.

Therefore when thou offerest thy gift at the altar, and there rememberest that thy brother hath ought against thee: leave there thine offering before the altar, and go thy way first and be reconciled to thy brother, and then come and offer thy gift. ⊦

Reconciling.

+ Agree with thine adversary quickly, whiles thou art in the way with him, lest that adversary deliver thee to the judge, and the judge deliver thee to the minister, and then thou be cast into prison. I say unto thee verily: thou shalt not come out thence till thou have paid the utmost farthing.

Luke 12. g.

Ye have heard how it was said to them of old time: Thou shalt not commit advoutry. But I say unto you, that whosoever looketh on a wife, lusting after her, hath committed advoutry with her already in his heart. **E**

Advoutry.
Exod. 20. c.
Eccl. 12. d.
Mark 9. g.
Right eye.

Wherefore if thy right eye offend thee, pluck him out, and cast him from thee. Better it is for thee that one of thy members perish, than that thy whole body should be cast into hell. Also if thy right hand offend thee, cut him off and cast him from thee. Better it is that one of thy members perish, than that all thy body should be cast into hell. ⊦

Right hand.

It is said, whosoever put away his wife, let him give her a testimonial also of the divorcement. But I say unto you: whosoever put away his wife, (except it be for fornication) causeth her to break matrimony. And whosoever marrieth her that is divorced, breaketh wedlock.

Divorcement.
Mark 10. b.
Luke 16. d.
1 Co. 7. b.

Again ye have heard how it was said to them of old time, thou shalt not **F** forswear thyself, but shalt perform thine oath to God. But I say unto you, swear not at all: neither by heaven, for it is God's seat: nor yet by the earth, for it is his footstool: neither by Jerusalem, for it is the city of that great king: neither shalt thou swear by thy head, because thou canst not make one white hair, or black: But your communication shall be, yea, yea: nay, nay. For whatsoever is more than that, cometh of evil.

Lev. 19. c.
Exod. 20. b.
Deut. 5. b.
Jas. 5. c.
Swear.

Ye have heard how it is said, an eye for an eye: a tooth for a tooth. But I say **G** to you, that ye resist not wrong. But whosoever give thee a blow on thy right cheek, turn to him the other. And if any man will sue thee at the law, and take

Exod. 31. c.
Deut. 19. c.
Lev. 24. c.
Luke 6. c.

away thy coat, let him have thy cloak also. And whosoever will compel thee to **Right cheek.**
go a mile, go with him twain. Give to him that asketh, and from him that
would borrow turn not away.

+ Ye have heard how it is said: thou shalt love thine neighbour, and hate
thine enemy. But I say unto you, love your enemies. Bless them that curse   *Lev. 19. d.*
you. Do good to them that hate you. Pray for them which do you wrong and   *Lev. 6. d.*
persecute you, that ye may be the children of your father that is in heaven: for
he maketh his sun to arise on the evil, and on the good, and sendeth his rain on
the just and unjust. For if ye love them, which love you: what reward shall ye   *Luke 6. f.*
have? Do not the publicans even so? And if ye be friendly to your brethren
only: what singular thing do ye? Do not the publicans likewise? Ye shall   **Publicans.**
therefore be perfect, even as your father which is in heaven, is perfect. +

CHAPTER SIX

A Take heed to your alms, that ye give it not in the sight of men, to the intent that   **Alms.**
ye would be seen of them. Or else ye get no reward of your father which is in
heaven. Whensoever therefore thou givest thine alms, thou shalt not make a
trumpet to be blown before thee, as the hypocrites do in the synagogues and in   **Trumpet.**
the streets, for to be praised of men. Verily I say unto you, they have their
reward. But when thou doest thine alms, let not thy left hand know, what thy
right hand doth, that thine alms may be secret: and thy father which seeth in
secret, shall reward thee openly. +

B And when thou prayest, thou shalt not be as the hypocrites are. For they love   **Prayer.**
to stand and pray in the synagogues, and in the corners of the streets, because
they would be seen of men. Verily I say unto you, they have their reward. But
when thou prayest, enter into thy chamber, and shut thy door to thee, and pray
to thy father which is in secret: and thy father which seeth in secret, shall
reward thee openly.

And when ye pray, babble not much, as the heathen do: for they think
that they shall be heard, for their much babbling's sake. Be ye not like them   **Babbling.**
therefore. For your father knoweth whereof ye have need, before ye ask of
him. After this manner therefore pray ye.   *Luke 11. a.*

O our father which art in heaven, hallowed be thy name. Let thy kingdom   **The Paternoster.**
come. Thy will be fulfilled, as well in earth, as it is in heaven. Give us this day
our daily bread. And forgive us our trespasses, even as we forgive our tres-   *Mark 11. c.*
passers. And lead us not into temptation: but deliver us from evil. For thine is   *Eccl. 28.*
the kingdom and the power, and the glory for ever. Amen. For and if ye shall   **Covenant.**
forgive other men their trespasses, your heavenly father shall also forgive you.
But and ye will not forgive men their trespasses, no more shall your father
forgive your trespasses.

C + Moreover when ye fast, be not sad as the hypocrites are. For they disfigure
their faces, that they might be seen of men how they fast. Verily I say unto
you, they have their reward. But thou, when thou fastest, anoint thine head,   **Fasting.**

and wash thy face, that it appear not unto men how that thou fastest: but unto
Luke 12. d. thy father which is in secret: and thy father which seeth in secret, shall reward
thee openly.

Luke 12. d. See that ye gather you not treasure upon the earth, where rust and moths
corrupt, and where thieves break through and steal. But gather ye treasure
Treasure. together in heaven, where neither rust nor moths corrupt, and where thieves
neither break up nor yet steal. For wheresoever your treasure is, there will your
hearts be also. ⊢

The light of the body is thine eye. Wherefore if thine eye be single, all thy
Luke 11. c. body shall be full of light. But and if thine eye be wicked then all thy body shall
Darkness. be full of darkness. Wherefore if the light that is in thee, be darkness: how great
is that darkness.

Two masters. + No man can serve two masters. For either he shall hate the one and love the
other: or else he shall lean to the one and despise the other: ye cannot serve God
Luke 16. e. and mammon. Therefore I say unto you, be not careful for your life, what ye
Luke 12. c. shall eat, or what ye shall drink, nor yet for your body, what ye shall put on. Is D
not the life more worth than meat, and the body more of value than raiment?
Fowls. Behold the fowls of the air: for they sow not, neither reap, nor yet carry into
the barns: and yet your heavenly father feedeth them. Are ye not much better
than they?

Which of you (though he took thought therefore) could put one cubit unto
Lilies. his stature? And why care ye then for raiment? Consider the lilies of the field,
how they grow. They labour not neither spin. And yet for all that I say unto
you, that even Solomon in all his royalty was not arrayed like unto one of
these.

Wherefore if God so clothe the grass, which is today in the field, and
tomorrow shall be cast into the furnace: shall he not much more do the same
unto you, o ye of little faith?

Therefore take no thought saying: what shall we eat, or what shall we drink,
or wherewith shall we be clothed? After all these things seek the Gentiles. For
your heavenly father knoweth that ye have need of all these things. But rather
Kingdom of heaven. seek ye first the kingdom of heaven and the righteousness thereof, and all these
things shall be ministered unto you. ⊢

Care not then for the morrow, but let the morrow care for itself: for the day
present hath ever enough of his own trouble.

CHAPTER SEVEN

Judge not. Judge not, that ye be not judged. For as ye judge so shall ye be judged. And A
with what measure ye mete, with the same shall it be measured to you again.
Luke 6. f. Why seest thou a mote in thy brother's eye, and perceivest not the beam that is
in thine own eye? Or why sayest thou to thy brother: suffer me to pluck out the
mote out of thine eye, and behold a beam is in thine own eye. Hypocrite, first
cast out the beam out of thine own eye, and then shalt thou see clearly to pluck
out the mote out of thy brother's eye.

Give not that which is holy, to dogs, neither cast ye your pearls before swine, lest they tread them under their feet, and the other turn again and all to-rend you.

Dogs and swine.

B Ask and it shall be given you. Seek and ye shall find. Knock and it shall be opened unto you. For whosoever asketh receiveth and he that seeketh findeth, and to him that knocketh, it shall be opened. Is there any man among you which if his son asked him bread, would offer him a stone? Or if he asked fish, would he proffer him a serpent? If ye then which are evil, can give to your children good gifts: how much more shall your father which is in heaven, give good things to them that ask him?

Covenants.

Luke 11. b.

Therefore whatsoever ye would that men should do to you, even so do ye to them. This is the law and the prophets.

Law and prophets.

Enter in at the strait gate: for wide is the gate, and broad is the way that leadeth to destruction: and many there be which go in thereat. But strait is the gate, and narrow is the way which leadeth unto life: and few there be that find it.

Luke 6.
Luke 12. c.

Strait gate. Narrow way.

C + Beware of false prophets, which come to you in sheep's clothing but inwardly they are ravening wolves. Ye shall know them by their fruits. Do men gather grapes of thorns? Or figs of briars? Even so every good tree bringeth forth good fruit. But a corrupt tree, bringeth forth evil fruit. A good tree cannot bring forth bad fruit: nor yet a bad tree can bring forth good fruit. Every tree that bringeth not forth good fruit, shall be hewn down, and cast into the fire. Wherefore by their fruits ye shall know them.

False prophets.

Luke 6. f.

Not all they that say unto me, Master, Master, shall enter in to the kingdom of heaven: but he that doth my father's will which is in heaven. ⊦ Many will say to me in that day, Master, master, have we not in thy name prophesied? And in thy name have cast out devils? And in thy name have done many miracles? And then will I knowledge unto them, that I never knew them. Depart from me, ye workers of iniquity.

Master: Master.

Luke 13. e. f.

Psa. 6.

Whosoever heareth of me these sayings and doeth the same, I will liken him unto a wise man which built his house on a rock: and abundance of rain descended, and the floods came, and the winds blew and beat upon that same house, and it fell not, because it was grounded on the rock. And whosoever heareth of me these sayings and doeth them not, shall be likened unto a foolish man which built his house upon the sand: and abundance of rain descended, and the floods came, and the winds blew and beat upon that house, and it fell, and great was the fall of it.

To build on the rock what it is.

To build on sand.

And it came to pass, that when Jesus had ended these sayings, the people were astonied at his doctrine. For he taught them as one having power, and not as the scribes.

Mark 1. c.
Luke 4. e.

CHAPTER EIGHT

A + When he was come down from the mountain, much people followed him. And lo, there came a leper and worshipped him saying: Master, if thou wilt,

Mark 1. d.
Luke 5. c.

A leper.

Lev. 14.

Luke 7. a.
Centurion.

Utter darkness.

Mark 1. c.
Luke 4. f.
Peter's mother-in-law.

Mark 1. d.

Luke 9. g.

Foxes and birds.

Bury.

Mark 4. d.
Luke 8. d.

Jesus sleepeth in the ship.

Mark 5. a.
Luke 8. d.

Gergesenes.

thou canst make me clean. And Jesus put forth his hand and touched him, saying: I will, be thou clean, and immediately his leprosy was cleansed. And Jesus said unto him. See thou tell no man, but go and shew thyself to the priest, and offer the gift that Moses commanded, in witness to them.

+ When Jesus was entered into Capernaum there came unto him a certain centurion, and besought him saying: Master my servant lieth sick at home of the palsy, and is grievously pained. And Jesus said unto him: I will come and heal him. The centurion answered and said: Sir I am not worthy that thou shouldest come under my roof, but speak the word only and my servant shall be healed. For I also myself am a man under power, and have soldiers under me, and I say to one, go, and he goeth, and to another come, and he cometh: **B** and to my servant, do this, and he doeth it. When Jesus heard that, he marvelled and said to them that followed him: Verily I say unto you, I have not found so great faith: no, not in Israel. I say therefore unto you that many shall come from the east and west, and shall rest with Abraham, Isaac and Jacob in the kingdom of heaven: and the children of the kingdom shall be cast out into utter darkness: there shall be weeping and gnashing of teeth. Then Jesus said unto the centurion, go thy way, and as thou believest so be it unto thee. And his servant was healed the self hour. ⊢

And then Jesus went to Peter's house, and saw his wife's mother lying sick of a fever, and touched her hand, and the fever left her: and she arose, and ministered unto them.

When the even was come, they brought unto him many that were possessed with devils. And he cast out the spirits with a word, and healed all that were sick, to fulfil that which was spoken by Esaias the prophet saying, he took on him our infirmities, and bare our sicknesses.

When Jesus saw much people about him, he commanded to go over the **C** water. And there came a scribe and said unto him: master, I will follow thee whithersoever thou goest. And Jesus said unto him: the foxes have holes, and the birds of the air have nests, but the son of the man hath not whereon to rest his head. Another that was one of his disciples said unto him: master, suffer me first, to go and bury my father. But Jesus said unto him: follow me, and let the dead bury their dead.

+ And he entered into a ship, and his disciples followed him. And behold there arose a great tempest in the sea, insomuch that the ship was covered with waves, and he was asleep. And his disciples came unto him, and awoke him saying: master save us, we perish. And he said unto them: why are ye fearful, o ye of little faith? Then he arose, and rebuked the winds and the sea, and there followed a great calm. And the men marvelled and said: what man is this, that both winds and sea obey him? ⊢

And when he was come to the other side, into the country of the Gerge- **D** senes, there met him two possessed of devils, which came out of the graves, and were out of measure fierce, so that no man might go by that way. And behold they cried out saying: O Jesu the son of God, what have we to do with thee? Art thou come hither to torment us before the time be come? And there was a good way off from them, a great herd of swine feeding. Then the devils besought him saying: if thou cast us out, suffer us to go our way into the herd of swine. And he said unto them: go your ways. Then went they out, and departed into the herd of swine. And behold the whole herd of swine was carried with violence headlong into the sea, and perished in the water. Then the herdmen fled and went their ways in to the city, and told everything, and what had fortuned unto the possessed of the devils. And behold all the city came out and met Jesus. And when they saw him, they besought him to depart out of their coasts.

CHAPTER NINE

A + Then he entered into a ship and passed over and came into his own city. And lo, they brought to him a man sick of the palsy, lying in his bed. And when Jesus saw the faith of them, he said to the sick of the palsy: son be of good cheer, thy sins be forgiven thee. And behold certain of the scribes said in themselves, this man blasphemeth. And when Jesus saw their thoughts, he said: wherefore think ye evil in your hearts? Whether is easier to say, thy sins be forgiven thee, or to say: arise and walk? That ye may know that the son of man hath power to forgive sins in earth, then said he unto the sick of the palsy: arise, take up thy bed, and go home to thine house. And he arose and departed to his own house. And when the people saw it, they marvelled and glorified God which had given such power to men. ⊦

B + And as Jesus passed forth from thence, he saw a man sit a-receiving of custom, named Matthew, and said to him: follow me. And he arose and followed him. And it came to pass as he sat at meat in the house: behold many publicans and sinners came and sat down also with Jesus and his disciples.

When the Pharisees saw that, they said to his disciples: why eateth your master with publicans and sinners? When Jesus heard that, he said unto them: The whole need not the physician, but they that are sick. Go and learn, what that meaneth: I have pleasure in mercy, and not in offering. For I am not come to call the righteous, but the sinners to repentance. ⊦

+ Then came the disciples of John to him saying: why do we and the Pharisees fast oft: but thy disciples fast not? And Jesus said unto them: Can the wedding children mourn as long as the bridegroom is with them? The time will come when the bridegroom shall be taken from them, and then shall they fast. No man pieceth an old garment with a piece of new cloth. For then taketh he away the piece again from the garment, and the rent is made greater. Neither do men put new wine into old vessels, for then the vessels break, and the wine runneth out, and the vessels perish. But they pour new wine into new vessels, and so are both saved together. ⊦

C + While he thus spake unto them, behold there came a certain ruler, and worshipped him saying: my daughter is even now deceased, but come and lay thy hand on her, and she shall live. And Jesus arose and followed him with his disciples. And behold, a woman which was diseased with an issue of blood

Mark 2. a
Luke 5. d.

Palsy.

This miracle shall be a sign to you, that I have power to forgive sins.

Mark 2. b.
Luke 5. f.

Matthew.

Publicans eat with Jesus.

Mercy and not sacrifice.

Hos. 6. e.

John's disciples fast.

New and old agree not.

The ruler's daughter.

Mark 5. b.
Luke 8. f.

Blood-issue.

31

twelve years, came behind him and touched the hem of his vesture. For she said in herself: if I may touch but even his vesture only, I shall be safe. Then Jesus turned him about, and beheld her saying: Daughter be of good comfort, thy faith hath made thee safe. And she was made whole even that same hour. ┝

And when Jesus came into the ruler's house, and saw the minstrels and the people raging, he said unto them: Get you hence, for the maid is not dead, but sleepeth. And they laughed him to scorn. As soon as the people were put forth, he went in and took her by the hand, and the maid arose. And this was noised throughout all that land.

And as Jesus departed thence, two blind men followed him crying and **D** saying: O thou son of David, have mercy on us. And when he was come to

Two blind are cured.

house, the blind came to him. And Jesus said unto them: Believe ye that I am able to do this? And they said unto him: yea Lord. Then touched he their eyes, saying: according to your faith, be it unto you. And their eyes were opened. And Jesus charged them saying: See that no man know of it. But they, as soon as they were departed, spread abroad his name throughout all the land.

Mark 7. c.
Luke 11. b.
Dumb.
Chief devil.

As they went out, behold, they brought to him a dumb man possessed of a devil. And as soon as the devil was cast out, the dumb spake: And the people marvelled, saying: it was never so seen in Israel. But the Pharisees said: he casteth out devils, by the power of the chief devil.

And Jesus went about all cities and towns, teaching in their synagogues and preaching the glad tidings of the kingdom, and healing all manner sickness and disease among the people. But when he saw the people, he had compassion on them, because they were pined away, and scattered abroad, even as sheep having no shepherd.

Harvest is great.

Then said he to his disciples: the harvest is great, but the labourers are few. Wherefore pray the Lord of the harvest, to send forth labourers into his harvest.

CHAPTER TEN

Mark 3. b.
Luke 6. b.

And he called his twelve disciples unto him, and gave them power over unclean **A** spirits, to cast them out, and to heal all manner of sicknesses, and all manner of diseases.

The apostles are sent.

The names of the twelve apostles are these. The first, Simon called also Peter: and Andrew his brother. James the son of Zebedee, and John his brother. Philip and Bartholomew. Thomas and Matthew the publican. James the son of Alphaeus, and Lebbaeus otherwise called Thaddaeus. Simon of Canaan, and Judas Iscariot, which also betrayed him.

Luke 9. a.

These twelve sent Jesus, and commanded them saying: Go not into the ways that lead to the gentiles, and into the cities of the Samaritans enter ye not. But go rather to the lost sheep of the house of Israel. Go and preach saying: that the kingdom of heaven is at hand. Heal the sick, cleanse the lepers, raise the dead, cast out the devils. Freely ye have received, freely give again. Possess not gold, nor silver, nor brass in your girdles, nor yet scrip towards your journey:

neither two coats, neither shoes, nor yet a staff. For the workman is worthy to have his meat. Into whatsoever city or town ye shall come, enquire who is worthy in it, and there abide till ye go thence.

Luke 10. c.

B And when ye come into an house salute the same. And if the house be worthy, your peace shall come upon it. But if it be not worthy, your peace shall return to you again.

And whosoever shall not receive you, nor will hear your preaching: when ye depart out of that house or that city, shake off the dust of your feet. Truly I say unto you: it shall be easier for the land of Sodom and Gomorrha in the day of judgement, than for that city.

Dust.

Behold I send you forth as sheep among wolves. Be ye therefore wise as serpents, and innocent as doves. Beware of men, for they shall deliver you up to the councils, and shall scourge you in their synagogues. And ye shall be brought to the head rulers and kings for my sake, in witness to them and to the gentiles.

Sheep among wolves.
Wise as serpents.
Innocent as doves.

But when they deliver you up, take no thought how or what ye shall speak, for it shall be given you, even in that same hour, what ye shall say. For it is not ye that speak, but the spirit of your father which speaketh in you.

The spirit speaketh in us.

The brother shall betray the brother to death, and the father the son. And the children shall arise against their fathers and mothers, and shall put them to death: and ye shall be hated of all men for my name. But he that endureth to the end, shall be saved.

John 5.

C When they persecute you in one city, fly into another. I tell you for a truth, ye shall not finish all the cities of Israel, till the son of man be come. The disciple is not above his master: nor yet the servant above his lord. It is enough for the disciple to be as his master is, and that the servant be as his lord is. If they have called the lord of the house Beelzebub: how much more shall they call them of his household so? Fear them not therefore.

Disciple.

There is nothing so close, that shall not be opened, and nothing so hid, that shall not be known.

Mark 4. c.
Luke 8. c.
and 12. a.

What I tell you in darkness, that speak ye in light. And what ye hear in the ear, that preach ye on the house-tops.

And fear ye not them which kill the body, and be not able to kill the soul. But rather fear him, which is able to destroy both soul and body into hell. Are not two sparrows sold for a farthing? And none of them doth light on the ground, without your father. And now are all the hairs of your heads numbered. Fear ye not therefore: ye are of more value than many sparrows.

Fear.

Sparrows.

Whosoever therefore shall knowledge me before men, him will I knowledge also before my father which is in heaven. But whosoever shall deny me before men, him will I also deny before my father which is in heaven.

Confess.
Mark 8. d.
Luke 9. c.
and 7. b.
Deny.

Think not, that I am come to send peace into the earth. I came not to send peace, but a sword. For I am come to set a man at variance against his father,

Luke 12. f.
A sword.

D and the daughter against her mother, and the daughter-in-law against her mother-in-law: And a man's foes shall be they of his own household.

Mic. 7. c

He that loveth his father or mother more than me, is not meet for me. And

33

Worthy of Christ, who.

Luke 14. f.

Cross.

Luke 14. f.

he that loveth his son, or daughter more than me, is not meet for me. And he that taketh not his cross and followeth me, is not meet for me. He that findeth his life, shall lose it: and he that loseth his life for my sake, shall find it.

Receive.

John 12. c.

Covenants.

Mark 9. f.

He that receiveth you, receiveth me: and he that receiveth me, receiveth him that sent me. He that receiveth a prophet in the name of a prophet, shall receive a prophet's reward. And he that receiveth a righteous man in the name of a righteous man, shall receive the reward of a righteous man. And whosoever shall give unto one of these little ones to drink, a cup of cold water only, in the name of a disciple: I tell you of a truth, he shall not lose his reward.

CHAPTER ELEVEN

And it came to pass when Jesus had made an end of commanding his twelve   **A**
disciples, that he departed thence, to teach and to preach in their cities.

Luke 7. c.

John sendeth to Christ.

+ When John being in prison heard the works of Christ, he sent two of his disciples and said unto him. Art thou he that shall come: or shall we look for another? Jesus answered and said unto them. Go and shew John what ye have heard and seen. The blind see, the halt go, the lepers are cleansed: the deaf hear, the dead rise again, and the glad tidings is preached to the poor. And happy is he that is not offended by me.

And as they departed Jesus began to speak unto the people of John. What for to see went ye out into the wilderness? Went ye out to see a reed shaken with the wind? Or what went ye out for to see? A man clothed in soft raiment? Behold they that wear soft clothing, are in kings' houses. But what went ye out for to see? A prophet? Yea I say to you, and more than a prophet. For this is he

Mal. 3. a.

of whom it is written, Behold, I send my messenger before thy face, which shall prepare thy way before thee. ⊦

Christ which humbled himself to the cross was less and etc.

Luke 16. d.

+ Verily I say unto you, among the children of women arose there not a   **B**
greater than John the Baptist. Notwithstanding he that is less in the kingdom of heaven, is greater than he. From the time of John Baptist hitherto, the kingdom of heaven suffereth violence, and they that go to it with violence pluck it unto them. For all the prophets and the law prophesied unto the time of John. Also if

Mal. 4. b.

ye will receive it, this is Elias which should come. He that hath ears to hear let him hear. ⊦

Luke 7. c.

But whereunto shall I liken this generation? It is like unto children which sit in the market and call unto their fellows, and say: we have piped unto you, and ye have not danced. We have mourned unto you, and ye have not sorrowed.   **C**
For John came neither eating nor drinking, and they say, he hath the devil. The son of man came eating and drinking, and they say, behold a glutton and drinker of wine, and a friend unto publicans and sinners. Nevethelater

Wisdom.

Luke 10. c.

wisdom is justified of her children.

Chorazin.
Bethsaida.
Sidon. Tyre.
Capernaum.

+ Then began he to upbraid the cities, in which most of his miracles were done, because they mended not. Woe be to thee Chorazin. Woe be to thee Bethsaida: for if the miracles which were shewed in you, had been done in Tyre and Sidon, they had repented long agone in sackcloth and ashes. Nevertheless I say to you: it shall be easier for Tyre and Sidon at the day of judgement, than for you. And thou Capernaum which art lift up unto heaven, shalt be brought down to hell. For if the miracles which have been done in thee, had been shewed in Sodom: they had remained to this day. Nevertheless I say unto you: it shall be easier for the land of Sodom in the day of judgement, than for thee. ⊦

D ⊦ At that time Jesus answered and said: I praise thee o father lord of heaven and earth, because thou hast hid these things from the wise and prudent, and hast opened them unto babes: even so father, for so it pleased thee. All things are given unto me of my father. And no man knoweth the son but the father: neither knoweth any man the father, save the son, and he to whom the son will open him.

Luke 10. c.

The wise knew not. Babes knew.

God is not known as a father, but through Christ.

Come unto me all ye that labour and are laden, and I will ease you. Take my yoke on you and learn of me, for I am meek and lowly in heart: and ye shall find rest unto your souls. For my yoke is easy, and my burden is light. ⊦

Yoke.

CHAPTER TWELVE

A ⊦ In that time went Jesus on the sabbath days through the corn and his disciples were an-hungered, and began to pluck the ears of corn, and to eat. When the Pharisees saw that, they said unto him: Behold, thy disciples do that which is not lawful to do upon the sabbath day. He said unto them: Have ye not read what David did, when he was an-hungered, and they also which were with him? How he entered into the house of God, and ate the hallowed loaves, which were not lawful, for him to eat, neither for them which were with him but only for the priests. Or have ye not read in the law, how that the priests in the temple break the sabbath day, and yet are blameless? But I say unto you: that here is one greater than the temple. Wherefore if ye had wist what this saying meaneth: I require mercy and not sacrifice; ye would never have condemned innocents. ⊦ For the son of man is lord even of the sabbath day.

Corn.

Sabbath.

1. Sam. 21. b.

Hallowed loaves.

Mercy and not sacrifice.

And he departed thence, and went into their synagogue: and behold there was a man, which had his hand dried up. And they asked him saying: is it lawful to heal upon the sabbath days? because they might accuse him. And he said unto them: which of you would it be, if he had a sheep fallen into a pit on the sabbath day, that would not take him and lift him out? And how much is a man better than a sheep? Wherefore it is lawful to do a good deed on the sabbath days. Then said he to the man: stretch forth thy hand. And he stretched it forth. And it was made whole again like unto the other.

Mark 3. a.

Luke 6. b.

Withered hand.

Sabbath.

B ⊦ Then the Pharisees went out, and held a council against him, how they might destroy him. When Jesus knew that, he departed thence, and much people followed him, and he healed them all, and charged them, that they should not make him known: to fulfil that which was spoken by Esaias the prophet, which sayeth, behold my child, whom I have chosen, my beloved, in whom my soul delighteth. I will put my spirit on him, and he shall shew judgement to the gentiles. He shall not strive, he shall not cry, neither shall any man hear his voice in the streets, a bruised reed shall he not break, and flax that

Isa. 12. a.

35

beginneth to burn, he shall not quench, till he send forth judgement unto
victory, and in his name shall the gentiles trust. ⊢

Mark 3. c.
Luke 6. b.

Then was brought to him, one possessed with a devil which was both blind C
and dumb: and he healed him, insomuch that he which was blind and dumb,

Blind and dumb.

both spake and saw. And all the people were amazed, and said: Is not this that
son of David? But when the Pharisees heard that, they said: This fellow driveth

Beelzebub.

the devils no other wise out but by the help of Beelzebub the chief of the devils.

But Jesus knew their thoughts, and said to them. Every kingdom divided within itself, shall be brought to naught. Neither shall any city or household divided against itself, continue. So if Satan cast out Satan, then is he divided against himself. How shall then his kingdom endure? Also if I by the help of Beelzebub cast out devils: by whose help do your children cast them out? Therefore they shall be your judges. But if I cast out the devils by the spirit of God: then is the kingdom of God come on you.

Either how can a man enter into a strong man's house, and violently take

Mark 3. d.

away his goods: except he first bind the strong man, and then spoil his house?

Luke 12. b.

+He that is not with me, is against me. And he that gathereth not with me,

Blasphemy.

scattereth abroad. Wherefore I say unto you, all manner of sin and blasphemy shall be forgiven unto men: but the blasphemy of the spirit, shall not be forgiven unto men. And whosoever speaketh a word against the son of man, it shall be forgiven him. But whosoever speaketh against the holy ghost, it shall not be forgiven him: no, neither in this world, neither in the world to come.

Either make the tree good, and his fruit good also: or else make the tree evil, and his fruit evil also. For the tree is known by his fruit. O generation of vipers,

Luke 6. b.

As the fruit is, such is the tree.

how can ye say well, when ye yourselves are evil? For of the abundance of the heart, the mouth speaketh. A good man out of the good treasure of his heart, bringeth forth good things. And an evil man out of his evil treasure, bringeth

Idle word.

forth evil things. But I say unto you, that of every idle word that men shall have spoken, they shall give accounts at the day of judgement. For by thy words thou shalt be justified: and by thy words thou shalt be condemned. ⊢

Luke 11. b

Sign.

John 2. a.

+Then answered certain of the scribes and of the Pharisees saying: Master, D
we would fain see a sign of thee. He answered and said to them: The evil and
advoutrous generation seeketh a sign, but there shall no sign be given to them,

Sign of Jonas.

save the sign of the prophet Jonas. For as Jonas was three days and three nights

Nineveh.

in the whale's belly: so shall the son of man be three days and three nights in the heart of the earth. The men of Nineveh shall rise at the day of judgement with

Jonah 3. b.

this nation, and condemn them: for they amended at the preaching of Jonas.

Queen of the south.

And behold, a greater than Jonas is here. The queen of the south shall rise at the day of judgement with this generation, and shall condemn them: for she came

1 Kin. 10. a.
2 Chr. 9. a.

from the utmost parts of the world to hear the wisdom of Solomon. And behold a greater than Solomon is here.

The unclean spirit cometh again.

When the unclean spirit is gone out of a man, he walketh throughout dry places, seeking rest, and findeth none. Then he sayeth: I will return again into my house, from whence I came out. And when he is come, he findeth the house, empty and swept and garnished. Then he goeth his way, and taketh unto him seven other spirits worse than himself, and so enter they in and dwell there. And the end of that man is worse than the beginning. Even so shall it be with this evil nation.

While he yet talked to the people, behold his mother and his brethren stood without, desiring to speak with him. Then one said unto him: behold thy mother and thy brethren stand without, desiring to speak with thee.

Mark 3. d.
Luke 8. c.

Mother and brethren.

He answered and said to him that told him: Who is my mother? or who are my brethren? And he stretched forth his hand over his disciples and said: behold my mother and my brethren. For whosoever doth my father's will which is in heaven, the same is my brother, sister and mother. ⊦

CHAPTER THIRTEEN

A The same day went Jesus out of the house, and sat by the sea side, and much people resorted unto him, so greatly that he went and sat in a ship, and all the people stood on the shore. And he spake many things to them in similitudes, saying: Behold, the sower went forth to sow. And as he sowed, some fell by the way's side, and the fowls came and devoured it up. Some fell upon stony ground where it had not much earth, and anon it sprang up, because it had no depth of earth: and when the sun was up, it caught heat, and for lack of rooting withered away. Some fell among thorns, and the thorns sprang up and choked it. Part fell in good ground, and brought forth good fruit: some an hundred-fold, some sixty-fold, some thirty-fold. Whosoever hath ears to hear, let him hear.

Mark 3. a.
Luke 8. a.

A sower.

B And the disciples came and said to him: Why speakest thou to them in parables? He answered and said unto them: it is given unto you to know the secrets of the kingdom of heaven, but to them it is not given*. For whosoever hath to him shall be given: and he shall have abundance. But whosoever hath not: from him shall be taken away even that he hath. Therefore speak I to them in similitudes: for though they see, they see not: and hearing they hear not: neither understand. And in them is fulfilled the prophecy of Esaias, which prophecy saith: with the ear ye shall hear and shall not understand, and with the eyes ye shall see, and shall not perceive. For this people's hearts are waxed gross, and their ears were dull of hearing, and their eyes have they closed, lest they should see with their eyes, and hear with their ears, and should understand with their hearts, and should turn, that I might heal them.

* A covenant to them that love the word of God to further it, that they shall increase therein, and another that they that love it not, shall lose it again, and wax blind.

Isa. 6. c.
Mark 4. b.
Luke 8. b.
John 12. f.
Acts 28.
Rom. 11. b.

C But blessed are your eyes, for they see: and your ears, for they hear. Verily I say unto you, that many prophets and perfect men have desired to see those things which ye see, and have not seen them: and to hear those things which ye hear, and have not heard them. Hear ye therefore the similitude of the sower. Whosoever heareth the word of the kingdom, and understandeth it not, there cometh the evil man and catcheth away that which was sown in his heart. And this is he which was sown by the way side. But he that was sown in the stony ground, is he which heareth the word of God, and anon with joy receiveth it, yet hath no roots in himself, and therefore dureth but a season: for as soon as

Luke 10. d.

Mark 4. b.
Luke 8. b.
The sower is expounded.

37

tribulation or persecution ariseth because of the word, by and by he falleth. He that was sown among thorns, is he that heareth the word of God: but the care of this world, and the deceitfulnes of riches choke the word, and so is he made unfruitful. He which is sown in the good ground, is he that heareth the word and understandeth it, which also beareth fruit and bringeth forth, some an hundred-fold, some sixty-fold, and some thirty-fold.`

Another similitude put he forth unto them saying: + The kingdom of heaven **D** is like unto a man which sowed good seed in his field. But while men slept, there came his foe and sowed tares among the wheat, and went his way. When the blade was sprung up and had brought forth fruit, then appeared the tares also. The servants came to the householder, and said unto him: Sir sowedst not thou good seed in thy close, from whence then hath it tares? He said to them, the envious man hath done this. Then the servants said unto him: wilt thou then that we go and gather them? But he said, nay, lest while ye go about to weed out the tares, ye pluck up also with them the wheat by the roots: let both grow together till harvest come, and in time of harvest, I will say to the reapers, gather ye first the tares, and bind them in sheaves to be burnt: but gather the wheat into my barn. ⊦

+ Another parable he put forth unto them saying. The kingdom of heaven is **E** like unto a grain of mustard seed, which a man taketh and soweth in his field, which is the least of all seeds. But when it is grown, it is the greatest among herbs, and it is a tree: so that the birds of the air come and build in the branches of it.

Another similitude said he to them. The kingdom of heaven is like unto leaven which a woman taketh and hideth in three pecks of meal, till all be leavened.

All these things spake Jesus unto the people by similitudes, and without similitudes spake he nothing to them, to fulfil that which was spoken by the prophet saying: I will open my mouth in similitudes, and will speak forth things which have been kept secret from the beginning of the world. ⊦

+ Then sent Jesus the people away, and came to house. And his disciples came unto him, saying: declare unto us the similitude of the tares of the field. Then answered he and said to them. He that soweth the good seed, is the son of man. And the field is the world. And the children of the kingdom, they are the good seed. And the tares are the children of the wicked. And the enemy that soweth them, is the devil. The harvest is the end of the world. And the reapers be the angels. For even as the tares are gathered and burnt in the fire: so shall it **F** be in the end of this world. The son of man shall send forth his angels, and they shall gather out of his kingdom all things that offend, and them which do iniquity, and shall cast them into a furnace of fire. There shall be wailing and gnashing of teeth. Then shall the just men shine as bright as the sun in the kingdom of their father. Whosoever hath ears to hear, let him hear. ⊦

+ Again the kingdom of heaven is like unto treasure hid in the field, the which a man findeth and hideth: and for joy thereof goeth and selleth all that he hath, and buyeth that field.

Tares.

Mark 4. b.
Luke 13. d.

Mustard seed.

Luke 13. c.

Leaven.

Mark 4. d.

Psa. 78.

Tares are expounded.

Rev. 14. c.

Wisdom 4. b.

Treasure.

Again the kingdom of heaven is like unto a merchant that seeketh good pearls, which when he had found one precious pearl, went and sold all that he had, and bought it. Pearls.

Again the kingdom of heaven is like unto a net cast into the sea, that gathereth of all kinds of fishes: which when it is full, men draw to land, and sit and gather the good into vessels, and cast the bad away. So shall it be at the end of the world. The angels shall come out, and sever the bad from the good, and shall cast them into a furnace of fire: there shall be wailing and gnashing of teeth. Net.

G Jesus said unto them: understand ye all these things? They said, yea Lord. Then said he unto them: Therefore every scribe which is taught unto the kingdom of heaven, is like an householder, which bringeth forth, out of his treasure, things both new and old. ⊦ New and old.

And it came to pass when Jesus had finished these similitudes, that he departed thence, and came in to his own country, and taught them in their synagogues, insomuch that they were astonied and said: whence cometh all this wisdom and power unto him? Is not this the carpenter's son? Is not his mother called Mary? and his brethren be called James and Joses and Simon and Judas? And are not his sisters all here with us? Whence hath he all these things? And they were offended by him. Then Jesus said to them, a prophet is not without honour, save in his own country, and among his own kin. And he did not many miracles there, for their unbelief's sake. *Mark 6. a. Luke 4. c. John 4. c. John 6. e.* Carpenter. Prophet.

CHAPTER FOURTEEN

A At that time Herod the tetrarch heard of the fame of Jesus, and said unto his servants: This is John the Baptist. He is risen again from death, and therefore are such miracles wrought by him. For Herod had taken John and bound him and put him in prison for Herodias' sake, his brother Philip's wife. For John said unto him: It is not lawful for thee to have her. And when he would have put him to death, he feared the people, because they counted him as a prophet. *Mark 6. b. Luke 9. a.* John Baptist is prisoned. *Mark 6. b. Luke 3. d.*

But when Herod's birthday was come, the daughter of Herodias danced before them, and pleased Herod. Wherefore he promised with an oath, that he would give her whatsoever she would ask. And she being informed of her mother before, said: give me here John Baptist's head in a platter. And the king sorrowed. Nevertheless for his oath's sake, and for their sakes which sat also at the table, he commanded it to be given her: and sent and beheaded John in the prison, and his head was brought in a platter and given to the damsel, and she brought it to her mother. And his disciples came and took up his body, and buried it: and went and told Jesus. John Baptist is beheaded.

B When Jesus heard that, he departed thence by ship into a desert place out of the way. And when the people had heard thereof, they followed him afoot out of their cities. And Jesus went forth and saw much people, and his heart did melt upon them, and he healed of them those that were sick. When even was come, his disciples came to him saying: This is a desert place, and the day is spent: let the people depart, that they may go into the towns, and buy them *Luke 9. b. Mark 6. b. John 6. a.*

victuals. But Jesus said unto them. They have no need to go away. Give ye them to eat. Then said they unto him: we have here but five loaves and two fishes. And he said: bring them hither to me. And he commanded the people to sit down on the grass: and took the five loaves, and the two fishes and looked up to heaven and blessed, and brake and gave the loaves to his disciples, and the disciples gave them to the people. And they did all eat, and were sufficed. And they gathered up of the gobbets that remained twelve baskets full. And they that ate, were in number about five thousand men, beside women and children.

And straightway Jesus made his disciples enter into a ship, and to go over **C** before him, while he sent the people away. And as soon as he had sent the people away, he went up into a mountain alone to pray. And when night was come, he was there himself alone. And the ship was now in the midst of the sea, and was tossed with waves, for it was a contrary wind. In the fourth watch of the night Jesus came unto them walking on the sea. And when his disciples saw him walking on the sea, they were troubled, saying: it is some spirit, and cried out for fear. And straightway Jesus spake unto them saying: be of good cheer, it is I, be not afraid.

Peter answered him, and said: Master, if thou be he, bid me come unto thee on the water. And he said, come. And when Peter was come down out of the ship, he walked on the water, to go to Jesus. But when he saw a mighty wind, he was afraid. And as he began to sink, he cried saying: Master save me. And immediately Jesus stretched forth his hand, and caught him, and said to him: O thou of little faith, wherefore didst thou doubt? And as soon as they were come into the ship, the wind ceased. Then they that were in the ship, came and worshipped him, saying: of a truth thou art the son of God. And when they were come over, they went in to the land of Gennesaret. And when the men of that place had knowledge of him, they sent out in to all that country round about, and brought unto him all that were sick, and besought him, that they might touch the hem of his vesture only. And as many as touched it were made safe.

CHAPTER FIFTEEN

+ Then came to Jesus scribes and Pharisees from Jerusalem, saying: why do **A** thy disciples transgress the traditions of the elders? for they wash not their hands, when they eat bread. He answered, and said unto them: why do ye also transgress the commandment of God, through your traditions? For God commanded, saying: honour thy father and mother, and he that curseth father or mother, shall suffer death. But ye say, every man shall say to his father or mother: That which thou desirest of me to help thee with is given God: and so shall he not honour his father or his mother. And thus have ye made, that the commandment of God is without effect, through your traditions. Hypocrites, well prophesied of you Esaias saying: This people draweth nigh unto me with their mouths, and honoureth me with their lips, howbeit their hearts are far

Five loaves and two fishes.

Mark 6. f.
John 6. b.

Jesus walked on the sea.

Peter walketh on the water.

Mark 6. g.

Gennesaret.

Hem.

Mark 7. a.

Traditions.

Exod. 20. e.
Deut. 5. b.
Eph. 6. a.
Exod. 21. e.
Lev. 20. b.
Prov. 20. c.

Isa. 29. d.

from me: but in vain they worship me teaching doctrines, which are nothing but men's precepts. Men's precepts.

B And he called the people unto him, and said to them: hear and understand. That which goeth into the mouth, defileth not the man: but that which cometh out of the mouth, defileth the man. *Mark* 7. *c* What defileth a man.

Then came his disciples, and said unto him. Perceivest thou not, how that the Pharisees are offended in hearing this saying? He answered, and said: all plants which my heavenly father hath not planted, shall be plucked up by the roots. Let them alone, they be the blind leaders of the blind. If the blind lead the blind, both shall fall into the ditch. Plants. *Luke* 6. *f.* Blind leaders.

Then answered Peter and said to him: declare unto us this parable. Then said Jesus: are ye yet without understanding? perceive ye not, that whatsoever goeth in at the mouth, descendeth down into the belly, and is cast out into the draught? But those things which proceed out of the mouth, come from the heart, and they defile the man. For out of the heart come evil thoughts, murder, breaking of wedlock, whoredom, theft, false witness-bearing, blasphemy. These are the things which defile a man. But to eat with unwashen hands, defileth not a man. ⊢ *Mark* 7. *c.* With what a man is defiled.

C + And Jesus went thence, and departed into the coasts of Tyre and Sidon. And behold a woman which was a Canaanite came out of the same coasts, and cried unto him, saying: have mercy on me Lord the son of David, my daughter is piteously vexed with a devil. And he gave her never a word to answer. Then came to him his disciples, and besought him saying: send her away, for she followeth us crying. He answered, and said: I am not sent, but unto the lost sheep of the house of Israel. Then she came and worshipped him, saying: Master help me. He answered and said: it is not good, to take the children's bread, and to cast it to whelps. She answered and said: truth Lord: nevertheless the whelps eat of the crumbs, which fall from their master's table. Then Jesus answered and said unto her. O woman great is thy faith, be it to thee, even as thou desirest. And her daughter was made whole even at that same hour. ⊢ *Mark* 7. *c.* The woman of Canaan.

Then Jesus went away from thence and came nigh unto the sea of Galilee, and went up into a mountain and sat down there. And much people came unto him, having with them, halt, blind, dumb, maimed, and other many: and cast them down at Jesus' feet. And he healed them, insomuch that the people wondered, to see the dumb speak, the maimed whole, the halt to go, and the blind to see. And they glorified the God of Israel. *Mark* 7. *d.*

Then Jesus called his disciples to him, and said: I have compassion on the people, because they have continued with me now three days, and have nought to eat: and I will not let them depart fasting, lest they perish in the way. And his disciples said unto him: whence should we get so much bread in the wilderness, as should suffice so great a multitude? And Jesus said unto them: how many loaves have ye? And they said: seven, and a few little fishes. And he commanded the people to sit down on the ground: and took the seven loaves, and the fishes, and gave thanks, and brake them, and gave to his disciples, and the disciples gave them to the people. And they did all eat and were sufficed. And *Mark* 7. *a.* Seven loaves.

they took up of the broken meat that was left seven baskets full. And yet they that ate were four thousand men, beside women and children. And he sent away the people, and took ship and came into the parts of Magdala.

CHAPTER SIXTEEN

Mark 8. b.
Luke 12. g.

+ Then came the Pharisees and Sadducees, and did tempt him, desiring him to shew them some sign from heaven. He answered and said unto them. At even ye say, we shall have fair weather, and that because the sky is red: and in the morning ye say, today shall be foul, and that because the sky is cloudy and red. O ye hypocrites, ye can discern the fashion of the sky: and can ye not discern the signs of the times? The froward nation and advoutrous seeketh a sign, and there shall none other sign be given unto them, but the sign of the prophet Jonas. So left he them and departed.

A

Sign of Jonas.

Jonah 2. a.

Mark 8. b.
Luke 12. a.

And when his disciples were come to the other side of the water, they had forgotten to take bread with them. Then Jesus said unto them: Take heed and beware of the leaven of the Pharisees and of the Sadducees. And they thought in themselves saying: because we have brought no bread with us. When Jesus understood that, he said unto them. O ye of little faith, why are your minds cumbered because ye have brought no bread? Do ye not yet perceive, neither remember those five loaves when there were five thousand men, and how many baskets took ye up? Neither the seven loaves, when there were four thousand and how many baskets took ye up? Why perceive ye not then, that I spake not unto you of bread, when I said, beware of the leaven of the Pharisees and of the Sadducees? Then understood they, how that he bade not them beware of the leaven of bread: but of the doctrine of the Pharisees, and of the Sadducees.

B

Leaven.

Mark 8. c.
Luke 9. c.

+ When Jesus came into coasts of the city which is called Cesarea Philippi, he asked his disciples saying: whom do men say that I the son of man am? They said, some say that thou art John Baptist, some Elias, some Jeremias, or one of the prophets. He said unto them: but whom say ye that I am? Simon Peter answered and said: Thou art Christ the son of the living God. And Jesus answered and said to him: happy art thou Simon the son of Jonas, for flesh and blood hath not opened unto thee that, but my father which is in heaven. And I say also unto thee, that thou art Peter: and upon this rock I will build my congregation. And the gates of hell shall not prevail against it. And I will give unto thee, the keys of the kingdom of heaven: and whatsoever thou bindest upon earth, shall be bound in heaven: and whatsoever thou loosest on earth, shall be loosed in heaven. ⊦

C

Keys.

Bind and loose.

Then he charged his disciples, that they should tell no man, that he was Jesus Christ. From that time forth, Jesus began to shew unto his disciples, how that he must go unto Jerusalem, and suffer* many things of the elders, and of the high priests, and of the scribes, and must be killed, and rise again the third day. But Peter took him aside, and began to rebuke him saying: Master, favour thyself, this shall not come unto thee. Then turned he about, and said unto

D

* When ought is said or done, that should move to pride: he dasheth them in the teeth with his death and passion.

Peter: come after me Satan, thou offendest me, because thou savourest not | Peter is Satan.
godly things, but worldly things.

Jesus then said to his disciples. If any man will follow me, let him forsake
himself, and take up his cross and follow me. For whosoever will save his life, | Christ's disciples.
shall lose it. And whosoever shall lose his life for my sake, shall find it. What | *Mark 8. d.*
shall it profit a man, though he should win all the whole world: if he lose his | *Luke 9. g.*
own soul? Or else what shall a man give to redeem his soul again withal? For | *John 12.*
the son of man shall come in the glory of his father, with his angels: and then | Judgement.
shall he reward every man according to his deeds. Verily I say unto you, some | Deeds.
there be among them that here stand, which shall not taste of death, till they | *Rom. 1. a.*
shall have seen the son of man come in his kingdom. | *Mark 9. a.*
| *Luke 9. c.*

CHAPTER SEVENTEEN

A + And after six days Jesus took Peter and James and John his brother, and | *Mark 9. a.*
brought them up into an high mountain out of the way, and was transfigured | *Luke 9. d.*
before them: and his face did shine as the sun, and his clothes were as white as
the light. And behold there appeared unto them, Moses and Elias, talking with | Transfiguration.
him. Then answered Peter, and said to Jesus: master here is good being for us.
If thou wilt, let us make here three tabernacles, one for thee, and one for
Moses, and one for Elias. While he yet spake, behold a bright cloud shadowed
them. And behold there came a voice out of the cloud saying: this is my dear | *2 Pet. 1. d.*
son, in whom I delight, hear him. And when the disciples heard that, they fell | Hear him.
on their faces, and were sore afraid. And Jesus came and touched them, and
said: arise and be not afraid. And when they looked up, they saw no man, save
Jesus only.

B   And as they came down from the mountain, Jesus charged them saying: see | *Mark 9. b.*
that ye shew the vision to no man, until the son of man be risen again from
death. ⊢ And his disciples asked of him, saying: Why then say the scribes, that | After the high vision he
Elias must first come? Jesus answered, and said unto them: Elias shall first | putteth them in mind of
his death.
come, and restore all things. And I say unto you that Elias is come already, and | *Mal. 4. b.*
they knew him not: but have done unto him whatsoever they lusted. In like
wise shall also the son of man suffer of them. Then the disciples perceived | John Baptist is Elias.
that he spake unto them of John Baptist.

C   And when they were come to the people, there came to him a certain man, | *Mark 9. c.*
and kneeled down to him, and said: Master have mercy on my son for he is | *Luke 9. c.*
frantic: and is sore vexed. And oft times he falleth into the fire, and oft into
the water. And I brought him to thy disciples, and they could not heal him.
Jesus answered and said: O generation faithless and crooked: how long shall I
be with you? how long shall I suffer you? bring him hither to me. And Jesus
rebuked the devil, and he came out of him. And the child was healed even that
same hour. ⊢

Then came the disciples to Jesus secretly and said: Why could not we cast | *Luke 17. d.*
him out? Jesus said unto them: Because of your unbelief. For I say verily unto
you: if ye had faith as a grain of mustard seed, ye should say unto this moun- | Unbelief.

tain, remove hence to yonder place, and he should remove: neither should any thing be impossible for you to do. Howbeit this kind goeth not out, but by prayer and fasting.

As they passed the time in Galilee, Jesus said unto them: the son of man shall **D** be betrayed into the hands of men, and they shall kill him, and the third day he shall rise again. And they sorrowed greatly.

+ And when they were come to Capernaum, they that were wont to gather poll money, came to Peter and said: Doth your master pay tribute? He said: yea. And when he was come into the house, Jesus spake first to him saying, what thinkest thou Simon? of whom do the kings of the earth take tribute or poll money? of their children, or of strangers? Peter said unto him: of strangers. Then said Jesus unto him again: Then are the children free. Nevertheless, lest we should offend them: go to the sea and cast in thine angle, and take the fish that first cometh up: and when thou hast opened his mouth, thou shalt find a piece of twenty pence: that take and pay for me and thee. ⊦

CHAPTER EIGHTEEN

+ The same time the disciples came unto Jesus saying: who is the greatest in the **A** kingdom of heaven? Jesus called a child unto him, and set him in the midst of them: and said. Verily I say unto you: except ye turn, and become as children, ye cannot enter into the kingdom of heaven. Whosoever therefore humble himself as this child, the same is the greatest in the kingdom of heaven. And whosoever receiveth such a child in my name, receiveth me. But whosoever offend one of these little ones, which believe in me: it were better for him, that a millstone were hanged about his neck, and that he were drowned in the depth of the sea. Woe be unto the world because of offences. Howbeit, it cannot be avoided but that offences shall be given. Nevertheless woe be to the man, by whom the offence cometh. ⊦

Wherefore if thy hand or thy foot offend thee, cut him off and cast him from **B** thee. It is better for thee to enter into life halt or maimed, rather than thou shouldest having two hands or two feet, be cast into everlasting fire. And if also thine eye offend thee, pluck him out and cast him from thee. It is better for thee to enter into life with one eye, than having two eyes to be cast into hell fire.

See that ye despise not one of these little ones. For I say unto you, that in heaven their angels always behold the face of my father, which is in heaven. Yea, and the son of man is come to save that which is lost. How think ye? If a man have an hundred sheep, and one of them be gone astray, doth he not leave ninety and nine in the mountains, and go and seek that one which is gone astray? If it happen that he find him, verily I say unto you: he rejoiceth more of that sheep, than of the ninety and nine which went not astray. Even so it is not the will of your father in heaven, that one of these little ones should perish.

+ Moreover if thy brother trespass against thee. Go and tell him his fault **C** between him and thee alone.* If he hear thee, thou hast won thy brother: But if he hear thee not, then take yet with thee one or two, that in the mouth of two

Marginal notes:

Prayer and fasting.

Mark 9. c.
Luke 9. c.

Passion.

Tribute.

Mark 9. e.
Luke 9. f.

Greatest.

Mark 9. f.
Luke 17. a.

Mark 9. g.

Luke 19. b.
Luke 15. a.

Hundred sheep.

* How men bind and loose.

or three witnesses, all things may be established. If he hear not them, tell it *Luke 17. a.*
unto the congregation. If he hear not the congregation, take him as an heathen
man, and as a publican. Verily I say unto you, whatsoever ye bind on earth,
shall be bound in heaven. And whatsoever ye loose on earth, shall be loosed in
heaven.

Again I say unto you, that if two of you shall agree in earth upon any manner *John 20. g.*
thing, whatsoever they shall desire: it shall be given them of my father which is
in heaven. For where two or three are gathered together in my name, there am *In the midst.*
I in the midst of them.

Then came Peter to him, and said: Master, how oft shall I forgive my *Luke 17. a.*
brother, if he sin against me, seven times? Jesus said unto him: I say not unto
thee seven times: but seventy times seven times. ⊦ + Therefore is the kingdom *Seven times.*
of heaven likened unto a certain king, which would take accounts of his
servants. And when he had begun to reckon, one was brought unto him,
which ought him ten thousand talents: whom because he had nought to pay his
master commanded him to be sold, and his wife, and his children, and all that
he had, and payment to be made. The servant fell down and besought him
saying: Sir, give me respite, and I will pay it every whit. Then had the lord pity
on that servant, and loosed him, and forgave him the debt.

D   And the said servant went out and found one of his fellows, which ought
him an hundred pence, and laid hands on him, and took him by the throat, *Covenant to the*
saying: pay me that thou owest. And his fellow fell down and besought him *unmerciful.*
saying: have patience with me, and I will pay thee all. And he would not, but
went and cast him into prison, till he should pay the debt. When his other
fellows saw what was done, they were very sorry, and came and told unto their
lord all that had happened. Then his lord called him, and said unto him: O evil
servant I forgave thee all that debt, because thou prayedst me: was it not meet
also that thou shouldest have had compassion on thy fellow, even as I had pity
on thee? And his lord was wroth, and delivered him to the jailers, till he should
pay all that was due to him. So likewise shall my heavenly father do unto you,
except ye forgive with your hearts, each one to his brother their trespasses. ⊦

CHAPTER NINETEEN

A And it came to pass, when Jesus had finished those sayings, he gat him from *Mark 10. a.*
Galilee, and came into the coasts of Jewry beyond Jordan, and much people
followed him, and he healed them there.

Then came unto him the Pharisees tempting him, and saying to him: Is it *Divorce.*
lawful for a man to put away his wife for all manner of causes? He answered *Gen. 1. d.*
and said unto them: Have ye not read, how that he which made man at the *Gen. 2. d.*
beginning, made them man and woman and said: for this thing, shall a man *Eph. 5.*
leave father and mother and cleave unto his wife, and they twain shall be one *1 Cor. 6. d.*
flesh. Wherefore now are they not twain, but one flesh. Let not man therefore
put asunder, that which God hath coupled together.

Then said they to him: why did Moses command to give a testimonial of
divorcement and to put her away? He said unto them: Moses, because of the

Mark 9. d.
Luke 16. d.

1 Cor. 7. d.

hardness of your hearts, suffered you to put away your wives: But from the beginning it was not so. I say therefore unto you, whosoever putteth away his wife (except it be for fornication) and marrieth another, breaketh wedlock. And whosoever marrieth her which is divorced, doth commit advoutry.

Then said his disciples to him: if the matter be so between man and wife, **B** then is it not good to marry? He said unto them: all men cannot away with that saying save they to whom it is given. There are chaste, which were so born out of their mother's belly. And there are chaste, which be made of men. And there be chaste, which have made themselves chaste for the kingdom of heaven's sake. He that can take it, let him take it.

Chaste.

Children.

Mark 10. b.
Luke 18. c.

Mark 10. b.
Luke 18. d.

Then were brought to him young children, that he should put his hands on them and pray. And the disciples rebuked them. But Jesus said: suffer the children and forbid them not to come to me: for of such is the kingdom of heaven. And when he had put his hands on them he departed thence.

And behold one came and said unto him: good master, what good thing shall **C** I do, that I may have eternal life? He said unto him: why callest thou me good? there is none good but one, and that is God. But if thou wilt enter into life, keep the commandments.

Commandments.

The other said to him, Which? And Jesus said: break no wedlock, kill not, steal not: bear not false witness: honour father and mother: and love thine neighbour as thy self. And the young man said unto him: I have observed all these things from my youth, what lack I yet? And Jesus said unto him: if thou wilt be perfect, go and sell that thou hast, and give it to the poor, and thou shalt have treasure in heaven, and come and follow me. When the young man heard that saying, he went away mourning. For he had great possessions.

Then Jesus said unto his disciples: Verily I say unto you: it is hard for a rich man to enter into the kingdom of heaven. And moreover I say unto you: it is easier for a camel to go through the eye of a needle, than for a rich man to enter into the kingdom of God. When his disciples heard that, they were exceedingly amazed, saying: who then can be saved? Jesus beheld them, and said unto them: with men this is impossible, but with God all things are possible.

Camel.

+ Then answered Peter, and said to him: Behold, we have forsaken all and **D** followed thee, what shall we have? Jesus said unto them: verily I say to you: when the son of man shall sit in the seat of his majesty, ye which follow me in the second generation shall sit also upon twelve seats, and judge the twelve tribes of Israel. And whosoever forsaketh houses, or brethren, or sisters, or father, or mother, or wife, or children, or lands, for my name's sake, the same shall receive an hundred-fold, and shall inherit everlasting life. ⊢ Many that are first shall be last, and the last shall be first.

Covenant.

An hundred-fold.

CHAPTER TWENTY

Mark 10. d.
Luke 13. f.

Vineyard.

+ For the kingdom of heaven is like unto an householder, which went out **A** early in the morning to hire labourers into his vineyard. And he agreed with the labourers for a penny a day, and sent them into his vineyard. And he went

out about the third hour, and saw other standing idle in the marketplace, and
said unto them, go ye also into my vineyard: and whatsoever is right, I will
give you. And they went their way. Again he went out about the sixth★ and
ninth hour, and did likewise. And he went out about the eleventh hour and
found other standing idle, and said unto them: Why stand ye here all the day
idle? They said unto him: because no man hath hired us. He said to them: go ye
also into my vineyard, and whatsoever is right, that shall ye receive.

★ The Jews reckon one, when the sun is up an hour.

B   When even was come, the lord of the vineyard said unto his steward: call the
labourers, and give them their hire, beginning at the last, till thou come to the
first. And they which were hired about the eleventh hour, came and received
every man a penny. Then came the first, supposing that they should receive
more: and they likewise received every man a penny. And when they had
received it, they murmured against the good man of the house saying: These
last have wrought but one hour, and thou hast made them equal unto us which
have borne the burden and heat of the day.

He answered to one of them saying: friend I do thee no wrong: didst thou
not agree with me for a penny? Take that which is thy duty, and go thy way. I
will give unto this last, as much as to thee. Is it not lawful for me to do as me
listeth with mine own? Is thine eye evil because I am good? So the last shall be
first, and the first shall be last. For many are called and few be chosen. ⊢

Last shall be first. Many called.

C   + And Jesus ascended to Jerusalem, and took the twelve disciples apart in the
way, and said to them. Behold we go up to Jerusalem, and the son of man shall
be betrayed unto the chief priests, and unto the scribes, and they shall condemn
him to death, and shall deliver him to the gentiles, to be mocked, to be
scourged, and to be crucified: and the third day he shall rise again. ⊢

Mark 10. d.
Luke 13. f.
Mark 10. e.
Luke 18. e.

Passion.

+ Then came to him the mother of Zebedee's children with her sons, worshipping him, and desiring a certain thing of him. And he said unto her: what
wilt thou have? She said unto him: Grant that these my two sons may sit, the
one on thy right hand, and the other on thy left hand in thy kingdom.

Mark 10. e.

Mother of Zebedee's children.

Jesus answered and said: Ye wot not what ye ask. Are ye able to drink of the
cup that I shall drink of, and to be baptised with the baptism that I shall be
baptised with? They answered to him, that we are. And he said unto them: Ye
shall drink of my cup, and shall be baptised with the baptism that I shall be
baptised with. But to sit on my right hand and on my left hand, is not mine to
give: but to them for whom it is prepared of my father. ⊢

D   And when the ten heard this, they disdained at the two brethren: But Jesus
called them unto him and said: Ye know that the lords of the gentiles have
domination over them. And they that are great, exercise power over them. It
shall not be so among you. But whosoever will be great among you, let him be
your minister: and whosoever will be chief, let him be your servant, even as the
son of man came, not to be ministered unto, but to minister, and to give his life
for the redemption of many. ⊢

Mark 10. g.
Luke 20. c.

Great.

And as they departed from Jericho, much people followed him. and behold
two blind men sitting by the wayside, when they heard Jesus pass by, cried
saying: Thou Lord the son of David have mercy on us. And the people rebuked

Jericho.
Mark 10. a.
Luke 18. c.

Two blind.

47

them, because they should hold their peace. But they cried the more, saying: have mercy on us thou Lord which art the son of David. Then Jesus stood still, and called them, and said: what will ye that I should do to you? They said to him: Lord that our eyes may be opened. Jesus had compassion on them, and touched their eyes. And immediately their eyes received sight. And they followed him.

CHAPTER TWENTY-ONE

Bethphage.

Mark 11. a.
Luke 19.

An ass and a colt.

Isa. 62. c.
Zech. 9. b.
John 12. b.

+ When they drew nigh unto Jerusalem, and were come to Bethphage, unto   **A** mount Olivet: then sent Jesus two of his disciples, saying to them. Go into the town that lieth over against you, and anon ye shall find an ass bound, and her colt with her: loose them and bring them unto me. And if any man say ought unto you, say ye that the lord hath need of them: and straight way he will let them go. All this was done, to fulfil that which was spoken by the prophet, saying: Tell ye the daughter of Sion: behold thy king cometh unto thee, meek, and sitting upon an ass and a colt, the foal of an ass used to the yoke. The disciples went and did as Jesus commanded them, and brought the ass and the colt, and put on them their clothes, and set him thereon. And many of the people spread their garments in the way. Other cut down branches from the trees, and strawed them in the way. Moreover the people that went before, and they also that came after, cried saying: Hosanna to the son of David. Blessed be he that cometh in the name of the Lord, Hosanna in the highest. ⊢

Hosanna.

Psa. 118. d.

Mark 11. b.
Luke 19. g.

Buyers and sellers.

Isa. 56. c.

Jer. 7. b.

And when he was come into Jerusalem, all the city was moved saying: who is this? And the people said: this is Jesus the Prophet of Nazareth a city of Galilee. And Jesus went in to the temple of God, and cast out all them that sold and bought in the temple, and overthrew the tables of the money-changers, and the seats of them that sold doves, and said to them: It is written, my house shall be called the house of prayer. But ye have made it a den of thieves. And the blind and the halt came to him in the temple, and he healed them.

Psa. 8. b.
Mark 11. b.

When the chief priests and scribes saw the marvels that he did, and the   **B** children crying in the temple and saying, Hosanna to the son of David, they disdained, and said unto him: hearest thou what these say? Jesus said unto them yea: have ye never read, of the mouth of babes and sucklings thou hast ordained praise? And he left them, and went out of the city unto Bethany, and had his abiding there. ⊢

Fig tree.

Mark 11. c.

In the morning as he returned into the city again, he hungered, and spied a fig tree in the way, and came to it, and found nothing thereon, but leaves only, and said to it, never fruit grow on thee henceforward. And anon the fig tree withered away. And when his disciples saw that, they marvelled saying: How soon is the fig tree withered away? Jesus answered, and said unto them: Verily I say unto you, if ye shall have faith and shall not doubt, ye shall not only do that which I have done to the fig tree: but also if ye shall say unto this mountain,   **C** take thyself away, and cast thyself into the sea, it shall be done. And whatsoever ye shall ask in prayer (if ye believe) ye shall receive it.

+ And when he was come into the temple, the chief priests and the elders of the people came unto him as he was teaching, and said: By what authority doest thou these things? and who gave thee this power? Jesus answered, and said unto them: I also will ask of you a certain question, which if ye assoil me, I in like wise will tell you by what authority I do these things. The baptism of John: whence was it? from heaven or of men? Then they reasoned among themselves saying: if we shall say from heaven, he will say unto us: why did ye not then believe him? But and if we shall say of men, then fear we the people. For all men held John as a prophet. And they answered Jesus and said: we cannot tell. And he likewise said unto them: neither tell I you by what authority I do these things. ⊦

Mark 11. d.
Luke 20. a.

Baptism of John, whence.

What say ye to this? + A certain man had two sons, and came to the elder and said: son go and work today in my vineyard. He answered and said, I will not: but afterward repented and went. Then came he to the second, and said likewise. And he answered and said: I will sir: yet went not. Whether of them twain did the will of the father? And they said unto him: the first. Jesus said unto them: verily I say unto you, that the publicans and the harlots shall come into the kingdom of God before you. For John came unto you in the way of righteousness, and ye believed him not. But the publicans and the harlots believed him. And yet ye (though ye saw it) were not yet moved with repentance, that ye might afterward have believed him. ⊦

Two sons.

Publicans.

Harlots.

D + Hearken another similitude. There was a certain householder, which planted a vineyard, and hedged it round about, and made a wine-press in it, and built a tower, and let it out to husbandmen, and went in to a strange country. And when the time of the fruit drew near, he sent his servants to the husbandmen, to receive the fruits of it. And the husbandmen caught his servants and beat one, killed another, and stoned another. Again, he sent other servants, more than the first: and they served them likewise. But last of all, he sent unto them his own son saying: they will fear my son. But when the husbandmen saw the son, they said among themselves: This is the heir: come, let us kill him, and let us take his inheritance to ourselves. And they caught him and thrust him out of the vineyard, and slew him. When the lord of the vineyard cometh, what will he do with those husbandmen? They said unto him: he will cruelly destroy those evil persons, and will let out his vineyard unto other husbandmen which shall deliver him the fruit at times convenient.

Mark 12. a.
Luke 20. b.
Isa. 5. c.
Jer. 2. d.

Vineyard that is let out hire.

Jesus said unto them: did ye never read in the scriptures? The stone which the builders refused the same is set in the principal part of the corner: this was the lord's doing, and it is marvellous in our eyes. Therefore say I unto you, the kingdom of God shall be taken from you, and shall be given to the gentiles, which shall bring forth the fruits of it. And whosoever shall fall on this stone, he shall be broken, but on whosoever it shall fall upon, it will grind him to powder. And when the chief priests and Pharisees heard these similitudes, they

Psa. 118. d.
Acts. 4. b.
1 Pet. 2. a.
Rom. 9. a.

Isa. 78. d.

perceived that he spake of them. And they went about to lay hands on him, but they feared the people, because they took him as a prophet. ⊢

CHAPTER TWENTY-TWO

Luke 14. d.
Rev. 19. b.

And Jesus answered and spake unto them again, in similitudes saying. + The kingdom of heaven is like unto a certain king, which married his son, and sent forth his servants, to call them that were bid to the wedding, and they would not come. Again he sent forth other servants, saying: Tell them which are bidden: behold I have prepared my dinner, mine oxen and my fatlings are killed, and all things are ready, come unto the marriage. But they made light of it, and went their ways: one to his farm place, another about his merchandise, the remnant took his servants and intreated them ungodly and slew them. When the king heard that, he was wroth, and sent forth his warriors and destroyed those murderers, and burnt up their city.

Marriage.

A

Then said he to his servants: the wedding was prepared. But they which were bidden, were not worthy. Go ye therefore out into the highways, and as many as ye find, bid them to the marriage. The servants went out into the highways, and gathered together as many as they could find, both good and bad, and the wedding was furnished with guests. Then the king came in, to visit the guests, and spied there a man which had not on a wedding garment, and said unto him: friend, how fortuned it that thou camest in hither and hast not on a wedding garment? And he was even speechless. Then said the king to his ministers: take and bind him hand and foot, and cast him into utter darkness, there shall be weeping and gnashing of teeth. For many are called and few be chosen. ⊢

Wedding garment.

Many are called.

B

+ Then went the Pharisees and took counsel how they might tangle him in his words. And they sent unto him their disciples with Herod's servants saying: Master, we know that thou art true, and teachest the way of God truly, neither carest for any man, for thou considerest not men's estate. Tell us therefore: how thinkest thou? Is it lawful to give tribute unto Caesar or not? Jesus perceived their wickedness, and said: Why tempt ye me, ye hypocrites? Let me see the tribute money. And they took him a penny★. And he said unto them: whose is this image and superscription? They said unto him: Caesar's. Then said he unto them: Give therefore to Caesar, that which is Caesar's: and give unto God, that which is God's. ⊢ When they heard that, they marvelled, and left him and went their way.

Mark 7. d.
Luke 20. d.

Tribute to Caesar.

★ A penny is ever taken for that the Jews call a sickle, and is worth 10 pence sterling.

The same day the Sadducees came to him (which say that there is no resurrection) and asked him saying: Master, Moses bade, if a man die having no children, that the brother marry his wife, and raise up seed unto his brother. There were with us seven brethren, and the first married and deceased without issue, and left his wife unto his brother. Like wise the second and the third, unto the seventh. Last of all the woman died also. Now in the resurrection, whose wife shall she be of the seven? For all had her. Jesus answered and said unto them: ye are deceived, and understand not the scriptures, nor yet the

Mark. 12.
Luke 20. d.
Acts 24.
Deut. 25.

Sadducees.

C

power of God. For in the resurrection they neither marry nor are married: but are as the angels of God in heaven.

As touching the resurrection of the dead: have ye not read what is said unto you of God, which sayeth: I am Abraham's God, and Isaac's God, and the God of Jacob? God is not the God of the dead: but of the living. And when the people heard that, they were astonied at his doctrine.

D + When the Pharisees had heard, how that he had put the Sadducees to silence, they drew together, and one of them which was a doctor of law, asked a question tempting him and saying: Master, which is the chief commandment in the law? Jesus said unto him: love the Lord thy God with all thine heart, with all thy soul, and with all thy mind. This is the first and the chief commandment. And there is another like unto this. Love thine neighbour as thyself. In these two commandments hang all the law and the prophets.

While the Pharisees were gathered together, Jesus asked them saying: what think ye of Christ? Whose son is he? They said unto him: the son of David. He said unto them: how then doth David in spirit, call him Lord saying: The Lord said to my Lord, sit on my right hand: till I make thine enemies thy footstool. If David call him Lord: how is he then his son? And none could answer him again one word: neither durst any from that day forth, ask him any more questions. ⊢

CHAPTER TWENTY-THREE

A + Then spake Jesus to the people, and to his disciples saying: The scribes and the Pharisees sit in Moses* seat. All therefore whatsoever they bid you observe, that observe and do: but after their works do not: For they say, and do not. Yea, and they bind heavy burdens and grievous to be borne, and lay them on men's shoulders: but they themselves will not heave at them with one of their fingers. All their works they do, for to be seen of men. They set abroad their phylacteries, and make large borders on their garments, and love to sit uppermost at feasts, and to have the chief seats in the synagogues, and greetings in the markets, and to be called of men Rabbi.

B But ye shall not suffer yourselves to be called Rabbi. For one is your master, that is to wit Christ, and all ye are brethren. And call no man your father upon the earth, for there is but one your father, and he is in heaven. Be not called masters, for there is but one your master, and he is Christ. He that is greatest among you, shall be your servant. But whosoever exalteth himself, shall be brought low. And he that humbleth himself, shall be exalted.

Woe be unto you scribes and Pharisees, hypocrites, for ye shut up the kingdom of heaven before men: ye yourselves go not in, neither suffer ye them that come, to enter in.

Woe be unto you scribes and Pharisees, hypocrites: ye devour widows' houses, and that under a colour of praying long prayers: wherefore ye shall receive greater damnation.

Woe be unto you scribes and Pharisees, hypocrites, which compass sea and

Marginal notes:

Exod. 3. b.
Resurrection.

Mark 7. c.
Luke 12. e.

Chief commandment.

Deut. 6. a.

Mark 12. d.
Luke 20. d.

David's son.

Psa. 110. a.

* Moses' seat is Moses' doctrine, as Christ's seat is Christ's doctrine.

Heavy burden.
Luke 11. g.
Phylacteries.
Chief seats.

Greetings.

Rabbi.

Great.
Exalt.
The kingdom is shut.

Widows' houses.

51

land, to bring one in to your belief: and when he is brought, ye make him two-fold more the child of hell, than ye yourselves are.

Temple.

Woe be unto you blind guides, which say whosoever swear by the temple, it is nothing: but whosoever swear by the gold of the temple, he offendeth. Ye fools and blind: whether is greater, the gold, or the temple that sanctifieth the

Altar.

gold? And whosoever sweareth by the altar, it is nothing: but whosoever sweareth by the offering that lieth on the altar, offendeth. Ye fools and blind: whether is greater the offering, or the altar which sanctifieth the offering? Whosoever therefore sweareth by the altar, sweareth by it, and by all that thereon is. And whosoever sweareth by the temple, sweareth by it, and by him that dwelleth therein. And he that sweareth by heaven, sweareth by the seat of God and by him that sitteth thereon.

Mint.
Annise.
Judgement and mercy.
Luke 11. f.
Blind guides.

Woe be to you scribes and Pharisees, hypocrites, which tithe mint, annise　　**C** and cummin, and leave the weightier matters of the law undone: judgement, mercy, and faith. These ought ye to have done, and not to have left the other undone. Ye blind guides which strain out a gnat and swallow a camel.

Inside.

Woe be to you scribes and Pharisees, hypocrites, which make clean the outer side of the cup, and of the platter: but within they are full of bribery and excess. Thou blind Pharisee, cleanse first, the outside of the cup and platter, that the inside of them may be clean also.[†]

Painted sépulchres.

Woe be to you scribes and Pharisees hypocrites, for ye are like unto painted tombs which appear beautiful outward: but are within full of dead bones and of all filthiness. So are ye, for outward ye appear righteous unto men, when within, ye are full of hypocrisy and iniquity.

Ye build the tombs.

Woe be unto you scribes and Pharisees hypocrites: ye build the tombs of the　　**D** prophets, and garnish the sepulchres of the righteous, and say: If we had been in the days of our fathers, we would not have been partners with them in the blood of the prophets. So then ye be witnesses unto yourselves, that ye are the children of them which killed the prophets. Fulfil ye likewise the measure of your fathers. Ye serpents and generation of vipers, how should ye scape the damnation of hell?

2 Chr. 24. f.

+ Wherefore, behold I send unto you, prophets, wise men and scribes, and of them ye shall kill and crucify: and of them ye shall scourge in your synagogues, and persecute from city to city, that upon you may come all the righteous blood that was shed upon the earth, from the blood of righteous Abel, unto the blood of Zacharias the son of Barachias, whom ye slew between the temple and

Innocent blood.

the altar. Verily I say unto you, all these things shall light upon this generation. Jerusalem, Jerusalem which killest prophets, and stonest them which are sent to thee: how often would I have gathered thy children together, as the hen

Luke 13. g.
2 Esdras 1. e.

gathereth her chickens under her wings, but ye would not: Behold your habitation shall be left unto you desolate. For I say to you, ye shall not see me henceforth, till that ye say: blessed is he that cometh in the name of the Lord. ⱶ

<hr>

[†] For Tyndale's correction, see above, p. 12.

CHAPTER TWENTY-FOUR

And Jesus went out and departed from the temple: and his disciples came to him, for to shew him the building of the temple. Jesus said unto them: see ye not all these things? Verily I say unto you: there shall not be here left one stone upon another, that shall not be cast down.

Mark 13. a.

Destruction of the temple.

And as he sat upon the mount Olivet, his disciples came unto him secretly saying. Tell us when these things shall be? and what sign shall be of thy coming, and of the end of the world? And Jesus answered, and said unto them: take heed that no man deceive you. For many shall come in my name saying: I am Christ, and shall deceive many.

Luke 19. g.

Eph. 5. b.
Col. 2. d.

Antichrist.

Ye shall hear of wars, and of the fame of wars: but see that ye be not troubled. For all these things must come to pass, but the end is not yet. For nation shall rise against nation, and realm against realm: and there shall be pestilence, hunger and earthquakes in all quarters. All these are the beginning of sorrows.

Then shall they put you to trouble, and shall kill you: and ye shall be hated of all nations for my name's sake. And then shall many be offended, and shall betray one another, and shall hate one the other. And many false prophets shall arise, and shall deceive many. And because iniquity shall have the upper hand, the love of many shall abate. But he that endureth to the end, the same shall be safe. And this glad tidings of the kingdom shall be preached in all the world, for a witness unto all nations: and then shall the end come.

John 15. c.
and 16. a.

False prophets.

When ye therefore shall see the abomination that betokeneth desolation, spoken of by Daniel the prophet, stand in the holy place: let him that readeth it, understand it. Then let them which be in Jewry, fly into the mountains. And let him which is on the house-top, not come down to fetch anything out of his house. Neither let him which is in the field, return back to fetch his clothes. Woe be in those days to them that are with child, and to them that give suck. But pray that your flight be not in the winter, neither on the sabbath day. For then shall be great tribulation, such as was not from the beginning of the world to this time, nor shall be. Yea and except those days should be shortened, there should no flesh be saved: but for the chosen's sake, those days shall be shortened.

Dan. 9.

Winter.

Elect.

Then if any man shall say unto you: lo, here is Christ, or there is Christ: believe it not. For there shall arise false christs, and false prophets, and shall do great miracles and wonders. Insomuch that if it were possible, the very elect should be deceived. Take heed, I have told you before. Wherefore if they shall say unto you: behold he is in the desert, go not forth: behold he is in the secret places, believe not. For as the lightning cometh out of the east and shineth unto the west: so shall the coming of the son of man be. For wheresoever a dead carcase is, even thither will the eagles resort.

Mark 13.
Luke 18. c.

Immediately after the tribulations of those days, shall the sun be darkened: and the moon shall not give her light, and the stars shall fall from heaven, and the powers of heaven shall move. And then shall appear the sign of the son of

Mark 13. c.
Luke 21. e.
Ezek. 32. b.
Isa. 13.
Joel 3. c.

man in heaven. And then shall all the kindreds of the earth mourn, and they shall see the son of man come in the clouds of heaven with power and great glory. And he shall send his angels with the great voice of a trumpet, and they shall gather together his chosen, from the four winds, and from the one end of the world to the other.

Fig tree.

Mark 13.
Luke 12.

Learn a similitude of the fig tree: when his branches are yet tender and his leaves sprung, ye know that summer is nigh. So likewise ye, when ye see all these things, be ye sure that it is near, even at the doors. Verily I say unto you, that this generation shall not pass till all these be fulfilled. Heaven and earth shall perish: but my words shall abide. But of that day and hour knoweth no man, no not the angels of heaven, but my father only.

Gen. 6. b.

Noe.

Luke 17. g.

As the time of Noe was, so likewise shall the coming of the son of man be. For as in the days before the flood, they did eat and drink, marry and were married, even unto the day that Noe entered in to the ship, and knew of nothing, till the flood came and took them all away: So shall also the coming of the son of man be. Then two shall be in the fields, the one shall be received, and the other shall be refused, two shall be grinding at the mill: the one shall be received, and the other shall be refused.

Mark 13. e.

Wake.
Luke 13. c.

Faithful servant.

Evil servant.

Wake therefore, because ye know not what hour your master will come. Of [
this be sure, that if the good man of the house knew what hour the thief would come: he would surely watch, and not suffer his house to be broken up. Therefore be ye also ready, for in the hour ye think he would not, will the son of man come. If there be any faithful servant and wise, whom his master hath made ruler over his household to give them meat in season covenient, happy is that servant whom his master (when he cometh) shall find so doing. Verily I say unto you, he shall make him ruler over all his goods. But and if that evil servant shall say in his heart, my master will defer his coming, and begin to smite his fellows, yea and to eat and to drink with the drunken: that servant's master will come in a day when he looketh not for him, and in an hour that he is not ware of, and will divide him, and give him his reward with hypocrites. There shall be weeping and gnashing of teeth.

CHAPTER TWENTY-FIVE

Virgins.

Then the kingdom of heaven shall be likened unto ten virgins, which took their lamps, and went to meet the bridegroom: five of them were foolish, and five were wise. The foolish took their lamps, but took none oil with them. But the wise took oil with them in their vessels with their lamps also. While the bridegroom tarried, all slumbered and slept. And even at midnight, there was a cry made: behold, the bridegroom cometh, go out against him. Then all those virgins arose, and prepared their lamps. And the foolish said to the wise: give us of your oil, for our lamps go out; but the wise answered saying: Not so, lest there be not enough for us and you: but go rather to them that sell, and buy for yourselves. And while they went to buy, the bridegroom came: and they that were ready, went in with him to the wedding, and the gate was shut up:

Afterwards came also the other virgins saying: master master, open to us. But he answered and said: verily I say unto you: I know not you. Watch therefore: for ye know neither the day not yet the hour, when the son of man shall come.

B   + Likewise as a certain man ready to take his journey to a strange country, called his servants and delivered to them his goods. And unto one he gave five talents, to another two and to another one: to every man after his ability, and straightway departed. Then he that had received the five talents, went and bestowed them, and won other five talents. Likewise he that received two gained other two. But he that received the one, went and digged a pit in the earth and hid his master's money. After a long season the lord of those servants came and reckoned with them. Then came he that had received five talents, and brought other five talents saying: master, thou deliveredst unto me five talents: behold I have gained with them five talents more. Then his master said unto him: well good servant and faithful. Thou hast been faithful in little, I will make thee ruler over much: enter in into thy master's joy. Also he that received two talents, came and said: master, thou deliveredest unto me two talents: behold, I have won two other talents with them. And his master said unto him, well good servant and faithful. Thou hast been faithful in little, I will make thee ruler over much: go in into thy master's joy. ⊢

C   Then he which had received the one talent, came, and said: master, I considered that thou wast an hard man, which reapest where thou sowedst not, and gatherest where thou strawedst not, and was therefore afraid, and went and hid thy talent in the earth: Behold, thou hast thine own. His master answered and said unto him: thou evil servant and slothful, thou knewest that I reap where I sowed not, and gather where I strawed not: thou oughtest therefore to have had my money to the changers, and then at my coming should I have received mine own with vantage. Take therefore the talent from him, and give it unto him which hath ten talents. For unto every man that hath shall be given, and he shall have abundance: and from him that hath not, shall be taken away, even that he hath. And cast that unprofitable servant into outer darkness: there shall be weeping and gnashing of teeth.

+ When the son of man cometh in his glory, and all the holy angels with him, then shall he sit upon the seat of his glory, and before him shall be gathered all nations. And he shall separate them one from another, as a shepherd divideth the sheep from the goats. And he shall set the sheep on his right hand, and the goats on the left. Then shall the king say to them on his right hand: Come ye blessed children of my father, inherit ye the kingdom prepared for you from the beginning of the world. For I was an-hungered, and ye gave me meat. I thirsted, and ye gave me drink. I was harbourless, and ye lodged me. I was naked and ye clothed me. I was sick and ye visited me. I was in prison and ye came unto me. Then shall the righteous answer him saying master, when saw we thee an-hungered, and fed thee? or a-thirst, and gave thee drink? when saw we thee harbourless, and lodged thee? or naked and clothed thee? or when saw we thee sick or in prison, and came unto thee? And the king shall answer and say unto them: verily I say unto you: inasmuch as ye have

Watch.

Luke 19. b.

Talents.

Mark 4. c.
Luke 8. c.
and 19. d.

Covenant.

The Judgement.

Sheep.
Goats.

Isa. 58. b.
Ezek. 18. b.

Eccl. 7. d.

done it unto one of the least of these my brethren, ye have done it to me.

Then shall the king say unto them that shall be on the left hand: depart from **D** me ye cursed, into everlasting fire, which is prepared for the devil and his angels. For I was an-hungered, and ye gave me no meat. I thirsted, and ye gave me no drink. I was harbourless, and ye lodged me not. I was naked, and ye clothed me not. I was sick and in prison, and ye visited me not.

Then shall they also answer him saying: master when saw we thee an-hungered, or a-thirst, or harbourless, or naked, or sick, or in prison, and did not minister unto thee? Then shall he answer them and say: Verily I say unto you, inasmuch as ye did it not to one of the least of these, ye did it not to me.

And these shall go into everlasting pain: And the righteous into life eternal. ⊦

Psa. 6. c.

Luke 13. f.

John 5. c.

Covenant.

CHAPTER TWENTY-SIX

The passion.

And it came to pass, when Jesus had finished all these sayings, he said unto his **A** disciples: + Ye know that after two days shall be Easter, and the son of man shall be delivered to be crucified.

Mark 14. a.
Luke 22. a.

Then assembled together the chief priests and the scribes and the elders of the people to the palace of the high priest, called Caiaphas, and held a counsel, how they might take Jesus by subtlety and kill him. But they said, not on the holy day, lest any uproar arise among the people.

Caiaphas.

When Jesus was in Bethany, in the house of Simon the leper, there came unto him a woman, which had an alabaster box of precious ointment, and poured it on his head, as he sat at the board. When his disciples saw that, they had indignation saying: what needed this waste? This ointment might have been well sold, and given to the poor. When Jesus understood that, he said unto them: why trouble ye the woman? She hath wrought a good work upon me. For ye shall have poor folk always with you: but me shall ye not have always. And in that she cast this ointment on my body, she did it to bury me withal. Verily I say unto you, wheresoever this gospel shall be preached throughout all the world, there shall also this that she hath done be told for a memorial of her.

He is anointed.

John 12. a.
Mark 14. a.

Then one of the twelve called Judas Iscariot, went unto the chief priests, **B** and said: what will ye give me, and I will deliver him unto you? And they appointed unto him thirty pieces of silver. And from that time he sought opportunity to betray him.

He is sold.

Mark 14. b.
Luke 22. a.

The first day of sweet bread the disciples came to Jesus saying unto him: where wilt thou that we prepare for thee to eat the paschal lamb? And he said: Go into the city, unto such a man, and say to him: the master saith, my time is at hand, I will keep mine Easter at thy house with my disciples. And the disciples did as Jesus had appointed them, and made ready the Easter lamb.

Mark 14. b.
Luke 22. a.

When the even was come, he sat down with the twelve. And as they did eat, he said: Verily I say unto you, that one of you shall betray me. And they were exceeding sorrowful, and began every one of them to say unto him: is it I master? He answered and said: he that dippeth his hand with me in the dish, the same shall betray me. The son of man goeth as it is written of him: but woe be

Mark 14.
Luke 22. b.
John 13. b.

Psa. 41. c.

to that man, by whom the son of man shall be betrayed. It had been good for that man, if he had never been born.

Then Judas which betrayed him, answered and said: is it I master? He said unto him: thou hast said. As they did eat, Jesus took bread and gave thanks, brake it, and gave it to the disciples, and said: Take, eat, this is my body. And he took the cup, and thanked, and gave it them, saying: drink of it every one. For this is my blood of the new testament, that shall be shed for many, for the remission of sins. I say unto you: I will not drink henceforth of this fruit of the vine tree, until that day, when I shall drink it new with you in my father's kingdom.

The institution of the sacrament.

1 Cor. 11. c.
Luke 22.

And when they had said grace, they went out into mount Olivet. Then said Jesus unto them: all ye shall be offended by me this night. For it is written: I will smite the shepherd, and the sheep of the flock shall be scattered abroad. But after I am risen again, I will go before you into Galilee. Peter answered, and said unto him: though all men should be offended by thee, yet would I never be offended. Jesus said unto him, Verily I say unto thee, that this same night before the cock crow thou shalt deny me thrice. Peter said unto him: If I should die with thee, yet would I not deny thee. Likewise also said all the disciples.

Mark 14. c.
Luke 22. b..
John 18. a.
Zech. 13. c.
Mark 14. e.
and 15. b.

Mark 14. c.

Luke 22. b.
John 13. d.

Then went Jesus with them into a place which is called Gethsemane, and said unto the disciples, sit ye here, while I go and pray yonder. And he took with him Peter and the two sons of Zebedee, and began to wax sorrowful and to be in an agony. Then said Jesus unto them: my soul is heavy even unto the death. Tarry ye here and watch with me. And he went a little apart, and fell flat on his face, and prayed saying: O my father, if it be possible, let this cup pass from me: nevertheless, not as I will, but as thou wilt. And he came unto the disciples, and found them asleep, and said to Peter: what, could ye not watch with me one hour? Watch and pray, that ye fall not into temptation. The spirit is willing, but the flesh is weak.

Mark 14. d.
Luke 22. d.

He armeth himself against the passion.

He went away once more, and prayed, saying: O my father, if this cup cannot pass away from me, but that I drink of it, thy will be fulfilled. And he came, and found them asleep again. For their eyes were heavy. And he left them and went again and prayed the third time saying the same words. Then came he to his disciples and said unto them: Sleep henceforth and take your rest. Take heed, the hour is at hand, and the son of man shall be betrayed into the hands of sinners. Rise, let us be going: behold, he is at hand that shall betray me. While he yet spake: lo, Judas one of the twelve came and with him a great multitude with swords and staves, sent from the chief priests and elders of the people. And he that betrayed him, had given them a token, saying: whosoever I kiss, that same is he, lay hands on him. And forthwithal he came to Jesus, and said: hail master, and kissed him. And Jesus said unto him: friend, wherefore art thou come? Then came they and laid hands on Jesus and took him.

Mark 14. c.
Luke 22. e.
John 18. b.

He is betrayed.

And behold, one of them which were with Jesus, stretched out his hand and drew his sword, and struck a servant of the high priest, and smote off his ear. Then said Jesus unto him: put up thy sword into his sheath. For all that lay

Gen. 9. a.
Rev. 13. c.

Isa. 54. c.

Lam. 4. d.

Mark 14. f.
Luke 22. g.
John 8. e.

He is taken.

He is falsely accused.

John 2. d.

Mark 14.
Luke 22. f.
John 18. c.

Peter denieth.

Mark 15. a.
Luke 24. a.

He is delivered to
Pilate.

Judas.

hand on the sword, shall perish with the sword. Either thinkest thou that I cannot now pray to my father, and he shall give me more than twelve legions of angels? But how then should the scriptures be fulfilled? For so must it be.

The same time said Jesus to the multitude: ye be come out as it were unto a thief, with swords and staves for to take me. I sat daily teaching in the temple among you and ye took me not. All this was done that the scriptures of the prophets might be fulfilled. Then all the disciples forsook him and fled. And they took Jesus and led him to Caiaphas the high priest, where the scribes and the elders where assembled. And Peter followed him afar off, unto the high priest's place: and went in, and sat with the servants, to see the end.

The chief priests and the elders, and all the council, sought false witness against Jesus, for to put him to death, but found none: insomuch that when many false witnesses came, yet found they none. At the last came two false witnesses and said: This fellow said: I can destroy the temple of God, and build it again in three days.

And the chief priest arose, and said to him: answerest thou nothing? How is it that these bear witness against thee? But Jesus held his peace: And the chief priest answered, and said to him: I charge thee in the name of the living God, that thou tell us, whether thou be Christ the son of God. Jesus said to him: thou hast said. Nevertheless I say unto you, hereafter shall ye see the son of man sitting on the right hand of power, and come in the clouds of the sky.

Then the high priest rent his clothes saying: He hath blasphemed: what need we of any more witnesses? Behold now ye have heard his blasphemy: what think ye? They answered and said: he is worthy to die. Then spat they in his face, and buffeted him with fists. And other smote him with the palm of their hands on the face, saying: tell us thou Christ, who is he that smote thee?

Peter sat without in the palace. And a damsel came to him saying: Thou also wast with Jesus of Galilee: but he denied before them all saying: I wot not what thou sayest. When he was gone out into the porch, another wench saw him, and said unto them that were there: This fellow was also with Jesus of Nazareth. And again he denied with an oath that he knew the man. And after a while came unto him they that stood by, and said unto Peter: surely thou art even one of them, for thy speech betrayeth thee. Then began he to curse and to swear, that he knew not the man. And immediately the cock crew. And Peter remembered the words of Jesus which said unto him: before the cock crow, thou shalt deny me thrice: and went out at the doors and wept bitterly.

CHAPTER TWENTY-SEVEN

When the morning was come, all the chief priests and the elders of the people held a counsel against Jesus, to put him to death, and brought him bound and delivered him unto Pontius Pilate the debite.

Then when Judas which betrayed him, saw that he was condemned, he repented himself, and brought again the thirty plates of silver to the chief priests and elders saying: I have sinned betraying the innocent blood. And they said: what is that to us? See thou to that. And he cast down the silver plates in the temple and departed, and went and hung himself.

And the chief priest took the silver plates and said: it is not lawful for to put them in to the treasury, because it is the price of blood. And they took counsel, and bought with them a potter's field to bury strangers in. Wherefore that field is called the field of blood, until this day. Then was fulfilled, that which was spoken by Jeremy the prophet saying: and they took thirty silver plates, the price of him that was valued, whom they bought of the children of Israel, and they gave them for the potter's field, as the Lord appointed me.

Jesus stood before the debite: and the debite asked him saying: Art thou the king of the Jews? Jesus said unto him: Thou sayest; and when he was accused of the chief priests and elders, he answered nothing. Then said Pilate unto him: hearest thou not how many things they lay against thee? And he answered him never a word: insomuch that the debite marvelled greatly.

At that feast, the debite was wont to deliver unto the people a prisoner, whom they would desire. He had then a notable prisoner, called Barabbas. And when they were gathered together, Pilate said unto them: whether will ye that I give loose unto you, Barabbas or Jesus which is called Christ? For he knew well, that for envy they had delivered him.

When he was set down to give judgement, his wife sent to him saying: have thou nothing to do with that just man. For I have suffered many things this day in a dream about him.

But the chief priests and the elders had persuaded the people, that they should ask Barabbas, and should destroy Jesus. Then the debite answered and said unto them: whether of the twain will ye that I let loose unto you? And they said, Barabbas. Pilate said unto them: what shall I do then with Jesus which is called Christ? They all said to him: let him be crucified. Then said the debite: what evil hath he done? And they cried the more saying: let him be crucified.

When Pilate saw that he prevailed nothing, but that more business was made, he took water and washed his hands before the people saying: I am innocent of the blood of this just person*, and that ye shall see. Then answered all the people and said: his blood be on us, and on our children. Then let he Barabbas loose unto them, and scourged Jesus and delivered him to be crucified.

Then the soldiers of the debite took Jesus unto the common hall, and gathered unto him all the company. And they stripped him and put on him a purple robe, and plaited a crown of thorns and put upon his head, and a reed in his right hand: and bowed their knees before him, and mocked him, saying: hail king of the Jews: and spitted upon him, and took the reed and smote him on the head.

And when they had mocked him, they took the robe off him again, and put his own raiment on him, and led him away to crucify him. And as they came out, they found a man of Cyrene, named Simon: him they compelled to bear his cross. And when they came to the place, called Golgotha (that is to say, a

Acts. i.

Zech. 11. e.

Mark 15. a.
Luke 23. a.

He holdeth his peace.

Barabbas.

Mark 15. b.
Luke 23. b.
John 18. g.
and 19. c.

* His judge confesseth him an innocent.

He is scourged.

Mark 15. b.
John 19. a.

He is crowned.

Mark 15. b.
Luke 23. d.

He drinketh vinegar
and gall.
John 19.

place of dead men's skulls) they gave him vinegar to drink mingled with gall. And when he had tasted thereof, he would not drink.

He is crucified.

When they had crucified him, they parted his garments, and did cast lots: to **B** fulfil that was spoken by the prophet: They divided my garments among them: and upon my vesture did cast lots. And they sat and watched him there. And they set up over his head the cause of his death written: This is Jesus the king of the Jews. And there were two thieves crucified with him, one on the right hand, and another on the left.

He is railed on.

They that passed by, reviled him wagging their heads and saying: Thou that destroyest the temple of God and buildest it in three days, save thyself. If thou be the son of God, come down from the cross. Likewise also the high priests mocking him with the scribes and elders said: He saved other, himself he cannot save. If he be the king of Israel, let him now come down from the cross, and we will believe him. He trusted in God, let him deliver him now, if he will have him: for he said, I am the son of God. That same also the thieves which were crucified with him, cast in his teeth.

From the sixth hour was there darkness over all the land unto the ninth hour. **F** And about the ninth hour Jesus cried with a loud voice, saying: Eli Eli lama

Psa. 22. a.

sabathani. That is to say, my God, my God, why hast thou forsaken me? Some of them that stood there, when they heard that, said: This man calleth for Elias. And straightway one of them ran and took a sponge and filled it full of vinegar, and put it on a reed, and gave him to drink. Other said, let be: let us see whether Elias will come and deliver him. Jesus cried again with a loud voice

He giveth up the ghost.

and yielded up the ghost.

The veil renteth.

And behold the veil of the temple did rent in twain from the top to the bottom, and the earth did quake, and the stones did rent, and graves did open:

Dead bodies arise.

and the bodies of many saints which slept, arose and came out of the graves after his resurrection, and came into the holy city, and appeared unto many.

When the centurion and they that were with him watching Jesus, saw the earthquake and those things which happened, they feared greatly saying, of a surety this was the son of God.

And many women were there, beholding him afar off, which followed Jesus from Galilee, ministering unto him. Among which was Mary Magdalene, and Mary the mother of James and Joses, and the mother of Zebedee's children.

Mark 15. d.
Luke 23. g.
John 19. g.

When the even was come, there came a rich man of Arimathæa named **C** Joseph, which same also was Jesus' disciple. He went to Pilate and begged the body of Jesus. Then Pilate commanded the body to be delivered. And Joseph

He is buried.

took the body, and wrapped it in a clean linen cloth, and put it in his new tomb, which he had hewn out, even in the rock, and rolled a great stone to the door of the sepulchre, and departed. And there was Mary Magdalene and the other Mary sitting over against the sepulchre. ⊢

The next day that followeth good friday, the high priests and Pharisees got themselves to Pilate and said: Sir, we remember, that this deceiver said while he was yet alive, after three days I will arise again. Command therefore that the

He is watched for rising
again.

sepulchre be made sure until the third day, lest peradventure his disciples come, and steal him away, and say unto the people, he is risen from death, and the last error be worse than the first. Pilate said unto them. Take watchmen: Go, and make it as sure as ye can. And they went and made the sepulchre sure with watchmen, and sealed the stone.

CHAPTER TWENTY-EIGHT

A   + The sabbath day at even which dawneth the morrow after the sabbath, Mary Magdalene and the other Mary came to see the sepulchre.

    Mark 16. b.
John 20. c.

And behold there was a great earthquake. For the angel of the lord descended from heaven: and came and rolled back the stone from the door, and sat upon it. His countenance was like lightning, and his raiment white as snow. And for fear of him the keepers were astonied, and became as dead men.

The angel answered, and said to the women, fear ye not. I know that ye seek Jesus which was crucified: he is not here: he is risen as he said. Come, and see the place where the Lord was put: and go quickly and tell his disciples that he is risen from death. And behold, he will go before you into Galilee, there ye shall see him. Lo I have told you. ⊢

+ And they departed quickly from the sepulchre with fear and great joy: and did run to bring his disciples word. And as they went to tell his disciples, behold, Jesus met them saying: All hail. And they came and held him by the feet and worshipped him. Then said Jesus unto them: be not afraid. Go and tell my brethren, that they go into Galilee, and there shall they see me.

C   When they were gone: behold, some of the keepers came in to the city, and shewed unto the high priests, all the things that were happened. And they gathered them together with the elders, and took counsel, and gave large money unto the soldiers saying: Say that his disciples came by night, and stole him away while ye slept. And if this come to the ruler's ears, we will pease him, and save you harmless. And they took the money and did as they were taught. And this saying is noised among the Jews unto this day. ⊢

D   + Then the eleven disciples went away into Galilee, into a mountain where Jesus had appointed them. And when they saw him, they worshipped him. But some of them doubted. And Jesus came and spake unto them saying: All power is given unto me in heaven, and in earth. Go therefore and teach all nations, baptising them in the name of the father, and the son, and the holy ghost: Teaching them to observe all things, whatsoever I commanded you. And lo I am with you always, even until the end of the world. ⊢

    Mark 16.

    All power.

Here endeth the Gospel of St Matthew.

THE GOSPEL OF ST MARK

1[1–21]

CHAPTER ONE +

Matt. 3. a. Luke 3. a. Mal. 3. a. Isa. 40. a. John 1. c.

The beginning of the gospel of Jesus Christ the son of God, as it is written A
in the prophets: behold I send my messenger before thy face, which shall prepare thy way before thee. The voice of a crier in the wilderness: prepare ye the way of the Lord, make his paths straight.

John baptised.

Matt. 3. a.

John did baptise in the wilderness, and preach the baptism of repentance, for the remission of sins. And all the land of Jewry and they of Jerusalem, went out unto him, and were all baptised of him in the river Jordan, confessing their sins.

Matt. 3. e. Luke 3. c. John 1. d.

John was clothed with camel's hair, and with a girdle of a skin about his loins. And he did eat locusts and wild honey, and preached saying: a stronger than I cometh after me, whose shoe latchet I am not worthy to stoop down and unloose. I have baptised you with water: but he shall baptise you with the holy ghost. ⊢

Jesus is baptised.

Matt. 3. d. Luke 3. d.

And it came to pass in those days, that Jesus came from Nazareth, a city of B
Galilee: and was baptised of John in Jordan. And as soon as he was come out of the water, John saw heaven open, and the holy ghost descending upon him, like a dove. And there came a voice from heaven: Thou art my dear son in whom I delight.

Jesus fasteth.

Matt. 4. a. Luke 5.

And immediately the spirit drave him into wilderness: and he was there in the wilderness forty days, and was tempted of Satan, and was with wild beasts. And the angels ministered unto him.

Matt. 4. b. Luke 4. e. John 4. f.

After John was taken, Jesus came into Galilee, preaching the gospel of the kingdom of God, and saying: the time is come, and the kingdom of God is at hand, repent and believe the gospel.

Matt. 4. c. Luke 5. a.

Simon. Andrew.

As he walked by the sea of Galilee, he saw Simon and Andrew his brother, casting nets into the sea, for they were fishers. And Jesus said unto them: follow me, and I will make you fishers of men. And straightway, they forsook their nets, and followed him.

James. John.

And when he had gone a little further thence, he saw James the son of Zebedee and John his brother, even as they were in the ship mending their nets. And anon he called them. And they left their father Zebedee in the ship with his hired servants, and went their way after him.

And they entered into Capernaum: and straightway on the sabbath days, he C entered into the synagogue and taught. And they marvelled at his learning. For he taught them as one that had power with him, and not as the scribes.

Matt. 8. d.
Luke 4. c.

And there was in their synagogue a man vexed with an unclean spirit, that cried saying: let be: what have we to do with thee thou Jesus of Nazareth? Art thou come to destroy us? I know thee what thou art, even that holy of God. And Jesus rebuked him saying: hold thy peace and come out of him. And the unclean spirit tare him, and cried with a loud voice, and came out of him. And they were all amazed, insomuch that they demanded one of another among themselves saying: what thing is this? what new doctrine is this? For he commandeth the foul spirits with power, and they obey him. And immediately his fame spread abroad throughout all the region bordering on Galilee.

The unclean spirit is cast out.

And forthwith, as soon as they were come out of the synagogue, they entered into the house of Simon and Andrew, with James and John. And Simon's mother-in-law lay sick of a fever. And anon they told him of her. And he came and took her by the hand and lifted her up: and the fever forsook her by and by: and she ministered unto them.

Matt. 8. b.
Luke 4. f.

Simon's mother-in-law.

D   And at even when the sun was down, they brought to him all that were diseased, and them that were possessed with devils. And all the city gathered together at the door, and he healed many that were sick of divers diseases. And he cast out many devils, and suffered not the devils to speak, because they knew him.

And in the morning very early, Jesus arose and went out into a solitary place, and there prayed. And Simon and they that were with him followed after him. And when they had found him, they said unto him: all men seek for thee. And he said unto them: let us go in to the next towns, that I may preach there also: for truly I came out for that purpose. And he preached in their synagogues, throughout all Galilee, and cast the devils out.

And there came a leper to him, beseeching him, and kneeled down unto him, and said to him: if thou wilt, thou canst make me clean. And Jesus had compassion on him, and put forth his hand, touched him, and said to him: I will, be thou clean. And as soon as he had spoken, immediately the leprosy departed from him, and was cleansed. And he charged him, and sent him away forthwith and said unto him: See thou say nothing to any man: but get thee hence and shew thyself to the priest, and offer for thy cleansing, those things which Moses commanded, for a testimonial unto them. But he (as soon as he was departed) began to tell many things, and to publish the deed: insomuch that Jesus could no more openly enter in to the city, but was without in desert places. And they came to him from every quarter.

A leper.

Matt. 8. a.
Luke 5. c.

CHAPTER TWO

A   After a few days, he entered into Capernaum again, and it was noised that he was in a house. And anon many gathered together, insomuch that now there was no room to receive them: no, not so much as about the door. And he preached the word unto them. And there came unto him that brought one sick

Matt. 9. a.
Luke 5. d.

Palsy.

of the palsy, borne of four men. And because they could not come nigh unto him for press, they uncovered the roof of the house where he was. And when they had broken it open, they let down the bed wherein the sick of the palsy lay. When Jesus saw their faith, he said to the sick of the palsy, son thy sins are forgiven thee.

And there were certain of the scribes sitting there, and reasoning in their **B** hearts: how doth this fellow so blaspheme? Who can forgiven sins, but God only? And immediately when Jesus perceived in his spirit, that they so reasoned in themselves, he said unto them: why think ye such things in your hearts? Whether is it easier to say to the sick of the palsy, thy sins are forgiven thee: or to say, arise take up thy bed, and walk? That ye may know that the son of man hath power in earth to forgive sins*, he spake unto the sick of the palsy: I say unto thee, arise and take up thy bed, and get thee hence into thine own house. And by and by he arose, took up the bed, and went forth before them all: insomuch that they were all amazed, and glorified God saying: we never saw it on this fashion.

And he went again unto the sea, and all the people resorted unto him, and he **C** taught them. And as Jesus passed by, he saw Levi the son of Alpheus, sit at the receipt of custom, and said unto him: follow me. And he arose and followed him. And it came to pass, as Jesus sat at meat in his house, many publicans and sinners sat at meat also with Jesus and his disciples. For there were many that followed him. And when the scribes and Pharisees saw him eat with publicans and sinners, they said unto his disciples: how is it, that he eateth and drinketh with publicans and sinners? When Jesus heard that, he said unto them, the whole have no need of the physician, but the sick. I came not to call the righteous, but the sinners to repentance.

And the disciples of John and the Pharisees did fast: and therefore came and said unto him, Why do the disciples of John and of the Pharisees fast, and thy disciples fast not? And Jesus said unto them: can the children of a wedding fast, while the bridegroom is with them? As long as they have the bridegroom with them, they cannot fast. But the days will come when the bridegroom shall be taken from them, and then shall they fast in those days.

Also no man soweth a piece of new cloth unto an old garment, for then **D** taketh he away the new piece from the old, and so is the rent worse.

In like wise, no man poureth new wine into old vessels: for if he do, the new wine breaketh the vessels, and the wine runneth out, and the vessels are marred. But new wine must be poured into new vessels.

And it chanced that he went through the corn fields on the sabbath day: and his disciples as they went on their way, began to pluck the ears of corn. And the Pharisees said unto him: behold, why do they on the sabbath days that which is not lawful? And he said to them: have ye never read what David did, when he had need, and was an-hungered, both he and they that were with him? How he went into the house of God in the days of Abiathar the high priest, and did eat the hallowed loaves, which is not lawful to eat, but for the priests only: and gave also to them which were with him? And he said to them: the sabbath day

*The visible miracle was a sign of the invisible power.

Matt. 9. a.
Luke 5. f.

Levi.

Publicans and sinners eat with Christ.

Christ's disciples fast not.

1 Tim. 1. c.
Matt. 9. b.
and Luke 5. f.

New and old agree not.

Matt. 12. a.
Luke 6. a.

They pluck the ears on the sabbath day.

1. Sam. 21. b.

was made for man, and not man for the sabbath day. Wherefore the son of man is lord even of the sabbath day.

The sabbath was made for man. Christ is Lord over the sabbath.

CHAPTER THREE

A + And he entered again into the synagogue, and there was a man there which had a withered hand. And they watched him to see, whether he would heal him on the sabbath day, that they might accuse him. And he said unto the man which had the withered hand: arise and stand in the midst. And he said to them: whether is it lawful to do a good deed on the sabbath days, or an evil? to save life or kill? But they held their peace. And he looked round about on them angerly, mourning on the blindness of their hearts, and said to the man: stretch forth thine hand. And he stretched it out. And his hand was restored, even as whole as the other. ⊦

Withered hand.

And the Pharisees departed, and straightway gathered a counsel with them that belonged to Herod against him, that they might destroy him. And Jesus avoided with his disciples to the sea. And a great multitude followed him from Galilee and from Jewry, and from Jerusalem, and from Idumea, and from beyond Jordan: and they that dwelled about Tyre and Sidon a great multitude: which when they had heard what things he did, came unto him.

B And he commanded his disciples, that a ship should wait on him, because of the people, lest they should throng him. For he had healed many, insomuch that they pressed upon him, for to touch him, as many as had plagues. And when the unclean spirits saw him, they fell down before him, and cried saying: thou art the son of God. And he straightly charged them that they should not utter him.

And he went up into a mountain, and called unto him whom he would, and they came unto him. And he ordained the twelve that they should be with him, and that he might send them to preach: and that they might have power to heal sicknesses, and to cast out devils. And he gave unto Simon, to name Peter.

Matt. 10. a.
Luke 1. b, c.

The apostles are chosen.

C And he called James the son of Zebedee and John James' brother, and gave them Boanerges to name, which is to say the sons of thunder. And Andrew, and Philip, and Bartholomew, and Matthew, and Thomas, and James the son of Alphæus, and Thaddeus, and Simon of Canaan, and Judas Iscariot, which same also betrayed him.

And they came unto house, and the people assembled together again, so greatly that they had not leisure so much as to eat bread. And when they that longed unto him heard of it, they went out to hold him. For they thought he had been beside himself. And the scribes which came from Jerusalem, said: he hath Beelzebub, and by the power of the chief devil, casteth out devils. And he called them unto him, and said unto them in similitudes.

Matt. 9. d.
and 12. b.

Luke 11. b.

Beelzebub.

How can Satan drive out Satan? For if a realm be divided against itself, that realm cannot endure. Or if a house be divided against itself, that house cannot continue: So if Satan make insurrection against himself and be divided, he cannot continue, but is at an end. No man can enter into a strong man's house, and take away his goods, except he first bind that strong man, and then spoil his house.

Matt. 12. a.
Luke 11. b.

Verily I say unto you, all sins shall be forgiven unto men's children, and **D** blasphemy wherewith they blaspheme. But he that blasphemeth the holy ghost, shall never have forgiveness, but is in danger of eternal damnation: because they said, he had an unclean spirit.

The sin of the holy ghost.

Matt. 12. d.
Luke 8. c.

Then came his mother and his brethren, and stood without, and sent unto him and called him. And the people sat about him, and said unto him: behold thy mother and thy brethren seek for thee without. And he answered them saying: who is my mother and my brethren? And he looked round about on his disciples which sat in compass about him, and said: behold my mother and my brethren. For whosoever doeth the will of God, he is my brother, my sister, and mother.

His mother seeketh him.

CHAPTER FOUR

Matt. 13. a.
Luke 8. a.

+ And he began again to teach by the sea side. And there gathered together **A** unto him much people, so greatly that he entered into a ship, and sat in the sea, and all the people was by the sea side on the shore. And he taught them many things in similitudes, and said unto them in his doctrine: Hearken to. Behold, There went out a sower to sow. And it fortuned as he sowed, that some fell by the way side, and the fowls of the air came and devoured it up. Some fell on stony ground, where it had not much earth: and by and by sprang up, because it had not depth of earth: but as soon as the sun was up it caught heat, and because it had not rooting, withered away.

Sower.

And some fell among the thorns, and the thorns grew up and choked it, so that it gave no fruit. And some fell upon good ground and did yield fruit that sprang and grew, and brought forth: some thirty-fold, some sixty-fold and some an hundred-fold. And he said unto them: he that hath ears to hear, let him hear. ⊦

The sower is expounded.

And when he was alone, they that were about him with the twelve asked **B** him of the similitude. And he said unto them. To you it is given to know the mystery of the kingdom of God. But unto them that are without, shall all things be done in similitudes: that when they see, they shall see, and not discern: and when they hear they shall hear, and not understand; lest at any time they should turn, and their sins should be forgiven them. And he said unto them: Perceive ye not this similitude? how then should ye understand all other similitudes?

Isa. 6. c.
Matt. 13. b.
Luke 8. b.
John 12. f.
Acts 28. f.
Rom. 11. b.

The sower soweth the word. And they that are by the way's side, where the word is sown, are they to whom as soon as they have heard it, Satan cometh immediately, and taketh away the word that was sown in their hearts. And likewise they that are sown on the stony ground, are they: which when they have heard the word, at once receive it with gladness, yet have no roots in themselves, and so endure but a time: and anon as trouble and persecution ariseth for the word's sake, they fall immediately. And they that are sown among the thorns, are such as hear the word: and the care of this world and the deceitfulness of riches and the lusts of other things, enter in and choke the word, and it is made unfruitful. And those that were sown in good ground, are they that hear the word and receive it, and bring forth fruit, some thirty-fold, some sixty-fold, some an hundred-fold.

C   And he said unto them: is the candle lighted, to be put under a bushel, or under the table, and not rather to be put on a candlestick? For there is nothing so privy, that shall not be opened: neither so secret, but that it shall come abroad. If any man have ears to hear, let him hear. And he said unto them: take heed what ye hear. With what measure ye mete, with the same shall it be measured unto you again. And unto you that hear shall more be given★. For unto him that hath, shall it be given: and from him that hath not, shall be taken away, even that he hath.

Matt. 5. b.
Luke 8. c.
and 11. e.
Matt. 10. c.
Luke 8. e.

Candle.

Measure

★ A covenant to them that love the word of God to win other with word and deed: and another to them that love it not, that it shall be their destruction.

And he said: so is the kingdom of God, even as if a man should sow seed in the ground, and should sleep and rise up night and day: and the seed should spring and grow up, he not ware. For the earth bringeth forth fruit of herself: first the blade, then the ears, after that full corn in the ears. And as soon as the fruit is brought forth, anon he thrusteth in the sickle, because the harvest is come.

And he said: whereunto shall we liken the kingdom of God? or with what comparison shall we compare it? It is like a grain of mustard seed, which when it is sown in the earth, is the least of all seeds that be in the earth: but after that it is sown, it groweth up, and is greatest of all herbs: and beareth great branches, so that the fowls of the air may dwell under the shadow of it.

Mustard seed.

Matt. 13. e.
Luke 13. d.

D   And with many such similitudes he preached the word unto them, after as they might hear it. And without similitude spake he nothing unto them. But when they were apart, he expounded all things to his disciples. And the same day when even was come, he said unto them: let us pass over unto the other side. And they left the people, and took him even as he was in the ship. And there were also with him other ships.

Matt. 8. d.
Luke 8. d.

And there arose a great storm of wind, and dashed the waves into the ship, so that it was full. And he was in the stern asleep on a pillow. And they awoke him, and said to him: Master, carest thou not that we perish? And he rose up, and rebuked the wind, and said unto the sea: peace and be still. And the wind allayed, and there followed a great calm. And he said unto them: why are ye so fearful? How is it that ye have no faith? And they feared exceedingly, and said one to another: what fellow is this? For both wind and sea obey him.

Jesus sleepeth in the ship.

CHAPTER FIVE

A   And they came over to the other side of the sea into the country of the Gadarenes. And when he was come out of the ship, there met him out of the graves a man possessed of an unclean spirit, which had his abiding among the graves. And no man could bind him: no not with chains, because that when he was often bound with fetters and chains, he plucked the chains asunder, and

Gadarenes.

Matt. 8. d.
Luke 8. d.

brake the fetters in pieces. Neither could any man tame him. And always both night and day, he cried in the mountains and in the graves, and beat himself with stones. When he had spied Jesus afar off, he ran and worshipped him, and cried with a loud voice and said: what have I to do with thee Jesus the son of the most highest God? I require thee in the name of God that thou torment me not. For he had said unto him: come out of the man thou foul spirit. And he asked him: what is thy name? And he answered saying: my name is Legion, for we are many. And he prayed him instantly that he would not send them away out of the country.

And there was there nigh unto the mountains a great herd of swine feeding, and all the devils besought him saying: send us into the herd of swine, that we may enter into them. And anon Jesus gave them leave. And the unclean spirits went out and entered into the swine. And the herd startled, and ran headlong into the sea. They were about two thousand swine, and they were drowned in the sea. And the swineherds fled, and told it in the city, and in the country. And they came out for to see what had happened: and came to Jesus, and saw him that was vexed with the fiend and had the legion, sit, both clothed and in his right mind, and were afraid. And they that saw it told them, how it had happened unto him that was possessed with the devil: and also of the swine. And they began to pray him, that he would depart from their coasts. And when he was come into the ship, he that had the devil, prayed him that he might be with him. Howbeit Jesus would not suffer him, but said unto him: go home into thine own house and to thy friends, and shew them what great things the Lord hath done unto thee, and how he had compassion on thee. And he departed, and began to publish in the ten cities, what great things Jesus had done unto him, and all men did marvel.

And when Jesus was come over again by ship unto the other side, much people gathered unto him, and he was nigh unto the sea. And behold, there came one of the rulers of the synagogue, whose name was Jairus: and when he saw him, he fell down at his feet, and besought him greatly saying: my daughter lieth at point of death, I would thou wouldst come and lay thy hand on her, that she might be safe and live. And he went with him, and much people followed him, and thronged him.

And there was a certain woman, which was diseased of an issue of blood twelve years and had suffered many things of many physicians, and had spent all that she had, and felt none amendment at all, but waxed worse and worse. When she had heard of Jesus: she came into the press behind him, and touched his garment. For she thought: if I may but touch his clothes, I shall be whole. And straightway her fountain of blood was dried up, and she felt in her body, that she was healed of the plague.

And Jesus immediately felt in himself, the vertue that went out of him, and turned him round about in the press, and said: who touched my clothes? And his disciples said unto him: seest thou the people thrust thee, and yet askest, who did touch me? And he looked round about, for to see her that had done that thing. The woman feared and trembled (for she knew what was done

Legion.

Swine.

B

Matt. 9. c.
Luke 8. f.

The ruler's daughter.

Bloody issue.

C

within her) and she came and fell down before him, and told him the truth of everything. And he said to her: Daughter, thy faith hath made thee whole: go in peace, and be whole of thy plague.

D While he yet spake, there came from the ruler of the synagogue's house, certain which said: thy daughter is dead: why diseasest thou the master any further? As soon as Jesus heard that word spoken, he said unto the ruler of the synagogue: be not afraid, only believe. And he suffered no man to follow him more than Peter and James and John the brother of James. And he came unto the house of the ruler of the synagogue, and saw the wondering, and them that wept and wailed greatly, and went in and said unto them: why make ye this ado and weep? The maiden is not dead, but sleepeth. And they laughed him to scorn. Then he put them all out, and took the father and the mother of the maiden, and them that were with him, and entered in where the maiden lay, and took the maiden by the hand, and said unto her: Tabitha,†† cumi: which is by interpretation: maiden I say unto thee, arise. And straight the maiden arose, and went on her feet. For she was of the age of twelve years. And they were astonied at it out of measure. And he charged them straitly that no man should know of it, and commanded to give her meat.

CHAPTER SIX

A + And he departed thence, and came into his own country, and his disciples followed him. and when the sabbath day was come, he began to teach in the synagogue. And many that heard him were astonied, and said: From whence hath he these things? and what wisdom is this that is given unto him? and such virtues that are wrought by his hands? Is not this that carpenter, Mary's son, the brother of James and Joses and of Juda and Simon? and are not his sisters here with us? And they were offended by him. And Jesus said unto them: a prophet is not despised but in his own country, and among his own kin, and among them that are of the same household. And he could there shew no miracles, but laid his hands upon a few sick folk and healed them. And he marvelled at their unbelief. ⊢

Matt. 13. g.
Luke 4. c.
John 4. f.

Carpenter.

A prophet is not honoured in his own country.

B And he went about by the towns that lay on every side, teaching. And he called the twelve and began to send them, two and two, and gave them power over unclean spirits. And commanded them, that they should take nothing unto their journey, save a rod only: Neither scrip, neither bread, neither money in their purses: but should be shod with sandals. And that they should not put on two coats. And he said unto them: wheresoever ye enter in to an house, there abide till ye depart thence. And whosoever shall not receive you, nor hear you, when ye depart thence, shake off the dust that is under your feet, for a witness unto them. I say verily unto you, it shall be easier for Sodom and Gomorrha at the day of judgement, than for that city.

Matt. 10. a.
Luke 9. a.

The apostles are sent forth.

Acts 13. g.

Dust.

And they went out and preached, that they should repent: and they cast out many devils. And they anointed many that were sick, with oil, and healed them.

Anoint.

69

Matt. 14. a.
Luke 9. a.

And king Herod heard of him (for his name was spread abroad) and said: **C**
John Baptist is risen again from death, and therefore miracles are wrought by
him. Other said, it is Elias: and some said: it is a prophet or as one of the
prophets. But when Herod heard of him, he said: it is John whom I beheaded,
he is risen from death again.

Matt. 14. a.
Luke 3. d.

+ For Herod himself, had sent forth and had taken John, and bound him and
cast him into prison for Herodias' sake which was his brother Philip's wife.
For he had married her. John said unto Herod: It is not lawful for thee to have
thy brother's wife. Herodias laid wait for him, and would have killed him, but
she could not. For Herod feared John, knowing that he was a just man and an
holy: and gave him reverence: and when he heard him, he did many things, and
heard him gladly.

But when a convenient day was come, Herod on his birthday made a supper **D**
to the lords, captains, and chief estates of Galilee. And the daughter of the said
Herodias came in and danced, and pleased Herod and them that sat at board
also. Then the king said unto the maiden: ask of me what thou wilt, and I will
give it thee. And he sware unto her, whatsoever thou shalt ask of me, I will
give it thee, even unto the one half of my kingdom. And she went forth and
said to her mother: what shall I ask? And she said: John Baptist's head. And she
came in straightway with haste unto the king, and asked saying: I will that
thou give me by and by in a charger the head of John Baptist. And the king was
sorry: howbeit for his oath's sake, and for their sakes which sat at supper also,
he would not put her beside her purpose. And immediately the king sent
the hangman and commanded his head to be brought in. And he went and
beheaded him in the prison, and brought his head in a charger, and gave it to

John Baptist is
beheaded.

the maiden, and the maiden gave it to her mother. And when his disciples
heard of it, they came and took up his body, and put it in a tomb. ⊢

Matt. 14. b.
Luke 9. b.

And the apostles gathered themselves together to Jesus, and told him all
things, both what they had done, and what they had taught. And he said unto
them: come ye apart into the wilderness, and rest awhile. For there were many
comers and goers, that they had no leisure so much as to eat. And he went by
ship out of the way into a desert place. But the people spied them when they
departed: and many knew him, and ran afoot thither out of all cities, and came
thither before them, and came together unto him. And Jesus went out and saw

Matt. 9. d.

much people, and had compassion on them, because they were like sheep
which had no shepherd. And he began to teach them many things.

Matt. 13. b.
Luke 9. b.
John 6. a.

And when the day was now far spent, his disciples came unto him saying: **B**
this is a desert place, and now the day is far passed, let them depart, that they
may go into the country round about, and into the towns, and buy them bread:
for they have nothing to eat. He answered and said unto them: give ye them to
eat. And they said unto him: shall we go and buy two hundred pennyworth of
bread, and give them to eat? He said unto them: how many loaves have ye? Go

Five loaves and two
fishes.

and look. And when they had searched, they said: five and two fishes. And he
commanded them to make them all sit down by companies upon the green
grass. And they sat down here a row and there a row, by hundreds and by
fifties. And he took the five loaves and the two fishes, and looked up to heaven **C**

and blessed and brake the loaves, and gave them to his disciples to put before them: and the fishes he divided among them all. And they all did eat, and were satisfied. And they took up twelve baskets full of the gobbets and of the fishes. And they that ate were about five thousand men.

And straightway he caused his disciples to go into the ship, and to go over the water before unto Bethsaida, while he sent away the people. And as soon as he had sent them away, he departed into a mountain to pray. And when even was come, the ship was in the midst of the sea, and he alone on the land, and he saw them troubled in rowing, for the wind was contrary unto them. And about the fourth quarter of the night, he came unto them, walking apon the sea, and would have passed by them. When they saw him walking apon the sea, they supposed it had been a spirit, and cried out: For they all saw him, and were afraid. And anon he talked with them, and said unto them: be of good cheer, it is I, be not afraid. And he went up unto them into the ship, and the wind ceased, and they were sore amazed in themselves beyond measure, and marvelled. For they remembered not, of the loaves, because their hearts were blinded.

And they came over, and went into the land of Gennesaret, and drew up into the haven. And as soon as they were come out of the ship, straight they knew him, and ran forth throughout all the region round about, and began to carry about in beds all that were sick, to the place where they heard tell that he was. And whithersoever he entered into towns, cities or villages, they laid their sick in the streets, and prayed him, that they might touch, and it were but the edge of his vesture. And as many as touched him were safe. ⊦

Matt. 14. c.
John. 6. b.

Jesus walketh on the sea.

Matt. 14. b.

Edge or hem.

CHAPTER SEVEN

A And the Pharisees came together unto him and divers of the scribes which came from Jerusalem. And when they saw certain of his disciples eat bread with common hands (that is to say, with unwashen hands) they complained. For the Pharisees and all the Jews, except they wash their hands oft, eat not, observing the traditions of the elders. And when they come from the market, except they wash, they eat not. And many other things there be, which they have taken upon them to observe, as the washing of cups and cruses, and of brazen vessels, and of tables.

B Then asked him the Pharisees and scribes, why walk not thy disciples according to the traditions of the elders, but eat bread with unwashen hands? He answered and said unto them: well prophesied Esaias of you hypocrites, as it is written: This people honoureth me with their lips, but their heart is far from me: In vain they worship me, teaching doctrines which are nothing but the commandments of men. For ye lay the commandment of God apart, and observe the traditions of men, as the washing of cruses and of cups, and many other such like things ye do.

And he said unto them: well, ye cast aside the commandment of God, to maintain your own traditions. For Moses said: Honour thy father and thy mother: and whosoever curseth father or mother, let him die for it. But ye say:

Matt. 15. a.

Unwashen hands.

Isa. 29. d.

Men's commandments.

Exod. 20. c.
Deut. 5. b.
Eph. 6. a.
Exod. 21. c.
Lev. 20. b.
Prov. 20.

71

a man shall say to father or mother Corban: which is: that thou desirest of me to help thee with, is given God. And so ye suffer him no more to do ought for his father or his mother, making the word of God of none effect, through your own traditions which ye have ordained. And many such things ye do.

Matt. 15. d.

And he called all the people unto him, and said unto them: Hearken unto me,   **C** every one of you and understand. There is nothing without a man that can

That goeth in, defileth not.

defile him when it entereth into him: but those things which proceed out of him are those which defile the man. If any man have ears to hear, let him hear. And when he came to house away from the people, his disciples asked him of the similitude. And he said unto them: Are ye so without understanding? Do ye not yet perceive, that whatsoever thing from without entereth into a man, it cannot defile him, because it entereth not in to his heart, but into the belly: and goeth out into the draught that purgeth out all meats.

That cometh out of a man defileth.

And he said: that defileth a man which cometh out of a man. For from within, even out of the heart of men, proceed evil thoughts: advoutry, fornication, murder, theft, covetousness, wickedness, deceit, uncleanness, and a wicked eye, blasphemy, pride, foolishness: all these evil things come from within, and defile a man.

Matt. 15. c.

The Syrophenician.

And from thence he rose and went into the borders of Tyre and Sidon, and entered into an house, and would that no man should have known: But he could not be hid. For a certain woman whose daughter had a foul spirit heard of him, and came and fell at his feet. The woman was a Greek out of Syrophenicia, and she besought him that he would cast out the devil out of her daughter. And Jesus said unto her: let the children first be fed. For it is not meet, to take the children's bread, and to cast it unto whelps. She answered and said unto him: even so master, nevertheless, the whelps also eat under the table of the children's crumbs. And he said unto her: for this saying go thy way, the devil is gone out of thy daughter. And when she was come home to her house, she found the devil departed, and her daughter lying on the bed.

Matt. 15. c.

+ And he departed again from the coasts of Tyre and Sidon, and came unto   **D** the sea of Galilee through the midst of the coasts of the ten cities. And they brought unto him one that was deaf and stammered in his speech, and prayed

The deaf and dumb.

him to lay his hand upon him. And he took him aside from the people, and put his fingers in his ears, and did spit and touched his tongue, and looked up to heaven and sighed, and said unto him: ephatha, that is to say, be opened. And straightway his ears were opened, and the string of his tongue was loosed, and he spake plain. And he commanded them that they should tell no man. But the more he forbade them, so much the more a great deal they published it: and were beyond measure astonied, saying: He hath done all things well, and hath

Gen. 1. d.
Eccl. 39. c.

made both the deaf to hear, and the dumb to speak. +

CHAPTER EIGHT

Matt. 15. d.

+ In those days when there was a very great company, and had nothing to eat,   **A** Jesus called his disciples to him and said unto them: I have compassion on this people, because they have now been with me three days and have nothing to eat: And if I should send them away fasting to their own houses, they should faint by the way. For divers of them came from far. And his disciples answered him: where should a man have bread here in the wilderness to satisfy these? And he asked them: how many loaves have ye? They said: seven. And he Seven loaves. commanded the people to sit down on the ground. And he took the seven loaves, gave thanks, brake, and gave to his disciples, to set before them. And they did set them before the people. And they had a few small fishes. And he blessed them and commanded them also to be set before them. And they ate and were sufficed: And they took up of the broken meat that was left seven baskets full. And they that ate, were in number about four thousand. And he sent them away. ⊦

B   And anon he entered into a ship with his disciples, and came into the parts of Matt. 16. a.
Luke 12. g. Dalmanutha. And the Pharisees came forth, and began to dispute with him, seeking of him a sign from heaven and tempting him. And he sighed in his A sign. spirit and said: why doth this generation seek a sign? Verily I say unto you, there shall no sign be given unto this generation. And he left them and went into the ship again, and departed over the water.

And they had forgotten to take bread with them, neither had they in the ship Matt. 16. a. with them more than one loaf. And he charged them saying. + Take heed, and beware of the leaven of the Pharisees, and of the leaven of Herod. And they Leaven. reasoned among themselves saying: we have no bread. And when Jesus knew that, he said unto them: why take ye thought because ye have no bread? perceive ye not yet, neither understand? Have ye your hearts yet blinded? Have ye eyes and see not? and have ye ears and hear not? Do ye not remember? When John. 6. b. I brake five loaves among five thousand: How many baskets full of broken meat took ye up? They said unto him twelve. When I brake seven among four thousand: How many baskets of the leavings of broken meat took ye up? they said seven. And he said unto them: how is it that ye understand not?

C   + And he came to Bethsaida, and they brought a blind man unto him and A blind is healed. desired him to touch him. And he caught the blind by the hand, and led him out of the town, and spat in his eyes and put his hands upon him, and asked him whether he saw ought. And he looked up and said: I see the men: For I see them walk, as they were trees. After that he put his hands again upon his eyes and made him see. And he was restored to his sight, and saw every man clearly. And he sent him home to his house saying: neither go into the town, nor tell it any in the town. ⊦

And Jesus went out and his disciples into the towns that belong to the city Matt. 16. b.
Luke 9. c. called Caesarea Philippi. And by the way he asked his disciples saying: whom do men say that I am? And they answered: some say that thou art John Baptist: some say Elias: and some, one of the prophets. And he said unto them: But Caesarea
Philippi whom say ye that I am? Peter answered and said unto him: Thou art very **D**   Christ. And he charged them, that they should tell no man of it. And he began to teach them, how that the son of man must suffer many things, and should be The passion. reproved of the elders and of the high priests and scribes, and be killed, and after three days arise again. And he spake that saying openly. And Peter took him aside, and began to chide him. Then he turned about and looked on his disciples, and rebuked Peter saying: Go after me Satan. For thou savourest not the things of God but the things of men.

Peter is Satan.

And he called the people unto him, with his disciples also, and said unto them: Whosoever will follow me, let him forsake himself, and take up his cross, and follow me. For whosoever will save his life, shall lose it. But whosoever shall lose his life for my sake and the gospel's, the same shall save it. What shall it profit a man, if he should win all the world and lose his own soul? or else what shall a man give, to redeem his soul again? Whosoever therefore shall be ashamed of me and of my words, among this advoutrous and sinful generation: of him shall the son of man be ashamed, when he cometh in the glory of his father with the holy angels. And he said unto them: Verily I say unto you: There be some of them that stand here, which shall not taste of death, till they have seen the kingdom of God come with power.

Matt. 16. d.
and 10. d.
Luke 9. c.
and 14. f.

Christ's disciple.

Matt. 10. d.
Luke 9. c.
and 12. b.

Matt. 16. d.
Luke 9. c.

CHAPTER NINE

And after six days Jesus took Peter, James, and John and led them up into an **A** high mountain out of the way alone, and he was transfigured before them. And his raiment did shine, and was made very white, even as snow: so white as no fuller can make upon the earth. And there appeared unto them Elias with Moses: and they talked with Jesus. And Peter answered and said to Jesus: Master, here is good being for us, let us make three tabernacles, one for thee, one for Moses, and one for Elias. And yet he wist not what he said: for they were afraid. And there was a cloud that shadowed them. And a voice came out of the cloud saying: This is my dear son, hear him. And suddenly, they looked round about them, and saw no man more than Jesus only with them.

Matt. 17. a.
Luke 9. d.

Transfiguration.

Hear him.

And as they came down from the hill, he charged them, that they should tell no man what they had seen, till the son of man were risen from death★ again. **B** And they kept that saying with them, and demanded one of another, what that rising from death again should mean? And they asked him saying: why then say the scribes, that Elias must first come? He answered and said unto them: Elias verily shall first come and restore all things. And also the son of man as it is written, shall suffer many things, and shall be set at nought. Moreover I say unto you, that Elias is come, and they have done unto him whatsoever pleased them, as it is written of him.

Matt. 17.

★ *Mention of the*
passion followeth the
high vision.

Mal. 4. b.
Isa. 53. b.
Matt. 22. c.
Luke 9. c.

And he came to his disciples, and saw much people about them, and the scribes disputing with them. And straightway all the people when they beheld him, were amazed, and ran to him and saluted him. And he said unto the scribes: what dispute ye with them? + And one of the company answered and said: Master, I have brought my son unto thee, which hath a dumb spirit. And **C** whensoever he taken him, he teareth him, and he foameth, and gnasheth with his teeth, and pineth away. And I spake to thy disciples that they should cast him out, and they could not.

He answered him and said: O generation without faith how long shall I be with you? How long shall I suffer you? Bring him unto me. And they brought him unto him. And as soon as the spirit saw him, he tare him. And he fell down on the ground wallowing and foaming. And he asked his father: how long is it ago, since this hath happened him? And he said, of a child: and oft-times casteth him into the fire, and also into the water, to destroy him. But if thou canst do any thing, have mercy on us, and help us. And Jesus said unto him: yea if thou couldest believe, all things are possible to him that believeth. And straight-way the father of the child cried with tears saying: Lord I believe, help mine unbelief.

Help mine unbelief.

D When Jesus saw, that the people came running together unto him, he rebuked the foul spirit, saying unto him: Thou dumb and deaf spirit, I charge thee come out of him, and enter no more into him. And the spirit cried, and rent him sore, and came out: And he was as one that had been dead, insomuch that many said, he is dead. But Jesus caught his hand, and lift him up: and he rose. And when he was come into the house, his disciples asked him secretly: why could not we cast him out? And he said unto them: this kind can by no other means come forth, but by prayer and fasting. ⊦

The dumb and deaf spirit is cast out.

Prayer and fasting.

E ⊦ And they departed thence, and took their journey through Galilee, and he would not that any man should have known it. For he taught his disciples, and said unto them: The son of man shall be delivered into the hands of men, and they shall kill him, and after that he is killed he shall arise again the third day. But they wist not what that saying meant, and were afraid to ask him.

Matt. 17. d.
Luke 9. e.

Passion.

B And he came to Capernaum. And when he was come to house, he asked them: what was it that ye disputed between you by the way? And they held their peace: for by the way they reasoned among themselves, who should be the chiefest. And he sat down and called the twelve unto him, and said to them: if any man desire to be first, the same shall be last of all, and servant unto all. And he took a child and set him in the midst of them, and took him in his arms and said unto them, Whosoever receive any such a child in my name, receiveth me. And whosoever receiveth me, receiveth not me, but him that sent me. ⊦

Matt. 18. a.
Luke. 9. f.

Chief or greatest.

John answered him saying: ⊦ Master, we saw one casting out devils in thy name, which followeth not us, and we forbade him, because he followeth us not. But Jesus said, ⋆ forbid him not. For there is no man that shall do a miracle in my name, that can lightly speak evil of me. Whosoever is not against you, is on your part. And whosoever shall give you a cup of water to drink for my name's sake, because ye belong to Christ, verily I say unto you, he shall not lose his reward. ⋆

C

⋆ *If he preach Christ truly, though he follow not with thee in thy ceremonies or traditions, let him alone.*

⋆ *Whatsoever is done for Christ's sake; shall be rewarded with the reward that Christ hath deserved for us.*

And whosoever shall offend one of these little ones, that believe in me, it were better for him, that a millstone were hanged about his neck, and that he were cast into the sea: wherefore if thy hand offend thee, cut him off. It is better for thee to enter into life maimed, than having two hands, go into hell, into fire that never shall be quenched, where their worm dieth not, and the fire never goeth out. Likewise if thy foot offend thee, cut him off. For it is better for thee

Offend.

to go halt into life, than having two feet to be cast into hell, into fire that never shall be quenched: where their worm dieth not, and the fire never goeth out. Even so if thine eye offend thee, pluck him out. It is better for thee to go into the kingdom of God with one eye, than having two eyes, to be cast into hell fire: where their worm dieth not, and the fire never goeth out. ⊢

Every man therefore shall be salted with fire★: and every sacrifice shall be seasoned with salt. Salt is good. But if the salt be unsavoury: what shall ye salt therewith? See that ye have salt in yourselves: and have peace among yourselves, one with another.

CHAPTER TEN

And he rose from thence, and went into the coasts of Jewry through the region   **A** that is beyond Jordan. And the people resorted unto him afresh: and as he was wont, he taught them again. And the Pharisees came and asked him a question: whether it were lawful for a man to put away his wife: to prove him. And he answered and said unto them: what did Moses bid you do? And they said: Moses suffered to write a testimonial of divorcement, and to put her away. And Jesus answered and said unto them: For the hardness of your hearts he wrote this precept unto you. But at the first creation, God made them man and woman. And for this thing's sake shall man leave his father and mother, and bide by his wife, and they twain shall be one flesh. So then are they now not twain, but one flesh. Therefore what God hath coupled, let not man separate.

And in the house his disciples asked him again of that matter. And he said   **B** unto them: Whosoever putteth away his wife and marrieth another, breaketh wedlock to her-ward. And if a woman forsake her husband and be married to another, she committeth advoutry.

+ And they brought children to him, that he should touch them. And his disciples rebuked those that brought them. When Jesus saw that, he was displeased, and said to them: Suffer the children to come unto me and forbid them not. For of such is the kingdom of God. Verily I say unto you, whosoever shall not receive the kingdom of God as a child, he shall not enter therein. And he took them up in his arms and put his hands upon them, and blessed them. ⊢

+ And when he was come into the way, there came one running and kneeled   **C** to him, and asked him: good master, what shall I do, that I may inherit eternal life? Jesus said to him: why callest thou me good? There is no man good but one, which is God. Thou knowest the commandments: break not matrimony: kill not: steal not: bear not false witness: defraud no man: honour thy father and mother. He answered and said to him: master, all these I have observed from my youth. Jesus beheld him and had a favour to him, and said unto him: one thing is lacking unto thee. Go and sell all that thou hast, and give to the poor, and thou shalt have treasure in heaven, and come and follow me, and take up thy cross★. ⊢ But he was discomforted with that saying, and went away mourning, for he had great possessions.

Isa. 66. g.

Fire and salt.

★ Fire is tribulation: and salt is God's word.

Divorcement.

Deut. 24.
Matt. 19. a.

Gen. 1, 2. d.
1 Cor. 6. b.

Eph. 5. g.

1 Cor. 7. b.

Matt. 19. b.
Luke 18. c.

Children.

Matt 19. b.
and Luke 18. d.

Exod. 20. c.

★ The rich men, may abide no cross: that is to say, persecution.

76

D And Jesus looked round about, and said unto his disciples: what an hard thing is it for them that have riches, to enter into the kingdom of God. And his disciples were astonished at his words. But Jesus answered again, and said unto them: children, how hard is it for them, that trust in riches, to enter into the kingdom of God. It is easier for a camel to go through the eye of an needle, than for a rich man to enter into the kingdom of God. And they were astonished out of measure, saying between themselves: who then can be saved? Jesus looked upon them, and said: with men it is impossible, but not with God: for with God all things are possible.

Camel.

And Peter began to say unto him: Lo, we have forsaken all, and have followed thee. Jesus answered and said: Verily I say unto you, there is no man that forsaketh house, or brethren, or sisters, or father, or mother, or wife, or children, or lands, for my sake and the gospel's, which shall not receive an hundred-fold now in this life: houses, and brethren, and sisters, and mothers, and children, and lands with persecutions: and in the world to come, eternal life. Many that are first, shall be last: and the last, first. And they were in the way going up to Jerusalem. And Jesus went before them: and they were amazed, and as they followed, were afraid.

Hundred-fold.

*Matt. 19. d.
and 20. b.
Luke 28. e.*

First and last.

E And Jesus took the twelve again, and began to tell them what things should happen unto him. Behold we go up to Jerusalem, and the son of man shall be delivered unto the high priests and unto the scribes: and they shall condemn him to death, and shall deliver him to the gentiles: and they shall mock him, and scourge him, and spit upon him, and kill him. And the third day he shall rise again.

Passion.

And then James and John the sons of Zebedee came unto him, saying: master, we would that thou shouldest do for us whatsoever we desire. He said unto them: what would ye I should do unto you? They said to him: grant unto us that we may sit one on thy right hand, and the other on thy left hand, in thy glory. But Jesus said unto them: Ye wot not what ye ask. Can ye drink of the **F** cup that I shall drink of, and be baptised in the baptism that I shall be baptised in? And they said unto him: that we can. Jesus said unto them: ye shall drink of the cup that I shall drink of, and be baptised with the baptism that I shall be baptised in: but to sit on my right hand and on my left hand is not mine to give, but to them for whom it is prepared.

The sons of Zebedee.

Matt. 20. c.

G And when the ten heard that, they began to disdain at James and John. But Jesus called them unto him, and said to them: ye know that they which seem to bear rule among the gentiles, reign as lords over them. And they that be great among them, exercise authority over them. So shall it not be among you, but whosoever of you will be great among you, shall be your minister. And whosoever will be chief, shall be servant unto all. For even the son of man came not to be ministered unto: but to minister, and to give his life for the redemption of many.

Matt. 22. c.

Great.

And they came to Jericho. And as he went out of Jericho with his disciples, and a great number of people: Bartimeus the son of Timeus which was blind, sat by the highway's side begging. And when he heard that it was Jesus of

*Jericho.
Bartimeus the blind.*

Matt. 20. d.
Luke 18. f.

Nazareth, he began to cry and to say: Jesus the son of David, have mercy on me. And many rebuked him, that he should hold his peace. But he cried the more a great deal, thou son of David have mercy on me. And Jesus stood still, and commanded him to be called. And they called the blind, saying unto him: Be of good comfort: rise, he called thee. And he threw away his cloak, and rose and came to Jesus. And Jesus answered and said unto him: what wilt thou that I do unto thee? The blind said unto him: master, that I might see. Jesus said unto him: go thy way, thy faith hath saved thee. And by and by he received his sight, and followed Jesus in the way.

CHAPTER ELEVEN

Matt. 21. a.
Luke 19. c.

Bethphage.

Colt.

And when they came nigh to Jerusalem unto Bethphage and Bethany, besides **A** mount Olivet, he sent forth two of his disciples, and said unto them: Go your ways into the town that is over against you. And as soon as ye be entered into it, ye shall find a colt bound, whereon never man sat: loose him and bring him. And if any man say unto you: why do ye so? Say that the Lord hath need of him: and straightway he will send him hither. And they went their way, and found a colt tied by the door without in a place where two ways met, and they loosed him. And divers of them that stood there, said unto them: what do ye

John. 12. b.

loosing the colt? And they said unto them even as Jesus had commanded them. And they let them go. And they brought the colt to Jesus, and cast their garments on him: and he sat upon him. And many spread their garments in the way. Other cut down branches of the trees, and strawed them in the way. And they that went before and they that followed, cried saying: Hosanna: blessed be

Hosanna.

he that cometh in the name of the Lord. Blessed be the kingdom that cometh in the name of him that is Lord of our father David. Hosanna in the highest.

Matt. 21. b.
Luke 19. g.

Fig tree.

And the Lord entered into Jerusalem, and into the temple. And when he had **B** looked round about upon all things, and now the eventide was come, he went out unto Bethany, with the twelve. And on the morrow when they were come out from Bethany, he hungered, and spied a fig tree afar off having leaves, and went to see whether he might find anything thereon. But when he came thereto, he found nothing but leaves: for the time of figs was not yet. And Jesus answered and said to it: never man eat fruit of thee hereafter while the world standeth. And his disciples heard it.

Sellers and buyers are cast out.

And they came to Jerusalem. And Jesus went into the temple, and began to cast out the sellers and buyers in the temple, and overthrew the tables of the money-changers, and the stools of them that sold doves: and would not suffer that any man carried a vessel through the temple. And he taught saying unto them, is it not written: my house shall be called the house of prayer unto all

Isa. 46. c.
Jer. 7. b.

nations? But ye have made it a den of thieves.

And the scribes and high priests heard it and sought how to destroy him. For **C** they feared him, because all the people marvelled at his doctrine. And when even was come, he went out of the city. And in the morning as they passed by,

Matt. 21. c.

they saw the fig tree dried up by the roots. And Peter remembered, and said unto him: master, behold, the fig tree which thou cursedst, is withered away. And Jesus answered, and said unto them: Have confidence in God. + Verily I say unto you, that whosoever shall say unto this mountain: take away thyself, and cast thyself in to the sea, and shall not waver in his heart, but shall believe that those things which he sayeth shall come to pass, whatsoever he sayeth, shall be done to him. Therefore I say unto you, whatsoever ye desire when ye pray, believe that ye shall have it, and it shall be done unto you. And when ye stand and pray, forgive, if ye have anything against any man, that your father also which is in heaven, may forgive you your trespasses. ⊦

Matt. 7. a.
and 22. c.
Matt. 6. b.
Luke 11. b.
Covenant

Eccl. 28.

D   And they came again to Jerusalem. And as he walked in the temple, there came to him the high priests, and the scribes, and the elders, and said unto him: by what authority doest thou these things? and who gave thee this authority, to do these things? Jesus answered and said unto them: I will also ask of you a certain thing: and answer ye me, and I will tell you by what authority I do these things. The baptism of John, was it from heaven or of men? Answer me. And they thought in themselves saying: if we shall say from heaven: he will say why then did ye not believe him? but if we shall say, of men: then fear we the people. For all men counted John, that he was a very prophet. And they answered and said unto Jesus: we cannot tell. And Jesus answered and said unto them: neither will I tell you, by what authority I do these things.

Matt. 21. c.
and Luke 20. b.

The baptism of John.

CHAPTER TWELVE

A   And he began to speak unto them in similitudes. A certain man planted a vineyard, and compassed it with an hedge, and ordained a wine-press, and built a tower in it. And let it out to hire unto husbandmen, and went into a strange country. And when the time was come, he sent to the tenants a servant, that he might receive of the tenants of the fruit of the vineyard. And they caught him and beat him and sent him again empty. And moreover he sent unto them another servant, and at him they cast stones and brake his head, and sent him again all to-reviled. And again he sent another, and him they killed: and many other, beating some, and killing some.

Matt. 21. d.

Vineyard.

Luke 20. b.
Isa. 50. a.
Jer. 2. d.

Yet had he one son whom he loved tenderly, him also he sent at the last unto them saying: they will fear my son. But the tenants said amongst themselves: this is the heir: come let us kill him, and the inheritance shall be ours. And they took him and killed him, and cast him out of the vineyard. What shall then the lord of the vineyard do? He will come and destroy the tenants, and let out the vineyard to other. Have ye not read this scripture? The stone which the builders did refuse, is made the chief stone in the corner: this was done of the Lord, and is marvellous in our eyes. And they went about to take him, but they feared the people. For they perceived that he spake that similitude against them. And they left him and went their way.

Psa. 118. d.
Isa. 28.
Acts 4. b.
Rom. 9. g.
1 Pet. 2. a.

B   And they sent unto him certain of the Pharisees with Herod's servants, to take him in his words. And as soon as they were come, they said unto him: master we know that thou art true, and carest for no man: for thou considerest

Matt. 23. b.
Luke 20. d.

Tribute to Caesar.

Rom. 13. c.

not the degree of men, but teachest the way of God truly: Is it lawful to pay tribute to Caesar, or not? Ought we to give, or ought we not to give? He understood their simulation, and said unto them: Why tempt ye me? Bring me a penny, that I may see it. And they brought. And he said unto them: Whose is this image and superscription? And they said unto him, Caesar's. And Jesus answered and said unto them: Then give to Caesar that which belongeth to Caesar: and to God, that which pertaineth to God. And they marvelled at him.

Matt. 22. c.
Luke 20. d.
Deut. 25. b.

Sadducees.

Then came the Sadducees unto him, which say, there is no resurrection. And they asked him saying: Master, Moses wrote unto us if any man's brother die, and leave his wife behind him, and leave no children: that then his brother should take his wife, and raise up seed unto his brother. There were seven brethren: and the first took a wife, and when he died left no seed behind him. And the second took her, and died: neither left any seed. And the third likewise. And seven had her, and left no seed behind them. Last of all the wife died also. In the resurrection then, when they shall rise again, whose wife shall she be of them? For seven had her to wife. Jesus answered and said unto them: Are ye not therefore deceived and understand not the scriptures, neither the power of God? For when they shall rise again from death, they neither marry, nor are

Resurrection.

Exod. 3. b.

Matt. 22. b.
Luke. 10. c.

married: but are as the angels which are in heaven. As touching the dead, that they shall rise again: have ye not read in the book of Moses, how in the bush God spake unto him saying: I am the God of Abraham, and God of Isaac, and the God of Jacob? He is not the God of the dead, but the God of the living. Ye are therefore greatly deceived.

First commandment.

Deut. 6. a.

Lev. 19. d
Matt. 22. d
Rom. 13. c.
Gal. 5. c.

And there came one of the scribes that had heard them disputing together, **C** and perceived that he had answered them well, and asked him: Which is the first of all the commandments? Jesus answered him: the first of all the commandments is: Hear Israel: The Lord God is one Lord. And thou shalt love the Lord thy God with all thy heart, and with all thy soul, and with all thy mind, and with all thy strength. This is the first commandment. And the second is like unto this: Thou shalt love thy neighbour as thy self. There is none other commandment greater than these.

And the scribe said unto him: well master, thou hast said the truth, that there is one God, and that there is none but he. And to love him with all the heart, and with all the mind, and with all the soul, and with all the strength: and to love a man's neighbour as himself, is a greater thing than all burnt offerings and sacrifices. And when Jesus saw that he answered discreetly, he said unto him: Thou art not far from the kingdom of God. And no man after that, durst ask him any question.

Matt. 22. d.
Luke 20. g.
David's son.

Psa. 110. a.

Matt. 23. a.
Luke 11. f.

And Jesus answered and said, teaching in the temple: how say the scribes that **D** Christ is the son of David? for David himself inspired with the holy ghost, said: The Lord said to my Lord, sit on my right hand, till I make thine enemies thy footstool. Then David himself calleth him Lord: and by what means is he then his son? And much people heard him gladly.

And he said unto them in his doctrine: beware of the scribes which love to go in long clothing: and love salutations in the market places, and the chief seats in the synagogues, and to sit in the uppermost rooms at feasts, and devour widows' houses, and that under colour of long praying. These shall receive greater damnation.

Long clothes.
Salutations.
Chief seats.
Widows' houses.

+ And Jesus sat over against the treasury, and beheld how the people put money into the treasury. And many that were rich, cast in much. And there came a certain poor widow, and she threw in two mites, which make a farthing. And he called unto him his disciples and said unto them: Verily I say unto you, that this poor widow hath cast more in, than all they which have cast into the treasury. For they all did cast in of their superfluity: but she of her poverty, did cast in all that she had, even all her living. ⊦

Luke 21. a.

Poor widow.

CHAPTER THIRTEEN

A And as he went out of the temple one of his disciples said unto him: Master, see what stones, and what buildings are here. And Jesus answered and said unto him: Seest thou these great buildings? There shall not be left one stone upon another, that shall not be thrown down.

Matt. 14. a.

The destruction of the temple.

And as he sat on mount Olivet, over against the temple, Peter, and James, and John, and Andrew asked him secretly: tell us, when shall these things be? And what is the sign when all these things shall be fulfilled? And Jesus answered them, and began to say: take heed lest any man deceive you. For many shall come in my name saying: I am Christ, and shall deceive many.

Antichrist.

When ye shall hear of war and tidings of war, be ye not troubled. For such things must needs be. But the end is not yet. For there shall nation arise against nation, and kingdom against kingdom. And there shall be earthquakes in all quarters, and famishment and troubles. These are the beginning of sorrows.

B But take ye heed to yourselves. For they shall bring you up to the councils and into the synagogues, and ye shall be beaten: yea and shall be brought before rulers and kings for my sake, for a testimonial unto them. And the gospel must first be published among all nations.

But when they lead you and present you, take no thought aforehand what ye shall say, neither imagine: but whatsoever is given you at the same time, that speak. For it shall not be ye that shall speak, but the holy ghost. Yea and the brother shall deliver the brother to death, and the father the son, and the children shall rise against their fathers and mothers, and shall put them to death. And ye shall be hated of all men for my name's sake. But whosoever shall endure unto the end, the same shall be safe.

Matt. 10. b.

The spirit answereth.

C Moreover when ye se the abomination that betokeneth desolation, whereof is spoken by Daniel the prophet, stand where it ought not, let him that readeth understand. Then let them that be in Jewry, flee to the mountains. And let him that is on the house-top, not descend down into the house, neither enter therein, to fetch anything out of his house. And let him that is in the field, not turn back again unto those things which he left behind him, for to take his clothes with him. Woe is then to them that are with child, and to them that give suck in those days. But pray, that your flight be not in the winter. For

Matt. 24.
Luke 21. d.
Daniel.

Dan. 9. a.

Winter.

81

there shall be in those days such tribulation, as was not from the beginning of creatures which God created, unto this time, neither shall be. And except that the Lord should shorten those days, no man should be saved. But for the elect's sake, which he hath chosen, he hath shortened those days.

Elect.

And then, if any man say to you: lo, here is Christ: lo, he is there, believe not. For false Christs shall arise, and false prophets and shall shew miracles and wonders, to deceive if it were possible, even the elect. But take ye heed: behold I have shewed you all things before.

Matt. 24.
Luke 21. b, c.

Moreover in those days, after that tribulation, the sun shall wax dark, and the moon shall not give her light, and the stars of heaven shall fall: and the powers which are in heaven, shall move. And then shall they see the son of **D** man coming in the clouds, with great power and glory. And then shall he send his angels, and shall gather together his elect from the four winds, and from the one end of the world to the other.

Ezek. 32. b.
Isa. 13. b.
Joel 3. c.

Learn a similitude of the fig tree. When his branches are yet tender, and hath brought forth leaves, ye know that summer is near. So in like manner when ye see these things come to pass: understand, that it is nigh even at the doors. Verily I say unto you, that this generation shall not pass, till all these things be done. Heaven and earth shall pass, but my words shall not pass. But of the day and the hour knoweth no man: no not the angels which are in heaven: neither the son himself, save the father only.

Fig tree.

That day knoweth no man.

Take heed, watch and pray, for ye know not when the time is. As a man which is gone into a strange country, and hath left his house, and given authority to his servants, and to every man his work, and commanded the porter to watch. Watch therefore, for ye know not when the master of the house will come, whether at even or at midnight, whether at the cock-crowing or in the dawning: lest if he come suddenly, he should find you sleeping. And that I say unto you, I say unto all men, watch.

Matt. 24.

Watch and pray.

CHAPTER FOURTEEN

After two days followed Easter, and the days of sweet bread. And the high **A** priests and the scribes sought means, how they might take him by craft and put him to death. But they said: not in the feast day, lest any business arise among the people.

Matt. 26. a.
and Luke 22. a.

When he was in Bethany, in the house of Simon the leper, even as he sat at meat, there came a woman having an alabaster box of ointment called nard, that was pure and costly: and she brake the box and poured it on his head. And there were some that were not content in themselves, and said: what needed this waste of ointment? For it might have been sold for more then three hundred pence, and been given unto the poor. And they grudged against her.

Matt. 26.
John 12. a.

Jesus is anointed.

And Jesus said: let her be in rest, why trouble ye her? She hath done a good work on me. For ye shall have poor with you always: and whensoever ye will, ye may do them good: but me ye shall not have always. She hath done that she could: she came aforehand to anoint my body to his burying-ward. Verily I say unto you: wheresoever this gospel shall be preached throughout the whole world: this also that she hath done, shall be rehearsed in remembrance of her.

B   And Judas Iscariot, one of the twelve, went away unto the high priests, to betray him unto them. When they heard that, they were glad, and promised that they would give him money. And he sought, how he might conveniently betray him.

Matt. 26.
Luke 22. a.

He is betrayed.

And the first day of sweet bread, when men offer the paschal lamb, his disciples said unto him: where wilt thou that we go and prepare, that thou mayest eat the Easter lamb? And he sent forth two of his disciples, and said unto them: Go ye into the city, and there shall a man meet you bearing a pitcher of water; follow him. And whithersoever he goeth in, say ye to the good man of the house: the master asketh where is the guest chamber, where I shall eat the Easter lamb with my disciples? And he will shew you a great parlour, paved and prepared: there make ready for us. And his disciples went forth and came to the city, and found as he had said unto them: and made ready the Easter lamb.

Matt. 26.
Luke 22. a.

Easter lamb.

C   And at even he came with the twelve. And as they sat at board and ate, Jesus said: Verily I say unto you: that one of you shall betray me, which eateth with me. And they began to mourn, and to say to him one by one: is it I? And another said: is it I? He answered and said unto them: It is one of the twelve and the same dippeth with me in the platter. The son of man goeth, as it is written of him: but woe be to that man, by whom the son of man is betrayed. Good were it for him, if that man had never been born.

Matt. 26.
Luke 26. b.
John 13.

Psa. 41. c.

And as they ate, Jesus took bread, blessed and brake and gave to them and said: Take, eat, this is my body. And he took the cup, gave thanks, and gave it to them, and they all drank of it. And he said unto them: This is my blood of the new testament which is shed for many. Verily I say unto you: I will drink no more of this fruit of the vine, until that day, that I drink it new in the kingdom of God. And when they had said grace, they went out to mount Olivet.

1 Cor. 11. c.

The institution of the sacrament.

And Jesus said unto them: All ye shall be offended through me this night. For it is written: I will smite the shepherd, and the sheep shall be scattered. But after that I am risen again, I will go into Galilee before you. Peter said unto him: And though all men should be offended, yet would not I. And Jesus said unto him: Verily I say unto thee, this day, even in this night, before the cock crow twice, thou shalt deny me thrice. And he spake boldlier: no, if I should die with thee, I will not deny thee. Likewise also said they all.

Matt. 26.
Zech. 13. c.

D   And they came into a place named Gethsemane. And he said to his disciples: Sit ye here, while I go apart and pray. And he took with him Peter, James and John, and he began to wax abashed and to be in an agony and said unto them: My soul is very heavy even unto the death, tarry here and watch. And he went forth a little and fell down on the ground and prayed: that if it were possible, the hour might pass from him. And he said: Abba father, all things are possible unto thee, take away this cup from me. Nevertheless not that I will, but that thou wilt, be done.

Luke 22. d.
John 28. a.
John 16. a.
Matt. 26.
Luke 22. d.

He armeth himself against his passion.

And he came and found them sleeping, and said to Peter: Simon, sleepest thou? Couldest not thou watch with me one hour? watch ye, and pray, lest ye enter into temptation: the spirit is ready, but the flesh is weak. And again he went away and prayed, and spake the same words. And he returned and found them asleep again, for their eyes were heavy: neither wist they what to answer him. And he came the third time, and said unto them: sleep henceforth and take your ease, it is enough. The hour is come, behold the son of man shall be delivered into the hands of sinners. Rise up, let us go. Lo he that betrayeth me, is at hand.

And immediately while he yet spake, came Judas one of the twelve, and with him a great number of people with swords and staves from the high priests and scribes and elders. And he that betrayed him, had given them a general token★　**E** saying: whosoever I do kiss, he it is: take him and lead him away warily. And as soon as he was come, he went straightway to him, and said unto him: Master, Master, and kissed him. And they laid their hands on him, and took him. And one of them that stood by, drew out a sword, and smote a servant of the high priest, and cut off his ear.

And Jesus answered and said unto them: ye be come out as unto a thief with swords and with staves, for to take me. I was daily with you in the temple teaching and ye took me not: but that the scriptures should be fulfilled. And they all forsook him and ran away. And there followed him a certain young man, clothed in linen upon the bare, and the young men caught him, and he left his linen and fled from them naked.

And they led Jesus away to the highest priest of all, and to him came all the high priests, and the elders, and the scribes. And Peter followed him a great way off, even into the palace of the high priest, and sat with the servants, and warmed himself at the fire.

And the high priests and all the council sought for witness against Jesus, to　**F** put him to death, and found none. Yet many bare false witness against him, but their witness agreed not together. And there arose certain and brought false witness against him, saying. We heard him say: I will destroy this temple made with hands, and within three days I will build another, made without hands. But their witness agreed not together.

And the highest priest stood up amongst them, and asked Jesus saying: answerest thou nothing? How is it that these bear witness against thee? And he held his peace, and answered nothing. Again the highest priest asked him, and said unto him: Art thou Christ the son of the blessed? And Jesus said: I am. And ye shall see the son of man sit on the right hand of power, and come in the clouds of heaven. Then the highest priest rent his clothes and said: what need we any further of witness? Ye have heard the blasphemy; what think ye? And they all gave sentence that he was worthy of death. And some began to spit at him, and to cover his face, and to beat him with fists, and to say unto him, arede unto us. And the servants buffeted him on the face.

And as Peter was beneath in the palace, there came one of the wenches of the　**G** highest priest: and when she saw Peter warming himself, she looked on him,

Matt. 26.
Luke 22. e.
John 28.

★ He is betrayed of
Judas, which also gave
them a token to know
him by.

Lam. 4. d.

The young man that
was clothed in linen.

Matt. 26.
Luke 22. f.
John 18.

He is falsely accused.

John 3.

He holdeth his peace.

He is mocked, spit on,
blindfolded and
buffeted.

Matt. 26. g.
Luke 22. f.
John 18. c.

and said: wast not thou also with Jesus of Nazareth? And he denied it saying: I
know him not, neither wot I what thou sayest. And he went out into the
porch, and the cock crew. And a damsel saw him, and again began to say to
them that stood by, this is one of them. And he denied it again. And anon after,
they that stood by, said again to Peter: surely thou art one of them, for thou art
of Galilee, and thy speech agreeth thereto. And he began to curse and to swear
saying: I know not this man of whom ye speak. And again the cock crew, and
Peter remembered the word that Jesus said unto him: before the cock crow
twice, thou shalt deny me thrice, and began to weep.

Peter denieth.

Matt. 22.
Luke 22. f, g.
John 18. e.

CHAPTER FIFTEEN

A And anon in the dawning the high priests held council with the elders and
the scribes, and the whole congregation, and bound Jesus and led him away,
and delivered him to Pilate. And Pilate asked him: art thou the king of the
Jews? And he answered and said unto him: thou sayest it. And the high
priests accused him of many things. Wherefore Pilate asked him again saying:
Answerest thou nothing? Behold how many things they lay unto thy charge.
Jesus yet answered never a word, so that Pilate marvelled.

Matt. 27.
Luke 23.
John 18.

He is delivered to Pilate

Matt. 27.
Luke 23. a.

He holdeth his peace.

At that feast Pilate was wont to deliver at their pleasure a prisoner: whomsoever they would desire. And there was one named Barabbas, which lay
bound with them that made insurrection, and in the insurrection committed
murder. And the people called unto him, and began to desire according as he
had ever done unto them. Pilate answered them and said: Will ye that I loose
unto you the king of the Jews? For he knew that the high priests had delivered
him of envy. But the high priests had moved the people, that he should rather
deliver Barabbas unto them.

Barabbas.

B And Pilate answered again, and said unto them: What will ye then that I do
with him whom ye call the king of the Jews? And they cried again: crucify
him. Pilate said unto them: What evil hath he done? And they cried the more
fervently: crucify him. And so Pilate willing to content the people, loosed them
Barabbas, and delivered Jesus when he had scourged him, for to be crucified.

Matt. 27. d.
Luke 23.
John 18. g.
and 19. c.

He is scourged and then
delivered to death.

And the soldiers led him away into the common hall, and called together the
whole multitude, and they clothed him with purple, and they plaited a crown
of thorns and crowned him withal, and began to salute him: Hail king of the
Jews. And they smote him on the head with a reed, and spat upon him, and
kneeled down and worshipped him.

Matt. 27.

He is crowned.

He is buffeted.

And when they had mocked him, they took the purple off him, and put his
own clothes on him, and led him out, to crucify him. And they compelled one
that passed by, called Simon of Cyrene (which came out of the field, and was
father of Alexander and Rufus) to bear his cross. And they brought him to a
place named Golgotha (which is by interpretation, the place of dead men's
skulls) and they gave him to drink, wine mingled with myrrh, but he received
it not.

Matt. 27.
Luke 23.

Golgotha.

Matt. 27.

C And when they had crucified him, they parted his garments, casting lots for

Luke 23. d.

85

His garments are
divided.

John 19. d.

He is crucified.

Isa. 53. d.

He is railed on.

John. 2. d.

Psa. 21.

Vinegar is offered
him to drink.

He giveth up his spirit.
The veil renteth.

Matt. 27.
Luke 23. g.
John 19. g.

He is buried.

Luke 24. a.
John 20. a.

Matt. 28.
John 20. c.

them, what every man should have. And it was about the third hour, and they
crucified him. And the title of his cause was written: The king of the Jews. And
they crucified with him two thieves: the one on the right hand, and the other
on his left. And the scripture was fulfilled which sayeth: he was counted among
the wicked.

And they that went by, railed on him: wagging their heads and saying: Ah,
wretch, that destroyest the temple and buildest it in three days: save thyself,
and come down from the cross. Likewise also mocked him the high priests
among themselves with the scribes and said: He saved other men, himself he
cannot save. Let Christ the king of Israel now descend from the cross, that we
may see and believe. And they that were crucified with him, checked him also.   **D**

And when the sixth hour was come, darkness arose over all the earth, until
the ninth hour. And at the ninth hour Jesus cried with a loud voice saying: Eloi,
Eloi, lama sabachthani, which is if it be interpreted: my God, my God, why
hast thou forsaken me? And some of them that stood by, when they heard
that, said: behold he calleth for Elias. And one ran and filled a sponge full of
vinegar, and put it on a reed, and gave him to drink, saying: let him alone, let
us see whether Elias will come and take him down.

But Jesus cried with a loud voice, and gave up the ghost. And the veil of the
temple did rent in two pieces, from the top to the bottom. And when the
centurion which stood before him, saw that he so cried and gave up the ghost,
he said: truly this man was the son of God. There were also women a good way
off beholding him: among whom was Mary Magdalene, and Mary the mother
of James the little and of Joses, and Mary Salome which also when he was in
Galilee, followed him and ministered unto him, and many other women which
came up with him to Jerusalem.

And now when night was come (because it was the even that goeth before   **E**
the sabbath) Joseph of Arimathæa a noble councillor which also looked for the
kingdom of God, came and went in boldly unto Pilate, and begged the body
of Jesus. And Pilate marvelled that he was already dead, and called unto him
the centurion, and asked of him, whether he had been any while dead. And
when he knew the truth of the centurion, he gave the body to Joseph. And he
bought a linen cloth, and took him down and wrapped him in the linen cloth,
and laid him in a tomb that was hewn out of the rock, and rolled a stone unto
the door of the sepulchre. And Mary Magdalene and Mary Joses beheld where
he was laid.

CHAPTER SIXTEEN

+ And when the sabbath day was past, Mary Magdalene, and Mary Jacobi, and   **A**
Salome, bought odours, that they might come and anoint him. And early in
the morning the next day after the sabbath day, they came unto the sepulchre,
when the sun was risen. And they said one to another: who shall roll us away
the stone from the door of the sepulchre? And when they looked, they saw
how the stone was rolled away: for it was a very great one. And they went into

the sepulchre, and saw a young man sitting on the right side, clothed in a long white garment, and they were abashed.

B   And he said unto them, be not afraid: ye seek Jesus of Nazareth which was crucified. He is risen, he is not here. Behold the place, where they put him. But go your way, and tell his disciples, and namely Peter: he will go before you into Galilee: there shall ye see him, as he said unto you. And they went out quickly and fled from the sepulchre. For they trembled and were amazed. Neither said they any thing to any man, for they were afraid. ⊦   *Matt. 28. c.*

+ When Jesus was risen the morrow after the sabbath day, he appeared first to Mary Magdalene, out of whom he cast seven devils. And she went and told them that were with him as they mourned and wept. And when they heard, that he was alive and he had appeared to her, they believed it not. After that, he appeared unto two of them in a strange figure, as they walked and went into the country. And they went and told it to the remnant. And they believed them neither. ⊦   *Mary Magdalenc.*   *Luke. 24. b.*

C   + After that he appeared unto the eleven as they sat at meat: and cast in their teeth their unbelief and hardness of heart: because they believed not them which had seen him after his resurrection. And he said unto them: Go ye in to all the world, and preach the glad tidings to all creatures: he that believeth and is baptised, shall be saved. But he that believeth not, shall be damned.   *Matt. 28.*   *Luke 24. f.*   *John 20. e.*   *Matt. 28.*

D   And these signs shall follow them that believe: In my name they shall cast out devils and shall speak with new tongues, and shall kill serpents. And if they drink any deadly thing, it shall not hurt them. They shall lay their hands on the sick, and they shall recover.

So then when the Lord had spoken unto them, he was received into heaven, and is set down on the right hand of God. And they went forth, and preached everywhere. And the Lord wrought with them, and confirmed the word with miracles that followed. ⊦   *Luke 24. g.*

The end of the gospel of St Mark.

THE GOSPEL OF ST LUKE

Forasmuch as many have taken in hand to compile a treatise of those things, which are surely known among us, even as they declared them unto us, which from the beginning saw them theirselves, and were ministers at the doing: I determined also, as soon as I had searched out diligently all things from the beginning, that then I would write unto thee, good Theophilus: that thou mightest know the certainty of those things, whereof thou art informed.

CHAPTER ONE

There was in the days of Herod king of Jewry, a certain priest named Zacharias, of the course of Abia. And his wife was of the daughters of Aaron: And her name was Elizabeth. Both were perfect before God, and walked in all the laws and ordinances of the Lord, that no man could find fault with them. And they had no child, because that Elizabeth was barren and both were well stricken in age.

And it came to pass, as he executed the priest's office before God, as his course came (according to the custom of the priest's office) his lot was to burn incense. And went into the temple of the Lord and the whole multitude of the people were without in prayer while the incense was a-burning. And there appeared unto him an angel of the lord standing on the right side of the altar of incense. And when Zacharias saw him, he was abashed, and fear came on him.

And the angel said unto him: fear not Zachary, for thy prayer is heard: And thy wife Elizabeth shall bear thee a son, and thou shalt call his name John, and thou shalt have joy and gladness, and many shall rejoice at his birth. For he shall be great in the sight of the lord, and shall neither drink wine nor strong drink. And he shall be filled with the holy ghost, even in his mother's womb: and many of the children of Israel shall he turn to their Lord God. And he shall go before him in the spirit and power of Elias to turn the hearts* of the fathers to the children, and the unbelievers to the wisdom of the just men: to make the people ready for the Lord.

And Zacharias said unto the angel: Whereby shall I know this? seeing that I am old and my wife well stricken in years. And the angel answered and said

A

B

Zacharias.

Elizabeth.

Lev. 11: d.

John.

* To make the children have such an heart to God as Abraham and the Fathers had.

Psa. 131.
Mal. 3. a.
Mal. 4. b.

A sign is asked.

unto him: I am Gabriel that stand in the presence of God, and am sent to speak unto thee: and to shew thee these glad tidings. And behold thou shalt be dumb, and not able to speak until the time that these things be performed, because thou believedst not my words which shall be fulfilled in their season.

And the people waited for Zacharias, and marvelled that he tarried in the temple. And when he came out, he could not speak unto them. Whereby they perceived that he had seen some vision in the temple. And he beckoned unto them, and remained speechless.

+ And it fortuned, as soon as the time of his office was out, he departed home into his own house. And after those days, his wife Elizabeth conceived, and hid herself five months saying: This wise hath God dealt with me in the days when he looked on me, to take from me the rebuke that I suffered among men.

+ And in the sixth month the angel Gabriel was sent from God unto a city of Galilee, named Nazareth, to a virgin spoused to a man whose name was Joseph, of the house of David, and the virgin's name was Mary. And the angel went in unto her, and said: Hail full of grace, the Lord is with thee: blessed art thou among women.

Mary.

When she saw him, she was abashed at his saying: and cast in her mind what manner of salutation that should be. And the angel said unto her: fear not Mary: for thou hast found grace with God. Lo: thou shalt conceive in thy womb, and shalt bear a son, and shalt call his name Jesus. He shall be great, and shall be called the son of the highest. And the lord God shall give unto him the seat of his father David, and he shall reign over the house of Jacob for ever, and of his kingdom shall be none end.

Isa. 7. d.
Jesus.

Dan. 7. d.
Mic. 4. e.

Then said Mary unto the angel: How shall this be, seeing I know not a man? And the angel answered and said unto her: The holy ghost shall come upon thee, and the power of the highest shall overshadow thee. Therefore also that holy thing which shall be born, shall be called the son of God. And behold thy cousin Elizabeth, she hath also conceived a son in her age. And this is her sixth month, though she be called barren: for with God can nothing be unpossible. And Mary said: behold the handmaiden of the lord, be it unto me even as thou hast said. ⊦ And the angel departed from her.

+ And Mary arose in those days, and went into the mountains with haste, into a city of Jewry and entered into the house of Zachary, and saluted Elizabeth. And it fortuned, as Elizabeth heard the salutation of Mary, the babe sprang in her belly. And Elizabeth was filled with the holy ghost, and cried with a loud voice, and said: Blessed art thou among women, and blessed is the fruit of thy womb. And whence happeneth this to me, that the mother of my Lord should come to me? For lo, as soon as the voice of thy salutation sounded in mine ears, the babe sprang in my belly for joy. And blessed art thou that believedst: for those things shall be performed which were told thee from the Lord. And Mary said:

Mary greeteth Elizabeth.

My soul magnifieth the Lord.

And my spirit rejoiceth in God my saviour. ⊦

Magnificat.

For he hath looked on the poor degree of his handmaiden. Behold now from henceforth shall all generations call me blessed.

For he that is mighty hath done to me great things, and holy is his name.

And his mercy is on them that fear him throughout all generations.

He sheweth strength with his arm, he scattereth them that are proud in the imagination of their hearts.

He putteth down the mighty from their seats, and exalteth them of low degree.

He filleth the hungry with good things: and sendeth away the rich empty.   **F**

Isa. 41. b.
Isa. 30. d.
and 54. b.
Jer. 31. a.
Psa. 131.
Gen. 22.

He remembereth mercy: and helpeth his servant Israel.

Even as he promised to our fathers, Abraham and to his seed for ever.

And Mary abode with her about a three months, and returned again to her own house.

John is born.

+ Elizabeth's time was come that she should be delivered, and she brought forth a son. And her neighbours and her cousins heard tell how the Lord had shewed great mercy upon her, and they rejoiced with her.

And it fortuned the eighth day: they came to circumcise the child: and called his name Zacharias, after the name of his father. Howbeit his mother answered, and said: not so, but he shall be called John. And they said unto her: There is none of thy kin, that is named with this name. And they made signs to his father, how he would have him called. And he asked for writing tables and wrote saying: his name is John. And they marvelled all. And his mouth was opened immediately, and his tongue also, and he spake lauding God. And fear came on all them that dwelt nigh unto them. And all these sayings were noised abroad throughout all the hill country of Jewry and all they that heard them laid them up in their hearts saying: What manner child shall this be? And the hand of the Lord was with him.

And his father Zacharias was filled with the holy ghost, and prophesied saying:

Benedictus.

Blessed be the Lord God of Israel, for he hath visited and redeemed his people. ⊦

Psa. 74.
and 132. d.
Jer. 23. a.
and 30. b.
Jer. 31. f.
Gen. 29. c.

And hath raised up an horn of salvation unto us, in the house of his servant   **G** David.

Even as he promised by the mouth of his holy prophets which were since the world began,

That we should be saved from our enemies and from the hands of all that hate us:

To fulfil the mercy promised to our fathers, and to remember his holy covenant.

And to perform the oath which he sware to our father Abraham, for to give us.

That we, delivered out of the hands of our enemies, might serve him without fear, all the days of our life, in such holiness and righteousness that are accept before him.

And thou child, shalt be called the prophet of the highest: for thou shalt go before the face of the lord, to prepare his ways:

And to give knowledge of salvation unto his people, for the remission of sins:

Through the tender mercy of our God, whereby the day-spring* from on high hath visited us.

To give light to them that sat in darkness and in shadow of death, and to guide our feet into the way of peace.

And the child grew and waxed strong in spirit, and was in wilderness, till the day came when he should shew himself unto the Israelites.

*Christ is the day-spring that giveth light to them that sit in darkness of the ignorance of God.

CHAPTER TWO

A + And it chanced in those days: that there went out a commandment from August the Emperor, that all the world should be taxed. And this taxing was the first and executed when Cyrenius was lieutenant in Syria. And every man went unto his own city to be taxed. And Joseph also ascended from Galilee, out of a city called Nazareth, into Jewry: unto the city of David which is called Bethlehem, because he was of the house and lineage of David, to be taxed with Mary his spoused wife which was with child.

And it fortuned while they were there, her time was come that she should be delivered. And she brought forth her first begotten son, and wrapped him in swaddling clothes, and laid him in a manger, because there was no room for them within in the inn.

Christ is born.

B And there were in the same region shepherds abiding in the field and watching their flock by night. And lo: the angel of the Lord stood hard by them, and the brightness of the Lord shone round about them, and they were sore afraid. But the angel said unto them: Be not afraid. For behold, I bring you tidings of great joy that shall come to all the people: for unto you is born this day in the city of David, a saviour which is Christ the Lord. And take this for a sign: ye shall find the child swaddled and laid in a manger. And straightway there was with the angel a multitude of heavenly soldiers, lauding God and saying: Glory to God on high, and peace on the earth: and unto men rejoicing. ⊢

Shepherds.

Sign.

C And it fortuned, as soon as the angels were gone away from them into heaven, + the shepherds said one to another: let us go even unto Bethlehem, and see this thing that is happened which the Lord hath shewed unto us. And they came with haste, and found Mary and Joseph and the babe laid in a manger. And when they had seen it, they published abroad the saying which was told them of that child. And all that heard it, wondered at those things which were told them of the shepherds. But Mary kept all those sayings, and pondered them in her heart. And the shepherds returned, praising and lauding God for all that they had heard and seen, even as it was told unto them. ⊢

+ And when the eighth day was come that the child should be circumcised, his name was called Jesus, which was named of the angel before he was conceived in the womb. ⊢

Lev. 12. a.

Christ is circumcised.

D + And when the time of their purification (after the law of Moses) was come, they brought him to Jerusalem, to present him to the Lord (as it is written in the law of the Lord: every man that first openeth the matrix, shall be called

Matt. 1. c.
Lev. 12. a.
Exod. 13. a.
Num. 8. c.
Lev. 12. c.

holy to the Lord) and to offer (as it is said in the law of the Lord) a pair of turtle-doves or two young pigeons.

Simeon.

And behold there was a man in Jerusalem whose name was Simeon. And the same man was just and feared God, and longed for the consolation of Israel, and the holy ghost was in him. And an answer was given him of the holy ghost, that he should not see death, before he had seen the Lord's Christ. And he came by inspiration into the temple.

And when the father and mother brought in the child Jesus, to do for him after the custom of the law, then took he him up in his arms and said,

Nunc dimittis.

Lord, now lettest thou thy servant depart in peace, according to thy promise.

For mine eyes have seen the saviour sent from thee,

Which thou hast prepared before the face of all people.

A light to lighten the gentiles, and the glory of thy people Israel. �   **E**

+ And his father and mother marvelled at those things which were spoken of him. And Simeon blessed them, and said unto Mary his mother: behold, this child shall be the fall and resurrection of many in Israel, and a sign which shall be spoken against. And moreover the sword shall pierce thy soul, that the thoughts of many hearts may be opened.

Isa. 8. c.
Rom. 10. g.
1 Pet. 2. b.

Anna.

And there was a prophetess, one Anna, the daughter of Phanuel of the tribe of Aser: which was of a great age, and had lived with an husband seven years from her virginity. And she had been a widow about four score and four years, which went never out of the temple, but served God with fasting and prayer night and day. And the same came forth that same hour, and praised the Lord, and spake of him to all that looked for redemption in Jerusalem.

And as soon as they had performed all things according to the law of the Lord, they returned into Galilee to their own city Nazareth. And the child grew and waxed strong in spirit, and was filled with wisdom, and the grace of God was with him. ⊢

+ And his father and mother went to Jerusalem every year at the feast of   **E** Easter. + And when he was twelve years old, they went up to Jerusalem after the custom of the feast. And when they had fulfilled the days, as they returned home, the child Jesus bode still in Jerusalem, unknowing to his father and mother. For they supposed he had been in the company, and therefore came a day's journey, and sought him among their kinsfolk and acquaintaunce. And when they found him not, they went back again to Jerusalem, and sought him.

Christ is found
disputing in the temple.

And it fortuned after three days, that they found him in the temple, sitting in the midst of the doctors, both hearing them and posing them. And all that heard him, marvelled at his wit and answers.

And when they saw him, they were astonied. And his mother said unto him: **C** son, why hast thou thus dealt with us? Behold thy father and I have sought thee, sorrowing. And he said unto them: how is it that ye sought me? Wist ye not that I must go about my father's business? And they understood not the saying that he spake to them. And he went with them, and came to Nazareth, and was obedient to them. But his mother kept all these things in her heart. And Jesus increased in wisdom and age, and in favour with God and man. ⊢

CHAPTER THREE   3¹⁻²³

A + In the fifteenth year of the reign of Tiberius the Emperor, Pontius Pilate
being lieutenant of Jewry, and Herod being Tetrarch of Galilee, and his brother
Philip Tetrarch in Iturea and in the region of Trachonitis, and Lysanias the
Tetrarch of Abilene, when Annas and Caiaphas were the high priests: the
word of God came unto John the son of Zacharias in the wilderness. And he
came into all the coasts about Jordan, preaching the baptism of repentance for
the remission of sins, as it is written in the book of the sayings of Esaias the
prophet which sayeth: The voice of a crier in wilderness, prepare the way of the
Lord, make his paths straight. Every valley shall be filled, and every mountain
and hill shall be brought low. And crooked things shall be made straight: and
the rough ways shall be made smooth: and all flesh shall see the saviour sent of
God. ⊦

Tetrarch.

John Baptist.

Matt. 3. a.
Mark. 1. a.

Isa. 11. a.
John. 1. c.

B   Then said he to the people that were come to be baptised of him: O
generation of vipers, who hath taught you to fly from the wrath to come?
Bring forth due fruits of repentance, and begin not to say in yourselves, we
have Abraham to our father. For I say unto you: God is able of these stones to
raise up children unto Abraham. Now also is the axe laid unto the root of the
trees: so that every tree which bringeth not forth good fruit, shall be hewn
down, and cast into the fire.

Mark 3. b.

The axe.

And the people asked him saying: What shall we do then? He answered and
said unto them: He that hath two coats, let him part with him that hath none:
and he that hath meat, let him do likewise.

Then came there publicans to be baptised, and said unto him: Master, what
shall we do? And he said unto them: require no more than that which is
appointed unto you.

Publicans.

C   The soldiers likewise demanded of him saying: and what shall we do? And
he said to them: Do violence to no man: neither trouble any man wrongfully:
but be content with your wages.

Soldiers.

As the people were in a doubt, and all men disputed in their hearts of John,
whether he were very Christ, John answered and said to them all: I baptise you
with water, but a stronger than I cometh after me, whose shoe-latchet I am not
worthy to unloose: he will baptise you with the holy ghost, and with fire:
which hath his fan in his hand, and will purge his floor, and will gather the corn
into his barn: but the chaff will he burn with fire that never shall be quenched.
And many other things in his exhortation preached he unto the people.

Matt. 3. b.
Mark 3. b.
John 1. d.

Fan.

Chaff.

D   Then Herod the Tetrarch (when he was rebuked of him for Herodias his
brother Philip's wife, and for all the evils which Herod had done) added this
above all, and laid John in prison.

Matt. 3. a.
Mark 1. b.

And it fortuned as all the people received baptism (and when Jesus was
baptised and did pray) that heaven was opened and the holy ghost came down
in a bodily shape like a dove upon him, and a voice came from heaven saying:
Thou art my dear son, in thee do I delight.

John is prisoned.

Christ is baptised.

E   And Jesus himself was about thirty years of age when he began, being as men
supposed the son of Joseph.

Genealogy.

which Joseph was the son of Heli:

which was the son of Matthat:

which was the son of Levi:

which was the son of Melchi:

which was the son of Janna:

which was the son of Joseph:

which was the son of Mattathias:

which was the son of Amos:

which was the son of Naum:

which was the son of Esli:

which was the son of Nagge:

which was the son of Maath:

which was the son of Mattathias:

which was the son of Semei:

which was the son of Joseph:

which was the son of Juda:

which was the son of Joanna:

which was the son of Rhesa:

which was the son of Zorobabel:

which was the son of Salathiel:

which was the son of Neri:

which was the son of Melchi:

which was the son of Addi:

which was the son of Cosam:

which was the son of Elmodam:

which was the son of Er:

which was the son of Jose:

which was the son of Eliezer:

which was the son of Jorim:

which was the son of Matthat:

which was the son of Levi:

which was the son of Simeon:

which was the son of Juda:

which was the son of Joseph:

which was the son of Jonan:

which was the son of Eliakim:

which was the son of Melea:

which was the son of Menan:

which was the son of Mattatha:

which was the son of Nathan:

which was the son of David:

which was the son of Jesse:

which was the son of Obed:

which was the son of Booz:

which was the son of Salmon:

which was the son of Naasson:
which was the son of Aminadab:
which was the son of Aram:
which was the son of Esrom:
which was the son of Phares:
which was the son of Juda:
which was the son of Jacob:
which was the son of Isaac:
which was the son of Abraham:
which was the son of Thara:
which was the son of Nachor:
which was the son of Saruch:
which was the son of Ragau:
which was the son of Phalec:
which was the son of Heber:
which was the son of Sala:
which was the son of Cainan:
which was the son of Arphaxad:
which was the son of Sem:
which was the son of Noe:
which was the son of Lamech:
which was the son of Mathusala:
which was the son of Enoch:
which was the son of Jared:
which was the son of Maleleel:
which was the son of Cainan:
which was the son of Enos:
which was the son of Seth:
which was the son of Adam:
which was the son of God.

CHAPTER FOUR

A Jesus then full of the holy ghost returned from Jordan, and was carried of the *Matt. 3. a.*
spirit into wilderness, and was forty days tempted of the devil. And in those *Mark 1. b.*
days ate he nothing. And when they were ended, he afterward hungered. And *Jesus fasteth forty days.*
the devil said unto him: if thou be the son of God, command this stone that it
be bread. And Jesus answered him saying: It is written: man shall not live by
bread only, but by every word of God. *Deut. 8. d*

And the devil took him up into an high mountain, and shewed him all the
kingdoms of the world, even in the twinkling of an eye. And the devil said
unto him: all this power will I give thee every whit and the glory of them: for
that is delivered to me, and to whosoever I will, I give it. If thou therefore wilt
worship me, they shall be all thine. Jesus answered him and said: hence from

95

Deut. 6. c. and 10. d.

me Satan. For it is written: Thou shalt honour the Lord thy God, and him only serve.

And he carried him to Jerusalem, and set him on a pinnacle of the temple, **B** and said unto him: If thou be the son of God, cast thyself down from hence. For it is written, he shall give his angels charge over thee, to keep thee, and with their hands they shall stay thee up that thou dash not thy foot against a stone. Jesus answered and said to him, it is said: thou shalt not tempt the Lord thy God. As soon as the devil had ended all his temptations, he departed from him, for a season.

Psa. 90. c.

Deut. 6 c.

Matt. 4. b.
Mark 1. b.
John 4. f.

+ And Jesus returned by the power of the spirit into Galilee, and there went a **C** fame of him throughout all the region round about. And he taught in their synagogues, and was commended of all men.

Matt. 13. b.
Mark 6. a.
John 4. b.
Isa. 51.

And he came to Nazareth where he was nursed, and as his custom was, went into the synagogue on the sabbath days, and stood up for to read. And there was delivered unto him the book of the prophet Esaias. And when he had opened the book, he found the place, where it was written, the spirit of the Lord upon me, because he hath anointed me: to preach the gospel to the poor he hath sent me: and to heal the broken-hearted: to preach deliverance to the captive, and sight to the blind, and freely to set at liberty them that are bruised, and to preach the acceptable year of the Lord.

And he closed the book, and gave it again to the minister, and sat down. And **D** the eyes of all that were in the synagogue, were fastened on him. And he began to say unto them. This day is this scripture fulfilled in your ears. And all bare him witness, and wondered at the gracious words which proceeded out of his mouth, ⊢ and said: Is not this Joseph's son?

Joseph's son.

And he said unto them: Ye may very well say unto me this proverb: Physician, heal thyself. + Whatsoever we have heard done in Capernaum, do the same here likewise in thine own country. And he said, verily I say unto you: No prophet is accepted in his own country.

John 4. f.

Prophet.

1 Kin. 17.
Jas. 5. d.

But I tell you of a truth, many widows were in Israel in the days of Elias, when heaven was shut three years and six months, when great famishment was throughout all the land, and unto none of them was Elias sent, save into Sarepta besides Sidon unto a woman that was a widow. And many lepers were in Israel in the time of Eliseus the prophet: and yet none of them was healed, saving Naaman of Syria.

The widow of Sarepta.

2 Kin. 5. d.

Naaman

And as many as were in the synagogue when they heard that, were filled **E** with wrath: and rose up, and thrust him out of the city, and led him even unto the edge of the hill, whereon their city was built, to cast him down headlong. But he went his way even through the midst of them; ⊢ + and came into Capernaum a city of Galilee, and there taught them on the sabbath days. And they were astonied at his doctrine: for his preaching was with power.

Matt. 4. b.
Mark 1. c.

And in the synagogue there was a man which had a spirit of an unclean devil, and cried with a loud voice saying: let me alone, what hast thou to do with us, **F** thou Jesus of Nazareth? Art thou come to destroy us? I know thee what thou art, even the holy of God. And Jesus rebuked him saying: hold thy peace, and

Matt. 7. d.
Mark 1. c.

come out of him. And the devil threw him in the midst of them and came out of him, and hurt him not. And fear came on them all, and they spake among themselves saying: what manner a thing is this? For with authority and power he commandeth the foul spirits, and they come out? And the fame of him spread abroad through all places of the country round about. ⊢

The unclean spirit is cast out.

+ And he rose up and came out of the synagogue, and entered into Simon's house. And Simon's mother-in-law was taken with a great fever, and they made intercession to him for her. And he stood over her, and rebuked the fever: and it left her. And immediately she arose and ministered unto them.

Matt. 8. b.
Mark 1. c.

Simon's mother-in-law.

G   When the sun was down, all they that had sick taken with divers diseases, brought them unto him: and he laid his hands on every one of them, and healed them. And devils also came out of many of them, crying and saying: thou art Christ the son of God. And he rebuked them, and suffered them not to speak: for they knew that he was Christ.

Laid his hand on them.

As soon as it was day, he departed and went away into a desert place, and the people sought him and came to him, and kept him that he should not depart from them. And he said unto them: I must to other cities also preach the kingdom of God: for therefore am I sent. ⊢ And he preached in the synagogues of Galilee.

Mark 1. d.

CHAPTER FIVE

A   + It came to pass as the people pressed upon him, to hear the word of God, that he stood by the lake of Gennesaret: and saw two ships stand by the lake-side, but the fishermen were gone out of them, and were washing their nets. And he entered into one of the ships, which pertained to Simon, and prayed him, that he would thrust out a little from the land. And he sat down and taught the people out of the ship.

Matt. 4. c.
Mark 1. b.

When he had left speaking, he said unto Simon: Launch out into the deep, and let slip your nets to make a draught. And Simon answered and said to him: Master, we have laboured all night, and have taken nothing. Nethelater at thy word I will loose forth the net. And when they had so done, they inclosed a great multitude of fishes. And their net brake: but they made signs to their fellows which were in the other ship, that they should come and help them. And they came: and filled both the ships that they sank again.

B

When Simon Peter saw that, he fell down at Jesus' knees saying: Lord go from me, for I am a sinful man. For he was utterly astonied and all that were with him, at the draught of fish which they took: and so was also James and John the sons of Zebedee which were partners with Simon. And Jesus said unto Simon: fear not, from henceforth thou shalt catch men. And they brought the ships to land, and forsook all, and followed him. ⊢

C   And it fortuned as he was in a certain city: behold, there was a man full of leprosy: and when he had spied Jesus, he fell on his face, and besought him saying: Lord, if thou wilt, thou canst make me clean. And he stretched forth the hand, and touched him saying: I will, be thou clean. And immediately the

Matt. 8. a.
Mark 1. d.

Leper.

leprosy departed from him. And he warned him, that he should tell no man: but that he should go and shew himself to the priest, and offer for his cleansing, according as Moses' commandment was, for a witness unto them.

But so much the more went there a fame abroad of him, and much people came together to hear, and to be healed of him, of their infirmities. And he kept himself apart in the wildernesses, and gave himself to prayer.

+ And it happened on a certain day, that he taught: and there sat the **D** Pharisees: and doctors of law, which were come out of all the towns of Galilee, Jewry, and Jerusalem. And the power of the Lord was to heal them. And behold, men brought a man lying in his bed which was taken with a palsy: and sought means to bring him in, and to lay him before him. And when they could not find by what way they might bring him in, because of the press, they went up on the top of the house, and let him down through the tiling, bed and all in the midst before Jesus. When he saw their faith, he said unto him: man, thy sins are forgiven thee. And the scribes and the Pharisees began to think saying: What fellow is this which speaketh blasphemy? Who can forgive sins but God only?

When Jesus perceived their thoughts, he answered and said unto them: What **E** think ye in your hearts? Whether is easier to say, thy sins are forgiven thee, or to say: rise and walk? But that ye may know that the son of man hath power to forgive sins on earth, he said unto the sick of the palsy: I say to thee, arise, take up thy bed and go home to thy house. And immediately he rose up before them, and took up his bed whereon he lay, and departed to his own house praising God. And they were all amazed and they lauded God, and were filled with fears saying: We have seen strange things today. ⊢

And after that he went forth and saw a publican named Levi, sitting at the **F** receipt of custom, and said unto him: follow me. And he left all, rose up, and followed him. And that same Levi made him a great feast at home in his own house. And there was a great company of publicans and of other that sat at meat with him. And the scribes and Pharisees murmured against his disciples saying: Why eat ye and drink ye with publicans and sinners? Jesus answered and said unto them: They that are whole, need not of the physician: but they that are sick. I came not to call the righteous, but sinners to repentance.

Then they said unto him: Why do the disciples of John fast often and pray, **G** and the disciples of the Pharisees also: and thine eat and drink? And he said unto them: Can ye make the children of the wedding fast, as long as the bridegroom is present with them? The days will come, when the bridegroom shall be taken away from them: then shall they fast in those days.

Then he spake unto them in a similitude: No man putteth a piece of a new garment, into an old vesture: for if he do, then breaketh he the new, and the piece that was taken out of the new, agreeth not with the old. Also, no man poureth new wine into old vessels. For if he do, the new wine breaketh the vessels, and runneth out itself, and the vessels perish: But new wine must be poured into new vessels, and both are preserved. Also, no man that drinketh old wine, straightway can away with new, for he sayeth the old is pleasanter. **D**

Lev. 13. a.

Matt. 9. a.
Mark 2. a.

Palsy.

Sign.

Matt. 9. a.
Mark 2. b.

Levi.

Publicans and sinners.

Matt. 9. b.
Mark 2. c.

The disciples fast not.

New and old agree not.

CHAPTER SIX 6^{1-25}

It happened on an after-sabbath, that he went through the corn-field, and that his disciples plucked the ears of corn, and ate, and rubbed them in their hands. And certain of the Pharisees said unto them: Why do ye that which is not lawful to do on the sabbath days? And Jesus answered them and said: Have ye not read what David did, when he himself was an-hungered and they which were with him: how he went into the house of God, and took and ate the loaves of hallowed bread, and gave also to them which were with him: which was not lawful to eat, but for the priests only. And he said unto them: The son of man is Lord of the sabbath day.

+ And it fortuned in another sabbath also, that he entered into the synagogue and taught. And there was a man whose right hand was dried up. And the scribes and Pharisees watched him, to see whether he would heal on the sabbath day, that they might find an accusation against him. But he knew their thoughts, and said to the man which had the withered hand: Rise up, and stand forth in the midst. And he arose and stepped forth. Then said Jesus unto them: I will ask you a question: Whether is it lawful on the sabbath days to do good or to do evil? to save life or for to destroy it? And he beheld them all in compass, and said unto the man: Stretch forth thy hand. And he did so and his hand was restored, and made as whole as the other. And they were filled full of madness, and communed one with another, what they might do to Jesus. +

C And it fortuned in those days, that he went out into a mountain for to pray, and continued all night in prayer to God. And as soon as it was day, he called his disciples, and of them he chose twelve, which also he called apostles. Simon whom he named Peter: and Andrew his brother. James and John, Philip and Bartholomew, Matthew and Thomas, James the son of Alpheus and Simon called Zelotes, and Judas, James' son, and Judas Iscariot, which same was the traitor.

+ And he came down with them and stood in the plain field with the company of his disciples, and a great multitude of people out of all parts of **D** Jewry and Jerusalem, and from the sea-coast of Tyre and Sidon, which came to hear him, and to be healed of their diseases: and they also that were vexed with foul spirits, and they were healed. And all the people pressed to touch him: for there went virtue out of him, and healed them all.

And he lifted up his eyes upon the disciples, and said: Blessed be ye poor: for yours is the kingdom of God. Blessed are ye that hunger now: for ye shall be satisfied. Blessed are ye that weep now: for ye shall laugh. Blessed are ye when men hate you, and thrust you out of their company, and rail, and abhor your name as an evil thing, for the son of man's sake. Rejoice ye then, and be glad: for behold, your reward is great in heaven. + After this manner their fathers entreated the prophets.

But woe be to you that are rich: for ye have therein your consolation. Woe be to you that are full: for ye shall hunger. Woe be to you that now laugh: for

Corn-field.

Matt. 22. d.
Mark 2. d.

The sabbath day is broken.

1 Sam. 21. g.

Matt. 12. a.
Mark 3. a.

Dried hand.

Madness.

Matt. 10. a.
Mark 3. b.

The twelve are chosen.

Matt. 5. a.

Covenants.

True prophets.

Amos 6. a.
Eccl. 31. a.

ye shall wail and weep. Woe be to you when all men praise you: for so did their fathers to the false prophets.

But I say unto you which hear: Love your enemies. Do good to them which **E** hate you. Bless them that curse you. And pray for them which wrongfully trouble you. And unto him that smiteth thee on the one cheek, offer also the other. And him that taketh away thy gown, forbid not to take thy coat also. Give to every man that asketh of thee. And of him that taketh away thy goods, ask them not again. And as ye would that men should do to you: so do ye to them likewise.

If ye love them which love you: what thank are ye worthy of? For the very sinners love their lovers. And if ye do for them which do for you: what thank are ye worthy of? For the very sinners do even the same. If ye lend to them of whom ye hope to receive: what thank shall ye have? For the very sinners lend to sinners, to receive as much again. Wherefore, love ye your enemies, do good and lend, looking for nothing again, and your reward shall be great, and ye shall be the children of the highest: for he is kind unto the unkind and to the evil.

+ Be ye therefore merciful, as your father is merciful. Judge not and ye shall **F** not be judged. Condemn not: and ye shall not be condemned. Forgive, and ye shall be forgiven. Give, and it shall be given unto you: good measure, pressed down, shaken together and running over, shall men give into your bosoms. For with what measure ye mete, with the same shall men mete to you again.

And he put forth a similitude unto them: Can the blind lead the blind? Do they not both then fall into the ditch? The disciple is not above his master. Every man shall be perfect, even as his master is. Why seest thou a mote in thy brother's eye, and considerest not the beam that is in thine own eye? Either how canst thou say to thy brother: Brother, let me pull out the mote that is in thine eye: when thou perceivest not the beam that is in thine own eye? Hypocrite, cast out the beam out of thine own eye first, and then shalt thou see perfectly, to pull out the mote out of thy brother's eye. +

It is not a good tree that bringeth forth evil fruit: neither is that an evil tree, **G** that bringeth forth good fruit. For every tree is known by his fruit. Neither of thorns gather men figs, nor of bushes gather they grapes. A good man out of the good treasure of his heart, bringeth forth that which is good. And an evil man out of the evil treasure of his heart, bringeth forth that which is evil. For of the abundance of the heart, his mouth speaketh.

Why call ye me Master, Master: and do not as I bid you? whosoever cometh to me and heareth my sayings, and doth the same, I will shew you to whom he is like. He is like a man which built an house: and digged deep, and laid the foundation on a rock. When the waters arose, the flood beat upon that house, and could not move it. For it was grounded upon a rock. But he that heareth and doth not, is like a man that without foundation built an house upon the earth, against which the flood did beat: and it fell by and by. And the fall of that house was great.

Covenants.

Love. Do good.
Bless. Pray.

Matt. 5. g.

All the law.

Matt. 7. b.
John 4. c.
Matt. 5. g.

Lend.

Covenants.

Matt. 7. a.

Judge not. Forgive.

Mark 12. a.
Mark 4. c.
Measure.

Matt. 15. b.
Matt. 10. c.
John 13. b.
Matt 7 a.

Mote.

Beam.

Matt. 7. a.
Matt. 12. c.

The tree is known by
his fruit.

The mouth speaketh of
the fulness of the heart.

To build on rock.

To build on sand.

A When he had ended all his sayings in the audience of the people, he entered into Capernaum. And a certain centurion's servant was sick and ready to die whom he made much of. And when he heard of Jesus, he sent unto him the elders of the Jews, beseeching him that he would come and heal his servant. And they came to Jesus and besought him instantly saying: He is worthy that thou shouldest do this for him. For he loveth our nation, and hath built us a synagogue. And Jesus went with them.

Matt. 8. a.

Centurion.

B And when he was not far from the house, the centurion sent friends to him saying unto him: Lord trouble not thyself: for I am not worthy that thou shouldest enter under my roof. Wherefore I thought not myself worthy to come unto thee: but say the word, and my servant shall be whole. For I likewise am a man under power, and have under me soldiers, and I say unto one, go: and he goeth. And to another, come: and he cometh. And to my servant, do this: and he doeth it. When Jesus heard this, he marvelled at him, and turned him about and said to the people that followed him: I say unto you, I have not found so great faith, no, not in Israel. And they that were sent, turned back home again, and found the servant that was sick, whole.

C + And it fortuned after that, that he went into a city called Nain, and many of his disciples went with him, and much people. When he came nigh to the gate of the city: behold, there was a dead man carried out which was the only son of his mother, and she was a widow, and much people of the city was with her. And when the Lord saw her, he had compassion on her, and said unto her: weep not. And he went and touched the coffin, and they that bare him, stood still. And he said: Young man, I say unto thee, arise. And the dead sat up and began to speak. And he delivered him to his mother. And there came a fear on them all. And they glorified God saying: a great prophet is risen among us, and God hath visited his people. ⊦ + And this rumour of him went forth throughout all Jewry, and throughout all the regions which lie round about.

The dead is raised.

Matt. 11. a.

And the disciples of John shewed him of all these things. And John called unto him two of his disciples, and sent them to Jesus saying: Art thou he that shall come: or shall we look for another? When the men were come unto him, they said: John Baptist sent us unto thee saying: Art thou he that shall come: or shall we wait for another? And at the same time he cured many of their infirmities and plagues, and of evil spirits, and unto many that were blind, he gave sight. And Jesus answered and said unto them: Go your ways and shew John, what things ye have seen and heard: how that the blind see, the halt go, the lepers are cleansed, the deaf hear, the dead arise, to the poor is the glad tidings preached, and happy is he, that is not offended by me.

John Baptist sendeth to Christ.

Isa. 60.

D When the messengers of John were departed, he began to speak unto the people of John. What went ye out into the wilderness for to see? Went ye to see a reed shaken with the wind? But what went ye out for to see? A man clothed in soft raiment? Behold they which are gorgeously apparelled, and live delicately, are in kings' courts. But what went ye forth to see? A prophet? Yea I say to you, and more than a prophet. This is he of whom it is written: Behold I send my messenger before thy face, to prepare thy way before thee. For I say unto you: a greater prophet than John among women's children is there none. Nevertheless one that is less in the kingdom of God, is greater than he. ⊢

And all the people that heard, and the publicans, justified God, and were baptised with the baptism of John. But the Pharisees and scribes despised the counsel of God against themselves, and were not baptised of him.

And the Lord said: Whereunto shall I liken the men of this generation, and **E** what thing are they like? They are like unto children sitting in the market-place, and crying one to another, and saying: We have piped unto you, and ye have not danced: we have mourned to you, and ye have not wept. For John Baptist came, neither eating bread nor drinking wine, and ye say: he hath the devil. The son of man is come and eateth and drinketh, and ye say: behold a man which is a glutton, and a drinker of wine, a friend of publicans and sinners. Yet is wisdom justified of all her children.

+ And one of the Pharisees desired him that he would eat with him. And he went into the Pharisee's house, and sat down to meat. And behold a woman in that city, which was a sinner, as soon as she knew that Jesus sat at meat in the Pharisee's house, she brought an alabaster box of ointment, and she stood at his feet behind him weeping, and began to wash his feet with tears, and did wipe them with the hairs of her head, and kissed his feet, and anointed them with ointment.

When the Pharisee which bade him, saw that, he spake within himself, **F** saying: If this man were a prophet, he would surely have known who and what manner woman this is which toucheth him, for she is a sinner. And Jesus answered and said unto him: Simon, I have somewhat to say unto thee. And he said, Master say on. There was a certain lender which had two debtors, the one ought five hundred pence, and the other fifty. When they had nothing to pay, he forgave them both. Which of them tell me, will love him most? Simon answered and said: I suppose, that he to whom he forgave most. And he said unto him: Thou hast truly judged.

And he turned to the woman, and said unto Simon: Seest thou this woman? I entered into thy house, and thou gavest me no water to my feet: but she hath washed my feet with tears, and wiped them with the hairs of her head. Thou gavest me no kiss: but she, since the time I came in, hath not ceased to kiss my feet. Mine head with oil thou didst not anoint: but she hath anointed my feet with ointment. Wherefore I say unto thee: many sins are forgiven her, for she loved* much. To whom less is forgiven, the same doth less love.

And he said unto her, thy sins are forgiven thee. And they that sat at meat with him, began to say within themselves: Who is this which forgiveth sins also? And he said to the woman: Thy faith hath saved thee, Go in peace. ⊢

CHAPTER EIGHT

And it fortuned after that, that he himself went throughout cities and towns, **A** preaching, and shewing the kingdom of God, and the twelve with him. And

Margin notes

Mal. 3. a.

Publicans justify God.
Pharisees despise the counsel of God.

Matt. 11. d.

Wisdom.

Mary of Bethany.

* Love is the sign that the sins are forgiven her.

also certain women, which were healed of evil spirits, and infirmities: Mary called Magdalene, out of whom went seven devils, and Joanna the wife of Chuza Herod's steward, and Susanna and many other: which ministered unto them of their substance. + When much people were gathered together, and were come to him out of all cities, he spake by a similitude. A sower went out to sow his seed: and as he sowed, some fell by the way-side, and it was trodden under feet, and the fowls of the air devoured it up. And some fell on stone, and as soon as it was sprung up, it withered away, because it lacked moistness. And some fell among thorns, and the thorns sprang up with it, and choked it. And some fell on good ground, and sprang up and bare fruit, an hundred-fold. And as he said these things, he cried: He that hath ears to hear, let him hear.

B And his disciples asked him saying: what manner similitude is this? And he said: unto you is it given to know the secrets of the kingdom of God: but to other in similitudes, that when they see, they should not see: and when they hear they should not understand.

The similitude is this. The seed is the word of God. Those that are beside the way, are they that hear, and afterward cometh the devil and taketh away the word out of their hearts, lest they should believe and be saved. They on the stones, are they which when they hear, receive the word with joy. But these have no roots, which for a while believe, and in time of temptation go away. And that which fell among thorns, are they which hear, and go forth, and are choked with cares and with riches, and voluptuous living, and bring forth no fruit. That in the good ground, are they which with a good and pure heart, hear the word and keep it, and bring forth fruit with patience. ⊦

C No man lighteth a candle, and covereth it under a vessel, neither putteth it under the table: but setteth it on a candlestick, that they that enter in, may see the light. Nothing is in secret, that shall not come abroad: Neither any thing hid, that shall not be known, and come to light. Take heed therefore how ye hear. For whosoever hath, to him shall be given: And whosoever hath not, from him shall be taken, even that same which he supposeth that he hath.

Then came to him his mother and his brethren, and could not come at him for press. And they told him saying: Thy mother and thy brethren stand without, and would see thee. He answered and said unto them: my mother and my brethren are these which hear the word of God and do it.

D + And it chanced on a certain day that he went into a ship, and his disciples also, and he said unto them: Let us go over unto the other side of the lake. And they launched forth. And as they sailed, he fell asleep, and there arose a storm of wind in the lake, and they were filled with water, and were in jeopardy. And they went to him and awoke him saying: Master Master, we are lost. Then he arose and rebuked the wind and the tempest of water, and they ceased, and it waxed calm. And he said unto them: where is your faith? They feared and wondered saying one to another: what fellow is this? for he commandeth both the winds and water, and they obey him? ⊦ And they sailed unto the region of the Gadarenites, which is over against Galilee.

And as he went out to land, there met him a certain man out of the city, which had a devil long time, and ware no clothes, neither abode in any house:

Sower.

Matt. 12. a.
Mark 4. a.

Isa. 7. e.
Matt. 13. b.
Mark 4. b.
John 13. f.
Rom. 11. b.

The sower is expounded.

Matt. 10. b.

Candle.

Mark 4. c.
Matt. 10. c.
Mark 3. c.
Matt. 13. b. and 25. c.
Mark 4. c.
Matt. 12. d.

Mark 3. d.

Mother and brethren.

Matt. 8. c.
Mark 4. d.

Jesus sleepeth in the ship.

Matt. 8. c.
Mark 5. a.

Gadarenites.

but among graves. When he saw Jesus, he cried, and fell down before him, and with a loud voice said: What have I to do with thee; Jesus the son of the God most highest? I beseech thee torment me not. Then he commanded the foul spirit to come out of the man. For oft-times he caught him, and he was bound with chains and kept with fetters: and he brake the bonds, and was carried of the fiend, into wilderness.

Legion.

And Jesus asked him saying: what is thy name? And he said; Legion, because **E** many devils were entered into him. And they besought him, that he would not command them to go out into the deep. And there was thereby an herd of *Swine.* many swine, feeding on an hill: and they besought him, that he would suffer them to enter into them. And he suffered them. Then went the devils out of the man, and entered into the swine: And the herd took their course and ran headlong into the lake, and were choked. When the herdmen saw what had chanced, they fled and told it in the city and in the villages.

And they came out to see what was done; and came to Jesus, and found the man, out of whom the devils were departed, sitting at the feet of Jesus, clothed and in his right mind, and they were afraid. They also which saw it, told them by what means he that was possessed of the devil was healed. And all the whole multitude of the country of the Gadarenites, besought him that he would depart from them: for they were taken with great fear. And he gat him into the ship and returned back again. Then the man out of whom the devils were departed, besought him that he might be with him: But Jesus sent him away saying: Go home again into thine own house, and shew what great things God hath done to thee. And he went his way, and preached throughout all the city what great things Jesus had done unto him. **F**

Matt. 9. c.
Mark 5. b.

The rulér's daughter is raised.

And it fortuned when Jesus was come again that the people received him. For they all waited for him. And behold there came a man named Jairus (and he was a ruler of the synagogue) and he fell down at Jesus' feet, and besought him that he would come into his house, for he had but a daughter only, upon a twelve years of age, and she lay a-dying. And as he went the people thronged him.

Issue of blood.

And a woman having an issue of blood twelve years (which had spent all her substance among physicians, neither could be holpen of any) came behind him, and touched the hem of his garment, and immediately her issue of blood stanched. And Jesus said: Who is it that touched me? when every man denied, Peter and they that were with him, said: Master, the people thrust thee and vex thee: and sayest thou, who touched me? And Jesus said: Somebody touched me. For I perceive that virtue is gone out of me. When the woman saw, that she was not hid, she came trembling, and fell at his feet, and told him before all the people for what cause she had touched him, and how she was healed immediately. And he said unto her: Daughter, be of good comfort, Thy faith hath made the whole, go in peace.

While he yet spake, there came one from the ruler's of the synagogue's house **G** which said to him: thy daughter is dead, disease not the master. When Jesus heard that, he answered the father, saying: Fear not, believe only, and she shall be made whole. And when he came to the house, he suffered no man to go in with him, save Peter, James and John, and the father and the mother of the maiden. Everybody wept and sorrowed for her. And he said: Weep not: for she is not dead, but sleepeth. And they laughed him to scorn. For they knew that she was dead. And he thrust them all out, and caught her by the hand, and cried saying: Maid arise. And her spirit came again, and she rose straightway. And he commanded to give her meat. And the father and the mother of her were astonied. But he warned them that they should tell no man, what was done.

Matt. 10. a.
Mark 3. b.

CHAPTER NINE

A + Then called he the twelve together, and gave them power, and authority over all devils, and that they might heal diseases. And he sent them to preach the kingdom of God, and to cure the sick. And he said to them: Take nothing to succour you by the way: neither staff, nor scrip, neither bread, neither money, neither have two coats. And whatsoever house★ ye enter into, there abide and thence depart. And whosoever will not receive you, when ye go out of that city, shake off the very dust from your feet, for a testimony against them. And they went out, and went through the towns, preaching the gospel and healing everywhere. +

The twelve are sent.

Matt. 10. a.
Mark 11. a.
Mark 6. a.
★ Go not from house to house as friars do.

Dust.

Acts 13.

And Herod the tetrarch heard of all that was done of him, and doubted, because that it was said of some, that John was risen again from death: and of some, that Elias had appeared: and of other, that one of the old prophets was risen again. And Herod said: John have I beheaded: who then is this of whom I hear such things? And he desired to see him.

Matt. 14. a.
Mark 6. b.

B And the apostles returned, and told him what great things they had done. And he took them and went aside into a solitary place, nigh to a city called Bethsaida. And the people knew of it, and followed him. And he received them, and spake unto them of the kingdom of God, and healed them that had need to be healed. And when the day began to wear away, then came the twelve and said unto him: send the people away, that they may go into the towns and villages round about, and lodge, and get meat, for we are here in a place of wilderness. But he said unto them: Give ye them to eat. And they said. We have no more but five loaves and two fishes, except we should go and buy meat for all this people. And they were about a five thousand men. And he said to his disciples: Cause them to sit down by fifties in a company. And they did so, and made them all sit down. And he took the five loaves, and the two fishes, and looked up to heaven, and blessed them, and brake, and gave to the disciples, to set before the people. And they ate, and were all satisfied. And there was taken up of that remained to them, twelve baskets full of broken meat.

Matt. 14. b.

Mark 6. d.

Five loaves and two fishes.

C And it fortuned as he was alone praying, his disciples were with him, and he asked them saying: Who say the people that I am? They answered and said: John Baptist. Some say Elias. And some say, one of the old prophets is risen again. He said unto them: Who say ye that I am? Peter answered and said: thou

Matt. 16. b.
Mark 8.

art the Christ of God. And he warned and commanded them, that they should tell no man that thing saying: that the son of man must suffer many things, and be reproved of the elders, and of the high priests and scribes, and be slain, and the third day rise again.

And he said to them all, if any man will come after me, let him deny himself, and take up his cross daily and follow me. Whosoever will save his life, shall lose it. And whosoever shall lose his life for my sake, the same shall save it. For what advantageth it a man, to win the whole world, if he lose himself or run in damage of himself? For whosoever is ashamed of me, and of my sayings: of him shall the son of man be ashamed, when he cometh in his own glory, and in the glory of his father, and of the holy angels. And I tell you of a surety: There be some of them that stand here, which shall not taste of death, till they see the kingdom of God.

And it followed about an eight days after those sayings, that he took Peter, **D** James, and John, and went up into a mountain to pray. And as he prayed, the fashion of his countenance was changed, and his garment was white and shone. And behold, two men talked with him, and they were Moses and Elias, which appeared gloriously, and spake of his departing, which he should end at Jerusalem. Peter and they that were with him, were heavy with sleep. And when they woke, they saw his glory, and two men standing with him.

And it chanced as they departed from him, Peter said unto Jesus: Master, it is good being here for us. Let us make three tabernacles, one for thee, and one for Moses, and one for Elias: and wist not what he said. While he thus spake, there came a cloud and shadowed them: and they feared when they were come under the cloud. And there came a voice out of the cloud saying: This is my dear son, hear him. And as soon as the voice was past, Jesus was found alone. And they kept it close, and told no man in those days any of those things which they had seen.

And it chanced on the next day as they came down from the hill, much **E** people met him. And behold a man of the company cried out saying: Master, I beseech thee behold my son, for he is all that I have: and see, a spirit taketh him, and suddenly he crieth, and he teareth him that he foameth again, and with much pain departeth from him, when he hath rent him, and I besought thy disciples to cast him out, and they could not. Jesus answered and said: O generation without faith, and crooked: how long shall I be with you? and shall suffer you? Bring thy son hither. As he yet was a-coming, the fiend rent him and tare him. And Jesus rebuked the unclean spirit, and healed the child, and delivered him to his father. And they were all amazed at the mighty power of God.

While they wondered every one at all things which he did, he said unto his disciples: Let these sayings sink down into your ears. The time will come, when the son of man shall be delivered into the hands of men. But they wist not what that word meant, and it was hid from them, that they understood it not. And they feared to ask him of that saying.

Then there arose a disputation among them, who should be the greatest. **F**

Passion.

Matt. 17. d.
Mark 8.

Christ's disciple.

Matt. 10. d.
and 16.
Mark 8. b.
John 12. d.

Matt. 10. d.
Mark 8. b.
Covenant.
Matt. 16. d.
Mark 9. a.

Matt. 17. a.
Mark 9. a.

Transfiguration.

Hear him.

Matt. 17. d.
Mark 9. c.

The spirit of the falling
sickness is cast out.

Passion.

Matt. 17. b.
Mark 9. c.

When Jesus perceived the thoughts of their hearts, he took a child, and set him hard by him, and said unto them: Whosoever receiveth this child in my name, receiveth me. And whosoever receiveth me, receiveth him that sent me. For he that is least among you all, the same shall be great.

Greatest.

And John answered and said: Master we saw one casting out devils in thy name, and we forbade him, because he followeth not with us. And Jesus said unto him: forbid ye him not. For he that is not against us, is with us.

Forbid.

And it followed when the time was come that he should be received up, then he set his face to go to Jerusalem, and sent messengers before him. And they went and entered into a city of the Samaritans to make ready for him. But they would not receive him, because his face was as though he would go to Jerusalem. When his disciples James and John saw that, they said: Lord, wilt thou that we command, that fire come down from heaven and consume them, even as Elias did? Jesus turned about, and rebuked them saying: ye wot not what manner spirit ye are of. The son of man is not come to destroy men's lives, but to save them. And they went to another town.

Fire from heaven.

G + And it chanced as he went in the way, a certain man said unto him: I will follow thee whithersoever thou go. Jesus said unto him: foxes have holes, and birds of the air have nests: but the son of man hath not whereon to lay his head.

Matt. 8. c.

Foxes.

And he said unto another: follow me. And the same said: Lord suffer me first to go and bury my father. Jesus said unto him: Let the dead, bury their dead: but go thou and preach the kingdom of God.

Bury his father.

And another said: I will follow thee Lord: but let me first go bid them farewell, which are at home at my house. Jesus said unto him: No man that putteth his hand to the plough, and looketh back, is apt to the kingdom of God. ⊦

Plough.

CHAPTER TEN

A + After these things, the Lord appointed other seventy also, and sent them, two and two before him into every city and place, whither he himself would come. And he said unto them, the harvest is great: but the labourers are few. Pray therefore the Lord of the harvest, to send forth labourers into his harvest. Go your ways: behold, I send you forth as lambs among wolves. Bear no wallet, neither scrip, nor shoes, and salute no man by the way. Into whatsoever house ye enter, first say: Peace be to this house. And if the son of peace be there, your peace shall rest upon him: if not, it shall return to you again. And in the same house tarry still eating and drinking such as they have. For the labourer is worthy of his reward. ⊦

Seventy are sent.

Matt. 9. a.

Harvest.
Lambs among wolves.
Matt. 10. a.
Matt. 6. a.

Faith shall minister all.

B Go not from house to house: and into whatsoever city ye enter, if they receive you, eat such things as are set before you, and heal the sick that are there, and say unto them: the kingdom of God is come nigh upon you. But into whatsoever city ye shall enter, if they receive you not, go your ways out into the streets of the same, and say: even the very dust, which cleaveth on us of your city, we wipe off against you: Notwithstanding, mark this: that the

Matt. 10. a.
1 Tim. 5. c.

Dust.

kingdom of God was come nigh upon you. Yea and I say unto you, that it shall be easier in that day for Sodom than for that city.

Chorazim.
Bethsaida.
Tyre.
Sidon.

Capernaum.

Matt. 10. d.
John 13. c.

Woe be to thee, Chorazin: woe be to thee, Bethsaida. For if the miracles had   C
been done in Tyre and Sidon, which have been done in you, they had a great while ago repented, sitting in hair and ashes. Nevertheless it shall be easier for Tyre and Sidon, at the judgement, than for you. And thou Capernaum which art exalted to heaven, shalt be thrust down to hell. He that heareth you, heareth me: and he that despiseth you, despiseth me: and he that despiseth me, despiseth him that sent me.

And the seventy returned again with joy saying: Lord even the very devils are subdued to us through thy name. And he said unto them: I saw Satan, as it had been lightning, fall down from heaven. Behold I give unto you power to tread on serpents and scorpions, and over all manner power of the enemy, and nothing shall hurt you. Nevertheless, in this rejoice not, that the spirits are under your power: but rejoice, because your names are written in heaven.

Rejoice.

Matt. 6. d.

That same time rejoiced Jesus in the spirit, and said: I confess unto thee   D
father, Lord of heaven and earth, that thou hast hid these things from the wise and prudent, and hast opened them to the babes. Even so father, for so pleased it thee. All things are given me of my father. And no man knoweth who the son is, but the father: neither who the father is, save the son, and he to whom the son will shew him.

Babes.
Matt. 6. d.

He only that is, taught of Christ, knoweth the father.

Matt. 13. b.

And he turned to his disciples, and said secretly: + Happy are the eyes, which see that ye see. For I tell you that many prophets and kings have desired to see those things which ye see, and have not seen them: and to hear those things which ye hear, and have not heard them.

And behold, a certain lawyer stood up, and tempted him saying: Master   E
what shall I do, to inherit eternal life? He said unto him: What is written in the law? How readest thou? And he answered and said: Love thy Lord God, with all thy heart, and with all thy soul, and with all thy strength, and with all thy mind: and thy neighbour as thyself. And he said unto him: Thou hast answered right. This do and thou shalt live. He, willing to justify himself, said unto Jesus: Who is then my neighbour?

Matt. 22. d.
Mark 12. e.
Eternal life.
Deut. 6. b.

Jesus answered and said: A certain man descended from Jerusalem into Jericho, and fell into the hands of thieves, which robbed him of his raiment and wounded him, and departed leaving him half dead. And by chance there came a certain priest that same way, and when he saw him, he passed by. And likewise   F
a Levite, when he was come nigh to the place, went and looked on him, and passed by. Then a certain Samaritan, as he journeyed, came nigh unto him, and when he saw him, had compassion on him, and went to and bound up his wounds, and poured in oil and wine, and put him on his own beast, and brought him to a common inn, and made provision for him. And on the morrow when he departed, he took out two pence and gave them to the host, and said unto him. Take care of him, and whatsoever thou spendest more, when I come again, I will recompense thee. Which now of these three, thinkest thou, was neighbour unto him that fell into the thieves' hands? And he said:

Samaritan.

A neighbour, who.

he that shewed mercy on him, Then said Jesus unto him, Go and do thou likewise. ⊦

G ⊦ It fortuned as they went, that he entered into a certain town. And a certain woman named Martha received him into her house. And this woman had a sister called Mary, which sat at Jesus' feet, and heard his preaching. And Martha was cumbered about much serving, and stood and said: Master, dost thou not care, that my sister hath left me to minister alone? Bid her therefore, that she help me. And Jesus answered, and said unto her: Martha, Martha, thou carest, and art troubled about many things: verily one is needful. Mary hath chosen her that good part, which shall not be taken away from her. ⊦

Martha.
Mary.

CHAPTER ELEVEN

A And it fortuned as he was praying in a certain place: when he ceased, one of his disciples said unto him: Master, teach us to pray, as John taught his disciples. And he said unto them: When ye pray, say: O our father which art in heaven, hallowed by thy name. Thy kingdom come. Thy will be fulfilled, even in earth as it is in heaven. Our daily bread give us evermore. And forgive us our sins: For even we forgive every man that trespasseth us. And lead us not into temptation. But deliver us from evil.

Matt. 6. b.

The paternoster.

And he said unto them: ⊦ if any of you should have a friend, and should go to him at midnight, and say unto him: friend lend me three loaves, for a friend of mine is come out of the way to me, and I have nothing to set before him: and he within should answer and say, trouble me not, the door is now shut, and my servants are with me in the chamber, I cannot rise and give them to thee. I say unto you, though he would not arise and give him, because he is his friend: yet because of his importunity he would rise, and give him as many as he needed.

Prayer what it doth.

B And I say unto you: ask, and it shall be given you. Seek, and ye shall find: knock, and it shall be opened unto you. For every one that asketh, receiveth: and he that seeketh, findeth: and to him that knocketh, shall it be opened. If the son shall ask bread of any of you that is a father: will he give him a stone? Or if he ask fish, will he for a fish give him a serpent? Or if he ask an egg: will he offer him a scorpion? If ye then which are evil, can give good gifts unto your children, how much more shall the father of heaven give an holy spirit to them, that desire it of him? ⊦

Covenant.

Matt. 7. a.
and 21. e.
Mark. 11. c.
John. 14. d.
and 16. c.

James 1. a.
Mark 7. b.
Matt. 9. d.
and 12. b.
Mark 3. c.

⊦ And he was a casting out a devil, which was dumb. And it followed when the devil was gone out, the dumb spake, and the people wondered. But some of them said: he casteth out devils by the power of Beelzebub, the chief of the devils. And other tempted him, seeking of him a sign from heaven. But he knew their thoughts and said unto them: Every kingdom divided within itself, shall be desolate: and one house shall fall upon another. So if Satan be divided within himself: how shall his kingdom endure? Because ye say that I cast out devils by the power of Beelzebub. If I, by the power of Beelzebub cast out devils: by whom do your children cast them out? Therefore shall they be your

The dumb spirit is cast out.

Beelzebub.

judges. But if I, with the finger of God cast out devils, no doubt the kingdom of God is come upon you.

When a strong man armed watcheth his house: that he possesseth is in peace. **D**◖ But when a stronger than he cometh upon him and overcometh him: he taketh from him his harness wherein he trusted, and divideth his goods. He that is not with me, is against me. And he that gathereth not with me, scattereth.

When the unclean spirit is gone out of a man, he walketh through waterless places, seeking rest. And when he findeth none, he sayeth: I will return again unto my house whence I came out. And when he cometh, he findeth it swept and garnished. Then goeth he and taketh to him seven other spirits worse than himself: and they enter in, and dwell there. And the end of that man, is worse than the beginning.

And it fortuned as he spake those things, a certain woman of the company lifted up her voice, and said unto him: Happy is the womb that bare thee, and the paps which gave thee suck. But he said: Yea, happy are they that hear the word of God, and keep it. ⊦

When the people were gathered thick together: he began to say. This is an evil nation: they seek a sign, and there shall no sign be given them, but the sign of Jonas the prophet. For as Jonas was a sign to the Ninevites, so shall the son of man be to this nation. The queen of the south shall rise at judgement with the men of this generation, and condemn them: for she came from the end of the world, to hear the wisdom of Solomon. And behold a greater than Solomon is here. The men of Nineveh shall rise at the judgement with this generation, and shall condemn them: for they repented at the preaching of Jonas. And behold, a greater than Jonas is here.

No man lighteth a candle, and putteth it in a privy place, neither under a **E** bushel, but on a candlestick, that they that come in may see the light. The light of thy body is the eye. Therefore when thine eye is single: then is all thy body full of light. But if thine eye be evil: then shall thy body also be full of darkness. Take heed therefore that the light which is in thee, be not darkness. For if all thy body shall be light, having no part dark: then shall all be full of light, even as when a candle doth light thee with his brightness. ⊦

And as he spake, a certain Pharisee besought him to dine with him: and he went in and sat down to meat. When the Pharisee saw that, he marvelled that **F** he had not first washed before dinner. And the Lord said to him: Now do ye Pharisees, make clean the outside of the cup, and of the platter: but your inward parts are full of ravening and wickedness. Ye fools, did not he that made that which is without: make that which is within also? Nevertheless give alms of that ye have, and behold all is clean to you.

But woe be to you Pharisees, for ye tithe the mint and rue, and all manner herbs, and pass over judgement and the love of God. These ought ye to have done, and yet not to have left the other undone.

Woe be to you, Pharisees: for ye love the uppermost seats in the synagogues, and greetings in the markets.

Woe be to you scribes and Pharisees, hypocrites, for ye are as graves which appear not, and the men that walk over them, are not ware of them.

Marginal notes (left column):

Seven worse than himself.

Happy, who.

Matt. 12. a.

Sign of Jonas.

Queen of the south.

1 Kin. 10. g.
2 Chr. 9.

Ninevites.

John 3. b.
Matt. 5. b.
Mark 4. 'c.
Matt. 6. c.

Eye.

Matt. 23.

Alms.

Tithe mint.

Matt. 24.

Uppermost seats.

Mark 12. d.

Then answered one of the lawyers, and said unto him: Master, thus saying, *Lawyers.*
thou puttest us to rebuke also. Then he said: Woe be to you also, ye lawyers:
for ye lade men with burdens grievous to be borne, and ye yourselves touch *Matt. 23.*
not the packs with one of your fingers.

Woe be to you: ye build the sepulchres of the prophets, and your fathers *Build seplulchres.*
killed them: truly ye bear witness, that ye allow the deeds of your fathers: for
they killed them, and ye build their sepulchres.

Therefore said the wisdom of God: I will send them prophets and apostles,
and of them they shall slay and persecute: that the blood of all prophets, which *Gen. 4.*
was shed from the beginning of the world, may be required of this generation, *2 Chron. 24. b.*
from the blood of Abel unto the blood of Zacharias, which perished between *Zacharias.*
the altar and the temple. Verily I say unto you: it shall be required of this
nation.

Woe be to you lawyers: for ye have taken away the key of knowledge; ye *Key.*
entered not in yourselves, and them that came in ye forbade.

When he thus spake unto them, the lawyers and the Pharisees began to wax
busy about him, and to stop his mouth with many questions, laying wait for
him, and seeking to catch something of his mouth, whereby they might accuse
him.

CHAPTER TWELVE

A   As there gathered together an innumerable multitude of people (insomuch *Matt. 16.*
that they trod one another) he began to say unto his disciples: First of all *Mark 8.*
beware of the leaven of the Pharisees, which is hypocrisy. For there is nothing *Matt. 10. c.* *Mark 4. c.*
covered, that shall not be uncovered: neither hid, that shall not be known. For *Leaven.*
whatsoever ye have spoken in darkness: that same shall be heard in light. And
that which ye have spoken in the ear, even in secret places, shall be preached
even on the top of the houses.

I say unto you my friends: Be not afraid of them that kill the body, and after
that have no more that they can do. But I will shew you, whom ye shall fear.
Fear him which after he hath killed, hath power to cast into hell. Yea, I say *Who is to be feared.*
unto you, him fear. Are not five sparrows bought for two farthings? And yet
not one of them is forgotten of God. Also even the very hairs of your heads are
numbered. Fear not therefore: Ye are more of value, than many sparrows.

B   I say unto you: Whosoever confesseth me before men, even him shall the son *Matt. 10. d.*
of man confess also before the angels of God. And he that denieth me before *Mark 3.*
men, shall be denied before the angels of God. And whosoever speaketh a *Covenants.*
word against the son of man, it shall be forgiven him. But unto him that
blasphemeth the holy ghost, it shall not be forgiven.

When they bring you unto the synagogues, and unto the rulers, and officers, *Matt. 12. e.*
take no thought how or what thing ye shall answer or what ye shall speak. For *Mark 3.*
the holy ghost shall teach you in the same hour, what ye ought to say. *A promise that the spirit shall teach us.*

+ One of the company said unto him: Master, bid my brother divide the
inheritance with me. And he said unto him: Man, who made me a judge or a *The life standeth not in riches but in keeping*
divider over you? Wherefore he said unto them: take heed, and beware of *God's commandments.*

111

covetousness. For no man's life standeth in the abundance of the things which he possesseth. And he put forth a similitude unto them saying:

Rich man.

The ground of a certain rich man brought forth fruits plenteously, and he thought in himself saying: what shall I do? because I have no room where to

Eccl. 11. c.

bestow my fruits? And he said: This will I do. I will destroy my barns, and build greater, and therein will I gather all my fruits, and my goods: and I will say to my soul: Soul thou hast much goods laid up in store for many years, take thine ease: eat, drink, and be merry. But God said unto him: Thou fool, this night will they fetch away thy soul again from thee. Then whose shall those things be which thou hast provided? So is it with him that gathered riches, and is not rich in God.

Matt. 6. c.
1 Pet. 10. b.
Psa. 55.

And he spake unto his disciples: Therefore I say unto you: Take no thought for your life, what ye shall eat, neither for your body, what ye shall put on. The life is more than meat, and the body is more than raiment. Consider the

Ravens.

ravens, for they neither sow nor reap, which neither have storehouse nor barn, and yet God feedeth them. How much are ye better than the fowls. ⊦

Which of you with taking thought can add to his stature one cubit? If ye **D** then be not able to do that thing which is least: why take ye thought for the

Lilies.

remnant? Consider the lilies how they grow: They labour not: they spin not: and yet I say unto you, that Solomon in all this royalty, was not clothed like to one of these.

If the grass which is today in the field, and tomorrow shall be cast into the furnace, God so clothe: how much more will he clothe you, o ye endued with little faith? And ask not what ye shall eat, or what ye shall drink, neither climb ye up on high, for all such things the heathen people of the world seek for.

Matt. 5. c.

Your father knoweth that ye have need of such things. Wherefore seek ye after the kingdom of God, and all these things shall be ministered unto you.

Little flock.

Fear not little flock, for it is your father's pleasure, to give you a kingdom. Sell that ye have, and give alms. And make you bags, which wax not old,

Alms.
Loins, lights.

and treasure that faileth not in heaven, where no thief cometh, neither moth corrupteth. For where your treasure is, there will your hearts be also.

Let your loins be girded about, and your lights burning, and ye yourselves **E** like unto men, that wait for their master, when he will return from a wedding: that as soon as he cometh and knocketh, they may open unto him. Happy are those servants, which the lord when he cometh, shall find waking. Verily I say unto you, he will gird himself about, and make them sit down to meat, and walk by, and minister unto them.

Matt. 24.

And if he come in the second watch, yea if he come in the third watch, and

Second watch.

shall find them so, happy are those servants.

This understand, that if the good man of the house knew what hour the thief would come, he would surely watch: and not suffer his house to be broken up. Be ye prepared therefore: for the son of man will come at an hour when ye think not.

Then Peter said unto him: Master, tellest thou this similitude unto us, or to **F** all men? And the Lord said: If there be any faithful servant and wise, whom his

lord shall make ruler over his household, to give them their duetie of meat at
due season: happy is that servant, whom his master when he cometh, shall find
so doing. Of a truth I say unto you: that he will make him ruler over all that he
hath. But and if the evil servant shall say in his heart: My master will defer his
coming, and shall begin to smite the servants, and maidens, and to eat and
drink, and to be drunken: the lord of that servant will come in a day, when he
thinketh not, and at an hour when he is not ware, and will divide him, and will
give him his reward with the unbelievers.

Rev. 16.

Evil servant.

The servant that knew his master's will, and prepared not himself, neither
did according to his will, shall be beaten with many stripes. But he that knew
not, and yet did commit things worthy of stripes, shall be beaten with few
stripes. For unto whom much is given, of him shall be much required. And to
whom men much commit, the more of him will they ask.

Covenant.

G I am come to send fire on earth: and what is my desire but that it were
already kindled? Notwithstanding I must be baptised with a baptism: and how
am I pained till it be ended? Suppose ye that I am come to send peace on earth? I
tell you, nay but rather debate. For from henceforth there shall be five in one
house divided, three against two, and two against three. The father shall be
divided against the son, and the son against the father. The mother against the
daughter, and the daughter against the mother. The mother-in-law against her
daughter-in-law, and the daughter-in-law against her mother-in-law.

Fire.

Baptism.
Baptise.
Peace.
Debate.

Matt. 10. d.

Then said he to the people: when ye see a cloud rise out of the west, straight
way ye say, we shall have a shower, and so it is. And when ye see the south
wind blow, ye say, we shall have heat, and it cometh to pass. Hypocrites, ye
can skill of the fashion of the earth, and of the sky: but what is the cause, that ye
cannot skill of this time? Yea, and why judge ye not of yourselves what is
right?

Matt. 16.
Mark 8.

While thou goest with thine adversary to the ruler: as thou art in the way,
give diligence that thou mayest be delivered from him, lest he bring thee to the
judge, and the judge deliver thee to the jailer, and the jailer cast thee in to
prison. I tell thee, thou departest not thence, till thou have made good the
utmost mite.

Adversary.

Matt. 5. d.

CHAPTER THIRTEEN

A There were present at the same season, that shewed him of the Galileans,
whose blood Pilate mingled with their own sacrifice. And Jesus answered, and
said unto them: Suppose ye that these Galileans were greater sinners then all the
other Galileans, because they suffered such punishment? I tell you nay: but
except ye repent, ye shall all in like wise perish. Or those eighteen upon which
the tower in Siloam fell, and slew them, think ye that they were sinners above
all men that dwell in Jerusalem? I tell you nay: But except ye repent, ye all shall
likewise perish.

Galileans.

Tower in Siloam.

B + He put forth this similitude, A certain man had a fig tree planted in his
vineyard, and he came and sought fruit thereon, and found none. Then said he

Fig tree.

to the dresser of his vineyard: Behold, this three year have I come and sought fruit in this fig tree, and find none: cut it down: why cumbereth it the ground? And he answered and said unto him: lord let it alone this year also, till I dig round about it, and dung it to see whether it will bear fruit: and if it bear not then, after that, cut it down.

The woman that was bowed together.

And he taught in one of their synagogues on the sabbath days. And behold **C** there was a woman which had a spirit of infirmity eighteen years: and was bowed together, and could not lift up herself at all. When Jesus saw her he called her to him, and said to her: woman, thou art delivered from thy disease. And he laid his hands on her, and immediately she was made straight, and glorified God. And the ruler of the synagogue answered with indignation (because that Jesus had healed on the sabbath day) and said unto the people, There are six

The sabbath is broken.

days in which men ought to work: in them come and be healed, and not on the sabbath day.

Then answered him the Lord and said: Hypocrite, doth not each one of you on the sabbath day, loose his ox or his ass from the stall, and lead him to the water? And ought not this daughter of Abraham, whom Satan hath bounde lo eighteen years, be loosed from this bond on the sabbath day? And when he thus said, all his adversaries were ashamed, and all the people rejoiced on all the excellent deeds, that were done by him. ⊦

Mustard seed.

Then said he: What is the kingdom of God like? or whereto shall I compare **D** it? Is is like a grain of mustard seed, which a man took and sowed in his garden: and it grew and waxed a great tree, and the fowls of the air made nests in the branches of it.

Matt. 13.

Leaven.

And again he said: whereunto shall I liken the kingdom of God? It is like leaven, which a woman took, and hid in three bushels of flour, till all was through leavened. And he went through all manner of cities and towns teaching, and journeying towards Jerusalem.

Matt. 7. b.
Matt. 12. d.

Strait gate.

Then said one unto him: Lord, are there few that shall be saved? And he said **E** unto them: strive with yourselves to enter in at the strait gate: For many I say unto you will seek to enter in, and shall not be able★. When the goodman of

★ When the covenant made in the blood of Christ, is blinded: then men pain themselves with holy works, trusting thereby to enter: but all in vain.

the house is risen up, and hath shut to the door, ye shall begin to stand without, and to knock at the door saying: Lord, lord, open unto us: and he shall answer and say unto you: I know you not whence ye are. Then shall ye begin to say: We have eaten in thy presence and drunk, and thou hast taught in our streets.

Psa. 6. c.
Matt. 7. c.
and 25.

And he shall say: I tell you, I know you not whence ye are: depart from me all **F** ye workers of iniquity. There shall be weeping and gnashing of teeth when ye shall see Abraham and Isaac and Jacob, and all the prophets in the kindgom of God, and yourselves thrust out at doors. And they shall come from the east and from the west, and from the north and from the south, and shall sit down in the kingdom of God. And behold, there are last, which shall be first: And there are first which shall be last.

The same day there came certain of the Pharisees and said unto him: Get thee **G** out of the way, and depart hence: for Herod will kill thee. And he said unto

Herod is a fox.

them, Go ye and tell that fox, behold I cast out devils and heal the people today and tomorrow, and the third day I make an end. Nevertheless, I must walk today and tomorrow, and the day following: For it cannot be, that a prophet perish any other where, save at Jerusalem.

O Jerusalem, Jerusalem, which killest prophets, and stonest them that are sent to thee: how often would I have gathered thy children together, as the hen gathereth her nest under her wings, but ye would not. Behold your habitation shall be left unto you desolate. For I tell you, ye shall not see me until the time come that ye shall say, blessed is he that cometh in the name of the Lord.

CHAPTER FOURTEEN

+ And it chanced that he went into the house of one of the chief Pharisees to eat bread, on a sabbath day: and they watched him. And behold there was a man before him which had the dropsy. And Jesus answered and spake unto the lawyers and Pharisees saying: is it lawful to heal on the sabbath day? And they held their peace. And he took him and healed him, and let him go: and answered them saying, which of you shall have an ass or an ox, fallen into a pit, and will not straightway pull him out on the sabbath day? And they could not answer him again to that.

B   He put forth a similitude to the guests, when he marked how they pressed to the highest rooms, and said unto them: When thou art bidden to a wedding of any man, sit not down in the highest room, lest a more honourable man than thou be bidden of him, and he that bade both him and thee, come and say to thee: give this man room, and thou then begin with shame to take the lowest room. But rather when thou art bidden, go and sit in the lowest room, that when he that bade thee cometh, he may say unto thee: friend sit up higher. Then shalt thou have worship in the presence of them that sit at meat with thee. For whosoever exalteth himself, shall be brought low. And he that humbleth himself, shall be exalted. ⊦

C   Then said he also to him that had desired to him to dinner: + When thou makest a dinner or a supper: call not thy friends, nor thy brethren neither thy kinsmen nor yet rich neighbours: lest they bid thee again, and a recompence be made thee. But when thou makest a feast, call the poor, the maimed, the lame and the blind, and thou shalt be happy, for they cannot recompense thee. But thou shalt be recompensed at the resurrection of the just men.

D   When one of them that sat at meat also heard that, he said unto him: happy is he that eateth bread in the kingdom of God. ⊦ Then said he to him. + A certain man ordained a great supper, and bade many, and sent his servant at supper time, to say to them that were bidden, come: for all things are now ready. And they all at once began to make excuse. The first said unto him: I have bought a farm, and I must needs go and see it, I pray thee have me excused. And another said: I have bought five yoke of oxen, and I go to prove them, I pray thee have me excused. The third said: I have married a wife, and therefore I cannot come. And the servant went, and brought his master word thereof.

E   Then was the good man of the house displeased, and said to his servant: Go

*Matt. 19. d.
and 20. b.*

Jerusalem killeth prophets.

Matt. 23.

Dropsy.

Prov. 25. a.

*Exalt.
Humble.*

Matt. 23.

*Tobit 4. a.
Prov. 3. b.*

Feast the poor.

Supper.

*Matt. 22. a.
Rev. 19.*

out quickly into the streets and quarters of the city, and bring in hither the poor and the maimed and the halt and the blind. And the servant said: lord it is done as thou commandedst, and yet there is room. And the lord said to the servant: Go out into the highways and hedges, and compel them to come in, that my house may be filled. For I say unto you, that none of those men which were bidden, shall taste of my supper. ⊢

Matt. 10. d.
and 16. d.
Christ's disciple.
Mark. 8. d.

There went a great company with him, and he turned and said unto them: + **D** If a man come to me, and hate not his father and mother, and wife, and children, and brethren, and sisters, moreover and his own life, he cannot be my disciple. And whosoever bear not his cross and come after me, cannot be my disciple.

Tower.

Which of you disposed to build a tower, sitteth not down before and counteth the cost, whether he have sufficient to perform it? Lest after he hath laid the foundation, and is not able to perform it, all that behold it, begin to mock him saying: this man began to build, and was not able to make an end. Or what king goeth to make battle against another king, and sitteth not down **E** first, and casteth in his mind, whether he be able with ten thousand, to meet him that cometh against him with twenty thousand? Or else while the other is yet a great way off, he will send ambassadors, and desire peace. So likewise

Christ's disciples.

none of you that forsaketh not all that he hath, can be my disciple. ⊢

Matt. 5. b.
Mark 9. g.

Salt is good, but if salt have lost her saltness, what shall be seasoned there- **F** with? It is neither good for the land nor yet for the dunghill, but men cast it out at the doors. He that hath ears to hear, let him hear.

CHAPTER FIFTEEN

Publicans.
Sinners.

+ Then resorted unto him all the publicans and sinners, for to hear him. And the Pharisees and scribes murmured saying: He received to his company sinners,

Hundred sheep.

and eateth with them. Then put he forth this similitude to them saying: What man of you having an hundred sheep, if he lose one of them, doth not leave

Matt. 17.

ninety and nine in the wilderness, and go after that which is lost, until he find him? And when he hath found him, he putteth him on his shoulders with joy: And as soon as he cometh home, he calleth together his lovers and neighbours saying unto them: rejoice with me, for I have found my sheep which was **B** lost. I say unto you, that likewise joy shall be in heaven over one sinner that repenteth, more then over ninety and nine just persons, which need no

Ten groats.

repentance. Either what woman having ten groats, if she lose one, doth not light a candle, and sweep the house, and seek diligently, till she find it? And when she hath found it she calleth her lovers and her neighbours saying: Rejoice with me, for I have found the groat which I had lost. Likewise I say unto you, joy is made in the presence of the angels of God over one sinner that repenteth. ⊢

The riotous son.

+ And he said: a certain man had two sons, and the younger of them said to **C** his father: father, give me my part of the goods that to me belongeth. And he divided unto them his substance. And not long after, the younger son gathered all that he had together, and took his journey into a far country, and there he wasted his goods with riotous living. And when he had spent all that he had, there rose a great dearth throughout all that same land, and he began to lack. And he went and clave to a citizen of that same country, which sent him to his field, to keep his swine. And he would fain have filled his belly with the cods that the swine ate: and no man gave him.

Then he came to himself and said: how many hired servants at my father's, have bread enough, and I die for hunger. I will arise, and go to my father and will say unto him: father, I have sinned against heaven and before thee, and am no more worthy to be called thy son; make me as one of thy hired servants. And he arose and went to his father. And when he was yet a great way off, his father saw him and had compassion, and ran and fell on his neck, and kissed him. And the son said unto him: father, I have sinned against heaven, and in thy sight, and am no more worthy to be called thy son. But his father said to his servants: bring forth that best garment and put it on him, and put a ring on his hand, and shoes on his feet. And bring hither that fatted calf, and kill him, and let us eat and be merry: for this my son was dead, and is alive again, he was lost, and is now found. And they began to be merry.

The elder brother was in the field, and when he came and drew nigh to the house, he heard minstrelsy and dancing, and called one of his servants, and asked what those things meant. And he said unto him: thy brother is come, and thy father had killed the fatted calf, because he hath received him safe and sound. And he was angry, and would not go in. Then came his father out, and entreated him. He answered and said to his father: Lo these many years have I done thee service, neither brake at any time thy commandment, and yet gavest thou me never so much as a kid to make merry with my lovers: but as soon as this thy son was come, which hath devoured thy goods with harlots, thou hast for his pleasure killed the fatted calf. And he said unto him: Son, thou wast ever with me, and all that I have, is thine: it was meet that we should make merry and be glad: for this thy brother was dead, and is alive again: and was lost, and is found.

CHAPTER SIXTEEN

And he said also unto his disciples. + There was a certain rich man, which had a steward, that was accused unto him, that he had wasted his goods. And he called him, and said unto him: How is it, that I hear this of thee? Give accounts of thy stewardship: for thou mayest be no longer steward. The steward said within himself: what shall I do? for my master will take away from me the stewardship. I cannot dig, and to beg, I am ashamed. I wot what to do, that when I am put out of the stewardship, they may receive me into their houses.

The unrighteous steward.

Then called he all his master's debtors, and said unto the first: how much owest thou unto my master? And he said: an hundred tuns of oil. And he said to him: take thy bill, and sit down quickly, and write fifty. Then said he to another: what owest thou? And he said: an hundred quarters of wheat. He said to him: Take thy bill, and write fourscore. And the lord commended the unjust steward, because he had done wisely. For the children of this world are in their kind, wiser than the children of light. And I say also unto you: make you friends of the wicked mammon, that when ye shall depart, they may receive you into everlasting habitations. ⊢

+ He that is faithful in that which is least, the same is faithful in much. And he that is unfaithful in the least: is unfaithful also in much. So then if ye have not been faithful in the wicked mammon, who will believe you in that which is true? And if ye have not been faithful in another man's business who shall give you your own? No servant can serve two masters, for either he shall hate the one and love the other, or else he shall lean to the one and despise the other. Ye cannot serve God and mammon.

All these things heard the Pharisees also which were covetous, and they **D** mocked him. And he said unto them: Ye are they which justify yourselves before men: but God knoweth your hearts. For that which is highly esteemed among men, is abominable in the sight of God. ⊢

The law and the prophets reigned until the time of John: and since that time, the kingdom of God is preached, and every man striveth to go in.

Sooner shall heaven and earth perish, than one tittle of the law shall perish. Whosoever forsaketh his wife and marrieth another, breaketh matrimony. And every man which marrieth her that is divorced from her husband, committeth advoutry also.

+ There was a certain rich man, which was clothed in purple and fine byss, **E** and fared deliciously every day. And there was a certain beggar, named Lazarus, which lay at his gate full of sores, desiring to be refreshed with the crumbs which fell from the rich man's board. Nevertheless, the dogs came and licked his sores. And it fortuned that the beggar died, and was carried by the angels into Abraham's bosom. The rich man also died, and was buried.

And being in hell in torments, he lift up his eyes and saw Abraham afar off, **F** and Lazarus in his bosom, and he cried and said: father Abraham, have mercy on me, and send Lazarus that he may dip the tip of his finger in water, and cool my tongue: for I am tormented in this flame. But Abraham said unto him, Son, remember that thou in thy lifetime, receivedst thy pleasure, and contrarywise Lazarus pain. Now therefore is he comforted, and thou art punished. Beyond all this, between you and us there is a great space set, so that they which would go from hence to you cannot: neither may come from thence to us.

Then he said: I pray thee therefore father, send him to my father's house. For **G** I have five brethren: for to warn them, lest they also come into this place of torment. Abraham said unto him: they have Moses★ and the prophets, let them hear them. And he said: nay father Abraham, but if one came unto them, from the dead, they would repent. He said unto him: If they hear not Moses and the prophets, neither will they believe, though one rose from death again. ⊢

CHAPTER SEVENTEEN

Then said he to the disciples, it cannot be avoided, but that offences will come. **A** Nevertheless woe be to him through whom they come. It were better for him that a millstone were hanged about his neck, and that he were cast into the sea,

Mammon.

Matt. 6. c.

Two masters.

Matt. 11. b.

Matt. 5. c.
Mark 10. b.
1 Cor. 7.

Byss.

The rich glutton and Lazarus.

★ Moses and the prophets is the old testament.

Matt. 18.
Mark 9. f.
Offence.
Millstone.

than that he should offend one of these little ones. Take heed to yourselves. If thy brother trespass against thee, rebuke him: and if he repent, forgive him. And though he sin against thee seven times in a day, and seven times in a day turn again to thee saying: it repenteth me; forgive him.

Matt. 18. Lev. 19. d. Eccl. 20. Matt. 18.

And the apostles said unto the Lord: increase our faith. And the Lord said: if ye had faith like a grain of mustard seed, and should say unto this sycamine tree, pluck thyself up by the roots, and plant thyself in the sea: he should obey you.

Sycamine tree.

Who is it of you if he had a servant ploughing or feeding cattle, that would say unto him when he were come from the field, Go quickly and sit down to meat: and would not rather say to him, dress wherewith I may sup, and gird up thyself and serve me, till I have eaten and drunken: and afterward, eat thou, and drink thou? Doth he thank that servant because he did that which was commanded unto him? I trow not. So likewise ye, when ye have done all those things which are commanded you: say, we are unprofitable* servants. We have done that which was our duty to do.

* In works may no faith be put, for by them no man is justified before God, but by Christ's blood only.

+ And it chanced as he went to Jerusalem, that he passed through Samaria and Galilee. And as he entered into a certain town, there met him ten men that were lepers. Which stood afar off, and put forth their voices and said: Jesus master, have mercy on us. When he saw them, he said unto them: Go and shew yourselves to the priests. And it chanced as they went, they were cleansed. And one of them, when he saw that he was cleansed, turned back again, and with a loud voice praised God, and fell down on his face at his feet, and gave him thanks. And the same was a Samaritan. And Jesus answered and said: are there not ten cleansed? But where are those nine? There are not found that returned again, to give God praise, save only this stranger. And he said unto him: arise, and go thy way, thy faith hath made thee whole. ⊦

Ten lepers.

E + When he was demanded of the Pharisees, when the kingdom of God should come: he answered them and said: The kingdom of God cometh not with waiting for. Neither shall men say: Lo here, lo there. For behold, the kingdom* of God is with in you.

* The kingdom of God is to love God with all thine heart, and to put thy whole trust in him according to the covenant, made in Christ: and for Christ's sake to love thy neighbour as Christ loved thee. And all this is within thee.

And he said unto the disciples: The days will come, when ye shall desire to see one day of the son of man, and ye shall not see it. And they shall say to you: See here, See there. Go not after them, nor follow them, for as the lightning that appeareth out of the one part of the heaven, and shineth unto the other part of heaven: So shall the son of man be in his days. But first must he suffer many things, and be refused of this nation.

See here: see there.

F As it happened in the time of Noah: So shall it be in the time of the son of man. They ate, they drank, they married wives and were married, even unto the same day that Noah went into the ark: and the flood came and destroyed them all. Likewise also, as it chanced in the days of Lot. They ate, they drank, they bought, they sold, they planted, they built. And even the same day that Lot went out of Sodom, it rained fire and brimstone from heaven, and destroyed them all. After these examples shall it be in the day when the son of man shall appear.

Matt. 24. Gen. 8.

Gen. 19.

G At that day he that is on the house-top, and his stuff in the house: let him not

Lot's wife.

come down to take it out. And likewise let not him that is in the fields, turn back again to that he left behind. Remember Lot's wife. Whosoever will go about to save his life, shall lose it: And whosoever shall lose his life, shall save it.

Matt. 10. e.
Mark 8.
John 12. d.
Matt. 24.

Eagles.

I tell you: In that night, there shall be two in one bed, the one shall be received, and the other shall be forsaken. Two shall be also a-grinding together: the one shall be received, and the other forsaken. And they answered, and said to him: where Lord? And he said unto them: wheresoever the body shall be, thither will the eagles resort. ⊦

CHAPTER EIGHTEEN

Eccl. 24. e.
1 Thes. 5.

Wicked judge.

+ And he put forth a similitude unto them, signifying that men ought always to **A** pray, and not to be weary saying: There was a judge in a certain city, which feared not God neither regarded man. And there was a certain widow in the same city, which came unto him saying: avenge me of mine adversary. And he would not for a while. But afterward he said unto himself: though I fear not God, nor care for man, yet because this widow troubleth me, I will avenge her lest at the last she come and hag on me.

And the Lord said: hear what the unrighteous judge saith. And shall not God **B** avenge his elect, which cry day and night unto him, yea though he defer them? I tell you he will avenge them, and that quickly. ⊦

Nevertheless, when the son of man cometh, suppose ye, that he shall find faith on the earth?

+ And he put forth this similitude, unto certain which trusted in themselves that they were perfect, and despised other. Two men went up into the temple to pray: the one a Pharisee, and the other a publican. The Pharisee stood and prayed thus with himself. God I thank thee that I am not as other men are, extortioners, unjust, advoutrers, or as this publican. I fast twice in the week. I give tithe of all that I possess. And the publican stood afar off, and would not lift up his eyes to heaven, but smote his breast saying: God be merciful to me a sinner. I tell you: this man departed home to his house justified more than the other. For every man that exalteth himself, shall be brought low: And he that

Exalt.

humbleth himself, shall be exalted. ⊦

Matt. 23.
Mark 19.
Mark 10. b.

They brought unto him also babes, that he should touch them. When his disciples saw that, they rebuked them. But Jesus called them unto him, and said: Suffer children to come unto me, and forbid them not. For of such is the kingdom of God. Verily I say unto you: whosoever receiveth not the kingdom of God as a child, he shall not enter therein.

And a certain ruler asked him saying: Good Master: what ought I to do, to obtain eternal life? Jesus said unto him: Why callest thou me good? No man is good, save God only. Thou knowest the commandments: Thou shalt not

Exod. 20.

commit advoutry: thou shalt not kill: thou shalt not steal: thou shalt not bear false witness: Honour thy father and thy mother. And he said: all these have I kept from my youth. When Jesus heard that, he said unto him: Yet lackest thou one thing. Sell all that thou hast, and distribute it unto the poor, and thou shalt have treasure in heaven, and come, and follow me. When he heard that, he was heavy: for he was very rich.

E When Jesus saw him mourn, he said: with what difficulty shall they that have riches, enter into the kingdom of God: it is easier for a camel to go through a needle's eye, than for a rich man to enter into the kingdom of God. Then said they that heard that: And who shall then be saved? And he said: Things which are unpossible with men are possible with God.

Then Peter said: Lo we have left all, and have followed thee. And he said unto them: Verily I say unto you, there is no man that leaveth house, or father and mother, or brethren or wife or children for the kingdom of God's sake, which same shall not receive much more in this world: and in the world to come, life everlasting.

F +He took unto him twelve, and said unto them. Behold we go up to Jerusalem, and all shall be fulfilled that are written by the prophets of the son of man. He shall be delivered unto the gentiles, and shall be mocked, and shall be despitefully entreated, and shall be spitted on: and when they have scourged him, they will put him to death, and the third day he shall arise again. But they understood none of these things. And this saying was hid from them. And they perceived not the things which were spoken. ⊦

G And it came to pass, as he was come nigh unto Jericho, a certain blind man sat by the way-side begging. And when he heard the people pass by, he asked what it meant. And they said unto him, that Jesus of Nazareth passed by. And he cried saying: Jesus the son of David, have thou mercy on me. And they which went before rebuked him, that he should hold his peace. But he cried so much the more, thou son of David have mercy on me. And Jesus stood still, and commanded him to be brought unto him. And when he was come near, he asked him, saying: What wilt thou that I do unto thee? And he said: Lord, that I may receive my sight. Jesus said unto him: receive thy sight: thy faith hath saved thee. And immediately he saw, and followed him, praising God. And all the people, when they saw it, gave laud to God.

CHAPTER NINETEEN

A + And he entered in, and went through Jericho. And behold, there was a man named Zaccheus, which was a ruler among the publicans, and was rich also. And he made means to see Jesus, what he should be: and could not for the press, because he was of a low stature. Wherefore he ran before, and ascended up, into a wild fig tree, to see him: for he should come that same way. And when Jesus came to the place, he looked up, and saw him, and said unto him: Zacche, at once come down, for today I must abide at thy house. And he came down hastily and received him joyfully. And when they saw that, they all grudged saying: He is gone in to tarry with a man that is a sinner.

B And Zaccheus stood forth and said unto the Lord: behold Lord, the half of my goods I give to the poor, and if I have done any man wrong, I will restore

Camel.

Covenant.

Matt. 20. b.

Mark 10. c.

Passion.

Matt. 20. d.
Mark 10. g.

Blind man.

Zaccheus.

him four-fold. And Jesus said to him: this day is health come unto this house, forasmuch as it also is become the child of Abraham. For the son of man is come to seek and to save that which was lost. ⊦

Matt. 18. and 25.

As they heard these things, he added thereto a similitude, because he was nigh to Jerusalem, and because also they thought that the kingdom of God should shortly appear. He said therefore: + a certain nobleman, went into a far country, to receive him a kingdom, and then to come again. And he called his ten servants, and delivered them ten pounds saying unto them: buy and sell till I come. But his citizens hated him, and sent messengers after him saying: We will not have this man to reign over us.

Ten pounds.

And it came to pass, when he was come again and had received his kingdom, he commanded these servants, to be called to him (to whom he gave his money) to wit what every man had done. Then came the first saying: Lord, thy pound hath increased ten pounds. And he said unto him: Well good servant, because thou wast faithful in a very little thing, take thou authority over ten cities. And the other came saying: Lord thy pound hath increased five pounds. And to the same he said: and be thou also ruler over five cities. C

And the third came and said: Lord, behold here thy pound, which I have kept in a napkin, for I feared thee, because thou art a strait man: thou takest up that thou laidst not down, and reapest that thou didst not sow. And he said unto him: Of thine own mouth, judge I thee, thou evil servant: knewest thou that I am a strait man, taking up that I laid not down, and reaping that I did not sow? Wherefore then gavest not thou my money into the bank, that at my coming I might have required mine own with vantage? D

And he said to them that stood by: take from him that pound, and give it him that hath ten pounds. And they said unto him: Lord he hath ten pounds. I say unto you, that unto all them that have, it shall be given: and from him that hath not, even that he hath shall be taken from him. Moreover those mine enemies, which would not that I should reign over them, bring hither, and slay them before me. And when he had thus spoken, he proceeded forth before, ascending up to Jerusalem. ⊦

To him that hath, it shall be given.

Matt. 13. b. and 25.
Mark 4. c.

Matt. 21. a.
Mark 11. a.
Colt.

And it fortuned, when he was come nigh to Bethphage and Bethany, besides mount Olivet, he sent two of his disciples saying: Go ye in to the town which is over against you. In the which as soon as ye are come, ye shall find a colt tied, whereon yet never man sat. Loose him and bring him hither. And if any man ask you, why that ye loose him: thus say unto him, the Lord hath need of him. E

Bethphage.
Bethany.

They that were sent, went their way, and found, even as he had said unto them. And as they were a-loosing the colt, the owners said unto them: why loose ye the colt? And they said: for the Lord hath need of him. And they brought him to Jesus. And they cast their raiment on the colt, and set Jesus thereon. And as he went, they spread their clothes in the way.

John 12. b.

And when he was now come, where he should go down from the mount Olivet, the whole multitude of the disciples began to rejoice, and to laud God with a loud voice, for all the miracles that they had seen saying: Blessed be the king that cometh in the name of the Lord: peace in heaven, and glory in the highest. And some of the Pharisees of the company said unto him: Master rebuke thy disciples. He answered, and said unto them: I tell you, if these should hold their peace, the stones would cry.

F + And when he was come near, he beheld the city, and wept on it saying: If thou hadst known those things which belong unto thy peace, even at this thy time. But now are they hid from thine eyes. For the days shall come upon thee, *Matt. 24.* that thy enemies shall cast a bank about thee, and compass thee round, and *Mark 13. a.* keep thee in on every side, and make thee even with the ground, with thy children which are in thee. And they shall not leave in thee one stone upon another, because thou knewest not the time of thy visitation.

G And he went into the temple, and began to cast out them that sold therein, *Sellers and buyers.* and them that bought, saying unto them, it is written: my house is the house of prayer: but ye have made it a den of thieves. And he taught daily in the *Matt. 21. b.* temple. ⊦ The high priests and the scribes and the chief of the people went about *Mark 11. b.* to destroy him: but could not find what to do. For all the people stuck by him, *Isa. 56.* and gave him audience. *Jer. 7. c.*

CHAPTER TWENTY

A + And it fortuned in one of those days, as he taught the people in the temple and preached the gospel: the high priests and the scribes came with the elders, and spake unto him saying, tell us by what authority thou doest these things? *Matt. 21. c.* Either who is he that gave thee this authority? He answered and said unto *Mark 11. d.* them: I also will ask you a question, and answer me. The baptism of John: was *Baptism of John.* it from heaven or of men? And they thought within themselves saying: if we shall say from heaven: he will say: why then believed ye him not? But and if we shall say of men, all the people will stone us. For they be persuaded that John is a prophet. And they answered that they could not tell whence it was. And Jesus said unto them: neither tell I you by what authority I do these things. ⊦

B Then began he to put forth to the people, this similitude. A certain man *Vineyard.* planted a vineyard, and let it forth to farmers, and went himself into a strange country for a great season. And when the time was come, he sent a servant to *Mark 12.* his tenants that they should give him of the fruits of the vineyard. And the *Isa. 5. a.* tenants did beat him, and sent him away empty. And again he sent yet another *Jer. 2. d.* servant. And they did beat him, and foul entreated him also, and sent him away empty. Moreover, he sent the third too, and him they wounded, and cast out. Then said the lord of the vineyard: what shall I do? I will send my dear son, him peradventure they will reverence, when they see him.

C But when the farmers saw him, they thought in themselves saying: this is the heir, come let us kill him, that the inheritance may be ours. And they cast him out of the vineyard, and killed him. Now what shall the lord of the vineyard do unto them? He will come and destroy those farmers, and will let out his vineyard to other. When they heard that, they said: God forbid.

D And he beheld them and said: what meaneth this then that is written: That *Psa. 118.* stone that the builders refused, the same is made the head corner-stone? whoso- *Acts 4. b.* ever stumble at that stone, shall be broken: but on whosoever it fall upon, it *Rom. 9. g.* will grind him to powder. And the high priests and the scribes the same hour *1 Pet. 3. a.* *Isa. 28.*

went about to lay hands on him, but they feared the people. For they perceived that he had spoken this similitude against them.

Matt. 22. b.
Mark 12. b.

And they watched him, and sent forth spies, which should feign themselves perfect, to take him in his words, and to deliver him unto the power and authority of the debite. And they asked him saying: Master, we know that thou sayest and teachest right, neither considerest thou any man's degree, but teachest the way of God truly. Is it lawful for us to give Caesar tribute or no?

Tribute to Caesar.

He perceived their craftiness, and said unto them: why tempt ye me? Shew me

Rom. 13. b.

a penny. Whose image and superscription hath it? They answered and said: Caesar's. And he said unto them: Give then unto Caesar, that which belongeth unto Caesar: and to God, that which pertaineth to God. And they could not reprove his saying before the people. But they marvelled at his answer, and held their peace.

Sadducees.

Then came to him certain of the Sadducees which deny that there is any resurrection. And they asked him saying: Master, Moses wrote unto us, if any

Matt. 22.
Mark 12.
Deut. 25. b.

man's brother die having a wife, and the same die without issue: that then his brother should take his wife, and raise up seed unto his brother. There were seven brethren, and the first took a wife, and died without children. And the second took the wife, and he died childless. And the third took her, and in like wise the residue of the seven, and left no children behind them, and died. Last of all the woman died also. Now at the resurrection whose wife of them shall she be? For seven had her to wife.

Jesus answered and said unto them. The children of this world marry wives, and are married, but they which shall be made worthy to enjoy that world and the resurrection from death, neither marry wives, neither are married, nor yet can die any more. For they are equal unto the angels: and are the sons of God,

Exod. 3. b.

inasmuch as they are the children of the resurrection. And that the dead shall rise again, even Moses signified besides the bush, when he said: the Lord God of Abraham, and the God of Isaac, and the God of Jacob. For he is not the God of the dead, but of them which live. For all live in him. Then certain of the Pharisees answered and said: Master thou hast well said. And after that durst they not ask him any question at all.

Then said he unto them: how say they that Christ is David's son? And David himself saith in the book of the Psalms: The Lord said unto my Lord, sit on my

Matt. 22. d.
Mark 12. d.
Psa. 110. a.

right hand, till I make thine enemies thy footstool. Seeing David calleth him Lord: How is he then his son?

Matt. 23.
Mark 12. d.

Then in the audience of all the people, he said unto his disciples, beware of the scribes, which desire to go in long clothing: and love greetings in the markets, and the highest seats in the synagogues, and chief rooms at feasts, which devour widows' houses, and that under a colour of long praying: the same shall receive greater damnation.

CHAPTER TWENTY-ONE

Matt. 12. d.

As he beheld, he saw the rich men, how they cast in their offerings into the treasury. And he saw also a certain poor widow, which cast in thither two mites. And he said: of a truth I say unto you, this poor widow hath put in more than they all. For they all have of their superfluity added unto the offering of God: but she, of her penury, hath cast in all the substance that she had.

Poor widow.

Matt. 24.
Mark 13.

As some spake of the temple, how it was garnished with goodly stones and jewels, he said: The days will come, when of these things which ye see, shall

B not be left stone upon stone, that shall not be thrown down. And they asked him saying: Master when shall these things be, and what sign will there be, when such things shall come to pass?

Destruction of the temple.

And he said: take heed, that ye be not deceived. For many will come in my name saying: I am he: and the time draweth near. Follow ye not them therefore. But when ye hear of war and of dissension: be not afraid. For these things must first come: but the end followeth not by and by. Then said he unto

C them: Nation shall rise against nation, and kingdom against kingdom, and great earthquakes shall be in all quarters, and hunger, and pestilence: and fearful things. And great signs shall there be from heaven.

But before all these, they shall lay their hands on you, and persecute you, delivering you up to the synagogues and into prison, and bring you before kings and rulers for my name's sake. And this shall chance you for a testimonial. Let it stick therefore fast in your hearts, not once to study before, what ye shall answer: for I will give you a mouth and wisdom, where against, all your adversaries shall not be able to speak nor resist. Yea and ye shall be betrayed of your fathers and mothers, and of your brethren, and kinsmen, and lovers, and some of you shall they put to death. And hated shall ye be of all men for my name's sake. Yet there shall not one hair of your heads perish. With your patience possess* your souls.

A promise.

★ Possess: win or save.

D And when ye see Jerusalem besieged with an host, then understand that the desolation of the same is nigh. Then let them which are in Jewry fly to the mountains. And let them which are in the midst of it, depart out. And let not them that are in other countries, enter therein. For these be the days of vengeance, to fulfil all that are written. But woe be to them that be with child, and to them that give suck in those days: for there shall be great trouble in the land, and wrath over all this people. And they shall fall on the edge of the sword, and shall be led captive, into all nations. And Jerusalem shall be trodden under foot of the gentiles, until the time of the gentiles be fulfilled.

Matt. 24.
Mark 13.
Dan. 9. g.

E + And there shall be signs in the sun, and in the moon, and in the stars: and in the earth the people shall be in such perplexity, that they shall not tell which way to turn themselves. The sea and the waters shall roar, and men's hearts shall fail them for fear, and for looking after those things which shall come on the earth. For the powers of heaven shall move. And then shall they see the son of man come in a cloud with power and great glory. When these things begin to come to pass: then look up, and lift up your heads for your redemption draweth nigh.

Matt. 24
Mark 13
Isa. 13 b.
Ezek. 32.
Joel 3. c.

And he shewed them a similitude: behold the fig tree, and all other trees, when they shoot forth their buds, ye see and know of your own selves that summer is then nigh at hand. So likewise ye (when ye see these things come to pass) understand, that the kingdom of God is nigh. Verily I say unto you: this generation shall not pass, till all be fulfilled. Heaven and earth shall pass: but my words shall not pass. ⊦

+ Take heed to yourselves, lest your hearts be overcome with surfeiting and G
drunkenness and cares of this world, and that that day come on you unawares. For as a snare shall it come on all them that sit on the face of the earth. Watch therefore continually and pray, that ye may obtain grace to fly all this that shall come, and that ye may stand before the son of man. ⊦

Watch.

In the daytime, he taught in the temple, and at night, he went out, and had abiding in the mount Olivet. And all the people came in the morning to him in the temple, for to hear him.

CHAPTER TWENTY-TWO

Matt. 26.
Mark 14.
Matt. 26.

+ The feast of sweet bread drew nigh which is called Easter, and the high A
priests and scribes sought how to kill him, but they feared the people. Then entered Satan into Judas, whose surname was Iscariot (which was of the number of the twelve) and he went his way and communed with the high priests and officers, how he might betray him to them. And they were glad: and promised to give him money. And he consented and sought opportunity to betray him unto them, when the people were away.

Christ is betrayed.

Matt. 26.
Mark 14.

Then came the day of sweet bread, when of necessity the Easter lamb must be offered. And he sent Peter and John saying: Go and prepare us the Easter lamb, that we may eat. They said to him. Where wilt thou, that we prepare? And he said unto them. Behold when ye be entered into the city, there shall a man meet you bearing a pitcher of water, him follow into the same house that he entereth in, and say unto the good man of the house: The master sayeth unto thee: where is the guest chamber, where I shall eat mine Easter lamb with my disciples? And he shall shew you a great parlour paved. There make ready. And they went and found as he had said unto them: and made ready the Easter lamb.

Easter lamb.

And when the hour was come, he sat down and the twelve apostles with B
him. And he said unto them: I have inwardly desired to eat this Easter lamb with you before that I suffer. For I say unto you: henceforth, I will not eat of it any more, until it be fulfilled in the kingdom of God. And he took the cup, and gave thanks, and said. Take this, and divide it among you. For I say unto you: I will not drink of the fruit of the vine, until the kingdom of God be come.

Matt. 26.
Mark 14.
1 Cor. 11.

And he took bread, gave thanks, and gave to them, saying: This is my body which is given for you. This do in the remembrance of me. Likewise also, when they had supped, he took the cup saying: This cup is the new testament, in my blood, which shall for you be shed.

The sacrament is instituted.

Matt. 26.
Mark 14.

Yet behold, the hand of him that betrayeth me, is with me on the table. And the son of man goeth as it is appointed: But woe be to that man by whom he is betrayed. And they began to enquire among themselves, which of them it should be, that should do that.

John 13. c.
Psa. 41. c.

C + And there was a strife among them, which of them should be taken for the greatest. And he said unto them: the kings of the gentiles reign over them, and they that bear rule over them, are called gracious lords. But ye shall not be so. But he that is greatest among you, shall be as the youngest: and he that is chief, shall be as the minister. For whether is greater, he that sitteth at meat: or he that serveth? Is not he that sitteth at meat? And I am among you, as he that ministereth. Ye are they which have bidden with me in my temptations. And I appoint unto you a kingdom, as my father hath appointed to me: that ye may eat and drink at my table in my kingdom, and sit on seats, and judge the twelve tribes of Israel. ⊦

And the Lord said: Simon, Simon behold Satan hath desired you, to sift you, as it were wheat: but I have prayed for thee, that thy faith fail not. And when thou art converted, strengthen thy brethren. And he said unto him. Lord I am ready to go with thee into prison, and to death. And he said: I tell thee Peter, the cock shall not crow this day, till thou have thrice denied that thou knewest me.

D And he said unto them: when I sent you without wallet and scrip and shoes, lacked ye anything? And they said, no. And he said to them: but now he that hath a wallet let him take it up and likewise his scrip. And he that hath no sword, let him sell his coat and buy one. For I say unto you that yet, that which is written, must be performed in me: Even with the wicked was he numbered. For those things which are written of me, have an end. And they said: Lord, behold here are two swords. And he said unto them: it is enough.

And he came out, and went as he was wont, to mount Olivet. And the disciples followed him. And when he came to the place, he said to them: pray lest ye fall into temptation.

E And he gat himself from them, about a stone's cast, and kneeled down, and prayed, saying: Father if thou wilt, withdraw this cup from me. Nevertheless, not my will, but thine be fulfilled. And there appeared an angel unto him from heaven, comforting him. And he was in agony, and prayed somewhat longer. And his sweat was like drops of blood, trickling down to the ground. And he rose up from prayer and came to his disciples, and found them sleeping for sorrow, and said unto them: Why sleep ye? Rise and pray, lest ye fall into temptation.

While he yet spake: behold, there came a company, and he that was called Judas, one of the twelve, went before them, and pressed nigh unto Jesus to kiss him. And Jesus said unto him: Judas, betrayest thou the son of man with a kiss? When they which were about him saw what would follow, they said unto him. Lord, shall we smite with sword? And one of them smote a servant of the highest priest of all, and smote off his right ear. And Jesus answered and said: Suffer ye thus far forth. And he touched his ear, and healed him.

F Then Jesus said unto the high priests and rulers of the temple and the elders which were come to him. Be ye come out, as unto a thief with swords and staves? When I was daily with you in the temple, ye stretched not forth hands against me. But this is even your very hour, and the power of darkness. Then

Greatest.

Matt. 20. d.
Mark 10. f.

Simon's faith faileth not.

Matt. 26.
Mark 14.

Buy a sword.

Isa. 54.

Two swords.

Matt. 26.
Mark 14.
John 18.

Christ armeth himself against his passion.

An angel comforteth him.

He sweateth blood.

Ear is smitten off.

Matt. 26.
Mark 14.
John 18.

took they him, and led him, and brought him to the high priest's house. And Peter followed afar off.

Matt. 16.
Mark 14.
John 18.

When they had kindled a fire in the midst of the palace, and were set down together Peter also sat down among them. And one of the wenches beheld him G as he sat by the fire, and set good eyesight on him and said: this same was also

Peter denieth.

with him. Then he denied him saying: woman I know him not. And after a little while, another saw him and said: thou art also of them. And Peter said, man I am not. And about the space of an hour after, another affirmed saying: verily even this fellow was with him, for he is of Galilee, and Peter said: man I wot not what thou sayest. And immediately while he yet spake, the cock crew. And the Lord turned back and looked upon Peter. And Peter remembered the words of the Lord, how he said unto him, before the cock crow, thou shalt deny me thrice. And Peter went out, and wept bitterly. G

Christ is mocked.

And the men that stood about Jesus, mocked him, and smote him, and blindfolded him, and smote his face. And asked him saying: arede, who it is that smote thee? And many other things despitefully said they against him.

Matt. 27.
Mark 15.
John 18.

And as soon as it was day, the elders of the people and the high priests and scribes, came together and led him into their council saying: art thou very Christ? tell us. And he said unto them: if I shall tell you, ye will not believe. And if also I ask you, ye will not answer me, or let me go. Hereafter shall the son of man sit on the right hand of the power of God. Then said they all: Art thou then the son of God? He said to them: ye say that I am. Then said they: what need we any further witness? We ourselves have heard of his own mouth.

CHAPTER TWENTY-THREE

Matt. 22.
Mark 12.
Mark 15. a.
John 18.

And the whole multitude of them arose, and led him unto Pilate. And they A began to accuse him saying: We have found his fellow perverting the people, and forbidding to pay tribute to Caesar: saying, that he is Christ a king. And

He is delivered to
Pilate.

Pilate opposed him saying: art thou the king of the Jews? He answered him and said: thou sayest it. Then said Pilate to the high priests, and to the people: I find no fault in this man. And they were the more fierce saying. He moveth the people, teaching throughout all Jewry, and began at Galilee, even to this place.

He is sent to Herod.

When Pilate heard mention of Galilee, he asked whether the man were of B Galilee. And as soon as he knew that he was of Herod's jurisdiction he sent him to Herod, which was also at Jerusalem in those days. And when Herod saw Jesus, he was exceedingly glad. For he was desirous to see him of a long season, because he had heard many things of him, and trusted to have seen some miracle done by him. Then questioned he with him of many things. But he

He holdeth his peace.

answered him not one word. The high priests and scribes, stood forth and accused him straitly. And Herod with his men of war, despised him, and mocked him, and arrayed him in white, and sent him again to Pilate. And the

Pilate and Herod are
become friends.

same day Pilate and Herod were made friends together. For before they were at variance.

And Pilate called together the high priests and the rulers, and the people, and said unto them: Ye have brought this man unto me, as one that perverted the people. And behold I have examined him before you, and have found no fault C in this man, of those things whereof ye accuse him. No nor yet Herod. For I sent you to him: and lo nothing worthy of death is done to him. I will therefore chasten him and let him loose. For of necessity, he must have let one loose unto them at that feast.

And all the people cried at once saying: away with him, and deliver to us Barabbas: which for insurrection made in the city, and murder, was cast into prison. Pilate spake again to them willing to let Jesus loose. And they cried saying: Crucify him, Crucify him. He said unto them the third time. What evil hath he done? I find no cause of death in him. I will therefore chasten him, and let him loose. And they cried with loud voice, and required that he might be crucified. And the voice of them and of the high priests prevailed.

D And Pilate gave sentence that it should be as they required, and let loose unto them him that for insurrection and murder, was cast into prison, whom they desired: and delivered Jesus to do with him what they would. And as they led him away, they caught one Simon of Cyrene, coming out of the field: and on him laid they the cross, to bear it after Jesus.

And there followed him a great company of people and of women, which women bewailed and lamented him. But Jesus turned back unto them, and said: Daughters of Jerusalem, weep not for me: but weep for yourselves and for your children. For behold, the days will come, when men shall say: happy are the barren and the wombs that never bare, and the paps which never gave suck. Then shall they begin to say to the mountains, fall on us: and to the hills, cover us. For if they do this to a green tree, what shall be done to the dry?

E And there were two evil-doers led with him to be slain. And when they were come to the place, which is called Calvary, there they crucified him, and the evil-doers, one on right hand, and the other on the left. Then said Jesus: father forgive them, for they wot not what they do. And they parted his raiment, and cast lots. And the people stood and beheld.

And the rulers mocked him with them saying: he holp other men, let him help himself, if he be Christ the chosen of God. The soldiers also mocked him, and came and gave him vinegar and said: if thou be that king of the Jews, save thyself. And his superscription was written over him, in Greek, in Latin and Hebrew: This is the king of the Jews.

F And one of the evil-doers which hanged, railed on him saying: If thou be Christ save thyself and us. The other answered and rebuked him saying, Neither fearest thou God, because thou art in the same damnation? We are righteously punished, for we receive according to our deeds: But this man hath done nothing amiss. And he said unto Jesus: Lord remember me when thou comest into thy kingdom. And Jesus said unto him: Verily I say unto thee, today shalt thou be with me in Paradise.

And it was about the sixth hour. And there came a darkness over all the land, until the ninth hour, and the sun was darkened. And the veil of the temple did rent even through the midst. And Jesus cried with a great voice and said:

Matt. 27.
Mark 15.

John 18. and 19. c.

Barabbas.

Simon of Cyrene.

Matt. 27.

Mark 15. b.
Isa. 54. a.
Gal. 4.

Isa. 2. a.
Hos. 10. b.
Rev. 9. b.

Matt. 27.
Mark 15. b.
John 19. b.
Matt. 27.
Mark 15. b.

He is mocked.

Paradise.

Veil.

Father, into thy hands I commend my spirit. And when he thus had said, he
gave up the ghost. When the centurion saw what had happened, he glorified
God saying: Of a surety this man was perfect. And all the people that came
together to that sight, beholding the things which were done: smote their
breasts, and returned home. And all his acquaintance, and the women, that
followed him from Galilee, stood afar off beholding these things. ⊢

And behold there was a man named Joseph, a councillor, and was a good **G**
man and a just, and did not consent to the counsel and deed of them, which was
of Arimathæa, a city of the Jews: which same also waited for the kingdom of
God: he went unto Pilate, and begged the body of Jesus, and took it down, and
wrapped it in a linen cloth, and laid it in an hewn tomb, wherein was never
man before laid. And that day was the sabbath even, and the sabbath drew on.
The women that followed after, which came with him from Galilee, beheld the
sepulchre and how his body was laid. And they returned and prepared odours
and ointments: but rested the sabbath day, according to the commandment.

CHAPTER TWENTY-FOUR

+ On the morrow after the sabbath, early in the morning, they came unto the **A**
tomb and brought the odours which they had prepared and other women with
them. And they found the stone rolled away from the sepulchre, and went in:
but found not the body of the Lord Jesus. And it happened, as they were
amazed thereat, behold two men stood by them in shining vestures. And as
they were afraid, and bowed down their faces to the earth, they said to them:
why seek ye the living among the dead? He is not here: but is risen. Remember
how he spake unto you, when he was yet with you in Galilee, saying: that the
son of man must be delivered into the hands of sinful men, and be crucified,
and the third day rise again.

And they remembered his words, and returned from the sepulchre, and told **B**
all these things unto the eleven, and to all the remnant. It was Mary Magdalene
and Joanna, and Mary Jacobi, and other that were with them, which told these
things unto the apostles, and their words seemed unto them feigned things,
neither believed they them. Then arose Peter and ran unto the sepulchre, and
stooped in and saw the linen clothes laid by themself, and departed wondering
in himself at that which had happened.

+ And behold, two of them went that same day to a town which was from **C**
Jerusalem about three score furlongs, called Emmaus: and they talked together
of all these things that had happened. And it chanced, as they communed
together and reasoned, that Jesus himself drew near, and went with them. But
their eyes were holden, that they could not know him. And he said unto them:
What manner of communications are these that ye have one to another as ye
walk, and are sad? And the one of them named Cleopas, answered and said
unto him: art thou only a stranger in Jerusalem, and hast not known the things
which have chanced therein in these days? To whom he said: what things?

And they said unto him: of Jesus of Nazareth which was a prophet, mighty

He giveth up the ghost.

His friends stand
afar off.

Joseph of Arimathæa.

Matt. 27.
Mark 15.
John 19. g.

Mark 16.
John 22. a.

Matt. 27. d.
Mark 9. a.

Peter runneth to
the grave.

Emmaus.

in deed, and word, before God, and all the people. And how the high priests, and our rulers delivered him to be condemned to death: and have crucified him. But we trusted that it should have been he that should have delivered Israel. And as touching all these things, today is even the third day, that they were done. ⊦

D   Yea, and certain women also of our company made us astonied, which came early unto the sepulchre, and found not his body: and came saying, that they had seen a vision of angels, which said that he was alive. And certain of them which were with us, went their way to the sepulchre, and found it even so as the women had said: but him they saw not.

And he said unto them: O fools and slow of heart to believe all that the prophets have spoken. Ought not Christ to have suffered these things, and to

D   enter into his glory? And he began at Moses, and at all the prophets, and interpreted unto them in all scriptures which were written of him. And they drew nigh unto the town which they went to. And he made as though he would have gone further. But they constrained him saying: abide with us, for it draweth towards night, and the day is far passed. And he went in to tarry with them.

And it came to pass as he sat at meat with them, he took bread, blessed it, brake and gave to them. And their eyes were opened, and they knew him: and

E   he vanished out of their sight. And they said between themselves: did not our hearts burn within us, while he talked with us by the way, and as he opened to us the scriptures? And they rose up the same hour, and returned again to Jerusalem, and found the eleven gathered together and them that were with them, which said: the Lord is risen indeed and hath appeared to Simon. And they told what things was done in the way, and how they knew him in breaking of bread. ⊦

F   As they thus spake ✠ Jesus himself stood in the midst of them, and said unto them: peace be with you. And they were abashed and afraid, supposing that they had seen a spirit. And he said unto them: Why are ye troubled, and why do thoughts arise in your hearts? Behold my hands and my feet, that it is even myself. Handle me and see: for spirits have not flesh and bones, as ye see me have. And when he had thus spoken, he shewed them his hands and his feet. And while they yet believed not for joy, and wondered, he said unto them: Have ye here any meat? And they gave him a piece of a broiled fish, and of an honeycomb. And he took it, and ate it before them.

Matt. 28.
Mark 16.
John 20. c.

G   And he said unto them. These are the words, which I spake unto you, while I was yet with you: that all must be fulfilled which were written of me in the law of Moses, and in the Prophets, and in the Psalms. Then opened he their wits, that they might understand the scriptures, and said unto them, Thus is it written, and thus it behoved Christ to suffer, and to rise again from death the third day, and that repentance and remission of sins should be preached in his name among all nations, and must begin at Jerusalem. And ye are witnesses of these things. And behold, I will send the promise of my father upon you. But tarry ye in the city of Jerusalem, until ye be endued with power from on high. ⊦

He giveth the keys.

Psa. 29.

Acts 1. a.
John 26.

131

Acts 1. a.
Mark 16. d.

And he led them out into Bethany, and lift up his hands, and blest them. And it came to pass, as he blessed them, he departed from them, and was carried up into heaven. And they worshipped him, and returned to Jerusalem with great joy, and were continually in the temple, praising and lauding God. Amen.

Here endeth the Gospel of Saint Luke.

THE GOSPEL OF SAINT JOHN

CHAPTER ONE +

A In the beginning was the word, and the word was with God: and the word was God. The same was in the beginning with God. All things were made by it, and without it, was made nothing, that was made. In it was life, and the life was the light of men, and the light shineth in the darkness, but the darkness comprehended it not.

There was a man sent from God, whose name was John. The same came as a witness to bear witness of the light, that all men through him might believe. He was not that light: but to bear witness of the light. That was a true light, which lighteth all men that come into the world. He was in the world, and the world was made by him: and yet the world knew him not.

B He came among his own* and his own received him not. But as many as received him, to them he gave power to be the sons of God in that they believed on his name: which were born, not of blood nor of the will of the flesh, nor yet of the will of man: but of God.

* Own is his own people.

Faith maketh us the sons of God.

And the word was made flesh and dwelt among us, and we saw the glory of it, as the glory of the only begotten son of the father, which word was full of grace and verity. ⊦

Matt. 1. c.
Luke 2. d.

+John bare witness of him and cried saying: This was he of whom I spake, he that cometh after me, was before me, because he was ere than I. And of his fulness have all we received, even grace for grace*. For the law was given by Moses, but grace and truth came by Jesus Christ. No man hath seen God at any time. The only begotten son, which is in the bosom of the father, he hath declared him. ⊦

John bare witness.

* Grace: all grace: and all that is pleasant in the sight of God, is given us for Christ's sake only: even out of the fulness and abundance of the favour that he receiveth with his father.

C + And this is the record of John: When the Jews sent priests and Levites from Jerusalem, to ask him, what art thou? And he confessed and denied not, and said plainly: I am not Christ. And they asked him: what then? art thou Elias? And he said: I am not. Art thou a Prophet? And he answered no. Then said they unto him: what art thou that we may give an answer to them that sent us: What sayest thou of thyself? He said: I am the voice* of a crier in the wilderness, make straight the way of the Lord, as said the Prophet Esaias.

* Voice: that is: I am that I preach. I am sent to prove you sinners and to cry on you to amend that ye may receive Christ and his grace.

D And they which were sent, were of the Pharisees. And they asked him, and said unto him: why baptisest thou then, if thou be not Christ nor Elias, neither a Prophet? John answered them saying: I baptise with water: but one is come among you, whom ye know not, he it is that cometh after me, which was before me, whose shoe latchet I am not worthy to unloose. These things were done in Bethabara beyond Jordan, where John did baptise. ⊢

Lamb.

⊦ The next day, John saw Jesus coming unto him, and said: behold the lamb of God, which taketh away the sin of the world. This is he of whom I said, After me cometh a man, which was before me, for he was ere than I, and I knew him not: but that he should be declared to Israel, therefore am I come baptising with water.

Matt. 3. d.
Mark 1. b.
Luke 3. d.

And John bare record saying: I saw the spirit descend from heaven, like unto a dove, and abide upon him, and I knew him not. But he that sent me to baptise in water, the same said unto me: upon whom thou shalt see the spirit descend and tarry still on him, the same is he which baptiseth with the holy ghost. And I saw and bare record, that this is the son of God. ⊦

E

The next day after, John stood again, and two of his disciples. And he beheld Jesus as he walked by, and said: behold the lamb of God. And the two disciples heard him speak, and followed Jesus. And Jesus turned about, and saw them follow, and said unto them: What seek ye? They said unto him: Rabbi (which is to say by interpretation, Master) where dwellest thou? He said unto them: come and see. They came and saw where he dwelt: and abode with him that day. For it was about the tenth hour.

Andrew.

Peter.

One of the two which heard John speak and followed Jesus was Andrew, Simon Peter's brother. The same found his brother Simon first, and said unto him: we have found Messias, which is by interpretation, anointed: and brought him to Jesus. And Jesus beheld him and said: thou art Simon the son of Jonas, thou shalt be called Cephas: which is by interpretation, a stone.

F

Philip.

Nathanael.

Gen. 49.
Deut. 18.
Isa. 40. c. and 45. b.

Jer. 23.
Ezek. 34. and 37.
Dan. 9. f.

The day following Jesus would go into Galilee, and found Philip, and said unto him, follow me. Philip was of Bethsaida the city of Andrew and Peter. And Philip found Nathanael, and said unto him. We have found him of whom Moses in the law, and the prophets did write. Jesus the son of Joseph of Nazareth. And Nathanael said unto him: can there any good thing come out of Nazareth? Philip said to him: come and see.

G

Jesus saw Nathanael coming to him, and said of him: Behold a right Israelite, in whom is no guile. Nathanael said unto him: where knewest thou me? Jesus answered, and said unto him: Before that Philip called thee, when thou wast under the fig tree, I saw thee. Nathanael answered and said unto him: Rabbi, thou art the son of God, thou art the king of Israel. Jesus answered and said unto him: Because I said unto thee, I saw thee under the fig tree, thou believest. Thou shalt see greater things than these. And he said unto him: Verily verily I say unto you: hereafter shall ye see heaven open, and the angels of God ascending and descending over the son of man.

CHAPTER TWO

A marriage in Cana of Galilee.

⊦ And the third day, was there a marriage in Cana a city of Galilee: and the mother of Jesus was there. And Jesus was called also and his disciples unto the

A

marriage. And when the wine failed, the mother of Jesus said unto him: they have no wine. Jesus said unto her: woman, what have I to do with thee? mine hour is not yet come. His mother said unto the ministers: whatsoever he sayeth unto you, do it. And there were standing there, six waterpots of stone after the manner of the purifying of the Jews, containing two or three firkins apiece.

B   And Jesus said unto them: fill the waterpots with water. And they filled them up to the brim. And he said unto them: draw out now, and bear unto the governor of the feast. And they bare it. When the ruler of the feast had tasted the water that was turned unto wine, and knew not whence it was (but the ministers which drew the water knew), he called the bridegroom, and said unto him, all men at the beginning set forth good wine, and when men be drunk, then that which is worse. But thou hast kept back the good wine, until now.   *Water into wine.*

This beginning of miracles did Jesus in Cana of Galilee, and shewed his glory, and his disciples believed on him. ⊦After that he descended into Capernaum, and his mother, and his brethren, and his disciples: but continued not many days there.

C   + And the Jews' Easter was even at hand, and Jesus went up to Jerusalem, and found sitting in the temple those that sold oxen and sheep and doves, and changers of money. And he made a scourge of small cords, and drave them all out of the temple, with the sheep and oxen, and poured out the changers' money, and overthrew the tables, and said unto them that sold doves: Have these things hence, and make not my father's house an house of merchandise. And his disciples remembered, how that it was written: the zeal of thine house hath even eaten me.   *Sellers in the temple are cast out.*

Psa. 58.

D   Then answered the Jews and said unto him: what token shewest thou unto us, seeing that thou dost these things? Jesus answered and said unto them: destroy this temple, and in three days I will rear it up again. Then said the Jews: forty-six years was this temple a-building: and wilt thou rear it up in three days? But he spake of the temple of his body. As soon therefore as he was risen from death again, his disciples remembered that he thus said. And they believed the scripture, and the words which Jesus had said.   *Matt. 21. and 27.*
Mark 14. f. and 15. c.

When he was at Jerusalem at Easter in the feast, many believed on his name, when they saw his miracles which he did. But Jesus put not himself in their hands, because he knew all men, and needed not, that any man should testify of man. For he knew what was in man. ⊦   *Psa. 3. b. and 57. c.*

CHAPTER THREE

A   + There was a man of the Pharisees named Nicodemus, a ruler among the Jews. The same came to Jesus by night, and said unto him: Rabbi, we know that thou art a teacher which art come from God. For no man could do such miracles as thou doest, except God were with him. Jesus answered and said unto him: Verily verily I say unto thee: except a man be born anew, he cannot see the kingdom of God. Nicodemus said unto him: how can a man be born   *Nicodemus.*

when he is old? can he enter into his mother's womb and be born again? Jesus answered: verily, verily I say unto thee: except that a man be born of water and of the spirit, he cannot enter into the kingdom of God. That which is born of the flesh, is flesh: and that which is born of the spirit, is spirit. Marvel not that I said to thee, ye must be born anew. The wind bloweth where he listeth, and thou hearest his sound: but canst not tell whence he cometh and whither he goeth. So is every man that is born of the spirit.

And Nicodemus answered and said unto him: how can these things be? Jesus **B** answered and said unto him: art thou a master in Israel, and knowest not these things? Verily verily, I say unto thee, we speak that we know, and testify that we have seen: and ye receive not our witness. If when I tell you earthly things, ye believe not: how should ye believe, if I shall tell you of heavenly things?

And no man ascendeth up to heaven, but he that came down from heaven, that is to say, the son of man which is in heaven.

Serpent. And as Moses lift up the serpent in the wilderness, even so must the son of man be lift up, that none that believeth in him perish: but have eternal life. ⊢

Num. 21. + For God so loveth the world, that he hath given his only son, that none **C** that believe in him, should perish: but should have everlasting life. For God

Faith. sent not his son into the world, to condemn the world: but that the world

1. John 4. through him might be saved. He that believeth on him, shall not be condemned. But he that believeth not, is condemned already, because he believeth not in the name of the only son of God. And this is the

Condemnation. condemnation: that light is come into the world, and the men loved darkness more than light, because their deeds were evil. For every man that evil doeth, hateth the light: neither cometh to light, lest his deeds should be reproved. But he that doth truth, cometh to the light, that his deeds might be known, how that they are wrought in God. ⊢

After these things came Jesus and his disciples into the Jews' land, and there he haunted with them and baptised. And John also baptised in Ænon besides Salim, because there was much water there, and they came and were baptised. For John was not yet cast into prison.

+ And there arose a question between John's disciples and the Jews about **D** purifying. And they came unto John, and said unto him: Rabbi, he that was with thee beyond Jordan, to whom thou barest witness. Behold the same baptiseth, and all men come to him. John answered, and said: a man can receive nothing at all except it be given him from heaven. Ye yourselves are witnesses, how that I said: I am not Christ but am sent before him. He that hath the bride, is the bridegroom. But the friend of the bridegroom which standeth by and heareth him, rejoiceth greatly of the bridegroom's voice. This my joy is fulfilled. He must increase: and I must decrease.

He that cometh from on high is above all: He that is of the earth, is of the earth, and speaketh of the earth. He that cometh from heaven, is above all, and what he hath seen and heard: that he testifieth: but no man receiveth his

Rom. 3. a. testimony. Howbeit he that hath received his testimony hath set to his seal that God is true. For he whom God hath sent, speaketh the words of God. For God giveth not the spirit by measure. The father loveth the son and hath given all things into his hand. He that believeth on the son, hath everlasting life: and he that believeth not the son, shall not see life, but the wrath of God abideth on him. ⊢

Measure

1 John 5. b.

CHAPTER FOUR

A As soon as the Lord had knowledge, how the Pharisees had heard, that Jesus made and baptised more disciples than John (though that Jesus himself baptised not: but his disciples) he left Jewry, and departed again into Galilee. And it was so that he must needs go through Samaria. + Then came he to a city of Samaria called Sychar, besides the possession that Jacob gave to his son Joseph. And there was Jacob's well. Jesus then wearied in his journey, sat thus on the well.

Gen. 48.

B And it was about the sixth hour: and there came a woman of Samaria to draw water. And Jesus said unto her: give me drink. For his disciples were gone away unto the town to buy meat. Then said the woman of Samaria unto him: how is it, that thou being a Jew, askest drink of me, which am a Samaritan? for the Jews meddle not with the Samaritans. Jesus answered and said unto her: if thou knewest the gift of God, and who it is that sayeth to thee give me drink, thou wouldest have asked of him, and he would have given thee water of life. The woman said unto him, Sir thou hast nothing to draw with, and the well is deep: from whence then hast thou that water of life? Art thou greater than our father Jacob which gave us the well, and he himself drank thereof, and his children, and his cattle?

The woman of Samaria.

Jesus answered and said unto her: whosoever drinketh of this water, shall thirst again. But whosoever shall drink of the water that I shall give him, shall never be more athirst: but the water that I shall give him, shall be in him a well of water, springing up into everlasting life. The woman said unto him: Sir give me of that water, that I thirst not, neither come hither to draw. Jesus said unto her. Go and call thy husband, and come hither. The woman answered and said to him: I have no husband. Jesus said to her: Thou hast well said, I have no husband. For thou hast had five husbands, and he whom thou now hast, is not thy husband. That saidst thou truly.

C The woman said unto him: Sir I perceive that thou art a prophet. Our fathers worshipped in this mountain: and ye say that in Jerusalem is the place where men ought to worship. Jesus said unto her: woman believe me, the hour cometh, when ye shall neither in this mountain nor yet at Jerusalem, worship the father. Ye worship, ye wot not what: we know what we worship. For salvation cometh of the Jews. But the hour cometh and now is, when the true worshippers shall worship the father in spirit and in truth. For verily such the father requireth to worship him. God is a spirit, and they that worship him, must worship him, in spirit and truth*.

* How and where God will be worshipped.

D The woman said unto him: I wot well Messias shall come, which is called

2. Cor. 3. d.

Christ. When he is come, he will tell us all things. Jesus said unto her: I that speak unto thee am he. And even at that point, came his disciples, and marvelled that he talked with the woman. Yet no man said unto him: what meanest thou, or why talkest thou with her? The woman then left her water-pot, and went her way into the city, and said to the men, Come see a man which told me all things that ever I did. Is not he Christ? Then they went out of the city, and came unto him.

And in the mean while his disciples prayed him saying: Master, eat. He   E
said unto them: I have meat to eat, that ye know not of. Then said the disciples between themselves: hath any man brought him meat? Jesus said unto them: my meat is to do the will of him that sent me. And to finish his work. Say not ye: there are yet four months, and then cometh harvest? Behold I say unto you, lift up your eyes, and look on the regions: for they are white already unto harvest. And he that reapeth receiveth reward, and gathereth fruit unto life eternal: that both he that soweth, and he that reapeth might rejoice together. And herein is the saying true, that one soweth, and another reapeth. I sent you to reap that whereon ye bestowed no labour. Other men laboured, and ye are entered into their labours.

Many of the Samaritans of that city believed on him, for the saying of the   F
woman, which testified: he told me all things that ever I did. Then when the Samaritans were come unto him, they besought him, that he would tarry with them. And he abode there two days. And many more believed because of his own words, and said unto the woman: Now we believe not because of thy saying. For we have heard him ourselves, and know that this is even indeed Christ the saviour of the world. ⊦

Matt. 13. a.
Mark 6. a.
Luke 4. c.
Matt. 4. b.

After two days he departed thence, and went away into Galilee. And Jesus himself testified, that a prophet hath none honour in his own country. Then as soon as he was come into Galilee, the Galileans received him which had seen all the things that he did at Jerusalem at the feast. For they went also unto the feast day. And Jesus came again into Cana of Galilee, where he turned water into wine.

Mark 1. d.
Luke 4. c.

Ruler.

+ And there was a certain ruler, whose son was sick at Capernaum. As soon   G
as the same heard that Jesus was come out of Jewry into Galilee, he went unto him, and besought him, that he would descend, and heal his son: For he was even ready to die. Then said Jesus unto him: except ye see signs and wonders, ye cannot believe. The ruler said unto him: Sir come away or ever that my child die. Jesus said unto him, go thy way, thy son liveth. And the man believed the words that Jesus had spoken unto him, and went his way. And anon as he went on his way, his servants met him, and told him saying: thy child liveth. Then enquired he of them the hour when he began to amend. And they said unto him: Yesterday the seventh hour, the fever left him. And the father knew that it was the same hour in which Jesus said unto him: Thy son liveth. And he believed, and all his household. This is again the second miracle, that Jesus did, after he was come out of Jewry into Galilee. ⊦

A + After that there was a feast of the Jews, and Jesus went up to Jerusalem. And there is at Jerusalem, by the slaughterhouse★, a pool called in the Hebrew tongue, Bethesda, having five porches, in which lay a great multitude of sick folk, of blind, halt and withered, waiting for the moving of the water. For an angel went down at a certain season into the pool and troubled the water. Whosoever then first after the stirring of the water, stepped in, was made whole of whatsoever disease he had. And a certain man was there, which had been diseased thirty-eight years. When Jesus saw him lie, and knew that he now long time had been diseased, he said unto him, Wilt thou be made whole? The sick answered him: Sir I have no man when the water is troubled, to put me into the pool. But in the mean time, while I am about to come, another steppeth down before me.

★ The Greek hath sheep house: a place where they killed the beasts that were sanctified.

The man that lay thirty-eight years by the pool is healed.

B And Jesus said unto him: rise, take up thy bed, and walk. And immediately the man was made whole, and took up his bed, and went. And the same day was the sabbath day. The Jews therefore said unto him that was made whole: It is the sabbath day, it is not lawful for thee to carry thy bed. He answered them: he that made me whole, said unto me: take up thy bed, and get thee hence. Then asked they him: what man is that which said unto thee, take up thy bed and walk? And he that was healed, wist not who it was. For Jesus had gotten himself away, because that there was press of people in the place.

The sabbath is broken.

C And after that, Jesus found him in the temple, and said unto him: behold thou art made whole, sin no more, lest a worse thing happen unto thee. The man departed, and told the Jews that it was Jesus, which had made him whole.⊢ And therefore the Jews did persecute Jesus and sought the means to slay him, because he had done these things on the sabbath day. And Jesus answered them: + my father worketh hitherto, and I work. Therefore the Jews sought the more to kill him, not only because he had broken the sabbath: but said also that God was his father, and made himself equal with God.

D Then answered Jesus and said unto them: verily verily, I say unto you: the son can do nothing of himself, but that he seeth the father do. For whatsoever he doeth, that doeth the son also. For the father loveth the son and sheweth him all things, whatsoever he himself doeth. And he will shew him greater works than these, because ye should marvel. For likewise as the father raiseth up the dead, and quickeneth them, even so the son quickeneth whom he will. Neither judgeth the father any man: but hath committed all judgement unto the son, because that all men should honour the son, even as they honour the father. He that honoureth not the son, the same honoureth not the father which hath sent him. Verily verily I say unto you: He that heareth my words, and believeth on him that sent me, hath everlasting life, and shall not come into damnation: but is scaped from death unto life.

Christ is judge over all.

Faith.

D Verily verily I say unto you: the time shall come, and now is, when the dead shall hear the voice of the son of God. And they that hear, shall live. For as the

Matt. 25.

father hath life in himself: so likewise hath he given to the son to have life in himself: and hath given him power also to judge, in that he is the son of man. Marvel not at this, the hour shall come in the which all that are in the graves, shall hear his voice, and shall come forth: they that have done good unto the resurrection of life: and they that have done evil, unto the resurrection of damnation.

Resurrection.

+I can of mine own self do nothing at all. As I hear, I judge, and my judgement is just, because I seek not mine own will*, but the will of the father which hath sent me. If I bear witness of myself, my witness is not true. There is another that beareth witness of me, and I am sure that the witness which he beareth of me, is true. E

* He that seeketh not his own will, judgeth truly.

Matt. 3. d.

Ye sent unto John, and he bare witness unto the truth. But I receive not the record of man. Nevertheless, these things I say, that ye might be safe. He was a burning and a shining light, and ye would for a season have rejoiced in his light. But I have greater witness than the witness of John. For the works which the father hath given me to finish: the same works which I do, bear witness of me, that the father sent me. And the father himself which hath sent me, beareth witness of me. Ye have not heard his voice at any time, nor ye have seen his shape: thereto his words have ye not abiding in you. For whom he hath sent: him ye believe not.

Matt. 3. b.

Search the scriptures, for in them ye think ye have eternal life: and they are they which testify of me. And yet will ye not come to me, that ye might have life. I receive not praise of men. But I know you, that ye have not the love of God in you. I am come in my father's name, and ye receive me not. If another shall come in his own name, him will ye receive. How can ye believe which receive honour* one of another, and seek not the honour that cometh of God only? G

Search the scripture.

* He that seeketh honour cannot believe.

Do not think that I will accuse you to my father. There is one that accuseth you, even Moses in whom ye trust. For had ye believed Moses, ye would have believed me: for he wrote of me. But now ye believe not his writing: how shall ye believe my words?⊢

Moses.

CHAPTER SIX

+After these things Jesus went his way over the sea of Galilee nigh to a city called Tiberias. And a great multitude followed him, because they had seen his miracles which he did on them that were diseased. And Jesus went up into a mountain, and there he sat with his disciples. And Easter, a feast of the Jews, was nigh.⊢+Then Jesus lift up his eyes, and saw a great company come unto him, and said unto Philip: whence shall we buy bread that these might eat? This he said to prove him: for he himself knew what he would do. A

Matt. 14. d.
Mark 6. c.
Luke 9. b.

Philip answered him, two hundred penny-worth of bread are not sufficient for them, that every man have a little. Then said unto him, one of his disciples, Andrew, Simon Peter's brother: There is a lad here, which hath five barley loaves and two fishes: but what is that among so many? And Jesus said, Make B

Five loaves and two fishes.

the people sit down: There was much grass in the place. And the men sat down, in number, about five thousand. And Jesus took the bread, and gave thanks, and gave to the disciples, and his disciples to them that were set down. And likewise of the fishes, as much as they would.

When they had eaten enough, he said unto his disciples: gather up the broken meat that remaineth: that nothing be lost. And they gathered it together, and filled twelve baskets with the broken meat, of the five barley loaves, which broken meat remained unto them that had eaten. Then the men, when they had seen the miracle that Jesus did, said: This is of a truth the prophet that should come into the world. ⊦

When Jesus perceived that they would come, and take him up, to make him king, he departed again into a mountain himself alone. *Matt. 14. Mark 6. f.*

And when even was come, his disciples went unto the sea and entered into a ship, and went over the sea unto Capernaum. And anon it was dark, and Jesus was not come to them. And the sea arose with a great wind that blew. And when they had rowed about a twenty-five or a thirty furlongs, they saw Jesus walk on the sea, and draw nigh unto the ship, and they were afraid. And he said unto them: It is I, be not afraid. Then would they have received him into the ship, and the ship was by and by at the land whither they went.

The day following, the people which stood on the other side of the sea, saw that there was none other ship there, save that one wherein his disciples were entered, and that Jesus went not in with his disciples into the ship: but that his disciples were gone away alone. Howbeit, there came other ships from Tiberias nigh unto the place, where they ate bread, when the Lord had blessed. Then when the people saw that Jesus was not there, neither his disciples, they also took shipping and came to Capernaum seeking for Jesus.

And when they had found him on the other side of the sea, they said unto him: Rabbi, when camest thou hither? Jesus answered them and said: verily verily I say unto you: ye seek me, not because ye saw the miracles: but because ye ate of the loaves, and were filled. + Labour, not for the meat which perisheth, but for the meat that endureth unto everlasting life, which meat the son of man shall give unto you. For him hath God the father sealed★.

★ Sealed: that is: he hath put his mark of the holy ghost on him which testifieth with miracles what he is.

Then said they unto him: what shall we do that we might work the works of God? Jesus answered and said unto them, This is the work of God, that ye believe on him, whom he hath sent. They said unto him: what sign shewest thou then, that we may see and believe thee? What dost thou work? Our fathers did eat manna in the desert, as it is written: He gave them bread from heaven to eat. Jesus said unto them: verily verily I say unto you: Moses gave you bread from heaven: but my father giveth you the true bread from heaven. For the bread of God is he which cometh down from heaven and giveth life unto the world. *Exod. 16. Num. 11. b. Psa. 78. Prov. 16.*

Then said they unto him: Lord, evermore give us this bread. And Jesus said unto them: I am that bread of life. He that cometh to me, shall not hunger: and he that believeth on me shall never thirst. ⊦ But I said unto you: that ye have seen me, and yet believe not. All that the father giveth me: shall come to me: *Eccl. 24.*

and him that cometh to me, I cast not away. For I came down from heaven: not
to do mine own will, but his will which hath sent me: And this is the father's
will which hath sent me, that of all which he hath given me, I should lose
nothing: but should raise it up again at the last day. And this is the will of him
that sent me: that every man which seeth the son and believeth on him, have
everlasting life. And I will raise him up at the last day.

The Jews then murmured at him, because he said: I am that bread which is   E
come down from heaven. And they said: Is not this Jesus the son of Joseph,

Matt. 13.

whose father and mother we know? How is it then that he sayeth, I came
down from heaven? Jesus answered and said unto them. Murmur not between
yourselves. + No man can come to me except the father which hath sent me,
draw him. And I will raise him up at the last day. It is written in the prophets,

Isa. 26.
Jer. 31.

that they shall all be taught of God. Every man therefore that hath heard and
hath learned of the father cometh unto me. Not that any man hath seen the
father, save he which is of God: the same hath seen the father.

Verily verily I say unto you, he that believeth on me, hath everlasting life. I

Exod. 16. a.

am that bread of life. Your fathers did eat manna in the wilderness and are
dead. This is that bread which cometh from heaven, that he which eateth of it,
should also not die. I am that living bread which came down from heaven. If
any man eat of this bread, he shall live forever. And the bread that I will give, is
my flesh, which I will give for the life of the world. +

And the Jews strove among themselves saying: How can this fellow give us
his flesh to eat? Then Jesus said unto them: Verily verily I say unto you, except
ye eat the flesh of the son of man, and drink his blood, ye shall not have life in
you. Whosoever eateth my flesh, and drinketh my blood, hath eternal life: and
I will raise him up at the last day. + For my flesh is meat indeed: and my blood   F
is drink indeed. He that eateth my flesh and drinketh my blood, dwelleth in me
and I in him. As the living father hath sent me, even so live I by my father: and
he that eateth me, shall live by me. This is the bread which came from heaven:
not as your fathers have eaten manna and are dead. He that eateth of this bread,
shall live ever. +

These things said he in the synagogue as he taught in Capernaum. Many of   C
his disciples, when they had heard this, said: this is an hard saying: who can
abide the hearing of it? Jesus knew in himself, that his disciples murmured at it,
and said unto them: Doth this offend you? What and if ye shall see the son of
man ascend up where he was before? It is the spirit that quickeneth, the flesh
profiteth nothing. The words that I speak unto you, are spirit and life. But
there are some of you that believe not. For Jesus knew from the beginning,
which they were that believed not, and who should betray him. And he said:
Therefore said I unto you: that no man can come unto me, except it were given
unto him of my father.

From that time many of his disciples went back, and walked no more with
him. Then said Jesus to the twelve: will ye also go away? Then Simon Peter
answered: Master to whom shall we go? Thou hast the words of eternal life,

Matt. 16.

and we believe and know, that thou art Christ the son of the living God. Jesus answered them: Have not I chosen you twelve, and yet one of you is the devil? He spake it of Judas Iscariot the son of Simon. For he it was that should betray him, and was one of the twelve. ⊢

CHAPTER SEVEN

C

+ After that, Jesus went about in Galilee and would not go about in Jewry, for the Jews sought to kill him. The Jews' tabernacle feast was at hand. His brethren therefore said unto him: get thee hence and go into Jewry that thy disciples may see thy works that thou doest. For there is no man that doeth anything secretly, and he himself seeketh to be known. If thou do such things, shew thyself to the world. For as yet his brethren believed not in him.

Then Jesus said unto them: My time is not yet come, your time is always ready. The world cannot hate you. Me it hateth: because I testify of it, that the works of it are evil. Go ye up unto this feast. I will not go up yet unto this feast, for my time is not yet full come. These words he said unto them and abode still in Galilee. But as soon as his brethren were gone up, then went he also up unto the feast: not openly but as it were privily. Then sought him the Jews at the feast, and said: Where is he? And much murmuring was there of him among the people. Some said: He is good. Other said nay, but he deceiveth the people. Howbeit no man spake openly of him, for fear of the Jews. ⊢

+ In the midst of the feast, Jesus went up into the temple and taught. And the Jews marvelled saying: How knoweth he the scriptures, seeing that he never learned? Jesus answered them, and said: My doctrine is not mine: but his that sent me. If any man will do his will*, he shall know of the doctrine, whether it be of God, or whether I speak of myself. He that speaketh of himself, seeketh his own praise. But he that seeketh his praise that sent him, the same is true, and no unrighteousness is in him.

D

Did not Moses give you a law, and yet none of you keepeth the law? Why go ye about to kill me? The people answered and said: thou hast the devil: who goeth about to kill thee? Jesus answered and said to them: I have done one work, and ye all marvel. Moses therefore gave unto you circumcision: not because it is of Moses, but of the fathers. And yet ye on the sabbath day, circumcise a man. If a man on the sabbath day receive circumcision without breaking of the law of Moses: disdain ye at me, because I have made a man every whit whole on the sabbath day? Judge not after the utter appearance: but judge righteous judgement.

Then said some of them of Jerusalem: Is not this he whom they go about to kill? Behold he speaketh boldly, and they say nothing to him. Do the rulers know indeed, that this is very Christ? Howbeit we know this man whence he is: but when Christ cometh, no man shall know whence he is.

Then cried Jesus in the temple as he taught saying: ye know me, and whence I am ye know. And yet I am not come of myself, but he that sent me is true, whom ye know not. I know him: for I am of him, and he hath sent me. Then they sought to take him: but no man laid hands on him, because his time was

* He that loveth the will of God to keep his law: the same understandeth the doctrine.

Praise.

Lev. 12. a.

Sabbath.

Deut. 1. c.

not yet come. Many of the people believed on him and said: when Christ cometh, will he do more miracles than this man hath done?

The Pharisees heard that the people murmured such things about him.   **E**
Wherefore the Pharisees and high priests sent ministers forth to take him. Then said Jesus unto them: Yet am I a little while with you, and then go I unto him that sent me. Ye shall seek me, and shall not find me: and where I am, thither can ye not come. Then said the Jews between themselves: whither will he go, that we shall not find him? Will he go among the gentiles which are scattered all abroad, and teach the gentiles? What manner of saying is this that he said: ye shall seek me, and shall not find me: and where I am, thither can ye not come?

In the last day, that great day of the feast, Jesus stood and cried saying: If any   **F**
man thirst, let him come unto me and drink. He that believeth on me, as sayeth the scripture, out of his belly shall flow rivers of water of life. This spake he of the spirit which they that believed on him, should receive. ⊢ For the holy ghost was not yet there, because that Jesus was not yet glorified.

＋ Many of the people, when they heard this saying said: of a truth this is a prophet. Other said: this is Christ. Some said: shall Christ come out of Galilee? Saith not the scripture that Christ shall come of the seed of David: and out of the town of Bethlehem where David was? So was there dissension among the people about him. And some of them would have taken him: but no man laid hands on him.

Then came the ministers to the high priests and Pharisees. And they said   **G**
unto them: why have ye not brought him? The servants answered; never man spake as this man doeth. Then answered them the Pharisees: are ye also deceived? Doth any of the rulers or of the Pharisees believe on him? But the common people which know not the law, are cursed. Nicodemus said unto them: He that came to Jesus by night, and was one of them: Doth our law judge any man, before it hear him, and know what he hath done? They answered and said unto him: art thou also of Galilee? Search and look, for out of Galilee ariseth no prophet. And every man went unto his own house. ⊢

CHAPTER EIGHT

＋ And Jesus went unto mount Olivet and early in the morning came again into   **A**
the temple and all the people came unto him, and he sat down and taught them. And the scribes and the Pharisees brought unto him a woman taken in advoutry, and set her in the midst and said unto him: Master, this woman was taken in advoutry, even as the deed was a-doing. Moses in the law commanded us that such should be stoned. What sayest thou therefore? And this they said to tempt him: that they might have whereof to accuse him. Jesus stooped down, and with his finger wrote on the ground. And while they continued asking him, he lifted himself up, and said unto them: let him that is among you without sin cast the first stone at her. And again he stooped down and wrote on the ground. And as soon as they heard that, they went out one by one, the eldest first. And Jesus was left alone, and the woman standing in the midst.

2. Chr. 16.

Mic. 5. a.
Matt. 2. a.

Rulers and Pharisees
believe not.

Lev. 21. a.

Deut. 17.

144

When Jesus had lifted up himself again, and saw no man but the woman, he said unto her: Woman, where are those thine accusers? Hath no man condemned thee? She said: No man Lord. And Jesus said: Neither do I condemn thee. Go, and sin no more. ⊢

B Then spake Jesus again unto them saying: I am the light of the world. He that followeth me shall not walk in darkness: but shall have the light of life. The Pharisees said unto him: Thou bearest record of thyself; thy record is not true. Jesus answered and said unto them: Though I bear record of myself yet my record is true: for I know whence I came and whither I go. But ye cannot tell whence I come, and whither I go. Ye judge after the flesh. I judge no man; though I judge, yet is my judgement true. For I am not alone; but I and the father that sent me. It is also written in your law, that the testimony of two men is true. I am one that bear witness of myself, and the father that sent me, beareth witness of me. Then said they unto him: where is thy father? Jesus answered: ye neither know me, nor yet my father. If ye had known me, ye should have known my father also. These words spake Jesus in the treasury, as

C he taught in the temple, and no man laid hands on him, for his time was not yet come. ⊢

Then said Jesus again unto them. + I go my way, and ye shall seek me, and shall die in your sins. Whither I go, thither can ye not come. Then said the Jews: will he kill himself, because he saith: whither I go, thither can ye not come? And he said unto them: ye are from beneath, I am from above. Ye are of this world, I am not of this world. I said therefore unto you, that ye shall die in your sins. For except ye believe that I am he, ye shall die in your sins.

) Then said they unto him, who art thou? And Jesus said unto them: Even the very same thing that I say unto you. I have many things to say, and to judge of you. But he that sent me is true. And I speak in the world, those things which I have heard of him. They understood not that he spake of his father.

Then said Jesus unto them: when ye have lift up on high the son of man, then shall ye know that I am he, and that I do nothing of myself: but as my father hath taught me, even so I speak: and he that sent me, is with me. The father hath not left me alone, for I do always those things that please him. ⊢As he spake these words, many believed on him.

+ Then said Jesus to those Jews which believed on him: If ye continue in my words, then are ye my very disciples, and shall know the truth: and the truth shall make you free. They answered him: We be Abraham's seed, and were never bond to any man: why sayest thou then, ye shall be made free?

Jesus answered them: Verily verily I say unto you, that whosoever committeth sin, is the servant of sin. And the servant abideth not in the house for ever: But the son abideth ever. If the son therefore shall make you free, then are ye free indeed. I know that ye are Abraham's seed: but ye seek means to kill me, because my sayings have no place in you. I speak that I have seen with my father: and ye do that which ye have seen with your father.

E They answered and said unto him: Abraham is our father. Jesus said unto them: If ye were Abraham's children, ye would do the deeds of Abraham. But

Light.

1. John. 1. b.

Deut. 19. b.

Matt. 18. a.
2. Cor. 13.
Heb. 10. e.

Christ is his doctrine.

Rom. 3. d.

Rom. 6. c.
2 Pet. 2. d.

Abraham.

145

now ye go about to kill me, a man that have told you the truth, which I have heard of God: this did not Abraham. Ye do the deeds of your father. Then said they unto him: we were not born of fornication. We have one father, which is God. Jesus said unto them: if God were your father, then would ye love me. For I proceeded forth and come from God. Neither came I of myself, but he sent me. Why do ye not know my speech? Even because ye cannot abide the hearing of my words.

1 John 3. b.

The devil.

Ye are of your father the devil, and the lusts of your father ye will follow. He was a murderer from the beginning, and abode not in the truth, because there is no truth in him. When he speaketh a lie, then speaketh he of his own. For he is a liar, and the father thereof. And because I tell you the truth, therefore ye believe me not.

F

+ Which of you can rebuke me of sin? If I say the truth, why do not ye believe me? He that is of God, heareth God's words. Ye therefore hear them not, because ye are not of God.

Thou art a Samaritan and hast the devil.

Then answered the Jews and said unto him: Say we not well that thou art a Samaritan, and hast the devil? Jesus answered: I have not the devil: but I honour my father, and ye have dishonoured me. I seek not mine own praise: but there is one that seeketh and judgeth.

Verily verily I say unto you, if a man keep my sayings, he shall never see death. Then said the Jews to him: Now know we that thou hast the devil. Abraham is dead, and also the prophets: and yet thou sayest, if a man keep my saying, he shall never taste of death. Art thou greater than our father Abraham which is dead? and the prophets are dead. Whom makest thou thyself?

G

Jesus answered: If I honour myself, mine honour is nothing worth. It is my father that honoureth me, which ye say, is your God, and ye have not known him: but I know him. And if I should say, I know him not, I should be a liar like unto you. But I know him, and keep his saying.

Your father Abraham was glad to see my day, and he saw it and rejoiced. Then said the Jews unto him: thou art not yet fifty years old, and hast thou seen Abraham? Jesus said unto them: Verily verily I say unto you: ere Abraham was, I am. Then took they up stones, to cast at him. But Jesus hid himself, and went out of the temple. ⊦

CHAPTER NINE

+ And as Jesus passed by, he saw a man which was blind from his birth. And his disciples asked him saying. Master, who did sin: this man or his father and mother, that he was born blind? Jesus answered: Neither hath this man sinned, nor yet his father and mother: but that the works of God should be shewed on him. I must work the works of him that sent me, while it is day. The night* cometh when no man can work. As long as I am in the world, I am the light of the world.

A

* Night, when the true knowledge of Christ, how he only justifieth, is lost: then can no man work a good work in the sight of God, how glorious soever his works appear.

As soon as he had thus spoken, he spat on the ground and made clay of the spittle, and rubbed the clay on the eyes of the blind, and said unto him: Go

B

wash thee in the pool of Siloam, which by interpretation, signifieth sent. He
went his way and washed, and came again seeing. The neighbours and they
that had seen him before how that he was a beggar, said: is not this he that sat
and begged? Some said: this is he. Other said: he is like him. But he himself
said: I am even he. They said unto him: How are thine eyes opened then? He
answered and said. The man that is called Jesus, made clay, and anointed mine
eyes, and said unto me: Go to the pool Siloam and wash. I went and washed
and received my sight. They said unto him: where is he? He said: I cannot tell.

C   Then brought they to the Pharisees, him that a little before was blind: for it
was the sabbath day when Jesus made the clay and opened his eyes. Then again
the Pharisees also asked him how he had received his sight. He said unto them:
He put clay upon mine eyes and I washed, and do see. Then said some of the
Pharisees: this man is not of God, because he keepeth not the sabbath day.
Other said: how can a man that is a sinner, do such miracles? And there was
strife among them. Then spake they unto the blind again: What sayest thou of
him, because he hath opened thine eyes? And he said: He is a prophet.

D   But the Jews did not believe of the fellow, how that he was blind and
received his sight, until they had called the father and mother of him that had
received his sight. And they asked them saying: Is this your son, whom ye say
was born blind? How doth he now see then? His father and mother answered
them and said: we wot well that this is our son, and that he was born blind:
but by what means he now seeth, that can we not tell, or who hath opened his
eyes, can we not tell. He is old enough, ask him, let him answer for himself.

E   Such words spake his father and mother, because they feared the Jews. For the
Jews had conspired already that if any man did confess that he was Christ, he
should be excommunicate out of the synagogue. Therefore said his father and
mother: he is old enough, ask him.

    Then again called they the man that was blind, and said unto him: Give God
the praise: we know that this man is a sinner. He answered and said: Whether
he be a sinner or no, I cannot tell: One thing I am sure of, that I was blind, and
now I see. Then said they to him again: What did he to thee? How opened
he thine eyes? He answered them, I told you erewhile, and ye did not hear.
Wherefore would ye hear it again? Will ye also be his disciples? Then rated they
him, and said: Thou art his disciple. We be Moses's disciples. We are sure that
God spake with Moses. This fellow we know not from whence he is.

F   The man answered and said unto them: this is a marvellous thing that ye wot
not whence he is, seeing he hath opened mine eyes. For we be sure that God
heareth not sinners. But if any man be a worshipper of God and do his will,
him heareth he. Since the world began was it not heard that any man opened
the eyes of one that was born blind. If this man were not of God, he could have
done nothing. They answered and said unto him: thou art altogether born in
sin: and dost thou teach us? And they cast him out.

    Jesus heard that they had excommunicated him: and as soon as he had found
him, he said unto him: dost thou believe on the son of God? He answered and
said: Who is it Lord, that I might believe on him? And Jesus said unto him:

Thou hast seen him, and he it is that talketh with thee. And he said: Lord I believe: and worshipped him. ⊦ Jesus said: I am come unto judgement into this world: that they which see not, might see, and they which see, might be made blind. And some of the Pharisees which were with him, heard these words and said unto him: are we then blind? Jesus said unto them: if ye were blind, ye should have no sin. But now ye say, we see, therefore your sin remaineth.

CHAPTER TEN

Door.

⊦ Verily verily I say unto you: he that entereth not in by the door, into the   **A** sheepfold, but climbeth up some other way: the same is a thief and a robber. He that goeth in by the door, is the shepherd of the sheep: to him the porter openeth, and the sheep hear his voice, and he calleth his own sheep by name, and leadeth them out. And when he hath sent forth his own sheep, he goeth before them, and the sheep follow him: for they know his voice. A stranger they will not follow, but will fly from him: for they know not the voice of strangers. This similitude spake Jesus unto them. But they understood not what things they were which he spake unto them.

Christ is the door.

Then said Jesus unto them again. Verily verily I say unto you: I am the door   **B** of the sheep. All, even as many as came before me, are thieves and robbers: but the sheep did not hear them. I am the door: by me if any man enter in, he shall be safe, and shall go in and out and find pasture. The thief cometh not but for to steal, kill and destroy. I am come that they might have life, and have it more abundantly. ⊦

Shepherd.

Isa. 40. c.
Ezek. 34. and 28.

⊦ I am the good shepherd. The good shepherd giveth his life for the sheep.   **C** An hired servant, which is not the shepherd, neither the sheep are his own, seeth the wolf coming, and leaveth the sheep, and flyeth, and the wolf catcheth them, and scattereth the sheep. The hired servant flyeth, because he is an hired servant, and careth not for the sheep. I am that good shepherd, and know mine, and am known of mine. As my father knoweth me: even so know I my

Ezek. 27.

father. And I give my life for the sheep: and other sheep I have, which are not of this fold. Them also must I bring, that they may hear my voice, and that there may be one flock and one shepherd. ⊦

Therefore doth my father love me, because I put my life from me, that I   **D** might take it again. No man taketh it from me: but I put it away of myself. I have power to put it from me, and have power to take it again: This commandment have I received of my father. And there was a dissension again among the Jews for these sayings, and many of them said, He hath the devil, and is mad: why hear ye him? Other said, these are not the words of him that hath the devil. Can the devil open the eyes of the blind?

1. Maccabees. 4.

⊦ And it was at Jerusalem the feast of the dedication, and it was winter: and   **E** Jesus walked in Solomon's porch. Then came the Jews round about him, and said unto him: How long dost thou make us doubt? If thou be Christ, tell us plainly. Jesus answered them: I told you and ye believe not. The works that I do in my father's name, they bear witness of me. But ye believe not, because ye are not of my sheep. As I said unto you: my sheep hear my voice, and I know them, and they follow me, and I give unto them eternal life, and they shall never perish, neither shall any man pluck them out of my hand. My father which gave them me, is greater than all, and no man is able to take them out of my father's hand. And I and my father are one.

F Then the Jews again took up stones, to stone him withal. Jesus answered them: many good works have I shewed you from my father: for which of them will ye stone me? The Jews answered him saying, for thy good works' sake we stone thee not: but for thy blasphemy, and because that thou being a man, *Isa. 44.*
G makest thyself God. Jesus answered them: Is it not written in your law: I say, ye are gods? If he called them gods unto whom the word of God was spoken *Psa. 82.* (and the scripture cannot be broken) say ye then to him, whom the father hath sanctified, and sent into the world, thou blasphemest, because I said I am the son of God? If I do not the works of my father, believe me not. But if I do, though ye believe not me, yet believe the works, that ye may know and believe that the father is in me, and I in him. ⊦

Again they went about to take him: but he escaped out of their hands, and went away again beyond Jordan, into the place where John before had baptised, and there abode. And many resorted unto him, and said, John did no miracle: but all things that John spake of this man are true. And many believed on him there.

CHAPTER ELEVEN

A + A certain man was sick, named Lazarus of Bethany the town of Mary and Lazarus.
her sister Martha. It was that Mary which anointed Jesus with ointment, and wiped his feet with her hair, whose brother Lazarus was sick, and his sisters sent unto him saying, Lord behold, he whom thou lovest, is sick. When Jesus heard that, he said: this infirmity is not unto death, but for the laud of God, that the son of God might be praised by the reason of it. Jesus loved Martha and her sister and Lazarus. After he heard, that he was sick, then abode he two days still in the same place where he was.

B Then after that said he to his disciples: let us go into Jewry again. His disciples said unto him, Master, the Jews lately sought means to stone thee, and wilt thou go thither again? Jesus answered: are there not twelve hours in the day? If a man walk in the day, he stumbleth not, because he seeth the light of this world. But if a man walk in the night, he stumbleth, because there is no light in him. This said he, and after that, he said unto them: our friend Lazarus sleepeth, but I go to wake him out of sleep. Then said his disciples: Lord if he sleep, he shall do well enough. Howbeit Jesus spake of his death: but they thought that he had spoken of the natural sleep. Then said Jesus unto them plainly, Lazarus is dead, and I am glad for your sakes, that I was not there, because ye may believe. Nevertheless let us go unto him. Then said Thomas which is called Didymus, unto the disciples: let us also go, that we may die with him.

Then went Jesus, and found that he had lain in his grave four days already.   C
Bethany was nigh unto Jerusalem, about fifteen furlongs off, and many of the
Jews were come to Martha and Mary, to comfort them over their brother.
Martha, as soon as she heard that Jesus was coming, went and met him: but
Mary sat still in the house.

+ Then said Martha unto Jesus: Lord if thou hadst been here, my brother had
not been dead: but nevertheless, I know that whatsoever thou askest of God,
God will give it thee. Jesus said unto her: Thy brother shall rise again. Martha
said unto him: I know that he shall rise again in the resurrection at the last day.
Jesus said unto her: I am the resurrection and the life: He that believeth on me,
yea though he were dead, yet shall he live. And whosoever liveth and believeth
on me, shall never die. Believest thou this? She said unto him: yea Lord, I
believe that thou art Christ the son of God which should come into the world. ⊢

And as soon as she had so said, she went her way and called Mary her sister   D
secretly saying: The master is come and calleth for thee. And she as soon as she
heard that, arose quickly, and came unto him. Jesus was not yet come into the
town: but was in the place where Martha met him. The Jews then which were
with her in the house and comforted her, when they saw Mary that she rose up
hastily, and went out, followed her, saying: She goeth unto the grave, to weep
there.

Then when Mary was come where Jesus was, and saw him, she fell down at
his feet, saying unto him: Lord if thou hadst been here, my brother had not
been dead.

When Jesus saw her weep, and the Jews also weep, which came with her, he   E
groaned in the spirit, and was troubled in himself and said: Where have ye laid
him? They said unto him: Lord come and see. And Jesus wept. Then said the
Jews: Behold how he loved him. And some of them said: could not he which
opened the eyes of the blind, have made also, that this man should not have
died? Jesus again groaned in himself, and came to the grave. It was a cave, and a
stone laid on it.

And Jesus said: take ye away the stone. Martha the sister of him that was
dead, said unto him: Lord by this time he stinketh. For he hath been dead
four days: Jesus said unto her: Said I not unto thee, that if thou didst believe,
thou shouldest see the glory of God? Then they took away the stone from the
place where the dead was laid. And Jesus lift up his eyes and said: Father I
thank thee because that thou hast heard me. I wot that thou hearest me always:
but because of the people that stand by I said it, that they may believe, that
thou hast sent me.

And when he thus had spoken, he cried with a loud voice, Lazarus come   F
forth. And he that was dead, came forth, bound hand and foot with grave
bonds, and his face was bound with a napkin. Jesus said unto them: loose him,
and let him go. Then many of the Jews which came to Mary, and had seen the
things which Jesus did, believed on him. ⊢ But some of them went their ways
to the Pharisees, and told them what Jesus had done.

+ Then gathered the high priests and the Pharisees a council, and said: what do we? This man doeth many miracles. If we let him scape thus, all men will believe on him, and the Romans shall come and take away our country and the people. And one of them named Caiaphas which was the high priest that same year, said unto them: Ye perceive nothing at all nor yet consider that it is expedient for us, that one man die for the people, and not that all the people perish. This spake he not of himself, but being high priest that same year, he prophesied that Jesus should die for the people, and not for the people only, but that he should gather together in one the children of God which were scattered abroad. From that day forth they held a counsel together, for to put him to death.

Jesus therefore walked no more openly among the Jews: but went his way thence unto a country nigh to a wilderness, into a city called Ephraim, and there haunted with his disciples. ⊦ And the Jews' Easter was nigh at hand, and many went out of the country up to Jerusalem before the Easter, to purify themselves. Then sought they for Jesus, and spake between themselves as they stood in the temple: What think ye, seeing he cometh not to the feast? The high priests and Pharisees had given a commandment, that if any man knew where he were, he should shew it, that they might take him.

CHAPTER TWELVE

A ⊦ Then Jesus six days before Easter, came to Bethany where Lazarus was, which was dead and whom Jesus raised from death. There they made him a supper, and Martha served: but Lazarus was one of them that sat at the table with him. Then took Mary a pound of ointment called Nardus, perfect and precious, and anointed Jesus' feet, and wiped his feet with her hair, and the house was filled of the savour of the ointment. Then said one of his disciples named Judas Iscariot Simon's son, which afterward betrayed him: why was not this ointment sold for three hundred pence, and given to the poor? This said he, not that he cared for the poor: but because he was a thief, and kept the bag, and bare that which was given. Then said Jesus: Let her alone, against the day of my burying she kept it. The poor always shall ye have with you, but me shall ye not have.

B Much people of the Jews had knowledge that he was there. And they came not for Jesus' sake only, but that they might see Lazarus also whom he raised from death. The high priests therefore held a council that they might put Lazarus to death also, because that for his sake many of the Jews went away, and believed on Jesus.

On the morrow, much people that were come to the feast, when they heard that Jesus should come to Jerusalem, took branches of palm trees and went and met him, and cried: Hosanna, blessed is he that in the name of the Lord, cometh king of Israel. And Jesus got a young ass and sat thereon, according to

C that which was written: fear not daughter of Sion, behold thy king cometh sitting on an ass's colt. These things understood not his disciples at the first: but

Matt. 26.
Mark 14.

Mary.

Hosanna.

Matt. 21.
Mark 14.
Luke 19. f.
Zech. 9. b.

when Jesus was glorified, then remembered they that such things were written of him, and that such things they had done unto him.

The people that was with him, when he called Lazarus out of his grave, and raised him from death, bare record. Therefore met him the people, because they heard that he had done such a miracle. The Pharisees therefore said among themselves: perceive ye how we prevail nothing? behold the world goeth away after him.

There were certain Greeks among them, that came to pray at the feast: the same came to Philip which was of Bethsaida a city in Galilee, and desired him saying: Sir we would fain see Jesus. Philip came and told Andrew. And again Andrew and Philip told Jesus. And Jesus answered them saying: the hour is come that the son of man must be glorified.

Mark 10. d. and 16.
Mark 8.

+ Verily verily I say unto you, except the wheat corn fall into the ground and **D** die, it bideth alone. If it die, it bringeth forth much fruit. He that loveth his life shall destroy it: and he that hateth his life in this world shall keep it unto life eternal. If any man minister unto me, let him follow me, and where I am there

Luke 9. c. and 17. g.

shall also my minister be. And if any man minister unto me, him will my father honour. ⊦

Now is my soul troubled, and what shall I say? Father deliver me from this hour: but therefore came I unto this hour. Father glorify thy name. Then came there a voice from heaven: I have glorified it, and will glorify it again. Then said the people that stood by and heard: it thundereth. Other said an angel spake to him. Jesus answered and said: this voice came not because of me, but for your sakes.

Psa. 110. b. and 116. a.
Isa. 40. c.
Ezek. 32.

+ Now is the judgement of this world: now shall the prince of this world be **E** cast out. And I, if I were lifted up from the earth, will draw all men unto me. This said Jesus, signifying what death he should die. The people answered him: We have heard of the law that Christ bideth ever: and how sayest thou

Light.

then that the son of man must be lifted up? who is that son of man? Then Jesus said unto them: yet a little while is the light with you. Walk while ye have light, lest the darkness come on you. He that walketh in the dark, wotteth not

Darkness.

whither he goeth. While ye have light, believe on the light, that ye may be the children of light.

Isa. 54. a.
Rom. 10. d.
Isa. 6. c.
Matt. 13.
Mark 4. b.
Luke 8. b.
Acts 28.
Rom. 11. b.

These things spake Jesus and departed, and hid himself from them. And **F** though he had done so many miracles before them, yet believed not they on him, that the saying of Esaias the prophet might be fulfilled, that he spake: Lord who shall believe our saying? And to whom is the arm of the Lord opened? Therefore could they not believe, because that Esaias saith again: he hath blinded their eyes and hardened their hearts, that they should not see with their eyes and understand with their hearts, and should be converted, and I should heal them. Such things said Esaias when he saw his glory and spake of him. Nevertheless among the chief rulers many believed on him. But because of the Pharisees they would not be a-known of it, lest they should be excommunicated. For they loved the praise that is given of men, more than the praise that cometh of God.

And Jesus cried and said: he that believeth on me, believeth not on me, but on him that sent me. And he that seeth me, seeth him that sent me. + I am come a light into the world, that whosoever believeth on me, should not bide in darkness. And if any man hear my words and believe not, I judge him not. For I came not to judge the world: but to save the world. He that refuseth me and receiveth not my words, hath one that judgeth him. The words that I have spoken, they shall judge him in the last day. For I have not spoken of myself: but the father which sent me, he gave me a commandment what I should say, and what I should speak. And I know that this commandment is life everlasting. Whatsoever I speak therefore, even as the father bade me, so I speak. ⊢

Light.

CHAPTER THIRTEEN

+ Before the feast of Easter when Jesus knew that his hour was come, that he should depart out of this world unto the father: When he loved his which were in the world, unto the end he loved them. And when supper was ended, after that the devil had put in the heart of Judas Iscariot Simon's son, to betray him: Jesus knowing that the father had given all things into his hands: And that he was come from God and went to God, he rose from supper, and laid aside his upper garments, and took a towel, and girt himself. After that poured he water into a basin, and began to wash his disciples' feet, and to wipe them with the towel, wherewith he was girt.

Matt. 27. a.
Luke 22.
Mark 14.

Jesus washeth his disciples' feet.

Then came he to Simon Peter. And Peter said to him: Lord shalt thou wash my feet? Jesus answered and said unto him: what I do, thou wottest not now, but thou shalt know hereafter. Peter said unto him: thou shalt not wash my feet while the world standeth. Jesus answered him: if I wash thee not, thou shalt have no part with me. Simon Peter said unto him: Lord, not my feet only: but also my hands and my head. Jesus said to him: he that is washed, needeth not save to wash his feet, and is clean every whit. And ye are clean: but not all. For he knew his betrayer. Therefore said he: ye are not all clean.

After he had washed their feet, and received his clothes, and was set down again, he said unto them, wot ye what I have done to you? Ye call me master and Lord, and ye say well, for so am I. If I then your Lord and master have washed your feet, ye also ought to wash one another's feet. For I have given you an example, that ye should do as I have done to you. Verily verily I say unto you, the servant is not greater than his master, neither the messenger greater than he that sent him.

Matt. 10. c.
Luke. 6. f.

If ye understand these things, happy are ye if ye do them. I speak not of you all, I know whom I have chosen. But that the scripture be fulfilled: he that eateth bread with me, hath lifted up his heel against me. Now tell I you before it come: that when it is come to pass, ye might believe that I am he. Verily verily I say unto you, he that receiveth whomsoever I send, receiveth me. And he that receiveth me, receiveth him that sent me.

Psa. 41. c.

Matt. 10. d.
Luke 10. c.

When Jesus had thus said, he was troubled in the spirit, and testified saying:

Matt. 26. b.
Mark 14.
Luke 22. b.

verily verily I say unto you, that one of you shall betray me. And then the disciples looked one on another doubting of whom he spake. There was one of his disciples, which leaned on Jesus' bosom, whom Jesus loved. To him beckoned Simon Peter that he should ask who it was of whom he spake. He then as he leaned on Jesus' breast, said unto him: Lord who is it? Jesus answered, he it is to whom I give a sop, when I have dipped it. And he wet a sop, and gave it to Judas Iscariot Simon's son. And after the sop, Satan entered into him.

Then said Jesus unto him: that thou dost, do quickly. That wist no man at the table, for what intent he spake unto him. Some of them thought, because Judas had the bag, that Jesus had said unto him, buy those things that we have need of against the feast: or that he should give something to the poor. As soon then as he had received the sop, he went immediately out. And it was night. When he was gone out, Jesus said: now is the son of man glorified. And God is glorified by him. If God be glorified by him, God shall also glorify him, in himself: and shall straightway glorify him.

New commandment.
1 John 2. b.

★ Christ's disciple is known.

+ Dear children, yet a little while am I with you. Ye shall seek me, and as I said unto the Jews, whither I go, thither can ye not come. Also to you say I now: A new commandment give I unto you, that ye love together, as I have loved you, that even so ye love one another. By this★ shall all men know that ye are my disciples, if ye shall have love one to another. Simon Peter said unto him: Lord whither goest thou? Jesus answered him: whither I go thou canst not follow me now, but thou shalt follow me afterwards. Peter said unto him:

Matt. 26.
Mark 14.
Luke 22.

Lord, why cannot I follow thee now? I will give my life for thy sake. Jesus answered him: wilt thou give thy life for my sake? Verily verily I say unto thee, the cock shall not crow, till thou have denied me thrice. ⊦

CHAPTER FOURTEEN

+ And he said unto his disciples: Let not your hearts be troubled. Believe in God and believe in me. In my father's house are many mansions. If it were not so, I would have told you. I go to prepare a place for you. And if I go to prepare a place for you, I will come again, and receive you even unto myself, that where I am, there may ye be also. And whither I go ye know, and the way ye know.

Thomas said unto him: Lord we know not whither thou goest. Also how is it possible for us to know the way? Jesus said unto him: I am the way, the truth and the life. And no man cometh unto the father, but by me. If ye had known me, ye had known my father also. And now ye know him, and have seen him.

Philip said unto him: Lord shew us the father, and it sufficeth us. Jesus said unto him: have I been so long time with you: and yet hast thou not known me? Philip, he that hath seen me, hath seen the father. And how sayest thou then: shew us the father? Believest thou not that I am in the father, and the father in me? The words that I speak unto you, I speak not of myself: but the father that dwelleth in me, is he that doeth the works. Believe me, that I am†† the father and the father in me. At the least believe me for the very works' sake.

Verily verily I say unto you: he that believeth on me, the works that I do, the same shall he do, and greater works than these shall he do, because I go unto my father. And whatsoever ye ask in my name, that will I do, that the father might be glorified by the son. If ye shall ask any thing in my name, I will do it. ⊦

Matt. 7. a.
Mark 11. c.

A promise.

⊦ If ye love me keep my commandments*, and I will pray the father, and he shall give you another comforter, that he may bide with you ever, which is the spirit of truth whom the world cannot receive, because the world seeth him not, neither knoweth him. But ye know him. For he dwelleth with you, and shall be in you. I will not leave you comfortless: but will come unto you.

* By the keeping the commandments is a man known that he loveth God.

Yet a little while and the world seeth me no more: but ye shall see me. For I live, and ye shall live. That day shall ye know that I am in my father, and you in me, and I in you.

He that hath my commandments and keepeth them, the same is he that loveth me. And he that loveth me, shall be loved of my father: and I will love him, and will shew mine own self unto him. ⊦ Judas said unto him (not Judas Iscariot) Lord what is the cause that thou wilt shew thyself unto us, and not unto the world? Jesus answered and said unto him: ⊦ if a man love me and will keep my sayings, my father also will love him, and we will come unto him, and will dwell with him. He that loveth me not, keepeth not my sayings. And the words which ye hear, are not mine, but the father's which sent me.

Who loveth Christ.

Who keepeth Christ's sayings.

This have I spoken unto you being yet present with you. But that comforter which is the holy ghost (whom my father will send in my name) he shall teach you all things, and bring all things to your remembrance whatsoever I have told you.

Peace I leave with you, my peace I give unto you. Not as the world giveth, give I unto you. Let not your hearts be grieved, neither fear ye. Ye have heard how I said unto you: I go and come again unto you. If ye loved me, ye would verily rejoice, because I said, I go unto the father. For the father is greater than I. And now have I showed you, before it come, that when it is come to pass, ye might believe.

Peace.

Hereafter will I not talk many words unto you. For the ruler of this world cometh, and hath nought in me. But that the world may know that I love the father: therefore as the father gave me commandment, even so do I. ⊦ Rise let us go hence.

CHAPTER FIFTEEN

⊦ I am the true vine, and my father is an husbandman. Every branch that beareth not fruit in me, he will take away. And every branch that beareth fruit, will he purge, that it may bring more fruit. Now are ye clean through the words which I have spoken unto you. Bide in me, and let me bide in you. As the branch cannot bear fruit of itself, except it bide in the vine: no more can ye, except ye abide in me.

Vine.

I am the vine, and ye are the branches. He that abideth in me, and I in him, the same bringeth forth much fruit. For without me can ye do nothing. If a

Matt. 21.
1. John 3. d.

Covenant.

man bide not in me, he is cast forth as a branch, and is withered: and men gather it, and cast it into the fire, and it burneth. If ye bide in me, and my words also bide in you: ask what ye will, and it shall be done to you. ⊦ Herein is my father glorified, that ye bear much fruit, and be made my disciples.

* To keep the law maketh us continue in the love and favour of Christ.

As the father hath loved me, even so have I loved you. Continue in my love. If ye shall keep* my commandments, ye shall bide in my love, even as I have kept my father's commandments, and bide in his love. These things have I spoken unto you, that my joy might remain in you, and that your joy might be full.

Eph. 4. a.
1 Thes. 4.
1. John 3. b. and 4. d.

+ This is my commandment, that ye love together as I have loved you. Greater love than this hath no man, than that a man bestow his life for his friends. Ye are my friends, if ye do whatsoever I command you. Henceforth call I you not servants: for the servant knoweth not what his Lord doeth. But you have I called friends: for all things that I have heard of my father, I have opened to you.

Ye have not chosen me, but I have chosen you and ordained you, that ye go and bring forth fruit, and that your fruit remain, that whatsoever ye shall ask of the father in my name, he should give it you. ⊦

1. John 3. d. and 4. d.

+ This command I you, that ye love together. If the world hate you, ye know that he hated me before he hated you. If ye were of the world, the world would love his own. Howbeit because ye are not of the world, but I have chosen you out of the world, therefore hateth you the world. Remember the saying that I said unto you: the servant is not greater than his lord. If they have persecuted me, so will they persecute you. If they have kept my saying, so will they keep yours.

Mark 10. c.
Matt. 23.

But all these things will they do unto you for my name's sake, because they have not known him that sent me. If I had not come and spoken unto them, they should not have had sin: but now have they nothing to cloak their sin withal. He that hateth me, hateth my father. If I had not done works among them which none other man did, they had not had sin. But now have they seen, and yet have hated both me and my father: even that the saying might be fulfilled that is written in their law: they hated me without a cause.⊦

Psa. 25.

Luke 24. g.

+ But when the comforter is come, whom I will send unto you from the father, which is the spirit of truth, which proceedeth of the father, he shall testify of me. And ye shall bear witness also, because ye have been with me from the beginning. ⊦

CHAPTER SIXTEEN

Matt. 24.

These things have I said unto you, because ye should not be offended. They shall excommunicate you: yea, the time shall come, that whosoever killeth you, will think that he doth God service. And such things will they do unto you, because they have not known the father neither yet me. But these things have I told you, that when that hour is come, ye might remember them, that I told you so. ⊦ These things said I not unto you at the beginning, because I was present with you.

B   + But now I go my way to him that sent me, and none of you asketh me:
whither goest thou? But because I have said such things unto you, your hearts
are full of sorrow. Nevertheless I tell you the truth, it is expedient for you that I
go away. For if I go not away, that comforter will not come unto you. But if I
depart, I will send him unto you. And when he is come, he will rebuke the
world of sin, and of righteousness, and of judgement. Of sin, because they
believe not on me: Of righteousness because I go to my father, and ye shall see
me no more: and of judgement, because the chief ruler of this world, is judged
already.

Sin.

Righteousness.

Judgement.

C   I have yet many things to say unto you: but ye cannot bear them away now.
Howbeit when he is come (I mean the spirit of truth) he will lead you into all
truth. He shall not speak of himself: but whatsoever he shall hear, that shall he
speak, and he will show you things to come. He shall glorify me, for he shall
receive of mine and shall show unto you. All things that the father hath are
mine. Therefore said I unto you, that he shall take of mine and show unto
you. ⊦

D   + After a while ye shall not see me, and again after a while ye shall see me:
For I go to the father. Then said some of his disciples between themselves:
what is this that he saith unto us, after a while ye shall not see me, and again
after a while ye shall see me? and that I go to the father? They said therefore:
what is this that he saith after a while? we cannot tell what he saith. Jesus perceived, that they would ask him, and said unto them: This is it that ye enquire
of between yourselves, that I said, after a while ye shall not see me, and again
after a while ye shall see me. Verily verily I say unto you: ye shall weep and
lament and the world shall rejoice. Ye shall sorrow: but your sorrow shall be
turned to joy.

E   A woman when she travaileth hath sorrow, because her hour is come: but as
soon as she is delivered of the child, she remembreth no more the anguish, for
joy that a man is born into the world. And ye now are in sorrow: but I will see
you again, and your hearts shall rejoice, and your joy shall no man take from
you. ⊦ And in that day shall ye ask me no question. + Verily verily I say unto
you, whatsoever ye shall ask the father in my name, he will give it you.
Hitherto have ye asked nothing in my name. Ask and ye shall receive it: that
your joy may be full.

Matt. 7. a. and 21. c.

Mark 11. c.
Luke 11. d.
Jas. 1. a.

F   These things have I spoken unto you in proverbs. The time will come when I
shall no more speak to you in proverbs: but I shall shew you plainly from my
father. At that day shall ye ask in mine name. And I say not unto you that I will
speak unto my father for you. For the father himself loveth you, because ye
have loved me, and have believed that I came out from God. I went out from
the father, and came into the world: and I leave the world again, and go to the
father.

Promise.

His disciples said unto him: lo now speakest thou plainly, and thou usest no
proverb. Now know we that thou understandest all things, and needest not
that any man should ask thee any question. Therefore believe we that thou
camest from God. ⊦ Jesus answered them: Now ye do believe. Behold the hour
draweth nigh, and is already come, that ye shall be scattered every man his

Matt. 26.
Mark 14.

ways, and shall leave me alone. And yet am I not alone. For the father is with me.

These words have I spoken unto you, that in me ye might have peace. For in the world shall ye have tribulation: but be of good cheer, I have overcome the world.

CHAPTER SEVENTEEN

+ These words spake Jesus and lifted up his eyes to heaven, and said: father the **A** hour is come: glorify thy son, that thy son may glorify thee: as thou hast given

Eternal life.   him power over all flesh, that he should give eternal life to as many as thou hast given him. This is life eternal, that they might know thee that only very God, and whom thou hast sent Jesus Christ.

I have glorified thee on the earth. I have finished the work which thou gavest **B** me to do. And now glorify me thou father with thine own self, with the glory which I had with thee ere the world was. I have declared thy name unto the men which thou gavest me out of the world. Thine they were, and thou gavest them me, and they have kept thy sayings. Now they know that all things whatsoever thou hast given me, are of thee. For I have given unto them the words which thou gavest me, and they have received them, and know surely that I came out from thee: and do believe that thou didst send me.

I pray for them, and pray not for the world: but for them which thou hast given me, for they are thine. And all mine are thine, and thine are mine, and I **C** am glorified in them. And now am I no more in the world, but they are in the world, and I come to thee. ⊢+ Holy father keep in thine own name, them which thou hast given me, that they may be one, as we are. While I was with them in the world, I kept them in thy name. Those that thou gavest me, have I

Psa. 109. b.   kept, and none of them is lost, but that lost child, that the scripture might be fulfilled.

Now come I to thee, and these words speak I in the world, that they might have my joy full in them. I have given them thy words, and the world hath hated them, because they are not of the world, even as I am not of the world. I desire not that thou shouldest take them out of the world: but that thou keep them from evil. ⊢ They are not of the world, as I am not of the world. Sanctify them with thy truth. Thy saying is truth. As thou didst sent me into the world, even so have I sent them into the world, and for their sakes sanctify I myself, that they also might be sanctified through the truth.

I pray not for them alone: but for them also which shall believe on me **D** through their preaching, that they all may be one, as thou father art in me, and I in thee, that they may be also one in us, that the world may believe that thou hast sent me. And that glory that thou gavest me, I have given them, that they may be one, as we are one, I in them and thou in me, that they may be made perfect in one, and that the world may know that thou hast sent me, and hast loved them, as thou hast loved me.

Father, I will that they which thou hast given me, be with me where I am, that they may see my glory which thou hast given me. For thou lovedest me before the making of the world. O righteous father, the very world hath not known thee: but I have known thee, and these have known that thou hast sent me. And I have declared unto them thy name, and will declare it, that the love wherewith thou hast loved me, be in them, and that I be in them.

CHAPTER EIGHTEEN

A + When Jesus had spoken these words, he went forth with his disciples over the brook Cedron, where was a garden, into the which he entered with his disciples. Judas also which betrayed him, knew the place: for Jesus oft-times resorted thither with his disciples. Judas then after he had received a band of **B** men, and ministers of the high priests and Pharisees, came thither with lanterns and firebrands and weapons. Then Jesus knowing all things that should come on him, went forth and said unto them: whom seek ye? They answered him: Jesus of Nazareth. Jesus said unto them: I am he.

B   Judas also which betrayed him, stood with them. But as soon as he had said unto them, I am he, they went backwards and fell to the ground. And he asked them again: whom seek ye? They said: Jesus of Nazareth. Jesus answered, I said unto you, I am he. If ye seek me, let these go their way. That the saying might be fulfilled which he spake: of them which thou gavest me, have I not lost one.

    Simon Peter had a sword, and drew it, and smote the high priest's servant, and cut off his right ear. The servant's name was Malchus. Then said Jesus unto Peter: put up thy sword into the sheath: shall I not drink of the cup which my **C** father hath given me? Then the company and the captain, and the ministers of the Jews, took Jesus and bound him, and led him away to Annas first: For he was father-in-law unto Caiaphas, which was the high priest that same year. Caiaphas was he that gave counsel to the Jews, that it was expedient that one man should die for the people.

    And Simon Peter followed Jesus and another disciple: that disciple was known of the high priest, and went in with Jesus into the palace of the high priest. But Peter stood at the door without. Then went out that other disciple which was known unto the high priest, and spake to the damsel that kept the door, and brought in Peter. Then said the damsel that kept the door, unto Peter: Art not thou one of this man's disciples? He said: I am not. The servants and the ministers stood there, and had made a fire of coals: for it was cold: and they warmed themselves. Peter also stood among them and warmed himself.

D   The high priest asked Jesus of his disciples and of his doctrine. Jesus answered him: I spake openly in the world. I ever taught in the synagogue and in the temple whither all the Jews resorted, and in secret have I said nothing: Why askest thou me? Ask them which heard me, what I said unto them. Behold they can tell what I said. When he had thus spoken, one of the ministers which stood by, smote Jesus on the face saying: answerest thou the high priest so? Jesus answered him. If I have evil spoken, bear witness of the evil: if I have

Matt. 26. c.
Mark 14. c.
Luke 22. d.

Matt. 26. c.
Mark 14. c.
Luke 22. c.

Malchus.

Matt. 26.
Mark 14.
Luke 22. f.

Matt. 26.
Mark 14.
Luke 22.

159

well spoken, why smitest thou me? And Annas sent him bound unto Caiaphas the high priest.

Simon Peter stood and warmed himself. And they said unto him: art not **E** thou also one of his disciples? He denied it, and said: I am not. One of the servants of the high priest (his cousin whose ear Peter smote off) said unto *Matt. 27.* him: did not I see thee in the garden with him? Peter denied it again: and *Mark 15. a.* immediately the cock crew.

Luke 22. g.

Then led they Jesus from Caiaphas into the hall of judgement. It was in the **F** morning, and they themselves went not into the judgement hall lest they should be defiled, but that they might eat the paschal lamb. Pilate then went out unto them and said: what accusation bring ye against this man? They answered and said unto him. If he were not an evil-doer, we would not have delivered him unto thee. Then said Pilate unto them: take ye him, and judge *Matt. 20. c.* him after your own law. Then the Jews said unto him. It is not lawful for us to put any man to death. That the words of Jesus might be fulfilled which he spake, signifying what death he should die.

Then Pilate entered into the judgement hall again, and called Jesus, and said *Matt. 27.* unto him: art thou the king of the Jews? Jesus answered: sayest thou that of *Mark 15. b.* thyself, or did other tell it thee of me? Pilate answered: Am I a Jew? Thine own *Luke 23.* nation and high priests have delivered thee unto me. What hast thou done? Jesus answered: my kingdom is not of this world. If my kingdom were of this world, then would my ministers surely fight, that I should not be delivered to the Jews, but now is my kingdom not from hence. Pilate said unto him: Art thou a king then? Jesus answered: Thou sayest that I am a king. For this cause **G** was I born, and for this cause came I into the world, that I should bear witness unto the truth. And all that are of the truth hear my voice. Pilate said unto him: what thing is truth? And when he had said that, he went out again unto the Jews, and said unto them: I find in him no cause at all. Ye have a custom, that I should deliver you one loose at Easter. Will ye that I loose unto you the king *Matt. 27.* of the Jews? Then cried they all again saying: Not him, but Barabbas: that *Mark 15. b.* Barabbas was a robber.

Luke 22.

CHAPTER NINETEEN

Then Pilate took Jesus and scourged him. And the soldiers wound a crown of **A** *Matt. 27.* thorns and put it on his head. And they did on him a purple garment, and said: *Mark 15. b.* hail king of the Jews: and they smote him on the face. Pilate went forth again, and said unto them: behold I bring him forth to you, that ye may know, that I find no fault in him. Then came Jesus forth wearing a crown of thorns and a robe of purple. And Pilate said unto them: behold the man. When the high priests and ministers saw him, they cried saying: crucify him, crucify him. Pilate said unto them. Take ye him and crucify him: for I find no cause in him. The Jews answered him, We have a law, and by our law he ought to die: because he made himself the son of God.

When Pilate heard that saying, he was the more afraid, and went again into **B** the judgement hall, and said unto Jesus: whence art thou? But Jesus gave him none answer. Then said Pilate unto him: Speakest thou not unto me? knowest thou not that I have power to crucify thee, and have power to loose thee? Jesus answered: Thou couldest have no power at all against me, except it were given thee from above. Therefore he that delivered me unto thee, is more in sin. And from thenceforth sought Pilate means to loose him: but the Jews cried saying: if thou let him go, thou art not Caesar's friend. For whosoever maketh himself a king, is against Caesar.

When Pilate heard that saying, he brought Jesus forth, and sat down to give sentence, in a place called the pavement: but in the Hebrew tongue, Gabbatha. It was the sabbath even which falleth in the Easter feast, and about the sixth hour. And he said unto the Jews: behold your king. They cried, away with him, away with him, crucify him. Pilate said unto them, Shall I crucify your king? The high priests answered: we have no king but Caesar. Then delivered he him unto them, to be crucified.

B And they took Jesus and led him away. And he bare his cross, and went forth into a place called the place of dead men's skulls, which is named in Hebrew, Golgotha. Where they crucified him and two other with him on either side one, and Jesus in the midst. And Pilate wrote his title, and put it on the cross. The writing was, Jesus of Nazareth, king of the Jews. This title read many of the Jews. For the place where Jesus was crucified, was nigh to the city. And it was written in Hebrew, Greek and Latin. Then said the high priests of the Jews to Pilate: write not, king of the Jews: but that he said, I am king of the Jews. Pilate answered: what I have written, that have I written.   *Matt. 27.*
Mark 15. b.
Luke 23. c:

E Then the soldiers, when they had crucified Jesus, took his garments and made four parts, to every soldier a part, and also his coat. The coat was without seam, wrought upon throughout. And they said one to another. Let us not divide it: but cast lots who shall have it. That the scripture might be fulfilled which saith: They parted my raiment among them, and on my coat did cast lots. And the soldiers did such things indeed.   *Matt. 27.*
Mark 15. b.
Luke 23.

Psa. 22.

There stood by the cross of Jesus his mother, and his mother's sister, Mary the wife of Cleophas, and Mary Magdalene. When Jesus saw his mother, and the disciple standing whom he loved, he said unto his mother: woman behold thy son. Then said he to the disciple: behold thy mother. And from that hour the disciple took her for his own.

F After that when Jesus perceived that all things were performed: that the scripture might be fulfilled, he said: I thirst. There stood a vessel full of vinegar by. And they filled a sponge with vinegar, and wound it about with hyssop, and put it to his mouth. As soon as Jesus had received of the vinegar, he said: It is finished, and bowed his head, and gave up the ghost.   *Psa. 69.*

The Jews then because it was the sabbath even, that the bodies should not remain upon the cross on the sabbath day (for that sabbath day was an high day) besought Pilate that their legs might be broken and that they might be taken down. Then came the soldiers and brake the legs of the first, and of the other which was crucified with Jesus. But when they came to Jesus, and saw that he was dead already they brake not his legs: but one of the soldiers with a spear, thrust him into the side, and forthwith came there out blood and water.

Exod. 12.
Num. 9. d.
Zech. 12.

And he that saw it, bare record, and his record is true. And he knoweth that he saith true, that ye might believe also. These things were done that the   **G** scripture should be fulfilled: Ye shall not break a bone of him. And again another scripture saith: They shall look on him, whom they pierced. ⊦

Matt. 27.
Mark 15. b.
Luke 23.
John 3. a.

After that, Joseph of Arimathæa (which was a disciple of Jesus: but secretly for fear of the Jews) besought Pilate that he might take down the body of Jesus. And Pilate gave him licence. And there came also Nicodemus which at the beginning came to Jesus by night, and brought of myrrh and aloes mingled together about an hundred pound weight. Then took they the body of Jesus and wound it in linen clothes with the odours as the manner of the Jews is to bury. And in the place where Jesus was crucified, was a garden, and in the garden a new sepulchre, wherein was never man laid. There laid they Jesus because of the Jews' sabbath even, for the sepulchre was nigh at hand.

CHAPTER TWENTY

Matt.
16. a.
Luke. 24.

⊦ The morrow after the sabbath day, came Mary Magdalene early, when it was   **A** yet dark, unto the sepulchre, and saw the stone taken away from the tomb. Then she ran, and came to Simon Peter and to the other disciple whom Jesus loved, and said unto them: They have taken away the Lord out of the tomb, and we cannot tell where they have laid him. Peter went forth and that other disciple, and came unto the sepulchre. They ran both together, and that other disciple did out-run Peter, and came first to the sepulchre. And he stooped   **B** down and saw the linen clothes lying, yet went he not in. Then came Simon Peter following him, and went into the sepulchre, and saw the linen clothes lie, and the napkin that was about his head, not lying with the linen cloth, but wrapped together in a place by itself. Then went in also that other disciple which came first to the sepulchre, and he saw and believed. For as yet they knew not the scriptures, that he should rise again from death. ⊦ And the disciples went away again unto their own home.

Matt. 28.
Mark 16. b.

⊦ Mary stood without at the sepulchre weeping. And as she wept, she   **C** bowed herself into the sepulchre and saw two angels in white sitting, the one at the head and the other at the feet, where they had laid the body of Jesus. And they said unto her: woman why weepest thou? She said unto them: For they have taken away my lord, and I wot not where they have laid him. When she had thus said, she turned herself back and saw Jesus standing, and knew not that it was Jesus. Jesus said unto her: woman why weepest thou? Whom seekest   **D** thou? She supposing that he had been the gardner, said unto him: Sir if thou have borne him hence tell me where thou hast laid him, that I may fetch him. Jesus said unto her: Mary. She turned herself, and said unto him: Rabboni, which is to say master. Jesus said unto her, touch me not, for I am not yet ascended to my father. But go to my brethren and say unto them, I ascend unto my father and your father: to my God and your God. Mary Magdalene came

and told the disciples that she had seen the Lord, and that he had spoken such
things unto her. ⊦

E + The same day at night, which was the morrow after the sabbath day, when
the doors were shut, where the disciples were assembled together for fear of the
Jews, came Jesus and stood in the midst, and said to them: peace be with you.
And when he had so said, he showed unto them his hands, and his side. Then
were the disciples glad when they saw the Lord. Then said Jesus to them again:
peace be with you. As my father sent me, even so send I you. And when he had
said that, he breathed on them and said unto them: Receive the holy ghost★.
Whosoever's sins ye remit they are remitted unto them. And whosoever's sins
ye retain, they are retained. ⊦

Matt. 28. Mark 16. c. Luke 28. 1 Cor. 15. a.

★ Here is paid that is promised Matt. 16. A covenant upon binding and loosing.

F + But Thomas one of the twelve, called Didymus, was not with them when
Jesus came. The other disciples said unto him: we have seen the Lord. And he
said unto them: except I see in his hands the print of the nails, and put my
finger in the holes of the nails, and thrust my hand into his side, I will not
believe.

And after eight days again, his disciples were within, and Thomas with
them. Then came Jesus when the doors were shut, and stood in the midst and
said: peace be with you.

G After that said he to Thomas: bring thy finger hither, and see my hands, and
bring thy hand and thrust it into my side, and be not faithless, but believing.
Thomas answered and said unto him: my Lord, and my God. Jesus said unto
him: Thomas, because thou hast seen me, therefore thou believest: Happy are
they that have not seen, and yet believe.

And many other signs did Jesus in the presence of his disciples, which are not
written in this book. These are written that ye might believe, that Jesus is
Christ the son of God, and that in believing ye might have life through his
name. ⊦

CHAPTER TWENTY-ONE

A + After that Jesus showed himself again, at the sea of Tiberias. And on this wise
showed he himself. There were together Simon Peter and Thomas, which is
called Didymus: and Nathanael of Cana a city of Galilee, and the sons of
Zebedee, and two other of the disciples. Simon Peter said unto them: I go a-
C fishing. They said unto him: we also will go with thee. They went their way
and entered into a ship straightway, and that night caught they nothing. But
when the morning was now come, Jesus stood on the shore: nevertheless the
disciples knew not that it was Jesus. Jesus said unto them: sirs, have ye any
meat? They answered him, no. And he said unto them: cast out the net on the
right side of the ship, and ye shall find. They cast out, and anon they were not
able to draw it for the multitude of fishes.

Then said the disciple whom Jesus loved, unto Peter: It is the Lord. When
Simon Peter heard that it was the Lord, he girded his mantle to him (for he was
naked) and sprang into the sea. The other disciples came by ship: for they were

not far from land, but as it were two hundred cubits, and they drew the net with fishes. As soon as they were come to land, they saw hot coals and fish laid thereon, and bread. Jesus said unto them: bring of the fish which ye have now caught. Simon Peter stepped forth and drew the net to land full of great fishes, an hundred and fifty-three. And for all there were so many, yet was not the net broken. Jesus said unto them: come and dine. And none of the disciples durst ask him: what art thou? For they knew that it was the Lord. Jesus then came and took bread, and gave them, and fish likewise. And this is now the third time that Jesus appeared to his disciples, after that he was risen again from death. ⊢

When they had dined, Jesus said to Simon Peter: Simon Joanna, lovest thou me more than these? He said unto him: yea Lord, thou knowest, that I love thee. He said unto him: feed my lambs★. He said to him again the second time: Simon Joanna, lovest thou me? He said unto him: yea lord thou knowest that I love thee. He said unto him: feed my sheep. He said unto him the third time: Simon Joanna lovest thou me? And Peter sorrowed because he said to him the third time, lovest thou me, and said unto him: Lord, thou knowest all things, thou knowest that I love thee. Jesus said unto him: feed my sheep. D

★ He loveth Christ that feedeth his lambs and sheep.

Verily verily I say unto thee, when thou wast young, thou girdedst thyself, and walkedst whither thou wouldest: but when thou art old, thou shalt stretch forth thy hands, and another shall gird thee, and lead thee whither thou wouldest not. That spake he signifying by what death he should glorify God. E

2. Pet. 1. c.

+ And when he had said thus, he said to him follow me. Peter turned about, and saw that disciple whom Jesus loved following: which also leaned on his breast at supper and said: Lord which is he that shall betray thee? When Peter saw him, he said to Jesus: Lord what shall he here do? Jesus said unto him, If I will have him to tarry till I come, what is that to thee? follow thou me. Then went this saying abroad among the brethren, that that disciple should not die. Yet Jesus said not to him, he shall not die: but if I will that he tarry till I come, what is that to thee? The same disciple is he, which testifieth of these things, and wrote these things. And we know, that his testimony is true. ⊢ There are also many other things which Jesus did: the which if they should be written every one I suppose the world could not contain the books that should be written. F

Here endeth the Gospel of Saint John.

THE ACTS OF THE APOSTLES

written by Saint Luke Evangelist which was present at the doings of them.

A In the former treatise (dear friend Theophilus) I have written of all that Jesus began to do and teach, until the day in the which he was taken up, after that he through the holy ghost, had given commandments unto the apostles, which he had chosen: to whom also he shewed himself alive, after his passion, by many tokens, appearing unto them forty days, and speaking of the kingdom of God, and gathered them together, and commanded them, that they should not depart from Jerusalem: but to wait for the promise of the father, whereof ye have heard of me. For John baptised with water: but ye shall be baptised with the holy ghost, and that within this few days. When they were come together, they asked of him saying: Lord wilt thou at this time restore again the kingdom to Israel? And he said unto them: It is not for you to know the times, or the seasons which the father hath put in his own power: but ye shall receive power of the holy ghost which shall come on you. And ye shall be witnesses unto me in Jerusalem, and in all Jewry and in Samaria, and even unto the world's end.

Luke 24. g.

B And when he had spoken these things, while they beheld, he was taken up, and a cloud received him up out of their sight. And while they looked steadfastly up to heaven as he went, behold two men stood by them in white apparel, which also said: ye men of Galilee, why stand ye gazing up into heaven? This same Jesus which is taken up from you into heaven, shall so come, even as ye have seen him go into heaven. ⊢

Then returned they unto Jerusalem from mount Olivet, which is nigh to Jerusalem, containing a sabbath day's journey. And when they were come in, they went up into a parlour, where abode both Peter and James, John and Andrew, Philip and Thomas, Bartholomew and Matthew, James the son of Alpheus, and Simon Zelotes, and Judas, James' son. These all continued with one accord in prayer and supplication with the women and Mary the mother of Jesus, and with his brethren.

Luke 24. g.

C ⊢ And in those days Peter stood up in the midst of the disciples and said (the number of names that were together, were about an hundred and twenty), Ye men and brethren, this scripture must have needs been fulfilled which the holy ghost through the mouth of David spake before of Judas, which was guide to them that took Jesus. For he was numbered with us and had obtained fellow-

Psa. 41. c.
John 18.

Matt. 27. a.

ship in this ministration. And the same hath now possessed a plot of ground with the reward of iniquity, and when he was hanged, burst asunder in the midst, and all his bowels gushed out. And it is known unto all the inhabiters of Jerusalem: insomuch that that field is called in their mother tongue, Acheldama, that is to say, the blood field.

Psa. 69.

It is written in the book of Psalms: His habitation be void, and no man be **I** dwelling therein: and his bishopric let another take. Wherefore of these men

Psa. 109.

which have companied with us, all the time that the Lord Jesus went in and out among us, beginning at the baptism of John unto that same day that he was taken up from us, must one be ordained to bear witness with us of his resurrection.

And they appointed two, Joseph called Barsabas (whose surname was Justus) and Matthias. And they prayed saying: thou Lord which knowest the hearts of all men, show whether of these two thou hast chosen that the one may take the room of this ministration, and apostleship from the which Judas by transgression fell, that he might go to his own place. And they gave forth their

Matthias.

lots, and the lot fell on Matthias, and he was counted with the eleven apostles. ⊢

CHAPTER TWO

+ When the fiftieth day was come, they were all with one accord together in **A** one place. And suddenly there came a sound from heaven, as it had been the coming of a mighty wind, and it filled all the house where they sat. And there

Tongues.

appeared unto them cloven tongues, like as they had been fire, and it sat upon each of them: and they were all filled with the holy ghost, and began to speak with other tongues, even as the spirit gave them utterance.

And there were dwelling at Jerusalem Jews, devout men, which were of **B** all nations under heaven. When this was noised about, the multitude came together and were astonied, because that every man heard them speak his own tongue. They wondered all and marvelled saying among themselves: Behold, are not all these which speak, of Galilee? And how hear we every man his own tongue wherein we were born? Parthians, Medes and Elamites, and the inhabiters of Mesopotamia, of Jewry, and of Cappadocia, of Pontus and Asia, Phrygia, Pamphylia, and of Egypt, and of the parts of Libya which is beside

* Converts: that is,
heathen or gentiles
converted to the
Jews' faith.

Cyrene, and strangers of Rome, Jews and converts*, Greeks and Arabians: we have heard them speak with our own tongues the great works of God. ⊢ They were all amazed, and wondered saying one to another: what meaneth this? Other mocked them saying: they are full of new wine.

+ But Peter stepped forth with the eleven, and lift up his voice, and said unto them: Ye men of Jewry, and all ye that inhabit Jerusalem: be this known unto you, and with your ears hear my words. These are not drunken, as ye suppose: for it is yet but the third hour of the day. But this is that which was spoken by **C**

Joel 2. g.

the prophet Joel: It shall be in the last days saith God: of my spirit I will pour out upon all flesh. And your sons and your daughters shall prophesy, and your young men shall see visions, and your old men shall dream dreams. And on my

servants, and on my handmaidens I will pour out of my spirit in those days,
and they shall prophesy. And I will show wonders in heaven above, and tokens
in the earth beneath, blood and fire, and the vapour of smoke. The sun shall be
turned into darkness, and the moon into blood before that great and notable
day of the Lord come. And it shall be, that whosoever shall call on the name of
the Lord shall be saved. ⊢

+ Ye men of Israel hear these words. Jesus of Nazareth, a man approved of *Rom. 10. c.*
God among you with miracles, wonders and signs which God did by him in
the midst of you, as ye yourselves know: him have ye taken by the hands of
unrighteous persons, after he was delivered by the determinate counsel and
foreknowledge of God, and have crucified and slain: whom God hath raised up
and loosed the sorrows of death, because it was impossible that he should be
D holden of it. For David speaketh of him: Aforehand I saw God always before Death.
me: For he is on my right hand, that I should not be moved. Therefore did my
heart rejoice, and my tongue was glad. Moreover, also my flesh shall rest in *Psa. 16. c.*
hope, because thou wilt not leave my soul in hell, neither wilt suffer thine holy Hell.
to see corruption. Thou hast shewed me the ways of life, and shalt make me
full of joy with thy countenance. ⊢

E Men and brethren, let me freely speak unto you of the patriarch David: For *1. Kin. 2. b.*
he is both dead and buried, and his sepulchre remaineth with us unto his day.
Therefore seeing he was a prophet, and knew that God had sworn with an oath
to him, that the fruit of his loins should sit on his seat (in that Christ should rise
again in the flesh) he saw before: and spake in the resurrection of Christ, that
his soul should not be left in hell: neither his flesh should see corruption. This
Jesus hath God raised up, whereof we all are witnesses.

Since now that he by the right hand of God exalted is, and hath received of
the father the promise of the holy ghost, he hath shed forth that which ye now
F see and hear. For David is not ascended into heaven: but he said, The Lord said *Psa. 110. a.*
to my Lord sit on my right hand, until I make thy foes thy footstool. So
therefore let all the house of Israel know for a surety, that God hath made the
same Jesus whom ye have crucified Lord and Christ.

When they heard this, they were pricked in their hearts, and said unto Peter
and unto the other apostles: Ye men and brethren, what shall we do? Peter said
unto them: repent and be baptised every one of you in the name of Jesus Christ,
for the remission of sins, and ye shall receive the gift of the holy ghost. For the
promise was made unto you and to your children, and to all that are afar, even
as many as the Lord our God shall call. And with many other words bare
he witness and exhorted them saying: Save yourselves from this untoward
generation. Then they that gladly received his preaching, were baptised: and
the same day, there were added unto them about three thousand souls.

G And they continued in the apostles' doctrine and fellowship, and in breaking
of bread, and in prayer. And fear came over every soul. And many wonders
and signs were showed by the apostles. And all that believed kept themselves
together, and had all things common, and sold their possessions and goods,
and departed them to all men, as every man had need. And they continued Common.

daily with one accord in the temple, and brake bread in every house, and did eat their meat together, with gladness and singleness of heart praising God, and had favour with all the people. And the Lord added to the congregation daily such as should be saved.

CHAPTER THREE

Peter and John went up together into the temple at the ninth hour of prayer. And there was a certain man halt from his mother's womb, whom they brought and laid at the gate of the temple called Beautiful, to ask alms of them that entered into the temple. Which same when he saw Peter and John, that they would in to the temple, desired to receive an alms. And Peter fastened his eyes on him with John and said: look on us. And he gave heed unto them, trusting to receive something of them. Then said Peter: Silver and gold have I none, such as I have, give I thee. In the name of Jesus Christ of Nazareth, rise up and walk. And he took him by the right hand, and lifted him up. And immediately his feet and anklebones received strength. And he sprang, stood and also walked, and entered with them into the temple, walking, and leaping and lauding God.

And all the people saw him walk and laud God. And they knew him, that it was he which sat and begged at the Beautiful gate of the temple. And they wondered and were sore astonied at that which had happened unto him. And as the halt which was healed, held Peter and John, all the people ran amazed unto them in Solomon's porch.

When Peter saw that, he answered unto the people, + Ye men of Israel, why marvel ye at this, or why look ye so steadfastly on us, as though by our own power or holiness, we had made this man go? The God of Abraham, Isaac and Jacob, the God of our fathers hath glorified his son Jesus, whom ye delivered, and denied in the presence of Pilate, when he had judged him to be loosed. But ye denied the holy and just, and desired a murderer to be given you, and killed the lord of life, whom God hath raised from death, of the which we are witnesses. And his name through the faith of his name, hath made this man sound, whom ye see and know. And the faith which is by him, hath given to him this health in the presence of you all.

And now brethren I wot well that through ignorance ye did it, as did also your heads. But those things which God before had showed by the mouth of all his prophets, how that Christ should suffer, he hath thus-wise fulfilled. Repent ye therefore and turn, that your sins may be done away, + when the time of refreshing cometh, which we shall have of the presence of the Lord, and when God shall send him, which before was preached unto you, that is to wit Jesus Christ, which must receive heaven until the time that all things, which God hath spoken by the mouth of all his holy prophets since the world began be restored again.

For Moses said unto the fathers: A prophet shall the Lord your God raise up unto you, even of your brethren, like unto me: him shall ye hear in all things

The halt is cured.

Matt. 27.
Mark 15. c.
Luke 23.
John 17. a.

Deut. 18.

whatsoever he shall say unto you. For the time will come, that every soul which shall not hear that same prophet, shall be destroyed from among the people. Also all the prophets from Samuel and thenceforth, as many as have spoken, have in like wise told of these days.

Ye are the children of the prophets, and of the covenant which God hath made unto our fathers saying to Abraham: Even in thy seed shall all the kindreds of the earth be blessed. First unto you hath God raised up his son Jesus, and him he hath sent to bless you, that every one of you should turn from your wickedness.

CHAPTER FOUR

A As they spake unto the people, the priests and the ruler of the temple, and the Sadducees came upon them, taking it grievously that they taught the people and preached in Jesus the resurrection from death. And they laid hands on them, and put them in hold until the next day: for it was now eventide. Howbeit many of them which heard the words, believed, and the number of the men was about five thousand.

And it chanced on the morrow that their rulers and elders and scribes, as Annas the chief Priest and Caiaphas and John and Alexander, and as many as were of the kindred of the high priests gathered together at Jerusalem, and set the other before them, and asked: by what power or what name have ye done **B** this, sirs? + Then Peter full of the holy ghost said unto them: ye rulers of the people, and elders of Israel, if we this day are examined of the good deed done to the sick man, by what means he is made whole: be it known unto you all, and to the people of Israel, that in the name of Jesus Christ of Nazareth, whom ye crucified, and whom God raised again from death: even by him doth this man stand here present before you whole. This is the stone cast aside of you builders which is set in the chief place of the corner. Neither is there salvation in any other. Nor yet also is there any other name given to men wherein we must be saved. +

C When they saw the boldness of Peter and John, and understood that they were unlearned men and lay people, they marvelled, and they knew them, that they were with Jesus: and beholding also the man which was healed standing with them, they could not say against it. But they commanded them to go aside out of the council, and counselled among themselves saying: what shall we do to these men? For a manifest sign is done by them and is openly known to all them that dwell in Jerusalem, and we cannot deny it. But that it be noised no farther among the people, let us threaten, and charge them that they speak henceforth to no man in this name.

D And they called them, and commanded them that in no wise they should speak or teach in the name of Jesus. But Peter and John answered unto them and said: whether it be right in the sight of God to obey you more than God, judge ye. For we cannot but speak that which we have seen and heard. So threatened they them and let them go, and found nothing how to punish them,

Sadducees.

Peter.

Psa. 118.
Matt. 21.
Mark 12. a.
Luke 20. c.

Salvation.

Rom. 9. g.

God is more to be
obeyed than man.

because of the people. For all men lauded God for the miracle which was done:
for the man was above forty years old, on whom this miracle of healing was
showed.

As soon as they were let go, they came to their fellows, and showed all that   E
the high priests and elders had said to them. And when they heard that, they
lifted up their voices to God with one accord, and said: Lord, thou art God
which hast made heaven and earth, the sea and all that in them is, which by the
mouth of thy servant David hast said: Why did the heathen rage, and the
people imagine vain things? The kings of the earth stood up and the rulers
came together, against the Lord and against his Christ.

Psa. 2. a.

For of a truth, against thy holy child Jesus whom thou hast anointed, both   F
Herod and also Pontius Pilate, with the gentiles and the people of Israel,
gathered themselves together, for to do whatsoever thy hand and thy counsel
determined before to be done. And now Lord, behold their threatenings, and
grant unto thy servants with all confidence to speak thy word. So that thou
stretch forth thy hand, that healing and signs and wonders be done by the name
of thy holy child Jesus. And as soon as they had prayed, the place moved where
they were assembled together, and they were all filled with the holy ghost, and
they spake the word of God boldly.

+ And the multitude of them that believed, were of one heart, and of one   G
soul. Also none of them said, that any of the things which he possessed, was
his own: but had all things common. And with great power gave the apostles
witness of the resurrection of the Lord Jesus. And great grace was with them

Common.

all. Neither was there any among them, that lacked. For as many as were pos-

Love.

sessors of lands or houses, sold them and brought the price of the things that
were sold, and laid it down at the apostles' feet. And distribution was made
unto every man according as he had need. ⊢

And Joses which was also called of the apostles Barnabas (that is to say the
son of consolation) being a Levite, and of the country of Cyprus, had land, and
sold it and laid the price down at the Apostles' feet.

CHAPTER FIVE

Ananias.

A certain man named Ananias with Sapphira his wife sold a possession, and   A

Sapphira.

kept away part of the price (his wife also being of counsel) and brought a certain part, and laid it down at the apostles' feet. Then said Peter: Ananias, how is
it that Satan hath filled thine heart, that thou shouldest lie unto the holy ghost,
and keep away part of the price of the livelihood: Pertained it not unto thee
only, and after it was sold, was not the price in thine own power? How is it that
thou hast conceived this thing in thine heart? Thou hast not lied unto men, but
unto God. When Ananias heard these words, he fell down and gave up the
ghost. And great fear came on all them that these things heard. And the young
men rose up, and put him apart, and carried him out, and buried him.

And it fortuned as it were about the space of three hours after, that his wife
came in, ignorant of that which was done. And Peter said unto her: Tell me,

gave ye the land for so much? And she said: yea for so much. Then Peter said unto her: why have ye agreed together, to tempt the spirit of the Lord? Behold the feet of them which have buried thy husband, are at the door, and shall carry thee out. Then she fell down straightway at his feet and yielded up the ghost. And the young men came in, and found her dead, and carried her out and buried her by her husband. And great fear came on all the congregation, and on as many as heard it.

C By the hands of the Apostles were many signs and wonders shewed among the people. And they were all together with one accord in Solomon's porch. And of other durst no man join himself to them: neverthelater the people magnified them. The number of them that believed in the Lord both of men and women, grew more and more: insomuch that they brought the sick into the streets, and laid them on beds and pallets, that at the least way the shadow of Peter when he came by, might shadow some of them. There came also a multitude out of the cities round about, unto Jerusalem, bringing sick folks, and them which were vexed with unclean spirits. And they were healed every one.

The shadow of Peter.

D Then the chief priest rose up and all they that were with him (which is the sect of the Sadducees) and were full of indignation, and laid hands on the apostles, and put them in the common prison. But the angel of the Lord by night opened the prison doors, and brought them forth, and said: go, step forth, and speak in the temple to the people all the words of this life. When they heard that, they entered into the temple early in the morning and taught.

Sadducees.

E The chief priest came and they that were with him, and called a council together, and all the elders of the children of Israel, and sent to the prison to fetch them. When the ministers came and found them not in the prison, they returned and told saying: the prison found we shut as sure as was possible, and the keepers standing without before the doors. But when we had opened, we found no man within. When the chief priest of all and the ruler of the temple and the high priests heard these things, they doubted of them, whereunto this would grow.

Then came one and showed them: behold the men that ye put in prison, stand in the temple, and teach the people. Then went the ruler of the temple with ministers, and brought them without violence. For they feared the people, lest they should have been stoned. And when they had brought them, they set them before the council. And the chief priest asked them saying: did not we straitly command you that ye should not teach in this name? And behold ye have filled Jerusalem with your doctrine, and ye intend to bring this man's blood upon us.

F Peter and the other apostles answered and said: We ought more to obey God than men. The God of our fathers raised up Jesus, whom ye slew and hanged on tree. Him hath God lift up with his right hand, to be a ruler and a saviour, for to give repentance to Israel and forgiveness of sins. And we are his records concerning these things and also the holy ghost whom God hath given to them that obey him. When they heard that, they clave asunder: and sought means to

God must be obeyed.

Gamaliel.

slay them. Then stood there up one in the council, a Pharisee named Gamaliel, a doctor of law, had in authority among all the people, and commanded to put the apostles aside a little space, and said unto them: Men of Israel take heed to yourselves what ye intend to do as touching these men. Before these days rose up one Theudas boasting himself, to whom resorted a number of men, about a four hundred, which was slain, and they all which believed him were scattered abroad and brought to nought. After this man arose there up one Judas of Galilee, in the time when tribute began, and drew away much people after him. He also perished: and all even as many as harkened to him, are scattered abroad.   **G**

And now I say unto you: refrain yourselves from these men, let them alone. For if the counsel or this work be of men, it will come to nought. But and if it be of God, ye cannot destroy it, lest haply ye be found to strive against God. And to him they agreed, and called the Apostles, and beat them, and commanded that they should not speak in the name of Jesus, and let them go.

And they departed from the council, rejoicing that they were counted worthy to suffer rebuke for his name. And daily in the temple and in every house they ceased not, teaching and preaching Jesus Christ.

Theudas.

Judas the Galilean.

CHAPTER SIX

In those days as the number of the disciples grew, there arose a grudge among   **A**
the Greeks against the Hebrews, because their widows were despised in the daily ministration. Then the twelve called the multitude of the disciples together and said: it is not meet that we should leave the word of God and serve at the tables. Wherefore brethren, look ye out among you seven men of honest report, and full of the holy ghost and wisdom, which we may appoint to this needful business. But we will give ourselves continually to prayer, and to the ministration of the word. And the saying pleased the whole multitude. And they chose Stephen a man full of faith and of the holy ghost, and Philip, and   **B**
Prochorus, and Nicanor, and Timon, and Parmenas, and Nicolas a convert of Antioch. Which they set before the apostles, and they prayed and laid their hands on them.

And the word of God increased, and the number of the disciples multiplied   **C**
in Jerusalem greatly, and a great company of the priests were obedient to the faith. + And Stephen full of faith and power, did great wonders and miracles among the people. Then there arose certain of the synagogue which are called Libertines, and Cyrenians, and of Alexandria, and of Cilicia, and Asia, and disputed with Stephen. And they could not resist the wisdom, and the spirit, with which he spake. Then sent they in men, which said: we have heard him speak blasphemous words against Moses, and against God. And they moved the people and the elders and the scribes: and came upon him and caught him, and brought him to the council, and brought forth false witnesses which said, this man ceaseth not to speak blasphemous words against this holy place and   **D**
the law: for we heard him say: this Jesus of Nazareth shall destroy this place, and shall change the ordinances which Moses gave us. And all that sat in the

Seven deacons.

Stephen.

council looked steadfastly on him, and saw his face as it had been the face of an angel. ⊦

CHAPTER SEVEN

A Then said the chief priest: is it even so? And he said: ye men, brethren and fathers, hearken to. The God of glory appeared unto our father Abraham while he was yet in Mesopotamia, before he dwelt in Charran, and said unto him: come out of thy country, and from thy kindred, and come into the land, which I shall show thee. Then came he out of the land of Chaldey, and dwelt in Charran. And after that, as soon as his father was dead, he brought him into this land, in which ye now dwell, and he gave him none inheritance in it, no not the breadth of a foot: but promised that he would give it to him to possess and to his seed after him, when as yet he had no child.

The sermon of Stephen.

Gen. 12. a.

God verily spake on this wise that his seed should be a dweller in a strange land and that they should keep them in bondage and entreat them evil four hundred years. But the nation to whom they shall be in bondage will I judge, said God. And after that shall they come forth and serve me in this place. And he gave him the covenant of circumcision. And he begat Isaac, and circumcised him the eighth day, and Isaac begat Jacob, and Jacob the twelve patriarchs.

Gen. 18.
Gen. 21.
Gen. 25.
Gen. 29.

B And the patriarchs having indignation sold Joseph into Egypt. And God was with him and delivered him out of all his adversities. And gave him favour and wisdom in the sight of Pharaoh king of Egypt which made him governor over Egypt, and over all his household.

Patriarchs.

Gen. 30. and 35.
Gen. 38.
Gen. 41. e.

Then came there a dearth over all the land of Egypt and Canaan, and great affliction, that our fathers found no sustenance. But when Jacob heard that there was corn in Egypt, he sent our fathers first, and at the second time, Joseph was known of his brethren, and Joseph's kindred was made known unto Pharaoh. Then sent Joseph and caused his father to be brought and all his kin, three score and fifteen souls. And Jacob descended into Egypt and died both he and our fathers, and were translated into Sychem, and were put in the sepulchre that Abraham bought for money of the sons of Emmor, at Sychem.

Gen. 44.
Gen. 45.

Gen. 46.
Gen. 49.
Gen. 50. b.

C When the time of the promise drew nigh (which God had sworn to Abraham) the people grew and multiplied in Egypt, till another king arose which knew not of Joseph. The same dealt subtly with our kindred, and evil intreated our fathers, and made them to cast out their young children, that they should not remain alive. The same time was Moses born, and was a proper child in the sight of God, which was nourished up in his father's house three months. When he was cast out, Pharaoh's daughter took him up, and nourished him up for her own son. And Moses was learned in all manner wisdom of the Egyptians, and was mighty in deeds and in words.

Exod. 1. a.

Exod. 2. a.

And when he was full forty year old, it came into his heart to visit his brethren, the children of Israel. And when he saw one of them suffer wrong, he defended him, and avenged his quarrel that had the harm done to him, and smote the Egyptian. For he supposed his brethren would have understood how that God by his hands should save them. But they understood not.

Exod. 2. c.

And the next day he shewed himself unto them as they strove, and would **D** have set them at one again saying: Sirs, ye are brethren, why hurt ye one another? But he that did his neighbour wrong, thrust him away saying: who made thee a ruler and a judge among us? What, wilt thou kill me, as thou didst the Egyptian yesterday? Then fled Moses at that saying, and was a stranger in the land of Madian, where he begat two sons.

Exod. 3. a.

And when forty years were expired, there appeared to him in the wilderness of mount Sina an angel of the Lord in a flame of fire in a bush. When Moses saw it, he wondered at the sight. And as he drew near to behold, the voice of the Lord came unto him: I am the God of thy fathers, the God of Abraham, the God of Isaac, and the God of Jacob. Moses trembled and durst not behold. Then said the Lord to him: Put off thy shoes from thy feet, for the place where thou standest, is holy ground. I have perfectly seen the affliction of my people which is in Egypt, and I have heard their groaning, and am come down to deliver them. And now come and I will send thee into Egypt.

This Moses whom they forsook saying: who made the a ruler and a judge? **E** the same God sent both a ruler and deliverer, by the hands of the angel which appeared to him in the bush. And the same brought them out showing wonders and signs in Egypt, and in the Red sea and in the wilderness forty

Exod. 7 and 8, 9, 10,
11, 14.

years. This is that Moses which said unto the children of Israel: A prophet shall the Lord your God raise up unto you of your brethren like unto me, him shall

Deut. 18.
Exod. 19.

ye hear.

This is he that was in the congregation, in the wilderness with the angel which spake to him in the mount Sina, and with our fathers. This man received the word of life to give unto us, to whom our fathers would not obey but cast

Exod. 32.

it from them, and in their hearts turned back again into Egypt, saying unto Aaron: Make us gods to go before us. For this Moses that brought us out of the land of Egypt, we wot not what is become of him. And they made a calf in those days, and offered sacrifice unto the image, and rejoiced in the works of their own hands.

Then God turned himself, and gave them up, that they should worship the

Amos. 5. g.

stars of the sky, as it is written in the book of the prophets: O ye of the house of Israel, gave ye to me sacrifices and meat offerings, by the space of forty years in the wilderness? And ye took unto you the tabernacle of Moloch, and the star of your god Remphan, figures which ye made to worship them. And I will translate you beyond Babylon.

Exod. 25. d.
Heb. 8. b.
Josh. 3. c.

Our fathers had the tabernacle of witness in the wilderness, as he had ap- **F** pointed them speaking unto Moses, that he should make it according to the fashion that he had seen. Which tabernacle our fathers received, and brought it

1 Sam. 16.
Psa. 131.

in with Joshua into the possession of the gentiles which God drave out before the face of our fathers unto the time of David, which found favour before God, and desired that he might find a tabernacle for the God of Jacob. But Solomon built him an house.

Howbeit he that is highest of all, dwelleth not in temple★ made with hands, as saith the prophet: Heaven is my seat, and earth is my footstool, what house will ye build for me saith the Lord? or what place is it that I should rest in? hath not my hand made all these things?

Ye stiffnecked and of uncircumcised hearts and ears: ye have always resisted the holy ghost: as your fathers did, so do ye. Which of the prophets have not your fathers persecuted? And they have slain them, which shewed before of the coming of that just, whom ye have now betrayed and murdered. And ye also have received a law by the ordinance of angels, and have not kept it.

G When they heard these things, their hearts clave asunder, and they gnashed on him with their teeth. But he being full of the holy ghost, looked up stead-fastly with his eyes into heaven and saw the glory of God, and Jesus standing on the right hand of God, and said: behold, I see the heavens open, and the son of man standing on the right hand of God. Then they gave a shout with a loud voice, and stopped their ears and ran upon him all at once, and cast him out of the city, and stoned him. And the witnesses laid down their clothes at a young man's feet named Saul. And they stoned Stephen calling on and saying: Lord Jesus receive my spirit. And he kneeled down and cried with a loud voice: Lord lay not this sin to their charge. And when he had thus spoken, he fell asleep. ⊢

CHAPTER EIGHT

A Saul had pleasure in his death. And at that time there was a great persecution against the congregation which was at Jerusalem, and they were all scattered abroad throughout the regions of Jewry and Samaria, except the apostles. Then devout men dressed Stephen, and made great lamentation over him. But Saul made havoc of the congregation entering into every house, and drew out both man and woman, and thrust them into prison. They that were scattered abroad, went everywhere preaching the word. + Then came Philip into a city of Samaria and preached Christ unto them. And the people gave heed unto those things which Philip spake, with one accord, in that they heard and saw

B the miracles which he did. For unclean spirits crying with loud voice, came out of many that were possessed of them. And many taken with palsies, and many that halted, were healed. And there was great joy in that city. And there was a certain man called Simon, which before time in the same city, used witchcraft and bewitched the people of Samaria, saying, that he was a man that could do great things. Whom they regarded, from the least to the greatest, saying: this fellow is the great power of God. And him they set much by, because of long time with sorcery he had mocked them. But as soon as they believed Philip's preaching of the kingdom of God and of the name of Jesus Christ, they were baptised both men and women. Then Simon himself believed also, and was baptised, and continued with Philip, and wondered beholding the miracles and signs, which were shewed. ⊢

C + When the apostles which were at Jerusalem heard say that Samaria had received the word of God: they sent unto them, Peter and John, which when

★ God dwelleth not in temples or churches made with hands.

Saul.

Saul.

Philip.

Simon Magus.

they were come, prayed for them, that they might receive the holy ghost. For as yet he was come on none of them: But they were baptised only in the name of Christ Jesus. Then laid they their hands on them, and they received the holy ghost. ⊢

Laying on of hands.

When Simon saw, that through laying on of the apostles' hands on them, the holy ghost was given: he offered them money saying: Give me also this power, that on whomsoever I put the hands, he may receive the holy ghost. Then said Peter unto him: thy money perish with thee, because thou weenest that the gift of God may be obtained with money. Thou hast neither part nor fellowship in this business. For thy heart is not right in the sight of God. Repent therefore of this thy wickedness, and pray God that the thought of thine heart may be forgiven thee. For I perceive that thou art full of bitter gall, and wrapped in iniquity.

Then answered Simon and said: Pray ye to the Lord for me that none of these **D** things which ye have spoken, fall on me. And they, when they had testified and preached the word of the Lord, returned toward Jerusalem, and preached the gospel in many cities of the Samaritans.

+ Then the angel of the Lord spake unto Philip saying: arise and go towards mid-day unto the way that goeth down from Jerusalem unto Gaza which is in the desert. And he arose and went on. And behold a man of Ethiopia which was a chamberlain, and of great authority with Candace queen of the Ethiopians, and had the rule of all her treasure, came to Jerusalem for to pray. And as he returned home again sitting in his chariot, he read Esaias the prophet.

Then the spirit said unto Philip: Go near and join thyself to yonder chariot. **E** And Philip ran to him, and heard him read the prophet Esaias and said: Understandest thou what thou readest? And he said: how can I, except I had a guide? And he desired Philip that he would come up and sit with him. The tenor of the scripture which he read, was this. He was led as a sheep to be slain: and like a lamb dumb before his shearer, so opened he not his mouth⋆. Because of his humbleness, he was not esteemed: who shall declare his generation? for his life is taken from the earth. The chamberlain answered Philip and said: I pray thee, of whom speaketh the prophet this? of himself, or of some other man?

⋆ Because he was of so low degree in this world: but a poor carpenter, and humbled himself unto all men, and was obedient even unto the most vile death of the cross: therefore cannot the Jews esteem him for the very Messias.

And Philip opened his mouth, and began at the same scripture, and preached **F** unto him Jesus. And as they went on their way, they came unto a certain water, and the chamberlain said: See here is water, what shall let me to be baptised? Philip said unto him: If thou believe with all thine heart, thou mayst. He answered and said: I believe that Jesus Christ is the son of God. And he commanded the chariot to stand still. And they went down both into the water: both Philip and also the chamberlain, and he baptised him. And as soon as they were come out of the water, the spirit of the Lord caught away Philip, that the chamberlain saw him no more. And he went on his way rejoicing: but Philip was found at Azotus. And he walked throughout the country preaching in their cities, till he came to Cesarea. ⊢

176

CHAPTER NINE

A + And Saul yet breathing out threatenings and slaughter against the disciples of the Lord, went unto the high priest, and desired of him letters to Damascus, to the synagogues: that if he found any of this way, whether they were men or women, he might bring them bound unto Jerusalem. But as he went on his journey, it fortuned that he drew nigh to Damascus, and suddenly there shined round about him a light from heaven. And he fell to the earth, and heard a voice saying to him: Saul, Saul, why persecutest thou me? And he said, what art thou Lord? And the Lord said, I am Jesus whom thou persecutest, it shall be hard for thee to kick against the pricks. And he both trembling and astonied said: Lord what wilt thou have me to do? And the Lord said unto him: arise and go into the city, and it shall be told thee what thou shalt do.

Gal. 1. b.

1 Cor. 15.
2 Cor. 12.

Saul is converted.

B The men which journeyed with him, stood amazed, for they heard a voice, but saw no man. And Saul arose from the earth, and opened his eyes, but saw no man. Then led they him by the hand, and brought him into Damascus. And he was three days without sight, and neither ate nor drank. And there was a certain disciple at Damascus named Ananias, and to him said the Lord in a vision: Ananias. And he said: behold I am here Lord. And the Lord said to him: arise and go into the street which is called Straight, and seek in the house of Judas, after one called Saul of Tarsus. For behold he prayeth, and hath seen in a vision a man named Ananias coming in to him, and putting his hands on him, that he might receive his sight.

Ananias.

C Then Ananias answered: Lord I have heard by many of this man, how much evil he hath done to thy saints at Jerusalem, and here he hath authority of the high priests to bind all that call on thy name. The Lord said unto him: Go thy ways: for he is a chosen vessel unto me, to bear my name before the gentiles and kings, and the children of Israel. For I will shew him how great things he must suffer for my name's sake.

Ananias went his way and entered into the house and put his hands on him and said: brother Saul, the Lord that appeared unto thee in the way as thou camest, hath sent me, that thou mightest receive thy sight and be filled with the holy ghost. And immediately there fell from his eyes as it had been scales, and he received sight, and arose and was baptised, and received meat and was comforted.

Then was Saul a certain day with the disciples which were at Damascus. And straightway he preached Christ in the synagogues, how that he was the son of God. All that heard him, were amazed and said: is not this he that spoiled them which called on this name in Jerusalem, and came hither for the intent that he should bring them bound unto the high priests? But Saul increased in strength, and confounded the Jews which dwelt at Damascus, affirming that this was very Christ. ⊦

Paul preacheth Christ.

And after a good while, the Jews took counsel together, to kill him. But their laying wait was known of Saul. And they watched at the gates day and night

Paul is persecuted.

to kill him. Then the disciples took him by night and put him through the wall and let him down in a basket.

2. Cor. 11.

And when Saul was come to Jerusalem, he assayed to couple himself with   **E** the disciples and they were all afraid of him and believed not that he was a disciple. But Barnabas took him and brought him to the apostles and declared to them how he had seen the Lord in the way and had spoken with him: and how he had done boldly at Damascus in the name of Jesus. And he had his conversation with them at Jerusalem, and quit himself boldly in the name of the Lord Jesus. And he spake and disputed with the Greeks: and they went about to slay him. But when the brethren knew of that, they brought him to Cesarea, and sent him forth to Tarsus. Then had the congregations rest throughout all Jewry and Galilee and Samaria, and were edified, and walked in the fear of the Lord, and multiplied by the comfort of the holy ghost.

And it chanced that as Peter walked throughout all quarters, he came to the   **F**

Eneas.

saints which dwelt at Lydda and there he found a certain man named Eneas, which had kept his bed eight years sick of the palsy. Then said Peter unto him: Eneas, Jesus Christ make thee whole: Arise and make thy bed. And he arose immediately. And all that dwelt at Lydda and Saron, saw him, and turned to the Lord.

Tabitha.
Dorcas.

There was at Joppa a certain woman (which was a disciple named Tabitha, which by interpretation is called Dorcas): the same was full of good works and alms-deeds, which she did. And it chanced in those days that she was sick and died. When they had washed her and laid her in a chamber: Because Lydda was nigh to Joppa, and the disciples had heard that Peter was there, they sent unto him, desiring him that he would not be grieved to come unto them.

Peter arose and came with them and when he was come, they brought him   **G** into the chamber. And all the widows stood round about him weeping and showing the coats and garments which Dorcas made while she was with them. And Peter put them all forth and kneeled down and prayed and turned him to the body, and said: Tabitha arise. And she opened her eyes, and when she saw Peter she sat up. And he gave her the hand and lift her up, and called the saints and widows, and showed her alive. And it was known throughout all Joppa, and many believed on the Lord. And it fortuned that he tarried many days in Joppa with one Simon a tanner.

CHAPTER TEN

Cornelius.

There was a certain man in Cesarea called Cornelius, a captain of the soldiers of   **A** Italy, a devout man, and one that feared God with all his household, which gave much alms to the people, and prayed God always. The same man saw in a vision, evidently, about the ninth hour of the day an angel of God coming into him, and saying unto him: Cornelius. When he looked on him, he was afraid, and said: what is it Lord? He said unto him: Thy prayers and thy alms are come up into remembrance before God.

And now send men to Joppa, and call for one Simon named also Peter. He lodgeth with one Simon a tanner, whose house is by the sea-side. He shall tell thee, what thou oughtest to do. When the angel which spake unto Cornelius was departed, he called two of his household servants, and a devout soldier of them that waited on him, and told them all the matter, and sent them to Joppa.

B   On the morrow as they went on their journey and drew nigh unto the city, Peter went up into the top of the house to pray, about the sixth hour. Then waxed he an-hungered, and would have eaten. But while they made ready, he fell into a trance, and saw heaven opened and a certain vessel come down unto him, as it had been a great sheet, knit at the four corners, and was let down to the earth, wherein were all manner of four-footed beasts of the earth and

Peter's vision.

C   vermin and worms, and fowls of the air. And there came a voice to him: rise Peter, kill and eat. But Peter said: God forbid Lord, for I have never eaten any thing that is common or unclean. And the voice spake unto him again the second time: what God hath cleansed, that make thou not common. This was done thrice, and the vessel was received up again into heaven.

While Peter mused in himself what this vision which he had seen meant,

D   behold, the men which were sent from Cornelius, had made inquirance for Simon's house, and stood before the door. And called out one and asked whether Simon which was also called Peter were lodged there. While Peter thought on this vision, the spirit said unto him: Behold, men seek thee: arise therefore, get thee down, and go with them, and doubt not. For I have sent them. Peter went down to the men which were sent unto him from Cornelius, and said, Behold, I am he whom ye seek, what is the cause wherefore ye are come? And they said unto him: Cornelius the captain, a just man, and one that feareth God, and of good report among all the people of the Jews was warned by an holy angel, to send for thee into his house, and to hear words of thee. Then called he them in, and lodged them.

D   And on the morrow Peter went away with them, and certain brethren from Joppa accompanied him. And the third day entered they into Caesarea. And Cornelius waited for them, and had called together his kinsmen, and special friends. And as it chanced Peter to come in, Cornelius met him, and fell down at his feet, and worshipped him. But Peter took him up saying: stand up: for even I myself am a man. And as he talked with him he came in, and found many that were come together. And he said unto them: Ye do know how that it is an unlawful thing for a man that is a Jew, to company or come unto an alien: But God hath shewed me that I should not call any man common or unclean: therefore came I unto you without saying nay as soon as I was sent for. I ask therefore, for what intent have ye sent for me?

E   And Cornelius said: This day now four days I fasted, and at the ninth hour I prayed in my house: and behold, a man stood before me in bright clothing, and said: Cornelius, thy prayer is heard, and thine alms-deeds are had in remembrance in the sight of God. Send therefore to Joppa, and call for Simon which is also called Peter. He is lodged in the house of one Simon a tanner by the sea-side, the which as soon as he is come, shall speak unto thee. Then sent I for thee immediately and thou hast well done for to come. Now are we all here present before God, to hear all things that are commanded unto thee of God.

Deut. 10. d 2 Chr. 19. Job 34. Prov. 6. b.

Then Peter opened his mouth and said: Of a truth I perceive, that God is not partial, but in all people he that feareth him and worketh righteousness, is accepted with him.

Eccl. 35. Rom. 2. b. Gal. 2. b. Eph. 6. b. Col. 3. d. 1 Pet. 1. c.

Ye know the preaching that God sent unto the children of Israel, preaching F
peace by Jesus Christ, (which is Lord over all things), + which preaching was published throughout all Jewry, and began in Galilee, after the baptism which John preached, how God had anointed Jesus of Nazareth with the holy ghost, and with power, which Jesus went about doing good, and healing all that were oppressed of the devils, for God was with him. And we are witnesses of all things which he did in the land of the Jews and at Jerusalem, whom they slew, and hung on tree. Him God raised up the third day, and showed him openly, not to all the people, but unto us witnesses chosen before of God, which ate
and drank with him, after he arose from death. + And he commanded us to G
preach unto the people and testify, that it is he that is ordained of God a judge of quick and dead. To him give all the prophets witness, that through his name shall receive remission of sins★ all that believe in him. ⊢

Jer. 31. Mic. 7.

★ Faith is the remission of sins.

While Peter yet spake these words, the holy ghost fell on all them which heard the preaching. And they of the circumcision which believed, were astonied, as many as came with Peter, because that on the Gentiles also was shed out the gift of the holy ghost★. For they heard them speak with tongues and magnify God. Then answered Peter: can any man forbid water that these should not be baptised, which have received the holy ghost as well as we? And he commanded them to be baptised in the name of the Lord. ⊢ Then prayed they him, to tarry a few days.

★ The holy ghost cometh without laying-on of hands.

CHAPTER ELEVEN

The Apostles were here first taught and certified by the holy ghost of the conversion of the gentiles.

And the apostles, and the brethren that were throughout Jewry, heard say that A
the heathen had also received the word of God. And when Peter was come up to Jerusalem, they of the circumcision reasoned with him saying: Thou wentest in to men uncircumcised, and atest with them.

Then Peter began and expounded the thing in order to them saying: I was in the city of Joppa praying, and in a trance I saw a vision, a certain vessel descend, as it had been a large linen cloth, let down from heaven by the four corners, and it came to me. Into the which when I had fastened mine eyes, I considered and saw fourfooted beasts of the earth, and vermin and worms, and fowls of the air. And I heard a voice saying unto me: arise Peter, slay and eat. And I said: God forbid Lord, for nothing common or unclean, hath at any time entered into my mouth. But the voice answered me again from heaven, count not thou those things common, which God hath cleansed. And this was done three times. And all were taken up again into heaven.

And behold immediately there were three men come unto the house where I B
was, sent from Caesarea unto me. And the spirit said unto me, that I should

go with them, without doubting. Moreover the six brethren accompanied me: and we entered into the man's house. And he shewed us, how he had seen an angel in his house, which stood and said to him: Send men to Joppa, and call for Simon, named also Peter: he shall tell thee words, whereby both thou and all thine house shall be saved. And as I began to preach, the holy ghost fell on them, as he did on us at the beginning. Then came to my remembrance the words of the Lord, how he said: John baptised with water, but ye shall be baptised with the holy ghost. Forasmuch then as God gave them like gifts, as he did unto us, when we believed on the Lord Jesus Christ: what was I that I should have withstood God? When they heard this, they held their peace and glorified God, saying: then hath God also to the gentiles granted repentance unto life.

They which were scattered abroad through the affliction that arose about Stephen, walked throughout till they came unto Phenice and Cyprus and Antioch, preaching the word to no man, but unto the Jews only. Some of them were men of Cyprus and Cyrene, which when they were come into Antioch, spake unto the Greeks, and preached the Lord Jesus. And the hand of the Lord was with them, and a great number believed and turned unto the Lord.

Tidings of these things came unto the ears of the congregation, which was in Jerusalem. And they sent forth Barnabas that he should go unto Antioch. Which when he was come, and had seen the grace of God, was glad, and exhorted them all, that with purpose of heart they would continually cleave unto the Lord. For he was a good man, and full of the holy ghost and of faith: and much people was added unto the Lord. Then departed Barnabas to Tarsus, for to seek Saul. And when he had found him, he brought him unto Antioch. And it chaunced that a whole year they had their conversation with the congregation there, and taught much people: insomuch that the disciples of Antioch were the first that were called Christian.

In those days came prophets from Jerusalem unto Antioch. And there stood up one of them, named Agabus, and signified by the spirit, that there should be great dearth throughout all the world, which came to pass in the Emperor Claudius' days. Then the disciples every man according to his ability, purposed to send succour unto the brethren which dwelt in Jewry. Which thing they also did, and sent it to the elders, by the hands of Barnabas and Saul.

CHAPTER TWELVE

+ In that time Herod the king stretched forth his hands to vex certain of the congregation. And he killed James the brother of John with the sword: and because he saw that it pleased the Jews, he proceeded further, and took Peter also. Then were the days of sweet bread. And when he had caught him, he put him in prison, and delivered him to four quaternions* of soldiers to be kept, intending after Easter to bring him forth to the people. Then was Peter kept in prison. But prayer was made without ceasing of the congregation unto God for him. And when Herod would have brought him out unto the people, the same

Barnabas is sent to Antioch.

Barnabas seeketh Paul.

James the brother of John is killed.

Peter is taken.

* Quaternions of soldiers is four companies of soldiers.

181

night slept Peter between two soldiers, bound with two chains, and the keepers before the door kept the prison.

Peter is loosed.

And behold the angel of the Lord was there present, and a light shined in the lodge. And his chains fell off from his hands. And the angel said unto him: gird

* Sandals are soles to be bound under the feet.

thyself and bind on thy sandals★. And so he did. And he said unto him: cast thy mantle about thee, and follow me. And he came out and followed him, and wist not, that it was truth which was done by the angel, but thought he had seen a vision. When they were past the first and the second watch, they came unto the iron gate, that leadeth unto the city, which opened to them by his own accord. And they went out and passed through one street, and by and by the angel departed from him.

And when Peter was come to himself, he said: now I know of a surety, that the Lord hath sent his angel, and hath delivered me out of the hand of Herod, and from all the waiting for of the people of the Jews. ⊦ + And as he considered the

* This John is the same Mark that writ the gospel of Mark.

thing, he came to the house of Mary the mother of one John★, which was called Mark also, where many were gathered together in prayer. As Peter knocked at the entry door, a damsel came forth to hearken, named Rhoda. And when she knew Peter's voice, she opened not the entry for gladness, but ran in and told how Peter stood before the entry. And they said unto her: thou art mad. And she bare them down that it was even so. Then said they: it is his angel. Peter continued knocking. When they had opened the door, and saw him, they were astonied. And he beckoned unto them with the hand to hold their peace, and told them by what means the Lord had brought him out of the prison. And said: go shew these things unto James and to the brethren. And he departed and went into another place. ⊦

As soon as it was day there was no little ado among the soldiers, what was become of Peter. When Herod had called for him, and found him not, he examined the keepers, and commanded to depart. And he descended from Jewry to Caesarea, and there abode. Herod was displeased with them of Tyre and Sidon. And they came all at once, and made intercession unto Blastus the king's chamberlain, and desired peace, because their country was nourished by the king's land. And upon a day appointed Herod arrayed him in royal apparel, and set him in his seat, and made an oration unto them. And the people gave a shout, saying: it is the voice of a god and not of a man. And immediately the

* Herod is slain and eaten of worms.

angel of the Lord★ smote him, because he gave not God the honour, and he was eaten of worms, and gave up the ghost.

* John is Mark the evangelist.

And the word of God grew and multiplied. And Barnabas and Paul returned to Jerusalem, when they had fulfilled their office, and took with them John★, which was also called Marcus.

CHAPTER THIRTEEN

There were at Antioch, in the congregation certain prophets and teachers: as Barnabas and Simeon called Niger, and Lucius of Cyrene, and Manaen Herod the tetrarch's nursefellow, and Saul. As they ministered to the Lord and fasted, the holy ghost said: separate me Barnabas and Saul, for the work whereunto I have called them. Then fasted they and prayed, and put their hands on them, and let them go. And they after they were sent of the holy ghost, came unto Seleucia, and from thence they sailed to Cyprus. And when they were come to Salamis, they showed the word of God in the synagogues, of the Jews. And they had John* to their minister.

Barnabas and Paul are sent to preach.

* This John is Mark the evangelist.

When they had gone throughout the isle unto the city of Paphos, they found a certain sorcerer, a false prophet which was a Jew, named Bar-jesus, which was with the ruler of the country, one Sergius Paulus, a prudent man. The same ruler called unto him Barnabas and Saul, and desired to hear the word of God. But Elymas the sorcerer (for so was his name by interpretation) withstood them: and sought to turn away the ruler from the faith. Then Saul which also is called Paul being full of the holy ghost, set his eyes on him, and said: O full of all subtlety and deceitfulness, and child of the devil, and the enemy of all righteousness, thou ceasest not to pervert the straight ways of the Lord. And now behold the hand of the Lord is upon thee, and thou shalt be blind and not see the sun for a season. And immediately there fell on him a mist and a darkness, and he went about seeking them that should lead him by the hand. Then the ruler when he saw what had happened, believed, and wondered at the doctrine of the Lord.

Bar-jesus.

Sergius Paulus.

Elymas.

Paul.

When they that were with Paul, were departed by ship from Paphos, they came to Perga a city of Pamphylia: and there John departed from them, and returned to Jerusalem. But they wandered through the countries, from Perga to Antioch a city of the country of Pisidia, and went in to the synagogue on the sabbath day, and sat down. And after the law and the prophets were read, the rulers of the synagogue sent unto them saying: Ye men and brethren, if ye have any sermon to exhort the people, say on.

Mark the evangelist otherwise called John breaketh company.

Then Paul stood up and beckoned with the hand, and said: Men of Israel, and ye that fear God, give audience. The God of this people chose our fathers, and exalted the people when they dwelt as strangers in the land of Egypt, and with a mighty arm brought them out of it, and about the time of forty years suffered he their manners in the wilderness. And he destroyed seven nations in the land of Canaan, and divided their land to them by lot. And afterward he gave unto them judges about the space of four hundred and fifty years unto the time of Samuel the prophet. And after that they desired a king, and God gave unto them Saul the son of Cis, a man of the tribe of Benjamin, by the space of forty years. And after he had put him down, he set up David to be their king, of whom he reported saying: I have found David the son of Jesse, a man after mine own heart, he shall fulfil all my will.

Exod. 1. a.
Exod. 13.

Exod. 16. a.

Josh. 14.
Judg. 3. d.

1 Sam. 8. a.
1 Sam. 9. c. and 10. a.

Psa. 89.
1 Sam. 16.

Of this man's seed hath God (according to his promise) brought forth to the people of Israel a saviour, one Jesus, when John had first preached before his coming the baptism of repentance to Israel. And when John had fulfilled his course, he said: whom ye think that I am, the same am I not. But behold there cometh one after me, whose shoes of his feet I am not worthy to loose.

Isa. 11. a.

Matt. 4. a.
Mark 1. a.
Luke 3. a.
Mark 1. a.

+ Ye men and brethren, children of the generation of Abraham, and whosoever among you feareth God, to you is this word of salvation sent. The inhabiters of Jerusalem and their rulers, because they knew him not, nor yet the

Matt. 27.
Mark 15.

voices of the prophets which are read every sabbath day, they have fulfilled
them in condemning him. And when they found no cause of death in him, yet
desired they Pilate to kill him. And when they had fulfilled all that were written

Luke 23.
John 19. c.
Matt. 28.
Mark 16.
Luke 24.
John 20.

of him, they took him down from the tree and put him in a sepulchre. But
God raised him again from death, and he was seen many days of them which
came with him from Galilee to Jerusalem. Which are his witnesses unto the
people.

And we declare unto you, how that the promise made unto the fathers, God

Psa. 2. b.
Heb. 1. b.

hath fulfilled unto us their children, in that he raised up Jesus again ⊦ even as it is
written in the second psalm: Thou art my son, this same day begat I thee.
As concerning that he raised him up from death, now no more to return to
corruption, he said on this wise: The holy promises made to David I will give

Isa. 55. b.
Psa. 16. d.
1 Sam. 1. b.

them faithfully to you. Wherefore he saith also in another place: Thou shalt not
suffer thine holy to see corruption. Howbeit David after he had in his time
fulfilled the will of God, he slept, and was laid with his fathers, and saw
corruption. But he whom God raised again, saw no corruption.

Be it known unto you therefore ye men and brethren, that through this man is

* Faith justifieth and
not the law.

preached unto you the forgiveness of sins, and that by him are all that believe*
justified from all things from the which ye could not be justified by the law

Hab. 1. b.

of Moses. Beware therefore lest that fall on you, which is spoken of in the
prophets: Behold ye despisers and wonder, and perish ye: for I do a work in
your days, which ye shall not believe, if a man would declare it you.

When they were come out of the synagogue of the Jews, the gentiles besought that they would preach the word to them between the sabbath days.
When the congregation was broken up, many of the Jews and virtuous converts followed Paul and Barnabas, which spake to them and exhorted them to
continue in the grace of God. + And the next sabbath day, came almost the
whole city together, to hear the word of God. When the Jews saw the people,
they were full of indignation and spake against those things which were spoken
of Paul, speaking against it, and railing on it. Then Paul and Barnabas waxed
bold, and said: it was meet that the word of God should first have been
preached to you. But seeing ye put it from you, and think yourselves unworthy of everlasting life: lo, we turn to the gentiles. For so hath the Lord
commanded us: I have made thee a light to the gentiles, that thou be salvation

Isa. 49.

unto the end of the world.

The gentiles heard and were glad and glorified the word of the Lord, and
believed: even as many as were ordained unto eternal life. And the word of
the Lord was published throughout all the region. But the Jews moved the
worshipful and honourable women, and the chief men of the city, and raised
persecution against Paul and Barnabas, and expelled them out of their coasts.

Matt. 10. b.
Mark 6. b.
Luke 9. a.

And they shook off the dust off their feet against them, and came unto
Iconium. And the disciples were filled with joy and with the holy ghost. ⊦

CHAPTER FOURTEEN

And it fortuned in Iconium that they went both together into the synagogue of the Jews, and so spake, that a great multitude both of the Jews and also of the Greeks believed. But the unbelieving Jews, stirred up and unquieted the minds of the gentiles against the brethren. Long time abode they there and quit themselves boldly with the help of the Lord, the which gave testimony unto the word of his grace, and caused signs and wonders to be done by their hands. The people of city were divided: and part held with the Jews, and part with the apostles.

When there was assault made both of the gentiles and also of the Jews with their rulers, to put them to shame and to stone them, they were ware of it, and fled unto Lystra and Derbe, cities of Lycaonia, and unto the region that lieth round about, and there preached the gospel. And there sat a certain man at Lystra weak in his feet, being cripple from his mother's womb, and never walked. The same heard Paul preach. Which beheld him and perceived that he had faith to be whole, and said with a loud voice: stand upright on thy feet. And he started up, and walked. And when the people saw what Paul had done, they lift up their voices, saying in the speech of Lycaonia: gods are come down to us in the likeness of men. And they called Barnabas Jupiter, and Paul Mercurius, because he was the preacher. Then Jupiter's priest, which dwelt before their city, brought oxen and garlands unto the church porch, and would have done sacrifice with the people.

But when the apostles, Barnabas and Paul heard that, they rent their clothes, and ran in among the people, crying and saying: sirs, why do ye this? We are mortal men like unto you, and preach unto you, that ye should turn from these vanities unto the living God, which made heaven and earth and the sea and all that in them is: the which in times past suffered all nations to walk in their own ways. Nevertheless he left not himself without witness, in that he showed his benefits, in giving us rain from heaven and fruitful seasons, filling our hearts with food and gladness. And with these sayings, scarce refrained they the people, that they had not done sacrifice unto them.

Thither came certain Jews from Antioch and Iconium, and obtained the people's consent and stoned Paul, and drew him out of the city, supposing he had been dead. Howbeit as the disciples stood round about him, he arose up and came into the city. And the next day he departed with Barnabas to Derbe. After they had preached to that city and had taught many, they returned again to Lystra, and to Iconium and Antioch, and strengthed the disciples' souls, exhorting them to continue in the faith, affirming that we must through much tribulation enter into the kingdom of God. And when they had ordained them elders by election in every congregation, after they had prayed and fasted, they commended them to God on whom they believed.

And they went throughout Pisidia and came into Pamphylia, and when they had preached the word of God in Perga, they descended into Attalia, and thence departed by ship to Antioch, from whence they were delivered unto the

A cripple is healed.

Gods.

Psa. 146. Rev. 14.

Paul is stoned.

Tribulation.

Prayer and fasting go together.

grace of God, to the work which they had fulfilled. When they were come and had gathered the congregation together, they rehearsed all that God had done by them, and how he had opened the door of faith unto the gentiles. And there they abode long time with the disciples.

CHAPTER FIFTEEN

Circumcision.

Then came certain from Jewry, and taught the brethren: except ye be circumcised after the manner of Moses, ye cannot be saved. And when there was risen dissension and disputing not a little unto Paul and Barnabas against them: They determined that Paul and Barnabas and certain other of them should ascend to Jerusalem unto the apostles and elders about this question. And after they were brought on their way by the congregation, they passed over Phenice and Samaria, declaring the conversion of the gentiles, and they brought great joy unto all the brethren. And when they were come to Jerusalem, they were received of the congregation and of the apostles and elders. And they declared what things God had done by them. Then arose there up certain that were of the sect of the Pharisees and did believe saying, that it was needful to circumcise them and to enjoin them to keep the law of Moses. And the apostles and elders came together to reason of this matter.

Council.

And when there was much disputing, Peter rose up and said unto them: Ye men and brethren, ye know how that a good while ago, God chose among us that the gentiles by my mouth should hear the word of the gospel and believe. And God which knoweth the heart, bare them witness, and gave unto them the holy ghost, even as he did unto us, and he put no difference between them and us, but with faith* purified their hearts. Now therefore why tempt ye God, that ye would put a yoke on the disciples' necks, which neither our fathers nor we were able to bear? But we believe that through the grace* of the Lord Jesus Christ we shall be saved, as they do. Then all the multitude was peaced and gave audience to Barnabas and Paul, which told what signs and wonders God had showed among the gentiles, by them.

* Faith purifieth the heart.

* The grace of Christ saveth.

And when they held their peace, James answered saying: Men and brethren hearken unto me. Simeon told how God at the beginning did visit the gentiles, and received of them, people unto his name. And to this agreeth the words of the prophets, as it is written: After this I will return, and will build again the tabernacle of David which is fallen down, and that which is fallen in decay of it, will I build again, and I will set it up, that the residue of men might seek after the Lord, and also the gentiles upon whom my name is named saith the Lord, which doth all these things: known unto God are all his works from the beginning of the world. Wherefore my sentence is, that we trouble not them which from among the gentiles, are turned to God: but that we write unto them that they abstain themselves from filthiness of images, from fornication, from strangled and from blood. For Moses of old time hath in every city that preach him, and he is read in the synagogues every sabbath day.

Amos 9.

Images.
Fornication.
Strangled.
Blood.

Then pleased it the apostles and elders with the whole congregation, to send chosen men of their own company to Antioch with Paul and Barnabas. They sent Judas called also Barsabas, and Silas, which were chief men among the brethren, and gave them letters in their hands after this manner.

The apostles, elders and brethren send greetings unto the brethren which are of the gentiles in Antioch, Syria and Cilicia. Forasmuch as we have heard that certain which departed from us, have troubled you with words, and cumbered your minds saying: Ye must be circumcised and keep the law, to whom we gave no such commandment. It seemed therefore to us a good thing, when we were come together with one accord, to send chosen men unto you, with our beloved Barnabas and Paul, men that have jeoparded their lives for the name of our Lord Jesus Christ. We have sent therefore Judas and Silas, which shall also tell you the same things by mouth. For it seemed good to the holy ghost and to us, to put no grievous thing to you more than these necessary things: that is to say, that ye abstain from things offered to images, from blood, from strangled and fornication. From which if ye keep yourselves, ye shall do well. So fare ye well.

When they were departed, they came to Antioch and gathered the multitude together and delivered the epistle. When they had read it, they rejoiced of that consolation. And Judas and Silas being prophets★, exhorted the brethren with much preaching, and strengthened them. And after they had tarried there a space, they were let go in peace of the brethren unto the apostles. Notwithstanding it pleased Silas to abide there still. Paul and Barnabas continued in Antioch teaching and preaching the word of the Lord with other many.

★ Prophets are here taken and in diverse places of the new testament for expounders of the scripture.

But after a certain space, Paul said unto Barnabas: Let us go again and visit our brethren in every city where we have shewed the word of the Lord, and see how they do. And Barnabas gave counsel to take with them John, called also Mark. But Paul thought it not meet to take him unto their company which departed from them at Pamphylia, and went not with them to the work. And the dissension was so sharp between them, that they departed asunder one from the other: so that Barnabas took Mark and sailed unto Cyprus. And Paul chose Silas and departed, delivered of the brethren unto the grace of God. And he went through all Syria and Cilicia, establishing the congregations.

Mark the evangelist.

CHAPTER SIXTEEN

Then came he to Derbe and to Lystra. And behold a certain disciple was there named Timotheus, a woman's son which was a Jewess and believed: but his father was a Greek. Of whom reported well, the brethren of Lystra and of Iconium. The same Paul would that he should go forth with him, and took and circumcised him because of the Jews which were in those quarters: for they knew all that his father was a Greek. As they went through the cities, they delivered them the decrees for to keep, ordained of the apostles and elders which were at Jerusalem. And so were the congregations established in the faith, and increased in number daily.

Timotheus.

When they had gone throughout Phrygia, and the region of Galatia, and were forbidden of the holy ghost to preach the word in Asia, they came to Mysia, and sought to go into Bithynia. But the spirit suffered them not. Then they went over Mysia, and came down to Troas. And a vision appeared to Paul in the night. There stood a man of Macedonia and prayed him saying: come into Macedonia and help us. After he had seen the vision, immediately we prepared to go into Macedonia, certified that the Lord had called us for to preach the gospel unto them. Then loosed we forth from Troas, and with a straight course came to Samothracia, and the next day to Neapolis, and from thence to Philippi, which is the chiefest city in the parts of Macedonia, and a free city.

We were in that city abiding a certain days. And on the sabbath days we went out of the city besides a river where men were wont to pray, and we sat down and spake unto the women which resorted thither: And a certain woman named Lydia, a seller of purple, of the city of Thyatira, which worshipped God, gave us audience. Whose heart the Lord opened that she attended unto the things which Paul spake. When she was baptised and her household, she besought us saying: If ye think that I believe on the Lord, come into my house, and abide there. And she constrained us.

And it fortuned as we went to prayer, a certain damsel possessed with a spirit that prophesied, met us, which brought her masters much vantage with prophesying. The same followed Paul and us and cried saying: these men are the servants of the most high God, which show unto us the way of salvation. And this did she many days. But Paul not content, turned about and said to the spirit: I command thee in the name of Jesus Christ, that thou come out of her. And he came out the same hour.

And when her masters saw that the hope of their gains was gone, they caught Paul and Silas, and drew them into the marketplace unto the rulers, and brought them to the officers saying: These men trouble our city, which are Jews and preach ordinances, which are not lawful for us to receive, neither to observe, seeing we are Romans. And the people ran on them, and the officers rent their clothes, and commanded them to be beaten with rods. And when they had beaten them sore, they cast them into prison, commanding the jailer to keep them surely. Which jailer when he had received such commandment, thrust them into the inner prison, and made their feet fast in the stocks.

At midnight Paul and Silas prayed, and lauded God. And the prisoners heard them. And suddenly there was a great earthquake, so that the foundation of the prison was shaken, and by and by all the doors opened, and every man's bonds were loosed. When the keeper of the prison waked out of his sleep and saw the prison doors open, he drew out his sword and would have killed himself, supposing the prisoners had been fled. But Paul cried with a loud voice saying: Do thyself no harm, for we are all here.

Then he called for a light and sprang in, and came trembling, and fell down before Paul and Silas, and brought them out and said: Sirs, what must I do to be saved? And they said: believe on the Lord Jesus, and thou shalt be saved and

Lydia.

A spirit is cast out.

Vantage.

1. Cor. 11. f.

thy household. And they preached unto him the word of the Lord, and to all that were in his house. And he took them the same hour of the night and washed their wounds, and was baptised with all that belonged unto him straightway. When he had brought them into his house, he set meat before them, and joyed that he with all his household, believed on God.

G   And when it was day, the officers sent the ministers saying: Let those men go. The keeper of the prison told this saying to Paul, the officers have sent word to loose you. Now therefore get you hence and go in peace. Then said Paul unto them: they have beaten us openly uncondemned, for all that we are Romans, and have cast us into prison: and now would they send us away privily? Nay not so, but let them come themselves and fetch us out. When the ministers told these words unto the officers, they feared when they heard that they were Romans, and came and besought them, and brought them out, and desired them to depart out of the city. And they went out of the prison and entered into the house of Lydia, and when they had seen the brethren, they comforted them and departed.

CHAPTER SEVENTEEN

A   As they made their journey through Amphipolis, and Apollonia, they came to Thessalonica where was a synagogue of the Jews. And Paul as his manner was, went in unto them, and three sabbath days declared out of the scripture unto them, opening and alleging that Christ must needs have suffered and risen again from death, and that this Jesus was Christ, whom (said he) I preach to you. And some of them believed and came and companied with Paul and Silas: also of the honourable Greeks a great multitude, and of the chief women, not a few.

B   But the Jews which believed not, having indignation, took unto them evil men which were vagabonds, and gathered a company, and set all the city on a roar, and made assault unto the house of Jason, and sought to bring them out to the people. But when they found them not, they drew Jason and certain brethren unto the heads of the city crying: these that trouble the world, are come hither also, which Jason hath received privily. And these all do contrary to the elders†† of Caesar, affirming another king, one Jesus. And they troubled the people and the officers of the city when they heard these things. And when they were sufficiently answered of Jason, and of the other, they let them go.

C   And the brethren immediately sent away Paul and Silas by night unto Berea. Which when they were come thither, they entered into the synagogue of the Jews. These were the noblest of birth among them of Thessalonica which received the word with all diligence of mind, and searched★ the scriptures daily whether those things were even so. And many of them believed: also of worshipful women which were Greeks, and of men not a few. When the Jews of Thessalonica had knowledge that the word of God was preached of Paul at Berea, they came there and moved the people. And then by and by the brethren sent away Paul to go as it were to the sea: but Silas and Timotheus abode there

★ Search the scriptures, for by them may ye try all doctrine.

still. And they that guided Paul, brought him unto Athens, and received a commandment unto Silas and Timotheus for to come to him at once, and came their way.

Athens.

While Paul waited for them at Athens, his spirit was moved in him, to see the city given to worshipping of images. Then he disputed in the synagogue **D** with the Jews, and with the devout persons, and in the market daily with them that came unto him. Certain philosophers of the Epicures and of the Stoics, disputed with him. And some there were which said: what will this babbler say? Other said: he seemeth to be a tidings-bringer of new devils, because he preached unto them Jesus and the resurrection. And they took him, and **E** brought him into Mars street saying: may we not know what this new doctrine whereof thou speakest, is? For thou bringest strange tidings to our ears. We would know therefore what these things mean. For all the Athenians and strangers which were there, gave themselves to nothing else, but either to tell or to hear new tidings.

Paul stood in the midst of Mars street and said: ye men of Athens, I perceive **F** that in all things ye are too superstitious. For as I passed by and beheld the manner how ye worship your gods, I found an altar wherein was written: unto the unknown god. Whom ye then ignorantly worship, him shew I unto you.

Unknown God.

God dwelleth not in the temple.

God that made the world and all that are in it, seeing that he is Lord of heaven and earth, he dwelleth not in temples made with hands, neither is worshipped with men's hands, as though he needed of any thing, seeing he himself giveth life and breath to all men everywhere, and hath made of one blood all nations of men, for to dwell on all the face of the earth, and hath assigned, before how long time, and also the ends of their inhabitation, that they should seek God, if they might feel and find him, though he be not far from every one of us. For in him we live, move and have our being, as certain of your own poets said. For we are also his generation. Forasmuch then as we are the generation of God, we ought not to think that the godhead is like unto gold, silver or stone, graven by craft and imagination of man.

And the time of this ignorance God regarded not: but now he biddeth all **G** men everywhere repent, because he hath appointed a day, in the which he will judge the world according to righteousness, by that man whom he hath appointed, and hath offered faith* to all men, after that he had raised him from death.

* Faith is here taken for the promises of mercy which through faith save us: which promises after the resurrection of Christ God commanded to be preached unto all nations and not to the Jews only, as before.

Dionysius.
Damaris.

When they heard of the resurrection from death, some mocked, and other said: we will hear thee again of this matter. So Paul departed from among them. Howbeit certain men clave unto Paul and believed, among the which was Dionysius a senator, and a woman named Damaris, and other with them.

CHAPTER EIGHTEEN

Corinth.

After that, Paul departed from Athens, and came to Corinth, and found a **A** certain Jew named Aquila, born in Pontus, lately come from Italy with his wife Priscilla (because that the Emperor Claudius had commanded all Jews to

depart from Rome) and he drew unto them. And because he was of the same
craft, he abode with them and wrought: their craft was to make tents. And he
preached in the synagogue every sabbath day, and exhorted the Jews and the
gentiles.

Tents.

B When Silas and Timotheus were come from Macedonia, Paul was constrained by the spirit to testify to the Jews that Jesus was very Christ. And
when they said contrary and blasphemed, he shook his raiment and said unto
them: your blood upon your own heads, and from henceforth I go blameless
unto the gentiles. And he departed thence, and entered into a certain man's
house named Justus a worshipper of God, whose house joined hard to the
synagogue. Howbeit one Crispus the chief ruler of the synagogue believed on
the Lord with all his household, and many of the Corinthians gave audience
and believed and were baptised.

Shook his raiment.

C Then spake the Lord to Paul in the night by a vision: be not afraid, but speak,
and hold not thy peace: for I am with thee, and no man shall invade thee that
shall hurt thee. For I have much people in this city. And he continued there a
year and six months, and taught them the word of God.

When Gallio was ruler of the country of Achaia, the Jews made insurrection
with one accord against Paul, and brought him to the judgement seat saying:
D this fellow counselleth men to worship God contrary to the law. And as Paul
was about to open his mouth, Gallio said unto the Jews: if it were a matter of
wrong, or an evil deed (o ye Jews) reason would that I should hear you: but if it
be a question of words, or of names, or of your law, look ye to it yourselves.
For I will be no judge in such matters, and he drave them from the seat. Then
took all the Greeks Sosthenes the chief ruler of the synagogue and smote him
before the judge's seat. And Gallio cared for none of those things.

E Paul after this, tarried there yet a good while, and then took his leave of the
brethren, and sailed thence into Syria, Priscilla and Aquila accompanying him.
And he shore his head in Cenchrea, for he had a vow. And he came to Ephesus
and left them there: but he himself entered into the synagogue, and reasoned
with the Jews. When they desired him to tarry longer time with them, he
consented not, but bade them farewell saying: I must needs at this feast that
cometh, be in Jerusalem; but I will return again unto you if God will. And he
departed from Ephesus and came unto Ceasarea: and ascended and saluted the
congregation, and departed unto Antioch, and when he had tarried there a
while, he departed. And went over all the country of Galatia and Phrygia by
order, strengthening all the disciples.

Ephesus.

Here went Paul to
Jerusalem.

And a certain Jew named Apollos, born at Alexandria, came to Ephesus, an
eloquent man, and mighty in the scriptures. The same was informed in the way
F of the Lord, and he spake fervently in the spirit, and taught diligently the things
of the Lord, and knew but the baptism of John only. And the same began to
speak boldly in the synagogue. And when Aquila and Priscilla had heard him:
they took him unto them, and expounded unto him the way of God more
perfectly.

Apollos.

And when he was disposed to go into Achaia, the brethren wrote exhorting the disciples to receive him. After he was come thither, he holp them much which had believed through grace. And mightily he overcame the Jews, and that openly, shewing by the scriptures that Jesus was Christ.

CHAPTER NINETEEN

+ It fortuned, while Apollo was at Corinthum, that Paul passed through the upper coasts and came to Ephesus, and found certain disciples and said unto them: have ye received the holy ghost since ye believed? And they said unto him: no we have not heard whether there be any holy ghost or no. And he said unto them: wherewith were ye then baptised? And they said: with John's baptism. Then said Paul: John verily baptised with the baptism of repentance, saying unto the people that they should believe on him which should come after him: that is on Christ Jesus. When they heard that, they were baptised in the name of the Lord Jesus. And Paul laid his hands upon them, and the holy ghost came on them, and they spake with tongues, and prophesied, and all the men were about twelve. ⊢

And he went into the synagogue, and behaved himself boldly for the space of three months, disputing and giving them exhortations of the kingdom of God. + When divers waxed hard-hearted and believed not, but spake evil of the way, and that before the multitude: he departed from them, and separated the disciples. And disputed daily in the school of one called Tyrannus. And this continued by the space of two years: so that all they which dwelt in Asia, heard the word of the Lord Jesus, both Jews and Greeks. And God wrought no small miracles by the hands of Paul: so that from his body, were brought unto the sick, napkins or partlets, and the diseases departed from them, and the evil spirits went out of them.

Then certain of the vagabond Jews, exorcists, took upon them to call over them which had evil spirits, the name of the Lord Jesus saying: We adjure you by Jesus whom Paul preacheth. And there were seven sons of one Sceva a Jew and chief of the priests which did so. And the evil spirit answered and said: Jesus I know, and Paul I know: but who are ye? And the man in whom the evil spirit was, ran on them, and overcame them, and prevailed against them, so that they fled out of that house naked and wounded. And this was known to all the Jews and Greeks also, which dwelt at Ephesus, and fear came on them all, and they magnified the name of the Lord Jesus.

And many that believed, came and confessed and shewed their works. Many of them which used curious crafts, brought their books and burned them before all men, and they counted the price of them and found it fifty thousand silverlings★. So mightily grew the word of God, and prevailed. After these things were ended, Paul purposed in the spirit, to pass over Macedonia and Achaia, and to go to Jerusalem saying: After I have been there, I must also see Rome. So sent he into Macedonia two of them that ministered unto him, Timotheus and Erastus: but he himself remained in Asia for a season.

The same time there arose no little ado about that way. For a certain man

Ephesus.

Matt. 3. c.

Laying on of hands.

Napkin.

Partlet.

★ These silverlings which we now and then call pence the Jews call sickles, and are worth ten pence sterling.

A

B

C

D

E

192

named Demetrius, a silversmith, which made silver shrines for Diana, was   Demetrius.
not a little beneficial unto the craftsmen. Which he called together with the
workmen of like occupation, and said: Sirs, ye know that by this craft we
have vantage. Moreover ye see and hear that not alone at Ephesus, but almost
throughout all Asia, this Paul hath persuaded and turned away much people,
saying that they be not gods which are made with hands. So that not only this
our craft cometh into peril to be set at nought: but also that the temple of the
great goddess Diana should be despised, and her magnificence should be
destroyed which all Asia, and the world worshippeth.

    When they heard these sayings, they were full of wrath, and cried out saying:
F Great is Diana of the Ephesians. And all the city was on a roar, and they rushed
into the common hall with one assent, and caught Gaius and Aristarchus, men
of Macedonia, Paul's companions. When Paul would have entered in unto the
people, the disciples suffered him not. Certain also of the chief of Asia which
were his friends, sent unto him, desiring him that he would not press into the
common hall. Some cried one thing and some another, and the congregation
was all out of quiet, and the more part knew not wherefore they were come
together.

G   Some of the company drew forth Alexander, the Jews thrusting him forwards. Alexander beckoned with the hand, and would have given the people
an answer. When they knew that he was a Jew, there arose a shout almost for
the space of two hours, of all men crying, great is Diana of the Ephesians.

    When the town clerk had ceased the people, he said: ye men of Ephesus,
what man is it that knoweth not how that the city of the Ephesians is a worshipper of the great goddess Diana, and of the image which came from heaven.
Seeing then that no man saith here against, ye ought to be content, and to do
nothing rashly: For ye have brought hither these men which are neither robbers
of churches, nor yet despisers of your goddess. Wherefore if Demetrius and the
craftsmen which are with him, have any saying to any man, the law is open,
and there are rulers, let them accuse one another. If ye go about any other
thing, it may be determined in a lawful congregation. For we are in jeopardy to
be accused of this day's business: forasmuch as there is no cause whereby we
may give a reckoning of this concourse of people. And when he had thus
spoken, he let the congregation depart.

CHAPTER TWENTY

A After the rage was ceased, Paul called the disciples unto him, and took his leave
of them, and departed for to go into Macedonia. And when he had gone over
those parts, and given them large exhortations, he came into Greece, and there
abode three months. And when the Jews laid wait for him as he was about to
sail into Syria, he purposed to return through Macedonia.

    There accompanied him into Asia, Sopater of Berea, and of Thessalonica
Aristarchus and Secundus, and Gaius of Derbe, and Timotheus: and out of Asia
Tychicus and Trophimus. These went before, and tarried us at Troas. And we

sailed away from Philippi after the Easter holy days, and came unto them to Troas in five days, where we abode seven days.

And on the morrow after the sabbath day the disciples came together for **B** to break bread and Paul preached unto them (ready to depart on the morrow) and continued the preaching unto midnight. And there were many lights in the chamber where they were gathered together, and there sat in a window

Eutychus.

a certain young man named Eutychus, fallen into a deep sleep. And as Paul declared, he was the more overcome with sleep, and fell down from the third loft, and was taken up dead. Paul went down and fell on him, and embraced him, and said: make nothing ado, for his life is in him. When he was come up again, he brake bread, and tasted, and communed a long while even till the **C** morning, and so departed. And they brought the young man alive, and were not a little comforted.

And we went afore to ship and loosed unto Assos, there to receive Paul. For so had he appointed, and would himself go afoot. When he was come to us unto Assos, we took him in, and came to Mitylene. And we sailed thence, and came the next day over against Chios. And the next day we arrived at Samos, and tarried at Trogyllium. The next day we came to Myletus: for Paul had determined to leave Ephesus as they sailed, because he would not spend the time in Asia. For he hasted to be (if he could possibly) at Jerusalem at the day of Pentecost. Wherefore from Myletus he sent to Ephesus, and called the elders of the congregation. And when they were come to him, he said unto them: Ye **D**

The sermon of Paul to the Ephesians.

know from the first day that I came unto Asia, after what manner I have been with you at all seasons, serving the Lord with all humbleness of mind, and with many tears, and temptations which happened unto me by the laying-wait of the Jews, and how I kept back nothing that was profitable: but that I have showed you and taught you openly and at home in your houses, witnessing both to the Jews, and also to the Greeks, the repentance toward God, and faith

Repentance and faith.

toward our Lord Jesus.

And now behold I go bound in the spirit unto Jerusalem, and know not what **E** shall come on me there, but that the holy ghost witnessth in every city saying: that bonds and trouble abide me. But none of those things move me: neither is my life dear unto myself, that I might fulfil my course with joy, and the ministration which I have received of the Lord Jesus, to testify the gospel of the grace of God.

And now behold, I am sure that henceforth ye all (through whom I have **F** gone preaching the kingdom of God) shall see my face no more. Wherefore I take you to record this same day, that I am pure from the blood of all men. For I have kept nothing back: but have shewed you all the counsel of God. Take heed therefore unto yourselves, and to all the flock, whereof the holy ghost hath made you overseers, to rule the congregation of God, which he hath purchased with his blood. For I am sure of this, that after my departing shall

Grievous wolves.

grievous wolves enter in among you, which will not spare the flock. Moreover of your own selves shall men arise speaking perverse things, to draw disciples after them. Therefore awake and remember, that by the space of three years I ceased not to warn every one of you, both night and day with tears.

G   And now brethren I commend you to God and to the word of his grace, which is able to build further, and to give you an inheritance among all them which are sanctified. I have desired no man's silver, gold, or vesture. Ye know well that these hands have ministered unto my necessities, and to them that were with me. I have shewed you all things, how that so labouring ye ought to receive the weak, and to remember the words of the Lord Jesus, how that he said: It is more blessed to give, than to receive.

When he had thus spoken, he kneeled down, and prayed with them all. And they wept all abundantly, and fell on Paul's neck, and kissed him, sorrowing most of all for the words which he spake, that they should see his face no more. And they accompanied him unto the ship.

1 Cor. 4.
1 Thess. 2. b.
2 Thess. 3.

CHAPTER TWENTY-ONE

A   And it chanced that as soon as we had launched forth, and were departed from them, we came with a straight course unto Coos, and the day following unto the Rhodes, and from thence unto Patara. And we found a ship ready to sail unto Phenicia, and went aboard and set forth. Then appeared unto us Cyprus, and we left it on the left hand, and sailed unto Syria, and came unto Tyre. For there the ship unladed her burden. And when we had found brethren, we tarried there seven days. And they told Paul through the spirit, that he should not go up to Jerusalem. And when the days were ended, we departed and went our ways, and they all brought us on our way, with their wives and children, till we were come out of the city. And we kneeled down in the shore and prayed. And when we had taken our leave one of another, we took ship, and they returned home again.

B   When we had full ended the course from Tyre, we arrived at Ptolemais, and saluted the brethren, and abode with them one day. The next day, we that were of Paul's company, departed and came unto Caesarea. And we entered into the house of Philip the evangelist, which was one of the seven deacons, and abode with him. The same man had four daughters, virgins, which did prophesy. And as we tarried there a good many days, there came a certain prophet from Jewry, named Agabus. When he was come unto us, he took Paul's girdle, and bound his hands and feet, and said: thus saith the holy ghost: so shall the Jews at Jerusalem bind the man that owneth this girdle, and shall deliver him into the hands of the gentiles.

Philip.

Agabus.

C   When we heard this, both we and other of the same place, besought him, that he would not go up to Jerusalem. Then Paul answered and said: what do ye weeping and breaking mine heart? I am ready not to be bound only, but also to die at Jerusalem for the name of the Lord Jesus. When we could not turn his mind, we ceased, saying: the will of the Lord be fulfilled. After those days we made ourselves ready, and went up to Jerusalem. There went with us also certain of his disciples of Caesarea, and brought with them one Mnason of Cyprus, an old disciple with whom we should lodge. And when we were come to Jerusalem, the brethren received us gladly. And on the morrow Paul went in with us unto James. And all the elders came together. And when he had saluted

them, he told by order all things that God had wrought among the gentiles by   **D**
his ministration. And when they heard it, they glorified the Lord, and said unto
him: thou seest brother, how many thousand Jews there are which believe,
and they are all zealous over the law. And they are informed of thee, that
thou teachest all the Jews which are among the gentiles, to forsake Moses, and
sayest that they ought not to circumcise their children, neither to live after the
customs. What is it therefore? The multitude must needs come together. For
they shall hear that thou art come. Do therefore this that we say to thee.

Num. 6.

We have four men, which have a vow on them. Them take, and purify   **E**
thyself with them, and do cost on them, that they may shave their heads, and
all shall know that those things which they have heard concerning thee, are
nothing: but that thou thyself also walkest and keepest the law. For as touching
the gentiles which believe, we have written and concluded, that they observe
no such things: but that they keep themselves from things offered to idols,
from blood, from strangled and from fornication. Then the next day Paul
took the men, and purified himself with them, and entered into the temple,
declaring that he observed the days of the purification, until that an offering
should be offered for every one of them.

And as the seven days should have been ended, the Jews which were of Asia
when they saw him in the temple, they moved all the people, and laid hands on
him crying: men of Israel help. This is the man that teacheth all men every
where against the people, and the law, and this place. Moreover also he hath
brought Greeks into the temple, and hath polluted this holy place. For they saw
one Trophimus an Ephesian with him in the city. Him they supposed Paul had
brought into the temple. And all the city was moved, and the people swarmed
together. And they took Paul and drew him out of the temple, and forthwith
the doors were shut to.

As they went about to kill him, tidings came unto the high captain of the   **F**
soldiers, that all Jerusalem was moved. Which immediately took soldiers and
undercaptains, and ran down unto them. When they saw the uppercaptain and
the soldiers, they left smiting of Paul. Then the captain came near and took
him, and commanded him to be bound with two chains, and demanded what
he was, and what he had done. And one cried this, another that among the
people. And when he could not know the certainty for the rage, he commanded him to be carried into the castle. And when he came unto a grece, it
fortuned that he was borne of the soldiers of the violence of the people. For the
multitude of the people followed after crying: away with him.

And as Paul should have been carried into the castle, he said unto the high   **G**
captain: may I speak unto thee? Which said: canst thou speak Greek? Art not
thou that Egyptian which before these days made an uproar and led out into the
wilderness four thousand men that were murderers? But Paul said: I am a man
which am a Jew of Tarsus a city in Cilicia a citizen of no vile city: I beseech thee
suffer me to speak unto the people. When he had given him licence, Paul stood
on the steps and beckoned with the hand unto the people, and there was made a
great silence. And he spake unto them in the Hebrew tongue saying:

A   Ye men, brethren and fathers, hear mine answer which I make unto you. When they heard that he spake in the Hebrew tongue to them, they kept the more silence. And he said: I am verily a man which am a Jew, born in Tarsus, a city in Cilicia: nevertheless yet brought up in this city, at the feet of Gamaliel and informed diligently in the law of the fathers, and was fervent-minded to God-ward, as ye all are this same day, and I persecuted this way unto the death, binding and delivering into prison both men and women, as the chief priest doth bear me witness, and all the elders: of whom also I received letters unto the brethren, and went to Damascus to bring them which were there, bound unto Jerusalem for to be punished.

B   And it fortuned, as I made my journey and was come nigh unto Damascus about noon, that suddenly there shone from heaven a great light round about me, and I fell unto the earth, and heard a voice saying unto me: Saul, Saul, why persecutest thou me? And I answered: what art thou Lord? And he said unto me: I am Jesus of Nazareth, whom thou persecutest. And they that were with me, saw verily a light and were afraid: but they heard not the voice of him that spake with me. And I said: what shall I do Lord? And the Lord said unto me: Arise and go into Damascus and there it shall be told thee of all things which are appointed for thee to do. And when I saw nothing for the brightness of that light, I was led by the hand of them that were with me, and came into Damascus.

C   And one Ananias, a perfect man, and as pertaining to the law, having good report of all the Jews which there dwelt, came unto me, and stood and said unto me: Brother Saul, look up. And that same hour I received my sight and saw him. And he said, the God of our fathers hath ordained thee before, that thou shouldest know his will, and shouldest see that which is rightful, and shouldest hear the voice of his mouth: for thou shalt be his witness unto all men of those things which thou hast seen and heard. And now: why tarriest thou? Baptism. Arise and be baptised, and wash away thy sins, in calling on the name of the Lord.

D   And it fortuned, when I was come again to Jerusalem and prayed in the temple, that I was in a trance, and saw him saying unto me: Make haste, and get thee quickly out of Jerusalem: for they will not receive thy witness that thou bearest of me. And I said: Lord they know that I prisoned, and beat in every synagogue them that believed on thee. And when the blood of thy witness Stephen was shed, I also stood by, and consented unto his death, and kept the raiment of them that slew him. And he said unto me: depart, for I will send thee afar hence unto the gentiles.

E   They gave him audience unto this word, and then lifted up their voices and said: away with such a fellow from the earth: it is pity that he should live. And as they cried and cast off their clothes, and threw dust into the air, the captain bade him to be brought into the castle, and commanded him to be scourged, and to be examined, that he might know wherefore they cried on him. And as they bound him with thongs, Paul said unto the centurion that stood by: Is it lawful for you to scourge a man that is a Roman and uncondemned? When the centurion heard that, he went, and told the uppercaptain saying: What intendest thou to do? This man is a Roman.

Then the uppercaptain came, and said to him: tell me, art thou a Roman? He **F** said: Yea. And the captain answered: with a great sum obtained I this freedom. And Paul said: I was free born. Then straightway departed from him, they which should have examined him. And the high captain also was afraid, after he knew that he was a Roman: because he had bound him. **G**

On the morrow because he would have known the certainty wherefore he was accused of the Jews, he loosed him from his bonds, and commanded the high priests and all the council to come together, and brought Paul, and set him before them.

CHAPTER TWENTY-THREE

Paul beheld the council and said: men and brethren, I have lived in all good **A** conscience before God until this day. The high priest Ananias commanded them that stood by to smite him on the mouth. Then said Paul to him: God smite thee, thou painted wall. Sittest thou and judgest me after the law? and commandest me to be smitten contrary to the law? And they that stood by, said: revilest thou God's high priest? Then said Paul: I wist not brethren, that he was the high priest. For it is written, thou shalt not curse the ruler of thy people.

Exod. 22.

Sadducees.

When Paul perceived that the one part were Sadducees, and the other **B** Pharisees: he cried out in the council, Men and brethren, I am a Pharisee, the son of a Pharisee. Of the hope, and resurrection from death, I am judged. And when he had so said, there arose a debate between the Pharisees and the Sadducees, and the multitude was divided. For the Sadducees say that there is no resurrection, neither angel, nor spirit. But the Pharisees grant both. And there arose a great cry, and the scribes which were of the Pharisees' part, arose and strove saying: we find none evil in this man. Though a spirit or an angel hath appeared to him, let us not strive against God.

Pharisees.
Phil. 3. b.

Matt. 22.

And when there arose great debate, the captain fearing lest Paul should have **C** been plucked asunder of them, commanded the soldiers to go down, and to take him from among them, and to bring him into the castle. The night following, God stood by him and said: Be of good cheer Paul: for as thou hast testified of me in Jerusalem, so must thou bear witness at Rome.

When day was come, certain of the Jews gathered themselves together, and **D** made a vow, saying that they would neither eat nor drink till they had killed Paul. They were about forty which had made this conspiration. And they came to the chief priests and elders, and said: we have bound ourselves with a vow, that we will eat nothing until we have slain Paul. Now therefore give ye knowledge to the uppercaptain and to the council, that he bring him forth unto us tomorrow, as though we would know something more perfectly of him. But we (or ever he come near) are ready in the mean season to kill him.

When Paul's sister's son heard of their laying wait, he went and entered into the castle, and told Paul. And Paul called one of the undercaptains unto him, and said: bring this young man unto the high captain: for he hath a certain thing to show him. And he took him, and said: Paul the prisoner called me unto him and prayed me to bring this young man unto thee, which hath a certain matter to show thee.

The high captain took him by the hand, and went apart with him out of the way: and asked him: what hast thou to say unto me? And he said: the Jews are determined to desire thee that thou wouldest bring forth Paul tomorrow into the council, as though they would enquire somewhat of him more perfectly. But follow not their minds: for there lie in wait for him of them, more than forty men, which have bound themselves with a vow, that they will neither eat nor drink till they have killed him. And now are they ready, and look for thy promise.

The uppercaptain let the young man depart and charged: see thou tell it out to no man that thou hast showed these things to me. And he called unto him two undercaptains, saying: make ready two hundred soldiers to go to Caesarea, and horsemen threescore and ten, and spearmen two hundred, at the third hour of the night. And deliver them beasts that they may put Paul on, and bring him safe unto Felix the high debite, and wrote a letter in this manner:

Claudius Lysias unto the most mighty ruler Felix, sendeth greetings. This man was taken of the Jews, and should have been killed of them. Then came I with soldiers, and rescued him, and perceived that he was a Roman. And when I would have known the cause, wherefore they accused him, I brought him forth into their council. There perceived I that he was accused of questions of their law: but was not guilty of any thing worthy of death or of bonds. Afterward when it was showed me how that the Jews laid wait for the man, I sent him straightway to thee, and gave commandment to his accusers, if they had ought against him, to tell it unto thee: farewell.

Then the soldiers as it was commanded them, took Paul, and brought him by night to Antipatris. On the morrow they left horsemen to go with him, and returned unto the castle. Which when they came to Caesarea, they delivered the epistle to the debite, and presented Paul before him. When the debite had read the letter, he asked of what country he was, and when he understood that he was of Cilicia, I will hear thee (said he) when thine accusers are come also: and commanded him to be kept in Herod's palace.

CHAPTER TWENTY-FOUR

After five days, Ananias the high priest descended, with elders and with a certain orator named Tertullus, and informed the ruler of Paul. When Paul was called forth, Tertullus began to accuse him saying: Seeing that we live in great

quietness by the means of thee, and that many good things are done unto this
nation through thy providence: that allow we, ever and in all places, most
mighty Felix with all thanks. Notwithstanding, that I be not tedious unto thee,
I pray thee, that thou wouldest hear us of thy courtesy a few words.

We have found this man a pestilent fellow, and a mover of debate unto all the   B
Jews throughout the world, and a maintainer of the sect of the Nazarites, and
hath also enforced to pollute the temple. Whom we took and would have
judged according to our law: but the high captain Lysias came upon us, and
with great violence took him away out of our hands, commanding his accusers
to come unto thee. Of whom thou mayest (if thou wilt enquire) know the
certain of all these things whereof we accuse him. The Jews likewise affirmed,
saying that it was even so.

Then Paul (after that the ruler himself had beckoned unto him that he should   C
speak) answered: I shall with a more quiet mind answer for myself, forasmuch
as I understand that thou hast been of many years a judge unto this people,
because that thou mayest know that there are yet twelve days since I went up to
Jerusalem for to pray, and that they neither found me in the temple disputing
with any man, or raising up the people, neither in the synagogues, nor in the
city. Neither can they prove the things whereof they accuse me.

But this I confess unto thee, that after that way (which they call heresy) so
worship I the God of my fathers, believing all things which are written in the
law and the prophets, and have hope towards God, that the same resurrection
from death (which they themselves look for also) shall be, both of just and
unjust. And therefore study I to have a clear conscience toward God, and
toward man also.

But after many years I came and brought alms to my people and offerings, in   E
the which they found me purified in the temple, neither with multitude, nor
yet with unquietness. Howbeit there were certain Jews out of Asia which
ought to be here present before thee, and accuse me, if they had ought against
me: or else let these same here say, if they have found any evil doing in me,
while I stand here in the council: except it be for this one voice, that I cried
standing among them, of the resurrection from death am I judged of you this
day.

When Felix heard these things he deferred them, for he knew very well of   F
that way and said: when Lysias the captain is come, I will know the utmost of
your matters. And he commanded an undercaptain to keep Paul, and that he
should have rest, and that he should forbid none of his aquaintance to minister
unto him, or to come unto him.

And after a certain days, came Felix and his wife Drusilla which was a   C
Jewess, and called forth Paul, and heard him of the faith which is toward
Christ. And as he preached of righteousness, temperance and judgement to
come, Felix trembled and answered: thou hast done enough at this time,
depart, when I have a convenient time, I will send for thee. He hoped also that
money should have been given him of Paul, that he might loose him: wherefore he called him the oftener and communed with him. But after two years,

Festus Porcius came into Felix' room. And Felix willing to show the Jews a pleasure, left Paul in prison bound.

CHAPTER TWENTY-FIVE

A When Festus was come into the province, after three days, he ascended from Caesarea unto Jerusalem. Then informed him the high priests and the chief of the Jews of Paul. And they besought him, and desired favour against him, that he would send for him to Jerusalem: and laid wait for him in the way to kill him. Festus answered, that Paul should be kept at Caesarea: but that he himself would shortly depart thither. Let them therefore (said he) which among you are able to do it, come down with us and accuse him, if there be any fault in the man.

B When he had tarried there more then ten days, he departed unto Caesarea, and the next day sat down in the judgement seat, and commanded Paul to be brought. When he was come, the Jews which were come from Jerusalem, came about him and laid many and grievous complaints against Paul, which they could not prove as long as he answered for himself, that he had neither against the law of the Jews, neither against the temple, nor yet against Caesar offended any thing at all.

C Festus, willing to do the Jews a pleasure, answered Paul and said: wilt thou go to Jerusalem, and there be judged of these things before me? Then said Paul: I stand at Caesar's judgement seat, where I ought to be judged. To the Jews have I no harm done, as thou verily well knowest. If I have hurt them, or committed any thing worthy of death, I refuse not to die. If none of these things are, whereof they accuse me, no man ought to deliver me to them. I appeal unto Caesar. Then spake Festus with deliberation, and answered: Thou hast appealed unto Caesar: unto Caesar shalt thou go.

D After a certain days, king Agrippa and Bernice came unto Caesarea to salute Festus. And when they had been there a good season, Festus rehearsed Paul's cause unto the king saying: there is a certain man left in prison of Felix, about whom when I came to Jerusalem, the high priests and elders of the Jews informed me, and desired to have judgement against him. To whom I answered: It is not the manner of the Romans to deliver any man, that he should perish, before that he which is accused, have the accusers before him, and have licence to answer for himself, concerning the crime laid against him:

E when they were come hither, without delay on the morrow I sat to give judgement, and commanded the man to be brought forth. Against whom when the accusers stood up, they brought none accusation of such things as I supposed: but had certain questions against him of their own superstition, and of one Jesus which was dead: whom Paul affirmed to be alive. And because I doubted of such manner questions, I asked him whether he would go to Jerusalem, and there be judged of these matters. Then when Paul had appealed to be kept unto the knowledge of Caesar, I commanded him to be kept, till I might send him to Caesar.

Festus.
Porcius.

Paul appealed.

Agrippa.

Agrippa said unto Festus: I would also hear the man myself. To morrow   F
(said he) thou shalt hear him. And on the morrow when Agrippa was come and
Bernice with great pomp, and were entered into the council-house with the
captains and chief men of the city, at Festus' commandment Paul was brought
forth. And Festus said: king Agrippa, and all men which are here present
with us: ye see this man about whom all the multitude of the Jews have been
with me, both at Jerusalem and also here, crying that he ought not to live
any longer. Yet found I nothing worthy of death that he had committed.   G
Nevertheless seeing that he hath appealed to Caesar, I have determined to send
him. Of whom I have no certain thing to write unto my lord. Wherefore I
have brought him unto you, and specially unto thee, king Agrippa, that after
examination had, I might have somewhat to write. For me thinketh it unreasonable, for to send a prisoner, and not to show the causes which are laid
against him.

CHAPTER TWENTY-SIX

Agrippa said unto Paul: thou art permitted to speak for thyself. Then Paul   A
stretched forth the hand, and answered for himself. I think myself happy king
Agrippa, because I shall answer this day before thee, of all the things whereof I
am accused of the Jews, namely because thou art expert in all customs and
questions, which are among the Jews. Wherefore I beseech thee to hear me
patiently.

My living of a child, which was at the first among mine own nation at   B
Jerusalem, know all the Jews which knew me from the beginning, if they
would testify it. For after the most straitest sect of our lay, lived I a Pharisee.
And now I stand and am judged for the hope of the promise made of God unto
our fathers: unto which promise, our twelve tribes instantly serving God day
and night, hope to come. For which hope's sake, king Agrippa, am I accused of
the Jews. Why should it be thought a thing incredible unto you, that God
should raise again the dead?

I also verily thought in myself, that I ought to do many contrary things,   C
clean against the name of Jesus of Nazareth: which things I also did in Jerusalem:
Where many of the saints I shut up in prison, and had received authority of the
high priests. And when they were put to death, I gave the sentence. And I
punished them oft in every synagogue, and compelled them to blaspheme: and
was yet more mad upon them, and persecuted them, even unto strange cities.
About the which things as I went to Damascus with authority and licence of
the high priests, even at midday (o king) I saw in the way a light from heaven,
above the brightness of the sun, shine round about me and them, which
journeyed with me.

When we were all fallen to the earth, I heard a voice speaking unto me, and   D
saying in the Hebrew tongue: Saul, Saul, why persecutest thou me? It is hard
for thee to kick against the pricks. And I said: Who art thou lord? And he said I
am Jesus whom thou persecutest. But rise and stand up on thy feet. For I have

appeared unto thee for this purpose, to make thee a minister and a witness, both of those things which thou hast seen, and of those things in thee which I will appear unto thee, delivering thee from the people, and from the gentiles unto which now I send thee, to open their eyes that they might turn from darkness unto light, and from the power of Satan unto God, that they may receive forgiveness of sins and inheritance among them which are sanctified by faith in me.

Faith.

E Wherefore king Agrippa, I was not disobedient unto the heavenly vision: but showed first unto them of Damascus, and at Jerusalem, and throughout all the coasts of Jewry, and to the gentiles, that they should repent, and turn to God, and do the right works of repentance. For this cause the Jews caught me in the temple, and went about to kill me. Nevertheless I obtained help of God, and

F continue unto this day witnessing both to small and to great saying none other things, than those which the prophets and Moses did say should come, that Christ should suffer, and that he should be the first that should rise from death, and should show light unto the poeple, and the gentiles.

As he thus answered for himself: Festus said with a loud voice: Paul, thou art besides thyself. Much learning hath made thee mad. And Paul said: I am not mad most dear Festus: but speak the words of truth and soberness. The king knoweth of these things, before whom I speak freely: neither think I that any of these things are hidden from him. For this thing was not done in a corner. King Agrippa believest thou the prophets? I wot well thou believest. Agrippa said unto Paul: Somewhat thou bringest me in mind for to become a Christian. And Paul said: I would to God that not only thou: but also all that hear me today, were, not somewhat only, but altogether such as I am, except these bonds. And when he had thus spoken, the king rose up, and the debite, and Bernice, and they that sat with them. And when they were gone apart, they talked between themselves saying: This man doth nothing worthy of death, nor of bonds. Then said Agrippa unto Festus: This man might have been loosed, if he had not appealed unto Caesar.

CHAPTER TWENTY-SEVEN

A When it was concluded that we should sail into Italy, they delivered Paul and certain other prisoners unto one named Julius, an undercaptain of Caesar's soldiers. And we entered into a ship of Adramyttium, and loosed from land, appointed to sail by the coasts of Asia, one Aristarchus out of Macedonia, of the country of Thessalonica, being with us. And the next day we came to Sidon. And Julius courteously entreated Paul, and gave him liberty to go unto his friends, and to refresh himself. And from thence launched we, and sailed hard by Cyprus, because the winds were contrary. Then sailed we over the sea of Cilicia, and Pamphylia, and came to Myra a city in Lycia.

2 Cor. 11.

B And there the undercaptain found a ship of Alexander ready to sail into Italy and put us therein. And when we had sailed slowly many days, and scarce were come over against Cnidus (because the wind withstood us) we sailed hard by

the coast of Candy, over against Salmone, and with much work sailed beyond
it, and came unto a place called Good Port. Nigh whereunto was a city called
Lasea. When much time was spent and sailing was now jeopardous, because
also that we had overlong fasted, Paul put them in remembrance, and said unto   C
them Sirs, I perceive that this voyage will be with hurt and much damage, not
of the lading and ship only: but also of our lives. Neverthelater the undercaptain believed the governor and the master, better than those things which
were spoken of Paul. And because the haven was not commodius to winter in,
many took counsel to depart thence, if by any means they might attain to
Phenice and there to winter, which is an haven of Candy, and serveth to the
southwest and northwest wind. When the south wind blew, they supposing to
obtain their purpose, loosed unto Asson, and sailed past all Candy.

But anon after, there arose against their purpose, a flaw of wind out of the   D
northeast. And when the ship was caught, and could not resist the wind, we let
her go and drave with the weather. And we came unto an isle named Clauda,
and had much work to come by a boat, which they took up and used help,
undergirding the ship, fearing lest we should have fallen into Syrtes, and we let
down a vessel and so were carried. The next day when we were tossed with an
exceeding tempest, they lightened the ship, and the third day we cast out with
our own hands, the tackling of the ship. When at the last neither sun nor star in
many days appeared, and no small tempest lay upon us, all hope that we should
be saved, was then taken away.

Then after long abstinence, Paul stood forth in the midst of them and said: E
Sirs ye should have hearkened to me, and not have loosed from Candy, neither
to have brought unto us this harm and loss. And now I exhort you to be of
good cheer. For there shall be no loss of any man's life among you, save of the
ship only. For there stood by me this night the angel of God, whose I am, and
whom I serve, saying; fear not Paul, for thou must be brought before Caesar.
And lo, God hath given unto thee all that sail with thee. Wherefore sirs be of
good cheer: for I believe God, that so it shall be even as it was told me.
Howbeit we must be cast into a certain island.

But when the fourteenth night was come, as we were carried in Adria about   F
midnight, the shipmen deemed that there appeared some country unto them:
and sounded, and found it twenty fathoms. And when they had gone a little
further, they sounded again, and found fifteen fathoms. Then fearing lest they
should have fallen on some rock, they cast four anchors out of the stern, and
wished for the day. As the shipmen were about to flee out of the ship, and had
let down the boat into the sea, under a colour as though they would have cast
anchors out of the foreship: Paul said unto the undercaptain and the soldiers:
except these abide in the ship, ye cannot be safe. Then the soldiers cut off the
rope of the boat, and let it fall away.

And in the meantime betwixt that and day Paul besought them all to take   G
meat, saying: this is the fourteenth day that ye have tarried and continued
fasting, receiving nothing at all. Wherefore I pray you to take meat: for this no
doubt is for your health: for there shall not an hair fall from the head of any of

you. And when he had thus spoken, he took bread and gave thanks to God in presence of them all, and brake it, and began to eat. Then were they all of good
G cheer, and they also took meat. We were altogether in the ship, two hundred three score and sixteen souls. And when they had eaten enough, they lightened the ship and cast out the wheat into the sea.

When it was day, they knew not the land but they spied a certain haven with a bank into the which they were minded (if it were possible) to thrust in the ship. And when they had taken up the anchors, they committed themselves unto the sea, and loosed the rudder bonds and hoised up the mainsail to the wind and drew to land. But they chanced on a place, which had the sea on both the sides, and thrust in the ship. And the fore part stuck fast and moved not, but the hinder brake with the violence of the waves.

The soldiers' counsel was to kill the prisoners, lest any of them, when he had swum out, should flee away. But the undercaptain, willing to save Paul, kept them from their purpose, and commanded that they that could swim, should cast themselves first in to the sea, and scape to land. And the other he commanded to go, some on boards, and some on broken pieces of the ship. And so it came to pass, that they came all safe to land.

CHAPTER TWENTY-EIGHT

A And when they were scaped, then they knew that the isle was called Mileta. And the people of the country shewed us no little kindness: for they kindled a fire and received us every one, because of the present rain, and because of cold. And when Paul had gathered a bundle of sticks, and put them into the fire, there came a viper out of the heat and leapt on his hand. When the men of the country saw the worm hang on his hand, they said among themselves: this man must needs be a murderer, whom (though he have escaped the sea) yet vengeance suffereth not to live. But he shook off the vermin into the fire, and felt no harm. Howbeit they waited when he should have swollen, or fallen down dead suddenly. But after they had looked a great while, and saw no harm come to him, they changed their minds, and said that he was a god.

B In the same quarters, the chief man of the isle whose name was Publius, had a lordship: the same received us, and lodged us three days courteously. And it fortuned that the father of Publius lay sick of a fever, and of a bloody flux. To whom Paul entered in and prayed, and laid his hand on him and healed him. When this was done, other also which had diseases in the isle, came and were healed. And they did us great honour. And when we departed, they laded us with things necessary.

Laying on of hands.

After three months we departed in a ship of Alexandria, which had wintred in the isle, whose badge was Castor and Pollux. And when we came to Syracuse, we tarried there three days. And from thence we fetched a compass and came to Rhegium. And after one day the south wind blew, and we came the next day to Puteoli: where we found brethren, and were desired to tarry with them seven days, and so came to Rome. And from thence, when the

brethren heard of us, they came against us to Appii forum, and to the three   **D**
taverns. When Paul saw them, he thanked God, and waxed bold. And when he
came to Rome, the undercaptain delivered the prisoners to the chief captain of
the host: but Paul was suffered to dwell by himself with one soldier that kept
him.

And it fortuned after three days, that Paul called the chief of the Jews
together. And when they were come, he said unto them: Men and brethren,   **E**
though I have committed nothing against the people or laws of our fathers: yet
was I delivered prisoner from Jerusalem into the hands of the Romans. Which
when they had examined me, would have let me go, because they found no
cause of death in me. But when the Jews cried contrary, I was constrained to
appeal unto Caesar: not because I had ought to accuse my people of. For this
cause have I called for you, even to see you and to speak with you: because that
for the hope of Israel, I am bound with this chain.

And they said unto him: We neither received letters out of Jewry pertaining
unto thee, neither came any of the brethren that showed or spake any harm   **F**
of thee. But we will hear of thee what thou thinkest. For we have heard of
this sect, that everywhere it is spoken against. And when they had appointed
him a day, there came many unto him into his lodging. To whom he
expounded and testified the kingdom of God, and preached unto them of
Jesus: both out of the law of Moses and also out of the prophets, even from
morning to night. And some believed the things which were spoken, and some
believed not.

When they agreed not among themselves, they departed, after that Paul had
spoken one word. Well spake the holy ghost by Esaias the prophet unto our
Isa. 6. c.
Matt. 13.
fathers, saying: Go unto this people and say: with your ears shall ye hear, and
shall not understand: and with your eyes shall ye see and shall not perceive.
Mark 4. b.
Luke 8. f.
John 12. f.
For the heart of this people is waxed gross, and their ears were thick of
Rom. 11. b.
hearing, and their eyes have they closed: lest they should see with their eyes,   **G**
and hear with their ears, and understand with their hearts, and should be converted, and I should heal them. Be it known therefore unto you, that this salvation of God is sent to the gentiles, and they shall hear it. And when he had said
that, the Jews departed, and had great despitions among themselves.

And Paul dwelt two years full in his lodging, and received all that came to
him, preaching the kingdom of God, and teaching those things which concerned the Lord Jesus, with all confidence, unforbidden.

Here endeth the Acts of the Apostles.

A PROLOGUE TO THE EPISTLE OF PAUL
TO THE ROMANS[†]

Forasmuch as this epistle is the principal and most excellent part of the new testament, and most pure evangelion, that is to say glad tidings and that we call gospel, and also a light and a way in unto the whole scripture, I think it meet, that every Christian man not only know it by rote and without the book, but also exercise himself therein evermore continually, as with the daily bread of the soul. No man verily can read it too oft or study it too well: for the more it is studied the easier it is, the more it is chewed the pleasanter it is, and the more groundly it is searched the preciouser things are found in it, so great treasure of spiritual things lieth hid therein.

I will therefore bestow my labour and diligence, through this little preface or prologue, to prepare a way in thereunto, so far forth as God shall give me grace, that it may be the better understood of every man, for it hath been hitherto evil darkened with glosses and wonderful dreams of sophisters, that no man could spy out the intent and meaning of it, which nevertheless of itself, is a bright light, and sufficient to give light unto all the scripture.

First we must mark diligently the manner of speaking of the apostle, and above all things know what Paul meaneth by these words, the law, sin, grace, faith, righteousness, flesh, spirit and such like, or else read thou it never so oft, thou shalt but lose thy labour. This word law may not be understood here after the common manner, and to use Paul's term, after the manner of men or after man's ways, that thou wouldest say the law here in this place were nothing but learning which teacheth what ought to be done and what ought not to be done, as it goeth with man's law where the law is fulfilled with outward works only, though the heart be never so far off. But God judgeth the ground of the heart, yea and the thoughts and the secret movings of the mind, and therefore his law requireth the ground of the heart and love from the bottom thereof, and is not content with the outward work only: but rebuketh those works most of all which spring not of love from the ground and low bottom of the heart, though they appear outward never so honest and good, as Christ in the gospel rebuketh the Pharisees above all other that were open sinners, and calleth them hypocrites, that is to say simulars, and painted sepulchres. Which Pharisees yet

How Paul useth certain words, must be diligently understood.

[†] This for the most part translates Luther's prologue. The last five paragraphs are Tyndale's.

lived no men so pure, as pertaining to the outward deeds and works of the law. Yea and Paul in the third chapter of his epistle unto the Philippians confesseth of himself, that as touching the law he was such a one as no man could complain on, and notwithstanding was yet a murderer of the Christians, persecuted them, and tormented them, so sore, that he compelled them to blaspheme Christ, and was altogether merciless, as many which now fain outward good work are.

For this cause the 116th Psalm calleth all men liars, because that no man keepeth the law from the ground of the heart, neither can keep it, though he appear outward full of good works.

For all men are naturally inclined unto evil and hate the law. We find in ourselves unlust and tediousness to do good, but lust and delectation to do evil. Now where no free lust is to do good, there the bottom of the heart fulfilleth not the law, and there no doubt is also sin, and wrath is deserved before God, though there be never so great an outward show and appearance of honest living.

For this cause concludeth saint Paul in the second chapter, that the Jews are all sinners and transgressors of the law, though they make men believe, through hypocrisy of outward works, how that they fulfil the law, and saith that he only which doeth the law, is righteous before God, meaning thereby that no man with outward works, fulfilleth the law.

Thou (saith he to the Jew) teachest, a man should not break wedlock, and yet breakest wedlock thyself. Wherein thou judgest another man, therein condemnest thou thyself, for thou thyself dost even the very same things which thou judgest. As though he would say, thou livest outwardly well in the works of the law, and judgest them that live not so.

Thou teachest other men: and seest a mote in another man's eye, but art not ware of the beam that is in thine own eye. For though thou keep the law outwardly with works for fear of rebuke, shame and punishment, other for love of reward, vantage and vainglory, yet dost thou all without lust and love toward the law, and hadst liefer a great deal otherwise do, if thou didest not fear the law. Yea, inwardly in thine heart, thou wouldest that there were no law, no nor yet God, the author and avenger of the law, if it were possible: so painful it is unto thee to have thine appetites refrained, and to be kept down.

Wherefore then it is a plain conclusion, that thou from the ground and bottom of thine heart, art an enemy to the law. What prevaileth it now, that thou teachest another man not to steal, when thou thine own self art a thief in thine heart, and outwardly would fain steal if thou durst? – though that the outward deeds abide not alway behind with such hypocrites and dissemblers, but break forth among, even as an evil scab or a pock cannot always be kept in with violence of medicine.

Thou teachest another man, but teachest not thyself, yea thou wotst not what thou teachest, for thou understandest not the law aright, how that it cannot be fulfilled and satisfied, but with an unfeigned love and affection, so greatly it cannot be fulfilled with outward deeds and works only. Moreover the law increaseth sin, as he saith in the fifth chapter, because that man is an enemy to the law, forasmuch as it requireth so many things clean contrary to his nature, whereof he is not able to fulfil one point or tittle, as the law requireth it. And therefore are we more provoked, and have greater lust to break it.

The law increaseth sin.

For which cause's sake he saith in the seventh chapter, that the law is spiritual: as though he would say, if the law were fleshly and but man's doctrine, it might be fulfilled, satisfied and stilled with outward deeds.

But now is the law ghostly, and no man fulfilleth it, except that all that he doth, spring of love from the bottom of the heart. Such a new heart and lusty courage unto the law-ward, canst thou never come by of the thine own strength and enforcement, but by the operation and working of the spirit.

The spirit is required, ere we can keep the law before God.

For the spirit of God only maketh a man spiritual and like unto the law, so that now henceforth he doth nothing of fear or for lucre or vantage's sake or of vainglory, but of a free heart, and of inward lust. The law is spiritual and will be both loved and fulfilled of a spiritual heart, and therefore of necessity requireth it the spirit that maketh a man's heart free, and giveth him lust and courage unto the law-ward. Where such a spirit is not, there remaineth sin, grudging and hatred against the law, which law nevertheless is good, righteous and holy.

Acquaint thyself therefore with the manner of speaking of the apostle, and let this now stick fast in thine heart, that it is not both one, to do the deeds and works of the law, and to fulfil the law. The work of the law is, whatsoever a man doth or can do of his own free will, of his own proper strength and enforcing, notwithstanding though there be never so great working, yet as long as there remaineth in the heart unlust, tediousness, grudging, grief, pain, loathsomeness, and compulsion toward the law, so long are all the works unprofitable, lost, yea and damnable in the sight of God. This meaneth Paul in the third chapter where he saith, by the deeds of the law shall no flesh be justified in the sight of God. Hereby perceivest thou, that those sophisters are but deceivers, which teach that a man may, and must prepare himself to grace and to the favour of God, with good works. How can they prepare themselves unto the favour of God, and to that which is good, when they themselves can do no good, no cannot once think a good thought or consent to do good, the devil possessing their hearts, minds and thoughts captive at his pleasure? Can those works please God, thinkest thou, which are done with grief, pain and tediousness, with an evil will, with a contrary and grudging mind?

To do the deeds of the law, and to fulfil the law, are two things.

O holy Saint Prosperus,[†] how mightily with the scripture of Paul, didst thou confound this heresy, about (I trow) a twelve hundred years ago, or thereupon.

Prosperus.

To fulfil the law is, to do the work thereof and whatsoever the law commandeth, with love, lust and inward affection and delectation: and to live godly and well, freely, willingly, and without compulsion of the law, even as

To fulfil the law, what it is.

[†] St Prosper of Aquitaine (c.390–c.463), influential in support for Augustine, against even a mild Pelagianism which allowed some place for human endeavour.

though there were no law at all. Such lust and free liberty to love the law, cometh only by the working of the spirit in the heart, as he saith in the first chapter.

The spirit cometh by faith.

Now is the spirit none otherwise given, than by faith only, in that we believe the promises of God, without wavering, how that God is true, and will fulfil all his good promises toward us, for Christ's blood's sake, as it is plain in the first chapter. I am not ashamed saith Paul, of Christ's glad tidings, for it is the power of God, unto salvation to as many as believe. For at once and together even as we believe the glad tidings preached to us, the holy ghost entereth into our hearts, and looseth the bonds of the devil, which before possessed our hearts in captivity, and held them that we could have no lust to the will of God in the law. And as the spirit cometh by faith only, even so faith cometh by hearing the word or glad tidings of God, when Christ is preached, how that he is God's son and man also, dead and risen again for our sakes, as he saith in the third, fourth and tenth chapters. All our justifying then cometh of faith, and faith and the spirit come of God and not of us.

Faith cometh by hearing the glad tidings.

Hereof cometh it, that faith only justifieth, maketh righteous, and fulfilleth the law, for it bringeth the spirit through Christ's deservings, the spirit bringeth lust, looseth the heart, maketh him free, setteth him at liberty, and giveth him strength to work the deeds of the law with love, even as the law requireth. Then at the last out of the same faith so working in the heart, spring all good works by their own accord. That meaneth he in the third chapter: for after he hath cast away the works of the law, so that he soundeth as though he would break and disannul the law through faith: he answereth to that might be laid against, saying: we destroy not the law through faith but maintain, further or establish the law through faith. That is to say, we fulfil the law through faith.

Faith only justifieth.

Works spring of faith.

Sin in the scripture is not called that outward work only committed by the body, but all the whole business and whatsoever accompanieth, moveth or strirreth unto the outward deed, and that whence the works spring: as unbelief, proneness and readiness unto the deed in the ground of the heart, with all the powers, affections and appetites wherewith we can but sin. So that we say, that a man then sinneth, when he is carried away headlong into sin, altogether as much as he is, of that poison inclination and corrupt nature wherein he was conceived and born. For there is none outward sin committed, except a man be carried away altogether, with life, soul, heart, body, lust and mind thereunto. The scripture looketh singularly unto the heart, and unto the root and original fountain of all sin, which is unbelief in the bottom of the heart. For as faith only justifieth and bringeth the spirit and lust unto the outward good works, even so unbelief only damneth and keepeth out the spirit, provoketh the flesh and stirreth up lust unto the evil outward works, as happened to Adam and Eve in Paradise (Gen. 3).

Sin.

Faith is the mother of all good works, and unbelief of evil.

For this cause Christ calleth sin unbelief, and that notably in the sixteenth chapter of John. The spirit, saith he, shall rebuke the world of sin, because they believe not in me. And (John 8) he saith: I am the light of the world.

And therefore in the twelfth of John he biddeth them, while they have light, to believe in the light, that ye may be the children of light: for he that walketh in darkness wotteth not whither he goeth. Now as Christ is the light, so is the ignorance of Christ that darkness whereof he speaketh, in which he that walketh wotteth not whither he goeth: that is, he knoweth not how to work a good work in the sight of God, or what a good work is. And therefore in the ninth he saith: as long as I am in the world, I am the light of the world: but there cometh night when no man can work. Which night is but the ignorance of Christ in which no man can see to do any work that pleaseth God. And Paul exhorteth (Eph. 4) that they walk not as other heathen which are strangers from the life of God, through the ignorance that is in them. And again in the same chapter, Put off (saith he) the old man which is corrupt through the lusts of error, that is to say ignorance. And (Rom. 13) Let us cast away the deeds of darkness: that is to say of ignorance and unbelief. And (1 Pet. 1) Fashion not yourselves unto your old lusts of ignorance. And (1 John 2) He that loveth his brother dwelleth in light: and he that hateth his brother walketh in darkness, and wotteth not whither he goeth, for darkness hath blinded his eyes. By light he meaneth the knowledge of Christ, and by darkness, the ignorance of Christ. For it is impossible that he that knoweth Christ truly, should hate his brother.

Furthermore, to perceive this thing more clearly, thou shalt understand, that it is impossible to sin any sin at all except a man break the first commandment before. Now is the first commandment divided into two verses. Thy Lord God is one God: and thou shalt love thy Lord God with all thine heart, with all thy soul, with all thy power and with all thy might. And the whole cause why I sin against any inferior precept, is that this love is not in mine heart: for were this law written in my heart and were full and perfect in my soul, it would keep mine heart from consenting unto any sin. And the whole and only cause why this love is written in our hearts, is that we believe not the first part, that our Lord God is one God. For wist I what these words, one Lord and one God meaneth: that is to say, if I understood that he made all, and ruleth all, and that whatsoever is done to me, whether it be good or bad, is yet his will, and that he only is the Lord that ruleth and doth it: and wist I thereto what this word mine meaneth, that is to say, if mine heart believed and felt the infinite benefits and kindness of God to me-ward, and understood and earnestly believed the manifold covenants of mercy wherewith God hath bound himself to be mine, wholly and altogether, with all his power, love, mercy and might, then should I love him with all mine heart, soul, power and might, and of that love ever keep his commandments. So see ye now that as faith is the mother of all goodness and of all good works, so is unbelief the ground and root of all evil and all evil works.

Finally, if any man hath forsaken sin and is converted to put his trust in Christ and to keep the law of God, doth fall at a time: the cause is, that the flesh through negligence hath choked the spirit and oppressed her and taken from her the food of her strength. Which food is her meditation in God and in his wonderful deeds, and in the manifold covenants of his mercy.

Wherefore then before all good works as good fruits, there must needs be faith in the heart whence they spring. And before all bad deeds as bad fruits, there must needs be unbelief in the heart as in the root, fountain, pith and strength of all sin. Which unbelief and ignorance is called the head of the serpent and of the old dragon, which the woman's seed Christ must tread under foot, as it was promised unto Adam.

Grace and gift have this difference. Grace properly is God's favour, benevolence or kind mind, which of his own self, without deserving of us, he beareth to us, whereby he was moved and inclined to give Christ unto us, with all his other gifts of grace. Gift is the holy ghost and his working whom he poureth into the hearts of them, on whom he hath mercy, and whom he favoureth. Though the gifts of the spirit increase in us daily, and have not yet their full perfection: yea and though there remain in us yet evil lusts and sin which fight against the spirit, as he saith here in the seventh chapter, and in the fifth to the Galatians, and as it was spoken before in the third chapter of Genesis of the debate between the woman's seed and the seed of the serpent: yet nevertheless God's favour is so great, and so strong over us for Christ's sake, that we are counted for full as whole and perfect before God. For God's favour toward us divideth not herself, increasing a little and a little, as do the gifts, but receiveth us whole and altogether in full love for Christ's sake our intercessor and mediator, and because that the gifts of the spirit and the battle between the spirit and evil lusts, are begun in us already.

Of this now understandest thou the seventh chapter where Paul accuseth himself as a sinner and yet in the eighth chapter saith, there is no damnation to them that are in Christ, and that because of the spirit, and because the gifts of the spirit are begun in us. Sinners we are because the flesh is not full killed and mortified. Nevertheless inasmuch as we believe in Christ, and have the earnest and beginning of the spirit, and would fain be perfect, God is so loving and favourable unto us that he will not look on such sin, neither will count it as sin, but will deal with us according to our belief in Christ, and according to his promises which he hath sworn to us, until the sin be full slain and mortified by death.

Faith is not man's opinion and dream, as some imagine and feign when they hear the story of the gospel: but when they see that there follow no good works nor amendment of living, though they hear, and yet can babble many things of faith, then they fall from the right way and say, faith only justifieth not, a man must have good works also, if he will be righteous and safe. The cause is when they hear the gospel or glad tidings, they fain of their own strength certain imaginations and thoughts in their hearts saying: I have heard the gospel, I remember the story, lo I believe. And that they count right faith, which nevertheless as it is but man's imagination and feigning even so profiteth it not, neither follow there any good works or amendment of living.

But right faith is a thing wrought by the holy ghost in us, which changeth us, turneth us into a new nature and begetteth us anew in God, and maketh us the sons of God, as thou readest in the first of John, and killeth the old

Grace.

Gift.

Faith is not the work of man.

Right faith is of the working of the spirit of God.

Adam, and maketh us altogether new in the heart, mind, will, lust and in all our affections and powers of the soul, and bringeth the holy ghost with her. Faith is a lively thing, mighty in working, valiant and strong, ever doing, ever fruitful, so that it is impossible that he which is endued therewith, should not work always good works without ceasing. He asketh not whether good works are to be done or not, but hath done them already, ere mention be made of them, and is always doing, for such is his nature now: quick faith in his heart and lively moving of the spirit drive him and stir him thereunto. Whosoever doeth not good works, is an unbelieving person and faithless, and looketh round about groping after faith and good works, and wot not what faith or good works mean, though he babble never so many things of faith and good works.

Faith is then a lively and steadfast trust in the favour of God, wherewith we commit ourselves altogether unto God, and that trust is so surely grounded and sticketh so fast in our hearts, that a man would not once doubt of it, though he should die a thousand times therefore. And such trust wrought by the holy ghost through faith, maketh a man glad, lusty, cheerful and true-hearted unto God and to all creatures. By the means whereof, willingly and without compulsion he is glad and ready to do good to every man, to do service to every man, to suffer all things, that God may be loved and praised, which hath given him such grace: so that it is impossible to separate good works from faith, even as it is impossible to separate heat and burning from fire. *Faith: what it is.*

Therefore take heed to thyself, and beware of thine own fantasies and imaginations, which to judge of faith and good works will seem wise, when indeed they are stark blind and of all things most foolish. Pray God that he will witesafe to work faith in thine heart, or else shalt thou remain evermore faithless, feign thou, imagine thou: enforce thou, wrestle with thyself, and do what thou wilt or canst.

Righteousness is even such faith, and is called God's righteousness, or righteousness that is of valour before God. For it is God's gift, and it altereth a man and changeth him to a new spiritual nature, and maketh him free and liberal to pay every man his duty. For through faith is a man purged of his sins, and obtaineth lust unto the law of God whereby he giveth God his honour and payeth him that he oweth him, and unto men he doeth service willingly wherewithsoever he can, and payeth every man his duty. Such righteousness can nature, freewill, and our own strength never bring to pass. For as no man can give himself faith, so can he not take away unbelief, how then can he take away any sin at all? Wherefore all is false hypocrisy and sin, whatsoever is done without faith or in unbelief, as it is evident in the fourteenth chapter unto the Romans, though it appear never so glorious or beautiful outwards. *Faith is righteousness.*

Flesh and spirit mayest thou not here understand, as though flesh were only that which pertaineth unto unchastity, and the spirit that which inwardly pertaineth to the heart: but Paul calleth flesh here as Christ doth (John 3) All that is born of flesh, that is to weet, the whole man with life, soul, body, wit, will, *Flesh: what it is.*

213

reason and whatsoever he is or doth within and without, because that these all, and all that is in man, study after the world and the flesh. Call flesh therefore whatsoever (as long as we are without the spirit of God) we think or speak of God, of faith of good works and of spiritual matters. Call flesh also all works which are done without grace and without the working of the spirit, howsoever good, holy and spiritual they seem to be, as thou mayest prove by the fifth chapter unto the Galatians, where Paul numbereth worshipping of idols, witchcraft, envy and hate among the deeds of the flesh, and by the eighth unto the Romans, where he saith that the law by the reason of the flesh is weak which is not understood of unchastity only, but of all sins, and most specially, of unbelief which is a vice most spiritual and ground of all sins.

And as thou callest him which is not renewed with the spirit and born again in Christ, flesh, and all his deeds, even the very motions of his heart and mind, his learning, doctrine and contemplation of high things, his preaching, teaching and study in scripture, building of churches, founding of abbeys, giving of alms, mass, matins and whatsoever he doeth, though it seem spiritual and after the law of God: So contrariwise call him spiritual which is renewed in Christ, and all his deeds which spring of faith, seem they never so gross as the washing of the disciples' feet, done by Christ, and Peter's fishing after the resurrection, yea and all the deeds of matrimony are pure spiritual, if they proceed of faith, and whatsoever is done within the laws of God, though it be wrought by the body, as the very wiping of shoes and such like, howsoever gross they appear outward. Without such understanding of these words canst thou never understand this epistle of Paul, neither any other place in the holy scripture. Take heed therefore, for whosoever understandeth these words otherwise, the same understandeth not Paul, whatsoever he be. Now will we prepare ourselves unto the epistle.

Spiritual.

The first chapter.

Forasmuch as it becometh the preacher of Christ's glad tidings, first through opening of the law, to rebuke all things and to prove all things sin, that proceed not of the spirit and of faith in Christ, and to prove all men sinners and children of wrath by inheritance, and how that to sin is their nature, and that by nature they can none otherwise do than to sin, and therewith to abate the pride of man, and to bring him unto the knowledge of himself, and of his misery and wretchedness, that he might desire help. Even so doeth saint Paul and beginneth in the first chapter to rebuke unbelief and gross sins which all men see, as the idolatry, and as the gross sins of the heathen were and as the sins now are of all them which live in ignorance without faith, and without the favour of God: and saith, the wrath of God of heaven appeareth through the gospel upon all men for their ungodly and unholy living. For though it be known and daily understood by the creatures, that there is but one God, yet is nature of herself without the spirit and grace so corrupt and so poisoned, that men neither can thank him, neither worship him, neither give him his due honour, but blind themselves and fall without ceasing into worse case, even until they come unto worshipping of images and working of shameful sins

which are abominable and against nature, and moreover suffer the same un-
rebuked in other, having delectation and pleasure therein.

In the second chapter he proceedeth further, and rebuketh all those holy
people also which without lust and love to the law, live well outwardly in
the face of the world and condemn other gladly, as the nature of all hypocrites
is, to think themselves pure in respect of open sinners, and yet hate the law
inwardly, and are full of covetousness and envy and of all uncleanness, (Matt.
23). These are they which despise the goodness of God, and according to the
hardness of their hearts, heap together for themselves the wrath of God.
Furthermore saint Paul as a true expounder of the law, suffereth no man to be
without sin, but declareth that all they are under sin which of freewill of nature,
will live well, and suffereth them not to be better than the open sinners, yea he
calleth them hard-hearted and such as cannot repent.

Second chapter.

In the third chapter he mingleth both together, both the Jews and the
Gentiles, and saith that the one is as the other, both sinners, and no difference
between them, save in this only, that the Jews had the word of God committed
unto them. And though many of them believed not thereon, yet is God's
truth and promise thereby neither hurt nor diminished: And he taketh in
his way and allegeth the saying of the fifty-first Psalm that God might abide
true in his words and overcome when he is judged. After that he returneth
to his purpose again, and proveth by the scripture, that all men without
difference or exception are sinners, and that by the works of the law no man is
justified: but that the law was given to utter and to declare sin only. Then he
beginneth and showeth the right way unto righteousness, by what means men
must be made righteous and safe, and saith: They are all sinners and without
praise before God, and must without their own deserving be made righteous
through faith in Christ, which hath deserved such righteousness for us, and is
become unto us God's mercystool for the remission of sins that are past, thereby proving that Christ's righteousness which cometh on us through faith,
helpeth us only. Which righteousness, saith he, is now declared through the
gospel and was testified of before by the law and the prophets. Furthermore
(saith he) the law is helped and furthered through faith, though that the works
thereof with all their boast are brought to nought and proved not to justify.

Third chapter.

The law justifieth not:
but uttereth the sin only
and condemneth.

In the fourth chapter (after that now by the three first chapters, the sins are
opened, and the way of faith unto righteousness laid) he beginneth to answer
unto certain objections and cavillations. And first he putteth forth those blind
reasons, which commonly they that will be justified by their own works, are
wont to make when they hear that faith only without works justifieth, saying,
shall men do no good works, yea and if faith only justifieth, what needeth a
man to study for to do good works? He putteth forth therefore Abraham for an
example, saying: What did Abraham with his works? was all in vain? came his
works to no profit? And so concludeth that Abraham without and before all
works was justified and made righteous. Insomuch that before the work of
circumcision he was praised of the scripture and called righteous by his faith
only, (Genesis 15). So that he did not the work of circumcision for to be helped

Fourth chapter.

thereby unto righteousness, which yet God commanded him to do, and was a good work of obedience, so in like wise no doubt none other works help anything at all unto a man's justifying: but as Abraham's circumcision was an outward sign whereby he declared his righteousness which he had by faith, and his obedience and readiness unto the will of God, even so are all other good works outward signs and outward fruit of faith and of the spirit, which justify not a man, but that a man is justified already before God inwardly in the heart, through faith and through the spirit purchased by Christ's blood.

Outward works are signs and witnesses of the inward faith.

Herewith now establisheth saint Paul his doctrine of faith afore rehearsed in the third chapter, and bringeth also testimony of David in the thirty-second Psalm, which calleth a man blessed not of works, but in that his sin is not reckoned and in that faith is imputed for righteousness, though he abide not afterward without good works, when he is once justified.

Blessed is he that hath his sins forgiven him.

For we are justified and receive the spirit for to do good works, neither were it otherwise possible to do good works, except we had first the spirit.

For how is it possible to do anything well in the sight of God, while we are yet in captivity and bondage under the devil, and the devil possesseth us altogether and holdeth our hearts, so that we cannot once consent unto the will of God. No man therefore can prevent the spirit in doing good: but the spirit must first come and wake him out of his sleep and with the thunder of the law fear him, and show him his miserable estate and wretchedness, and make him abhor, and hate himself and to desire help, and then comfort him again with the pleasant rain of the gospel, that its to say, with the sweet promises of God in Christ, and stir up faith in him to believe the promises. Then when he believeth the promises, as God was merciful to promise, so is he true to fulfil them, and will give him the spirit and strength, both to love the will of God and to work thereafter. So see we that God only (which according to the scripture worketh all in all things) worketh a man's justifying, salvation and health, yea and poureth faith and belief, lust to love God's will, and strength to fulfil the same, into us, even as water is poured into a vessel, and that of his good will and purpose, and not of our deservings and merits. God's mercy in promising and truth in fulfilling his promises saveth us and not we ourselves. And therefore is all laud, praise and glory, to be given unto God for his mercy and truth, and not unto us for our merits and deservings. After that, he stretcheth his example out against all other good work of the law, and concludeth that the Jews cannot be Abraham's heirs because of blood and kindred only, and much less by the works of the law, but must inherit Abraham's faith, if they will be the right heirs of Abraham forasmuch as Abraham before the law, both of Moses and also of circumcision, was through faith made righteous and called the father of all them that believe, and not of them that work. Moreover the law causeth wrath, inasmuch as no man can fulfil it with love and lust, and as long as such grudging, hate and indignation against the law remaineth in the heart, and is not taken away by the spirit that cometh by faith, so long (no doubt) the works of the law, declare evidently that the wrath of God is upon us and not favour. Wherefore faith only receiveth the grace promised unto Abraham. And these examples were not written for Abraham's sake only (saith he) but for ours also to whom if we believe, faith shall be reckoned likewise for righteousness, as he saith in the end of the chapter.

In the fifth chapter he commendeth the fruits and works of faith, as are peace, rejoicing in the conscience, inward love, to God and man: moreover, boldness, trust, confidence and a strong and a lusty mind and steadfast hope in tribulation and suffering. For all such follow, where the right faith is, for the abundant grace's sake and gifts of the spirit, which God hath given us in Christ, in that he gave him to die for us yet his enemies. Now have we then that faith only before all works justifieth, and that it followeth not yet therefore that a man should do no good works but that the right shapen works abide not behind, but accompany faith, even as brightness doth the sun, and are called of Paul the fruits of the spirit. Where the spirit is, there it is always summer and there are always good fruits, that is to say: good works. This is Paul's order, that good works spring of the spirit, the spirit cometh by faith and faith cometh by hearing the word of God, when the glad tidings and promises which God hath made to us in Christ, are preached truly, and received in the ground of the heart without wavering or doubting after that the law hath passed upon us and hath damned our consciences. Where the word of God is preached purely and received in the heart, there is faith and the spirit of God, and there are also good works of necessity whensoever occasion is given. Where God's word is not purely preached, but men's dreams, traditions, imaginations, inventions, ceremonies and superstition, there is no faith and consequently no spirit that cometh of God. And where God's spirit is not, there can be no good works, even as where an apple tree is not, there can grow no apples, but there is unbelief, the devil's spirit and evil works. Of this God's spirit and his fruit, have our holy hypocrites not once known, neither yet tasted how sweet they are, though they feign many good works of their own imagination, to be justified withal, in which is not one crumb of true faith or spiritual love, or of inward joy, peace and quietness of conscience, forasmuch as they have not the word of God for them, that such works please God, but they are even the rotten fruits of a rotten tree.

After that he breaketh forth, and runneth at large, and showeth whence both sin and righteousness, death and life come. And he compareth Adam and Christ together, thuswise reasoning and disputing, that Christ must needs come as a second Adam to make us heirs of his righteousness, through a new spiritual birth, without our deservings: even as the first Adam made us heirs of sin, through the bodily generation, without our deserving. Whereby is evidently known and proved to the uttermost, that no man can bring himself out of sin unto rightousness, no more than he could have withstood that he was born bodily. And that is proved herewith, forasmuch as the very law of God, which of right should have helped if anything could have helped, not only came and brought no help with her, but also increased sin, because that the evil and poisoned nature is offended and utterly displeased with the law, and the more she is forced by the law, the more is she provoked and set afire to fulfil and satisfy her lusts. By the law then we see clearly that we must needs have Christ to justify us with his grace, and to help nature.

In the sixth he setteth forth the chief and principal work of faith, the battle of the spirit against the flesh, how the spirit laboureth and enforceth to kill the remnant of sin and lust which remain in the flesh, after our justifying. And this chapter teacheth us, that we are not so free from sin through faith, that we should henceforth go up and down idle careless and sure of ourselves, as though there were now no more sin in us. Yes there is sin remaining in us, but it is not reckoned, because of faith and of the spirit, which fight against it. Wherefore we have enough to do all our lives long, to tame our bodies, and to compel the members to obey the spirit and not the appetites, that thereby we might be like unto Christ's death and resurrection, and might fulfil our baptism, which signifieth the mortifying of sins, and the new life of grace. For this battle ceaseth not in us until the last breath, and until that sin be utterly slain by the death of the body.

This thing (I mean to tame the body and so forth) we are able to do (saith he) seeing we are under grace and not to be under the law, what it is, not to be under the law, he himself expoundeth. For not to be under the law is not so to be understood, that every man may do what him lusteth. But not to be under the law, is to have a free heart renewed with the spirit, so that thou hast lust inwardly of thine own accord to do that which the law commandeth, without compulsion, yea though there were no law. For grace, that is to say God's favour bringeth us the spirit, and maketh us love the law, so is there now no more sin, neither is the law now any more against us, but at one and agreed with us and we with it.

But to be under the law, is to deal with the works of the law, and to work without the spirit and grace: for so long no doubt sin reigneth in us through the law, that is to say, the law declareth that we are under sin and that sin hath power and dominion over us, seeing we cannot fulfil the law, namely within, in the heart, forasmuch as no man of nature favoureth the law, consenteth thereunto and therein. Which thing is exceeding great sin, that we cannot consent to the law which law is nothing else save the will of God.

This is the right freedom and liberty from sin and from the law whereof he writeth unto the end of this chapter, that it is a freedom to do good only with lust, and to live well without compulsion of the law. Wherefore this freedom is a spiritual freedom, which destroyeth not the law, but ministreth that which the law requireth, and wherewith the law is fulfilled, that is to understand, lust and love, wherewith the law is stilled and accuseth us no more, compelleth us no more, neither hath ought to crave of us any more. Even as though thou were in debt to another man, and were not able to pay, two manner ways mightest thou be loosed. One way, if he would require nothing of thee, and break thine obligation. Another way, if some other good man would pay for thee, and give thee as much as thou mightest satisfy thine obligation withal. Of this wise hath Christ made us free from the law: and therefore is this no

The sixth chapter.

Baptism is a witness between God and us that we have promised to mortify the lusts and sin that remaineth in the flesh and etc.

Not to be under the law, what it meaneth.

To be under the law; what it is.

wild fleshly liberty, that should do nought, but that doeth all things, and is free from the craving and debt of the law.

In the seventh he confirmeth the same with a similitude of the state of matrimony. As when the husband dieth the wife is at her liberty, and the one loosed and departed from the other, not that the woman should not have power to marry unto another man, but rather now first of all is she free and hath power to marry unto another man which she could not do before, till she was loosed from her first husband. Even so are our consciences bound and in danger to the law under old Adam the flesh, as long as he liveth in us. For the law declareth that our hearts are bound and that we cannot disconsent from him. But when he is mortified and killed by the spirit, then is the conscience free and at liberty: not so that the conscience shall now nought do, but now first of all cleaveth unto another, that is to wit Christ, and bringeth forth the fruits of life. So now to be under the law, is not to be able to fulfil the law, but to be debtor to it and not able to pay that which the law requireth. And to be loose from the law, is to fulfil it and to pay that which the law demandeth, so that it can now henceforth ask thee nought.

Consequently Paul declareth more largely the nature of sin and of the law, how that through the law sin reviveth, moveth herself, and gathereth strength. For the old man and corrupt nature, the more he is forbidden and kept under of the law, is the more offended and displeased therewith, forasmuch as he cannot pay that which is required of the law. For sin is his nature and of himself, he cannot but sin. Therefore is the law death to him, torment and martyrdom. Not that the law is evil, but because that the evil nature cannot suffer that which is good, cannot abide that the law should require of him any good thing. Like as a sick man cannot suffer that a man should desire of him to run, to leap and to do other deeds of an whole man.

For which cause Saint Paul concludeth, that where the law is understood and perceived of the best wise, there it doeth no more but utter sin, and bring us unto the knowledge of our selves, and thereby kill us and make us bond unto eternal damnation and debtors of the everlasting wrath of God, even as he well feeleth and understandeth whose conscience is truly touched of the law. In such danger were we ere the law came, that we knew not what sin meant, neither yet know we the wrath of God upon sinners, till the law had uttered it. So seest thou that a man must have some other thing, yea and a greater and a more mighty thing than the law, to make him righteous and safe. They that understand not the law on this wise, are blind and go to work presumptuously, supposing to satisfy the law with works. For they know not that the law requireth a free, a willing, a lusty and a loving heart. Therefore they see not Moses right in the face, the veil hangeth between and hideth his face so that they cannot behold the glory of his countenance, how that the law is spiritual and requireth the heart. I may of mine own strength refrain that I do mine enemy no hurt, but to love him with all mine heart, and to put away wrath clean out of my mind can I not of mine own strength. I may refuse money of mine own strength, but to put away love unto riches out of mine heart can I

The seventh chapter.

To be under the law.

To be loose from the law.

not do of mine own strength. To abstain from adultery as concerning the deed can I do of mine own strength, but not to desire in mine heart is as unpossible unto me as is to chose whether I will hunger or thirst, and yet so the law requireth. Wherefore of a man's own strength is the law never fulfilled, we must have there unto God's favour and his spirit, purchased by Christ's blood.

Nevertheless when I say a man may do many things outwardly clean against his heart, we must understand that man is but driven of divers appetites, and the greatest appetite overcometh the less and carrieth the man away violently with her.

As when I desire vengeance, and fear also the inconvenience that is like to follow, if fear be greater, I abstain and if the appetite that desireth vengeance be greater, I cannot but prosecute the deed, as we see by experience in many murderers and thieves, which though they be brought into never so great peril of death, yet after they have escaped, do even, the same again. And common women prosecute their lusts because fear and shame are away, when other which have the same appetites in their hearts, abstain at the least way outwardly or work secretly being overcome of fear and of shame, and so likewise is it of all other appetites.

Flesh and spirit fight together.

Furthermore he declareth, how the spirit and the flesh fight together in one man, and maketh an example of himself, that we might learn to know that work aright, I mean to kill sin in ourselves. He calleth both the spirit and also the flesh a law, because that like as the nature of God's law is to drive, to compel, and to crave, even so the flesh driveth, compelleth, craveth and rageth, against the spirit, and will have her lusts satisfied.

On the other side driveth the spirit, crieth and fighteth against the flesh, and will have his lust satisfied. And this strife dureth in us, as long as we live: in some more and in some less as the spirit or the flesh is stronger, and the very man his own self is both the spirit and the flesh, which fighteth with his own self until sin be utterly slain and he altogether spiritual.

The eighth chapter.

In the eighth chapter he comforteth such fighters that they despair not because of such flesh, or think that they are less in favour with God. And he sheweth how that the sin remaining in us, hurteth not, for there is no danger to them that are in Christ which walk not after the flesh, but fight against it. And he expoundeth more largely what the nature of the flesh and of the spirit is, and how the spirit cometh by Christ, which spirit maketh us spiritual, tameth, subdueth and mortifieth the flesh, and certifieth us that we are nevertheless the sons of God, and also beloved, though that sin rage never so much in us, so long as we follow the spirit and fight against sin to kill and mortify it. And because the chastising of the cross and suffering are nothing pleasant, he comforteth us in our passions and afflictions by the assistance of the spirit which maketh intercession to God for us, mightily with groanings that pass man's utterance, so that man's speech cannot comprehend them, and the creatures mourn also with us of great desire that they have, that we were loosed from sin and corruption of the flesh. So see we that these three chapters, the sixth, seventh and eighth, do none other thing so much as to drive us unto the right work of faith, which is to kill the old man and mortify the flesh.

In the ninth, tenth and eleventh chapters he treateth of God's predestination, whence it springeth altogether, whether we shall believe or not believe, be loosed from sin or not be loosed. By which predestination our justifying and salvation are clean taken out of our hands, and put in the hands of God only, which thing is most necessary of all. For we are so weak and so uncertain, that if it stood in us, there would of a truth no man be saved, the devil no doubt would deceive us. But now is God sure, that his predestination cannot deceive him, neither can any man withstand or let him, and therefore have we hope and trust against sin. The ninth, tenth and eleventh chapters.

But here must a mark be set unto those unquiet, busy and high-climbing spirits how far they shall go, which first of all bring hither their high reasons and pregnant wits, and begin first from on high to search the bottomless secrets of God's predestination, whether they be predestinate or not. These must needs either cast themselves down headlong into desperation or else commit themselves to free chance careless. But follow thou the order of this epistle, and noosell thyself with Christ, and learn to understand what the law and the gospel mean, and the office of both two, that thou mayst in the one know thyself, and how that thou hast of thyself no strength, but to sin: and in the other the grace of Christ. And then see thou fight against sin and the flesh as the seven first chapters teach thee. After that when thou art come to the eighth chapter, and art under the cross and suffering of tribulation, the necessity of predestination will wax sweet and thou shalt well feel how precious a thing it is. For except thou have borne the cross of adversity and temptation, and hast felt thyself brought unto the very brim of desperation, yea and unto hell gates, thou canst never meddle with the sentence of predestination without thine own harm, and without secret wrath and grudging inwardly against God, for otherwise it shall not be possible for thee to think that God is righteous and just. Therefore must Adam be well mortified and the fleshly wit brought utterly to nought, ere that thou mayst away with this thing, and drink so strong wine. Take heed therefore unto thyself, that thou drink not wine, while thou art yet but a suckling. For every learning hath her time, measure and age, and in Christ is there a certain childhood, in which a man must be content with milk for a season, until he wax strong and grow up unto a perfect man in Christ, and be able to eat of more strong meat. This do if thou wilt understand.

In the twelfth chapter he giveth exhortations. For this manner observeth Paul in all his epistles, first he teacheth Christ and the faith, then exhorteth he to good works, and unto continual mortifying of the flesh. So here teacheth he good works indeed, and the true serving of God, and maketh all men priests, to offer up not money and beasts, as the manner was in the time of the law, but their own bodies, with killing and mortifying of the lusts of the flesh. After that he describeth the outward conversation of Christian men, how they ought to behave themselves in spiritual things, how to teach, preach and rule in the congregation of Christ, to serve one another, to suffer all things patiently, and to commit the wreak and vengeance to God, in conclusion how a Christian man ought to behave himself unto all men, to friend, foe or whatsoever he be. These are the right works of a Christian man which spring out of faith. For The twelfth chapter.

faith keepeth not holiday neither suffereth any man to be idle, wheresoever he dwelleth.

The thirteenth chapter. In the thirteenth he teacheth to honour the wordly and temporal sword. For though that man's law and ordinance make not a man good before God, neither justify him in the heart, yet are they ordained for the furtherance of the commonwealth, to maintain peace, to punish the evil and to defend the good. Therefore ought the good to honour the temporal sword and to have it in reverence, though as concerning themselves they need it not, but would abstain from evil of their own accord, yea and do good without man's law, but by the law of the spirit which governeth the heart, and aideth it unto all that is Love is the fulfilling of the law. the will of God. Finally he comprehendeth and knitteth up all in love. Love of her own nature bestoweth all that she hath and even her own self on that which is loved. Thou needest not to bid a kind mother to be loving unto her only son. Much less spiritual love. Which hath eyes given her of God, needeth man's law to teach her to do her duty?

And as in the beginning he did put forth Christ as the cause and author of our righteousness and salvation, even so here setteth he him forth as an example to counterfeit that as he hath done to us, even so should we do one to another.

The fourteenth chapter. In the fourteenth chapter he teacheth to deal soberly with the consciences of the weak in the faith, which yet understand not the liberty of Christ perfectly enough and to favour them of Christian love, and not to use the liberty of the faith unto hindrance. But unto the furtherance and edifying of the weak. For where such consideration is not, there followeth debate and despising of the gospel. It is better therefore to forbear the weak a while, until they wax strong, than that learning of the gospel should come altogether underfoot. And such work is singular work of love, and where love is perfect, there must needs be such a respect unto the weak, a thing that Christ commanded and charged to be had above all things.

The fifteenth chapter. In the fifteenth chapter he setteth forth Christ again to be followed, that we also by his example, should suffer other that are yet weak, as them that are frail, open sinners, unlearned, unexpert, and of loathsome manners, and not to cast them away forthwith, but to suffer them till they wax better and exhort them in the meantime. For so dealt Christ in the gospel and now dealeth with us daily, suffering our unperfectness, weakness, conversation and manners, not yet fashioned after the doctrine of the gospel, but smell of the flesh, yea and sometime break forth into outward deeds.

After that to conclude withal he wisheth them increase of faith, peace, and joy of conscience, praiseth them and comitteth them to God and magnifieth his office and administration in the gospel, and soberly and with great discretion desireth succour and aid of them for the poor saints of Jerusalem, and it is all pure love that he speaketh or dealeth withal. So find we in this epistle plenteously, unto the utmost, whatsoever a Christian man or woman ought to know, that is to wit what the law, the gospel, sin, grace, faith, righteousness, Christ, God, good works, love, hope, and the cross are, and even wherein the pith of all that pertaineth to the Christian faith standeth and how a

Christian man ought to behave himself unto every man, be he perfect or a sinner, good or bad, strong or weak, friend or foe, and in conclusion how to behave ourselves both toward God and toward ourselves also. And all things are profoundly grounded in the scriptures, and declared with examples of himself, of the fathers and of the prophets, that a man can here desire no more.

Wherefore it appeareth evidently, that Paul's mind was to comprehend briefly in this epistle all the whole learning of Christ's gospel, and to prepare an introduction unto all the old testament. For without doubt whosoever hath this epistle perfectly in his heart, the same hath the light and the effect of the old testament with him. Wherefore let every man without exception exercise himself therein diligently, and record it night and day continually, until he be full acquainted therewith.

This epistle to the Romans is the door into all the scripture: yea, and the key that openeth it and bringeth men to the true understanding of it.

The last chapter is a chapter of recommendation, wherein he yet mingleth a good admonition, that we should beware of the traditions and doctrine of men which beguile the simple with sophistry and learning that is not after the gospel, and draw them from Christ, and noosell them in weak and feeble and (as Paul calleth them in the epistle to the Galatians) in beggarly ceremonies, for the intent that they would live in fat pastures and be in authority, and be taken as Christ, yea and above Christ, and sit in the temple of God, that is to wit in the consciences of men, where God only, his word, and his Christ ought to sit. Compare therefore all manner doctrine of men unto the scripture, and see whether they agree or not. And commit thyself whole and altogether unto Christ, and so shall he with his holy spirit and with all his fulness dwell in thy soul.

The last chapter.

The sum and whole cause of the writings of this epistle, is, to prove that a man is justified by faith only: which proposition whoso denieth, to him is not only this epistle and all that Paul writeth, but also the whole scripture so locked up, that he shall never understand it to his soul's health. And to bring a man to the understanding and feeling that faith only justifieth: Paul proveth that the whole nature of man is so poisoned and so corrupt, yea and so dead concerning godly living or godly thinking, that it is impossible for her to keep the law in the sight of God: that is to say, to love it, and of love and lust to do it as naturally as a man eateth or drinketh, until she be quickened again and healed through faith.

And by justifying, understand none other thing than to be reconciled to God and to be restored unto his favour, and to have thy sins forgiven thee. As when I say God justifieth us, understand thereby, that God for Christ's sake, merits and deservings only, receiveth us unto his mercy, favour and grace, and forgiveth us our sins. And when I say Christ justifieth us, understand thereby that Christ only hath redeemed us, bought and delivered us out of the wrath of God and damnation, and hath with his work only, purchased us the mercy, the favour and grace of God, and the forgiveness of our sins. And when I say that faith only justifieth, understand thereby that faith and trust in the truth of God and in the mercy promised us for Christ's sake, and for his deserving and

223

works only, doth quiet the conscience and certify her that our sins be forgiven and we in the full favour of God.

Furthermore, set before thine eyes Christ's works and thine own works. Christ's works only justifieth and make satisfaction for thy sin, and thine own works not: that is to say, quieteth thy conscience and make thee sure that thy sins are forgiven thee, and not thine own works. For the promise of mercy is made thee for Christ's works' sake, and not for thine own works' sake. Wherefore, seeing God hath not promised that thine own works shall save thee, therefore faith in thine own works can never quiet thy conscience nor certify thee before God (when God cometh to judge and to take a reckoning) that thy sins are forgiven thee. Beyond all this, mine own works can never satisfy the law or pay her that I owe her. For I owe the law to love her with all mine heart, soul, power and might. Which thing to pay I am never able while I am compassed with flesh. No, I cannot once begin to love the law, except I be first sure by faith that God loveth me and forgiveth me.

Finally that we say faith only justifieth, ought to offend no man. For if this be true, that Christ only redeemed us, Christ only bare our sins, made satisfaction for them and purchased us the favour of God, then must it needs be true, that the trust only in Christ's deserving and in the promises of God the father made us for Christ's sake, doth only quiet the conscience and certify her that the sins are forgiven. And when they say, a man must repent, forsake sin, and have a purpose to sin no more as nigh as he can and love the law of God: Ergo faith alone justifieth not: I answer, that and all like arguments are nought, and like to this. I must repent and be sorry, the Gospel must be preached me, and I must believe it or else I cannot be partaker of the mercy which Christ hath deserved for me, Ergo Christ only justifieth me not, or Christ only hath not made satisfaction for my sins. As this is a naughty argument so is the other.

Now go to reader, and according to the order of Paul's writing, even so do thou. First behold thyself diligently in the law of God, and see there thy just damnation. Secondarily turn thine eyes to Christ, and see there the exceeding mercy of thy most kind and loving father. Thirdly remember that Christ made not this atonement that thou shouldest anger God again: neither died he for thy sins, that thou shouldest live still in them: neither cleansed he thee, that thou shouldest return (as a swine) unto thine old puddle again: but that thou shouldest be a new creature and live a new life after the will of God and not of the flesh. And be diligent lest through thine own negligence and unthankfulness thou lose this favour and mercy again.

Farewell.

W.T.

THE EPISTLE OF THE APOSTLE ST PAUL TO THE ROMANS

CHAPTER ONE+ 1[1–20]

Paul the servant of Jesus Christ, called to be an apostle, put apart to preach the gospel of God, which he promised afore by his prophets, in the holy scriptures that make mention of his son, the which was begotten of the seed of David, as pertaining to the flesh: and declared to be the son of God with power of the holy ghost that sanctifieth, since the time that Jesus Christ our Lord rose again from death, by whom we have received grace and apostleship, to bring all manner heathen people unto obedience of the faith, that is in his name: of the which heathen are ye a part also, which are Jesus Christ's by vocation. ⊦

To all you of Rome beloved of God and saints by calling, grace be with you and peace from God our father, and from the Lord Jesus Christ.

First verily I thank my God through Jesus Christ for you all, because your faith is published throughout all the world. For God is my witness, whom I serve with my spirit in the gospel of his son, that without ceasing I make mention of you always in my prayers, beseeching that at one time or another, a prosperous journey (by the will of God) might fortune me, to come unto you. For I long to see you, that I might bestow among you some spiritual gift, to strength you withal: that is, that I might have consolation together with you, through the common faith, which both ye and I have.

Hab. 2. a.
Heb. 10.
Gal. 3.

I would that ye should know brethren, how that I have often times purposed to come unto you (but have been let hitherto) to have some fruit among you, as I have among other of the gentiles. For I am debtor both to the Greeks and to them which are no Greeks, unto the learned and also unto the unlearned. Likewise, as much as in me is, I am ready to preach the gospel to you of Rome also.

For I am not ashamed of the gospel of Christ, because it is the power of God unto salvation to all that believe, namely to the Jew, and also to the gentile. For by it the righteousness which cometh of God, is opened, from faith to faith★. As it is written: The just shall live by faith.

★ From faith to faith: that is from a weak faith to a stronger, or from one battle of faith to another, for as we have escaped one jeopardy through faith, another invadeth us, through which we must wade by the help of faith also.

For the wrath of God appeareth from heaven against all ungodliness and unrighteousness of men which withhold the truth in unrighteousness: seeing, what may be known of God, that same is manifest among them. For God did shew it unto them. So that his invisible things: that is to say, his eternal power and Godhead are understood and seen, by the works from the creation of the

Eph. 4.

What followeth when men know the truth and love it not.

world. So that they are without excuse, inasmuch as when they knew God, they glorified him not as God, neither were thankful, but waxed full of vanities in their imaginations, and their foolish hearts were blinded. When they counted themselves wise, they became fools and turned the glory of the immortal God, unto the similitude of the image of mortal man, and of birds, and fourfooted beasts, and of serpents. Wherefore God likewise gave them up unto their heart's lusts, unto uncleanness, to defile their own bodies between themselves: which turned his truth unto a lie, and worshipped and served the creatures more than the maker, which is blessed for ever. Amen. For this cause God gave them up unto shameful lusts. For even their women did change the natural use unto the unnatural. And likewise also the men left the natural use of the woman, and burned in their lusts one on another. And man with man wrought filthiness, and received in themselves the reward of their error, as it was according.

And as it seemed not good unto them to be a-known of God, even so God delivered them up unto a lewd mind, that they should do those things which were not comely, being full of all unrighteous doing, of fornication, wickedness, covetousness, maliciousness, full of envy, murder, debate, deceit, evil conditioned, whisperers, backbiters, haters of God, doers of wrong, proud, boasters, bringers-up of evil things, disobedient to father and mother, without understanding, covenant-breakers, unloving, truce-breakers and merciless.

To have pleasure in another man's sin is greater wickedness than to sin thyself.

Which men though they knew the righteousness of God, how that they which such things commit, are worthy of death, yet not only do the same, but also have pleasure in them that do them.

CHAPTER TWO

Therefore art thou inexcusable o man, whosoever thou be that judgest. For in the same wherein thou judgest another, thou condemnest thyself. For thou that judgest, doest even the same self things. But we are sure that the judgement of God is according to truth, against them which commit such things. Thinkest thou this O thou man that judgest them which do such things and yet doest even the very same, that thou shalt escape the judgement of God? Either despisest thou the riches of his goodness, patience and long-sufferance? and rememberest not how that the kindness of God leadeth thee to repentance?

Matt. 16. d.

* The deserving of Christ is promised to be the reward of our good deeds: which reward yet our deeds deserve not.

But thou after thine hard heart that cannot repent, heapest thee together the treasure of wrath against the day of vengeance, when shall be opened the righteous judgement of God, which will reward every man according to his deeds*: that is to say, praise, honour and immortality, to them which continue in good doing, and seek eternal life. But unto them that are rebellious and disobey the truth, yet follow iniquity, shall come indignation and wrath, tribulation and anguish, upon the soul of every man that doth evil: of the Jew first, and also of the gentile. To every man that doth good, shall come praise, honour and peace, to the Jew first, and also to the gentile. For there is no partiality with God. But whosoever hath sinned without law, shall perish

Deut. 10. d.
2 Chr. 19.
Job 27.
Acts 10. c.
Matt. 7. d.
Jas. 1. d.

without law. And as many as have sinned under the law, shall be judged by the law. For before God they are not righteous which hear the law: but the doers* of the law shall be justified. For if the gentiles which have no law, do of nature the things contained in the law: then they having no law, are a law unto themselves, which shew the deed of the law written in their hearts: while their conscience beareth witness unto them, and also their thoughts, accusing one another or excusing, at the day when God shall judge the secrets of men by Jesus Christ, according to my gospel.

Behold, thou art called a Jew, and trustest in the law, and rejoicest in God, and knowest his will, and hast experience of good and bad, in that thou art informed by the law: and believest that thou thyself art a guide unto the blind, a light to them which are in darkness, an informer of them which lack discretion, a teacher of unlearned, which hast the example of that which ought to be known, and of the truth, in the law. But thou which teachest another teachest not thyself. Thou preachest, a man should not steal: and yet thou stealest. Thou sayest, a man should not commit advoutry: and thou breakest wedlock. Thou abhorrest images, and robbest God of his honour. Thou rejoicest in the law, and through breaking the law dishonourest God. For the name of God is evil spoken of among the gentiles through you, as it is written.

Circumcision* verily availeth, if thou keep the law. But if thou break the law, thy circumcision is made uncircumcision. Therefore if the uncircumcised keep the right things contained in the law: shall not his uncircumcision be counted for circumcision? And shall not uncircumcision which is by nature (if it keep the law) judge thee, which being under the letter and circumcision, dost transgress the law? For he is not a Jew, which is a Jew outward. Neither is that thing circumcision, which is outward in the flesh. But he is a Jew which is hid within and the circumcision of the heart is the true circumcision, which is in the spirit, and not in the letter, whose praise is not of men, but of God.

CHAPTER THREE

What preferment than hath the Jew? or what advantageth circumcision? Surely very much. First unto them was committed the word of God. What then though some of them did not believe? shall their unbelief make the promise of God without effect? God forbid. Let God be true, and all men liars, as it is written: That thou mightest be justified in thy saying and shouldest overcome when thou art judged.

If our unrighteousness make the righteousness of God more excellent: what shall we say? Is God unrighteous which taketh vengeance? I speak after the manner of men. God forbid. For how then shall God judge the world? If the verity of God appear more excellent through my life, unto his praise, why am I henceforth judged as a sinner? and say not rather (as men evil speak of us, and as some affirm that we say) let us do evil, that good may come thereof. Whose damnation is just.

What say we then? Are we better than they? No, in no wise. For we have

Marginal notes:

* Deeds are an outward righteousness before the world and testify what a man is within: but justify not the heart before God: nor certify the conscience that the fore-sins are forgiven.

Isa. 54. b.
Ezek. 36.

* Circumcision was a witness of the covenant between them and God and holp not but after as it put them in remembrance to believe in God and to keep the law.

John 3. d.
Psa. 116.
Psa. 51.

227

Gal. 3. d.
Psa. 14. a.
Psa. 5. c. and 14. b.
Psa. 120. and 10. c.
Isa. 59. b.
Psa. 14. b.

already proved how that both Jews and gentiles are all under sin, as it is
written: There is none righteous, no not one: there is none that understandeth,
there is none that seeketh after God, they are all gone out of the way, they are
all made unprofitable, there is none that doeth good, no not one. Their throat
is an open sepulchre, with their tongues they have deceived: the poison of asps
is under their lips. Whose mouths are full of cursing and bitterness. Their feet
are swift to shed blood. Destruction and wretchedness are in their ways. And
the way of peace they have not known. There is no fear of God before their
eyes.

Gal. 2. d.

* The law justifieth not
before God but uttereth
sin only.

+ Yea and we know that whatsoever the law saith, he saith it to them which
are under the law. That all mouths may be stopped and all the world be subdued to God, because that by the deeds of the law*, shall no flesh be justified in
the sight of God. For by the law cometh the knowledge of sin.

Justifying cometh
by faith.

Now verily is the righteousness that cometh of God declared without the
fulfilling of the law, having witness yet of the law and of the prophets. The
righteousness no doubt which is good before God, cometh by the faith of Jesus
Christ unto all and upon all that believe.

There is no difference: for all have sinned, and lack the praise that is of valour
before God: but are justified freely by his grace, through the redemption that
is in Christ Jesus, whom God hath made a seat of mercy through faith in his
blood, to shew the righteousness which before him is of valour, in that he forgiveth the sins that are passed, which God did suffer to show at this time, the
righteousness that is allowed of him, that he might be counted just, and a
justifier of him which believeth on Jesus.+

Where is then thy rejoicing? It is excluded. By what law? by the law of
works? Nay: but by the law of faith.

Faith justifieth.

* Faith maintaineth the
law, because thereby
we obtain power to
love it and to keep it.

For we suppose that a man is justified by faith without the deeds of the law.
Is he the God of the Jews only? Is he not also the God of the gentiles? Yes, even
of the gentiles also. For it is God only which justifieth circumcision which is of
faith, and uncircumcision through faith. Do we then destroy the law through
faith? God forbid. But we rather maintain* the law.

CHAPTER FOUR

* Deeds justify not
before God: neither
may a man before God
put trust in them.

What shall we say then, that Abraham our father as pertaining to the flesh, did
find? If Abraham were justified by deeds*, then hath he wherein to rejoice: but
not with God. For what saith the scripture? Abraham believed God, and it was
counted unto him for righteousness. To him that worketh, is the reward not
reckoned of favour: but of duty. To him that worketh not, but believeth on
him that justifieth the ungodly, is his faith counted for righteousness. Even as
David describeth the blessedfulness of the man unto whom God ascribeth
righteousness without deeds. Blessed* are they, whose unrighteousnesses are
forgiven, and whose sins are covered. Blessed is that man to whom the Lord
imputeth not sin.

Psa. 32.

* Blessedfulness: what
it is.

Came this blessedness then upon the circumcised or upon the uncircumcised?

We say verily how that faith was reckoned to Abraham for righteousness. How was it reckoned? in the time of circumcision? or in the time before he was circumcised? Not in time of circumcision: but when he was yet uncircumcised. And he received the sign of circumcision, as a seal of the righteousness which is by faith, which faith he had yet being uncircumcised: that he should be the father of all them that believe, though they be not circumcised, that righteousness might be imputed to them also: and that he might be the father of the circumcised, not because they are circumcised only: but because they walk also in the steps of that faith that was in our father Abraham before the time of circumcision.

For the promise that he should be heir of the world, was not given to Abraham or to his seed through the law: but through the righteousness which cometh of faith. For if they which are of the law, be heirs, then is faith but vain, and the promise of none effect. Because the law causeth wrath. For where no law is, there is no transgression. Therefore by faith is the inheritance given, that it might come of favour: and the promise might be sure to all the seed. Not to them only which are of the law: but also to them which are of the faith of Abraham, which is the father of us all. As it is written: I have made thee a father to many nations, even before God whom thou hast believed, which quickeneth the dead, and called those things which be not, as though they were.

Which Abraham, contrary to hope, believed in hope, that he should be the father of many nations, according to that which was spoken: So shall thy seed be. And he fainted not in the faith, nor yet considered his own body which was now dead, even when he was almost an hundred year old: neither yet that Sara was past childbearing. He staggered not at the promise of God through unbelief: but was made strong in the faith, and gave honour to God, full certified, that what he had promised that he was able to make good. And therefore was it reckoned to him for righteousness.

It is not written for him only, that it was reckoned to him for righteousness: but also for us, to whom it shall be counted for righteousness, so we believe on him that raised up Jesus our Lord from death. Which was delivered for our sins, and rose again for to justify us.

CHAPTER FIVE

Because therefore that we are justified by faith, we are at peace with God through our Lord Jesus Christ: by whom we have a way in through faith unto this grace wherein we stand and rejoice in hope of the praise that shall be given of God. Neither do we so only: but also we rejoice in tribulation. For we know that tribulation bringeth patience, patience bringeth experience, experience bringeth hope. And hope★ maketh not ashamed, for the love of God is shed abroad in our hearts, by the holy ghost, which is given unto us.

For when we were yet weak, according to the time: Christ died for us which were ungodly. Yet scarce will any man die for a righteous man. Peradventure for a good man durst a man die. + But God setteth out his love that he hath to

Marginal notes:

Circumcision is the seal.

The promise cometh by faith.

The law causeth wrath.

Gen. 17.

Gen. 13. and 15. b.

Christ justifieth us.

Faith setteth us at peace with God.

James 1. b.

★ We are not ashamed of our hope for we are sure by the death of Christ that God loveth us and will being our hope to pass.

us, seeing that while we were yet sinners, Christ died for us. Much more than now (seeing we are justified in his blood) shall we be saved from wrath, through him.

For if when we were enemies, we were reconciled to God by the death of his son: much more, seeing we are reconciled, we shall be preserved by his life. Not only so, but we also joy in God by the means of our Lord Jesus Christ, by whom we have received the atonement. ⊢

Wherefore as by one man sin entered into the world, and death by the means of sin: And so death went over all men, insomuch that all men sinned. For even unto the time of the law was sin in the world: but sin was not regarded, as long as there was no law: nevertheless death reigned from Adam to Moses, even over them also that sinned not, with like transgression as did Adam: which is the similitude of him that is to come.

But the gift is not like as the sin. ⊢ For if through the sin of one, many be **C** dead: much more plenteous upon many was the grace of God and gift by grace: which grace was given by one man Jesus Christ.

And the gift is not over one sin, as death came through one sin of one that sinned. For damnation came of one sin unto condemnation: but the gift came to justify from many sins. For if by the sin of one, death reigned by the means of one, much more shall they which receive abundance of grace and of the gift of righteousness reign in life by the means of one (that is to say) Jesus Christ. ⊢

⊢ Likewise then as by the sin of one, condemnation came on all men: even so **D** by the justifying of one cometh the righteousness that bringeth life, upon all men. For as by one man's disobedience many became sinners: so by the obedience of one shall many be made righteous.

But the law* in the meantime entered in, that sin should increase. Neverthelater where abundance of sin was, there was more plenteousness of grace. That as sin had reigned unto death, even so might grace reign through righteousness unto eternal life, by the help of Jesus Christ. ⊢

CHAPTER SIX

What shall we say then? Shall we continue in sin, that there may be abundance **A** of grace? God forbid. How shall we that are dead as touching sin, live any longer therein? ⊢ Remember ye not that all we which are baptised in the name of Jesus Christ, are baptised to die with him? We are buried with him by baptism, for to die, that likewise as Christ was raised up from death by the glory of the father: even so we also should walk in a new life. For if we be graft in death like unto him: even so must we be in the resurrection. This we must remember, that our old man is crucified with him also, that the body of sin **B** might utterly be destroyed, that henceforth we should not be servants of sin. For he that is dead, is justified from sin.

Wherefore if we be dead with Christ, we believe that we shall live with him: remembering that Christ, once raised from death, dieth no more. Death hath no more power over him. For as touching that he died, he died concerning sin, once. And as touching that he liveth, he liveth unto God. Likewise imagine ye also, that ye are dead concerning sin: but are alive unto God through Jesus Christ our Lord. ⊢ Let not sin reign therefore in your mortal bodies, that ye should thereunto obey in the lusts of it. Neither give ye your members as instruments of unrighteousness unto sin: but give yourselves unto God, as they that are alive from death. And give your members as instruments of righteousness unto God. Let not sin have power over you. For ye are not under the law, but under grace.

C What then? Shall we sin, because we are not under the law: but under grace? God forbid. + Remember ye not how that to whomsoever ye commit yourselves as servants to obey, his servants ye are to whom ye obey: whether it be of sin unto death, or of obedience unto righteousness? God be thanked, that though ye were once the servants of sin, ye have yet obeyed with heart unto the form of doctrine whereunto ye were delivered. Ye are then made free from sin, and are become the servants of righteousness. ⊢ *John 8. d. 2 Pet. 2. d.*

D + I will speak grossly because of the infirmity of your flesh. As ye have given your members servants to uncleanness and to iniquity, from iniquity unto iniquity: even so now give your members servants unto righteousness, that ye may be sanctified. For when ye were servants of sin, ye were not under righteousness. What fruit had ye then in those things, whereof ye are now ashamed? For the end of those things is death. But now are ye delivered from sin, and made the servants of God, and have your fruit that ye should be sanctified, and the end everlasting life. For the reward of sin is death: but eternal★ life is the gift of God, through Jesus Christ our Lord. ⊢ Eternal life is the serving of Christ.

CHAPTER SEVEN

A + Remember ye not brethren (I speak to them that know the law) how that the law hath power over a man as long as it endureth? For the woman which is in subjection to a man, is bound by the law to the man, as long as he liveth. If the man be dead, she is loosed from the law of the man. So then if while the man liveth she couple herself with another man, she shall be counted a wedlock-breaker. But if the man be dead, she is free from the law: so that she is no wedlock-breaker, though she couple herself with another man. *1 Cor. 7.*

B Even so ye my brethren, are dead concerning the law by the body of Christ, that ye should be coupled to another (I mean to him that is risen again from death) that we should bring forth fruit unto God. For when we were in the flesh, the lusts of sin which were stirred up by the law, reigned in our members, to bring forth fruit unto death. But now are we delivered from the law, and dead, from that whereunto we were in bondage, that we should serve in a new conversation of the spirit, and not in the old conversation of the letter.

What shall we say then? is the law sin? God forbid: but I knew not what sin meant but by the law. For I had not known what lust had meant, except the law had said, thou shalt not lust. But sin took an occasion by the means of the commandment, and wrought in me all manner of concupiscence. For without Law maketh sin to be known. *Exod. 20. c. Deut. 5. 6.*

the law, sin was dead. I once lived without law. But when the commandment came, sin revived, and I was dead. And the very same commandment which was ordained unto life, was found to be unto me an occasion of death. For sin took occasion by the means of the commandment and so deceived me, and by the self commandment slew me. Wherefore the law is holy, and the commandment holy, just and good.

1 Tim. 1. b.

Was that then which is good, made death unto me? God forbid. Nay, sin was death unto me, that it might appear, how that sin by the means of that which is good, had wrought death in me: that sin which is under the commandment, might be out of measure sinful. For we know that the law is spiritual: but I am carnal, sold* under sin, because I wot not what I do. For what I would, that do I not: but what I hate, that do I. If I do now that which I would not, I grant to the law that it is good. So then now, it is not I that do it, but sin that dwelleth in me. For I know that in me (that is to say in my flesh) dwelleth no good thing. To will is present with me: but I find no means to perform that which is good. For I do not that good thing which I would: but that evil do I, which I would not. Finally, if I do that I would not, then is it not I that do it, but sin that dwelleth in me, doeth it. I find then by the law that when I would do good, evil is present with me. I delight in the law of God, concerning the inner man. But I see another law in my members rebelling against the law of my mind, and subduing me unto the law of sin, which is in my members. O wretched man that I am: who shall deliver me from this body of death? I thank God through Jesus Christ our Lord. So then I myself in my mind serve the law of God, and in my flesh the law of sin.

C

* Sold under sin is to be made a bondman to do the will of sin only.

D

CHAPTER EIGHT

+ There is then no damnation to them which are in Christ Jesus, which walk not after the flesh: but after the spirit. For the law of the spirit that bringeth life through Jesus Christ, hath delivered me from the law of sin and death. For what the law could not do inasmuch it was weak because of the flesh: that performed God, and sent his son in the similitude of sinful flesh, and by sin* damned sin in the flesh: that the righteousness required of the law might be fulfilled in us, which walk not after the flesh, but after the spirit.

A

* Sin is taken here for a sin-offering after the use of the Hebrew tongue.

For they that are carnal, are carnally minded. But they that are spiritual, are ghostly minded. To be carnally minded, is death. But to be spiritually minded is life and peace. ⊦ Because that the fleshly mind is enmity against God: for it is not obedient to the law of God, neither can be. So then they that are given to the flesh, cannot please God.

B

* Christ's spirit is in all his, and the spirit is life because it consenteth unto the law. And the body that is dead because it consenteth to sin, will that spirit quicken at the last: give him lust to do the law, and will not suffer him to remain in sin.

But ye are not given to the flesh, but to the spirit: if so be that the spirit of God dwell in you. If there be any man that hath not the spirit of Christ*, the same is none of his. If Christ be in you, the body is dead because of sin: but the spirit is life for righteousness' sake. Wherefore if the spirit of him that raised up Jesus from death, dwell in you: even he that raised up Christ from death, shall quicken your mortal bodies, because that this spirit dwelleth in you.

C + Therefore brethren we are now debtors, not to the flesh, to live after the flesh. For if ye live after the flesh, ye must die. But if ye mortify the deeds of the body, by the help of the spirit, ye shall live. For as many as are led by the spirit of God: they are the sons of God. For ye have not received the spirit of bondage to fear any more, but ye have received the spirit of adoption whereby we cry Abba father. The same spirit certifieth our spirit that we are the sons of God. If we be sons, we are also heirs, the heirs I mean of God, and heirs annexed with Christ: if so be that we suffer★ together, that we may be glorified together. ⊢

The spirit that maketh us sons and heirs by grace.

★ We must suffer with Christ if we shall reign with him in glory.

D + For I suppose that the afflictions of this life, are not worthy of the glory which shall be showed upon us. Also the fervent desire of the creatures abideth looking when the sons of God shall appear, because the creatures are subdued to vanity against their will: but for his will which subdueth them in hope. For the very creatures shall be delivered from the bondage of corruption, into the glorious liberty of the sons of God. For we know that every creature groaneth with us also, and travaileth in pain even unto this time.

E Not they only, but even we also which have the first fruits★ of the spirit, mourn in ourselves and wait for the adoption★ and look for the deliverance of our bodies. ⊢ For we are saved by hope★. But hope that is seen is no hope. For how can a man hope for that which he seeth? But and if we hope for that we see not, then do we with patience abide for it.

★ First-fruits: a taste and a certain portion and not the full gift of the spirit.

★ Adoption: that is, the inheritance promised by grace.

★ We are saved by hope: that is, we hope to be delivered out of the corruption of our bodies into the glory that Christ now is in: and therefore faint not in our tribulations.

Likewise the spirit also helpeth our infirmities. For we know not what to desire as we ought: but the spirit maketh intercession mightily for us with groanings which cannot be expressed with tongue. And he that searcheth the hearts, knoweth what is the meaning of the spirit: for he maketh intercession for the saints according to pleasure of God. + For we know that all things work for the best unto them that love God, which also are called★ of purpose. For those which he knew before, he also ordained before, that they should be like fashioned unto the shape of his son, that he might be the first begotten son among many brethren. Moreover which he appointed before, them he also called. And which he called, them also he justified, which he justified, them he also glorified.

★ God chooseth of his own goodness and mercy: calleth through the gospel: justifieth through faith and glorifieth through good works.

F What shall we then say unto these things? If God be on our side: who can be against us? which spared not his own son, but gave him for us all: how shall he not with him give us all things also? Who shall lay anything to the charge of God's chosen? it is God that justifieth: who then shall condemn? it is Christ which is dead, yea rather which is risen again, which is also on the right hand of God, and maketh intercession for us.

Who shall separate us from the love★ of God? shall tribulation? or anguish? or persecution? or hunger? or nakedness? or peril? or sword? As it is written: For thy sake are we killed all day long, and are counted as sheep appointed to be slain.

★ He that seeth what Christ hath done for him cannot but believe that God loveth him and will love God again.

G Nevertheless in all these things we overcome strongly through his help that loved us. Yea and I am sure that neither death, neither life, neither angels, nor rule, neither power, neither things present, neither things to come, neither height, neither lowth, neither any other creature shall be able to depart us from the love of God, showed in Christ Jesus our Lord. ⊢

CHAPTER NINE

I say the truth in Christ and lie not, in that whereof my conscience beareth **A**
me witness in the holy ghost, that I have great heaviness and continual sorrow
in my heart. For I have wished myself to be cursed from Christ, for my
brethren and my kinsmen as pertaining to the flesh, which are the Israelites. To
whom pertaineth the adoption, and the glory, and the covenants, and the law
that was given, and the service of God, and the promises: whose also are the
fathers, and they of whom (as concerning the flesh) Christ came, which is God
over all things blessed for ever Amen.

I speak not these things as though the words of God had taken none effect. **B**
For they are not all Israelites which came of Israel: neither are they all children
straightway, because they are the seed of Abraham. But in Isaac shall thy seed
be called: that is to say, they which are the children of the flesh, are not the
children of God. But the children of promise are counted the seed. For this is a
word of promise, about this time will I come, and Sara shall have a son.

Neither was it so with her only: but also when Rebecca was with child by **C**
one, I mean by our father Isaac, ere the children were born, when they had
neither done good neither bad: that the purpose of God which is by election,
might stand, it was said unto her, not by the reason of works, but by grace of
the caller: the elder shall serve the younger. As it is written: Jacob he loved, but
Esau he hated.

What shall we say then? is there any unrighteousness with God? God forbid. **D**
For he saith to Moses: I will show mercy to whom I shew mercy: and will have
compassion on whom I have compassion. So lieth it not then in a man's will
or cunning, but in the mercy of God. For the scripture saith unto Pharaoh:
Even for this same purpose have I stirred thee up, to show my power on thee,
and that my name might be declared throughout all the world. So hath he
mercy on whom he will, and whom he will, he maketh hard-hearted.

Thou wilt say then unto me: why then blameth he us yet? For who can **E**
resist his will? But o man, what art thou which disputest with God★? Shall the
work say to the workman: why hast thou made me on this fashion? Hath not
the potter power over the clay, even of the same lump to make one vessel unto
honour, and another unto dishonour? Even so, God willing to show his wrath,
and to make his power known, suffered with long patience the vessels of
wrath, ordained to damnation, that he might declare the riches of his glory on
the vessels of mercy, which he had prepared unto glory: that is to say, us which
he called, not of the Jews only, but also of the gentiles. As he saith in Osee: I
will call them my people which were not my people: and her beloved which
was not beloved. And it shall come to pass in the place where it was said unto
them, ye are not my people: that there shall [they] be called the children of the
living God.

But Esaias crieth concerning Israel, though the number of the children of **F**
Israel be as the sand of the sea, yet shall a remnant be saved. He finisheth the

---

What love doth.

Adoption is an
inheritance by grace.

Gen. 21.

Gal. 4. d.
Gen. 18.

Gen. 25.
Mal. 1. a.

Exod. 23.

Exod. 9. d.

Isa. 45. c.
Jer. 18.
Prov. 15. b.

★ The fleshly and proud
mind that will be as
wise as God must be
mortified to learn to
fear God and to obey
him and to leave
disputing with him.

Hos. 2. d.
1 Pet. 2. d.

Hos. 2. d.

Isa. 10. e.

work[†] verily and maketh it short in righteousness. For a short work[†] will God make on earth. And as Esaias said before: Except the Lord of Sabaoth had left us seed, we had been made as Sodom, and had been likened to Gomorrha.

Isa. i. c.

G　　What shall we say then? We say that the gentiles which followed not righteousness have overtaken righteousness: I mean the righteousness which cometh of faith. But Israel which followed the law of righteousness, could not attain unto the law of righteousness. And wherefore? Because they sought it not by faith: but as it were by the works of the law. For they have stumbled at the stumbling-stone. As it is written: Behold I put in Sion a stumbling-stone, and a rock which shall make men fall. And none that believe on him, shall be ashamed.

Isa. 27.
1 Pet. 2. b.
Isa. 8. c.
Isa. 28.

CHAPTER TEN

A　　+ Brethren, my heart's desire and prayer to God for Israel is that they might be saved. For I bear them record that they have a fervent mind to Godward, but not according to knowledge. For they are ignorant of the righteousness which is allowed before God, and go about to establish their own righteousness and therefore are not obedient unto the righteousness which is of value before God. For Christ is the end of the law, to justify all that believe. ⊢

The law driveth to Christ to be justified.

B　　Moses describeth the righteousness which cometh of the law, how that the man which doth the things of the law, shall live therein. But the righteousness which cometh of faith, speaketh on this wise. Say not in thine heart who shall ascend into heaven? (that is nothing else than to fetch Christ down). Or who shall descend into the deep? (that is nothing else but to fetch up Christ from death). But what saith the scripture? The word is nigh thee, even in thy mouth and in thine heart.

Lev. 18.
Ezek. 20. b.
Deut. 30.

C　　This word is the word of faith which we preach. For if thou shalt knowledge with thy mouth that Jesus is the Lord, and shalt believe with thine heart that God raised him up from death, thou shalt be safe. + For the belief of the heart justifieth: and to knowledge with the mouth maketh a man★ safe. For the scripture saith: whosoever believeth on him, shall not be ashamed.

D　　There is no difference between the Jew and the gentile. For one is Lord of all, which is rich unto all that call on him. For whosoever shall call on the name of the Lord, shall be safe. But how shall they call on him, on whom they believed not? how shall they believe on him of whom they have not heard? how shall they hear without a preacher? And how shall they preach except they be sent? As it is written: how beautiful are the feet of them which bring glad tidings of peace, and bring glad tidings of good things. But they have not all obeyed to the gospel. For Esaias saith: Lord who shall believe our sayings? So then faith cometh by hearing, and hearing cometh by the word of God. But I

★ Though faith justify from sin, and though Christ deserved the reward promised, yet is the promise made on the condition that we embrace Christ's doctrine and confess him with word and deed. So that we are justified to do good works, and in them to walk to the salvation promised.

Isa. 42.
Isa. 53. a.
John 12. f.

E

† Tyndale prints 'word'.

ask: have they not heard? No doubt their sound went out into all lands: and their words into the ends of the world. ⊦

Deut. 22. c.
But I demand whether Israel did know or not? First Moses saith: I will provoke you for to envy, by them that are no people, and by a foolish nation I *Isa. 65. a.* will anger you. Esaias after that, is bold and saith, I am found of them that sought me not, and have appeared to them that asked not after me. And against Israel he saith: All day long have I stretched forth my hands unto a people that believeth not, but speaketh against me.

CHAPTER ELEVEN

I say then: hath God cast away his people? God forbid. For even I verily am an   **A** Israelite, of the seed of Abraham, and of the tribe of Benjamin: God hath not cast away his people which he knew before. Either wot ye not what the scripture saith by the mouth of Elias, how he maketh intercession to God *1 Kin. 19.* against Israel, saying: Lord they have killed thy prophets and digged down thine altars: and I am left only, and they seek my life. But what saith the answer of God to him again? I have reserved unto me seven thousand men which have not bowed the knee to Baal. Even so at this time is there a remnant left * Grace and works are through the election of grace. If it be of grace★, then is it not of works. For contrary things. then were grace no more grace. If it be of works, then is it no more grace. For then were deserving no longer deserving.

What then? Israel hath not obtained that, that he sought. No but yet the   **B** election hath obtained it. The remnant are blinded, according as it is written: God hath given them the spirit of unquietness: eyes that they should not see, and ears that they should not hear even unto this day. And David saith: Let *Isa. 6. c.* their table be made a snare to take them withal, and an occasion to fall, and a *Matt. 13.* reward unto them. Let their eyes be blinded that they see not: and ever bow *John 12. f.* down their backs.
Acts 28. f.
Psa. 19.
I say then: Have they therefore stumbled that they should but fall only? God forbid: but through their fall is salvation happened unto the gentiles, for to provoke them withal. Wherefore if the fall of them, be the riches of the world: and the minishing of them the riches of the gentiles: How much more should it be so, if they all believed? I speak to you gentiles, inasmuch as I am the apostle   **C** of the gentiles I will magnify mine office, that might provoke them which are my flesh, and might save some of them. For if the casting-away of them, be the Do it with all diligence. reconciling of the world: what shall the receiving of them be, but life again from death? For if one piece be holy, the whole heap is holy. And if the root be holy, the branches are holy also.

Though some of the branches be broken off, and thou being a wild olive   **C** tree, art graft in among them, and made partaker of the root and fatness of the olive tree, boast not thyself against the branches. For if thou boast thyself, remember that thou bearest not the root, but the root thee. Thou wilt say then: the branches are broken off, that I might be graft in. Thou sayest well: because of unbelief they are broken off, and thou standest steadfast in faith. Be not high-minded, but fear seeing that God spared not the natural branches, lest haply he also spare not thee.

Behold the kindness and rigorousness of God: on them which fell, rigorousness: but towards thee, kindness, if thou continue in his kindness. Or else thou shalt be hewn off, and they if they bide not still in unbelief, shall be graffed in again. For God is of power to graff them in again. For if thou wast cut out of a natural wild olive tree, and wast graffed contrary to nature in a true olive tree: how much more shall the natural branches be graffed in their own olive tree again?

D I would not that this secret should be hid from you my brethren (lest ye shoud be wise in your own conceits) that partly blindness is happened in Israel, until the fullness of the gentiles be come in: and so all Israel shall be saved. As it is written: There shall come out of Sion he that doth deliver, and shall turn away the ungodliness of Jacob. And this is my covenant unto them, when I shall take away their sins. As concerning the gospel, they are enemies for your sakes: but as touching the election, they are loved for the fathers' sakes.

Isa. 59. d.

For verily the gifts and calling of God are such, that it cannot repent him of them: for like, as ye in time passed have not believed God, yet have now obtained mercy through their unbelief: even so now have they not believed the mercy which is happened unto you, that they also may obtain mercy. God hath wrapped all nations in unbelief, that he might have mercy on all.

O the deepness of the abundant wisdom and knowledge of God: how unsearchable are his judgements, and his ways past finding out. For who hath known the mind of the Lord? or who was his counsellor? or who hath given unto him first, that he might be recompensed again? For of him, and through him, and for him, are all things. To him be glory for ever Amen.

Prov. 9. c.
Isa. 40. d.
1 Cor. 2. d.

CHAPTER TWELVE

A + I beseech you therefore brethren, by the mercifulness of God, that ye make your bodies a quick sacrifice holy and acceptable unto God which is your reasonable serving of God. And fashion not yourselves like unto this world: But be ye changed in your shape, by the renewing of your wits that ye may feel what thing that good, that acceptable, and perfect will of God is. For I say (through the grace that unto me given is) to every man among you that no man esteem of himself more than it becometh him to esteem: but that he discreetly judge of himself, according as God hath dealt to every man the measure of faith.

Phil. 4. c.

True serving of God is to bring the body into the obedience of the law of God.

B As we have many members in one body, and all members have not one office: so we being many are one body in Christ and every man (among ourselves) one another's members ⊦. + Seeing that we have divers gifts according to the grace that is given unto us: if any man have the gift of prophecy*, let him have it that it be agreeing unto the faith. Let him that hath an office, wait on his office. Let him that teacheth, take heed to his doctrine. Let him that exhorteth, give attendance to his exhortation. If any man give, let him do it with single-

1 Cor. 12. b.
Eph. 4. b.

* Prophecy is taken here for the expounding of scriptures: which in dark places must be expounded that it agree to the open places and general articles of the faith.

237

ness. Let him that ruleth, do it with diligence. If any man show mercy, let him do it with cheerfulness.

Amos 5.
Eph. 4. a.
1 Pet. 5. b.

Let love be without dissimulation. Hate that which is evil, and cleave unto **C** that which is good. Be kind one to another with brotherly love. In giving honour, go one before another. Let not the business which ye have in hand, be tedious to you. Be fervent in the spirit. Apply yourselves to the time. Rejoice in hope. Be patient in tribulation. Continue in prayer. Distribute unto the

Heb. 13.
1 Pet. 4. a.

necessity of the saints and diligently to harbour. Bless them which persecute you: bless but curse not. Be merry with them that are merry. Weep with them that weep. Be of like affection one towards another. Be not high-minded: but

Prov. 3. a.
1 Pet. 3. d.
2 Cor. 8.
Heb. 12. d.

make yourselves equal to them of the lower sort. ⊢ + Be not wise in your own **D** opinions. Recompence to no man evil for evil. Provide afore-hand things honest in the sight of all men. If it be possible, howbeit of your part, have peace with all men. Dearly beloved avenge not yourselves, but give room unto the

Deut. 32.
Heb. 10. e.
Prov. 25.

wrath of God. For it is written: vengeance is mine, and I will reward saith the Lord.

* Coals: this thou shalt kindle him and make him to love.

Therefore if thine enemy hunger, feed him: if he thirst, give him drink. For in so doing thou shalt heap coals★ of fire on his head: Be not overcome of evil: But overcome evil with goodness. ⊢

CHAPTER THIRTEEN

Obedience.

+ Let every soul submit himself unto the authority of the higher powers. For **A** there is no power but of God. The powers that be, are ordained of God. Whosoever therefore resisteth power, resisteth the ordinance of God. And they that resist, shall receive to themselves damnation. For rulers are not to be feared for good works, but for evil. Wilt thou be without fear of the power? Do well **B** then: and so shalt thou be praised of the same. For he is the minister of God, for thy wealth. But and if thou do evil, then fear: for he beareth not a sword for nought: but is the minister of God, to take vengeance on them that do evil.

* Though thou were of power to resist the power, yet were thou damned in thy conscience if thou didest it, because it is against God's commandment.

Wherefore ye must needs obey, not for fear of vengeance only: but also because of conscience★. And even for this cause pay ye tribute. For they are God's ministers, serving for the same purpose. ⊢

Exod. 20. c.
Deut. 5. b.

Give to every man therefore his duetie: Tribute to whom tribute belongeth: Custom to whom custom is due: fear to whom fear belongeth: Honour to whom honour pertaineth. + Owe nothing to any man: but to love one another. For he that loveth another, fulfilleth the law. For these commandments: Thou **C** shalt not commit advoutry: Thou shalt not kill: Thou shalt not steal: Thou shalt not bear false witness: Thou shalt not desire and so forth (if there be any other commandment), they are all comprehended in this saying: Love thine

Love is the fulfilling of the law.

neighbour as thy self. Love hurteth not his neighbour. Therefore is love the fulfilling of the law. ⊢

* Christ which is our salvation is now nearer than when we looked for him in the old testament.

+ This also we know, I mean the season, how that it is time that we should **D** now awake out of sleep. For now is our salvation★ nearer than when we believed. The night is passed and the day is come nigh. Let us therefore cast away the deeds of darkness, and let us put on the armour★ of light. Let us walk honestly as it were in the daylight: not in eating and drinking: neither in chambering and wantonness: neither in strife and envying: but put ye on the Lord Jesus Christ. ⊦ And make not provision for the flesh, to fulfil the lusts of it.

★ Armour of light: faith, hope, love, the fear of God. truth and all that the light of God's word teacheth.

CHAPTER FOURTEEN

A Him that is weak in the faith, receive unto you, not in disputing and troubling his conscience. One believeth that he may eat all things. Another which is weak, eateth herbs. Let not him that eateth, despise him that eateth not. And let not him which eateth not judge him that eateth. For God hath received him. What art thou that judgest another man's servant? Whether he stand or fall, that pertaineth unto his master: yea, he shall stand. For God is able to make him stand.

Jas. 4. d.

B This man putteth difference between day and day. Another man counteth all days alike. See that no man waver in his own meaning. He that observeth one day more than another, doth it for the Lord's pleasure. And he that observeth not one day more than another, doth it to please the Lord also. He that eateth, doth it to please the Lord, for he giveth God thanks. And he that eateth not, eateth not to please the Lord withal, and giveth God thanks. For none of us liveth his own servant: neither doth any of us die his own servant. If we live, we live to be at the Lord's will. And if we die, we die at the Lord's will. Whether we live therefore or die, we are the Lord's. For Christ therefore died and rose again, and revived, that he might be Lord both of dead and quick.

How weak so ever we be, we be Christ's. And therefore to be favoured for his sake.

C But why dost thou then judge thy brother? Or why dost thou despise thy brother? We shall all be brought before the judgement seat of Christ. For it is written: as truly as I live saith the Lord, all knees shall bow to me, and all tongues shall give a knowledge to God. So shall every one of us give accounts of himself to God. Let us not therefore judge one another any more.

1 Cor. 5. b.
Isa. 45. d.
Phil. 2.

But judge this rather, that no man put a stumbling-block or an occasion to fall in his brother's way. + For I know and am full certified in the Lord Jesus, that there is nothing common of itself: but unto him that judgeth it to be common: to him it is common. If thy brother be grieved with thy meat, now walkest thou not charitably. Destroy not him with thy meat, for whom Christ died. Cause not your treasure to be evil spoken of. For the kingdom of God is not meat and drink: but righteousness, peace and joy in the holy ghost. For whosoever in these things serveth Christ, pleaseth well God, and is commended of men.

Common: that is to say unclean.

Our treasure is our knowledge.

Kingdom of God: what it is.

D Let us follow those things which make for peace, and things wherewith one may edify another. Destroy not the work of God for a little meat's sake. All things are pure: but it is evil for that man, which eateth with hurt of his conscience. It is good neither to eat flesh, neither to drink wine, neither any thing, whereby thy brother stumbleth, either falleth, or is made weak. Hast

Tit. 1. d.

thou faith? have it with thyself before God. Happy is he that condemneth not himself in that thing which he alloweth. For he that maketh conscience, is damned if he eat: because he doth it not of faith. For whatsoever is not of faith, that same is sin. ⊢

To do against conscience is damnable. And all that is not of faith is sin.

CHAPTER FIFTEEN

He is strong that can bear another man's weakness.

A We which are strong, ought to bear the frailness of them which are weak, and not to stand in our own conceits. Let every man please his neighbour unto his wealth and edifying. For Christ pleased not himself: but as it is written, the rebukes of them which rebuked thee, fell on me. + Whatsoever things are written aforetime, are written for our learning, that we through patience and comfort of the scripture, might have hope.

Psa. 119.

B The God of patience and consolation, give unto every one of you, that ye be like-minded one towards another after the example of Christ: that ye all agreeing together, may with one mouth praise God the father of our Lord Jesus. Wherefore receive ye one another as Christ received us, to the praise of God.

1 Cor. 1. b.

And I say that Jesus Christ was a minister of the circumcision for the truth of God, to confirm the promises made unto the fathers. And let the gentiles praise God for his mercy, as it is written: For this cause I will praise thee among the gentiles, and sing in thy name. And again he saith: rejoice ye gentiles with his people. And again, praise the Lord all ye gentiles, and laud him all nations.
C And in another place Esaias saith: there shall be the root of Jesse, and he that shall rise to reign over the gentiles: in him shall the gentiles trust. The God of hope fill you with all joy and peace in believing: that ye may be rich in hope through the power of the holy ghost. ⊢

Psa. 18.
2. Sam. 22.
Psa. 117.
Isa. 11. c.

I myself am full certified of you my brethren, that ye yourselves are full of goodness and filled with all knowledge, and are able to exhort one another.
D Nevertheless brethren I have somewhat boldly written unto you, as one that putteth you in remembrance, through the grace that is given me of God, that I should be the minister of Jesus Christ among the gentiles, and should minister the glad tidings of God, that the gentiles might be an acceptable offering, sanctified by the holy ghost. I have therefore whereof I may rejoice in Christ Jesus, in those things which pertain to God. For I dare not speak of any of those things which Christ hath not wrought by me, to make the gentiles obedient, with word and deed, in mighty signs and wonders, by the power of the spirit of God: so that from Jerusalem and the coast round about unto Illyricum, I have filled all countries with glad tidings of Christ.

E So have I enforced myself to preach the gospel, not where Christ was named, lest I should have built on another man's foundation: but as it is written: To whom he was not spoken of, they shall see: and they that heard not, shall understand. For this cause I have been often let to come unto you: but now seeing I have no more to do in these countries, and also have been desirous many years to come unto you, when I shall take my journey into Spain, I will

Isa. 53. d.

come to you. I trust to see you in my journey, and to be brought on my way thither-ward by you after that I have somewhat enjoyed you.

Now go I unto Jerusalem, and minister unto the saints. For it hath pleased them of Macedonia and Achaia to make a certain distribution upon the poor saints which are at Jerusalem. It hath pleased them verily, and their debtors are they. For if the gentiles be made partakers of their spiritual things, their duty is to minister unto them in carnal things. When I have performed this, and have brought them this fruit sealed, I will come back again by you into Spain. And I am sure when I come, that I shall come with abundance of the blessing of the gospel of Christ.

+ I beseech you brethren for our Lord Jesus Christ's sake, and for the love of the spirit, that ye help me in my business, with your prayers to God for me, that I may be delivered from them which believe not in Jewry, and that this my service, which I have to Jerusalem, may be accepted of the saints, that I may come unto you with joy, by the will of God, and may with you be refreshed. The God of peace be with you. Amen. ⊦

1 Cor. 9. b.

CHAPTER SIXTEEN

I commend unto you Phebe our sister (which is a minister of the congregation of Cenchrea) that ye receive her in the Lord as it becometh saints, and that ye assist her in whatsoever business she needeth of your aid. For she hath succoured many, and mine own self also. Greet Prisca and Aquila my helpers in Christ Jesus, which have for my life laid down their own necks. Unto which not I only give thanks but also the congregation of the gentiles. Likewise greet all the company that is in her house. Salute my wellbeloved Epenetus, which is the first fruit among them of Achaia. Greet Mary which bestowed much labour on us. Salute Andronicus and Junia my cousins, which were prisoners with me also, which are well taken among the apostles, and were in Christ before me. Greet Amplias my beloved in the Lord. Salute Urban our helper in Christ, and Stachys my beloved. Salute Apelles approved in Christ. Salute them which are of Aristobolus' household. Salute Herodion my kinsman. Greet them of the household of Narcissus which are in the Lord. Salute Tryphena and Tryphosa, which women did labour in the Lord. Salute the beloved Persis, which labour-ed in the Lord. Salute Rufus chosen in the Lord, and his mother and mine. Greet Asincritus, Phlegon, Hermas, Patrobas, Hermes, and the brethren which are with them. Salute Philologus and Julia, Nereus and his sister, and Olympas, and all the saints which are with them. Salute one another with an holy kiss. The congregations of Christ salute you.

I beseech you brethren, mark them which cause division and give occasions of evil, contrary to the doctrine which ye have learned: and avoid them. For they that are such serve not the Lord Jesus Christ: but their own bellies, and with sweet preachings and flattering word deceive the hearts of the innocents. For your obedience★ extendeth to all men. I am glad no doubt of you. But yet I would have you wise unto that which is good, and to be innocents concerning

Acts 18.

First fruit: that is, the first that was converted to God.

★ Paul would have the lay people learned to judge the prophets and to obey them according to knowledge only: for all, obedience that is not after true knowledge is disallowed of God.

241

evil. The God of peace tread Satan under your feet shortly. The grace of our Lord Jesus Christ be with you.

Timotheus my workfellow, and Lucius and Jason and Sosipater my kinsmen, salute you. I Tertius salute you, which wrote this epistle in the Lord. Gaius mine host and the host of all the congregations, saluteth you. Erastus the chamberlain of the city saluteth you. And Quartus a brother saluteth you. The grace of our Lord Jesus Christ be with you all. Amen.

To him that is of power to establish you according to my gospel and preaching of Jesus Christ, in uttering of the mystery which was kept secret since the world began, but now is opened by the scriptures of prophecy, at the commandment of the everlasting God, to stir up obedience to the faith published among all nations: To the same God, which alone is wise, be praise through Jesus Christ for ever. Amen.

To the Romans.

Sent from Corinth by Phebe, she that was the minister
unto the congregation at Cenchrea.

THE PROLOGUE UPON THE FIRST EPISTLE
OF ST PAUL TO THE CORINTHIANS

This epistle declareth itself from chapter to chapter, that it needeth no prologue or introduction to declare it. When Paul had converted a great number at Corinth, as ye read (Acts 18) and was departed, there came immediately false apostles and sectmakers and drew every man disciples after him, so that the people were whole unquieted, divided and at variance among themselves, every man for the zeal of his doctor, those new apostles not regarding what division, what uncleanness of living, or what false opinions were among the people, as long as they might be in authority and well at ease in their bellies.

But Paul in the four first chapters with great wisdom and soberness, rebuketh, first the division and the authors thereof, and calleth the people to Christ again and teacheth how and for what the preacher is to be taken.

In the fifth he rebuketh the uncleanness that was amongst them.

In the sixth he rebuketh the debate and going to law together, pleading their causes before the heathen.

In the seventh he informeth them concerning chastity and marriage.

In the eighth, ninth, tenth and eleventh he teacheth the strong to forbear the weak that yet understood not the liberty of the gospel, and that with the example of himself. Which though he were an apostle and had authority, yet of love he abstained, to win other. And he feareth them with the examples of the old testament and rebuketh diverse disorders that were among them concerning the sacrament and the going bare-headed of married women.

In the twelfth, thirteenth and fourteenth, he teacheth of the manifold gifts of the spirit, and proveth by a similitude of the body, that all gifts are given that each should help other, and through love do service to other, and proveth that where love is not, there is nothing that pleaseth God. For that one should love another, is all that God requireth of us. And therefore if we desire spiritual gifts he teacheth those gifts to be desired that help our neighbours.

In the fifteenth he teacheth of the resurrection of the body.

And in the last he exhorteth to help the poor saints.

THE FIRST EPISTLE
OF ST PAUL THE APOSTLE
TO THE CORINTHIANS

1^{1–20} CHAPTER ONE

Paul by vocation an apostle of Jesus Christ through the will of God, and brother Sosthenes.

Unto the congregation of God which is at Corinth. To them that are sanctified in Christ Jesus, saints by calling, with all that call on the name of our Lord Jesus Christ in every place, both of theirs and of ours:

Grace be with you and peace from God our father, and from the Lord Jesus Christ.

+ I thank my God always on your behalf for the grace of God which is given you by Jesus Christ, that in all things ye are made rich by him in all learning and in all knowledge even as the testimony of Jesus Christ was confirmed in you, so that ye are behind in no gift, and wait for the appearing of our Lord Jesus Christ which shall strength you unto the end, that ye may be blameless in the day of our Lord Jesus Christ. ⊦ For God is faithful, by whom ye are called unto the fellowship of his son Jesus Christ our Lord.

I beseech you brethren in the name of our Lord Jesus Christ, that ye all speak one thing and that there be no dissension among you: but be ye knit together in one mind and in one meaning. It is showed unto me (my brethren) of you by them that are of the house of Chloe, that there is strife among you. And this is it that I mean: how that commonly among you, one sayeth: I hold of Paul: another I hold of Apollos: the third I hold of Cephas: the fourth that I hold of Christ. Is Christ divided? was Paul crucified for you? either were ye baptised in the name of Paul? I thank God that I christened none of you, but Crispus and Gaius, lest any should say that I had baptised in mine own name. I baptised also the house of Stephanas. Furthermore know I not whether I baptised any man or no.

For Christ sent me not to baptise, but to preach the gospel, not with wisdom of words, lest the cross of Christ should have been made of none effect. For the preaching of the cross is to them that perish foolishness: but unto us which are saved, it is the power of God. For it is written: I will destroy the wisdom of the wise, and will cast away the understanding of the prudent. Where is the wise? Where is the scribe? Where is the searcher of this world? Hath not God made the wisdom of this world foolishness?

1 Thes. 5.

Preaching of the cross is the power of God.

Isa. 29.
Ob. 1. c.
Isa. 33. c.

B

C

For when the world through wisdom knew not God, in the wisdom of God: it pleased God through foolishness of preaching to save them that believe. For the Jews require a sign, and the Greeks seek after wisdom. But we preach

D Christ crucified, unto the Jews an occasion of falling, and unto the Greeks foolishness: but unto them which are called both of Jews and Greeks, we preach Christ the power of God, and the wisdom of God. For the foolishness of God is wiser than men: and the weakness of God is stronger than men.

Brethren look on your calling, how that not many wise men after the flesh, not many mighty, not many of high degree are called: but God hath chosen the foolish things of the world, to confound the wise. And God hath chosen the weak things of the world, to confound things which are mighty. And vile things of the world, and things which are despised, hath God chosen, yea and things of no reputation, for to bring to nought things of reputation, that no flesh should rejoice in his presence. And unto him pertain ye, in Christ Jesus, which of God is made unto us wisdom★, and also righteousness, and sanctifying and redemption. That according as it is written: he which rejoiceth, should rejoice in the Lord.

Sign.

Christ is the power and wisdom of God.

★ *Christ is wisdom and etc. And of him only ought we to hold, and in him only to rejoice.*

CHAPTER TWO

A And I brethren when I came to you, came not in gloriousness of words or of wisdom, showing unto you the testimony of God. Neither showed I myself that I knew any thing among you save Jesus Christ, even the same that was crucified. And I was among you in weakness, and in fear, and in much trembling. And my words and my preaching were not with enticing words of man's wisdom: but in showing of the spirit and of power, that your faith should not stand in the wisdom of men, but in the power of God.

B That we speak of, is wisdom among them that are perfect: not the wisdom of this world, neither of the rulers of this world (which go to nought), but we speak the wisdom of God, which is in secret and lieth hid, which God ordained before the world unto our glory: which wisdom none of the rulers of the world knew. For had they known it, they would not have crucified the Lord of glory. But as it is written: The eye hath not seen, and the ear hath not heard, neither have entered into the heart of man, the things which God hath prepared for them that love him.

Perfect are they that understand the law, faith and works truly, and profess them.

Isa. 64.

C But God hath opened them unto us by his spirit. For the spirit searcheth all things, yea the bottom of God's secrets. For what man knoweth the things of a man: save the spirit of a man which is within him? Even so the things of God knoweth no man, but the spirit of God. And we have not received the spirit of

D the world: but the spirit which cometh of God, for to know the things that are given to us of God, which things also we speak, not in the cunning words of man's wisdom, but with the cunning words of the holy ghost, making spiritual comparisons of spiritual things. For the natural man perceiveth not the things of the spirit of God. For they are but foolishness unto him. Neither can he perceive them, because he is spiritually examined. But he that is spiritual,

The spirit understandeth godly things. The natural man that is not renewed in Christ cannot perceive the things of God.

discusseth all things: yet he himself is judged of no man. For who knoweth the mind of the Lord, or who shall inform him? But we understand the mind of Christ.

Isa. 40. d.
Isa. 9. c.
Rom. 11. d.

CHAPTER THREE

And I could not speak unto you brethren as unto spiritual: but as unto carnal, **A** even as it were unto babes in Christ. I gave you milk to drink and not meat. For ye then were not strong, no neither yet are. For ye are yet carnal. As long verily as there is among you envying, strife, and dissension: are ye not carnal, and walk after the manner of men? As long as one saith, I hold of Paul, and another, I am of Apollos, are ye not carnal? What is Paul? What thing is Apollos? Only ministers* are they by whom ye believed, even as the Lord gave every man grace. I have planted: Apollos watered: but God gave increase. So then, neither is he that planteth any thing, neither he that watereth: but God which gave the increase.

He that planteth and he that watereth, are neither better than the other. Every man yet shall receive his reward according to his labour. We are God's labourers, ye are God's husbandry, ye are God's building. According to the grace of God given unto me, as a wise builder have I laid the foundation: And another built thereon. But let every man take heed how he buildeth upon. For other foundation can no man lay, than that which is laid, which is Jesus Christ. If any man build on this foundation, gold, silver, precious stones, timber, hay or stubble: every man's work shall appear. For the day shall declare it, and it shall be showed in fire. And the fire shall try every man's work, what it is. If any man's work that he hath built upon, bide, he shall receive a reward. If any man's work burn he shall suffer loss: but he shall be safe himself: nevertheless yet as it were through fire.

+ Are ye not ware that ye are the temple of God, and how that the spirit of **D** God dwelleth in you? If any man defile the temple of God him shall God destroy. For the temple of God is holy, which temple ye are. Let no man deceive himself. If any man seem wise among you, let him be a fool in this world, that he may be wise. For the wisdom of this world is foolishness with God. For it is written: he compasseth the wise in their craftiness. And again, God knoweth the thoughts of the wise that they be vain. Therefore let no man rejoice in men. For all things are yours, whether it be Paul, or Apollos, or Cephas: whether it be the world, or life, or death, whether they be present things or things to come: all are yours, and ye are Christ's, and Christ is God's. ⊦

* The apostles and prelates are servants to preach Christ unto which doctrine only ought all obedience to be given.

Psa. 62. d.
Gal. 5.

Christ is the foundation that beareth all.

Day.

Temple.

2 Cor. 6.

Job 5. c.
Psa. 94. b.

In the Kingdom of Christ we are subjects to none save to Christ and his doctrine.

CHAPTER FOUR

+ Let men this wise esteem us, even as the ministers of Christ, and disposers of **A** the secrets of God. Furthermore it is required of the disposers that they be found faithful*. With me is it but a very small thing, that I should be judged of

The apostles are ministers.

you, either of man's day★. No, I judge not mine own self. I know nought by
myself: yet am I not thereby justified. It is the Lord that judgeth me. Therefore
judge nothing before the time, until the Lord come, which will lighten things
that are hid in darkness and open the counsels of the hearts. And then shall
every man have praise of God. ⊢

★ Faithful is he that
preacheth his master
and not himself.

★ Man's day is
man's wisdom.

B   These things brethren I have described in mine own person and Apollos, for
your sakes, that ye might learn by us, that no man count of himself beyond that
which is above written: that one swell not against another for any man's cause.
For who preferreth thee? What hast thou, that thou hast not received? If thou
have received it, why rejoicest thou as though thou haddest not received it?
Now ye are full: now ye are made rich: ye reign as kings without us: and I
would to God ye did reign, that we might reign with you.

Me thinketh that God hath set forth us which are apostles, for the lowest of
C   all, as it were men appointed to death. For we are a gazingstock unto the
world, and to the angels, and to men. We are fools for Christ's sake, and ye are
wise through Christ. We are weak, and ye are strong. Ye are honourable and
we are despised. Even unto this day we hunger and thirst, and are naked, and
are buffeted with fists, and have no certain dwelling place, and labour working
with our own hands. We are reviled, and yet we bless. We are persecuted, and
suffer it. We are evil spoken of, and we pray. We are made as it were the
filthiness of the world, the off-scouring of all things, even unto this time.

The fashion of
true apostles.

Acts 20. g.
1 Thes. 2. b.
2 Thes. 3.

I write not these things to shame you: but as my beloved sons I warn you.
For though ye have ten thousand instructors in Christ: yet have ye not many
fathers. In Christ Jesus, I have begotten you through the gospel. Wherefore I
D   desire you to follow me. For this cause have I sent unto you Timotheus, which
is my dear son, and faithful in the Lord, which shall put you in remembrance
of my ways which I have in Christ, even as I teach everywhere in all congregations. Some swell as though I would come no more at you. But I will come
to you shortly, if God will: and will know, not the words of them which swell,
but the power: for the kingdom of God is not in words, but in power. What
will ye? Shall I come unto you with a rod, or else in love and in the spirit of
meekness?

CHAPTER FIVE

A   There goeth a common saying that there is fornication among you, and such
fornication as is not once named among the gentiles: that one should have his
father's wife. And ye swell and have not rather sorrowed, that he which hath
done this deed, might be put from among you. For I verily as absent in body,
B   even so present in spirit, have determined already (as though I were present) of
him that hath done this deed, in the name of our Lord Jesus Christ, when ye are
gathered together, and my spirit, with the power of the Lord Jesus Christ, to
deliver him unto Satan★, for the destruction of the flesh, that the spirit may be
saved in the day of the Lord Jesus.

C   Your rejoicing is not good: know ye not that a little leaven soureth the whole

Fornication.

Col. 2. a.

★ Excommunication is
to destroy fleshly
wisdom that the spirit
may be found in the
doctrine of Christ.

lump of dough? + Purge therefore the old leaven, that ye may be new dough, as ye are sweet bread. For Christ our Easter lamb is offered up for us. Therefore let us keep holy day, not with old leaven, neither with the leaven of maliciousness and wickedness: but with the sweet bread of pureness and truth. ⊢

If any that professeth Christ be such: no other Christian man may bear his company.

I wrote unto you in an epistle that ye should not company with fornicators. And I meant not at all of the fornicators of this world, either of the covetous, or of extortioners, either of the idolaters: for then must ye needs have gone out of the world. But now I write unto you, that ye company not together, if any that is called a brother, be a fornicator, or covetous, or a worshipper of images, either a railer, either a drunkard, or an extortioner: with him that is such see that ye eat not.

For what have I to do, to judge them which are without? Do ye not judge them that are within? Them that are without, God shall judge. Put away from among you, that evil person.

CHAPTER SIX

To go to law.

How dare one of you having business with another, go to law under the **A**
wicked, and not rather under the saints? Do ye not know that the saints shall judge the world? If the world shall be judged by you: are ye not good enough to judge small trifles? know ye not how that we shall judge the angels? How much more may we judge things that pertain to the life? If ye have judgements of worldly matters, take them which are despised in the congregation, and make them judges. This I say to your shame. Is there utterly no wise man among you? What not one at all, that can judge between brother and brother, **B**
but one brother goeth to law with another: and that under the unbelievers?

Now therefore there is utterly a fault among you, because ye go to law one with another. Why rather suffer ye not wrong? why rather suffer ye not yourselves to be robbed? Nay ye yourselves do wrong, and rob: and that the brethren. Do ye not remember how that the unrighteous shall not inherit the kingdom of God? Be not deceived. For neither fornicators, neither wor-

These and suchlike have no part in Christ.

shippers of images, neither whoremongers, neither weaklings, neither abusers of themselves with the mankind, neither thieves, neither the covetous, neither drunkards, neither cursed speakers, neither pillers, shall inherit the kingdom of

Sanctifying and justifying come by Christ and his spirit.

God. And such were ye verily: but ye are washed: ye are sanctified: ye are justified by the name of the Lord Jesus, and by the spirit of our God.

All things are lawful unto me: but all things are not profitable. I may do all **C**
things: but I will be brought under no man's power. Meats are ordained for the belly, and the belly for meats: but God shall destroy both it and them. Let not the body be applied unto fornication, but unto the Lord, and the Lord unto the body. God hath raised up the Lord, and shall raise us up by his power. + Either

* Our bodies are the members of Christ.

remember ye not, that your bodies* are the members of Christ? Shall I now take the members of Christ, and make them the members of an harlot? God forbid. Do ye not understand that he which coupleth himself with an harlot, is become one body? For two (saith he) shall be one flesh. But he that is joined

He that is of Christ: hath his spirit.

unto the Lord, is one spirit.

D Flee fornication. All sins that a man doth, are without the body. But he that is a fornicator, sinneth against his own body. Either know ye not how that your bodies are the temple of the holy ghost, which is in you, whom ye have of God, and how that ye are not your own? For ye are dearly bought. Therefore glorify ye God in your bodies⊦ and in your spirits, for they are God's.

Rom. 8.

1 Pet. 1. d.

CHAPTER SEVEN

A ⊦ As concerning the things whereof ye wrote unto me: it is good for a man, not to touch a woman. Nevertheless to avoid fornication, let every man have his wife: and let every woman have her husband. Let the man give unto the wife due benevolence. Likewise also the wife unto the man. The wife hath not power over her own body: but the husband. and likewise the man hath not power over his own body: but the wife. Withdraw not yourselves one from another, except it be with consent for a time, for to give yourselves to fasting and prayer. And afterward come again to the same thing, lest Satan tempt you for your incontinence. ⊦

Of wedlock and virginity.

1 Pet. 3. b.

B This I say of favour, not of commandment. For I would that all men were as I myself am: but every man hath his proper gift of God, one after this manner, another after that. I say unto the unmarried men and widows: it is good for them if they abide even as I do. But and if they cannot abstain, let them marry. For it is better to marry than to burn.

Unto the married command not I, but the Lord: that the wife separate not herself from the man. If she separate herself, let her remain unmarried, or be reconciled unto her husband again. And let not the husband put away his wife from him.

Matt. 5. c. and 9. b.
Mark 10. b.

Luke 16. d.

C To the remnant speak I, and not the Lord. If any brother have a wife that believeth not, if she be content to dwell with him, let him not put her away. And the woman which hath to her husband an infidel, if he consent to dwell with her, let her not put him away. For the unbelieving husband is sanctified by the wife: and the unbelieving wife is sanctified by the husband. Or else were your children unclean: but now are they pure. But and if the unbelieving depart, let him depart. A brother or a sister is not in subjection to such. God hath called us in peace. For how knowest thou o woman, whether thou shalt save that man or no? Or how knowest thou o man, whether thou shalt save that woman or no? but even as God hath distributed to every man.

D As the Lord hath called every person, so let him walk: and so ordain I in all congregations. If any man be called being circumcised, let him add nothing thereto. If any be called uncircumcised: let him not be circumcised. Circumcision is nothing, uncircumcision is nothing: but the keeping of the commandments of God is altogether. ⊦ Let every man abide in the same state wherein he was called. Art thou called a servant? care not for it. Nevertheless if thou mayst be free, use it rather. For he that is called in the Lord being a servant, is the Lord's freeman. Likewise he that is called being free, is Christ's servant. Ye are dearly bought, be not men's servants. Brethren let every man wherein he is called, therein abide with God. ⊦

Circumcision.

As concerning virgins, I have no commandment of the Lord: yet give I **E**
counsel, as one that hath obtained mercy of the Lord to be faithful. I suppose
that it is good for the present* necessity. For it is good for a man so to be. Art
thou bound unto a wife? seek not to be loosed. Art thou loosed from a wife?
seek not a wife. But and if thou take a wife thou sinnest not. Likewise if a
virgin marry, she sinneth not. Nevertheless such shall have trouble in their
flesh: but I favour you.

* If a man have the
gift, chastity is good,
the more quietly to
serve God. For the
married have oft much
trouble: but if the mind
of the chaste be
cumbered with other
worldly business, what
helpeth it? and if the
married be the more
quiet-minded thereby,
what hurteth it?
Neither of itself is
better than the other, or
pleaseth God more than
the other. Neither is
outward circumcision
or outward baptism
worth a pin of
themselves, save that
they put us in
remembrance to keep
the covenant made
between us and God.

This say I brethren: the time is short. It remaineth that they which have
wives, be as though they had none, and they that weep be as though they wept
not: and they that rejoice, be as though they rejoiced not: and they that buy be
as though they possessed not: and they that use this world, be as though they
used it not. For the fashion of this world goeth away.

I would have you without care: the single man careth for the things of the **F**
Lord, how he may please the Lord. But he that hath married, careth for the
things of the world how he may please his wife. There is difference between a
virgin and a wife. The single woman careth for the things of the Lord, that she
may be pure both in body and also in spirit. But she that is married, careth for
the things of the world, how she may please her husband. This speak I for your
profit, not to tangle you in a snare: but for that which is honest and comely
unto you, and that ye may quietly cleave unto the Lord without separation.

If any man think that it is uncomely for his virgin if she pass the time of **G**
marriage, and if so need require, let him do what he listeth, he sinneth not: let
them be coupled in marriage. Nevertheless, he that purposeth surely in his
heart, having none need: but hath power over his own will: and hath so decreed
in his heart that he will keep his virgin, doth well. So then he that joineth his
virgin in marriage doth well. But he that joineth not his virgin in marriage
doth better. The wife is bound to the law as long as her husband liveth. If her
husband sleep, she is at liberty to marry with whom she will, only in the Lord.
But she is happier if she so abide, in my judgement. And I think verily that I
have the spirit of God.

Rom. 7.

CHAPTER EIGHT

A little love is better
than much knowledge.

To speak of things dedicate unto idols, we are sure that we all have knowledge. **A**
Knowledge maketh a man swell: but love edifieth. If any man think that he
knoweth any thing, he knoweth nothing yet as he ought to know. But if any
man love God, the same is known of him.

To speak of meat dedicate unto idols, we are sure that there is none idol in
the world and that there is none other God but one. And though there be that
are called gods, whether in heaven or in earth (as there be gods many and lords
many) yet unto us is there but one God, which is the father, of whom are all
things, and we in him: and one Lord Jesus Christ by whom are all things, and
we by him.

One God.
One Lord.

But every man hath not knowledge. For some suppose that there is an idol,
until this hour, and eat as of a thing offered unto the idol, and so their con-

sciences being yet weak, are defiled. Meat maketh us not acceptable to God. Neither if we eat, are we the better. Neither if we eat not, are we the worse.

D But take heed that your liberty cause not the weak to fall. For if some man see thee which hast knowledge sit at meat in the idol's temple, shall not the conscience of him which is weak, be boldened to eat those things which are offered unto the idol? And so through thy knowledge shall the weak brother perish for whom Christ died. When ye sin so against the brethren and wound their weak consciences ye sin against Christ. Wherefore if meat hurt my brother, I will eat no flesh while the world standeth, because I will not hurt my brother.

In all our deeds we must have a respect to our neighbour's wealth.

Charity: what it doeth.

CHAPTER NINE

A Am I not an apostle? am I not free? have I not seen Jesus Christ our Lord? Are not ye my work in the Lord? If I be not an apostle unto other, yet am I unto you. For the seal of mine apostleship are ye in the Lord. Mine answer to them that ask me, is this. Have we not power to eat and to drink? Either have we not power to lead about a sister to wife as well as other apostles, and as the brethren of the Lord, and Cephas? Either only I and Barnabas have not power this to do? Who goeth a warfare any time at his own cost? Who planteth a vineyard and eateth not of the fruit? Who feedeth a flock and eateth not of the milk?

Paul proveth himself an apostle equal to the best: in that the spirit beareth record to his preaching, and as many were by him converted as by the apostles.

B Say I these things after the manner of men? Or saith not the law the same also? For it is written in the law of Moses, Thou shall not muzzle the mouth of the ox that treadeth out the corn. Doth God take thought for oxen? Either saith he it not all together for our sakes? For our sakes no doubt this is written: that he which eareth, should ear in hope: and that he which thresheth in hope, should be partaker of his hope. If we sow unto you spiritual things: is it a great thing if we reap your carnal things? If other be partakers of this power over you, wherefore are not we rather?

The preacher hath right to challenge a living for his labour.

Nevertheless we have not used this power: but suffer all things lest we should hinder the gospel of Christ. Do ye not understand how that they which minister in the temple, have their finding of the temple? And they which wait at the altar, are partakers with the altar? Even so also did the Lord ordain, that they which preach the gospel, should live of the gospel. But I have used none of these things.

C Neither wrote I these things that it should be so done unto me. For it were better for me to die, than any man should take this rejoicing from me. In that I preach the gospel, I have nothing to rejoice of. For necessity is put unto me. Woe is it unto me if I preach not the gospel. If I do it with a good will, I have a reward. But if I do it against my will, an office is committed unto me. What is my reward then? Verily that when I preach the gospel, I make the gospel of Christ free, that I misuse not mine authority in the gospel.

He that worketh of love to his neighbour hath his reward.

For though I be free from all men, yet have I made myself servant unto all men, that I might win the more. Unto the Jews, I became as a Jew, to win the Jews. To them that were under the law, was I made as though I had been under

What love maketh a man do.

the law, to win them that were under the law. To them that were without law, became I as though I had been without law (when I was not without law as pertaining to God, but under a law as concerning Christ) to win them that were without law. To the weak became I as weak, to win the weak. In all things I fashioned myself to all men, to save at the least way some. And this I do for the gospel's sake, that I might have my part thereof.

+ Perceive ye not how that they which run in a course, run all, yet but one **E** receiveth the reward? So run that ye may obtain. Every man that proveth masteries, abstaineth from all things. And they do it to obtain a corruptible crown: but we to obtain an uncorruptible crown: I therefore so run, not as at an uncertain thing. So fight I, not as one that beateth the air: but I tame my body and bring it into subjection, lest after that I have preached to others, I myself should be a castaway. ⊢

CHAPTER TEN

Num. 9. d.
Exod. 13. d.
Exod. 13. e.
Exod. 16. d.
Exod. 17. b.

Brethren I would not that ye should be ignorant of this, how that our fathers **A** were all under a cloud, and all passed through the sea, and were all baptised under Moses, in the cloud, and in the sea: and did all eat of one spiritual meat, and did all drink of one manner of spiritual drink. And they drank of that spiritual rock that followed them, which rock was Christ. ⊢ But in many of them had God no delight. For they were overthrown in the wilderness.

As it went in the old testament; so shall it do in the new.

Num. 20. b.
Num. 26. g.
Exod. 32.
Num. 25. b.
Num. 21. b.
Exod. 14. f.
Judg. 8. c.

These are examples to us + that we should not lust after evil things, as they **B** lusted: Neither be ye worshippers of images as were some of them according as it is written: The people sat down to eat and drink, and rose up again to play. Neither let us commit fornication as some of them committed fornication, and were destroyed in one day twenty-three thousand. Neither let us tempt Christ, as some of them tempted, and were destroyed of serpents. Neither murmur ye as some of them murmured, and were destroyed of the destroyer.

All these things happened upon them for example, and were written to put **C** us in remembrance, whom the ends of the world are come upon. Wherefore let him that thinketh he standeth, take heed lest he fall. There hath none other temptation taken you, but such as followeth the nature of man. But God is faithful, which shall not suffer you to be tempted above your strength: but shall in the midst of the temptation make a way to escape out. ⊢ Wherefore my dear beloved, flee from worshipping of idols.

Cup.

Bread.

I speak as unto them which have discretion, judge ye what I say. Is not the **D** cup of blessing which we bless, partaking of the blood of Christ? Is not the bread which we break, partaking of the body of Christ? Because that we (though we be many) yet are one bread, and one body inasmuch as we all are partakers of one bread. Behold Israel which walketh carnally: Are not they which eat of the sacrifice, partakers of the altar?

What say I then? that the image is anything? or that it which is offered to images is anything? Nay, but I say, that those things which the gentiles offer, they offer to devils, and not to God. + And I would not that ye should have fellowship with the devils. Ye cannot drink of the cup of the Lord, and of the cup of the devils. Ye cannot be partakers of the Lord's table, and of the table of devils. Either shall we provoke the Lord? Or are we stronger than he? All things are lawful unto me, but all things are not expedient. All things are lawful to me, but all things edify not. Let no man seek his own profit: but let every man seek another's wealth.

Whatsoever is sold in the market, that eat, and ask no questions for conscience sake. For the earth is the Lord's, and all that therein is. If any of them which believe not, bid you to a feast, and if ye be disposed to go, whatsoever is set before you: eat, asking no question for conscience sake. But and if any man say unto you: this is dedicate unto idols, eat not of it for his sake that showed it, and for hurting of conscience. The earth is the Lord's and all that therein is. Conscience I say, not thine: but the conscience of that other*. For why should my liberty be judged of another man's conscience? For if I take my part with thanks: why am I evil spoken of for that thing wherefore I give thanks?

Whether therefore ye eat or drink, or whatsoever ye do, do all to the praise of God. ⊢ See that ye give occasion of evil, neither to the Jews, nor yet to the gentiles, neither to the congregation of God: even as I please all men in all things, not seeking mine own profit, but the profit of many, that they might be saved. Follow me as I do Christ.

CHAPTER ELEVEN

I commend you brethren that ye remember me in all things, and keep the ordinances even as I delivered them to you. I would ye knew that Christ is the head of every man. And the man is the woman's head. And God is Christ's head. Every man praying or prophesying having any thing on his head, shameth his head. Every woman that prayeth or prophesieth bare-headed, dishonesteth her head. For it is even all one, and the very same thing, even as though she were shaven. If the woman be not covered, let her also be shorn. If it be shame for a woman to be shorn or shaven, let her cover her head.

A man ought not to cover his head, forasmuch as he is the image and glory of God. The woman is the glory of the man. For the man is not of the woman, but the woman of the man. Neither was the man created for the woman's sake: but the woman for the man's sake. For this cause ought the woman to have power* on her head, for the angels' sakes. Nevertheless, neither is the man without the woman neither the woman without the man in the Lord. For as the woman is of the man, even so is the man by the woman: but all is of God.

Judge in yourselves whether it be comely that a woman pray unto God bare-headed. Or else doth not nature teach you, that it is a shame for a man, if he have long hair: and a praise to a woman, if she have long hair? For her hair is given her to cover her withal. If there be any man among you that lusteth to strive let him know that we have no such custom, neither the congregations of God.

This I warn you of, and commend not that ye come together: not after a

Ecclesiasticus 36.

We have professed every man to seek another's wealth.

* We should be so full of love and so circumspect, that we should give none occasion unto the ignorant for to speak evil on us for our liberty, and fordoing that which we may lawfully do before God.

Love seeketh her neighbour's profit.

Gen. 2. d.

* Power is as much to say as a sign that the woman is in subjection, and hath an head over her.

253

better manner but after a worse. First of all when ye come together in the congregation, I hear that there is dissension among you: and I partly believe it. For there must be sects among you, that they which are perfect among you, might be known. + When ye come together a man cannot eat the Lord's supper. For every man beginneth afore to eat his own supper. And one is hungry, and another is drunken. Have ye not houses to eat and to drink in? Or else despise ye the congregation of God and shame them that have not? What shall I say unto you? shall I praise you? In this praise I you not. ⊦

The Lord's supper.

+ That which I delivered unto you, I received of the Lord. For the Lord Jesus the same night in which he was betrayed, took bread: and thanked and brake, and said, Take ye, and eat ye: this is my body which is broken for you. This do ye in the remembrance of me. After the same manner he took the cup, when supper was done, saying, This cup is the new testament in my blood. This do as oft as ye drink it, in the remembrance of me. For as often as ye shall eat this bread, and drink this cup, ye shall show the Lord's death till he come. Wherefore whosoever shall eat of this bread, or drink of the cup unworthily, shall be guilty of the body and blood of the Lord. Let a man therefore examine himself, and so let him eat of the bread and drink of the cup. For he that eateth or drinketh unworthily, eateth and drinketh his own damnation, because he maketh no difference of the Lord's body. ⊦

The institution of the sacrament.

Matt. 26.

Mark 14.

Luke 22.

For this cause many are weak and sick among you, and many sleep. If we had truly judged ourselves, we should not have been judged. But when we are judged of the Lord we are chastened, because we should not be damned with the world. Wherefore my brethren when ye come together to eat, tarry one for another. If any man hunger, let him eat at home, that ye come not together unto condemnation. Other things will I set in order when I come.

CHAPTER TWELVE

Only the spirit teacheth that Christ is the Lord.

In spiritual things brethren I would not have you ignorant. + Ye know that ye were gentiles, and went your ways unto dumb idols, even as ye were led. Wherefore I declare unto you that no man speaking in the spirit of God, defieth Jesus. Also no man can say that Jesus is the Lord: but by the holy ghost.

One spirit.
One Lord.
One God.

There are diversities of gifts verily, yet but one spirit. And there are differences of administrations, and yet but one Lord. And there are divers manners of operations, and yet but one God, which worketh all things that are wrought, in all creatures. The gifts* of the spirit are given to every man to profit the congregation. To one is given through the spirit the utterance of wisdom: To another is given the utterance of knowledge by the same spirit. To another is given faith, by the same spirit. To another the gifts of healing by the same spirit. To another power to do miracles. To another prophecy. To another judgement of spirits. To another divers tongues. To another the interpretation of tongues. And these all worketh even the self-same spirit, dividing to every man several gifts, even as he will. ⊦

* The gifts of the spirit are given us to as service to our brethren.

Rom. 12. a.
Eph. 3. b.

For as the body is one, and hath many members, and all the members of one body though they be many, yet are but one body: even so is Christ. For in one spirit are we all baptised to make one body, whether we be Jews or gentiles, whether we be bond or free: and have all drunk of one spirit. For the body is not one member, but many. If the foot say: I am not the hand, therefore I am not of the body: is he therefore not of the body? And if the ear say, I am not the eye: therefore I am not of the body: is he therefore not of the body? If all the body were an eye, where were then the ear? If all were hearing: where were the smelling?

But now hath God disposed the members every one of them in the body, at his own pleasure. If they were all one member: where were the body? Now are there many members, yet but one body. And the eye cannot say unto the hand, I have no need of thee: nor the head also to the feet, I have no need of you. Yea rather a great deal those members of the body which seem to be most feeble, are most necessary. And upon those members of that body which we think least honest, put we most honesty on. And our ungodly parts have most beauty on. For our honest members need it not. But God hath so disposed the body, and hath given most honour to that part which lacked, lest there should be any strife in the body: but that the members should indifferently care one for another. And if one member suffer, all suffer with him: if one member be had in honour, all members be glad also.

Ye are the body of Christ, and members one of another. And God hath also ordained in the congregation, first the apostles, secondarily prophets, thirdly teachers, then them that do miracles: after that, the gifts of healing, helpers, governors, diversity of tongues.

Are all apostles? Are all prophets? Are all teachers? Are all doers of miracles? Have all the gifts of healing? Do all speak with tongues? Do all interpret? Covet after the best gifts. And yet show I unto you a more excellent way.

Eph. 4.

CHAPTER THIRTEEN

+ Though I spake with the tongues of men and angels, and yet had no love, I were even as sounding brass: or as a tinkling cymbal. And though I could prophesy, and understood all secrets, and all knowledge: yea, if I had all faith★ so that I could move mountains out of their places, and yet had no love, I were nothing. And though I bestowed all my goods to feed the poor, and though I gave my body even that I burned, and yet had no love, it profiteth me nothing.

★ All faith is as much to say as so strong a faith.

Love.

Love suffereth long, and is courteous. Love envieth not. Love doth not frowardly, swelleth not, dealeth not dishonestly, seeketh not her own, is not provoked to anger, thinketh not evil, rejoiceth not in iniquity: but rejoiceth in the truth, suffereth all things, believeth all things, hopeth all things, endureth in all things. Though that prophesying fail, or tongues shall cease, or knowledge vanish away, yet love falleth never away.

Phil. 2. c.

For our knowledge is imperfect, and our prophesying is imperfect. But when that which is perfect is come, then that which is imperfect shall be done away. When I was a child, I spake as a child, I understood as a child, I imagined as a child. But as soon as I was a man, I put away childishness. Now we see in a glass even in a dark speaking: but then shall we see face to face. Now I know imperfectly: but then shall I know even as I am known. Now abideth faith, hope, and love, even these three: but the chief of these is love. ⊦

CHAPTER FOURTEEN

Prophesying is here taken for expounding.

Labour for love and covet spiritual gifts: and most chiefly for to prophesy. For he that speaketh with tongues speaketh not unto men, but unto God, for no man heareth him, howbeit in the spirit he speaketh mysteries. But he that prophesieth, speaketh unto men, to edifying, to exhortation and to comfort. He that speaketh with tongues, profiteth himself: he that prophesieth edifieth the congregation. I would that ye all spake with tongues: but rather that ye prophesied. For greater is he that prophesieth than he that speaketh with tongues, except he expound it also, that the congregation may have edifying. Now brethren if I come unto you speaking with tongues: what shall I profit you, except I speak unto you, either by revelation or knowledge, or prophesying, or doctrine?

Words that are not understood profit not.

Moreover when things without life, give sound: whether it be a pipe or an harp: except they make a distinction in the sounds: how shall it be known what is piped or harped? And also if the trumpet give an uncertain voice, who shall prepare himself to fight? Even so likewise when ye speak with tongues, except ye speak words that have signification, how shall it be understood what is spoken? For ye shall but speak in the air.

Many kinds of voices are in the world and none of them are without signification. If I know not what the voice meaneth, I shall be unto him that speaketh, an alien: and he that speaketh shall be an alien unto me: Even so ye (forasmuch as ye covet spiritual gifts) seek that ye may have plenty unto the edifying of the congregation.

Wherefore let him that speaketh with tongues, pray that he may interpret also. If I pray with tongues, my spirit prayeth: but my mind is without fruit. What is it then? I will pray with the spirit, and will pray with the mind also. I will sing with the spirit, and will sing with the mind also.

★ To speak with tongues or with the spirit, is to speak that others understand not, as priests say their service. To speak with the mind is to speak that others understand, as when the preacher preacheth.

For else when thou blessest with the spirit★, how shall he that occupieth the room of the unlearned, say amen at thy giving of thanks, seeing he understandeth not what thou sayest? Thou verily givest thanks well, but the other is not edified. I thank my God, I speak with tongues more than ye all. Yet had I liefer in the congregation, to speak five words with my mind to the information of others, rather than ten thousand words with the tongue.

★ All deeds must be sauced with the doctrine of God, and not with good meaning only.

Brethren be not children in wit★. Howbeit as concerning maliciousness be children: but in wit be perfect. In the law it is written, with other tongues, and with other lips will I speak unto this people, and yet for all that will they not hear me, saith the Lord. Wherefore, tongues are for a sign, not to them that believe: but to them that believe not. Contrariwise, prophesying serveth not for them that believe not: but for them which believe.

If therefore when all the congregation is come together, and all speak with tongues, there come in they that are unlearned, or they which believe not: will **E** they not say that ye are out of your wits? But and if all prophesy, and there come in one that believeth not, or one unlearned, he is rebuked of all men, and is judged of every man: and so are the secrets of his heart opened and so falleth he down on his face, and worshippeth God, and saith that God is with you indeed.

How is it then brethren? When ye come together, every man hath his song, hath his doctrine, hath his tongue, hath his revelation, hath his interpretation. Let all things be done unto edifying. If any man speak with tongues, let it be two at once or at the most three at once and that by course: and let another interpret it. But if there be no interpreter, let him keep silence in the congregation, and let him speak to himself and to God.

F Let the prophets speak two at once, or three at once, and let other judge. If any revelation be made to another that sitteth by, let the first hold his peace. For ye may all prophesy one by one, that all may learn, and all may have comfort. For the spirits of the prophets are in the power of the prophets. For God is not causer of strife: but of peace, as he is in all other congregations of the saints.

G Let your wives keep silence in the congregations. For it is not permitted unto them to speak: but let them be under obedience, as saith the law. If they will learn any thing, let them ask their husbands at home. For it is a shame for women to speak in the congregation. Sprang the word of God from you? Either came it unto you only? If any man think himself a prophet either spiritual: let him understand, what things I write unto you. For they are the commandments of the Lord. But and if any man be ignorant, let him be ignorant. Wherefore brethren covet to prophesy, and forbid not to speak with tongues. And let all things be done honestly and in order.

1 Tim. 2.
Gen. 3. c.

The woman must be in subjection to her husband.

CHAPTER FIFTEEN

A + Brethren as pertaining to the gospel which I preached unto you, which ye have also accepted, and in the which ye continue, by which also ye are saved: I do you to wit, after what maner I preached unto you if ye keep it, except ye have believed in vain.

B For first of all I delivered unto you that which I received: how that Christ died for our sins, agreeing to the scriptures: and that he was buried, and that he arose again the third day according to the scriptures: and that he was seen of Cephas, then of the twelve. After that he was seen of more than five hundred brethren at once: of which many remain unto this day, and many are fallen asleep. After that appeared he to James, then to all the apostles.

The first principle of our faith.

Isa. 53. b.
Jonah 2. a.
Hos. 6. a.
John 20. c.
Acts 9. a.
Eph. 3. b.

And last of all he was seen of me, as of one that was born out of due time. For I am the least of all the apostles, which am not worthy to be called an apostle, because I persecuted the congregation of God. But by the grace of God I am that I am. And his grace which is in me, was not in vain: ⊦ but I laboured

more abundantly than they all, not I, but the grace of God which is with me.   **C**
Whether it were I or they, so we preach, and so have ye believed.

+ If Christ be preached how that he rose from death: how say some that are
among you, that there is no resurrection from death? If there be no rising again
from death: then is Christ not risen. If Christ be not risen, then is our preaching
vain, and your faith is also in vain. Yea and we are found false witnesses of
God. For we have testified of God, how that he raised up Christ, whom he
raised not up, if it be so that the dead rise not up again. For if the dead rise not
again, then is Christ not risen again. If it be so that Christ rose not, then is your
faith in vain and yet are ye in your sins. And thereto they which are fallen
asleep in Christ, are perished. If in this life only we believe on Christ, then are
we of all men the miserablest.

But now is Christ risen from death, and is become the first fruits of them
that slept. For by a man came death, and by a man came resurrection from
death. For as by Adam all die: even so by Christ, shall all be made alive, and
every man in his own order. ⊦ The first is Christ, then they that are Christ's at
his coming. Then cometh the end, when he hath delivered up the kingdom to   **D**
God the father, when he hath put down all rule, authority and power. For he

must reign till he have put all his enemies under his feet.

The last enemy that shall be destroyed is death. For he hath put all things
under his feet. But when he saith, all things are put under him, it is manifest
that he is excepted, which did put all things under him. When all things are
subdued unto him: then shall the son also himself be subject unto him that put
all things under him, that God may be all in all things.

Either else what do they which are baptised over the dead, if the dead rise
not at all? Why are they then baptised over the dead? Yea and why stand we
in jeopardy every hour? By our rejoicing which I have in Christ Jesus our Lord,

I die daily. That I have fought with beasts at Ephesus after the manner of
men, what advantageth it me, if the dead rise not again? Let us eat and drink,   **E**
tomorrow we shall die. Be not deceived: malicious speakings corrupt good
manners. Awake truly out of sleep, and sin not. For some have not the
knowledge of God. I speak this unto your rebuke.

But some man will say: how arise the dead? with what bodies come they in?
Thou fool, that which thou sowest, is not quickened except it die. And what
sowest thou? Thou sowest not that body that shall be: but bare corn (I mean
either of wheat, or of some other) and God giveth it a body at his pleasure, to
every seed a several body.

+ All flesh is not one manner of flesh: but there is one manner flesh of men,
another manner flesh of beasts, another manner flesh of fishes, and another of
birds. There are celestial bodies, and there are bodies terrestrial. But the glory
of the celestial is one, and the glory of the terrestrial is another. There is one   **F**
manner glory of the sun, and another glory of the moon, and another glory of
the stars. For one star differeth from another in glory. So is the resurrection of
the dead. It is sown in corruption, and riseth in incorruption. It is sown in
dishonour, and riseth in honour. It is sown in weakness, and riseth in power. It
is sown a natural body, and riseth a spiritual body.

There is a natural body and there is a spiritual body: as it is written: the first man Adam was made a living soul: and the last Adam was made a quickening spirit. Howbeit that is not first which is spiritual: but that which is natural, and then that which is spiritual. ⊦

The first man is of the earth, earthy: the second man is the Lord from heaven. As is the earthy, such are they that are earthy. And as is the heavenly, such are they that are heavenly. And as we have borne the image of the earthy, so shall we bear the image of the heavenly.

This say I brethren, that flesh and blood cannot inherit the kingdom of God: Neither corruption inherit incorruption. Behold I show you a mystery. We shall not all sleep: but we shall all be changed, and that in a moment, and in the twinkling of an eye, at the sound of the last trumpet. For the trumpet shall blow, and the dead shall rise incorruptible, and we shall be changed. For this corruptible must put on incorruptibility: and this mortal must put on immortality.

When this corruptible hath put on incorruptibility, and this mortal hath put on immortality: then shall be brought to pass the saying that is written: Death is consumed into victory. Death where is thy sting? Hell where is thy victory? The sting of death is sin: and the strength of sin is the law. But thanks be unto God, which hath given us victory, through our Lord Jesus Christ. Therefore my dear brethren, be ye steadfast and unmoveable, always rich in the works of the Lord, forasmuch as ye know how that your labour is not in vain in the Lord.

CHAPTER SIXTEEN

Of the gathering for the saints, as I have ordained in the congregations of Galatia, even so do ye. Upon some Sunday let every one of you put aside at home and lay up whatsoever he thinketh meet, that there be no gatherings when I come.

When I am come, whosoever ye shall allow by your letters, them will I send to bring your liberality unto Jerusalem. And if it be meet that I go, they shall go with me. I will come unto you after I have gone over Macedonia. For I will go throughout Macedonia. With you peradventure I will abide a while: or else winter, that ye may bring me on my way whithersoever I go.

I will not see you now in my passage: but I trust to abide a while with you, if God shall suffer me. I will tarry at Ephesus until Whitsuntide. For a great door and a fruitful is opened unto me: and there are many adversaries. If Timotheus come, see that he be without fear with you. For he worketh the work of the Lord as I do. Let no man despise him: but convey him forth in peace, that he may come unto me. For I look for him with the brethren.

To speak of brother Apollos: I greatly desired him to come unto you with the brethren, but his mind was not at all to come at this time. Howbeit he will come when he shall have convenient time. Watch ye, stand fast in the faith, quit you like men, and be strong. Let all your business be done in love.

Brethren (ye know the house of Stephanas, how that they are the first fruits

Marginal notes:
Gen. 2. b.

Image of Christ.

Corruptible flesh and blood cannot and etc.

Hos. 13. b.
Heb. 2. d.

The law is the strength of sin.

First fruits.

of Achaia, and that they have appointed themselves to minister unto the saints) I beseech you that ye be obedient unto such, and to all that help and labour. I am glad of the coming of Stephanas, Fortunatus and Achaicus: for that which was lacking on your part, they have supplied. They have comforted my spirit and yours. Look therefore that ye know them that are such.

The congregation of Asia salute you. Aquila and Priscilla salute you much in the Lord, and so doth the congregation that is in their house. All the brethren greet you. Greet ye one another with an holy kiss. The salutation of me Paul with mine own hand. If any man love not the Lord Jesus Christ, the same be anathema maranatha★. The grace of the Lord Jesus Christ be with you all. My love be with you all in Christ Jesus. Amen.

★ The same be accursed at the Lord's coming. Or as some will: the same be excommunicate and accursed to death.

The epistle unto the Corinthians sent from Philippi,
by Stephanas, and Fortunatus, and Achaicus, and Timotheus.

THE PROLOGUE UPON
THE SECOND EPISTLE OF SAINT PAUL
TO THE CORINTHIANS

As in the first epistle he rebuketh the Corinthians sharply, so in this he comforteth them and praiseth them, and commandeth him that was excommunicate to be received lovingly into the congregation again.

And in the first and second chapters he sheweth his love to them-ward, how that all that he spake, did or suffered, was for their sakes and for their salvation.

Then in the third, fourth and fifth he praiseth the office of preaching the gospel above the preaching of the law, and sheweth that the gospel groweth through persecution and through the cross, which maketh a man sure of eternal life: and here and there he toucheth the false prophets, which studied to turn the faith of the people from Christ unto the works of the law.

In the sixth and seventh chapters he exhorteth them to suffer with the gospel, and to live as it becometh the gospel, and praiseth him in the latter end.

In the eighth and ninth chapters he exhorteth them to help the poor saints that were at Jerusalem.

In the tenth, eleventh and twelfth he envieth against the false prophets.

And in the last chapter he threateneth them that had sinned and not amended themselves.

THE SECOND EPISTLE
OF ST PAUL THE APOSTLE
TO THE CORINTHIANS

CHAPTER ONE

Paul an apostle of Jesus Christ by the will of God, and brother Timotheus.   A
Unto the congregation of God, which is at Corinth, with all the saints
which are in all Achaia. Grace be with you and peace from God our father, and
from the Lord Jesus Christ.

Blessed be God the father of our Lord Jesus Christ, the father of mercy, and
the God of all comfort, which comforteth us in all our tribulation, insomuch
that we are able to comfort them which are troubled, in whatsoever tribulation
it be, with the same comfort wherewith we ourselves are comforted of God.
For as the afflictions★ of Christ are plenteous in us even so is our consolation
plenteous by Christ.

★ Afflictions or
passions of Christ are
such sufferings as
Christ suffered.

Whether we be troubled for your consolation and salvation, which salvation
sheweth her power in that ye suffer the same afflictions which we also suffer: or
whether we be comforted for your consolation and salvation: yet our hope is
steadfast for you, inasmuch as we know how that as ye have your part in
afflictions, so shall ye be partakers of consolation.

Brethren I would not have you ignorant of our trouble, which happened
unto us in Asia. For we were grieved out of measure passing strength, so
greatly that we despaired even of life. Also we received an answer of death in
ourselves, and that because we should not put our trust in ourselves: but in
God, which raiseth the dead to life again, and which delivered us from so great
a death, and doth deliver. On whom we trust, that yet hereafter he will deliver,
by the help of your prayer for us: that by the means of many occasions, thanks
may be given of many on our behalf, for the grace given unto us.

Conscience.

Our rejoicing is this, the testimony of our conscience, that in singleness and   C
godly pureness and not in fleshly wisdom, but by the grace of God, we have
had our conversation in the world, and most of all to you-wards. We write no
other things unto you, than that ye read and also know. Yea and I trust ye shall
find us unto the end even as ye have found us partly: for we are your rejoicing,
even as ye are ours, in the day of the Lord Jesus.

And in this confidence was I minded the other time to have come unto you,   D
that ye might have had yet one pleasure more: and to have passed by you into
Macedonia, and to have come again out of Macedonia unto you, and to have
been led forth to Jewry-ward of you.

When I thus-wise was minded: did I use lightness? Or think I carnally those things which I think? that with me should be yea yea, and nay nay. God is faithful: For our preaching unto you, was not yea and nay. For God's son Jesus Christ which was preached among you by us (that is to say by me and Silvanus and Timotheus) was not yea and nay: but in him it was yea. For all the promises* of God, in him are yea: and are in him Amen, unto the laud of God through us. For it is God which stablisheth us and you in Christ, and hath anointed us, which hath also sealed us, and hath given the earnest of the spirit into our hearts.

* All the promises of God are given us only for Christ's sake.

CHAPTER TWO

A + I call God for a record unto my soul, that for to favour you withal, I came not any more unto Corinth. Not that we be lords over your faith: but helpers of your joy. For by faith ye stand.† But I determined this in my self, that I would not come again to you in heaviness. For if I make you sorry, who is it that should make me glad, but the same which is made sorry by me? And I wrote this same epistle unto you, lest if I came I should take heaviness of them of **B** whom I ought to rejoice. Certainly this confidence have I in you all, that my joy is the joy of you all. For in great affliction and anguish of heart I wrote unto you with many tears: not to make you sorry, but that ye might perceive the love which I have most specially unto you.

If any man hath caused sorrow, the same hath not made me sorry, but partly: lest I should grieve you all. It is sufficient unto the same man that he was **C** rebuked of many. So that now contrariwise ye ought to forgive him and comfort him: lest that same person should be swallowed up with overmuch heaviness. Wherefore I exhort you, that love may have strength over him. For this cause verily did I write, that I might know the proof of you, whether ye should be obedient in all things. To whom ye forgive any thing, I forgive also. And verily if I forgive any thing, to whom I forgave it, for your sakes forgave I it, in the room of Christ, lest Satan should prevent us. For his thoughts are not unknown unto us. ⊢

When I was come to Troas for Christ's gospel's sake (and a great door was opened unto me of the Lord) I had no rest in my spirit, because I found not Titus my brother: but took my leave of them and went away into Macedonia. **D** Thanks be unto God which always giveth us the victory in Christ, and openeth the savour of his knowledge by us in every place. For we are unto God the sweet savour of Christ, both among them that are saved, and also among them which perish. To the one part are we the savour of death unto death. And unto the other part are we the savour of life unto life. And who is meet unto these things? For we are not as many are, which chop and change with the word of God: but even out of pureness, and by the power of God, and in the sight of God, so speak we in Christ.

Savour.

† The second chapter more correctly begins here.

3^1–4^6 CHAPTER THREE

We begin to praise ourselves again. Need we as some other, of epistles of **A**
recommendation unto you? or letters of recommendation from you? Ye are
our epistle written in our hearts, which is understood and read of all men, in
that ye are known, how that ye are the epistle of Christ, ministered by us and
written, not with ink: but with the spirit of the living God, not in tables of
stone, but in fleshly tables of the heart. + Such trust have we through Christ to
Heb. 4. God-ward, not that we are sufficient of ourselves to think anything as it were of
ourselves: but our ableness cometh of God, which hath made us able to
minister the new testament, not of the letter, but of the spirit. For the letter
killeth, but the spirit giveth life.

If the ministration of death through the letters figured in stones was glorious, **B**
so that the children of Israel could not behold the face of Moses for the glory of
Exod. 34. his countenance (which glory nevertheless is done away) why shall not the
ministration of the spirit be much more glorious? For if the ministering of
condemnation be glorious: much more doth the ministration of righteousness
exceed in glory. + For no doubt that which was there glorified, is not once
glorified in respect of this exceeding glory. Then if that which is destroyed,
was glorious, much more shall that which remaineth, be glorious.

Seeing then that we have such trust, we use great boldness, and do not as **C**
Moses, which put a veil over his face that the children of Israel should not
see for what purpose that served which is put away. But their minds were
blinded. For until this day remaineth the same covering untaken away in the
old testament when they read it, which in Christ is put away. But even unto
★ Liberty: there the this day, when Moses is read, the veil hangeth before their hearts. Nevertheless
heart is not in bondage when they turn to the Lord, the veil shall be taken away. The Lord no doubt is
to dumb ceremonies, a spirit. And where the spirit of the Lord is, there is liberty★. But we all behold
but knoweth how to the glory of the Lord with his face open, and are changed unto the same
use all things, and
understandeth that love similitude, from glory to glory, even of the spirit of the Lord.
is the end and the
fulfilling of all laws.

CHAPTER FOUR

Therefore seeing that we have such an office, even as mercy is come on us, we **A**
faint not: but have cast from us the cloaks of unhonesty, and walk not in
craftiness, neither corrupt we the word of God: but walk in open truth, and
report ourselves to every man's conscience in the sight of God.

+ If our gospel be yet hid, it is hid among them that are lost, in whom the
God of this world. god of this world hath blinded the minds of them which believe not, lest the
light of the glorious gospel of Christ which is the image of God, should shine
unto them.

The apostles and + For we preach not ourselves, but Christ Jesus to be the Lord, and ourselves **B**
servants. your servants, for Jesus' sake. For it is God that commanded the light to shine
out of darkness, which hath shined in our hearts, for to give the light of the
knowledge of the glory of God, in the face of Jesus Christ.

But we have this treasure in earthen vessels, that the excellent power of it might appear to be of God, and not of us. We are troubled on every side, yet are we not without shift. We are in poverty: but not utterly without somewhat.

C We are persecuted: but are not forsaken. We are cast down: nevertheless we perish not. And we always bear in our bodies the dying of the Lord Jesus, that the life of Jesus might appear in our bodies. ⊦

For we which live, are always delivered unto death for Jesus' sake, that the life also of Jesus might appear in our mortal flesh. So then death worketh in us, and life in you. ⊦

⊦ Seeing then that we have the same spirit of faith, according as it is written: I believed and therefore have I spoken. We also believe, and therefore speak. *Psa. 116.* For we know that he which raised up the Lord Jesus, shall raise up us also by the means of Jesus, and shall set us with you. For all things do I for your sakes, that the plenteous grace by thanks given of many, may redound to the praise of God.

D Wherefore we are not wearied, but though our outward man perish, yet the inward man is renewed day by day. For our exceeding tribulation, which is momentary and light, prepareth an exceeding and an eternal weight of glory unto us, while we look not on the things which are seen, but on the things which are not seen. For things which are seen, are temporal: but things which are not seen, are eternal. ⊦

CHAPTER FIVE

A We know surely if our earthy mansion wherein we now dwell were destroyed, that we have a building ordained of God, an habitation not made with hands, but eternal in heaven. And herefore sigh we, desiring to be clothed with our mansion which is from heaven: so yet if that we be found clothed, and not naked. For as long as we are in this tabernacle, we sigh and are grieved for we would not be unclothed but would be clothed upon, that mortality might be *Rev. 16.* swallowed up of life. He that hath ordained us for this thing, is God which very same hath given unto us the earnest of the spirit.

B Therefore we are always of good cheer, and know well that as long as we are at home in the body, we are absent from God. For we walk in faith and see not. Nevertheless we are of good comfort, and had liefer to be absent from the body and to be present with the Lord. Wherefore, whether we be at home or from home we endeavour ourselves to please him. For we must all appear before the judgement seat of Christ, that every man may receive the works of his body *Rom. 14.* according to that he hath done, whether it be good or bad. ⊦ Seeing then that we know, how the Lord is to be feared*, we fare fair with men. For we are known well enough unto God. I trust also that we are known in your consciences.

* Give all diligence that no man be offended or hurt by us or our example.

C We praise not ourselves again unto you, but give you an occasion to rejoice of us, that ye may have somewhat against them, which rejoice in the face, and not in the heart. For if we be too fervent, to God are we too fervent. If we keep

Christ's servants seek
Christ's will, and not
live at their our pleasure
but at his.

measure, for your cause keep we measure. For the love of Christ constraineth us, because we thus judge, if one be dead for all, that then are all dead, and that he died for all, that they which live, should not henceforth live unto themselves but unto him which died for them and rose again. ⊢

Wherefore henceforth know we no man after the flesh. Insomuch though we have known Christ after the flesh, now henceforth know we him so no more. Therefore if any man be in Christ, he is a new creature. Old things are passed away, behold all things are become new. Nevertheless all things are of **D** God, which hath reconciled us unto himself by Jesus Christ★, and hath given unto us the office to preach the atonement. For God was in Christ, and made agreement between the world and himself, and imputed not their sins unto them: and hath committed to us the preaching of the atonement. Now then are we messengers in the room of Christ: even as though God did beseech you through us: So pray we you in Christ's stead, that ye be at one with God: for he hath made him to be sin for us, which knew no sin, that we by his means should be that righteousness which before God is a-loved.

A new creature.

★ The atonement
between God and man
in Christ is the apostles'
office to preach.

Sin is an offering for
sin, as afore, Rom. 8.

CHAPTER SIX

⊢ We as helpers therefore exhort you, that ye receive not the grace of God in **A** vain★. For he saith: I have heard thee in a time accepted: and in the day of salvation, have I succoured thee. Behold now is that well-accepted time: behold now is the day of salvation. Let us give no man occasion of evil, that in our office be found no fault: but in all things let us behave ourselves as the ministers of God.

★ Vain that the word
sown in your heart
should be fruitless to
your greater
damnation.

In much patience, in afflictions, in necessity, in anguish, in stripes, in pri- **B** sonment, in strife, in labour, in watching, in fasting, in pureness, in know-ledge, in long-suffering, in kindness, in the holy ghost, in love unfeigned, in the words of truth, in the power of God, by the armour★ of righteousness on the right hand and on the left, in honour and dishonour, in evil report and good report, as deceivers and yet true, as unknown, and yet known: as dying, and behold we yet live: as chastened, and not killed: as sorrowing, and yet always merry: as poor, and yet make many rich: as having nothing, and yet possessing all things. ⊢

1 Cor. 4.

★ Armour of
righteousness: is the
word of God with
hope, love, fear, and
etc. which Paul calleth
the armour of light,
Rom 13.

O ye Corinthians, our mouth is open unto you. Our heart is made large: ye **C** are in no strait in us, but are in a strait in your own bowels†: I promise you like reward with me as to my children. Set yourselves therefore at large, and ⊢ bear not a stranger's yoke with the unbelievers. For what fellowship hath righteousness with unrighteousness? What company hath light with darkness? What concord hath Christ with Belial? Either what part hath he that believeth with an infidel? how agreeth the temple of God with images? And ye are the **D** temple of the living God, as said God: I will dwell among them and walk among them, and will be their God: and they shall be my people. Wherefore come out from among them, and separate yourselves (saith the Lord) and

Temple.
Covenant.
Lev. 26.
Isa. 52.

† That is, the restraint is in your own feelings.

touch none unclean thing: so will I receive you, and will be a father unto you,
and ye shall be unto me sons and daughters, saith the Lord almighty. ⊢

CHAPTER SEVEN

A Seeing that we have such promises dearly beloved, let us cleanse ourselves
from all filthiness of the flesh and spirit, and grow up to full holiness in the fear
of God. Understand us: we have hurt no man: we have corrupted no man: we
have defrauded no man. I speak not this to condemn you: for I have shewed
you before that ye are in our hearts to die and live with you. I am very bold
over you, and rejoice greatly in you. I am filled with comfort and am exceeding
joyous in all our tribulations. For when we were come into Macedonia, our
flesh had no rest, but we were troubled on every side. Outward was fighting,
inward was fear. Nevertheless God that comforteth the abject, comforted us at
the coming of Titus.

B And not with his coming only: but also with the consolation wherewith
he was comforted of you. For he told us your desire, your mourning, your
fervent mind to me-ward: so that I now rejoice the more. Wherefore though I
made you sorry with a letter, I repent not: though I did repent. For I perceive
that that same epistle made you sorry, though it were but for a season. But I
now rejoice, not that ye were sorry, but that ye so sorrowed, that ye repented.
For ye sorrowed godly: so that in nothing ye were hurt by us. For godly   *1 Pet. 2.*
sorrow causeth repentance unto salvation not to be repented of: when worldly
sorrow causeth death.

C Behold what diligence this godly sorrow that ye took, hath wrought in you:
yea it caused you to clear yourselves. It caused indignation, it caused fear, it
caused desire, it caused a fervent mind, it caused punishment. For in all things
ye have shewed yourselves that ye were clear in that matter. Wherefore though
I wrote unto you, I did it not for his cause that did hurt, neither for his cause
that was hurt: but that our good mind which we have toward you in the sight
of God, might appear unto you.

D Therefore we are comforted, because ye are comforted: yea and excedingly
the more joyed we, for the joy that Titus had: because his spirit was refreshed
of you all. I am therefore, not now ashamed, though I boasted myself to him
of you. For as all things which I preached unto you are true, even so is our
boasting, that I boasted myself to Titus withal, found true. And now is his
inward affection more abundant toward you, when he remembereth the obedience of every one of you: how with fear and trembling ye received him. I
rejoice that I may be bold over you in all things.

CHAPTER EIGHT

A I do you to wit, brethren, of the grace of God which is given in the congregations of Macedonia, how that the abundance of their rejoicing is, that they
are tried with much tribulation. And thereto though they were exceeding
poor, yet have they given exceeding richly, and that in singleness. For to their

powers (I bear record) yea and beyond their power, they were willing of their own accord, and prayed us with great instance that we would receive their benefit, and suffer them to be partakers with others in ministering to the saints. And this they did, not as we looked for: but gave their own selves first to the Lord, and after unto us by the will of God: so that we could not but desire Titus to accomplish the same benevolence among you also, even as he had begun.

Now therefore, as ye are rich in all parts in faith, in word, in knowledge,   **B** in all ferventness, and in love, which ye have to us: even so see that ye be plenteous in this benevolence. This say I not as commanding: but because others are so fervent, therefore prove I your love, whether it be perfect or no. Ye know the liberality of our Lord Jesus Christ, which though he were rich, yet for your sakes became poor: that ye through his poverty, might be made rich.

And I give counsel hereto. For this is expedient for you, which began, not to do only: but also to will, a year ago. Now therefore perform the deed: that as there was in you a readiness to will, even so ye may perform the deed, of that which ye have. For if there be first a willing mind, it is accepted according to that a man hath, and not according to that he hath not.

It is not my mind that others be set at ease, and ye brought into cumbrance: **C** but that there be egalness now at this time, that your abundance succour their *Exod. 16.*   lack: that their abundance may supply your lack: that there may be equality, agreeing to that which is written: He that gathered much, had never the more abundance, and he that gathered little had never the less. Thanks be unto God, which put in the heart of Titus the same good mind toward you. For he accepted the request: yea rather he was so well willing that of his own accord came unto you.

We have sent with him that brother whose laud is in the gospel throughout all the congregations: and not so only, but is also chosen of the congregations to be a fellow with us in our journey concerning this benevolence that is   **D** ministered by us unto the praise of the Lord, and to stir up your prompt mind.

For this we eschew, that any man should rebuke us in this plenteous distribution that is ministered by us, and therefore make provision for honest things, not in the sight of God only, but also in the sight of men.

We have sent with them a brother of ours whom we have oft-times proved diligent in many things, but now much more diligent. The great confidence which I have in you hath caused me this to do: partly for Titus' sake which is my fellow and helper as concerning you, partly because of others which are our brethren, and the messengers of the congregations, and the glory of Christ. Wherefore show unto them the proof of your love, and of the rejoicing that we have of you, that the congregations may see it.

CHAPTER NINE

Of the ministering to the saints, it is but superfluous for me to write unto you: **A** for I know your readiness of mind, whereof I boast myself unto them of

Macedonia, and say that Achaia was prepared a year ago, and your ferventness hath provoked many. Nevertheless yet have I sent these brethren, lest our rejoicing over you should be in vain in this behalf, and that ye (as I have said) prepare yourselves, lest peradventure if they of Macedonia come with me and find you unprepared, the boast that I made in this matter, should be a shame to us: I say not unto you.

B Wherefore I thought it necessary to exhort the brethren, to come beforehand unto you for to prepare your good blessing promised afore, that it might be ready: so that it be a blessing, and not a defrauding. + This yet remember, how that he which soweth little, shall reap little: and he that soweth plenteously shall reap plenteously. And let every man do according as he hath purposed in his heart, not grudgingly, or of necessity. For God loveth a cheerful giver.   *Ecclesiasticus 35.*

C God is able to make you rich in all grace that ye in all things having sufficient unto the utmost, may be rich unto all manner good works, as it is written: He   *Psa. 112.* that dispersed abroad and hath given to the poor, his righteousness remaineth for ever. He that findeth the sower seed, shall minister bread for food, and shall multiply your seed and increase the fruits of your righteousness that on all parts, ye may be made rich in all singleness, which causeth through us, thanksgiving unto God. +

D For the office of this ministration, not only supplieth the need of the saints: but also is abundant herein, that for this laudable ministering, thanks might be given to God of many, which praise God for the obedience of your professing the gospel of Christ, and for your singleness in distributing to them and to all men: and in their prayers to God for you, long after you, for the abundant grace of God given unto you. Thanks be unto God for his unspeakable gift.

CHAPTER TEN

A I Paul myself beseech you by the meekness and softness of Christ, which when I am present among you, am of no reputation, but am bold toward you being absent. I beseech you that I need not to be bold when I am present (with that same confidence, wherewith I am supposed to be bold) against some which repute us as though we walked carnally. Nevertheless though we walk

B compassed with the flesh, yet we war not fleshly. For the weapons of our war are not carnal things, but things mighty in God to cast down strongholds, wherewith we overthrow imaginations, and every high thing that exalteth itself against the knowledge of God and bring into captivity all understanding to the obedience of Christ, and are ready to take vengeance on all disobedience, when your obedience is fulfilled. Look ye on things after the outer appearance?

C If any man trust in himself that he is Christ's, let the same also consider of himself, that as he is Christ's, even so are we Christ's. And though I should boast myself somewhat more of our authority which the Lord hath given us to edify and not to destroy you, it should not be to my shame. This say I, lest I should seem as though I went about to make you afraid with letters. For the epistles (saith he) are sore and strong: but his bodily presence is weak, and his speech rude. Let him that is such think on this wise, that as we are in words by letters when we are absent, such are we in deeds when we are present.

For we cannot find in our hearts to make ourselves of the number of them, or to compare ourselves to them, which laud themselves nevertheless while they measure themselves with themselves, and compare themselves with themselves, they understand nought. But we will not rejoice above measure: **D** but according to the quantity of the measure which God hath distributed unto us, a measure that reacheth even unto you. For we stretch out ourselves beyond measure as though we had not reached unto you. For even unto you have we come with the gospel of Christ, and we boast not ourselves out of measure in other men's labours. Yea and we hope, when your faith is increased among you, to be magnified according to our measure more largely, and to preach the gospel in those regions which are beyond you: and not to rejoice of that which is by another man's measure prepared already. Let him that rejoiceth, rejoice in the Lord★. For he that praiseth himself, is not allowed: but he whom the Lord praiseth.

Eph. 4. b.

★ Let every man rejoice in that Christ died for him and not in the holiness of his own works.

CHAPTER ELEVEN

Would to God, ye could suffer me a little in my foolishness; yea, and I pray you **A** forbear me. For I am jealous over you with godly jealousy. For I coupled you to one man, to make you a chaste virgin to Christ. But I fear lest as the serpent beguiled Eve, through his subtlety, even so your wits should be corrupt from the singleness that is in Christ. For if he that cometh preach another Jesus than him whom we preached: or if ye receive another spirit than that which ye have received: or another gospel than that ye have received, ye might right well have been content.

We be married to Christ and not to the preacher.

I suppose that I was not behind the chief apostles. Though I be rude in speaking, yet I am not so in knowledge. Howbeit among you we are known to **B** the utmost what we are in all things. Did I therein sin, because I submitted myself, that ye might be exalted, and because I preached to you the gospel of God free? I robbed other congregations, and took wages of them, to do you service withal. And when I was present with you and had need, I was grievous to no man, for that which was lacking unto me, the brethren which came from Macedonia, supplied: and in all things I kept myself that I should not be grievous to you: and so will I keep myself.

If the truth of Christ be in me, this rejoicing shall not be taken from me in **C** the regions of Achaia. Wherefore? Because I love you not? God knoweth. Nevertheless what I do, that will I do, to cut away occasion from them which desire occasion, that they might be found like unto us in that wherein they rejoice. For these false apostles are deceitful workers, and fashion themselves **D** like unto the apostles of Christ. And no marvel, for Satan himself is changed into the fashion of an angel of light. Therefore it is no great thing, though his ministers fashion themselves as though they were the ministers of righteousness: whose end shall be according to their deeds.

I say again, lest any man think that I am foolish: or else even now take me as a fool, that I may boast myself a little. That I speak, I speak it not after the ways of the Lord: but as it were foolishly, while we are now come to boasting.

E Seeing that many rejoice after the flesh I will rejoice also. + For ye suffer fools gladly, because that ye yourselves are wise. For ye suffer even if a man bring you into bondage*: if a man devour: if a man take: if a man exalt himself: if a man smite you on the face. I speak as concerning rebuke, as though we had been weak.

* Too much meekness and obedience is not allowed in the kingdom of God but all must be according to knowledge.

Howbeit wheresoever any man dare be bold (I speak foolishly) I dare be bold also. They are Hebrews, so am I: They are Israelites, even so am I. They are the seed of Abraham, even so am I. They are the ministers of Christ (I speak as a fool) I am more: In labours more abundant: In stripes above measure: In prison more plenteously: In death oft. Of the Jews five times received I every

F time forty stripes save one. Thrice was I beaten with rods. I was once stoned. I suffered thrice shipwreck. Night and day have I been in the deep of the sea. In journeying often: In perils of waters: In perils of robbers: In jeopardies of mine own nation: In jeopardies among the heathen. I have been in perils in cities, in perils in wilderness, in perils in the sea, in perils among false brethren, in labour and travail, in watching often, in hunger, in thirst, in fastings often, in cold and in nakedness.

Acts 16.
Acts 14. c.
Acts 27.

And beside the things which outwardly happen unto me, I am cumbered daily, and do care for all congregations. Who is sick, and I am not sick? Who is hurt in the faith and my heart burneth not? If I must needs rejoice, I will rejoice of mine infirmities.

CHAPTER TWELVE

A The God and father of our Lord Jesus Christ, which is blessed for evermore, knoweth that I lie not. + In the city of Damascus, the governor of the people under king Aretas, laid watch in the city of the Damascenes, and would have caught me, and at a window was I let down in a basket through the wall, and so escaped his hands.

Acts 9. d.

†It is not expedient for me no doubt to rejoice. Nevertheless I will come to visions and revelations of the Lord. I know a man in Christ above fourteen years ago (whether he were in the body I cannot tell, or whether he were out

B of the body I cannot tell, God knoweth) which was taken up into the third heaven. And I know the same man (whether in the body, or out of the body, I cannot tell: God knoweth) how that he was taken up into paradise, and heard words not to be spoken, which no man can utter. Of this man will I rejoice, of myself will I not rejoice, except it be of mine infirmities. And yet though I would rejoice, I should not be a fool: for I would say the truth. Nevertheless I spare, lest any man should think of me above that he seeth me to be, or heareth of me.

Acts 9. a

† The twelfth chapter more correctly begins here.

And lest I should be exalted out of measure through the abundance of revelations, there was given unto me unquietness of the flesh, the messenger of Satan to buffet me: because I should not be exalted out of measure. For this **C** thing besought I the Lord thrice, that it might depart from me. And he said unto me: my grace is sufficient for thee. For my strength is made perfect through weakness. Very gladly therefore will I rejoice of my weakness, that the strength of Christ may dwell in me. ⊦ Therefore have I delectation in infirmities, in rebukes, in need, in persecutions, in anguish, for Christ's sake. For when I am weak, then am I strong.

Paul proveth by his sign that his authority was as great as the authority of the high apostles.
I am made a fool in boasting myself. Ye have compelled me: I ought to have been commended of you. For in nothing was I inferior unto the chief apostles. Though I be nothing, yet the tokens of an apostle were wrought among you with all patience: with signs, and wonders, and mighty deeds. For what is it **D** wherein ye were inferiors unto other congregations except it be therein that I was not grievous unto you. Forgive me this wrong done unto you. Behold now the third time I am ready to come unto you: and yet will I not be grievous unto you. For I seek not yours, but you. Also the children ought not to lay up for the fathers and mothers: but the fathers and mothers for the children.

I will very gladly bestow, and will be bestowed for your souls: though the more I love you, the less I am loved again. But be it that I grieved you not: nevertheless I was crafty and took you with guile. Did I pill you by any of them which I sent unto you? I desired Titus, and with him I sent a brother. Did Titus defraud you of any thing? walked we not in one spirit? walked we not in like steps? Again, think ye that we excuse ourselves? We speak in Christ in the sight of God.

But we do all things dearly beloved for your edifying. For I fear lest it come **E** to pass, that when I come, I shall not find you such as I would: and I shall be found unto you such as ye would not: I fear lest there be found among you debate, envying, wrath, strife, backbitings, whisperings, swellings and discord. I fear lest when I come again, God bring me low among you, and I be constrained to bewail many of them which have sinned already, and have not repented of the uncleanness, fornication and wantonness which they have committed.

CHAPTER THIRTEEN

Deut. 19.
Matt. 17.
John 8.
Heb. 10. c.
Now come I the third time unto you. In the mouth of two or three witnesses **A** shall everything stand. I told you before, and tell you before: and as I said when I was present with you the second time, so write I now being absent, to them which in time past have sinned, and to all other: that if I come again, I will not spare, seeing that ye seek experience of Christ which speaketh in me, which among you is not weak, but is mighty in you. And verily though it came of weakness that he was crucified, yet liveth he through the power of God. And we no doubt are weak in him: but we shall live with him, by the might of God among you.

B   Prove yourselves whether ye are in the faith or not. Examine your own selves: know ye not your own selves, how that Jesus Christ is in you except ye be castaways? I trust that ye shall know that we are not castaways. I desire before God that ye do none evil, not that we should seem commendable: but that ye should do that which is honest: and let us be counted as lewd persons.

C   We can do nothing against the truth, but for the truth. We are glad when we are weak, and ye strong. This also we wish for, even that ye were perfect. Therefore write I these things being absent, lest when I am present, I should use sharpness according to the power which the Lord hath given me, to edify, and not to destroy.

D   Finally brethren, fare ye well, be perfect, be of good comfort, be of one mind, live in peace, and the God of love and peace, shall be with you. Greet one another in an holy kiss. All the saints salute you. The grace of our Lord Jesus Christ, and the love of God, and the fellowship of the holy ghost, be with you all. Amen

The second epistle to the Corinthians.
Sent from Philippi a city in Macedonia, by Titus and Lucas.

THE PROLOGUE UPON THE EPISTLE OF
ST PAUL TO THE GALATIANS

As ye read (Acts 15) how certain came from Jerusalem to Antioch and vexed the disciples there, affirming that they could not be saved except they were circumcised.

Even so after Paul had converted the Galatians and coupled them to Christ, to trust in him only for the remission of sin, and hope of grace and salvation, and was departed: there came false apostles unto them (as unto the Corinthians, and unto all places where Paul had preached) and that in the name of Peter, James and John, whom they called the apostles, and preached circumcision and the keeping of the law, to be saved by, and minished Paul's authority.

To the confounding of those, Paul magnifieth his office and apostleship in the two first chapters and maketh himself equal unto the high apostles, and concludeth that every man must be justified without deservings, without works, and without help of the law: but alone by Christ.

And in the third and fourth, he proveth the same with scripture, examples and similitudes, and showeth that the law is cause of more sin and bringeth the curse of God upon us, and justifieth us not: but that justifying cometh by grace promised us of God through the deserving of Christ, by whom (if we believe) we are justified without help of the works of the law.

And in the fifth and sixth he exhorteth unto the works of love which follow faith and justifying. So that in all his epistle he observeth this order. First he preacheth the damnation of the law: then the justifying of faith, and thirdly the works of love. For on that condition that we love and work, is the mercy given us.

THE EPISTLE OF ST PAUL UNTO THE GALATIANS

CHAPTER ONE 1^{1-22}

A   Paul an apostle, not of men, neither by man, but by Jesus Christ, and by God the father which raised him from death: and all the brethren which are with me.

Unto the congregations of Galatia.

Grace be with you and peace from God the father, and from our Lord Jesus Christ, which gave himself for our sins, to deliver us from this present evil world, through the will of God our father, to whom be praise for ever and ever. Amen.

B   I marvel that ye are so soon turned from him that called you in the grace of Christ, unto another gospel: which is nothing else, but that there be some which trouble you, and intend to pervert the gospel of Christ. Nevertheless though we ourselves, or an angel from heaven, preach any other gospel unto you than that which we have preached unto you, hold him as accursed. As I said before, so say I now again, if any man preach any other thing unto you, than that ye have received, hold him accursed. Preach I man's doctrine or God's? Either go I about to please men? If I studied to please men, I were not the servant of Christ.

C   + I certify you brethren, that the gospel which was preached of me, was not after the manner of men, neither received I it of man, neither was I taught it: but received it by the revelation of Jesus Christ. For ye have heard of my conversation in time past, in the Jew's ways, how that beyond measure I persecuted the congregation of God, and spoiled it: and prevailed in the Jew's law, above many of my companions, which were of mine own nation, and was a much more fervent maintainer of the traditions of the elders.

But when it pleased God, which separated me from my mother's womb, and called me by his grace, for to declare his son by me, that I should preach him among the heathen: immediately I communed not of the matter with flesh and blood, neither returned to Jerusalem to them which were apostles before me: but went my ways into Arabia, and came again unto Damascus. Then after

D   three years I returned to Jerusalem to see Peter, and abode with him fifteen days: no other of the apostles saw I, save James the Lord's brother. The things which I write, behold, God knoweth I lie not.

After that I went into the coasts of Syria and Cilicia: and was unknown as

Paul, though he came long after the apostles, yet had he not his authority of Peter or of any that went before him. Neither brought he with him letters of recommendation or bulls of confirmation. But the confirmation of his apostleship was the word of good conscience of men and the power of the spirit that testified with him by miracles and manifold gifts of grace.

Paul's gospel was not confirmed by the authority of man: but by the miracles of the spirit.

275

touching my person, unto the congregations of Jewry, which were in Christ. But they heard only, that he which persecuted us in time past, now preacheth the faith which before he destroyed. And they glorified God on my behalf. ⊦

CHAPTER TWO

Paul defendeth the liberty of the gospel.

Then fourteen years after that, I went up again to Jerusalem with Barnabas, and **A** took with me Titus also. Yea and I went up by revelation, and communed with them of the gospel which I preach among the gentiles: but apart with them which were counted chief, lest it should have been thought that I should run or had run in vain. Also Titus which was with me, though he were a Greek, yet was not compelled to be circumcised, and that because of incomers, being false brethren, which came in among others to spy out our liberty which we have in Christ Jesus, that they might bring us into bondage. To whom we gave no room, no not for the space of an hour, as concerning to be brought into subjection: and that because that the truth of the gospel might continue with you.

Paul is of as high authority as Peter, James or John.

Deut. 10. d.
2 Chron. 19.
Job 34.
Wisdom 6. b.
Rom. 2. b.
Eph. 6. b.

* Circumcision are the Jews and uncircumcision are the gentiles.

Col. 3. b.
Acts 10. c.
1 Pet. 1. c.

Paul rebuketh Peter in the face.

Of them which seem to be great (what they were in time passed it maketh **B** no matter to me: God looketh on no man's person) nevertheless they which seem great, added nothing to me. But contrariwise, when they saw that the gospel over the uncircumcision was committed unto me, as the gospel over the circumcision★ was unto Peter: for he that was mighty in Peter in the apostleship over the circumcision, the same was mighty in me among the gentiles: and therefore when they perceived the grace that was given unto me, then James, Cephas and John, which seemed to be pillars, gave to me and Barnabas the right hands, and agreed with us, that we should preach among the heathen, and they among the Jews: warning only that we should remember the poor. Which thing also I was diligent to do.

And when Peter was come to Antioch, I withstood him in the face, for he **C** was worthy to be blamed. For ere that certain came from James, he ate with the gentiles. But when they were come, he withdrew and separated himself, fearing them which were of the circumcision. And the other Jews dissembled likewise, insomuch that Barnabas was brought into their simulation also. But when I saw, that they went not the right way after the truth of the gospel, I said unto Peter before all men, if thou being a Jew, livest after the manner of the gentiles, and not as do the Jews: why causest thou the gentiles to live as **D** do the Jews? We which are Jews by nature, and not sinners of the gentiles,

* Deeds of the law justify not: but faith justifieth. The law uttereth my sin and damnation, and maketh me flee to Christ for mercy and life. As the law roared unto me that I was damned for my sins: so faith certifieth me that I am forgiven and shall live through Christ.

know that a man is not justified by the deeds★ of the law: but by the faith of Jesus Christ. And therefore we have believed on Jesus Christ, that we might be justified by the faith of Christ, and not by the deeds of the law: because that by the deeds of the law no flesh shall be justified.

If then while we seek to be made righteous by Christ, we ourselves are found sinners, is not then Christ the minister of sin? God forbid. For if I build again that which I destroyed: then make I myself a trespasser. But I through the law am dead to the law: that I might live unto God. I am crucified with

Christ. I live verily: yet now not I, but Christ liveth in me. For the life which I now live in the flesh, I live by the faith of the son of God, which loved me, and gave himself for me. I despise not the grace of God. For if righteousness come of the law, then Christ died in vain.

CHAPTER THREE

A   O foolish Galatians: who hath bewitched you, that ye should not believe the truth? To whom Jesus Christ was described before the eyes, and among you crucified. This only would I learn of you: received ye the spirit by the deeds of the law, or else by preaching of the faith? Are ye so unwise, that after ye have begun in the spirit, ye would now end in the flesh? So many things there ye suffered in vain, if that be vain. Which ministered to you the spirit, and worketh miracles among you, doth he it through the deeds of the law, or by preaching of the faith? Even as Abraham believed God, and it was ascribed to him for righteousness. Understand therefore, that they which are of faith, the same are the children of Abraham.

Gen. 25.
Rom. 4. a.
Jas. 2. d.

B   For the scripture saw aforehand, that God would justify the heathen through faith, and therefore showed beforehand glad tidings unto Abraham: In thee shall all nations be blessed. So then they which be of faith, are blessed with faithful Abraham. For as many as are under the deeds of the law, are under malediction. For it is written: cursed is every man that continueth not in all things which are written in the book of the law, to fulfil them. That no man is justified by the law in the sight of God, is evident. For the just shall live by faith. The law is not of faith: but the man that fulfilleth the things contained in the law shall live in them. But Christ hath delivered us from the curse of the law, and was made accursed* for us. For it is written: cursed is every one that hangeth on tree, that the blessing of Abraham might come on the gentiles through Jesus Christ, and that we might receive the promise of the spirit through faith.

Gen. 22.
Eccl. 24.

The law curseth: but faith blesseth. For faith only maketh the conscience alive.

* Christ was accursed for our sakes: that is he was punished and slain for our sins.

C   Brethren I will speak after the manner of men. Though it be but a man's testament, yet no man despiseth it, or addeth any thing thereto when it is once allowed. + To Abraham and his seed were the promises made. He saith not, in the seeds as in many: but in the seed, as in one, which is Christ. This I say, that the law which began afterward, beyond four hundred and thirty years, doth not disannul the testament, that was confirmed afore of God unto Christ-ward, to make the promise of none effect. For if the inheritance come of the law, it cometh not of promise. But God gave it unto Abraham by promise.

Wherefore then serveth the law? The law was added because of transgression (till the seed came to which the promise was made) and it was ordained by angels in the hand of a mediator. A mediator is not a mediator of one. But

The law.

D   God is one. Is the law then against the promise of God? God forbid. Howbeit if there had been a law given which could have given life: then no doubt righteousness should have come by the law. But the scripture concluded all

The law giveth no life but threateneth death.

things under sin, that the promise by the faith of Jesus Christ should be given unto them that believe.⊢ Before that faith came, we were kept and shut up under the law, unto the faith which should afterward be declared.

Wherefore the law was our schoolmaster unto the time of Christ, that we might be made righteous by faith. But after that faith is come, now are we no longer under a schoolmaster. For ye are all the sons⋆ of God, by the faith which is in Christ Jesus. For all ye that are baptised, have put on Christ. Now is there no Jew neither gentile: there is neither bond nor free: there is neither man nor woman: but ye are all one thing in Christ Jesus. If ye be Christ's, then are ye Abraham's seed, and heirs by promise.

> ⋆ Faith maketh us sons and of the nature of Christ, and bindeth each to have other in the same reverence that he hath Christ.

CHAPTER FOUR

⊦ And I say that the heir as long as he is a child, differeth not from a servant, **A** though he be lord of all, but is under tutors and governors, until the time appointed of the father. Even so we, as long as we were children, were in bondage under the ordinances of the world. But when the time was full come, God sent his son born of a woman and made bond unto the law, to redeem them which were under the law: that we through election might receive the inheritance that belongeth unto the natural sons. Because ye are sons, God hath sent the spirit of his son into our heart, which crieth Abba father. Wherefore now, thou art not a servant, but a son. If thou be the son, thou art also the heir of God through Christ. ⊢

Notwithstanding, when ye knew not God, ye did service unto them, which **B** by nature were no gods. But now seeing ye know God (yea rather are known of God) how is it that ye turn again unto the weak and beggarly ceremonies, wherunto again ye desire afresh to be in bondage? Ye observe days, and months, and times, and years. I am in fear of you, lest I have bestowed on you labour in vain.

> Beggarly ceremonies.

Brethren I beseech you, be ye as I am: for I am as ye are. You have not hurt me at all. Ye know, how through infirmity of the flesh, I preached the gospel unto you at the first. And my temptation which I suffered by reason of my flesh, ye despised not, neither abhorred: but received me as an angel of God: yea as Christ Jesus. How happy were ye then? for I bear you record that if it had been possible, ye would have plucked out your own eyes, and have given them to me. Am I therefore become your enemy, because I tell you the truth?

> Infirmity and temptation are persecution, rebuke, and the cross.

They are jealous over you amiss. Yea, they intend to exclude you, that ye **C** should be fervent to them-ward. It is good always to be fervent, so it be in a good thing, and not only when I am present with you.

My little children (of whom I travail in birth again until Christ be fashioned in you) I would I were with you now, and could change my voice: for I stand in a doubt of you.

Tell me ye that desire to be under the law, have ye not heard of the law? ⊦ For it is written that Abraham had two sons, the one by a bondmaid, the other by a free woman. Yea and he which was of the bondwoman was born

> *Gen. 21.*

after flesh: but he which was of the free woman, was born by promise. Which things betoken mystery. For these women are two testaments, the one from the mount Sinai which gendereth unto bondage, which is Agar. For mount Sinai is called Agar in Arabia, and bordereth upon the city which is now Jerusalem, and is in bondage with her children.

D   But Jerusalem, which is above, is free: which is the mother of us all. For it is written: rejoice thou barren, that bearest no children: break forth and cry, thou that travailest not. For the desolate hath many more children than she which hath an husband. Brethren we are after the manner of Isaac, children of promise. But as then he that was born carnally, persecuted him that was born spiritually, even so is it now. Nevertheless what saith the scripture: put away the bondwoman and her son. For the son of the bondwoman shall not be heir with the son of the free woman. So then brethren we are not children of the bondwoman: but of the free woman.⊢

Isa. 55.

Rom. 9. b.

Gen. 21. a.

CHAPTER FIVE

A   Stand fast therefore in the liberty wherewith Christ hath made us free, and wrap not yourselves again in the yoke of bondage. Behold I Paul say unto you, that if ye be circumcised, Christ shall profit you nothing at all. I testify again to every man which is circumcised that he is bound to keep the whole law. Ye are gone quite from Christ, as many as are justified by the law, and are fallen from grace. We look for and hope in the spirit, to be justified through faith. For in Jesus Christ, neither is circumcision any thing worth, neither yet uncircumcision, but faith★ which by love is mighty in operation. Ye did run well: who was a let unto you, that ye should not obey the truth? Even that counsel that is not of him that called you. A little leaven doth leaven the whole lump of dough.

The liberty and freedom that we have in Christ ought every man to stand by.

★ Faith which worketh through love is the true faith and all that God requireth of us.

B   ⊢I have trust toward you in the Lord, that ye will be none otherwise minded. He that troubleth you shall bear his judgement, whatsoever he be. Brethren if I yet preach circumcision: why do I then yet suffer persecution? For then had the offence which the cross giveth, ceased. I would to God they were separated from you which trouble you. Brethren ye were called into liberty★: only let not your liberty be an occasion unto the flesh, but in love serve one another. For all the law is fulfilled in one word, which is this: thou shalt love thine neighbour as thyself. If ye bite and devour one another: take heed lest ye be consumed one of another. ⊢

★ Christ's liberty is a liberty of conscience and not of the flesh.

Lev. 9. d.
Matt. 22.
Mark 12. c.
Rom. 13.
Jas. 2. b.
1 Pet. 2. c.

C   ⊢I say walk in the spirit, and fulfil not the lusts of the flesh. For the flesh lusteth contrary to the spirit, and the spirit contrary to the flesh. These are contrary one to the other, so that ye cannot do that which ye would. But and if ye be led of the spirit, then are ye not under the law. The deeds of the flesh are manifest, which are these, advoutry, fornication, uncleanness, wantonness, idolatry, witchcraft, hatred, variance, zeal, wrath, strife, sedition, sects, envying, murder, drunkenness, gluttony, and suchlike: of the which I tell you before as I have told you in time past, that they which commit such things, shall not inherit the kingdom of God. But the fruit★ of spirit is, love, joy,

Flesh and spirit fight together.

Deeds of the flesh: to commit such deeds maketh us under the damnation of the law.

★ The fruit of the spirit.

These deeds testify that we are not under the damnation of the law.

peace, longsuffering, gentleness, goodness, faithfulness, meekness, temper-   **D**
ance. Against such there is no law. They that are Christ's, have crucified the
flesh with the appetites and lusts: ⊢ + If we live in the spirit, let us walk in the
spirit. Let us not be vainglorious, provoking one another, and envying one
another.

CHAPTER SIX

The duty of every christian man.

1 Cor. 3. b.

Brethren, if any man be fallen by chance into any fault: ye which are spiritual   **A**
help to amend him, in the spirit of meekness: considering thyself, lest thou
also be tempted. Bear ye one another's burden and so fulfil the law of Christ.
If any man seem to himself that he is somewhat, when indeed he is nothing,
the same deceiveth himself in his imagination. Let every man prove his own
work, and then shall he have rejoicing in his own self, and not in another. For
every man shall bear his own burden.

★ The covenant of mercy in Christ is made only to them that will work.

2 Thes. 3.

Let him that is taught in the word minister unto him that teacheth him in all   **B**
good things. Be not deceived★, God is not mocked. For whatsoever a man
soweth, that shall he reap. He that soweth in his flesh, shall of the flesh reap
corruption. But he that soweth in the spirit, shall of the spirit reap life
everlasting. Let us not be weary of well-doing. For when the time is come,
we shall reap without weariness. While we have therefore time, let us do good
unto all men, and specially unto them which are of the household of faith. ⊢

Behold how large a letter I have written unto you with mine own hand. As   **C**
many as desire with outward appearance to please carnally, they constrain you
to be circumcised, only because they would not suffer persecution with the
cross of Christ. For they themselves which are circumcised, keep not the law:
but desire to have you circumcised, that they might rejoice in your flesh.

★ Nothing helpeth save to be a new creature.

God forbid that I should rejoice but in the cross of our Lord Jesus Christ,
whereby the world is crucified as touching me, and I as concerning the world.
For in Christ Jesus neither circumcision availeth anything at all nor uncircumcision: but a new creature★. And as many as walk according to this rule, peace
be on them, and mercy, and upon Israel that pertaineth to God. From hence-   **D**
forth, let no man put me to business. For I bear in my body the marks of the
Lord Jesus. Brethren the grace of our Lord Jesus Christ be with your spirit.
Amen.

Unto the Galatians written from Rome.

THE PROLOGUE UPON THE EPISTLE OF
ST PAUL TO THE EPHESIANS

In this epistle, and namely in the three first chapters Paul sheweth that the gospel and grace thereof was foreseen and predestinate of God from before the beginning, and deserved through Christ, and now at the last sent forth that all men should believe thereon, thereby to be justified, made righteous, living and happy, and to be delivered from under the damnation of the law and captivity of ceremonies.

And in the fourth he teacheth to avoid traditions and men's doctrines, and to beware of putting trust in anything save Christ, affirming that he only is sufficient, and that in him we have all things, and beside him need nothing.

In the fifth and sixth he exhorteth to exercise the faith and to declare it abroad through good works, and to avoid sin, and to arm them with spiritual armour against the devil that they might stand fast in time of tribulation and under the cross.

THE EPISTLE OF ST PAUL TO
THE EPHESIANS

CHAPTER ONE

P aul an apostle of Jesus Christ, by the will of God.   **A**
     To the saints which are at Ephesus, and to them which believe on Jesus
Christ.

Grace be with you and peace from God our father, and from the Lord Jesus
Christ.

Blessed be God the father of our Lord Jesus Christ, which hath blessed us
with all manner of spiritual blessing in heavenly things by Christ, according as
he had chosen us in him, before the foundation of the world was laid, that we
should be saints, and without blame before him, through love. And ordained
us before through Jesus Christ to be heirs unto himself, according to the
pleasure of his will, to the praise of the glory of his grace wherewith he hath
made us accepted in the beloved.

By whom we have redemption through his blood even the forgiveness of   **A**
sins, according to the riches of his grace, which grace he shed on us abundantly
in all wisdom, and perceivance. And hath opened unto us the mystery★ of
his will according to his pleasure, and purposed the same in himself to have
it declared when the time were full come, that all things, both the things
which are in heaven, and also the things which are in earth, should be gathered
together, even in Christ: that is to say, in him in whom we are made heirs,
and were thereto predestinate according to the purpose of him which worketh
all things after the purpose of his own will: that we which before believed in
Christ should be unto the praise of his glory.

In whom also ye (after that ye heard the word of truth, I mean the gospel **C**
of your salvation, wherein ye believed) were sealed with the holy spirit of
promise, which is the earnest of our inheritance, to redeem the purchased
possession and that unto the laud of his glory.

Wherefore even I (after that I heard of the faith which ye have in the Lord **D**
Jesus, and love unto all the saints) cease not to give thanks for you, making
mention of you in my prayers, that the God of our Lord Jesus Christ and the
father of glory, might give unto you the spirit of wisdom, and open to you
the knowledge of himself, and lighten the eyes of your minds, that ye might
know what that hope is, whereunto he hath called you, and what the riches
of his glorious inheritance is upon the saints, and what is the exceeding

2 Cor. 1. a.
1 Pet. 1.,a.

Predestination.

Redemption is the
forgiveness of sins.

★ Mystery is secret
counsel.

Predestination.

Where faith to Christ
is, there is love to all
that are sanctified in
his blood.

Hope.

greatness of his power to us-ward which believe★ according to the working of that his mighty power, which he wrought in Christ, when he raised him from death, and set him on his right hand in heavenly things, above all rule, power, and might and domination, and above all names that are named, not in this world only, but also in the world to come: and hath put all things under his feet, and hath made him above all things, the head of the congregation which is his body and the fulness of him that filleth all in all things.

★ Faith is the work of God only, even as was the raising up of Christ.

CHAPTER TWO

A And hath quickened you also that were dead in trespass and sin, in the which in time past ye walked, according to the course of this world, and after the governor that ruleth in the air, the spirit that now worketh in the children of unbelief, among which we also had our conversation in time past, in the lusts of our flesh, and fulfilled the will of the flesh and of the mind: and were naturally★ the children of wrath, even as well as other.

Col. 2. b.

★ We be all by nature the children of wrath and heirs of damation.

But God which is rich in mercy through his great love wherewith he loved us, even when we were dead by sin, hath quickened us together in Christ (for by grace are ye saved) and hath raised us up together and made us sit together in heavenly things through Christ Jesus, for to show in times to come the
B exceeding riches of his grace, in kindness to us-ward in Christ Jesus. For by grace are ye made safe through faith, and that not of yourselves. For it is the gift of God, and cometh not of works, lest any man should boast himself. For we are his workmanship, created in Christ Jesus unto good works, unto the which God ordained us before, that we should walk in them.

The promises of mercy in Christ's blood, are made us on that condition that we keep the law and love one another as Christ loved us.

Wherefore remember that ye being in time past gentiles in the flesh, and were called uncircumcision to them which are called circumcision in the flesh, which circumcision is made by hands: Remember I say, that ye were at that time without Christ, and were reputed aliens from the commonwealth of Israel, and were strangers from the testaments★ of promise, and had no hope,
C and were without God in this world. But now in Christ Jesus, ye which a while ago were far off, are made nigh by the blood of Christ.

★ The gentiles till Christ came were not under the covenant of mercy: but the Jews only.

For he is our peace, which hath made of both one, and hath broken down the wall★ that was a stop between us, and hath also put away through his flesh, the cause of hatred (that is to say, the law of commandments contained in the law written) for to make of twain one new man in himself, so making peace:
D and to reconcile both unto God in one body through his cross, and slew hatred thereby: and came and preached peace to you which were afar off, and to them that were nigh. For through him we both have an open way in, in one spirit unto the father.

★ Moses' law, that was the wall and cause of hate between the Jews and gentiles, is taken away. In whose stead is love come, to love one another as Christ loved us.

✝ Now therefore ye are no more strangers and foreigners: but citizens with the saints, and of the household of God: and are built upon the foundation of the apostles and prophets, Jesus Christ being the head corner-stone, in whom every building coupled together, groweth unto an holy temple in the Lord, in whom ye also are built together, and made an habitation for God in the spirit. ✝

Foundation is the word of God.

CHAPTER THREE

Paul was an apostle to the heathen and learned his gospel by revelation.

For this cause I Paul am in the bonds of Jesus Christ for your sakes which are **A** heathen: If ye have heard of the ministration of the grace of God which is given me to you-ward. For by revelation showed he this mystery unto me, as I wrote above in few words, whereby when ye read ye may know mine understanding in the mystery of Christ, which mystery in times past was not opened unto the sons of men, as it is now declared unto his holy apostles and prophets by the spirit: that the gentiles should be inheritors also, and of the same body, and partakers of his promise that is in Christ, by the means of the gospel, whereof I am made a minister, by the gift of the grace of God given unto me through the working of his power.

Unto me the least of all saints is this grace given, that I should preach among **B** the gentiles the unsearchable riches of Christ, and to make all men see what the fellowship of the mystery is, which from the beginning of the world hath been hid in God which made all things through Jesus Christ, to the intent, that now unto the rulers and powers in heaven might be known by the congregation the manifold wisdom of God, according to that eternal purpose, which he purposed in Christ Jesus our Lord, by whom we are bold to draw nigh in that trust, which we have by faith on him. + Wherefore I desire that ye faint not because of my tribulations for your sakes: which is your praise.

★ Where true faith in Christ is, there is love to thy neighbour. And faith and love maketh us understand all things. Faith understandeth the secrets of God and the mercy that is given her in Christ: And love knoweth her duty to her neighbour, and can interpret all laws and ordinances and knoweth how far forth they are to be kept and when to be dispensed with.

For this cause I bow my knees unto the father of our Lord Jesus Christ, **C** which is father over all that is called father†† in heaven and in earth, that he would grant you according to the riches of his glory, that ye may be strengthened with might by his spirit in the inner man, that Christ may dwell in your hearts by faith★, that ye being rooted and grounded in love, might be able to comprehend with all saints, what is that breadth and length, depth and height: and to know what is the love of Christ, which love passeth knowledge: that ye might be fulfilled with all manner of fullness which cometh of God.

Unto him that is able to do exceeding abundantly above all that we ask or think, according to the power that worketh in us, be praise in the congregation by Jesus Christ, throughout all generations from time to time. Amen. ⊦

CHAPTER FOUR

The living of a true believer.

Rom. 12.
1 Cor. 12.

One God.
One Lord.
One faith.
One baptism.

+ I therefore which am in bonds for the Lord's sake, exhort you, that ye walk **A** worthy of the vocation wherewith ye are called, in all humbleness of mind and meekness, and long-suffering, forbearing one another through love, and that ye be diligent to keep the unity of the spirit in the bond of peace, being one body, and one spirit, even as ye are called in one hope of your calling. Let there be but one Lord, one faith, one baptism: one God and father of all, which is above all, through all and in you all. ⊦

Rom 12.
1 Cor. 12.
2 Cor. 10.
Psa. 68.

+ Unto every one of us is given grace according to the measure of the gift **B** of Christ. Wherefore he saith: He is gone up on high, and hath led captivity captive, and hath given gifts unto men. That he ascended: what meaneth it, but that he also descended first into the lowest parts of the earth? He that descended, is even the same also that ascended up, even above all heavens, to fulfil all things.

And the very same made some apostles, some prophets, some evangelists, some shepherds, some teachers: that the saints might have all things necessary to work and minister withal, to the edifying of the body of Christ, till we every one (in the unity of faith, and knowledge of the son of God) grow up unto a perfect man, after the measure of age* of the fulness of Christ. ⊢ That we henceforth be no more children, wavering and carried with every wind of doctrine, by the wiliness of men and craftiness, whereby they lay wait for us to deceive us.

1 Col. 12.

* Wherefore the true ministers of the congregation serve. Even to make us perfect men in the full knowledge of Christ.

B   But let us follow the truth in love, and in all things grow in him which is the head, that is to say Christ, in whom all the body is coupled and knit together in every joint wherewith one ministereth to another (according to the operation as every part hath his measure) and increaseth the body, unto the edifying of itself in love.

 ⊢ This I say therefore and testify in the Lord, that ye henceforth walk not as other gentiles walk, in vanity of their mind, blinded in their understanding, being strangers from the life which is in God through the ignorancy that is in them, because of the blindness of their hearts: which being past repentance, have given themselves unto wantonness, to work all manner of uncleanness,

Ignorance is cause of evil living.

C   even with greediness. But ye have not so learned Christ, if so be ye have heard of him, and are taught in him, even as the truth is in Jesus. So then as concerning the conversation in time past, lay from you that old man, which is corrupt through the deceivable lusts ⊢ and be ye renewed in the spirit of your minds, and put on that new man, which after the image of God is shapen

Rom 6. a.
Col. 3. b.
Heb. 12.
1 Pet. 2. a. and 3. a.

F   in righteousness and true holiness. ⊢ Wherefore put away lying, and speak every man truth unto his neighbour, forasmuch as we are members one of another. Be angry but sin not: let not the sun go down upon your wrath neither give place unto the backbiter. Let him that stole, steal no more, but let him rather labour with his hands some good thing that he may have to give unto him that needeth. ⊢

Avenge not.
Psa. 4. b.

Steal not.

Let no filthy communication proceed out of your mouths: but that which is good to edify withal, when need is: that it may have favour with the hearers. And grieve not the holy spirit of God, by whom ye are sealed unto the day of redemption. Let all bitterness, fierceness and wrath, roaring and cursed speaking, be put away from you, with all maliciousness. Be ye courteous one to another, and merciful, forgiving one another, even as God for Christ's sake forgave you.

Filthy communication.

They that have the spirit of God shall be grieved to hear such things.

CHAPTER FIVE

A   ⊢ Be ye followers of God as dear children, and walk in love even as Christ loved us and gave himself for us, an offering and a sacrifice of a sweet savour to God. So that fornication and all uncleanness, or covetousness be not once

Ungodly communication strengtheneth the body against the spirit.

named among you, as it becometh saints: neither filthiness, neither foolish talking, neither jestings which are not comely: but rather giving of thanks. For this ye know, that no whoremonger, or unclean person, or covetous person which is the worshipper of images, hath any inheritance in the kingdom of Christ and of God.

These have no part with Christ.

Let no man deceive you with vain words. For through such things cometh the wrath of God upon the children of unbelief. Be not therefore companions with them. Ye were once darkness, but are now light in the Lord. **B**

2 Thes. 2. a.
Matt. 22.
Mark 13.
Luke 21. b.

Walk as children of light. For the fruit of the spirit is in all goodness, righteousness and truth. ⊢ Accept that which is pleasing to the Lord: and have no fellowship with the unfruitful works of darkness: but rather rebuke them. For it is shame even to name those things which are done of them in secret: but all things, when they are rebuked of the light, are manifest. For whatsoever is manifest, that same is light. Wherefore he saith: awake thou that sleepest, and stand up from death, and Christ shall give thee light. **C**

Ignorance is cause of evil doing.

+ Take heed therefore that ye walk circumspectly: not as fools: but as wise redeeming the time★: for the days are evil. Wherefore, be ye not unwise, but understand what the will of the Lord is, and be not drunk with wine, wherein is excess: but be fulfilled with the spirit, speaking unto yourselves in psalms, and hymns, and spiritual songs, singing and making melody to the Lord in your hearts, giving thanks always for all things unto God the father, in the name of our Lord Jesus Christ: submitting yourselves one to another in the fear of God. ⊢ **D**

★ Redeeming the time: that is, spending the time well.

Col. 4.
Rom. 7.
1 Thes. 3.

Col. 3.

Women submit yourselves unto your own husbands, as unto the Lord. For the husband is the wife's head, even as Christ is the head of the congregation, and the same is the saviour of the body. Therefore as the congregation is in subjection to Christ, likewise let the wives be in subjection to their husbands in all things. Husbands love your wives, even as Christ loved the congregation, and gave himself for it, to sanctify it, and cleansed it in the fountain★ of water through the word, to make it unto himself, a glorious congregation without spot or wrinkle, or any such thing: but that it should be holy and without blame. **E** **F**

1 Cor. 11. a.

Col. 3. c.
1 Pet. 3.
Husbands.

★ Baptism saveth through the word: that is through faith in the word according to the covenant made in Christ.

So ought men to love their wives, as their own bodies. He that loveth his wife, loveth himself. For no man ever yet, hated his own flesh: but nourisheth and cherisheth it even as the Lord doth the congregation. For we are members of his body, of his flesh, and of his bones. For this cause shall a man leave father and mother, and shall continue with his wife, and two shall be made one flesh. This is a great secret, but I speak between Christ and the congregation. Nevertheless do ye so that every one of you love his wife truly even as himself. And let the wife see that she fear her husband. **G**

Gen. 2. d.
Matt. 19.
Mark 10. a.
1 Cor. 6. d.

CHAPTER SIX

Children obey your fathers and mothers in the Lord: for so is it right. Honour thy father and mother, that is the first commandment that hath any promise, **A**

Children.

B that thou mayst be in good estate, and live long on the earth. And ye fathers, move not your children to wrath: but bring them up with the nurture and information of the Lord. Servants be obedient unto your carnal masters, with fear and trembling, in singleness of your hearts, as unto Christ: not with service in the eye-sight, as men-pleasers: but as the servants of Christ, doing the will of God from the heart with good will serving the Lord, and not men. And remember that whatsoever good thing any man doeth, that shall he receive again of the Lord, whether he be bond or free. And ye masters, do even the same things unto them, putting away threatenings: and remember

C that even your master also is in heaven, neither is there any respect of person with him.

+ Finally my brethren, be strong in the Lord, and in the power of his might. Put on the armour of God, that ye may stand steadfast against the crafty assaults of the devil. For we wrestle not against flesh and blood: but against rule, against power, and against worldly rulers of the darkness of this world, against spiritual wickedness for heavenly things.

D For this cause take unto you the armour* of God, that ye may be able to resist in the evil day, and to stand perfect in all things.

Stand therefore and your loins girt about with verity, having on the breast-plate of righteousness, and shod with shoes prepared by the gospel of peace. Above all take to you the shield of faith, wherewith ye may quench all the fiery darts of the wicked. And take the helmet of salvation, and the sword of the spirit, which is the word of God. ⊢ And pray always with all manner prayer and supplication: and that in the spirit: and watch thereunto with all instance and supplication for all saints, and for me, that utterance may be given unto me, that I may open my mouth boldly, to utter the secrets of the gospel, whereof I am a messenger in bonds, that therein I may speak freely, as it becometh me to speak.

D But that ye may also know that condition I am in and what I do, Tychicus my dear brother and faithful minister in the Lord, shall show you of all things, whom I sent unto you for the same purpose, that ye might know what case I stand in, and that he might comfort your hearts.

Peace be with the brethren, and love with faith, from God the father and from the Lord Jesus Christ. Grace be with all them which love our Lord Jesus Christ in pureness. Amen.

Sent from Rome unto the Ephesians by Tychicus.

Col. 3. d.
Exod. 20.
Deut. 6. c.
Eccl. 3. b.
Matt. 11.
Mark 7.
Col. 3. d.
Tit. 2. c.
1 Pet. 2. c.

Masters: Christ hath purchased a reward for all things.

* The armour of God followeth: verity, the shoes of a steadfast purpose to follow the gospel: faith, the helmet of salvation: the word of God which is the sword, and etc.

THE PROLOGUE UPON THE EPISTLE OF
ST PAUL TO THE PHILIPPIANS

Paul praiseth the Philippians, and exhorteth them to stand fast in the true faith, and to increase in love. And because that false prophets study always to impugn and destroy the true faith, he warneth them of such work-learners or teachers of works, and praiseth Epaphroditus. And all this doth he in the first and second chapters.

In the third he reproveth faithless and man's righteousness, which false prophets teach and maintain. And he setteth him for an example, how that he himself had lived in such false righteousness and holiness unrebukable, that was so that no man could complain on him, and yet now setteth nought thereby, for Christ's righteousness' sake. And finally affirmeth that such false prophets are the enemies of the cross, and make their bellies their god. Further than they may safely and without all peril and suffering, will they not preach Christ.

THE EPISTLE OF ST PAUL UNTO THE PHILIPPIANS

CHAPTER ONE 1^{1-22}

A Paul and Timotheus the servants of Jesus Christ, to all the saints in Christ Jesus which are at Philippi, with the bishops and deacons. Bishops. Deacons.

Grace be with you and peace from God our father, and from the Lord Jesus Christ.

I thank my God with all remembrance of you, always in all my prayers for you and pray with gladness, because of the fellowship which ye have in the gospel from the first day unto now: + and am surely certified of this, that he which began a good work in you, shall go forth with it until the day of Jesus Christ, as it becometh me so to judge of you all, because I have you in my heart, and have you also every one companions of grace with me, even in my bonds, as I defend and establish the gospel.

B For God beareth me record how greatly I long after you all from the very heart root in Jesus Christ. And this I pray, that your love may increase more and more in knowledge, and in all feeling, that ye might accept things most excellent, that ye might be pure and such as should hurt no man's conscience, until the day of Christ, filled with the fruits of righteousness, which fruits come by Jesus Christ unto the glory and laud of God. ⊢

I would ye understood brethren that my business is happened unto the greater furthering of the gospel. So that my bonds in Christ are manifest throughout all the judgement-hall and in all other places: Insomuch that many of the brethren in the Lord are boldened through my bonds, and dare more largely speak the word without fear. Some there are which preach Christ of envy and strife, and some of goodwill. The one part preacheth Christ of strife and not purely, supposing to add more adversity to my bonds. The other part of love, because they see that I am set to defend the gospel.

C What then? So that Christ be preached all manner ways, whether it be by occasion, or of true meaning, I therein joy: yea and will joy. For I know that this shall chance to my salvation, through your prayer and ministering of the spirit of Jesus Christ, as I heartily look for and hope, that in nothing I shall be ashamed: but that with all confidence, as always in times past, even so now Christ shall be magnified in my body, whether it be through life, or else death. For Christ is to me life, and death is to me advantage.

D If it chance me to live in the flesh, that is to me fruitful for to work, and what to choose I wot not. I am constrained of two things: I desire to be loosed and to be with Christ, which thing is best of all. Nevertheless to abide in the flesh is more needful for you. And this am I sure of, that I shall abide, and with you all continue, for the furtherance and joy of your faith, that ye may more abundantly rejoice in Jesus Christ through me, by my coming to you again.

Only let your conversation be, as it becometh the gospel of Christ: that whether I come and see you, or else be absent, I may yet hear of you, that ye continue in one spirit, and in one soul, labouring as we do, to maintain the faith of the gospel, and in nothing fearing your adversaries: which is to them a token of perdition, and to you of salvation, and that of God. For unto you

★ Tribulation is a token of salvation to the true believers.

it is given, that not only ye should believe on Christ: but also suffer★ for his sake, and have even the same fight which ye saw me have and now hear of me.

CHAPTER TWO

If there be among you any consolation in Christ, if there be any comfortable   **A** love, if there be any fellowship of the spirit, if there be any compassion or mercy: fulfil my joy, that ye draw one way, having one love, being of one accord, and of one mind, that nothing be done through strife or vainglory, but that in meekness of mind every man esteem other better than himself, and that no man consider his own, but what is meet for other.

To follow Christ is our profession and so to humble ourselves, that we may be so exalted.

Heb. 2. b.

Rom. 14.

Isa. 45.

+ Let the same mind be in you that was in Christ Jesus: Which being in the shape of God, and thought it not robbery to be equal with God. Nevertheless he made himself of no reputation, and took on him the shape of a servant, and became like unto men, and was found in his apparel as a man. He humbled   **B** himself and became obedient unto the death, even the death of the cross. Wherefore God hath exalted him, and given him a name above all names: that in the name of Jesus should every knee bow, both of things in heaven and things in earth and things under earth, and that all tongues should confess that Jesus Christ is the Lord unto the praise of God the father. +

★ As ye be saved from sin through faith so work according to the covenant until ye come to the salvation of glory. For if ye cease working, the spirit quencheth again and ye cease to be partakers of the promise.

Wherefore my dearly beloved, as ye have always obeyed, not when I was present only, but now much more in mine absence, even so work out your own salvation★ with fear and trembling. For it is God which worketh in you, both the will and also the deed, even of good will.

Do all things without murmuring and disputing, that ye may be faultless   **C** and pure, and the sons of God without rebuke, in the midst of a crooked and a perverse nation, among which see that ye shine as lights in the world, holding fast the word of life, unto my rejoicing in the day of Christ, that I have not run in vain, neither have laboured in vain. Yea and though I be offered up upon the offering and sacrifice of your faith: I rejoice, and rejoice with you all. For the same cause also, rejoice ye, and rejoice ye with me.

I trust in the Lord Jesus for to send Timotheus shortly unto you, that I also   **D** may be of good comfort, when I know what case ye stand in. For I have no man that is so like-minded to me, which with so pure affection careth for your matters. For all others seek their own, and not that which is Jesus Christ's. Ye

D know the proof of him, how that as a son with the father, so with me bestowed he his labour upon the gospel. Him I hope to send as soon as I know how it will go with me. I trust in the Lord I also myself shall come shortly.

I supposed it necessary to send brother Epaphroditus unto you, my companion in labour and fellow-soldier, your apostle and my minister at my needs. For he longed after you and was full of heaviness, because that ye had heard say that he should be sick. And no doubt he was sick, and that nigh unto death. But God had mercy on him: not on him only, but on me also, lest I should have had sorrow upon sorrow.

I sent him therefore the diligentlier, that when ye should see him, ye might rejoice again, and I might be the less sorrowful. Receive him therefore in the Lord with all gladness, and make much of such: because that for the work of Christ he went so far, that he was nigh unto death, and regarded not his life, to fulfil that service which was lacking on your part toward me.

CHAPTER THREE

A Moreover my brethren, rejoice in the Lord. It grieveth me not to write one thing often to you. For to you it is a sure thing. Beware of dogs, beware of evil workers. Beware of dissension. For we are circumcision which worship God in the spirit*, and rejoice in Christ Jesus, and have no confidence in the flesh: though I have whereof I might rejoice in the flesh. If any other man thinketh that he hath whereof he might trust in the flesh: much more I: circumcised the eighth day, of the kindred of Israel, of the tribe of Benjamin, an Hebrew born of the Hebrews: as concerning the law, a Pharisee, and as con-

B cerning ferventness, I persecuted the congregation, and as touching the righteousness which is in the law I was unrebukable.

But the things that were vantage unto me I counted loss for Christ's sake, Yea I think all things but loss for that excellent knowledge's sake of Christ

C Jesus my Lord. For whom I have counted all things loss, and do judge them but dung, that I might win Christ, and might be found in him, not having mine own righteousness which is of the law: But that which springeth of the faith which is in Christ. I mean the righteousness which cometh of God through faith in knowing him and the virtue of his resurrection, and the fellowship of his passions, that I might be conformable unto his death* if by any means I might attain unto the resurrection from death.

Not as though I had already attained to it, either were already perfect: but I follow, if that I may comprehend that, wherein I am comprehended of Christ Jesus. Brethren I count not myself that I have gotten it: but one thing I say: I forget* that which is behind and stretch myself unto that which is before and press unto that mark appointed, to obtain the reward of the high calling of God in Christ Jesus. Let us therefore as many as be perfect be thuswise minded: and if ye be otherwise minded, I pray God open even this unto you. Nevertheless in that whereunto we are come, let us proceed by one rule, that we may be of one accord.

* We worship God in spirit through faith and love. We rejoice that Christ hath redeemed us and trust not in our works.

Christ only is our righteousness: for his sake our sins are forgiven us. And for his sake our sins are accepted. Which else were damnable for the sin that is in them.

* Death: we must die with Christ if we will live with him.

* I look not on the works that I have done, but what I lack of the perfectness of Christ.

291

+ Brethren be followers of me and look on them which walk even so, as ye have us for an example. For many walk (of whom I have told you often, and now tell you weeping) that they are the enemies of the cross of Christ, whose end is damnation, whose God is their belly, and whose glory is to their shame, which are worldly-minded. But our conversation is in heaven, from whence we look for a saviour even the Lord Jesus Christ, which shall change our vile bodies, that they may be fashioned like unto his glorious body, according to the working whereby he is able to subdue all things unto himself. ⊦

Rom. 16.

If we be like Christ in conversation, we shall be like him in glory.

CHAPTER FOUR

A Therefore my brethren dearly beloved and longed for, my joy and crown, so continue in the Lord ye beloved. I pray Euodias, and beseech Syntyche that they be of one accord in the Lord. Yea and I beseech thee, faithful yokefellow, help the women which laboured with me in the gospel, and with Clement also, and with other my labour-fellows, whose names are in the book of life. + Rejoice in the Lord always, and again I say rejoice. Let your softness be known unto all men. The Lord is even at hand. Be not careful: but in all things show your petition unto God in prayer and supplication with giving of thanks. And the peace of God which passeth all understanding, keep your hearts and minds in Christ Jesus. ⊦

B Furthermore brethren, whatsoever things are true, whatsoever things are honest, whatsoever things are just, whatsoever things are pure, whatsoever things pertain to love, whatsoever things are of honest report: if there be any virtuous thing, if there be any laudable thing, those same have ye in your mind, C which ye have both learned and received, heard and also seen in me: those things do, and the God of peace shall be with you. I rejoice in the Lord greatly, that now at the last ye are revived again to care for me, in that wherein ye were also careful, but ye lacked opportunity. I speak not because of necessity. For I have learned in whatsoever estate I am therewith to be content. I can both cast down myself, I can also exceed. Everywhere and in all things I am instructed, both to be full, and to be hungry: to have plenty, and to suffer need. I can do all things through the help of Christ which strengtheneth me. Notwithstanding ye have well done, that ye bare part with me in my tribulation.

D Ye of Philippi know that in the beginning of the gospel, when I departed from Macedonia, no congregation bare part with me as concerning giving and receiving, but ye only. For when I was in Thessalonica, ye sent once and afterward again unto my needs: not that I desire gifts: but I desire abundant fruit on your part. I received all, and have plenty. I was even filled after that I have received of Epaphroditus, that which came from you, an odour that smelleth sweet, a sacrifice accepted and pleasant to God. My God fulfil all your needs through his glorious riches in Jesus Christ. Unto God and our father be praise for evermore. Amen. Salute all the saints in Christ Jesus. The brethren

Rom. 12.

which are with me greet you. All the saints salute you: and most of all they which are of the Emperor's household. The grace of our Lord Jesus Christ be with you all. Amen.

Sent from Rome by Epaphroditus.

THE PROLOGUE UPON THE EPISTLE OF
ST PAUL TO THE COLOSSIANS

As the epistle to the Galatians holdeth the manner and fashion of the epistle to the Romans, briefly comprehending all that is therein at length disputed: Even so this epistle followeth the example of the epistle to the Ephesians, containing the tenor of the same epistle with fewer words.

In the first chapter, he praiseth them and wisheth that they continue in the faith, and grow perfecter therein, and then describeth he the gospel, how that it is a wisdom that confesseth Christ to be the Lord and God, crucified for us, and a wisdom that hath been hid in Christ since afore the beginning of the world, and now first begun to be opened through the preaching of the apostles.

In the second, he warneth them of men's doctrine, and describeth the false prophets to the uttermost and rebuketh them according.

In the third, he exhorteth to be fruitful in the pure faith with all manner of good works one to another, and describeth all degrees and what their duties are.

In the fourth he exhorteth to pray, and also to pray for him, and saluteth them.

THE EPISTLE OF ST PAUL TO
THE COLOSSIANS

CHAPTER ONE

A Paul an apostle of Jesus Christ by the will of God, and brother Timotheus. To the saints which are at Colosse, and brethren that believe in Christ. Grace be with you and peace from God our father, and from the Lord Jesus Christ.

We give thanks to God the father of our Lord Jesus Christ, always praying for you, since we heard of your faith* which ye have in Christ Jesus and of the love which ye bear to all saints for the hope's sake which is laid up in store for you in heaven, of which hope ye have heard before by the true word of the gospel, which is come unto you, even as it is into all the world, and is fruitful, as it is among you, from the first day in the which ye heard of it, and had experience in the grace of God in the truth, as ye learned of Epaphras our dear fellowservant, which is for you a faithful minister of Christ, which also declared unto us your love which ye have in the spirit.

* Where the faith of Christ is: there is love to the brethren.

B + For this cause we also, since the day we heard of it have not ceased praying for you and desiring that ye might be fulfilled with the knowledge of his will, in all wisdom and spiritual understanding, that ye might walk worthy of the Lord in all things that please, being fruitful in all good works and increasing in the knowledge of God, strengthed with all might, through his glorious power, unto all patience and longsuffering with joyfulness⊦ giving thanks into the father which hath made us meet to be partakers of the inheritance of saints in light.

C Which hath delivered us from the power of darkness, and hath translated us into the kingdom of his dear son, in whom we have redemption through his blood, that is to say forgiveness of sins, which is the image of the invisible God, first begotten of all creatures. For by him were all things created, things that are in heaven, and things that are in earth: things visible and things invisible: whether they be majesty or lordship, either rule or power. All things are created by him, and in him, and he is before all things, and in him all things have their being.

Our redemption is the forgiveness of our sins.

And he is the head of the body, that is to wit of the congregation: he is the beginning and first* begotten of the dead, that in all things he might have the pre-eminence. For it pleased the father that in him should all fulness dwell, and by him to reconcile all things unto himself, and to set at peace by him through the blood of his cross, both things in heaven and things in earth.

* He is the first that hath the glory and new life of the resurrection.

And you (which were in times past strangers and enemies, because your minds were set in evil works) hath he now reconciled in the body of his flesh through death, to make you holy, unblameable and without fault in his own sight, if ye continue grounded and stablished in the faith, and be not moved away from the hope of the gospel, whereof ye have heard, how that it is preached among all creatures which are under heaven, whereof I Paul am made a minister.

★ Passions or sufferings of Christ: is the passions which we must suffer for his sake. For we have professed and are appointed to suffer with Christ. John 20, as my father sent me, so send I you.

Now joy I in my sufferings★ which I suffer for you, and fulfil that which is behind of the passions of Christ in my flesh for his body's sake, which is the congregation, whereof I am made a minister according to the ordinance of God, which ordinance was given me unto you-ward, to fulfil the word of God, that mystery hid since the world began, and since the beginning of generations: but now is opened to his saints, to whom God would make known the glorious riches of this mystery among the gentiles, which riches is Christ in you, the hope of glory, whom we preach, warning all men, and teaching all men in all wisdom, to make all men perfect in Christ Jesus. Wherein I also labour and strive, even as far forth as his working worketh in me mightily. **D**

A true apostle would have all men perfect in the knowlege of Christ and of his doctrine.

CHAPTER TWO

I would ye knew what fighting I have for your sakes and for them of Laodicea, and for as many as have not seen my person in the flesh, that their hearts might be comforted and knit together in love, and in all riches of full understanding, for to know the mystery of God the father and of Christ, in whom are hid all the treasures of wisdom and knowledge. This I say lest any man should beguile you with enticing words. For though I be absent in the flesh, yet am I present with you in the spirit, joying and beholding the order that ye keep, and your steadfast faith in Christ. As ye have therefore received Christ Jesus the Lord, even so walk, rooted and built in him and steadfast in the faith, as ye have learned: and therein be plenteous in giving thanks. **A**

1 Cor. 5. b.

Philosophy and traditions of men.

Christ is sufficient.

Faith is the working of God.

Eph. 2. a.

+ Beware lest any man come and spoil you through philosophy and deceitful vanity, through the traditions of men, and ordinances after the world, and not after Christ. For in him dwelleth all the fulness of the Godhead bodily, and ye are complete in him which is the head of all rule and power, in whom also ye are circumcised with circumcision made without hands, by putting off the sinful body of the flesh, through the circumcision that is in Christ, in that ye are buried with him through baptism, in whom ye are also risen again through faith, that is wrought by the operation of God which raised him from death. **B**

★ The law is our handwriting in that the conscience setteth to her seal, subscribeth and consenteth that the law is just and we sinners, which law concerning damnation is taken away through faith in Chirst.

And ye which were dead in sin through the uncircumcision of your flesh, hath he quickened with him and hath forgiven us all our trespasses+ and hath put out the handwriting★ that was against us, contained in the law written, and that hath he taken out of the way and hath fastened it to his cross, and hath spoiled rule and power and hath made a shew of them openly, and hath triumphed over them in his own person. **C**

Let no man therefore trouble your consciences about meat and drink or for a piece of an holy day, as the holy day of the new moon or of the sabbath days, which are nothing but shadows of things to come: but the body is in Christ. Let no man make you shoot at a wrong mark*, which after his own imagination walketh in the humbleness and holiness of angels, things which he never saw: causeless puffed up with his fleshly mind, and holdeth not the head, whereof all the body by joints and couples receiveth nourishment, and is knit together, and increaseth with the increasing that cometh of God.

* Mark: there is none other mark than Christ, nor other name to be saved by.

D Wherefore if ye be dead with Christ from ordinances of the world, why as though ye yet lived in the world, are ye led with traditions of them that say Touch not, taste not, handle not? which all perish with the using of them and are after the commandments and doctrines of men, which things have the similitude of wisdom in chosen holiness and humbleness, and in that they spare not the body, and do the flesh no worship unto his need.

CHAPTER THREE

A + If ye be then risen again with Christ, seek those things which are above, where Christ sitteth on the right hand of God. Set your affection on things that are above, and not on things which are on the earth. For ye are dead, and your life is hid with Christ in God. When Christ which is our life, shall shew himself, then shall ye also appear with him in glory. ⊢

All the mercy that is set forth in the two upper chapters, is promised to them only that will follow Christ and live as hereafter followeth.

Mortify therefore your members which are on the earth, fornication, uncleanness, unnatural lust, evil concupiscence, and covetousness which is worshipping of idols: for which things' sakes the wrath of God cometh on the children of unbelief. In which things ye walked once when ye lived in them.

These members must be slain.

B But now put ye also away from you all things, wrath, fierceness, maliciousness, cursed speaking, filthy speaking out of your mouths. Lie not one to another that the old man with his works be put off, and the new put on, which is renewed in knowledge after the image of him that made him, where is neither gentile nor Jew, circumcision nor uncircumcision, Barbarous or Scythian, bond or free: but Christ is all in all things.

Rom. 6. b.
Eph. 4.
Heb. 12.
1 Pet. 2. a.

Every man is Christ to another.

+ Now therefore as elect of God, holy and beloved, put on tender mercy, kindness, humbleness of minds, meekness, longsuffering, forbearing one another, and forgiving one another, if any man have a quarrel to another, even **C** as Christ forgave you, even so do ye. Above all these things put on love, which is the bond of perfectness. And the peace of God rule in your hearts, to the which peace ye are called in one body. And see that ye be thankful. Let the word of Christ dwell in you plenteously in all wisdom. Teach and exhort your own selves, in psalms, and hymns, and spiritual songs which have favour with them singing in your hearts to the Lord. And all things (whatsoever ye do in word or deed) do in the name of the Lord Jesus, giving thanks to God the father by him. ⊢

Eph. 4. b.

Christ's example, of love.

1 Cor. 10. g.

Wives, submit yourselves unto your own husbands, as it is comely in the Lord. Husbands love your wives and be not bitter unto them. Children, obey

Wives.

Husbands.

Children and fathers.

Eph. 5. e.
1 Pet. 3. a.
Eph. 6. a.
Tit. 2. e.
1 Pet. 2. c.

Wisdom 6. b.
Rom. 2. b.

Masters.

your fathers and mothers, in all things, for that is well pleasing unto the Lord. Fathers, rate not your children, lest they be of a desperate mind. Servants, be obedient unto your bodily masters in all things: not with eye-service as men-pleasers, but in singleness of heart, fearing God. And whatsoever ye do, do it heartily as though ye did it to the Lord, and not unto men, forasmuch as ye know that of the Lord ye shall receive the reward of inheritance, for ye serve the Lord Christ. But he that doth wrong, shall receive for the wrong that he hath done: for there is no respect of persons. †Ye masters, do unto your servants that which is just and egal seeing ye know that ye also have a master in heaven.

CHAPTER FOUR

Eph. 5. d.

Continue in prayer and watch in the same with thanksgiving, praying also for **A** us, that God open unto us the door of utterance, that we may speak the mystery of Christ, wherefore I am in bonds: that I may utter it, as it becometh me to speak. Walk wisely to them that are without, and redeem the time. Let * Salt is the wisdom of God's word. your speech be always well-favoured and be powdered with salt*, that ye may know how to answer every man.

The dear brother Tychicus shall tell you of all my business, which is a **B** faithful minister and fellowservant in the Lord, whom I have sent unto you for the same purpose, that he might know how ye do, and might comfort your hearts, with one Onesimus a faithful and a beloved brother, which is one of you. They shall shew you of all things which are a-doing here.

Mark the evangelist.

Aristarchus my prison-fellow saluteth you, and Marcus, Barnabas' sister's **C** son: touching whom, ye received commandments. If he come unto you receive him: and Jesus which is called Justus, which are of the circumcision. These only are my work-fellows unto the kingdom of God, which were unto my consolation. Epaphras the servant of Christ, which is one of you, saluteth you, and always laboureth fervently for you in prayers, that ye may stand perfect and full in all that is the will of God. I bear him record that he hath a fervent Luke the evangelist. mind toward you and toward them of Laodicea and them of Hieropolis. Dear **D** 2 Tim. 4. Luke the physician greeteth you, and Demas. Salute the brethren which are of Laodicea, and salute Nymphas and the congregation which is in his house. And when the epistle is read of you, make that it be read in the congregation of the Laodiceans also: and that ye likewise read the epistle of Laodicea. And say to Archippus: take heed to the office that thou hast received in the Lord, that thou fulfil it. The salutation by the hand of me Paul. Remember my bonds. Grace be with you. Amen.

Sent from Rome by Tychicus, and Onesimus.

† The fourth chapter more correctly begins here.

A PROLOGUE TO THE FIRST EPISTLE OF
ST PAUL TO THE THESSALONIANS

This epistle did Paul write of exceeding love and care: and praiseth them in the two first chapters, because they did receive the gospel earnestly, and had in tribulation and persecution continued therein steadfastly, and were become an example unto all congregations, and hath thereto suffered of their own kinsmen as Christ and his apostles did of the Jews, putting them thereto in mind, how purely and godly he had lived among them to their example, and thanketh God that his gospel had brought forth such fruit among them.

In the third chapter, he sheweth his diligence and care, lest his so great labour and their so blessed a beginning should have been in vain, Satan and his apostles vexing them with persecution, and destroying their faith with men's doctrine. And therefore he sent Timothy to them to comfort them and strength them in the faith, and thanketh God that they had so constantly endured, and desired God to increase them.

In the fourth he exhorteth them to keep themselves from sin, and to do good one to another. And thereto be informeth them concerning the resurrection.

In the fifth he writeth of the last day, that it should come suddenly, exhorting to prepare themselves thereafter and to keep a good order concerning obedience and rule.

THE FIRST EPISTLE OF ST PAUL UNTO THE THESSALONIANS

1^{1}–2^{5}

CHAPTER ONE

Paul, Silvanus and Timotheus. A
Unto the congregation of the Thessalonians, in God the father, and in
the Lord Jesus Christ.

Grace be with you, peace from God our father, and from the Lord Jesus Christ.

We give God thanks always for you all, making mention of you in our
prayers without ceasing, and call to remembrance your work in the faith, and
labour in love and perseverance in the hope of our Lord Jesus Christ, in the B
sight of God our father: + because we know brethren beloved of God, how that
ye are elect. For our gospel came not unto you in word only, but also in
power, and also in the holy ghost and in much certainty, as ye know after
what manner we behaved ourselves among you, for your sakes.

And ye became followers of us and of the lord, and received the word in
much affliction, with joy of the holy ghost: so that ye were an example to all C
that believe in Macedonia and Achaia. For from you sounded out the word
of the Lord, not in Macedonia and in Achaia only: but your faith also which
ye have unto God, spread herself abroad in all quarters, so greatly that it
needeth not us to speak anything at all. For they themselves shew of you what
manner of entering in we had unto you and how ye turned to God from
images, for to serve the living and true God, and for to look for his son from
heaven, whom he raised from death: I mean Jesus which delivereth us from
wrath to come. ⊦

CHAPTER TWO

For ye yourselves know brethren of our entrance in unto you, how that it was A
not in vain: but even after that we had suffered before and were shamefully
entreated at Philippi (as ye well know) then were we bold in our God to speak
unto you the gospel of God, with much striving. Our exhortation was not to
bring you to error, nor yet to uncleanness, neither was it with guile: but as we
were allowed of God, that the gospel should be committed unto us: even so
we speak, not as though we intended to please men, but God, which trieth
our hearts.

Neither was our conversation at any time with flattering words, as ye well B know neither in cloaked covetousness, God is record: neither sought we praise of men, neither of you, nor yet of any other, when we might have been chargeable as the apostles of Christ, but we were tender among you, even as a nurse cherisheth her children, so was our affection toward you, our good will was to have dealt unto you, not the gospel of God only: but also our own souls, because ye were dear unto us.

+ Ye remember brethren our labour and travail. For we laboured day and night, because we would not be grievous unto any of you, and preached unto you the gospel of God. Ye are witnesses, and so is God, how holily and justly and unblameable we behaved ourselves among you that believe: as ye know how that we exhorted and comforted and besought every one of you, as a father his children, that ye would walk worthy of God, which hath called you unto his kingdom and glory.

A sure token of a true apostle.

Acts 20.
1 Cor. 4.
2 Thes. 3.

C For this cause thank we God without ceasing, because that when ye received of us the word wherewith God was preached, ye received it not as the word of man: but even as it was in deed, the word of God, which worketh in you that believe. ⊢ For ye brethren became followers of the congregations of God which in Jewry are in Christ Jesus: for ye have suffered like things of your kinsmen as we ourselves have suffered of the Jews. Which as they killed the **D** Lord Jesus and their own prophets, even so have they persecuted us, and God they please not, and are contrary to all men and forbid us to preach unto the gentiles, that they might be saved, to fulfil their sins all way. For the wrath of God is come on them, even to the utmost.

Forasmuch brethren as we are kept from you for a season, as concerning the bodily presence, but not in the heart, we enforced the more to see you personally with great desire. And therefore we would have come unto you, I Paul once and again: but Satan withstood us. For what is our hope or joy, or crown of rejoicing? are not ye it in the presence of our Lord Jesus Christ at his coming? yes ye are our glory and joy.

CHAPTER THREE

A Wherefore since we could no longer forbear, it pleased us to remain at Athens alone, and sent Timotheus our brother and minister of God, and our labour-fellow in the gospel of Christ, to establish you and to comfort you over your faith, that no man should be moved in these afflictions. For ye yourselves **B** know that we are even appointed thereunto. For verily when I was with you, I told you before that we should suffer tribulation, even as it came to pass, and as ye know. For this cause, when I could no longer forbear, I sent, that I might have knowledge of your faith, lest haply the tempter had tempted you, and that our labour had been bestowed in vain.

But now lately when Timotheus came from you unto us, and declared to us your faith and your love and how that ye have good remembrance of us **C** always, desiring to see us as we desire to see you: Therefore brethren we had consolation in you, in all our adversity and necessity, through your faith. For

Acts 16.

now are we alive, if ye stand steadfast in the Lord. For what thanks can we
recompense to God again for you, over all the joy that we joy for your sakes
before our God, while we, night and day pray exceedingly that we might see
you presently, and might fulfil that which is lacking in your faith.
God himself our father and our Lord Jesus Christ guide our journey unto D
you: and the Lord increase you and make you flow over in love one toward
another, and toward all men, even as we do toward you, to make your hearts
stable and unblameable, in holiness before God our father, at the coming of
our Lord Jesus Christ, with all his saints.

CHAPTER FOUR

+ Furthermore we beseech you brethren, and exhort you in the Lord Jesus, that A
ye increase more and more, even as ye have received of us, how ye ought to
walk and to please God. Ye remember what commandments we gave you in
Rom. 12. Eph. 5. a.
our Lord Jesus Christ. For this is the will of God, even that ye should be holy,
and that ye should abstain from fornication, that every one of you should know
how to keep his vessel in holiness and honour, and not in the lust of concupiscence, as do the heathen which know not God, that no man go too far and
defraud his brother in bargaining: because the Lord is avenger of all such things
as we told you beforetime and testified. For God hath not called us unto
uncleanness: but unto holiness. He therefore that despiseth, despiseth not man,
but God, which hath sent his holy spirit among you. ⊢
John 13. d. and 15. b. 1 John 2. b. 1 John 4. b.
But as touching brotherly love, ye need not that I write unto you. For ye B
are taught of God to love one another. Yea and that thing verily ye do unto all
the brethren which are thoughout all Macedonia. We beseech you brethren
A good lesson for monks and idle friars.
that ye increase more and more, and that ye study to be quiet, and to meddle
with your own business, and to work with your own hands, as we commanded you: that ye may behave yourselves honestly toward them that are
without, and that nothing be lacking unto you.
Resurrection.
+ I would not brethren have you ignorant concerning them which are fallen
asleep, that ye sorrow not as other do which have no hope. For if we believe C
that Jesus died and rose again: even so them also which sleep by Jesus, will
God bring again with him. And this say we unto you in the word of the Lord,
that we which live and are remaining in the coming of the Lord, shall not
come ere they which sleep. For the Lord himself shall descend from heaven
1 Cor. 15. d.
with a shout and the voice of the archangel and trumpet of God. And the dead
in Christ shall arise first: then shall we which live and remain, be caught up
with them also in the clouds, to meet the Lord in the air. And so shall we ever
be with the Lord. Wherefore comfort yourselves one another with these
words. ⊢

CHAPTER FIVE

Of the times and seasons brethren ye have no need that I write unto you: for ye A
yourselves know perfectly, that the day of the Lord shall come even as a thief in

the night. When they shall say peace and no danger, then cometh on the sudden destruction, as the travailing of a woman with child, and they shall not escape. But ye brethren are not in darkness, that that day should come on you as it were a thief. + Ye are all the children of light, and the children of the day. We are not of the night neither of darkness.

2 Pet. 3.
Rev. 3. a. and 16.

B Therefore let us not sleep as do other: but let us watch and be sober. For they that sleep sleep in the night: and they that be drunken, are drunken in the night. But let us which are of the day, be sober, armed with the breast-plate of faith and love, and with hope of salvation as an helmet. For God hath not appointed us unto wrath: but to obtain salvation by the means of our Lord Jesus Christ which died for us: that whether we wake or sleep, we should live together with him.

Isa. 59. c.
Eph. 6. c.

Faith is the breast plate and hope is the helmet.

C Wherefore comfort yourselves together, and edify one another, even as ye do. ⊦

We beseech you brethren, that ye know them which labour among you and have the oversight of you in the Lord and give you exhortation, that ye have them the more in love, for their works' sake, and be at peace with them. + We desire you brethren, warn them that are unruly, comfort the feeble-minded, forbear the weak, have continual patience toward all men. See that none re-compense evil for evil unto any man: but ever follow that which is good, both among yourselves, and to all men. Rejoice ever. Pray continually. In all things give thanks. For this is the will of God in Christ Jesus toward you.

Quench not the spirit★. Despise not prophesying. Examine all things, and keep that which is good. Abstain from all suspicious things. The very God of peace sanctify you throughout. And I pray God that your whole spirit, soul and body, be kept faultless unto the coming of our Lord Jesus Christ ⊦. Faithful is he which called you: which will also do it. Brethren, pray for us. Greet all the brethren with an holy kiss. I charge you in the Lord, that this epistle be read unto all the holy brethren. The grace of the Lord Jesus Christ be with you. Amen.

★ The spirit whereby we believe in Christ and consent to the law, is quenched again with evil conversation and lewd communication.

Examine all manner of learning.

1 Cor. 1. b.

The first epistle unto the Thessalonians sent from Athens.

THE PROLOGUE TO THE SECOND EPISTLE OF
ST PAUL TO THE THESSALONIANS

Because in the fore-epistle he had said that the last day should come suddenly, the Thessalonians thought that it should have come shortly. Wherefore in this epistle he declareth himself.

And in the first chapter he comforteth them with the everlasting reward of their faith and patience in suffering for the gospel, and with the punishment of their persecutors in everlasting pain.

In the second he sheweth that the last day should not come, till there were first a departing (as some men think) from under the obedience of the Emperor of Rome, and that Antichrist should set up himself in the same place, as God: and deceive the unthankful world with false doctrine, and with false and lying miracles wrought by the working of Satan, until Christ should come and slay him with his glorious coming and spiritual preaching of the word of God.

In the third he giveth them exhortation and warneth them to rebuke the idle that would not labour with their hands, and avoid their company, if they would not mend.

THE SECOND EPISTLE OF ST PAUL
TO THE THESSALONIANS

CHAPTER ONE 1^1–2^3

A Paul, Sylvanus and Timotheus.
Unto the congregation of the Thessalonians which are in God our father,
and in the Lord Jesus Christ.

Grace be with you and peace from God our father, and from the Lord Jesus
Christ.

We are bound to thank God always for you brethren, as it is meet, because
that your faith groweth exceedingly, and every one of you swimmeth in love
toward another between yourselves, so that we ourselves rejoice of you in the
B congregations of God over your patience and faith in all your persecutions and
tribulations that ye suffer, which is a token* of the righteous judgement of God   ⋆ Tribulation is a token
that ye are counted worthy of the kingdom of God, for which ye also suffer.   of salvation.
It is verily a righteous thing with God to recompense tribulation to them that
trouble you: and to you which are troubled, rest with us, when the Lord Jesus
shall shew himself from heaven with his mighty angels, in flaming fire, render-
C ing vengeance unto them that know not God, and to them that obey not unto
the gospel of our Lord Jesus Christ, which shall be punished with everlasting
damnation, from the presence of the Lord, and from the glory of his power,
when he shall come to be glorified in his saints, and to be made marvellous in
all them that believe: because our testimony that we had unto you, was believed
D even the same day that we preached it. Wherefore we pray always for you that
our God make you worthy of the calling, and fulfil all delectation of goodness
and the work of faith, with power: that the name of our Lord Jesus Christ may
be glorified in you, and ye in him, through the grace of our God, and of the
Lord Jesus Christ.

CHAPTER TWO

A We beseech you brethren by the coming of our Lord Jesus Christ, and in that
we shall assemble unto him, that ye be not suddenly moved from your mind,
and be not troubled, neither by spirit, neither by words, nor yet by letter
which should seem to come from us, as though the day of Christ were at   *Eph. 5. b.*
hand. Let no man deceive you by any means, for the Lord cometh not, except
there come a departing first, and that that sinful man be opened, the son of   Antichrist:

305

perdition which is an adversary, and is exalted above all that is called God, or that is worshipped: so that he shall sit as God in temple of God, and shew himself as God.

Remember ye not, that when I was yet with you, I told you these things?   **B**
And now ye know what withholdeth: even that he might be uttered at his time. For the mystery of that iniquity doth he already work which only locketh, until it be taken out of the way. And then shall that wicked be uttered, whom the Lord shall consume with the spirit of his mouth, and shall destroy with the appearance of his coming, ⊦even him whose coming is by the working of Satan, with all lying★ power, signs and wonders: and in all   **C**
deceivableness of unrighteousness, among them that perish: because they received not the love★ of the truth, that they might have been saved. And therefore God shall send them strong delusion, that they should believe lies: that all they might be damned which believed not the truth but had pleasure in unrighteousness.

But we are bound to give thanks always to God for you brethren beloved of the Lord, for because that God hath from the beginning chosen you to salvation, through sanctifying of the spirit, and through believing the truth: whereunto he called you by our gospel, to obtain the glory that cometh of our Lord Jesus Christ.

⊦Therefore brethren stand fast and keep the ordinances which ye have   **D**
learned: whether it were by our preaching, or by epistle. Our Lord Jesus Christ himself, and God our father which hath loved us and hath given us everlasting consolation and good hope through grace, comfort your hearts, and establish you in all doctrine and good doing.

CHAPTER THREE

Furthermore brethren pray for us, that the word of God may have free passage   **A**
and be glorified, as it is with you: and that we may be delivered from unreasonable and evil men. For all men have not faith: but the Lord is faithful, which shall establish you, and keep you from evil. We have confidence through the Lord to you-ward, that ye both do, and will do, that which we command you. And the Lord guide your hearts unto the love of God and patience of Christ. ⊦

We require you brethren in the name of our Lord Jesus Christ, that ye   **B**
withdraw yourselves from every brother that walketh inordinately, and not after the institution which ye received of us. Ye yourselves know how ye ought to follow us. For we behaved not ourselves inordinately among you. Neither took we bread of any man for nought: but wrought with labour and travail night and day, because we would not be grievous to any of you: not but that we had authority: but to make ourselves an example unto you, to follow us. For when we were with you, this we warned you of, that if there were any which would not work, that the same should not eat.

We have heard say no doubt that there are some which walk among you   **C**

Isa. 11. a.

★ Lying miracles because they testify a false faith.

★ Where no love is to the truth, on them doth God let slip false prophets to deceive them.

306

D inordinately and work not at all, but are busybodies. Them that are such, we command and exhort by our Lord Jesus Christ, that they work with quietness, and eat their own bread. Brethren be not weary in well doing. If any man obey not our sayings, send us word of him by a letter: and have no company with him that he may be ashamed. And count him not as an enemy: but warn him as a brother.

Excommunication.

The very Lord of peace give you peace always, by all means. The Lord be with you all. The salutation of me Paul with mine own hand. This is the token in all epistles. So I write. The grace of our Lord Jesus Christ be with you all Amen.

Sent from Athens.

THE PROLOGUE UPON THE FIRST EPISTLE OF
ST PAUL TO TIMOTHY

This epistle writeth St Paul to be an example unto all bishops, what they should **A** teach, and how they should govern the congregation of Christ in all degrees, that it should be no need to govern Christ's flock with the doctrine of their own good meanings.

In the first chapter, he commandeth that the bishop shall maintain the right faith and love, and resist false preachers which make the law and works equal with Christ and his gospel. And he maketh a short conclusion of all Christian learning, whereto the law serveth and what the end thereof is, also what the gospel is, and setteth himself for a comfortable example unto all sinners and troubled consciences.

In the second he commandeth to pray for all degrees, and chargeth that the women shall not preach nor wear costly apparel, but to be obedient unto the men.

In the third he describeth, what manner persons the bishops or priests and their wives should be, and also the deacons and their wives: and commendeth it, if any man desire to be a bishop after that manner.

In the fourth he prophesieth and sheweth before of the false bishops and spiritual officers that should arise among the Christian people, and be, do and preach clean contrary to the fore-described example, and should depart from the faith in Christ and forbid to marry and to eat certain meats, teaching to put trust therein, both of justifying and forgiveness of sins and also of deserving of eternal life.

In the fifth he teacheth how a bishop should use himself toward young and old and concerning widows what is to be done, and which should be found of the common cost: and teacheth also how men should honour the virtuous bishops and priests, and how to rebuke the evil.

In the sixth he exhorteth the bishop to cleave to the gospel of Christ and true doctrine, and to avoid vain questions and superfluous disputings which gender strife and quencheth truth, and by which also the false prophets get them authority and seek to satisfy their insatiable covetousness.

THE FIRST EPISTLE OF
ST PAUL UNTO TIMOTHY

CHAPTER ONE

1^{1-17}

A Paul an apostle of Jesus Christ, by the commandment of God our saviour, and Lord Jesus Christ, which is our hope.

Hope.

Unto Timothy his natural son in the faith.

Grace, mercy and peace from God our father and Lord Jesus Christ our Lord.

Acts 16.

As I besought thee to abide still in Ephesus when I departed into Macedonia, even so do, that thou command some that they teach no other wise: neither give heed to fables and genealogies which are endless, and breed doubts more than godly edifying which is by faith: for the end of the commandment is love* that cometh of a pure heart and of a good conscience, and of faith unfeigned: from the which things some have erred, and have turned unto vain jangling, because they would be doctors of the scripture, and yet understand not what they speak, neither whereof they affirm.

* Love is the end of the commandment and must interpret it.

B + We know that the law is good, if a man use it lawfully, understanding this, how that the law is not given unto a righteous man, but unto the unrighteous and disobedient, to the ungodly and to sinners, to unholy and unclean, to murderers of fathers and murderers of mothers, to manslayers and whoremongers: to them that defile themselves with mankind: to mensteolers: to liars and to perjured, and so forth if there be any other thing that is contrary to wholesome doctrine, according to the gospel of the glory of the blessed God, which gospel is committed unto me.

Rom. 7.

C And I thank Christ Jesus our Lord which hath made me strong: for he counted me true, and put me in office, when before I was a blasphemer, and a persecuter, and a tyrant. But I obtained mercy, because I did it ignorantly through unbelief. Neverthelater the grace of our Lord was more abundant with faith and love which is in Christ Jesus. +

+ This is a true saying and by all means worthy to be received, that Christ Jesus came into the world to save sinners, of whom I am chief. Notwithstanding for this cause was mercy given unto me that Jesus Christ should first shew on me all long patience, unto the example of them which shall in time to come believe on him unto eternal life. So then unto God, king everlasting, immortal, invisible, and wise only, be honour and praise for ever and ever Amen. +

The ground of the faith.
Matt. 9. b.
Mark 2. c.
Paul is an example that none despaireth that can repent.

This commandment commit I unto thee son Timothy, according to the **D** prophecies which in time past were prophesied of thee, that thou in them shouldest fight a good fight, having faith and good conscience which some have put away from them, and as concerning faith have made shipwreck. Of whose number is Hymenæus and Alexander which I have delivered unto Satan, that they might be taught not to blaspheme.

Hymenæus.
Alexander.

CHAPTER TWO

+ I exhort therefore, that above all things, prayers, supplications, intercessions, **A** and giving of thanks be had for all men: for kings, and for all that are in authority, that we may live a quiet and a peaceable life, in all godliness and honesty. For that is good and accepted in the sight of God our saviour, which will★ have all men saved, and to come unto the knowledge of the truth. For **B** there is one God, and one mediator★ between God and man, which is the man Christ Jesus which gave himself a ransom for all men, that it should be testified at his time, whereunto I am ordained a preacher and an apostle: I tell the truth in Christ and lie not, being the teacher of the gentiles in faith and verity. �muⱶ

★ Will and etc. that is: will have the gospel preached to all men without exception, and offereth all men repentance and will have all men prayed for.

★ Christ is the only mediator.

I will therefore that the men pray everywhere, lifting up pure hands without **C** wrath, or doubting. Likewise also the women that they array themselves in comely apparel with shamefastness and discreet behaviour, not with broided hair, or gold, or pearls, or costly array: but with such as becometh women that profess the worshipping of God through good works. Let the woman learn in silence with all subjection. I suffer not a woman to teach, neither to have authority over a man: but for to be in silence. For Adam was first formed, and then Eve. Also Adam was not deceived, but the woman was deceived, and was in transgression. Notwithstanding through bearing of children they shall be saved, so they continue in faith, love and holiness with discretion.

Prayer.

Women.

1 Pet. 3. a.
1 Cor. 14.

CHAPTER THREE

This is a true saying. If a man covet the office of a bishop, he desireth a good **A** work. Yea and a bishop must be faultless, the husband of one wife, sober, discreet, honestly apparelled, harbourous, apt to teach, not drunken, no fighter, not given to filthy lucre: but gentle, abhorring fighting, abhorring covetousness, and one that ruleth his own house honestly, having children under obedience, with all honesty. For if a man cannot rule his own house, **B** how shall he care for the congregation of God. He may not be a young scholar lest he swell and fall into the judgment of the evil speaker. He must also be well reported of among them which are withoutforth, lest he fall into rebuke and snare of the evil speaker.

A bishop or an overseer what he ought to be.

Likewise must the deacons be honest, not double-tongued, not given unto much drinking, neither unto filthy lucre: but having the mystery of the faith in pure conscience. And let them first be proved, and then let them minister, if they be found faultless.

Deacons.

310

C   Even so must their wives be honest, not evil speakers: but sober and faithful
in all things. Let the deacons be the husbands of one wife, and such as rule their
children well, and their own households. For they that minister well, get
themselves good degree and great liberty in the faith, which is in Christ Jesus.

D   These things write I unto thee, trusting to come shortly unto thee: but and
if I tarry long, that then thou mayst yet have knowledge how thou oughtest to
behave thyself in the house of God, which is the congregation of the living
God, the pillar and ground of truth. And without nay, great is that mystery of
godliness: God was showed in the flesh, was justified in the spirit, was seen
of angels, was preached unto the gentiles, was believed on in earth and received
up in glory.

The wives of the
priests and deacons.

CHAPTER FOUR

A   The spirit speaketh evidently that in the latter times some shall depart from
the faith, and shall give heed unto spirits of error, and devilish doctrine of them
which speak false through hypocrisy, and have their consciences marked with
an hot iron, forbidding to marry, and commanding to abstain from meats
which God hath created to be received with giving thanks, of them which
B   believe and know the truth. For all the creatures of God are good and nothing
to be refused, if it be received with thanksgiving. For it is sanctified by the
word of God and prayer. If thou shalt put the brethren in remembrance of these
things, thou shalt be a good minister of Jesus Christ, which hast been
nourished up in the words of the faith and good doctrine, which doctrine thou
hast continually followed. But cast away unghostly and old wives' fables.

Exercise thyself unto godliness. For bodily exercise profiteth little: But
godliness is good unto all things, as a thing which hath promises of the life that
is now, and of the life to come. This is a sure saying and of all parties worthy
to be received. For therefore we labour and suffer rebuke, because we believe
in the living God, which is the saviour of all men: but specially of those that
believe. Such things command and teach. Let no man despise thy youth: but
be unto them that believe, an example, in word in conversation, in love, in
spirit, in faith and in pureness.

D   Till I come, give attendance to reading, to exhortation and to doctrine.
Despise not the gift that is the thee, which was given thee through prophecy and
with laying on of the hands of an elder. These things exercise, and give thyself
unto them, that it may be seen how thou profitest in all things. Take heed unto
thyself and unto learning, and continue therein. For if thou shalt so do, thou
shalt save thyself and them that hear thee.

2 Tim. 3.
2 Pet. 3.
Jude 2. f.

Hot iron.

2 Tim. 3.
Tit. 4. c.

CHAPTER FIVE

A   Rebuke not an elder: but exhort him as a father, and the younger men as
brethren, the elder women as mothers, the younger as sisters, with all pureness. Honour widows which are true widows. If any widow have children or

The wives of the

How a bishop or priest
should behave himself
in exhorting
or rebuking.

Widows.

nephews, let them learn first to rule their own houses godly, and to recompense their elders. For that is good and acceptable before God. She that is a very widow and friendless, putteth her trust in God, and continueth in supplication and prayer night and day. But she that liveth in pleasure, is dead even yet alive. And these things command, that they may be without fault. If there be any that provideth not for his own, and namely for them of his household, the same denieth the faith, and is worse than an infidel.

Widows.

Let no widow be chosen under threescore year old, and such a one as was **B** the wife of one man, and well reported of in good works: if she have nourished children, if she have been liberal to strangers, if she have washed the saints' feet, if she have ministered unto them which were in adversity, if she were continually given unto all manner good works. The younger widows refuse. For when they have begun to wax wanton, to the dishonour of Christ, then will they marry, having damnation*, because they have broken their first faith. And also they learn to go from house to house idle, yea not idle only, but also trifling and busybodies, speaking things which are not comely.

* Whatsoever be used amongst us, if God be thereby dishonoured it ought to be broken.

I will therefore that the younger women marry and bear children, and guide **C** the house, and give none occasion to the adversary to speak evil. For many of them are already turned back, and are gone after Satan. And if any man or woman that believeth have widows, let them minister unto them, and let not the congregation be charged: that it may have sufficient for them that are widows indeed.

The elders that rule well, are worthy of double honour, most specially they which labour in the word and in teaching. For the scripture saith: Thou shalt not muzzle the mouth of the ox that treadeth out the corn. And the labourer is worthy of his reward. Against an elder receive none accusation: but under two or three witnesses. Them that sin, rebuke openly, that other may fear.

Deut. 25.
1 Cor. 9. a.
Matt. 10. b.
Luke 10. b.

I testify before God and the Lord Jesus Christ, and the elect angels, that thou **D** observe these things without hasty judgement, and do nothing partially. Lay hands suddenly on no man neither be partaker of other men's sins: keep thyself pure. Drink no longer water, but use a little wine for thy stomach's sake and thine often diseases.

Some men's sins are open beforehand and go before unto judgement: some mens' sins follow after. Likewise also good works are manifest beforehand and they that are otherwise, cannot be hid.

CHAPTER SIX

Servants.

Let as many servants as are under the yoke, count their masters worthy of all **A** honour, that the name of God and his doctrine be not evil spoken of. See that they which have believing masters, despise them not because they are brethren: but so much the rather do service, forasmuch as they are believing and beloved and partakers of the benefits.

These things teach and exhort. If any man teach otherwise, and is not content with the wholesome words of our Lord Jesus Christ, and with the doctrine

B of godliness, he is puffed up and knoweth nothing: but wasteth his brains about questions and strife of words, whereof spring envy, strife, railings, evil surmisings and vain disputations of men with corrupt minds and destitute of the truth, which think that lucre is godliness. From such separate thyself. Godliness is great riches, if a man be content with that he hath. For we brought nothing into the world, and it is a plain case that we can carry nothing out.

Job. 1. d.
Eccl. 5. c.

When we have food and raiment, let us therewith be content. They that will be rich, fall into temptation and snares, and into many foolish and noisome lusts, which drown men in perdition and destruction. For covetousness is root

C of all evil, which while some lusted after, they erred from the faith, and tangled themselves with many sorrows. But thou which art the man of God, fly such things. Follow righteousness, godliness, love, patience and meekness. Fight the good fight of faith. Lay hand on eternal life, whereunto thou art called, and hast professed a good profession before many witnesses.

Covetousness.
O that we at a lawful age might confess and profess openly the faith and life of a Christian man.

I give thee charge in the sight of God, which quickeneth all things, and before Jesus Christ which under Pontius Pilate witnessed a good witnessing, that thou keep the commandment, and be without spot and unrebukable until the appearing of our Lord Jesus Christ, which appearing (when the time is come) he shall show that is blessed and mighty only, king of kings and lord of lords, which only hath immortality, and dwelleth in light that no man can attain, whom never man saw, neither can see: unto whom be honour and rule everlasting. Amen.

Rev. 17. and 19. c.

John 1. b.
1 John 1. c.

D Charge them that are rich in this world, that they be not exceeding wise, and that they trust not in the uncertain riches, but in the living God, which giveth us abundantly all things to enjoy them, and that they do good and be rich in good works, and ready to give and to distribute, laying up in store for themselves a good foundation against the time to come that they may obtain eternal life.

Rich.

John 1. b.

O Timothy save that which is given thee to keep, and avoid unghostly vanities of voices and oppositions of science falsely so called, which science while some professed, they have erred as concerning the faith. Grace be with thee. Amen.

Sent from Laodicea, which is the chiefest city of Phrigia Pacatiana.

THE PROLOGUE TO THE SECOND EPISTLE OF
ST PAUL UNTO TIMOTHY

In this epistle Paul exhorteth Timothy to go forward as he had begun, and to preach the gospel with all diligence, as it need was, seeing many were fallen away, and many false spirits and teachers were sprung up already. Wherefore a bishop's part is, ever to watch and to labour in the gospel.

In the third and fourth he showeth before and that notably, of the jeopardous time toward the end of the world, in which a false spiritual living should deceive the whole world with outward hypocrisy and appearance of holiness, under which all abominations should have their free passage and course, as we (alas) have seen this prophecy of St Paul fulfilled in our spiritualty unto the uttermost jot.

THE SECOND EPISTLE OF
ST PAUL UNTO TIMOTHY

CHAPTER ONE 1¹⁻¹⁷

A Paul an apostle of Jesus Christ, by the will of God, to preach the promise of life, which life is in Christ Jesus.

To Timothy his beloved son.

Grace, mercy and peace, from God the Father, and from Christ Jesus our Lord.

I thank God, whom I serve from mine elders with pure conscience, that without ceasing I make mention of thee in my prayers night and day, desiring to see thee, mindful of thy tears: so that I am filled with joy, when I call to remembrance the unfeigned faith that is in thee which dwelt first in thy grandmother Lois, and in thy mother Eunice: and am assured that it dwelleth in thee also.

B Wherefore I warn thee that thou stir up the gift of God which is in thee, by the putting on of my hands. For God hath not given to us the spirit of fear: but of power, and of love, and of soberness of mind. Be not ashamed to testify our Lord, neither be ashamed of me, which am bound for his sake: but suffer adversity with the gospel also through the power of God, which saved us and

C called us with an holy calling, not according to our deeds, but according to his own purpose and grace, which grace was given us through Christ Jesus before the world was, but is now declared openly by the appearing of our saviour Jesus Christ, which hath put away death, and hath brought life and immortality unto light through the gospel, whereunto I am appointed a preacher, and an apostle, and a teacher of the gentiles: for the which cause I also suffer these things. Nevertheless I am not ashamed. For I know whom I have believed, and am sure that he is able keep that which I have committed to his keeping, against that day.

D See thou have the example of the wholesome words which thou heardest of me, in faith and love which is in Jesus Christ. That good thing, which was committed to thy keeping, keep in the holy ghost which dwelleth in us. This thou knowest, how that all they which are in Asia, be turned from me. Of which sort are Phygellus and Hermogenes. The Lord give mercy unto the house of Onesiphorus, for he oft refreshed me, and was not ashamed of my chains: but when he was at Rome, he sought me out very diligently, and found

Rom. 9.

Putting on of hands.

Tit. 3. d.

Purpose and grace.

1 Tim. 2. b.

me. The Lord grant unto him that he may find mercy with the Lord at that day. And in how many things he ministered unto me at Ephesus thou knowest very well.

CHAPTER TWO

+ Thou therefore my son, be strong in the grace that is in Christ Jesus. And   A
what things thou hast heard of me many bearing witness, the same deliver to
faithful men, which are apt to teach other. Thou therefore suffer affliction as a
good soldier of Jesus Christ. No man that warreth, entangleth himself with
worldly business, and that because he would please him that hath chosen him
to be a soldier. And though a man strive for a mastery, yet is he not crowned,
except he strive lawfully. The husbandman that laboureth must first receive
of the fruits. Consider what I say. The Lord give thee understanding in all
things. ⊦

Remember that Jesus Christ being of the seed of David, rose again from   B
death according to my gospel, wherein I suffer trouble as an evil-doer, even
unto bonds. But the word of God was not bound. Herefore I suffer all things,

Elect.

for the elect's sakes, that they might also obtain that salvation which is in
Christ Jesus, with eternal glory.

It is a true saying, if we be dead with him, we also shall live with him. If we

Covenants.

be patient, we shall also reign with him. If we deny him, he also shall deny us.
If we believe not, yet abideth he faithful. He cannot deny himself. Of these
things put them in remembrance, and testify before the Lord, that they strive
not about words which is to no profit, but to pervert the hearers.

Study to shew thyself laudable unto God a workman that needeth not to be   C
ashamed, dividing the word of truth justly. Unghostly and vain voices pass
over. For they shall increase unto greater ungodliness, and their words shall

Hymenæus.
Philetus.

fret even as doth a canker: of whose number is Hymenæus and Philetus, which
as concerning the truth have erred, saying that the resurrection is past already,
and do destroy the faith of divers persons.

But the sure ground of God remaineth, and hath this seal: the Lord knoweth
them that are his, and let every man that calleth on the name of Christ, depart
from iniquity. Notwithstanding in a great house are not only vessels of gold
and of silver: but also of wood and of earth, some for honour, and some unto
dishonour. But if a man purge himself from such fellows, he shall be a vessel
sanctified unto honour, meet for the Lord and prepared unto all good works.

Lusts of youth avoid, and follow righteousness, faith, love and peace, with   D
them that call on the Lord with pure heart. Foolish and unlearned questions put

1 Tim. 1. c.
Tit. 3. c.

from thee, remembering that they do but gender strife. But the servant of the
Lord must not strive: but must be peaceable unto all men, and apt to teach, and
one that can suffer the evil in meekness, and can inform them that resist, if that
God at any time will give them repentance for to know the truth: that they may
come to themselves again out of the snare of the devil, which are now taken of
him at his will.

CHAPTER THREE

A This understand, that in the last days shall come parlous times. For the men shall be lovers of their own selves, covetous, boasters, proud, cursed speakers, disobedient to father and mother, unthankful, unholy, unkind, trucebreakers, stubborn, false accusers, rioters, fierce despisers of them which are good, traitors, heady, high-minded, greedy upon voluptuousness more than the lovers of God, having a similitude* of godly living, but have denied the power thereof and such abhor. Of this sort are they which enter into houses, and bring into bondage women laden with sins, which women are led of divers lusts, ever learning and never able to come unto the knowledge of the truth.

C As Jannes and Jambres withstood Moses, even so do these resist the truth, men they are of corrupt minds, and lewd as concerning the faith: but they shall prevail no longer. For their madness shall be uttered unto all men as theirs was. But thou hast seen the experience of my doctrine, fashion of living, purpose, faith, longsuffering, love, patience, persecutions, and afflictions which happened unto me at Antioch, at Iconium and at Lystra: which persecutions I suffered patiently. And from them all the Lord delivered me. Yea and all that will live godly in Christ Jesus, must suffer persecutions. But the evil men and deceivers shall wax worse and worse, while they deceive and are deceived themselves.

D But continue thou in the things which thou hast learned, which also were committed unto thee seeing thou knowest of whom thou hast learned them and forasmuch also as thou hast known holy scripture of a child, which is able to make the wise unto salvation through the faith which is in Christ Jesus. For all scripture given by inspiration of God, is profitable to teach, to improve, to amend and to instruct in righteousness, that the man of God may be perfect and prepared unto all good works.

CHAPTER FOUR

A I testify therefore before God, and before the Lord Jesus Christ, which shall judge quick and dead at his appearing in his kingdom, preach the word, be fervent, be it in season or out of season. Improve, rebuke, exhort with all longsuffering and doctrine. For the time will come, when they will not suffer wholesome doctrine: but after their own lusts shall they (whose ears itch) get them an heap of teachers, and shall turn their ears from the truth, and shall be given unto fables. But watch thou in all things, and suffer adversity, and do the work of an evangelist, fulfil thine office unto the utmost.

C For I am now ready to be offered, and the time of my departing is at hand. I have fought a good fight, and have fulfilled my course, and have kept the faith. From henceforth is laid up for me a crown of righteousness which the Lord that is a righteous judge shall give me at that day: not to me only but unto all them that love his coming. Make speed to come unto me at once.

For Demas hath left me and hath loved this present world, and is departed

Marginal notes:

1 Tim. 4.
2 Pet. 3.
Jude 1. f.

* This was prophesied of them that should pretend holiness.

Jannes.
Jambres.

Exod. 7. b.

Persecution.

2 Pet. 1. d.

Scripture.

They that have no true faith, nor lust to live godly, seeketh ever new doctors.

Col. 4.

into Thessalonica. Crescens is gone to Galatia, and Titus unto Dalmatia. Only Luke is with me. Take Mark and bring him with thee, for he is necessary unto me for to minister. And Tychicus have I sent to Ephesus. The cloak that I left at Troas with Carpus, when thou comest, bring with thee, and the books, but specially the parchment. Alexander the coppersmith did me much evil; the Lord reward him according to his deeds, of whom be thou ware also. For he withstood our preaching sore.

At my first answering, no man assisted me, but all forsook me. I pray God, that it may not be laid to their charges: + not withstanding the Lord assisted me, and strengthed me, that by me the preaching should be fulfilled to the utmost, and that all the gentiles should hear. And I was delivered out of the mouth of the lion. And the Lord shall deliver me from all evil doing, and shall keep me unto his heavenly kingdom. To whom be praise for ever and ever. Amen. +

Salute Prisca and Aquila, and the household of Onesiphorus. Erastus abode at Corinth. Trophimus I left at Miletum sick. Make speed to come before winter. Eubulus greeteh thee, and Pudens, and Linus, and Claudia, and all the brethren. The Lord Jesus Christ be with thy spirit. Grace be with you. Amen.

The second epistle written from Rome unto Timothy, when Paul was presented the second time up before the Emperor Nero.

THE PROLOGUE UNTO THE EPISTLE OF
ST PAUL TO TITUS

A   This is a short epistle: wherein yet is contained all that is needful for a Christian
to know.

   In the first chapter he sheweth what manner a man a bishop or curate ought
to be: that is to wit, virtuous and learned, to preach and defend the gospel, and
to confound the doctrine of trusting in works and men's traditions which ever
fight against the faith and carry away the conscience captive from the freedom
that is in Christ into the bondage of their own imaginations and inventions, as
though those things should make a man good in the sight of God which are to
no profit at all.

   In the second he teacheth all degrees, old, young, men, women, masters,
and servants how to behave themselves, as they which Christ hath bought with
his blood, to be his proper or peculiar people, to glorify God with good works.

   In the third he teacheth to honour temporal rulers and to obey them, and yet
bringeth to Christ again and to the grace that he hath purchased for us, that no
man should think that the obedience of princes, laws or any other work should
justify us before God. And last of all he chargeth to avoid the company of the
stubborn and of the heretics.

THE EPISTLE OF ST PAUL
UNTO TITUS

CHAPTER ONE

Paul the servant of God, and an apostle of Jesus Christ, to preach the faith of God's elect, and the knowledge of that truth, which is after godliness upon the hope of eternal life, which life God that cannot lie, hath promised before the world began: but hath opened his word at the time appointed through preaching, which preaching is committed unto me, by the commandment of God our saviour.

To Titus his natural son in the common faith.

Grace mercy and peace from God the father, and from the Lord Jesus Christ our saviour.

For this cause left I thee in Crete, that thou shouldest perform that which was lacking, and shouldest ordain elders in every city as I appointed thee. If any be faultless, the husband of one wife, having faithful children, which are not slandered of riot, neither are disobedient. For a bishop★ must be faultless, as it becometh the minister of God: not stubborn, not angry, no drunkard, no fighter, not given to filthy lucre: but harbourous, one that loveth goodness, sober-minded, righteous, holy, temperate, and such as cleaveth unto the true word of doctrine, that he may be able to exhort with wholesome learning, and to improve them that say against it.

For there are many disobedient and talkers of vanity and deceivers of minds, namely they of the circumcision, whose mouths must be stopped, which pervert whole houses teaching things which they ought not, because of filthy lucre. One being of themselves, which was a poet of their own, said: The Cretans are always liars, evil beasts, and slow bellies. This witness is true, wherefore rebuke them sharply, that they may be sound in the faith, and not taking heed to Jews' fables and commandments of men that turn from the truth. Unto the pure, are all things pure: but unto them that are defiled and unbelieving, is nothing pure: but even the very minds and consciences of them are defiled. They confess that they know God: but with the deeds they deny him, and are abominable and disobedient, and unto all good works discommendable.

CHAPTER TWO

But speak thou that which becometh wholesome learning. That the elder men be sober, honest, discreet, sound in the faith in love and in patience. And the

Elders which
Timotheus calleth
overseers.

1 Tim. 3.

★ Bishops and elders is
all one and an officer
chosen to govern the
congregation in
doctrine and living.

Rom. 14.

Old men.

B

C

D

A

elder women likewise, that they be in such raiment as becometh holiness, not   *Old women.*
false accusers, not given to much drinking, but teachers of honest things, to
make the young women sober-minded, to love their husbands, to love their   *Young women.*
children, to be discreet, chaste, housewifely, good and obedient unto their own
husbands that the word of God be not evil spoken of. Young men likewise   *Young men.*
exhort that they be sober-minded.

B   Above all things shew thyself an example of good works with uncorrupt
doctrine, with honesty, and with the wholesome word which cannot be
rebuked, that he which withstandeth, may be ashamed, having nothing in you
that he may dispraise. The servants exhort to be obedient unto their own   *Servants.*
masters, and to please in all things, not answering again, neither be pickers, but
that they shew all good faithfulness, that they may do worship to the doctrine
C   of our saviour God in all things. + For the grace of God, that bringeth salvation
unto all men, hath appeared and teacheth us that we should deny ungodliness
and worldly lusts, and that we should live sober-minded, righteously and
godly in this present world, looking for that blessed hope and glorious appearing of the mighty God, and of our saviour Jesus Christ which gave himself
for us, to redeem us from all unrighteousness, and to purge us a peculiar people
unto himself, fervently given unto good works. These things speak, and
exhort, ⊢ and rebuke, with all commanding. See that no man despise thee.

CHAPTER THREE

A   Warn them that they submit themselves to rule and power, to obey the   *Officers must*
officers, that they be ready unto all good works, that they speak evil of no man,   *be obeyed.*
that they be no fighters, but soft, showing all meekness unto all men. For we
ourselves also were in times past, unwise, disobedient, deceived, in danger to
lusts, and to divers manners of voluptuousness, living in maliciousness and
envy, full of hate, hating one another.

B   + But after that the kindness and love of our saviour God to man-ward   *2 Tim. 1. a.*
appeared, not of the deeds of righteousness which we wrought but of his
mercy he saved us, by the fountain of the new birth, and with the renewing of   *Mercy saveth.*
the holy ghost, which he shed on us abundantly, through Jesus Christ our
saviour, that we, once justified by his grace, should be heirs of eternal life,
through hope. ⊢ This is a true saying.

C   Of these things I would thou shouldest certify, that they which believe God,
might be diligent to go forward in good works. These things are good and
profitable unto men. Foolish questions, and genealogies, and brawlings and   *1 Tim. 1. b.*
strife about the law, avoid, for they are unprofitable and superfluous. A man   *2 Tim. 2. d.*
that is given to heresy, after the first and the second admonition, avoid, remembering that he that is such, is perverted, and sinneth, even damned by
his own judgement.

D   When I shall send Artemas unto thee or Tychicus, be diligent to come to me
unto Nicopolis. For I have determined there to winter. Bring Zenas the lawyer
and Apollos on their journey diligently, that nothing be lacking unto them.

And let ours also learn to excel in good works as far forth, as need requireth, that they be not unfruitful. All that are with me, salute thee. Greet them that love us in the faith. Grace be with you all, Amen.

Written from Nicopolis a city of Macedonia.

THE PROLOGUE TO THE EPISTLE OF
ST PAUL UNTO PHILEMON

In this epistle St Paul showeth a godly example of Christian love. Herein we
see how Paul taketh poor Onesimus unto him and maketh intercession for
him unto his master and helpeth him with all that he may, and behaveth
himself none otherwise than as though he himself were the said Onesimus.
Which thing yet he doth not with power and authority, as he well might have
done: but putteth off all authority and whatsoever he might of right do, that
Philemon might do likewise toward Onesimus, and with great meekness and
wisdom teacheth Philemon to see his duty in Christ Jesus.

THE EPISTLE OF ST PAUL
UNTO PHILEMON

Paul the prisoner of Jesus Christ, and brother Timothy. **A**
Unto Philemon the beloved, and our helper, and to the beloved Apphia, and to Archippus our fellow-soldier, and to the congregation of thy house.

Grace be with you and peace, from God our father, and from the Lord Jesus Christ.

I thank my God, making mention always of thee in my prayers, when I hear of thy love and faith, which thou hast toward the Lord Jesus, and toward all saints: so that the fellowship that thou hast in the faith, is fruitful through knowledge of all good things, which are in you by Jesus Christ. And we have great joy, and consolation over thy love: For by thee (brother) the saints' hearts are comforted.

Wherefore though I be bold in Christ to enjoin thee, that which becometh **B** thee: yet for love's sake I rather beseech thee, though I be as I am, even Paul aged, and now in bonds for Jesus Christ's sake. I beseech thee for my son Onesimus, whom I begat in my bonds, which in time passed was to thee unprofitable: but now profitable both to thee and also to me, whom I have sent home again. Thou therefore receive him, that is to say mine own bowels, whom I would fain have retained with me, that in thy stead he might have ministered unto me in the bonds of the gospel. Nevertheless, without thy mind, would I do nothing, that that good which springeth of thee, should not be as it were of necessity, but willingly.

Haply he therefore departed for a season, that thou shouldest receive him for **C** ever, not now as a servant: but above a servant, I mean a brother beloved, specially to me: but how much more unto thee, both in the flesh, and also in the Lord? If thou count me a fellow, receive him as myself. If he have hurt thee or oweth thee ought, that lay to my charge. I Paul have written it with mine own hand. I will recompense it. So that I do not say to thee, how that thou owest unto me even thine own self. Even so brother, let me enjoy thee in the Lord. Comfort my bowels in the Lord. Trusting in thine obedience, I wrote unto thee, knowing that thou wilt do more than I say for. Moreover prepare me lodging: for I trust through the help of your prayers, I shall be given unto you. There salute thee, Epaphras my fellow-prisoner in Christ Jesus, Marcus,

Aristarchus, Demas, Lucas, my helpers. The grace of our Lord Jesus Christ be with your spirits. Amen.

Mark and Luke the evangelists.

Sent from Rome by Onesimus a servant.

A PROLOGUE TO THE FIRST EPISTLE OF
SAINT PETER

This epistle did saint Peter write to the heathen that were converted and exhorteth them to stand fast in the faith, to grow therein and to wax perfect, through all manner of suffering and also good works.

In the first he declareth the justifying of faith through Christ's blood, and comforteth them with the hope of the life to come, and sheweth that we have not deserved it, but that the prophets prophesied it should be given us, and as Christ which redeemed us out of sin and all uncleanness is holy, so he exhorteth to lead an holy conversation: and because we be richly bought and made heirs of a rich inheritance, to take heed that we lose it not again through our own negligence.

In the second chapter he sheweth that Christ is the foundation and head corner-stone, whereon all are built through faith, whether it be Jew or gentile, and how that in Christ they are made priests, to offer themselves to God (as Christ did himself) and to flee the lusts of the flesh that fight against the soul. And first he teacheth them in general to obey the worldly rulers and then in special he teacheth the servants to obey their masters be they good or bad, and to suffer wrong of them as Christ suffered wrong for us.

In the third he teacheth the wives to obey their husbands, yea though they be unbelievers and to apparel themselves godly and as it becometh holiness. And thereto that the husbands suffer and bear the infirmity of their wives and live according to knowledge with them. And then in general he exhorteth them to be soft, courteous, patient and friendly one to another, and to suffer for righteousness after the example of Christ.

In the fourth he exhorteth to flee sin and to tame the flesh with soberness, watching and prayer, and to love each other, and to know that all good gifts are of God and every man to help his neighbour with such as he hath received of God, and finally not to wonder, but to rejoice though they must suffer for Christ's name's sake, seeing as they be here partakers of his afflictions, so shall they be partakers of his glory to come.

In the fifth he teacheth the bishops and priests how they should live and feed Christ's flock: and warneth us of the devil which on every side lieth in wait for us.

THE FIRST EPISTLE OF
ST PETER THE APOSTLE

A Peter an apostle of Jesus Christ, to them that dwell here and there as strangers throughout Pontus, Galatia, Cappadocia, Asia, and Bithynia, elect by the foreknowledge of God the father, through the sanctifying of the spirit, unto obedience and sprinkling of the blood of Jesus Christ.

Grace be with you and peace be multiplied.

Blessed be God the father of our Lord Jesus Christ, which through his abundant mercy begat us again unto a lively hope, by the resurrection of Jesus Christ from death, to enjoy an inheritance immortal and undefiled, and that putrifieth not, reserved in heaven for you, which are kept by the power of God through faith, unto salvation, which salvation, is prepared all ready to be **B** shewed in the last time, in the which time ye shall rejoice, though now for a season (if need require) ye are in heaviness, through manifold temptations, that your faith once tried, being much more precious than gold that perisheth (though it be tried with fire) might be found unto laud, glory, and honour at the appearing of Jesus Christ: whom ye have not seen and yet love him, in whom even now, though ye see him not, ye yet believe, and rejoice with joy unspeakable and glorious: receiving the end of your faith, the salvation of your souls.

Of which salvation have the prophets enquired and searched, which prophesied of the grace that should come unto you, searching when or at what time the spirit of Christ which was in them should signify, which spirit testified before, the passions that should come unto Christ, and the glory that should follow after: unto which prophets it was declared, that not unto themselves, but unto us, they should minister the things which are now shewed unto you of them which by the holy ghost sent down from heaven, have preached unto you the things which the angels desire to behold.

C Wherefore gird up the loins of your minds, be sober, and trust perfectly on the grace that is brought unto you, by the declaring of Jesus Christ, as obedient children, not fashioning yourselves unto your old lusts of ignorance: but as he which called you is holy, even so be ye holy in all manner of conversation, because it is written. Be ye holy, for I am holy.

And if so be that ye call on the father which without respect of person judgeth according to every man's work*, see that ye pass the time of your

Here Peter (as other true apostles do) first setteth forth the treasure of mercy which God hath bound himself to give us, for Christ's sake: and then our duty: what we are bound to do again if we will be partakers of the mercy.

Our duty again.

Ignorance is cause of evil living.

* By our works shall we be judged: for as the invisible faith is, such are the works by which the faith is seen.

pilgrimage in fear. + Forasmuch as ye know how that ye were not redeemed with corruptible silver and gold from your vain conversation which ye received by the traditions of the fathers: but with the precious blood of Christ, as of a lamb undefiled, and without spot, which was ordained before the world **D** was made: but was declared in the last times for your sakes, which by his means have believed on God that raised him from death, and glorified him, that your faith and hope might be in God.

And forasmuch as ye have purified your souls through the spirit, in obeying the truth for to love brotherly without feigning, see that ye love one another with a pure heart fervently: for ye are born anew, not of mortal seed, but of immortal, by the word of God which liveth, and lasteth for ever. For all flesh is as grass, and all the glory of man is as the flower of grass. The grass withereth, and the flower falleth away, but the word of the Lord endureth ever. ⊢ And this is the word which by the gospel was preached among you.

CHAPTER TWO

+ Wherefore lay aside all maliciousness and all guile, and dissimulation, and **A** envy, and all backbiting: and as new-born babes, desire that reasonable milk which is without corruption, that ye may grow therein. If so be that ye have tasted how pleasant the Lord is, to whom ye come as unto a living stone disallowed of men, but chosen of God and precious: and ye as living stones, are made a spiritual house*, and an holy priesthood, for to offer up spiritual sacrifice, acceptable to God by Jesus Christ.

Wherefore it is contained in the scripture: behold, I put in Sion an head **B** corner-stone, elect and precious: and he that believeth on him shall not be ashamed. Unto you therefore which believe, he is precious: but unto them which believe not, the stone which the builders refused the same is made the head stone in the corner, and a stone to stumble at, and a rock to offend them which stumble at the word, and believe not that whereon they were set. But ye are a chosen generation, a royal priesthood, an holy nation, and a peculiar people, that ye should shew the virtues of him that called you out of darkness into his marvellous light which in time past were not a people, yet are now the people of God: which were not under mercy but now have obtained mercy. ⊢

+ Dearly beloved, I beseech you as strangers and pilgrims, abstain from **C** fleshly lusts which fight against the soul, and see that ye have honest conversation among the gentiles that they which backbite you as evildoers may see your good works and praise God in the day of visitation.

Submit yourselves unto all manner ordinance of man for the Lord's sake, whether it be unto the king as unto the chief head: or unto rulers, as unto them that are sent of him, for the punishment of evildoers: but for the laud of them that do well. For so is the will of God, that ye put to silence the ignorance of the foolish men: as free, and not as having the liberty for a cloak of maliciousness but even as the servants of God. Honour all men. Love brotherly fellowship. Fear God and honour the king. ⊢

Marginal notes

1 Cor. 6. and 7. d.
1 John 1. d.
Rev. 1.

We be purified freely in believing the trust of Christ for to love one another.

Isa. 40. b.
Rev. 14.
Jas. 1. b.

* We be the church: and the obedience of the heart is the spiritual sacrifice, Bodily sacifice must be offered to our neighbours, for if thou offerest it to God thou makest a bodily idol of him.

Isa. 28.
Rom. 9. g.

Psa. 118.
Matt. 21.
Acts 4. b.
Isa. 8. c.

Exod. 19.

Hos. 2. d.
Rom. 9. e.

Gal. 5. c.
Rom. 13.

Rom. 13.

Obedience to rulers.

Rom. 12. c.

Servants obey your masters with all fear, not only if they be good and courteous: but also though they be froward. For it is thankworthy if a man for conscience toward God endure grief, suffering wrongfully. For what praise is it, if when ye be buffeted for your faults, ye take it patiently? But and if when ye do well, ye suffer wrong and take it patiently, then is there thank with God.

For hereunto verily were ye called*: for + Christ also suffered for us leaving us an example that ye should follow his steps, which did no sin, neither was there guile found in his mouth: which when he was reviled, reviled not again: when he suffered, he threatened not: but committed the cause to him that judgeth righteously, which his own self bare our sins in his body on the tree, that we should be delivered from sin and should live in righteousness. By whose stripes ye were healed. For ye were as sheep going astray: but are now returned unto the shepherd and bishop of your souls. ⊦

Servants.

Eph. 6. a.
Col. 3. d.
2 Cor. 7.

★ Our calling is to follow Christ.

Isa. 53. c.
1 John 3. a.

Isa. 53. b.

CHAPTER THREE

A Likewise let the wives be in subjection to their husbands, that even they which believe not the word, may without the word be won by the conversation of the wives: while they behold your pure conversation coupled with fear. Whose apparel shall not be outward with broided hair, and hanging on of gold, or in putting on of gorgeous apparel: but let the hid man of the heart be incorrupt, with a meek and a quiet spirit, which spirit is before God a thing much set by. For after this manner in the old time did the holy women which trusted in God, attire themselves, and were obedient to their husbands, even as Sara obeyed Abraham and called him Lord: whose daughters ye are as long as ye do well, and be not afraid of every shadow.

Wives.

1. Tim. 3. c.

Gen. 16.

B Likewise ye men dwell with them according to knowledge, giving honour unto the wife, as unto the weaker vessel, and as unto them that are heirs also of the grace of life, that your prayers be not let.

Husbands.

1 Cor. 7. a.

+ In conclusion, be ye all of one mind, one suffer with another, love as brethren, be pitiful, be courteous, not rendering evil for evil, neither rebuke for rebuke: but contrariwise, bless, remembering that ye are thereunto called, even that ye should be heirs of blessing. If any man long after life, and loveth to see good days, let him refrain his tongue from evil, and his lips that they speak not guile. Let him eschew evil and do good: let him seek peace, and ensue it. For the eyes of the Lord are over the righteous, and his ears are open unto their prayers. But the face of the Lord beholdeth them that do evil.

Prov. 17. and 21.
Rom. 16.
1 Thes. 5. d.
Psa. 34.

C Moreover who is it that will harm you if ye follow that which is good? Notwithstanding happy are ye if ye suffer for righteousness' sake. Yea and fear not though they seem terrible unto you, neither be troubled: but sanctify the Lord God in your hearts. ⊦ Be ready always to give an answer to every man that asketh you a reason of the hope that is in you, and that with meekness and fear: having a good conscience, that when they backbite you as evildoers, they may be ashamed, forasmuch as they have falsely accused your good conversation in Christ.

Give a reason of your doctrine.

Heb. 9. d.
Rom. 5. b.

It is better (if the will of God be so) that ye suffer for well doing, than for evil doing. + Forasmuch as Christ hath once suffered for sins, the just for the unjust, for to bring us to God, and was killed, as pertaining to the flesh: but was quickened in the spirit.

In which spirit, he also went and preached unto the spirits that were in **D** prison, which were in time past disobedient, when the longsuffering of God abode exceeding patiently in the days of Noah, while the ark was a–preparing, wherein few (that is to say, eight souls) were saved by water, which signifieth baptism that now saveth us, not the putting away of the filth of the flesh, but in that a good conscience consenteth to God, by the resurrection of Jesus Christ, which is our right hand of God + and is gone into heaven, angels, power and might subdued unto him.

Gen. 6. b.
Matt. 19.
Luke 17. f.

CHAPTER FOUR

We must be partakers
with Christ in suffering
if we will have our part
with him in his glory.

Forasmuch as Christ hath suffered for us in the flesh, arm yourselves likewise **A** with the same mind: for he which suffereth in the flesh ceaseth from sin, that he henceforward should live as much time as remaineth in the flesh: not after the lusts of men, but after the will of God. For it is sufficient for us that we have spent the time that is past of the life, after the will of the gentiles, walking in wantonness, lusts, drunkenness, in eating, drinking and in abominable idolatry.

And it seemeth to them a strange thing that ye run not also with them unto **B** the same excess of riot, and therefore speak they evil of you, which shall give accompts to him that is ready to judge quick and dead. For unto this purpose verily was the gospel preached unto the dead* that they should be condemned of men in the flesh, but should live before God in the spirit. The end of all things is at hand.

* The dead are the
ignorant of God, for
they that be dead from
this world have no
flesh.

+ Be ye therefore discreet and sober, that ye may be apt to prayers. But above all things have fervent love among you. For love* covereth the multitude of sins. Be ye harbourous one to another, and that without grudging. As every man hath received the gift, minister the same one to another as good ministers of the manifold grace of God. If any man speak, let him talk as **C** though he spake the words of God. If any man minister, let him do it as of the ability which God ministreth unto him. That God in all things may be glorified through Jesus Christ +, to whom be praise and dominion for ever and while the world standeth. Amen.

* Hate maketh sin of
every trifle: but love
looketh not on small
things: but suffereth
all things.

Dearly beloved, be not troubled in this heat, which now is come among you to try you as though some strange thing had happened unto you: but rejoice inasmuch as ye are partakers of Christ's passions, that when his glory appeareth, ye may be merry and glad.

He that suffereth with
Christ, shall reign with
Christ.

If ye be railed upon for the name of Christ happy are ye. For the spirit of **D** glory and the spirit of God resteth upon you. On their part he is evil spoken of: but on your part he is glorified.

See that none of you suffer as a murderer, or as a thief, or an evildoer, or as a busybody in other men's matters. If any man suffer as a Christian man, let him not be ashamed: but let him glorify God on his behalf. For the time is come that judgement must begin at the house of God*. If it first begin at us, what shall the end be of them which believe not the gospel of God? And if the righteous scarcely be saved: where shall the ungodly and the sinner appear? Wherefore let them that suffer according to the will of God, commit their souls to him with well doing, as unto a faithful creator.

* If the sons of God must be all scourged and none may be saved but through the same fire that Christ were through: what shall the damnation of the disobedient and unbelievers be?

CHAPTER FIVE

A The elders which are among you, I exhort, which am also an elder and a witness of the afflictions of Christ, and also a partaker of the glory that shall be opened: see that ye feed Christ's flock which is among you, taking the oversight of them, not as though ye were compelled thereto, but willingly: not for the desire of filthy lucre, but of a good mind: not as though ye were lords over the parishes*: but that ye be an example to the flock. And when the chief shepherd shall appear, ye shall receive an incorruptible crown of glory.

* Parishes: the Greek hath lots: that is, they to whom any lot chance or election is to preach Gods word.

Likewise ye younger submit yourselves unto the elder. Submit yourselves every man, one to another, knit yourselves together in lowliness of mind. For **B** God resisteth the proud and giveth grace to the humble. ⊢ Submit yourselves therefore under the mighty hand of God, that he may exalt you, when the time is come. Cast all your care to him: for he careth for you.

C Be sober and watch, for your adversary the devil as a roaring lion walketh about, seeking whom he may devour: whom resist steadfast in the faith, remembering that ye do but fulfil the same afflictions which are appointed* to your brethren that are in the world. The God of all grace, which called you unto his eternal glory by Christ Jesus, shall his own self after ye have suffered a little affliction make you perfect: shall settle strength and establish you. To him be glory and dominion for ever, and while the world endureth. Amen. ⊢

Matt. 6. c.
Luke 12. c.
Rom. 12.
Psa. 55. d.

* We be appointed to suffer in this world.

By Silvanus a faithful brother unto you (as I suppose) have I written briefly, exhorting and testifying how that this is the true grace of God, wherein ye stand. The companions of your election that are at Babylon, saluteth you, and Marcus my son. Greet ye one another with the kiss of love. Peace be with you all which are in Christ Jesus. Amen.

Mark the evangelist.

A PROLOGUE TO THE SECOND EPISTLE OF
ST PETER

This epistle was written against them which thought that Christian faith might be idle and without works, when yet the promise of Christ is made us upon that condition, that we henceforth work the will of God and not of the flesh. Therefore he exhorteth them to exercise themselves diligently in virtue and all good works, thereby to be sure that they have the true faith, as a man knoweth the goodness of a tree by his fruit. Then he commendeth and magnifieth the gospel, and willeth that men hearken to that only, and to men's doctrine not at all. For as he saith, there came no prophetical scripture by the will of man, but by the will of the holy ghost which only knoweth the will of God, neither is any scripture of private interpretation: that is to say, may be otherwise expounded than agreeing to the open places and general articles and to the covenants of God and all the rest of the scripture.

And therefore in the second he warneth them of false teachers that should come, and through preaching confidence in false works to satisfy their covetousness withal, should deny Christ. Which he threateneth with three terrible examples, with the fall of the angels, the flood of Noah and overthrowing of Sodom and Gomorrah, and so describeth them with their insatiable covetousness, pride, stubborn and disobedience to all temporal rule and authority, with their abominable whoredom and hypocrisy that a blind man may see that he prophesied it of the popes' holy spirituality which devoured the whole world with their covetousness, living in all lust and pleasure and reigning as temporal tyrants.

In the third he sheweth that in the latter days, the people through unbelief and lack of fear of the judgement of the last day, shall be even as Epicures, wholly given to the flesh. Which last day shall yet surely and shortly come saith he: for a thousand years and one day is with God all one. And he showeth also how terrible that day shall be, and how suddenly it shall come: and therefore exhorteth all men to look earnestly for it, and to prepare themselves against it with holy conversation and godly living.

Finally: The first chapter sheweth how it should go in the time of the pure and true gospel. The second how it should go in the time of the pope and men's doctrine. The third how at the last men should believe nothing nor fear God at all.

THE SECOND EPISTLE OF
ST PETER

A   Simon Peter a servant and an apostle of Jesus Christ, to them which have obtained like precious faith with us in the righteousness that cometh of our God and saviour Jesus Christ.

Grace with you, and peace be multiplied in the knowledge of God and of Jesus our Lord. According as his godly power hath given unto us all things that pertain unto life and godliness, through the knowledge of him that hath called us by virtue and glory, by the means whereof, are given unto us excellent and most great promises, that by the help of them ye should be partakers of the godly nature, in that ye fly the corruption of worldy lust.

B   And hereunto give all diligence: in your faith minister virtue, and in virtue knowledge, and in knowledge temperance, and in temperance patience, in patience godliness, in godliness brotherly kindness, in brotherly kindness love. For if these things be among you and are plenteous, they will make you that ye neither shall be idle nor unfruitful in the knowledge of our Lord Jesus Christ. But he that lacketh these things is blind and gropeth for the way with his hand, and hath forgotten that he was purged from his old sins.

He that lacketh these and such like works is blind and understandeth not what the faith of Christ meaneth.

C   Wherefore brethren, give the more diligence for to make your calling and election sure. For if ye do such things, ye shall never err. Yea and by this means an entering in shall be ministered unto you abundantly into the everlasting kingdom of our Lord and saviour Jesus Christ.

He that hath such works may be sure that he is elect and that he hath the true faith.

Wherefore I will not be negligent to put you always in remembrance of such things, though that ye know them yourselves and be also established in the present truth. Notwithstanding I think it meet (as long as I am in this tabernacle) to stir you up by putting you in remembrance, for as much as I am sure how that the time is at hand that I must put off my tabernacle, even as our Lord Jesus Christ hath shewed me. I will enforce therefore, that on every side ye might have wherewith to stir up the remembrance of these things after my departing.

John 21.

+ For we followed not deceivable fables when we opened unto you the power and coming of our Lord Jesus Christ, but with our eyes we saw his majesty: even then verily when he received of God the father honour and

Matt. 17.

D   glory, and when there came such a voice to him from excellent glory: This is my dear beloved son, in whom I have delight. This voice we heard when it came from heaven, being with him in the holy mount.

We have also a right sure word of prophecy whereunto if ye take heed, as unto a light that shineth in a dark place, ye do well, until the day dawn and the day star arise in your hearts. ⊦ So that ye first know this: That no prophecy in the scripture hath any private interpretation. For the scripture came never by the will of man: but holy men of God spake as they were moved by the holy ghost.

2 Tim. 3.

CHAPTER TWO

False prophets must needs be amongst us and also prevail, and that because we have no love to the truth.

2 Thes. 2.

★ And covetousness is the father of them: and their preaching confidence in works is the denying of Christ.

There were false prophets among the people, even as there shall be false **A** teachers among you: which privily shall bring in damnable sects, even denying the Lord that hath bought them, and bring upon themselves swift damnation, and many shall follow their damnable ways, by which the way of truth shall be evil spoken of, and through covetousness★ shall they with feigned words make merchandise of you, whose judgement is not far off, and their damnation sleepeth not.

For if God spared not the angels that sinned, but cast them down into hell, **B** and delivered them in chains of darkness, to be kept unto judgement: Neither spared the old world but saved Noah the right preacher of righteousness, and brought in the flood upon the world of the ungodly, and turned the cities of Sodom and Gomorrha into ashes: overthrew them, damned them, and made of them an example unto all that after should live ungodly. And just Lot vexed with the uncleanly conversation of the wicked, delivered he. For he being righteous and dwelling among them, in seeing and hearing, vexed his righteous soul from day to day with their unlawful deeds. The Lord knoweth how to deliver the godly out of temptation, and how to reserve the unjust unto the day of judgement for to be punished: namely them that walk after the flesh in the lust of uncleanness, and despise the rulers. Presumptious are they, and stubborn and fear not to speak evil of them that are in authority. When the angels which are greater both in power and might, receive not of the Lord **C** railing judgement against them. But these as brute beasts, naturally made to be taken and destroyed, speak evil of that they know not, and shall perish through their own destruction, and receive the reward of unrighteousness.

They count it pleasure to live deliciously for a season. Spots they are and filthiness, living at pleasure and in deceivable ways feasting with you: having eyes full of advoutry and that cannot cease to sin, beguiling unstable souls. Hearts they have exercised with covetousness. They are cursed children, and have forsaken the right way, and are gone astray following the way of Balaam the son of Bosor, which loved the reward of unrighteousness: but was rebuked of his iniquity. The tame and dumb beast, speaking with man's voice, forbade the foolishness of the prophet.

Balaam.

Num. 22.

These are wells without water, and clouds carried about of a tempest, to whom the mist of darkness is reserved for ever. For when they have spoken the **D**

swelling words of vanity, they beguile with wantonness through the lusts of
the flesh, them that were clean escaped: but now are wrapped in errors. They
promise them liberty, and are themselves the bond-servants of corruption. For
of whomsoever a man is overcome, unto the same is he in bondage. For if they,
after they have escaped from the filthiness of the world through the knowledge
of the Lord and of the saviour Jesus Christ, they are yet tangled again therein
and overcome: then is the latter end worse with them than the beginning. For it
had been better for them, not to have known★ the way of righteousness than
after they have known it, to turn from the holy commandment given unto
them. It is happened unto them according to the true proverb: The dog is
turned to his vomit again, and the sow that was washed, to her wallowing in
the mire.

Jude 1. d.

John 8.
Rom. 6. c.
Heb. 6. a.
Matt. 12.

★ It is better not to
have known the truth,
than not to live
thereafter.

Prov. 21.

CHAPTER THREE

A This is the second epistle that I now write unto you, beloved, wherewith I stir
up and warn your pure minds, to call to remembrance the words which were
told before of the holy prophets, and also the commandment of us the apostles
of the Lord and saviour.

This first understand, that there shall come in the last days mockers, which
will walk after their own lusts and say, Where is the promise of his coming?
B For since the fathers died, all things continue in the same estate wherein they
were at the beginning. This they know not (and that willingly) how that the
heavens a great while ago were, and the earth that was in the water, appeared
up out of the water by the word of God: by the which things, the world that
then was, perished overflowen with the water. But the heavens verily and earth
which are now, are kept by the same word in store, and reserved unto fire,
against the day of judgement and perdition of ungodly men.

Dearly beloved, be not ignorant of this one thing, how that one day is with
C the Lord, as a thousand year, and a thousand year as one day. The Lord is not
slack to fulfil his promise, as some men count slackness: but is patient to us-
ward and would have no man lost, but would receive all men to repentance.
Nevertheless the day of the Lord will come as a thief in the night, in the which
day, the heavens shall perish with terrible noise, and the elements shall melt
with heat, and the earth with the works that are therein shall burn.

If all these things shall perish, what manner persons ought ye to be in holy
conversation and godliness: looking for and hasting unto the coming of the day
of God, in which the heavens shall perish with fire, and the elements shall be
consumed with heat. Nevertheless we look for a new heaven and a new earth,
according to his promise, wherein dwelleth righteousness.

Wherefore dearly beloved, seeing that ye look for such things, be diligent
D that ye may be found of him in peace, without spot and undefiled. And suppose that the longsuffering of the Lord is salvation, even as our dearly beloved
brother Paul, according to the wisdom given unto him, wrote to you, yea,
almost in every epistle speaking of such things: among which are many things

1 Tim. 4.
2 Tim. 3.
Jude 1. f.
Ezek. 12. f.

1 Thes. 5.
Rev. 3. a. and 16.

Rev. 21.
Isa. 65. c. and 66. g.

hard to be understood, which they that are unlearned and unstable, pervert, as they do other scriptures unto their own destruction. Ye therefore beloved, seeing ye know it beforehand, beware lest ye be also plucked away with the error of the wicked, and fall from your own steadfastness: but grow in grace, and in the knowledge of our Lord and saviour Jesus Christ. To whom be glory both now and for ever. Amen.

A PROLOGUE UPON THE
THREE EPISTLES OF ST JOHN

This first epistle of saint John containeth the doctrine of a very apostle of Christ, and ought of right to follow his gospel. For as in his epistle he setteth out the true faith, and teacheth by it only all men to be saved and restored unto the favour of God again: even so here in this epistle he goeth against them that boast themselves of faith and yet continue without good works and teacheth many ways that where true faith is, there the works tarry not behind, and contrary that where the works follow not, there is no true faith but a false imagination and utter darkness.

And he writeth sore against a certain sect of heretics which then began to deny that Christ was come in the flesh, and calleth them very antichrists. Which sect goeth now in their full swing. For though they deny not openly with the mouth that Christ is come in the flesh: yet they deny it in the heart with their doctrine and living. For he that will be justified and saved through his own works, the same doth as much as he that denieth Christ to be come in the flesh seeing that Christ came only therefore in the flesh, that he should justify us, or purchase us pardon of our sins, bring us into the favour of God again and make us heirs of eternal life, with his works only and with his bloodshedding, without and before all our works.

So fighteth this epistle both against them that will be saved by their own good works, and also against them that will be saved by a faith that hath no lust to do works at all, and keepeth us in the middle way, that we believe in Christ to be saved by his works only, and then to know that it is our duty for that kindness, to prepare ourselves to do the commandment of God, and to love every man his neighbour as Christ loved him, seeking with our own works God's honour and our neighbours' wealth only, and trusting for eternal life and for all that God hath promised us for Christ's sake.

The two last epistles though they be short, yet are goodly examples of love and faith and do savour of the spirit of a true apostle.

THE FIRST EPISTLE OF
ST JOHN THE APOSTLE

1^1–2^9 CHAPTER ONE

John, here as in his
gospel, and as Paul and
Peter in their epistles,
teacheth first the
justifying of faith and
that all mercy cometh
by Christ only without
all other respect and
then-what.

John 8.

That which was from the beginning, concerning which we have heard, **A**
which we have seen with our eyes, which we have looked upon, and our
hands have handled, of the word of life. For the life appeared, and we have
seen, and bear witness, and shew unto you that eternal life, which was with the
father, and appeared unto us. That which we have seen and heard declare we
unto you, that ye may have fellowship with us, and that our fellowship may be
with the father and his son Jesus Christ. And this write we unto you, that our
joy may be full.

⋆ Light is the doctrine
of Christ.

Heb. 9. d.
1 Pet. 1. d.

⋆ If we confess our sins
God which cannot lie,
hath promised to
forgive them.

And this is the tidings which we have heard of him, and declare unto you, **B**
that God is light, and in him is no darkness at all. If we say that we have
fellowship with him, and yet walk in darkness, we lie, and do not the truth:
but and if we walk in light⋆ even as he is in light, then have we fellowship with
him, and the blood of Jesus Christ his son cleanseth us from all sin.

If we say that we have no sin, we deceive ourselves, and truth is not in us. If
we knowledge⋆ our sins, he is faithful and just, to forgive us our sins, and to
cleanse us from all unrighteousness. If we say we have not sinned, we make
him a liar, and his word is not in us.

CHAPTER TWO

⋆ He that keepeth the
commandments
knoweth God: and he
that keepeth it not,
knoweth not God.

⋆ He that keepeth
God's word loveth God
and is in God and
walketh as Christ did.

+ My little children, these things write I unto you, that ye sin not: if any man **A**
sin, yet we have an advocate with the father, Jesus Christ, which is righteous:
and he it is that obtaineth grace for our sins: not for our sins only: but also for
the sins of all the world. + And hereby we are sure that we know him, if we
keep his commandments⋆. He that saith I know him, and keepeth not his
commandments is a liar, and the verity is not in him. Whosoever keepeth his
word⋆, in him is the love of God perfect in deed. And thereby know we that
we are in him. He that saith he bideth in him ought to walk even as he
walked. +

Brethren I write no new commandment unto you: but that old command- **B**
ment which ye heard from the beginning. The old commandment is the word
which ye heard from the beginning. Again a new commandment I write unto
you, a thing that is true in him, and also in you: for the darkness is past, and the
true light now shineth. He that saith how that he is in the light, and yet hateth

his brother, is in darkness even until this time. He that loveth his brother, abideth in the light and there is none occasion of evil in him. He that hateth★ his brother is in darkness, and walketh in darkness: and cannot tell whither he goeth, because that darkness hath blinded his eyes.

> ★ He that hateth is in darkness and knoweth not what Christ hath done for him: but he that loveth is in light and wotteth what Christ hath done.

C   Babes I write unto you how that your sins are forgiven you for his name's sake. I write unto you fathers, how that ye have known him that was from the beginning. I write unto you young men, how that ye have overcome the wicked. I write unto you little children, how that ye have known the father. I write unto you fathers, how that ye have known him that was from the beginning. I write unto you young men, how that ye are strong: and the word of God abideth in you and ye have overcome that wicked.

See that ye love not the world, neither the things that are in the world. If any man love the world, the love of the father is not in him. For all that is in the world (as the lust of the flesh, the lust of the eyes, and the pride of goods) is not of the father: but of the world. And the world vanisheth away, and the lust thereof: but he that fulfilleth the will of God, abideth ever.

> He that loveth the world, loveth not God.

Little children it is the last time, and as ye have heard how that Antichrist shall come: even now are there many antichrists come already. Whereby we know that it is the last time. They went out from us but they were not of us. For if they had been of us, they would no doubt, have continued with us. But that fortuned that it might appear, that they were not of us.

> Antichrist.

D   And ye have an ointment★ of the holy ghost, and ye know all things. +I wrote not unto you, as though ye knew not the truth: but as though ye knew it and know also that no lie cometh of truth. Who is a liar: but he that denieth that Jesus is Christ? The same is the antichrist that denieth the father and the son. Whosoever denieth the son the same hath not the father. Let therefore abide in you that same which ye heard from the beginning. If that which ye heard from the beginning, shall remain in you, ye also shall continue in the son, and in the father. And this is the promise that he hath promised us, even eternal life.

> ★ Ointment: that is knowledge of the truth and all the gifts of the spirit.

This have I written unto you, concerning them that deceive you. And the anointing which ye have received of him, dwelleth in you. And ye need not that any man teach you: but as the annointing teacheth you all things, and is true, and is no lie: and as it taught you, even so bide therein. And now babes abide in him that when he shall appear, we may be bold and not be made ashamed of him at his coming. If ye know that he is righteous, know also that he which followeth righteousness, is born of him. ⊦

> Here ye se that Christ and sin cannot dwell together for Christ's spirit fighteth against sin.

CHAPTER THREE

A   Behold what love the father hath shewed on us, that we should be called the sons of God. For this cause the world knoweth you not because it knoweth not him. Dearly beloved, now are we the sons of God, and yet it doth not appear what we shall be. But we know that when it shall appear, we shall be like him. For we shall see him as he is. And every man that hath this hope in him purgeth himself, even as he is pure. Whosoever committeth sin, committeth unrighteousness also, for sin is unrighteousness*. And ye know that he appeared to take away our sins, and in him is no sin. As many as bide in him sin not: whosoever sinneth hath not seen him, neither hath known him.

Babes let no man deceive you, He that doth righteousness, is righteous, **B** even as he is righteous. He that committeth sin, is of the devil: for the devil sinneth since the beginning. For this purpose appeared the son of God, to loose the works of the devil. Whosoever is born of God, sinneth not: for his seed remaineth in him, and he cannot sin, because he is born of God. In this are the children of God known, and the children of the devil. Whosoever doth not righteousness, is not of God, neither he that loveth not his brother.

For this is the tidings, that ye heard from the beginning, that we should love one another: not as Cain which was of the wicked and slew his brother. And wherefore slew he him? Because his own works were evil, and his brother's good. + Marvel not my brethren though the world hate you. We know that we are translated from death* unto life, because we love the brethren. He that loveth not his brother, abideth in death. Whosoever hateth his brother, is a man-slayer. And ye know that no man-slayer, hath eternal life abiding in him.

Hereby perceive we love: that he gave his life for us: and therefore ought we **D** also to give our lives for the brethren. Whosoever hath this world's good and seeth his brother have need: and shutteth up his compassion from him: how dwelleth the love of God in him? My babes, let us not love in word, neither in tongue: but with deed and in verity: + for thereby* we know that we are of the verity, and can before him quiet our hearts. But if our hearts condemn us, God is greater than our hearts, and knoweth all things. Beloved, if our hearts condemn us not, then have we trust to God-ward: and whatsoever we ask, we shall receive of him: because we keep his commandments, and do those things which are pleasing in his sight.

And this is his commandment, that we believe* on the name of his son Jesus Christ, and love one another, as he gave commandment. And he that keepeth his commandments dwelleth in him, and he in him: and thereby we know that there abideth in us of the spirit which he gave us.

CHAPTER FOUR

Ye beloved, believe not every spirit: but prove the spirits whether they are of God or no: for many false prophets are gone out into the world. Hereby shall ye know the spirit of God. Every spirit that confesseth that Jesus Christ is come in the flesh is of God. And every spirit which confesseth not that Jesus Christ is come in the flesh, is not of God. And this is that spirit of antichrist, of whom ye have heard, how that he should come: and even now already is he in the world.

Little children, ye are of God, and have overcome them: for greater is he that **B** is in you, then he that is in the world. They are of the world, and therefore speak they of the world, and the world heareth them. We are of God. He that knoweth God, heareth us: he that is not of God, heareth us not. Hereby know we the spirit of verity, and the spirit of error.

Beloved, let us love one another: for love cometh of God. And every one that loveth, is born of God, and knoweth God. He that loveth not, knoweth not God: + for God is love. In this appeared the love of God to us-ward because that God sent his only begotten son into the world, that we might live through him. Herein is love, not that we loved God, but that he loved us, and sent his son to make agreement for our sins.

God hath shewed us a token of love.

Beloved, if God so loved us, we ought also to love one another. No man hath seen God at any time. If we love one another, God dwelleth in us, and his love is perfect in us. Hereby know we, that we dwell in him, and he in us: because he hath given us of his spirit. And we have seen and do testify that the father sent the son, which is the saviour of the world. Whosoever confesseth that Jesus is the son of God, in him dwelleth God, and he in God. And we have known and believed the love that God hath to us.

Love is commanded.

John 1. b.
1 Tim. 6.

D God is love, and he that dwelleth in love dwelleth in God, and God in him. Herein is the love perfect in us, that we should have trust in the day of judgement: For as he is, even so are we in this world. There is no fear in love, but perfect love casteth out all fear, for fear hath painfulness. He that feareth, is not perfect in love.

We love him, for he loved us first. If a man say, I love God, and yet hate his brother he is a liar. For how can he that loveth not his brother whom he hath seen, love God whom he hath not seen? And this commandment have we of him: that he which loveth God, should love his brother also. +

He that loveth not his brother, loveth not God.

CHAPTER FIVE

A Whosoever believeth that Jesus is Christ, is born of God. And every one that loveth him which begat, loveth him also which was begotten of him. In this we know that we love the children of God, when we love God, and keep his commandments. This is the love of God, that we keep his commandments, and his commandments are not grievous. + For all that is born of God, overcometh the world. And this is the victory that overcometh the world, even our faith★. Who is it that overcometh the world: but he which believeth that Jesus is the son of God?

John 13. d. and 15. b.
Eph. 5. a.

1 Cor. 15. c.

★ Faith is our victory.

B This Jesus Christ is he that came by water and blood, not by water only: but by water and blood. And it is the spirit that beareth witness, because the spirit is truth. (For there are three which bear record in heaven, the father, the word, and the holy ghost. And these three are one). For there are three which bear record (in earth:) the spirit, and water, and blood: and these three are one. If we receive the witness of men, the witness of God is greater. For this is the witness of God, which he testified of his son. He that believeth on the son of God, hath the witness in himself. + He that believeth not God, hath made him a liar, because he believed not the record that God gave of his son. And this is that record, how that God hath given unto us eternal life, and this life is in his son. He that hath the son, hath life: and he that hath not the son of God, hath not life.

John 3. d.

In Christ is the life eternal.

These things have I written unto you that believe on the name of the son of God, that ye may know how that ye have eternal life, and that ye may believe on the name of the son of God. And this is the trust that we have in him: that if we ask anything according to his will he heareth us. And if we know that he hear us whatsoever we ask, we know that we shall have the petitions that we desire of him.

D

Sin into death.

If any man see his brother sin a sin that is not unto death, let him ask, and he shall give him life for them that sin not unto death. There is a sin unto death, for which say I not that a man should pray. All unrighteousness is sin, and there is sin not unto death.

He that is born of God, sinneth not.

We know that whosoever is born of God, sinneth not: but he that is begotten of God keepeth himself, and that wicked toucheth him not. We know that we are of God, and that the world is altogether set on wickedness. We know that the son of God is come, and hath given us a mind to know him which is true: and we are in him that is true, through his son Jesus Christ. This same is very God, and eternal life. Babes keep yourselves from images. Amen.

THE SECOND EPISTLE OF
ST JOHN

A The elder to the elect lady and her children which I love in the truth: and not I only, but also all that have known the truth, for the truth's sake, which dwelleth in us, and shall be in us for ever.

With you be grace, mercy, and peace from God the father, and from the Lord Jesus Christ the son of the father, in truth and love.

B I rejoiced greatly, that I found of thy children walking in truth, as we have received a commandment of the father. And now beseech I thee lady, not as though I wrote a new commandment unto thee, but that same which we had from the beginning, that we should love* one another. And this is the love, that we should walk after his commandments.

* Love is the first commandment.

This commandment is (that as ye have heard from the beginning) ye should walk in it. For many deceivers are entered into the world, which confess not **C** that Jesus Christ is come in the flesh. This is a deceiver and an antichrist. Look on yourselves, that we lose not that we have wrought: but that we may have a full reward. Whosoever transgresseth and bideth not in the doctrine of Christ, hath not God. He that endureth in the doctrine of Christ, hath both the father and the son.

If there come any unto you and bring not this learning, him receive not to house: neither bid him God speed. For he that biddeth him God speed, is partaker of his evil deeds. I had many things to write unto you, nevertheless I would not write with paper and ink: but I trust to come unto you, and speak with you mouth to mouth, that our joy may be full. The sons of thy elect sister greet thee. Amen.

THE THIRD EPISTLE OF
ST JOHN

The elder unto the beloved Gaius, whom I love in the truth. Beloved, I wish **A**
in all things that thou prosperedest and faredest well even as thy soul
prospereth. I rejoiced greatly when the brethren came, and testified of the truth
that is in thee, how thou walkest in truth. I have no greater joy than for to
hear how that my sons walk in verity.

Beloved, thou dost faithfully whatsoever thou dost to the brethren, and to **B**
strangers, which bare witness of thy love before all the congregation. Which
brethren when thou bringest forwards on their journey (as it beseemeth God)
thou shalt do well: because that for his name's sake they went forth, and took
nothing of the gentiles. We therefore ought to receive such, that we also might
be helpers to the truth.

I wrote unto the congregation: but Diotrephes which loveth to have the
pre-eminence among them, receiveth us not. Wherefore if I come, I will
declare his deeds which he doeth, jesting on us with malicious words, neither is
therewith content. Not only he himself receiveth not the brethren: but also he
forbiddeth them that would, and thrusteth them out of the congregation.

Beloved, follow not that which is evil, but that which is good. He that doeth
well is of God: but he that doeth evil seeth not God. Demetrius hath good
report of all men, and of the truth: yea and we ourselves also bear record, and **D**
ye know that our record is true. I have many things to write: but I will not with
ink and pen write unto thee. For I trust I shall shortly see thee, and we shall
speak mouth to mouth. Peace be with thee. The lovers salute thee. Greet the
lovers by name.

THE PROLOGUE TO THE EPISTLE OF
ST PAUL TO THE HEBREWS

About this epistle hath ever been much doubting and that among great learned men who should be the author thereof: divers affirming that it was not Paul's, partly because the style so disagreeth and is so unlike his other epistles, and partly because it standeth in the second chapter, this learning was confirmed to usward: that is to say taught us by them that heard it themselves of the Lord. Now Paul testifieth (Gal. 1) that he received not his gospel of man nor by man but immediately of Christ and that by revelation. Wherefore say they, seeing this man confesseth that he received his doctrine of the apostles, it cannot be Paul's, but some disciple of the apostles. Now whether it were Paul's or no I say not, but permit it to other men's judgements, neither think I it to be an article of any man's faith, but that a man may doubt of the author.

Moreover, many there hath been which not only have denied this epistle to have been written by any of the apostles, but have also refused it altogether as no catholic or godly epistle, because of certain texts written therein. For first it saith in the sixth: it is impossible that they which were once lighted, and have tasted of the heavenly gift and were become partakers of the holy ghost, and have tasted of the good word of God and of the power of the world to come, if they fall, should be renewed again to repentance or conversion. And in the tenth it saith, if we sin willingly after we have received the knowledge of the truth, there remaineth no more sacrifice for sins, but a fearful looking for judgment and violent fire which shall destroy the adversaries. And in the twelfth it saith that Esau found no way to repentance or conversion, no though he sought it with tears. Which texts say they, sound: that if a man sin any more after he is once baptised, he can be no more forgiven, and that is contrary to all the scripture, and therefore to be refused to be catholic and godly.

Unto which I answer: if we should deny this epistle for those text's sakes, so should we deny first Matthew which in his twelfth chapter affirmeth that he which blasphemeth the holy ghost, shall neither be forgiven here nor in the world to come. And then Mark which in his third chapter saith that he that blasphemeth the holy ghost, shall never have forgiveness, but shall be in danger of eternal damnation. And thirdly Luke which saith there shall be no remission to him that blasphemeth the spirit of God. Moreover John in his first epistle saith there is a sin unto death, for which a man should not pray. And

2 Pet. 2 saith: if a man be fled from the uncleanness of the world through the knowledge of the saviour Jesus Christ, and then be wrapt in again, his end is worse than the beginning and that it had been better for him never to have known the truth. And Paul (2 Tim. 3) curseth Alexander the coppersmith, desiring the Lord to reward him according to his deeds. Which is a sign that either the epistle should not be good, or that Alexander had sinned past forgiveness, no more to be prayed for. Wherefore seeing no scripture is of private interpretation: but must be expounded according to the general articles of our faith and agreeable to other open and evident texts, and confirmed or compared to like sentences, why should we not understand these places with like reverence as we do the other, namely when all the remnant of the epistle is so godly and of so great learning?

The first place in the sixth chapter will no more than that they which know the truth, and yet willingly refuse the light, and chose rather to dwell in darkness, and refuse Christ and make a mock of him (as the Pharisees which when they were overcome with scripture and miracles that Christ was the very Messiah, yet had such lust in iniquity that they forsook him, persecuted him, slew him and did all the shame that could be imagined to him) cannot be renewed (*eis metanoian*† saith the Greek), to be converted: that is to say, such malicious unkindness which is none other than the blaspheming of the holy ghost, deserveth that the spirit shall never come more at them to convert them, which I believe to be as true as any other text in all the scripture.

And what is meant by that place in the tenth chapter where he saith, if we sin willingly after we have received the knowledge of the truth, there remaineth no more sacrifice for sin, is declared immediately after. For he maketh a comparison between Moses and Christ, saying: if he which despised Moses' law died without mercy: how much worse punishment is he worthy of, that treadeth the son of God under foot and counteth the blood of the covenant, by which blood he was sanctified, as an unholy thing and blasphemeth the spirit of grace. By which words it is manifest that he meaneth none other by the fore words, than the sin of blasphemy of the spirit.

For them that sin of ignorance or infirmity, there is remedy, but for him that knoweth the truth, and yet willingly yieldeth himself to sin, and consenteth unto the life of sin with soul and body, and had liefer lie in sin than have his poisoned nature healed by the help of the spirit of grace, and maliciously persecuteth the truth: for him I say there is no remedy: the way to mercy is locked up and the spirit is taken from him for his unthankfulness' sake, no more to be given him. Truth it is if a man can turn to God and believe in Christ, he must be forgiven how deep soever he hath sinned: but that will not be without the spirit, and such blasphemers shall no more have the spirit offered them. Let every man therefore fear God and beware that he yield not himself to serve sin, but how oft soever he sin let him begin again and fight afresh, and no doubt he shall at the last overcome, and in the meantime yet be under mercy for

† To repentance

Christ's sake because his heart worketh and would fain be loosed from under the bondage of sin.

And that it saith in the twelfth, Esau found no way (*eis metanoian*) to be converted and reconciled unto God and restored unto his birthright again, though he sought it with tears, that text must have a spiritual eye. For Esau in selling his birthright despised not only that temporal promotion, that he should have been lord over all his brethren and king of that country: but he also refused the grace and mercy of God and the spiritual blessings of Abraham and Isaac and all the mercy that is promised us in Christ which should have been his seed. Of this ye see that this epistle ought no more to be refused for holy, godly and catholic than the other authentic scriptures.

Now therefore to come to our purpose again, though this epistle (as it saith in the sixth) lay not the ground of the faith of Christ, yet it buildeth cunningly thereon pure gold, silver and precious stones, and proveth the priesthood of Christ with scriptures inevitable. Moreover there is no work in all scripture that so plainly declareth the meaning and significations of the sacrifices, ceremonies and figures of the old testament, as this epistle: in so much that if wilful blindness and malicious malice were not the cause, this epistle only were enough to weed out of the hearts of the papists that cankered heresy of justifying of works, concerning our sacraments, ceremonies and all manner traditions of their own invention.

And finally in that ye see in the tenth that he had been in bonds and prison for Christ's sake, and in that he so mightily driveth all to Christ to be saved through him, and so cared for the flock of Christ that he both wrote and sent, where he heard that they began to faint, to comfort, encourage and strengthen them with the word of God, and in that also that he sent Timothy, Paul's disciple both virtuous, well-learned and had in great reverence, it is easy to see that he was a faithful servant of Christ's and of the same doctrine that Timothy was of, yea and Paul himself was, and that he was an apostle or in the apostles' time or near thereunto. And seeing the epistle agreeth to all the rest of the scripture, if it be indifferently looked on, how should it not be of authority and taken for holy scripture?

THE EPISTLE OF ST PAUL
UNTO THE HEBREWS

1^1–2^4 CHAPTER ONE +

God in time past diversely and many ways, spake unto the fathers by   A
prophets: but in these last days he hath spoken unto us by his son, whom
he hath made heir of all things: by whom also he made the world. Which son
being the brightness of his glory, and very image of his substance, bearing up
all things with the word of his power, hath in his own person purged our sins,

Christ hath purged and is sitten on the right hand of the majesty on high, and is more excellent   B
òur sin. than the angels, inasmuch as he hath by inheritance obtained an excellenter
name than have they.

Psa. 2. b.· For unto which of the angels said he at any time: Thou art my son, this day
2 Sam. 7. begat I thee? And again: I will be his father, and he shall be my son. And again
Psa. 27. when he bringeth in the first begotten son into the world, he saith: And all the   C
Psa. 104. angels of God shall worship him. And of the angels he saith: He maketh his
angels spirits, and his ministers flames of fire. But unto the son he saith: God
Psa. 45. thy seat shall be for ever and ever. The sceptre of thy kingdom is a right
sceptre. Thou hast loved righteousness and hated iniquity. Wherefore God
Oil of gladness, is the which is thy God, hath anointed thee with the oil of gladness above thy
holy ghost. fellows.

And thou Lord in the beginning hast laid the foundation of the earth. And
the heavens are the works of thy hands. They shall perish, but thou shalt   D
endure. They all shall wax old as doth a garment: and as a vesture shalt thou
change them, and they shall be changed. But thou art always, and thy years
shall not fail. ⊦ Unto which of the angels said he at any time: Sit on my right
Psa. 110. hand, till I make thine enemies thy footstool. Are they not all ministering
1 Cor. 15. spirits, sent to minister for their sakes which shall be heirs of salvation?

CHAPTER TWO

If the despisers of Wherefore we ought to give the more heed to the things we have heard lest we   A
Moses were so perish. For if the word which was spoken by angels was steadfast: so that every
grievously punished: transgression and disobedience received a just recompense to reward: how shall
what shall become of we escape, if we despise so great salvation which at the first began to be
of Christ. preached of the Lord himself, and afterward was confirmed unto us-ward, by
them that heard it, God bearing witness thereto, both with signs and wonders

348

also, and with divers miracles*, and gifts of the holy ghost, according to his own will.

He hath not unto the angels put in subjection the world to come, whereof we speak. But one in a certain place witnessed, saying. What is man, that thou art mindful of him? After thou hadst for a season made him lower than the angels: thou crownedst him with honour and glory, and hast set him above the works of thy hands. Thou hast put all things in subjection under his feet. In that he put all things under him, he left nothing that is not put under him. Nevertheless we yet see not all things subdued but him that was made less than the angels: we see that it was Jesus which is crowned with glory and honour for the suffering of death: that he by the grace of God, should taste of death for all men.

For it became him, for whom are all things and by whom are all things, after that he had brought many sons unto glory, that he should make the lord of their salvation perfect through suffering. For he that sanctifieth, and they which are sanctified, are all of one. For which cause's sake, he is not ashamed to call them brethren saying: I will declare thy name unto my brethren, and in the midst of the congregation will I praise thee. And again: I will put my trust in him. And again: behold here am I and the children which God hath given me.

For as much then as the children were partakers of flesh and blood, he also himself likewise took part with them, for to put down through death, him that had lordship over death, that is to say the devil, and that he might deliver them which through fear of death were all their lifetime in danger of bondage. For he in no place taketh on him the angels: but the seed of Abraham taketh he on him. Wherefore in all things it became him to be made like unto his brethren, that he might be merciful, and a faithful high priest in things concerning God, for to purge the people's sins. For in that he himself suffered and was tempted, he is able to succour them that are tempted.

CHAPTER THREE

Wherefore holy brethren, partakers of the celestial calling, consider the ambassador and high priest of our profession, Christ Jesus which was faithful to him that made him, even as was Moses in all his house. And this man was counted worthy of more glory than Moses: Inasmuch as he which hath prepared the house hath most honour in the house. Every house is prepared of some man. But he that ordained all things is God. And Moses verily was faithful in all his house as a minister, to bear witness of those things which should be spoken afterward. But Christ as a son hath rule over the house, whose house are we, so that we hold fast the confidence and the rejoicing of that hope, unto the end.

Wherefore as the holy ghost saith: today if ye shall hear his voice, harden not your hearts, after the rebellion in the day of temptation in the wilderness, where your fathers tempted me, proved me, and saw my works forty years long. Wherefore I was grieved with that generation and said: They err ever in

* Miracles are called signs because they be a sign-token and an evident proof that the thing that is preached is Gods word.

Psa. 22.
Psa. 18.
Isa. 8. d.

Hosea 13.
1 Cor. 15.

Num. 12.

Psa. 95.

their hearts: they verily have not known my ways, so that I sware in my wrath, that they should not enter into my rest. Take heed brethren that there be in none of you an evil heart in unbelief, that he should depart from the living God: but exhort one another daily, while it is called today, lest any of you wax hard-hearted through the deceitfulness of sin.

We are partakers of Christ if we keep sure unto the end the first substance, so long as it is said: today if ye hear his voice, harden not your hearts, as when ye rebelled. For some, when they heard, rebelled: howbeit not all that came out of Egypt under Moses. But with whom was he displeased forty years? Was he not displeased with them that sinned: whose carcases were overthrown in the desert? To whom sware he that they should not enter into his rest: but unto them that believed not? And we see that they could not enter in, because of unbelief*.

First substance is faith.

Num. 14. c.

★ As faith is the ground of all grace: even so is unbelief the root of all sin.

CHAPTER FOUR

Let us fear therefore lest any of us forsaking the promise of entering into his rest, should seem to come behind. For unto us was it declared, as well as unto them. But it profited not them that they heard the word, because they which heard it, coupled it not with faith. But we which have believed, do enter into his rest, as contrariwise he said to the other: I have sworn in my wrath, they shall not enter into my rest. And that spake he verily long after that the works were made and the foundation of the world laid. For he spake in a certain place of the seventh day, on this wise: And God did rest the seventh day from all his works. And in this place again: They shall not come into my rest.

Seeing therefore it followeth that some must enter thereinto, and they to whom it was first preached, entered not therein for unbelief's sake. Again he appointeth in David a certain present day after so long a time, saying as it is rehearsed: this day if ye hear his voice, be not hard-hearted. For if Joshua had given them rest, then would he not afterward have spoken of another day. There remaineth therefore yet a rest to the people of God. For he that is entered into his rest doth cease* from his own works, as God did from his.

Let us study therefore to enter into that rest, lest any man fall after the same example, into unbelief. For the word of God is quick, and mighty in operation, and sharper than any two-edged sword: and entereth through, even unto the dividing asunder of the soul and the spirit, and of the joints and the mary: and judgeth the thoughts and the intents of the heart: neither is there any creature invisible in the sight of it. For all things are naked and bare unto the eyes of him, of whom we speak.

Psa. 95.

Gen. 2. a.

★ Sin is our work, from which all must cease that enter into the rest of a quiet conscience in Christ.

Eccl. 15. d.
Psa. 34.

CHAPTER FIVE

Seeing then that we have a great high priest which is entered into heaven (I mean Jesus the son of God) let us hold our profession. For we have not an high priest, which cannot have compassion on our infirmities: but was in all points

1 Cor. 3. b.

tempted, like as we are: but yet without sin. Let us therefore go boldly unto the seat of grace, that we may receive mercy, and find grace to help in time of need.

† + For every high priest that is taken from among men, is ordained for men, in things pertaining to God: to offer gifts and sacrifices for sin: which can have compassion on the ignorant, and on them that are out of the way, because that he himself also is compassed with infirmity: For the which infirmity's sake, he is bound to offer for sins, as well for his own part, as for the people's. And no man taketh honour unto himself, but he that is called of God, as was Aaron.   *1 Chr. 2. b.*

Even so likewise, Christ glorified not himself, to be made the high priest: but he that said unto him: thou art my son, this day begat I thee, glorified him. As he also in another place speaketh: Thou art a priest for ever after the order of Melchisedec. ⊢ Which in the days of his flesh, did offer up prayers and supplications, with strong crying and tears, unto him that was able to save him from death: and was also heard, because of his godliness. And though he were God's son, yet learned he obedience, by those things which he suffered, and was made perfect, and the cause of eternal salvation unto all them that obey him: and is called of God an high priest, after the order of Melchisedec.   *Psa. 2. b.*

    Psa. 110.

Whereof we have many things to say which are hard to be uttered: because ye are dull of hearing. For when as concerning the time, ye ought to be teachers, yet have ye need again that we teach you the first principles of the word of God: and are become such as have need of milk, and not of strong meat: For every man that is fed with milk, is inexpert in the word of righteousness. For he is but a babe. But strong meat belongeth to them that are perfect which through custom have their wits exercised, to judge both good and evil also.

CHAPTER SIX

Wherefore let us leave the doctrine pertaining to the beginning of a Christian man, and let us go unto perfection, and now no more lay the foundation of repentance from dead works, and of faith toward God, of baptism, of doctrine, and of laying on of hands, and of resurrection from death, and of eternal judgement. And so will we do, if God permit. For it is not possible that they, which were once lighted, and have tasted of the heavenly gift, and were become partakers of the holy ghost, and have tasted of the good word of God, and of the power of the world to come: if they fall, should be renewed again unto repentance: for as much as they have (as concerning themselves) crucified the son of God afresh, making a mock of him.   *2 Pet. 2. d.*

For that earth which drinketh in the rain which cometh oft upon it, and bringeth forth herbs meet for them that dress it, receiveth blessing of God. But that ground, which beareth thorns and briars, is reproved, and is nigh unto cursing: whose end is to be burned. Nevertheless dear friends, we trust to see

---

† The fifth chapter more correctly begins here.

better of you and things which accompany salvation, though we thus speak.
For God is not unrighteous that he should forget your work and labour that
proceedeth of love, which love showed in his name, which have ministered
unto the saints, and yet minister. Yea, and we desire that every one of you
show the same diligence, to the establishing of hope, even unto the end: that
ye faint not, but follow them, which through faith and patience inherit the
promises.

Gen. 22.

For when God made promise to Abraham, because he had no greater thing
to swear by he sware by himself saying: Surely I will bless thee and multiply
thee indeed. And so after that he had tarried a long time, he enjoyed the promise. Men verily swear by him that is greater than themselves, and an oath to
confirm the thing, is among them an end of all strife. So God willing very
abundantly to show unto the heirs of promise, the stableness of his counsel, he

★ Two immutable
things: the promise and
the oath.

added an oath, that by two immutable things★ (in which it was impossible that
God should lie) we might have perfect consolation, which have fled, for to hold
fast the hope that is set before us, which hope we have as an anchor of the soul
both sure and steadfast. Which hope also entereth in, into those things which
are within the veil, whither the forerunner is for us entered in, I mean Jesus that
is made an high priest for ever, after the order of Melchisedec.

CHAPTER SEVEN

Gen. 14.

This Melchisedec king of Salem (which being priest of the most high God met
Abraham, as he returned again from the slaughter of the kings, and blessed
him: to whom also Abraham gave tithes of all things) first is by interpretation
king of righteousness: after that he is king of Salem, that is to say king of peace,
without father, without mother, without kin, and hath neither beginning of
his time, neither yet end of his life: but is likened unto the son of God and
continueth a priest for ever.

Consider what a man this was, unto whom the patriarch Abraham gave
tithes of the spoils. And verily those children of Levi, which receive the office
of the priests, have a commandment to take according to the law, tithes of the
people, that is to say, of their brethren, yea though they sprang out of the loins
of Abraham. But he whose kindred is not counted among them, received tithes
of Abraham, and blessed him that had the promises. And no man denieth but
that which is less, receiveth blessing of that which is greater. And here men that
die receive tithes. But there he receiveth tithes of whom it is witnessed, that
he liveth. And to say the truth, Levi himself also which receiveth tithes, paid
tithes in Abraham. For he was yet in the loins of his father Abraham when
Melchisedec met him.

If now therefore perfection came by the priesthood of the Levites (for under
that priesthood the people received the law) what needed it furthermore that
another priest should rise, after the order of Melchisedec, and not after the
order of Aaron? Now no doubt, if the priesthood be translated, then of
necessity must the law be translated also.

For he of whom these things are spoken, pertaineth unto another tribe, of which never man served at the altar. For it is evident that our Lord sprang of the tribe of Juda, of which tribe spake Moses nothing concerning priesthood.

And it is yet a more evident thing, if after the similitude of Melchisedec, there arise another priest, which is not made after the law of the carnal commandment: but after the power of the endless life (For he testifieth: Thou art a priest for ever, after the order of Melchisedec). Then the commandment that went afore, is disanulled, because of her weakness and unprofitableness. For the law made nothing perfect: but was an introduction of a better hope, by which hope, we draw nigh unto God. *Psa. 110.*

D And for this cause it is a better hope, that it was not promised without an oath. Those priests were made without an oath: but this priest with an oath, by him that said unto him: The Lord sware, and will not repent: Thou art a priest for ever after the order of Melchisedec. And for that cause was Jesus a stablisher of a better testament. *Psa. 110.*

And among them many were made priests, because they were not suffered to endure by the reason of death. But this man, because he endureth ever, hath an everlasting priesthood. Wherefore he is able also ever to save them that come unto God by him, seeing he ever liveth, to make intercession for us.

Such an high priest it became us to have, which is holy, harmless, undefiled, separate from sinners, and made higher than heaven. Which needeth not daily (as yonder high priests) to offer up sacrifice, first for his own sins, and then for the people's sins. For that did he at once for all when he offered up himself. For the law maketh men priests, which have infirmity: but the word of the oath that came since the law, maketh the son priest, which is perfect for ever more. *Christ once sacrificed, purged all sins.*

CHAPTER EIGHT

A Of the things which we have spoken, this is the pith: that we have such an high priest that is sitten on the right hand of the seat of majesty in heaven, and is a minister of holy things, and of the very tabernacle, which God pyght, and not man. For every high priest is ordained to offer gifts and sacrifices, wherefore it is of necessity, that this man have somewhat also to offer. For he were not a priest, if he were on the earth where are priests that according to the law, offer **B** gifts, which priests serve unto the example and shadow of heavenly things: even as the answer of God was given unto Moses when he was about to finish the tabernacle: Take heed (said he) that thou make all things according to the pattern shewed to thee in the mount. *Exod. 25. Acts 7. f.*

C Now hath he obtained a more excellent office, inasmuch as he is the mediator of a better testament, which was made for better promises. For if that first testament had been faultless: then should no place have been sought for the second. For in rebuking them he saith: Behold the days will come (saith the Lord) and I will finish upon the house of Israel, and upon the house of Judah, a new testament: not like the testament that I made with their fathers at that time, when I took them by the hands, to lead them out of the land of Egypt, *Jer. 31.*

Covenant.

for they continued not in my testament, and I regarded them not saith the Lord.

For this is the testament that I will make with the house of Israel: After those **D** days saith the Lord: I will put my laws in their minds, and in their hearts I will write them, and I will be their God, and they shall be my people. And they shall not teach, every man his neighbour, and every man his brother, saying: know the Lord: For they shall know me, from the least to the most of them: For I will be merciful over their unrighteousness, and on their sins and on their iniquities. In that he saith a new testament he hath abrogated the old. Now that which is disannulled and waxed old, is ready to vanish away.

CHAPTER NINE

That first tabernacle verily had ordinances, and servings of God, and wordly **A** holiness. + For there was a fore-tabernacle made, wherein was the candlestick, and the table, and the shewbread, which is called holy. But within the second veil was there a tabernacle, which is called holiest of all, which had the golden censer, and the ark of the testament overlaid round about with gold, wherein was the golden pot with manna, and Aaron's rod that sprang, and the tables of the testament. Over the ark were the cherubims of glory shadowing the seat of grace. Of which things, we will not now speak particularly.

When these things were thus ordained, the priests went always into the first **B** tabernacle and executed the service of God. But into the second went the high priest alone, once every year: and not without blood, which he offered for himself, and for the ignorance of the people. Wherewith the holy ghost this signifying, that the way of holy things, was not yet opened, while as yet the **C** first tabernacle was standing. Which was a similitude for the time then present, and in which were offered gifts and sacrifices that could not make them that minister perfect, as pertaining to the conscience, with only meats and drinks, and divers washings and justifyings of the flesh, which were ordained until the time of reformation.

+ But Christ being an high priest of good things to come, came by a greater and a more perfect tabernacle, not made with hands: that is to say, not of this manner building, neither by the blood of goats and calves: but by his own blood we†† entered once for all into the holy place, and found eternal

Lev. 16. c. redemption. ⊢ For if the blood of oxen and of goats and the ashes of an heifer, **D** when it was sprinkled, purified the unclean, as touching the purifying of the
1 Pet. 1. d. flesh: How much more shall the blood of Christ (which through the eternal
1 John 1. d. spirit, offered himself without spot to God) purge your consciences from dead
Rev. 1. d.
1 Pet. 3. works for to serve the living God?
Rom. 5. b.

And for this cause is he the mediator of the new testament (that through **E** death which chanced for the redemption of those transgressions that were in the first testament) they which were called, might receive the promise of eternal inheritance. ⊢ For wheresoever is a testament, there must also be the
Gal. 3. b. death of him that maketh the testament. For the testament taketh authority

when men are dead: For it is of no value as long as he that made it is alive. For
which cause also, neither that first testament was ordained without blood. For   **F**
when all the commandments were read of Moses unto all the people, he took
the blood of calves and of goats, with water and purple wool and hyssop, and
sprinkled both the book and all the people, saying: this is the blood of the
testament which God hath appointed unto you. Moreover, he sprinkled the
tabernacle with blood also, and all the ministering vessels. And almost all
things, are by the law, purged with blood, and without effusion of blood, is no
remission.

G   It is then need that the similitudes of heavenly things be purified with such   *Gen. 24.*
things: but the heavenly things themselves are purified with better sacrifices
D than are those. For Christ is not entered into the holy places that are made with
hands, which are but similitudes of true things: but is entered into very heaven,
for to appear now in the sight of God for us: not to offer himself often, as the
high priest entereth into the holy place every year with strange blood, for then
must he have often suffered since the world began. But now in the end of
the world, hath he appeared once, to put sin to flight, by the offering up of
himself. And as it is appointed unto men that they shall once die, and then
cometh the judgement, even so Christ was once offered to take away the sins of   *Rom. 5. b.*
many, and unto them that look for him, shall he appear again without sin, unto   *1 Pet. 3. c.*
salvation.

CHAPTER TEN

A   For the law which hath but the shadow of good things to come, and not the
things in their own fashion, can never with the sacrifices which they offer year
by year continually, make the comers thereunto perfect. For would not then   *Lev. 16.*
those sacrifices have ceased to have been offered, because that the offerers once
purged, should have had no more consciences of sins. Nevertheless in those
sacrifices is there mention made of sins every year. For it is unpossible that the
blood of oxen, and of goats should take away sins.

B   Wherefore when he cometh into the world, he saith: Sacrifice and offering   *Psa. 40.*
thou wouldest not have: but a body hast thou ordained me. In sacrifices and
sin-offerings thou hast no lust. Then I said: Lo I come, in the chiefest of the   *Psa. 1.*
book it is written of me, that I should do thy will, o God. Above when he had
said sacrifice and offering, and burnt sacrifices and sin-offerings thou wouldest
not have, neither hast allowed (which yet are offered by the law) and then said:
Lo I come to do thy will o God: he taketh away the first to establish the latter.
By the which will we are sanctified, by the offering of the body of Jesus Christ   *Christ's body is but*
once for all.   *once offered.*

C   And every priest is ready daily ministering, and oft-times offereth one
manner of offering, which can never take away sins. But this man after he had
offered one sacrifice for sins, sat him down for ever on the right hand of God,   *Psa. 110. a.*
and from henceforth tarrieth till his foes be made his footstool. For with one   *1 Cor. 15.*
offering hath he made perfect for ever them that are sanctified. And the holy

Jer. 31.

ghost also beareth us record of this, even when he told before: This is the testament that I will make unto them after those days saith the lord. I will put my laws in their hearts and in their mind I will write them and their sins and iniquities will I remember no more. And where remission of these things is, there is no more offering for sin.

Here followeth our duty, if we will be partakers of the mercy before rehearsed.

Seeing brethren that by the means of the blood of Jesus, we may be bold to enter into that holy place, by the new and living way, which he hath prepared for us, through the veil, that is to say by his flesh. And seeing also that we have an high priest which is ruler over the house of God, let us draw nigh with a true heart in a full faith, sprinkled in our hearts from an evil conscience, and washed in our bodies with pure water, and let us keep the profession of our hope,

We ought to care each for other's salvation, as we should if we truly loved each other.

without wavering (for he is faithful that promised) and let us consider one another to provoke unto love, and to good works: and let us not forsake the fellowship that we have among ourselves, as the manner of some is: but let us exhort one another, and that so much the more, because ye see that the day draweth nigh.

For if we sin willingly after that we have received the knowledge of the truth, there remaineth no more sacrifice for sins but a fearful looking for judgement, and violent fire which shall devour the adversaries. He that de-

Deut. 17.
Matt. 17.
John 8. c.
1 Cor. 13.

spiseth Moses' law, dieth without mercy under two or three witnesses. Of how much sorer punishment suppose ye shall he be counted worthy, which treadeth under foot the son of God: and counteth the blood of the testament as an unholy thing wherewith he was sanctified, and doth dishonour to the spirit of grace. For we know him that hath said, vengeance belongeth unto me, I will

Deut. 32.
Rom. 12.

recompense saith the Lord. And again: the Lord shall judge his people. It is a fearful thing to fall into the hands of the living God.

Call to remembrance the days that are passed, in the which after ye had received light, ye endured a great fight in adversities, partly while all men wondered and gazed at you for the shame and tribulation that was done unto you, and partly while ye became companions of them which so passed their time. For ye suffered also with my bonds, and took as worth the spoiling of your goods, and that with gladness, knowing in yourselves how that ye had in heaven a better and an enduring substance. Cast not away therefore your confidence, which hath great reward to recompense. For ye have need of patience, that after ye have done the will of God, ye might receive the promise. For yet a very little while, and he that shall come will come, and will not tarry.

Hab. 2. a.
Rom. 1. b.
Gal. 3. b.

But the just shall live by faith. And if he withdraw himself, my soul shall have no pleasure in him. We are not which withdraw ourselves unto damnation, but pertain to faith to the winning of the soul.

CHAPTER ELEVEN

Faith and trust in Christ only, is the life and quietness of the conscience, and not trust in works, how holy soever they appear.

Faith is a sure confidence of things which are hoped for, and a certainty of things which are not seen. By it the elders were well reported of. Through faith we understand that the world was ordained by the word of God: and that things which are seen, were made of things which are not seen. By faith Abel offered unto God a more plenteous sacrifice than Cain: by which, he obtained witness that he was righteous, God testifying of his gifts: by which also he being dead, yet speaketh.

Matt. 18. d.

B   By faith was Enoch translated that he should not see death: neither was he found: for God had taken him away. Before he was taken away, he was reported of, that he had pleased God: but without faith it is unpossible to please him. For he that cometh to God, must believe that God is, and that he is a rewarder of them that seek him.

Gen. 5. c.
Ecclesiastes 44.

By faith Noah honoured God, after that he was warned of things which were not seen, and prepared the ark to the saving of his household, through the which ark, he condemned the world, and became heir of the righteousness which cometh by faith.

Gen. 6. c.
Ecclesiastes 44.

By faith Abraham, when he was called obeyed, to go out into a place, which he should afterward receive to inheritance, and he went out not knowing whither he should go.

Gen. 12. a.

C   By faith he removed into the land that was promised him, as into a strange country, and dwelt in tabernacles: and so did Isaac and Jacob, heirs with him of the same promise. For he looked for a city having a foundation, whose builder and maker is God.

Through faith Sara also received strength to be with child, and was delivered of a child when she was past age, because she judged him faithful which had promised.

Gen. 21.

And therefore sprang thereof one (and of one which was as good as dead) so many in multitude, as the stars of the sky, and as the sand of the seashore which is innumerable.

Gen. 17. and 18.

D   And they all died in faith, and received not the promises: but saw them afar off, and believed them, and saluted them: and confessed that they were strangers and pilgrims on the earth. They that say such things, declare that they seek a country. Also if they had been mindful of that country, from whence they came out, they had leisure to have returned again. But now they desire a better, that is to say a heavenly. Wherefore God is not ashamed of them even to be called their God: for he hath prepared for them a city.

In faith Abraham offered up Isaac, when he was tempted, and he offered him being his only begotten son, which had received the promises of whom it was said, in Isaac shall thy seed be called: for he considered, that God was able to raise up again from death. Wherefore received he him, for an example. In faith Isaac blessed Jacob and Esau, concerning things to come.

Gen. 22
Ecclesiastes 44.
Gen. 21.
Rom. 9. b.
Gen. 27.

F   By faith Jacob when he was a-dying, blessed both the sons of Joseph, and bowed himself toward the top of his sceptre.

Gen. 29.

By faith Joseph when he died, remembered the departing of the children of Israel, and gave commandment of his bones.

Gen. 50. d.

By faith Moses when he was born, was hid three months of his father and mother, because they saw he was a proper child: neither feared they the king's commandment.

Exod. 2. a.
Exod 1. c.

Exod. 2. b.

By faith Moses when he was great, refused to be called the son of Pharaoh's daughter, and chose rather to suffer adversity with the people of God, than to enjoy the pleasures of sin for a season, and esteemed the rebuke of Christ greater riches than the treasure of Egypt. For he had a respect unto the reward.

By faith he forsook Egypt, and feared not the fierceness of the king. For he endured, even as he had seen him which is invisible.

Exod. 12. d.

Through faith he ordained the Easter lamb, and the effusion of blood, lest he that destroyed the first-born, should touch them.

Exod. 13. c.

By faith they passed through the Red Sea as by dry land, which when the Egyptians had assayed to do, they were drowned.

Josh. 6. c.

By faith the walls of Jericho fell down after they were compassed about, seven days.

Josh. 6. d. and 2. b.

By faith the harlot Rahab perished not with the unbelievers, when she had **F** received the spies to lodging peaceably.

And what shall I more say? The time would be too short for me to tell of Gideon, of Barak and of Samson, and of Jephtha: also of David and Samuel, and of the prophets: + which through faith subdued kingdoms, wrought righteousness, obtained the promises, stopped the mouths of lions, quenched the violence of fire, escaped the edge of the sword, of weak were made strong, waxed valiant in fight, turned to flight the armies of the aliens. And the women received their dead raised to life again.

Others were racked, and would not be delivered, that they might receive a better resurrection. Others tasted of mockings and scourgings, moreover of bonds and prisonment: were stoned, were hewn asunder, were tempted, were slain with swords, walked up and down in sheepskins, in goatskins, in need, tribulation, and vexation, which the world was not worthy of: they wandered in wilderness, in mountains, in dens and caves of the earth.

And these all through faith obtained good report ⊦ and received not the promise, God providing a better thing for us, that they without us should not be made perfect.

CHAPTER TWELVE

Rom. 6. a.
Col. 3. b.
Eph. 4. e.
1 Pet. 2. a. and 4. a.

Wherefore let us also (seeing that we are compassed with so great a multitude **A** of witnesses) lay away all that presseth down, and the sin that hangeth on, and let us run with patience unto the battle that is set before us, looking unto Jesus,

We be called to suffer. For without suffering no man can be the son of God.

the author and finisher of our faith, which for the joy that was set before him, abode the cross, and despised the shame, and is set down on the right hand of the throne of God. Consider therefore how that he endured such speaking against him of sinners, lest ye should be wearied and faint in your minds. For ye have not yet resisted unto blood-shedding, striving against sin. And ye have **B** forgotten the consolation, which speaketh unto you, as unto children: My son despise not the chastening of the Lord, neither faint when thou art rebuked of him: For whom the Lord loveth, him he chasteneth★: yea, and he scourgeth every son that he receiveth.

If ye endure chastening, God offereth himself unto you, as unto sons. What son is that whom the father chasteneth not? If ye be not under correction (whereof all are partakers) then are ye bastards and not sons. Moreover seeing we had fathers of our flesh which corrected us, and we gave them reverence:

C should we not much rather be in subjection unto the father of spiritual gifts, that we might live? And they verily for a few days, nurtured us after their own pleasure: but he learneth us unto that which is profitable, that we might receive of his holiness. No manner chastising for the present time seemeth to be joyous, but grievous: nevertheless afterward it bringeth the quiet fruit of righteousness unto them which are therein exercised.

D Stretch forth therefore again the hands which were let down, and the weak knees, and see that ye have straight steps unto your feet, lest any halting turn out of the way: yea, let it rather be healed. Embrace peace with all men, and holiness: without the which, no man shall see the Lord. And look to, that no man be destitute of the grace of God, and that no root of bitterness spring up and trouble, and thereby many be defiled: and that there be no fornicator, or unclean person, as Esau, which for one breakfast sold his birthright. Ye know how that afterward when he would have inherited the blessing, he was put by, and he found no means to come thereby again: no though he desired it with tears.

E For ye are not come unto the mount that can be touched, and unto burning fire, nor yet to mist and darkness and tempest of weather, neither unto the sound of a trumpet and the voice of words: which voice they that heard it, wished away, that the communication should not be spoken to them. For they were not able to abide that which was spoken. If a beast had touched the

F mountain, it must have been stoned, or thrust through with a dart: even so terrible was the sight which appeared. Moses said, I fear and quake. But ye are come unto the mount Sion, and to the city of the living God, the celestial Jerusalem: and to an innumerable sight of angels, and unto the congregation of the first born sons★, which are written in heaven, and to God the judge of all, and to the spirits of just and perfect men, and to Jesus the mediator of the new testament, and to the sprinkling of blood that speaketh better than the blood of Abel.

G See that ye despise not him that speaketh. For if they escaped not which refused him that spake on earth: much more shall we not escape, if we turn away from him that speaketh from heaven: whose voice then shook the earth, and now declareth saying: yet once more will I shake not the earth only, but also heaven. No doubt the same that he sayeth, yet once more, signifieth the removing away of those things which are shaken, as of things which have ended their course: that the things which are not shaken may remain. Wherefore if we receive a kingdom which is not moved, we have grace, whereby we may serve God and please him with reverence and godly fear. For our God is a consuming fire.

CHAPTER THIRTEEN

Our duty if we will
have our part with
Christ.

Let brotherly love continue. Be not forgetful to lodge strangers. For thereby **A** have divers received angels into their houses unawares. Remember them that are in bonds, even as though ye were bound with them. Be mindful of them which are in adversity, as ye which are yet in your bodies. Let wedlock be had in price in all points, and let the chamber be undefiled: for whorekeepers and advoutrers God will judge. Let your conversation be without covetousness and be content with that ye have already. For he verily said: I will not fail thee, neither forsake thee: that we may boldly say: the Lord is my helper, and I will not fear what man doeth unto me. Remember them which have the oversight of you, which have declared unto you the word of God. The end of whose conversation see that ye look upon, and follow their faith.

Josh. 1. a.
Psa. 128.

Jesus Christ yesterday and today, and the same continueth for ever. Be not carried about with divers and strange learning. For it is a good thing that the heart be stablished with grace, and not with meats, which have not profited them that have had their pastime in them. We have an altar whereof they may not eat which serve in the tabernacle. For the bodies of those beasts whose **C** blood is brought into the holy place by the high priest to purge sin, are burnt without the tents. Therefore Jesus to sanctify the people with his own blood, suffered without the gate. Let us go forth therefore out of the tents, and suffer rebuke with him. For here have we no continuing city: but we seek one to come.

Num. 19.

Mic. 2. c.

For by him offer we the sacrifice of laud always to God: that is to say, the fruit of those lips, which confess his name. To do good, and to distribute forget not, for with such sacrifices God is pleased. + Obey them that have the oversight of you, and submit yourselves to them, for they watch for your souls, even as they that must give accounts: that they may do it with joy, and not with grief. For that is an unprofitable thing for you. Pray for us. We have confidence because we have a good conscience in all things, and desire to live honestly. I desire you therefore somewhat the more abundantly, that ye so do, that I may be restored to you quickly.

The God of peace that brought again from death our Lord Jesus, the great **D** shepherd of the sheep, through the blood of the everlasting testament, make you perfect in all good works, to do his will, working in you that which is pleasant in his sight through Jesus Christ. To whom be praise for ever while the world endureth. Amen. ⊦

I beseech you brethren, suffer the words of exhortation: For we have written unto you in few words: know the brother Timothy, whom we have sent from us, with whom (if he come shortly) I will see you. Salute them that have the oversight of you, and all the saints. They of Italy salute you. Grace be with you all. Amen.

Sent from Italy by Timothy.

THE PROLOGUE UPON THE EPISTLES OF
SAINTS JAMES AND JUDAS

Though this epistle were refused in the old time and denied of many to be the epistle of a very apostle, and though also it lay not the foundation of the faith of Christ, but speaketh of a general faith in God, neither preacheth his death and resurrection, either the mercy that is laid up in store for us in him, or everlasting covenant made us in his blood, which is the office and duty of a very apostle, as Christ sayeth (John 15) ye shall testify of me: yet because it setteth up no man's doctrine, but crieth to keep the law of God, and maketh love which is without partiality the fulfilling of the law, as Christ and all the apostles did, and hath thereto many good and godly sentences in it: and hath also nothing that is not agreeable to the rest of the scripture, if it be looked indifferently on: me thinketh it ought of right to be taken for holy scripture. For as for that place for which haply it was at the beginning refused of holy men (as it ought, if it had meant as they took it, and for which place only, for the false understanding, it hath been chiefly received of the papists) yet if the circumstances be well pondered it will appear that the author's intent was far otherwise than they took him for.

For where he saith in the second chapter faith without deeds is dead in itself, he meaneth none other thing than all the scripture doth: how that faith which hath no good deeds following, is a false faith and none of that faith justifieth or receiveth forgiveness of sins. For God promised them only forgiveness of their sins which turn to God, to keep his laws. Wherefore they that purpose to continue still in sin have no part in that promise: but deceive themselves, if they believe that God hath forgiven them their old sins for Christ's sake. And after when he saith that a man is justified by deeds and not of faith only, he will no more than that faith doth not so justify everywhere, that nothing justifieth save faith. For deeds also do justify. And as faith only justifieth before God, so do deeds only justify before the world, whereof is enough spoken, partly in the prologue on Paul to the Romans, and also in other places. For as Paul affirmeth (Rom. 4) that Abraham was not justified by works afore God, but by faith only as Genesis beareth record, so will James that deeds only justified him before the world, and faith wrought with his deeds: that is to say, faith wherewith he was righteous before God in the heart did cause him to work the will of God outwardly, whereby he was righteous before the world, and whereby the world perceived that he believed in God loved and feared God. And as (Hebrews 11) the scripture affirmeth that Rahab was justified before God through faith, so doth James affirm that through works by which she shewed her faith, she was justified before the world, and it is true.

And as for the epistle of Judas, though men have and yet do doubt of the author, and though it seem also to be drawn out of the second epistle of St Peter, and thereto allegeth scripture that is nowhere found, yet seeing the matter is so godly and agreeing to other places of holy scripture, I see not but that it ought to have the authority of holy scripture.

THE EPISTLE OF ST JAMES

A James the servant of God and of the Lord Jesus Christ, sendeth greeting to the twelve tribes which are scattered here and there. + My brethren, count it exceeding joy when ye fall into divers temptations, for as much as ye know how that the trying of your faith bringeth patience: and let patience have her perfect work, that ye may be perfect and sound, lacking nothing.

Rom. 5. a.

If any of you lack wisdom, let him ask of God which giveth to all men indifferently, and casteth no man in the teeth: and it shall be given him. But let him ask in faith and waver not. For he that doubteth is like the waves of the sea, tossed of the wind and carried with violence. Neither let that man think that he shall receive any thing of the Lord. A wavering-minded man is unstable in all his ways.

Matt. 7. a. and 21. c.
Mak 11. c.
Luke 11. b.
John 16. b. and 16. e.

B Let the brother of low degree rejoice in that he is exalted, and the rich in that he is made low. For even as the flower of the grass, shall he vanish away. The sun riseth with heat, and the grass withereth, and his flower falleth away, and the beauty of the fashion of it perisheth: even so shall the rich man perish with his abundance.

In Christ we be all like good, and even servants each to other for Christ's sake, every man in his office. And he that taketh more on him than that, of what soever degree he be of is a false christian and an apostate from Christ.

Happy is the man that endureth in temptation, for when he is tried he shall receive the crown of life, which the Lord hath promised to them that love him. +

Let no man say when he is tempted that he is tempted of God. For God tempteth not unto evil, neither tempteth he any man. But every man is tempted, drawn away, and enticed of his own concupiscence. Then when lust hath conceived, she bringeth forth sin, and sin when it is finished bringeth forth death.

C Err not my dear brethren. + Every good gift, and every perfect gift, is from above and cometh down from the father of light, with whom is no variableness, neither is he changed unto darkness. Of his own will begat he us with the word of life, that we should be the first fruits of his creatures.

Wherefore dear brethren, let every man be swift to hear, slow to speak, and slow to wrath. For the wrath of man worketh not that which is righteous before God.

Wherefore lay apart all filthiness, all superfluity of maliciousness, and receive with meekness the word that is grafted in you, which is able to save your souls ⊦. + And see that ye be doers of the word and not hearers only, deceiving your own selves with sophistry. For if any hear the word, and do it not, he is like unto a man that beholdeth his bodily face in a glass. For as soon as he hath **D** looked on himself, he goeth his way, and forgetteth immediately what his fashion was. But whoso looketh in the perfect law of liberty, and continueth therein (if he be not a forgetful hearer, but a doer of the work) the same shall be happy in his deed.

Pure devotion.

If any man among you seem devout, and refrain not his tongue: but deceive his own heart, this man's devotion is in vain. Pure devotion and undefiled before God the father, is this: to visit the friendless and widow in their adversity, and to keep himself unspotted of the world. ⊦

CHAPTER TWO

+ Brethren have not the faith of our Lord Jesus Christ the lord of glory in **A** respect of persons. If there come into your company a man with a golden ring and in goodly apparel and there come in also a poor man in vile raiment, and ye have a respect to him that weareth the gay clothing and say unto him: Sit thou here in a good place: and say unto the poor, stand thou there or sit here under my footstool: are ye not partial in yourselves, and have judged after evil thoughts?

Hearken my dear beloved brethren. Hath not God chosen the poor of this world, which are rich in faith, and heirs of the kingdom which he promised to them that love him? But ye have despised the poor. Are not the rich they which **B** oppress you: and they which draw you before judges? Do not they speak evil of that good name after which ye be named?

If ye fulfil the royal law according to the scripture which saith: Thou shalt love thine neighbour as thyself, ye do well. But if ye regard one person more than another, ye commit sin, and are rebuked of the law as transgressors. Whosoever shall keep the whole law, and yet fail in one point, he is guilty in all. For he that said: Thou shalt not commit adultery, said also: thou shalt not kill. Though thou do none adultery, yet if thou kill, thou art a transgressor of the law. So speak ye, and so do as they that shall be judged by the law* of liberty. For there shall be judgement merciless to him that showeth no mercy, and mercy rejoiceth against judgement: ⊦

* To work of fear and compulsion is bondage; but to love is liberty and the fulfilling of the law before God and maketh a man merciful to work of his own accord. And to the merciful hath God bound himself to show mercy. And contrary unto the unmerciful he threateneth judgement without mercy. And mercy rejoiceth and triumpheth over judgment. For where mercy is, there hath damnation no place by God's promise. God hath promised all mercy to the merciful only.

What availeth it my brethren, though a man say he hath faith, when he hath **C** no deeds? Can faith save him? If a brother or a sister be naked or destitute of daily food, and one of you say unto them: Depart in peace, God send you warmness and food: not withstanding ye give them not those things which are needful to the body: what helpeth it them? Even so faith, if it have no deeds, is dead in itself.

Yea and a man might say: Thou hast faith, and I have deeds: Show me thy faith by thy deeds: and I will show thee my faith by my deeds. Believest thou that there is one God? Thou doest well. The devils also believe and tremble.

Wilt thou understand o thou vain man, that faith without deeds is dead? Was **D** not Abraham our father justified through works when he offered Isaac his son upon the altar? Thou seest how that faith wrought with his deeds, and through the deeds was the faith made perfect: and the scripture was fulfilled which saith: Abraham believed God, and it was reputed unto him for righteousness: and he was called the friend of God. + Ye see then how that of deeds a man is justified, and not of faith only. Likewise also was not Rahab the harlot justified through works, when she received the messengers, and sent them out another way? For as the body, without the spirit is dead, even so faith without deeds is dead. ⊢

Now if any that is not merciful believeth to have mercy of God he deceiveth himself: because he hath no God's word for him. For God's promise pertaineth to the merciful only: and true faith therefore is known by her deeds.

Jos. 2. *e.*

CHAPTER THREE

A My brethren, be not every man a master★, remembering how that we shall receive the more damnation: for in many things we sin all. If a man sin not in word, the same is a perfect man, and able to tame all the body. Behold we put bits into the horses' mouths that they should obey us, and we turn about all the body. Behold also the ships, which though they be so great, and are driven of fierce winds, yet are they turned about with a very small helm, whithersoever the violence of the governor will. Even so the tongue is a little member, and boasteth great things.

Behold how great a thing a little fire kindleth, and the tongue is fire, and a world of wickedness. So is the tongue set among our members, that it defileth the whole body, and setteth afire all that we have of nature, and is itself set afire even of hell.

★ He that taketh authority to rebuke other of that wherein he sinneth himself, the same shall have the greater damnation. He must be without sin that will cast the first stone.

B All the natures of beasts, and of birds, and of serpents, and things of the sea, are meeked and tamed of the nature of man. But the tongue can no man tame. It is an unruly evil full of deadly poison. Therewith bless we God the father, and therewith curse we men which are made after the similitude of God. Out of one mouth proceedeth blessing and cursing. My brethren these things ought not so to be. Doth a fountain send forth at one place sweet water and bitter also? Can the fig tree, my brethren, bear olive berries: or a vine bear figs? So can no fountain give both salt water and fresh also. If any man be wise and endued with learning among you let him shew the works of his good conversation in meekness that is coupled with wisdom★.

★ Wisdom: all meekness and obedience must be according to the wisdom, and word of God.

C But if ye have bitter envying and strife in your hearts, rejoice not: neither be liars against the truth. This wisdom descendeth not from above: but is earthy,

A and natural★, and devilish. For where envying and strife is, there is stableness and all manner of evil works. But the wisdom that is from above, is first pure, then peaceable, gentle, and easy to be entreated, full of mercy and good fruits, without judging, and without simulation: yea, and the fruit of righteousness is sown in peace, of them that maintain peace.

Godly wisdom: how it is known.

★ Natural: that is all that a man doth without the spirit of God.

CHAPTER FOUR

A From whence cometh war and fighting among you: come they not here hence? even of your voluptuousness that reign in your members. Ye lust, and have

Strife: whence it cometh.

not. Ye envy and have indignation, and cannot obtain. Ye fight and war and have not, because ye ask not. Ye ask and receive not, because ye ask amiss: even to consume it upon your voluptuousness. Ye advouterers, and women

that break matrimony: know ye not how that the friendship of the world is enmity to God-ward? Whosoever will be friend of the world, is made the enemy of God. Either do ye think that the scripture saith in vain: The spirit★

that dwelleth in you, lusteth even contrary to envy: but giveth more grace.   B

Submit yourselves to God, and resist the devil, and he will fly from you. Draw nigh to God and he will draw nigh to you. Cleanse your hands ye sinners, and purge your hearts ye wavering-minded. Suffer afflictions: sorrow ye and weep. Let your laughter be turned to mourning, and your joy to heaviness. Cast down yourselves before the Lord, and he shall lift you up.

Backbite not one another, brethren. He that★ backbiteth his brother, and he that judgeth his brother, backbiteth the law, and judgeth the law. But and if thou judge the law, thou art not an observer of the law: but a judge. There is one law-giver, which is able to save and to destroy. What art thou that judgest   D another man?

Go to now ye that say: today and tomorrow let us go into such a city and continue there a year and buy and sell, and win: and yet cannot tell what shall happen tomorrow. For what thing is your life? It is even a vapour that appeareth for a little time, and then vanisheth away: For that ye ought to say: if the Lord will and if we live, let us do this or that. But now ye rejoice in your boastings. All such rejoicing is evil. Therefore to him that knoweth how to do good, and doth it not, to him it is sin.

CHAPTER FIVE

Go to now ye rich men. Weep, and howl on your wretchedness that shall come   A upon you. Your riches is corrupt, your garments are motheaten. Your gold and your silver are cankered, and the rust of them shall be a witness unto you, and shall eat your flesh, as it were fire. Ye have heaped treasure together in your last days: Behold the hire of the labourers which have reaped down your fields (which hire is of you kept back by fraud) crieth: and the cries of them which have reaped, are entered into the ears of the lord Sabaoth. Ye have lived in pleasure on the earth and in wantonness. Ye have nourished your hearts, as in a day of slaughter★. Ye have condemned and have killed the just, and he hath not resisted you.

+ Be patient therefore brethren, unto the coming of the Lord. Behold the   B husbandman waiteth for the precious fruit of the earth, and hath long patience thereupon, until he receive (the early and the latter rain.) Be ye also patient therefore, and settle your hearts, for the coming of the Lord draweth nigh. Grudge not one against another brethren, lest ye be damned. Behold the judge standeth before the door. Take (my brethren) the prophets for an example of suffering adversity, and of long patience, which spake in the name of the

lord. ⊢ Behold we count them happy which endure. Ye have heard of the patience of Job, and have known what end the Lord made. For the Lord is very pitiful and merciful.

C   But above all things my brethren, swear not, neither by heaven, neither by earth, neither by any other oath. Let your yea be yea★, and your nay nay: lest ye fall into hypocrisy. If any of you be evil vexed, let him pray. If any of you be merry, let him sing psalms. If any be diseased among you, let him call for the elders of the congregation, and let them pray over him, and anoint him with oil in the name of the Lord: and the prayer of faith shall save the sick, and the Lord shall raise him up: and if he have committed sins, they shall be forgiven him.

D   ✝ Knowledge your faults one to another: and pray one for another, that ye may be healed. The prayer of a righteous man availeth much, if it be fervent. Elias was a man mortal even as we are, and he prayed in his prayer, that it might not rain: and it rained not on the earth by the space of three years and six months. And he prayed again, and the heaven gave rain and the earth brought forth her fruit.

    Brethren if any of you err from the truth and another convert him, let the same know that he which converted the sinner from going astray out of his way, shall save a soul from death, and shall hide the multitude of sins. ✝

The end of the epistle of Saint James.

★ Whether ye say yea or nay: see it be so. For if ye have one thing in the heart and another in the mouth or deed, in vesture or gesture: it is hypocrisy or dissimulation.

1 Kin. 16.
Luke 4. d.

Matt. 13.

THE EPISTLE OF SAINT JUDE

Jude the servant of Jesus Christ, the brother of James. To them which are **A** called and sanctified in God the father, and preserved in Jesus Christ. Mercy unto you, and peace and love be multiplied.

Beloved, when I gave all diligence to write unto you of the common salvation: it was needful for me to write unto you, to exhort you, that ye should continually labour in the faith which was once given unto the saints. For there are certain craftily crept in, of which it was written aforetime unto such **B** judgement. They are ungodly and turn the grace of our God unto wantonness, and deny God the only Lord, and our Lord Jesus Christ.

Num. 13.

Gen. 19.

My mind is therefore to put you in remembrance, forasmuch as ye once know this, how that the Lord (after that he had delivered the people out of Egypt) destroyed them which afterward believed not. The angels also which kept not their first estate: but left their own habitation, he hath reserved in everlasting chains under darkness unto the judgment of the great day: even as **C** Sodom and Gomorrha, and the cities about them (which in like manner defiled themselves with fornication and followed strange flesh★) are set forth for an example, and suffer the vengeance of eternal fire. Likewise these dreamers defileth flesh, despise rulers and speak evil of them that are in authority.

★ Strange flesh: that is turning the natural use unto the unnatural. *Rom. 1.*

Yet Michael the archangel when he strove against the devil, and disputed about the body of Moses, durst not give railing sentence, but said: the Lord rebuke thee. But these speak evil of those things which they know not: and **D** what things they know naturally, as beasts which are without reason, in those things they corrupt themselves. Woe be unto them, for they have followed the way of Cain, and are utterly given to the error of Balaam for lucre's sake, and perish in the treason of Core.

Gen. 4.
Num. 16. a.
Num. 22.

2 Pet. 2.

These are spots which of your kindness feast together, without fear, feeding **E** themselves. Clouds they are without water, carried about of winds, and trees without fruit at gathering time, twice dead and plucked up by the roots. They are the raging waves of the sea, foaming out their own shame. They are wandering stars to whom is reserved the mist of darkness for ever.

Rev. 1. b.

Enoch the seventh from Adam prophesied before of such, saying: Behold, the Lord shall come with thousands of saints, to give judgement against all men, and to rebuke all that are ungodly among them, of all their ungodly deeds, which they have ungodly committed, and of all their cruel speakings, which ungodly sinners have spoken against him.

F   These are murmurers, complainers, walking after their own lusts, whose mouths speak proud things. They have men in great reverence because of advantage. But ye beloved, remember the words which were spoken before of the apostles of our Lord Jesus Christ, how that they told you that there should be beguilers in the last time, which should walk after their own ungodly lusts. These are makers of sects fleshly, having no spirit.

1 Tim. 3.
2 Tim. 3.
2 Pet. 3.

G   But ye dearly beloved, edify yourselves in your most holy faith, praying in the holy ghost, and keep yourselves in the love of God, looking for the mercy of our Lord Jesus Christ, unto eternal life. And have compassion on some, separating them: and other save with fear, pulling them out of the fire, and hate the filthy vesture of the flesh.

Unto him that is able to keep you, that ye fall not, and to present you faultless before the presence of his glory with joy, that is to say, to God our saviour which only is wise, be glory, majesty, dominion, and power, now and for ever. Amen.

Hereafter followeth the Apocalypse.

THE REVELATION OF
ST JOHN THE DIVINE

CHAPTER ONE   **A**

The revelation of Jesus Christ, which God gave unto him, for to show unto his servants things which must shortly come to pass. + And he sent and showed by his angel unto his servant John, which bare record of the word of God, and of the testimony of Jesus Christ, and of all things that he saw. Happy is he that readeth, and they that hear the words of the prophecy, and keep those things which are written therein. For the time is at hand.

The seven churches in Asia.

John to the seven congregations in Asia. Grace be with you and peace, from **B** him which is and which was, and which is to come, and from the seven spirits which are present before his throne, and from Jesus Christ which is a faithful witness, and first begotten of the dead: and Lord over the kings of the earth. Unto him that loved us and washed us from sins in his own blood, + and made us kings and priests unto God his father, be glory, and dominion for ever more. Amen. Behold he cometh with clouds, and all eyes shall see him: and they also which pierced him. And all kindreds of the earth shall wail. Even so. Amen. I am Alpha and Omega, the beginning and the ending, saith the Lord almighty, which is and which was and which is to come.

Col. 1. c.
1 Cor. 15.
Heb. 9. d.
1 Pet. 1. b.
1 John 1. d.
Isa. 3. d.
Matt. 24.
Jude 1. c.

Patmos.

I John your brother and companion in tribulation, and in the kingdom and **C** patience which is in Jesus Christ, was in the isle of Patmos for the word of God, and for the witnessing of Jesus Christ. I was in the spirit on a Sunday, and heard behind me, a great voice, as it had been of a trumpet saying: I am Alpha and Omega, the first and the last. That thou seest write in a book, and send it unto the congregations which are in Asia, unto Ephesus and unto Smyrna, and unto Pergamos, and unto Thyatira, and unto Sardis, and unto Philadelphia, and unto Laodicea.

Sunday.

Seven golden candlesticks.

And I turned back to see the voice that spake to me. And when I was turned: **D** I saw seven golden candlesticks, and in the midst of the candlesticks, one like unto the son of man clothed with a linen garment down to the ground, and girt about the paps with a golden girdle. His head, and his hairs were white, as white wool, and as snow: and his eyes were as a flame of fire: and his feet like unto brass, as though they burnt in a furnace: and his voice as the sound of many waters. And he had in his right hand seven stars. And out of his mouth went a sharp two-edged sword. And his face shone even as the sun in his strength.

Seven stars.

E   And when I saw him, I fell at his feet, even as dead. And he laid his right hand upon me, saying unto me: fear not. I am the first, and the last, and am alive, and was dead. And behold I am alive for evermore, and have the keys of hell and of death. Write therefore the things which thou hast seen, and the things which are, and the things which shall be fulfilled hereafter: and the mystery of the seven stars which thou sawest in my right hand, and the seven golden candlesticks. The seven stars are the messengers of the seven congregations: And the seven candlesticks which thou sawest are the seven congregations.

Isa. 41. b. and 44.

CHAPTER TWO

A   Unto the messenger of the congregation of Ephesus write: These things saith he that holdeth the seven stars in his right hand, and walketh in the midst of the seven golden candlesticks. I know thy works, and thy labour, and thy patience, and how thou canst not forbear them which are evil: and examinedst them which say they are apostles, and are not: and hast found them liars and didst wash thyself. And hast patience: and for my name's sake hast laboured and hast not fainted. Nevertheless I have somewhat against thee, for thou hast left thy first love. Remember therefore from whence thou art fallen, and **B** repent, and do the first works. Or else I will come unto thee shortly, and will remove thy candlestick out of his place, except thou repent. But this thou hast because thou hatest the deeds of the Nicolaitans, which deeds I also hate. Let him that hath ears hear, what the spirit saith unto the congregations. To him that overcometh, will I give to eat of the tree of life, which is in the midst of the paradise of God.

Messenger is the preacher of the congregation.

C   And unto the angel of the congregation of Smyrna write: These things saith he that is first, and the last, which was dead and is alive. I know thy works and tribulation and poverty, but thou art rich: And I know the blasphemy of them which call themselves Jews and are not: but are the congregation of Satan. Fear none of those things which thou shalt suffer. Behold, the devil shall cast of you into prison, to tempt you, and ye shall have tribulation ten days. Be faithful unto the death and I will give thee a crown of life. Let him that hath ears hear, what the spirit saith to the congregations: He that overcometh shall not be hurt of the second death.

The congregation of Smyrna.

D   And to the messenger of the congregation in Pergamos write: This saith he which hath the sharp sword with two edges. I know thy works and where thou dwellest, even where Satan's seat is, and thou keepest my name and hast not denied my faith. And in my days Antipas was a faithful witness of mine, which was slain among you where Satan dwelleth. But I have a few things against thee: that thou hast there, they that maintain the doctrine of Balaam which taught in Balak,†† to put occasion of sin before the children of Israel, that they should eat of meat dedicated unto idols, and to commit fornication. Even so hast thou them that maintain the doctrine of the Nicolaitans, which thing I hate. But be converted or else I will come unto thee shortly and will fight

The congregation of Pergamos.

Num. 24.

against them with the sword of my mouth. Let him that hath ears hear what the spirit saith unto the congregations: To him that overcometh will I give to eat manna that is hid, and will give him a white stone, and in the stone a new name written, which no man knoweth, saving he that receiveth it.

And unto the messenger of the congregation of Thyatira write: This saith the   **E** son of God, which hath his eyes like unto a flame of fire, whose feet are like brass: I know thy works and thy love, service, and faith, and thy patience, and thy deeds, which are more at the last than at the first. Notwithstanding I have few things against thee, that thou sufferest that woman Jezebel, which called   **F** herself a prophetess to teach and to deceive my servants, to make them commit

fornication, and to eat meats offered up unto idols. And I gave her space to repent of her fornication and she repented not. Behold I will cast her into a bed, and them that commit fornication with her into great adversity, except they turn from their deeds. And I will kill her children with death. And all the congregations shall know that I am he which searcheth the reins and hearts.

And I will give unto every one of you according unto your works.

Unto you I say, and unto other of them of Thyatira as many as have not this   **G** learning and which have not known the deepness of Satan (as they say) I will put upon you none other burden, but that which ye have already. Hold fast till I come, and whosoever overcometh and keepeth my works unto the end, to

him will I give power over nations, and he shall rule them with a rod of iron: and as the vessels of a potter, shall he break them to shivers. Even as I received of my father, even so will I give him the morning star. Let him that hath ears hear what the spirit saith to the congregations.

CHAPTER THREE

And write unto the messenger of the congregation of Sardis: this saith he that   **A** hath the spirit of God, and the seven stars. I know thy works, thou hast a name that thou livest, and thou art dead. Be awake and strengthen the things which remain, that are ready to die. For I have not found thy works perfect before God. Remember therefore how thou hast received and heard, and hold fast,

and repent. If thou shalt not watch, I will come on thee as a thief, and thou shalt not know what hour I will come upon thee. Thou hast a few names in Sardis, which have not defiled their garments: and they shall walk with me in white, for they are worthy. He that overcometh shall be clothed in white array, and I will not put out his name out of the book of life, and I will confess his name before my father, and before his angels. Let him that hath ears hear what the spirit saith unto the congregations.

And write unto the tidings-bringer of the congregation of Philadelphia: this   **B**

saith he that is holy and true, which hath the key of David: which openeth and no man shutteth, and shutteth and no man openeth. I know thy works. Behold I have set before thee an open door, and no man can shut it, for thou hast a little strength and hast kept my sayings: and hast not denied my name. Behold I make them of the congregation of Satan, which call themselves Jews and are not, but do lie: Behold: I will make them that they shall come and worship before thy feet: and shall know that I love thee.

D   Because thou hast kept the words of my patience, therefore I will keep thee from the hour of temptation, which will come upon all the world, to tempt them that dwell upon the earth. Behold I come shortly. Hold that which thou hast, that no man take away thy crown. Him that overcometh, will I make a pillar in the temple of my God, and he shall go no more out. And I will write upon him, the name of my God, and the name of the city of my God, new Jerusalem, which cometh down out of heaven from my God, and I will write upon him my new name. Let him that hath ears hear, what the spirit saith unto the congregations.

A   And unto the messenger of the congregation which is in Laodicea write: This saith (amen) the faithful and true witness, the beginning of the creatures of God. I know thy works that thou art neither cold nor hot: I would thou were cold or hot. So then because thou art between both, and neither cold nor hot, I will spew thee out of my mouth: because thou sayst thou art rich and increased with goods and hast need of nothing, and knowest not how thou art wretched **B** and miserable, poor, blind, and naked. I counsel thee to buy of me gold tried in the fire, that thou mayst be rich, and white raiment, that thou mayst be clothed, that thy filthy nakedness do not appear: and anoint thine eyes with eye-salve, that thou mayst see.

The congregation of Laodicea.

D   As many as I love, I rebuke and chasten. Be fervent therefore and repent. Behold I stand at the door and knock. If any man hear my voice and open the door, I will come in unto him and will sup with him, and he with me. To him that overcometh will I grant to sit with me in my seat, even as I overcame and have sitten with my father, in his seat. Let him that hath ears hear what the spirit saith unto the congregations.

Whom God loveth them he chasteneth.

CHAPTER FOUR

A   + After this I looked, and behold a door was open in heaven, and the first voice which I heard, was as it were of a trumpet talking with me, which said: come up hither, and I will show thee things which must be fulfilled hereafter. And immediately I was in the spirit: and behold a seat was put in heaven and one **B** sat on the seat. And he that sat was to look upon like unto a jasper stone, and a sardine stone: And there was a rainbow about the seat, in sight like to an emerald. And about the seat were twenty-four seats. And upon the seats twenty-four elders sitting clothed in white raiment, and had on their heads crowns of gold.

Rainbow.

And out of the seat proceeded lightnings, and thunderings, and voices, and there were seven lamps of fire, burning before the seat, which are the seven spirits of God. And before the seat there was a sea of glass like unto crystal, and in the midst of the seat, and round about the seat, were four beasts full of eyes

Seven lamps.

Four beasts.

373

before and behind. And the first beast was like a lion, the second beast like a **C**
calf, and the third beast had a face as a man and the fourth beast was like a flying
eagle. And the four beasts had each one of them six wings about him, and they
were full of eyes within. And they had no rest day neither night saying: holy,
holy, holy, Lord God almighty, which was, and is, and is to come.

And when those beasts gave glory and honour and thanks to him that sat on **D**
the seat which liveth for ever and ever: the twenty-four elders fell down before
him that sat on the throne, and worshipped him that liveth for ever, ⊦ and cast
their crowns before the throne saying: thou art worthy Lord to receive glory,
and honour, and power, for thou hast created all things, and for thy will's sake
they are, and were created.

CHAPTER FIVE

The book sealed with
seven seals.

And I saw in the right hand of him, that sat in the throne, a book written **A**
within and on the backside, sealed with seven seals. And I saw a strong angel
which cried with a loud voice: Who is worthy to open the book, and to loose
the seals thereof? And no man in heaven nor in earth, neither under the earth,
was able to open the book, neither to look thereon. And I wept much, because
no man was found worthy to open and to read the book, neither to look
thereon.

A lion obtained to open
the book.

And one of the elders said unto me: weep not: Behold a lion being of the **B**
tribe of Juda, the root of David, hath obtained to open the book, and to loose
the seven seals thereof.

And I beheld, and lo, in the midst of the seat, and of the four beasts, and in
the midst of the elders, stood a lamb as though he had been killed, which had
seven horns and seven eyes, which are the spirits of God, sent into all the
world. And he came and took the book out of the right hand of him that sat
upon the seat.

And when he had taken the book, the four beasts and twenty-four elders fell
down before the lamb, having harps and golden vials full of odours which are
the prayers of saints and they sang a new song saying: thou art worthy to take
the book and to open the seals thereof: for thou wast killed and hast redeemed
us by thy blood, out of all kindreds, and tongues, and people, and nations, and
hast made us unto our God, kings and priests and we shall reign on the earth.

And I beheld, and I heard the voice of many angels about the throne, and **D**
about the beasts and the elders, and I heard thousand thousands, saying with a
Dan. 7. c.   loud voice: Worthy is the lamb that was killed to receive power, and riches and
wisdom, and strength, and honour and glory, and blessing. And all creatures,
which are in heaven, and on the earth, and under the earth, and in the sea, and
all that are in them heard I saying: blessing, honour, glory, and power, be unto
him, that sitteth upon the seat, and unto the lamb for evermore. And the four
beasts said: Amen. And the twenty-four elders fell upon their faces, and worshipped him that liveth for evermore.

CHAPTER SIX

A   And I saw when the lamb opened one of the seals, and I heard one of the four The lamb opened
the seals.
beasts say, as it were the noise of thunder, come and see. And I saw, and behold
there was a white horse, and he that sat on him had a bow, and a crown was
given unto him, and he went forth conquering and for to overcome. And when
he opened the second seal, I heard the second beast say: come and see. And
there went out another horse that was red, and power was given to him that sat
thereon, to take peace from the earth, and that they should kill one another.
And there was given unto him a great sword.

B   And when he opened the third seal, I heard the third beast say: come and see.
And I beheld, and lo, a black horse: and he that sat on him, had a pair of
balances in his hand. And I heard a voice in the midst of the four beasts say: a
measure of wheat for a penny, and three measures of barley for a penny: and oil
and wine see thou hurt not.

C   And when he opened the fourth seal, I heard the voice of the fourth beast say:
come and see. And I looked: and behold a green horse, and his name that sat on
him was death, and hell followed after him, and power was given unto them
over the fourth part of the earth, to kill with sword, and with hunger, and with
death, that cometh of vermin of the earth.

D   And when he opened the fifth seal, I saw under the altar, the souls of them
that were killed for the word of God, and for the testimony which they had,
and they cried with a loud voice saying: How long tarriest thou Lord holy and
true, to judge and to avenge our blood on them that dwell on the earth? And
long white garments were given unto every one of them. And it was said unto
them that they should rest for a little season until the number of their fellows, *Isa. 2. b.*
Hos. 10. b.
Luke 23.
and brethren, and of them that should be killed as they were, were fulfilled.

D   And I beheld when he opened the sixth seal, and lo there was a great earthquake and the sun was as black as sack-cloth made of hair. And the moon
waxed even as blood: and the stars of heaven fell unto the earth, even as a fig
tree casteth from her her figs, when she is shaken of a mighty wind. And
heaven vanished away, as a scroll when it is rolled together. And all mountains
and isles, were moved out of their places.

And the kings of the earth, and the great men, and the rich men, and the
chief captains, and the mighty men, and every bondman, and every free man,
hid themselves in dens, and in rocks of the hills, and said to the hills, and rocks:
fall on us, and hide us from the presence of him that sitteth on the seat, and
from the wrath of the lamb, for the great day of his wrath is come: And who
can endure it?

CHAPTER SEVEN

A   And after that I saw four angels stand on the four corners of the earth, holding
the four winds of the earth, that the winds should not blow on the earth,
neither on the sea, neither on any tree. + And I saw another angel ascend from
the rising of the sun: which had the seal of the living God, and he cried with a

loud voice to the four angels (to whom power was given to hurt the earth and the sea) saying: Hurt not the earth neither the sea, neither the trees, till we have sealed the servants of our God in their foreheads.

And I heard the number of them which were sealed, and there were sealed an **B** hundred and forty-four thousand of all the tribes of the children of Israel. Of the tribe of Juda were sealed twelve thousand. Of the tribe of Reuben were sealed twelve thousand. Of the tribe of Gad were sealed twelve thousand. Of the tribe of Aser were sealed twelve thousand. Of the tribe of Nephtalim were sealed twelve thousand. Of the tribe of Manasses were sealed twelve thousand. Of the tribe of Simeon were sealed twelve thousand. Of the tribe of Levi were sealed twelve thousand. Of the tribe of Issachar were sealed twelve thousand. Of the tribe of Zabulon were sealed twelve thousand. Of the tribe of Joseph were sealed twelve thousand. Of the tribe of Benjamin were sealed twelve thousand.

After this I beheld, and lo a great multitude (which no man could number) of **C** all nations and people, and tongues, stood before the seat, and before the lamb, clothed with long white garments, and palms in their hands, and cried with a loud voice, saying: salvation be ascribed to him that sitteth upon the seat of our God, and unto the lamb. And all the angels stood in the compass of the seat, and of the elders and of the four beasts, and fell before the seat on their faces, and worshipped God, saying, amen: Blessing and glory, wisdom and thanks, and honour, and power and might, be unto our God for evermore, Amen. ⊢

And one of the elders answered, saying unto me: what are these which are **D** arrayed in long white garments, and whence came they? And I said unto him: Lord thou wottest. And he said unto me: these are they which came out of great tribulation and made their garments large and made them white in the blood of the lamb: therefore are they in the presence of the seat of God and serve him day and night in his temple, and he that sitteth in the seat will dwell among them. They shall hunger no more neither thirst, neither shall the sun light on them, neither any heat: For the lamb which is in the midst of the seat shall feed them, and shall lead them unto fountains of living water, and God shall wipe away all tears from their eyes.

CHAPTER EIGHT

And when he had opened the seventh seal, there was silence in heaven about **A** the space of half an hour. And I saw angels standing before God, and to them were given seven trumpets. And another angel came and stood before the altar having a golden censer, and much of odours was given unto him, that he should offer of the prayers of all saints upon the golden altar, which wax before the seat. And the smoke of the odours which came of the prayers of all saints, ascended up before God out of the angel's hand. And the angel took the censer and filled it with fire of the altar and cast it into the earth, and voices were made, and thunderings and lightnings, and earthquake.

† That is, in the woodcuts which illustrate Revelation in Tyndale's volume.

And the seven angels which had the seven trumpets prepared themselves to blow. The first angel blew, and there was made hail and fire, which were mingled with blood, and they were cast into the earth: and the third part of trees was burnt, and all green grass was burnt. And the second angel blew: and

C as it were a great mountain burning with fire was cast in to the sea, and the third part of the sea turned to blood, and the third part of the creatures which had life, died, and the third part of ships were destroyed.

And the third angel blew, and there fell a great star from heaven burning as it were a lamp, and it fell into the third part of the rivers, and into fountains of waters, and the name of the star is called wormwood. And the third part was

D turned to wormwood. And many men died of the waters because they were made bitter. And the fourth angel blew, and the third part of the sun was smitten and the third part of the moon, and the third part of stars: so that the third part of them was darkened. And the day was smitten that the third part of it should not shine, and likewise the night. And I beheld and heard an angel flying through the midst of heaven, saying with a loud voice: Woe, woe to the inhabiters of the earth because of the voices to come of the trumpet of the three angels which were yet to blow.

CHAPTER NINE

A And the fifth angel blew, and I saw a star fall from heaven unto the earth. And to him was given the key of the bottomless pit. And he opened the bottomless pit, and there arose the smoke of a great furnace. And the sun, and the air were darkened by the reason of the smoke of the pit. And there came out of the smoke locusts upon the earth: and unto them was given power as the scorpions of the earth have power. And it hurt [not] the grass of the earth: neither any green thing: neither any tree: but only those men which have not the seal in their foreheads, and to them was commanded that they should not kill them, but that they should be vexed five months, and their pain was as the pain that cometh of a scorpion, when he hath stung a man. And in those days shall men *Isa. 2. d.* seek death, and shall not find it, and shall desire to die, and death shall fly from *Hos. 10. b.* *Luke 23.* them. *Wisdom 16.*

B And the similitude of the locusts was like unto horses prepared unto battle, and on their heads were as it were crowns, like unto gold: and their faces were as it had been the faces of men. And they had hair as the hair of women. And their teeth were as the teeth of lions. And they had habergeons, as it were habergeons of iron. And the sound of their wings, was as the sound of chariots when many horses run together to battle. And they had tails like unto scorpions, and there were stings in their tails. And their power was to hurt men five months. And they had a king over them, which is the angel of the bottomless pit, whose name in the Hebrew tongue, is Abaddon: but in the *Abaddon is as much as* Greek tongue, Apollyon. One woe is past, and behold two woes come after *to say a destroyer.* this.

C And the sixth angel blew, and I heard a voice from the four corners of the golden altar which is before God, saying to the sixth angel, which had the trumpet: Loose four angels, which are bound in the great river Euphrates. And the four angels were loosed which were prepared for an hour, for a day, for a month, and for a year, for to slay the third part of men. And the number of horsemen of war, were twenty times ten thousand. And I heard the number of them. And thus I saw the horses in a vision and them that sat on them having fiery habergeons of a jacinth colour, and brimstone, and the heads of the horses were as the heads of lions. And out of their mouths went forth fire and smoke, and brimstone. And of these three was the third part of men killed: that is to say, of fire, smoke, and brimstone, which proceeded out of the mouths of them: For their power was in their mouths and in their tails: for their tails were like unto serpents, and had heads, and with them they did hurt: And the remnant of the men which were not killed by these plagues, repented not of the deeds of their hands that they should not worship devils, and images of gold, and silver, and brass, and stone, and of wood, which neither can see, neither hear, neither go. Also they repented not of their murder, and of their sorcery neither of their fornication neither of their theft.

CHAPTER TEN

And I saw another mighty angel come down from heaven, clothed with a   **A**
cloud, and the rainbow upon his head. And his face as it were the sun, and his feet as it were pillars of fire and he had in his hand a little book open: and he put his right foot upon the sea, and his left foot on the earth. And cried with a loud voice, as when a lion roareth. And when he had cried, seven thunders spake their voices. And when the seven thunders had spoken their voices, I was about to write. And I heard a voice from heaven saying unto me, seal up those

Dan. 12. c.   things which the seven thunders spake, and write them not.

And the angel which I saw stand upon the sea, and upon the earth, lifted up   **B**
his hand to heaven, and sware by him that liveth for evermore, which created heaven, and the things that therein are, and the sea, and the things which therein are: that there should be no longer time: but in the days of the voice of the seventh angel, when he shall begin to blow: even the mystery of God shall be finished as he preached by his servants the prophets.

And the voice which I heard from heaven spake unto me again, and said: go   **C**
and take the little book which is open in the hand of the angel, which standeth upon the sea, and upon the earth. And I went unto the angel, and said to him: give me the little book, and he said unto me: take it, and eat it up, and it shall

Ezek. 3. c.   make thy belly bitter, but it shall be in thy mouth as sweet as honey. And I
took the little book out of his hand, and ate it up, and it was in my mouth   **D**
as sweet as honey, and as soon as I had eaten it, my belly was bitter. And he said unto me: thou must prophesy again among the people, and nations, and tongues, and to many kings.

CHAPTER ELEVEN

And then was given me a reed like unto a rod, and it was said unto me: Rise and   **A**
mete the temple of God, and the altar, and them that worship therein and the

choir which is within the temple cast out and mete it not: for it is given unto the gentiles and the holy city shall they tread under foot forty-two months. And I will give power unto my two witnesses, and they shall prophesy one thousand three hundred and sixty days, clothed in sackcloth. These are two olive trees, and two candlesticks, standing before the God of the earth.

B   And if any man will hurt them, fire shall proceed out of their mouths, and consume their enemies. And if any man will hurt them this wise must he be killed. These have power to shut heaven, that it rain not in the days of their prophesying: and have power over waters to turn them to blood, and to smite the earth with all manner plagues, as often as they will.

And when they have finished their testimony, the beast that came out of the bottomless pit shall make war against them and shall overcome them, and kill them. And their bodies shall lie in the streets of the great city, which spiritually is called Sodom and Eygpt, where our Lord was crucified. And they of the people and kindreds, and tongues, and they of the nations, shall see their bodies three days and an half, and shall not suffer their bodies to be put in graves. And they that dwell upon the earth, shall rejoice over them and be glad, and shall send gifts one to another for these two prophets vexed them that dwelt on the earth.

C   And after three days and an half the spirit of life from God, entered into them. And they stood up upon their feet: and great fear came upon them which saw them. And they heard a great voice from heaven, saying unto them. Come up hither. And they ascended up into heaven in a cloud, and their enemies saw them. And the same hour was there a great earthquake, and the tenth part of the city fell, and in the earthquake were slain names of men seven thousand and the remnant were feared, and gave glory to God of heaven. The second woe is past, and behold the third woe will come anon.

D   And the seventh angel blew, and there were made great voices in heaven, saying: the kingdoms of this world are our Lord's and his Christ's, and he shall reign for evermore. And the twenty-four elders, which sit before God on their seats, fell upon their faces, and worshipped God saying: we give thee thanks Lord God almighty: which art and wast, and art to come, for thou hast received thy great might, and hast reigned. And the nations were angry, and thy wrath is come, and the time of the dead that they should be judged and that thou shouldest give reward unto thy servants the prophets and saints, and to them that fear thy name small and great and shouldest destroy them, which destroy the earth. And the temple of God was opened in heaven, and there was seen in his temple, the ark of his testament: and there followed lightnings, and voices, and thunderings and earthquake, and much hail.

CHAPTER TWELVE

A   And there appeared a great wonder in heaven. A woman clothed with the sun, and the moon under her feet, and upon her head a crown of twelve stars. And she was with child and cried travailing in birth, and pained ready to be delivered. And there appeared another wonder in heaven, for behold a great red dragon, having seven heads, and ten horns and crowns upon his heads: and his tail drew the third part of the stars, and cast them to the earth.

And the dragon stood before the woman which was ready to be delivered: **B** for to devour her child as soon as it were born. And she brought forth a man child, which should rule all nations with a rod of iron. And her son was taken up unto God, and to his seat. And the woman fled into wilderness, where she had a place, prepared of God, that they should feed her there one thousand two hundred and sixty days.

And there was great battle in heaven, Michael and his angels fought with the dragon and the dragon fought and his angels, and prevailed not: neither was their place found any more in heaven. And the great dragon, that old serpent called the devil and Satan was cast out. Which deceiveth all the world. And he was cast into the earth, and his angels were cast out also.

And İ heard a loud voice saying: in heaven is now made salvation and **C** strength and the kingdom of our God, and the power of his Christ. For he is cast down which accused them before God day and night. And they overcame him by the blood of the lamb, and by the word of their testimony, and they loved not their lives unto the death. Therefore rejoice heavens, and ye that dwell in them.

Woe to the inhabiters of the earth, and of the sea: for the devil is come down unto you which hath great wrath, because he knoweth that he hath but a short time.

And when the dragon saw, that he was cast unto the earth, he persecuted the **D** woman which brought forth the man child. And to the woman were given two wings of a great eagle, that she might fly into the wilderness, into her place, where she is nourished for a time, times, and half a time, from the presence of the serpent. And the dragon cast out of his mouth water after the woman as it had been a river because she should have been caught of the flood. And the earth helped the woman, and the earth opened her mouth, and swallowed up the river which the dragon cast out of his mouth. And the dragon was wroth with the woman: and went and made war with the remnant of her seed, which keep the commandments of God, and have the testimony of Jesus Christ. And I stood on the sea sand.

CHAPTER THIRTEEN

And I saw a beast rise out of the sea, having seven heads, and ten horns, and **A** upon his horns ten crowns, and upon his head, the name of blasphemy. And the beast which I saw, was like a cat of the mountain, and his feet were as the feet of a bear, and his mouth as the mouth of a lion. And the dragon gave him his power and his seat, and great authority: and I saw one of his heads as it were wounded to death, and his deadly wound was healed. And all the world wondered at the beast, and they worshipped the dragon which gave power unto the beast, and they worshipped the beast saying: who is like unto the beast? who is able to war with him?

B   And there was a mouth given unto him that spake great things and blasphemies, and power was given unto him, to do forty-two months. And he opened his mouth unto blasphemy against God, to blaspheme his name, and his tabernacle and them that dwell in heaven. And it was given unto him to make war with the saints, and to overcome them. And power was given him over all kindred, tongue, and nation: and all that dwell upon the earth worshipped him: whose names are not written in the book of life of the lamb, which was killed from the beginning of the world. If any man have an ear, let him hear. He that leadeth into captivity, shall go into captivity: he that killeth with a sword, must be killed with a sword. Here is the patience, and the faith of the saints.

C   And I beheld another beast coming up out of the earth, and he had two horns like a lamb, and he spake as did the dragon. And he did all that the first beast could do in his presence, and he caused the earth, and them which dwell therein, to worship the first beast, whose deadly wound was healed. And he did great wonders, so that he made fire come down from heaven in the sight of men. And deceived them that dwelt on the earth by the means of those signs which he had power to do in the sight of the beast, saying to them that dwelt on the earth: that they should make an image unto the beast, which had the wound of a sword, and did live.

Gen. 9. a.
Matt. 26.

D   And he had power to give a spirit unto the image of the beast, and that the image of the beast should speak, and should cause that as many as would not worship the image of the beast, should be killed. And he made all both small and great, rich and poor, free and bond, to receive a mark in their right hands, or in their foreheads. And that no man might buy or sell, save he that had the mark, or the name of the beast, or the number of his name. Here is wisdom. Let him that hath wit count the number of the beast. For it is the number of a man, and his number is six hundred, three score and six.

CHAPTER FOURTEEN

A   + And I looked, and lo a lamb stood on the mount Sion, and with him a hundred and forty-four thousand having his father's name written in their foreheads. And I heard a voice from heaven, as the sound of many waters, and as the voice of a great thunder, And I heard the voice of harpers harping with their harps. And they sang as it were a new song, before the seat, and before the four beasts, and the elders, and no man could learn that song, but the hundred and forty-four thousand which were redeemed from the earth. These are they, which were not defiled with women, for they are virgins. These follow the lamb whithersoever he goeth. These were redeemed from men being the first fruits unto God and to the lamb, and in their mouths was found no guile. For they are without spot before the throne of God. +

E   And I saw an angel fly in the midst of heaven having an everlasting gospel, to preach unto them that sit and dwell on the earth, and to all nations, kindreds, and tongues and people saying with a loud voice: Fear God and give honour

Psa. 46.
Acts 14.
Isa. 16.
Jer. 51. a.

to him, for the hour of his judgement is come: and worship him, that made heaven and earth, and the sea, and fountains of water. And there followed another angel, saying: Babylon is fallen, is fallen, that great city, for she made all nations drink of the wine of her fornication.

And the third angel followed them saying with a loud voice: If any man worship the beast and his image, and receive his mark in his forehead, or on his hand, the same shall drink of the wine of the wrath of God which is poured in the cup of his wrath. And he shall be punished in fire and brimstone, before the holy angels, and before the lamb.

And the smoke of their torment ascendeth up evermore. And they have no rest day nor night, which worship the beast and his image, and whosoever receiveth the print of his name. Here is the patience of saints. Here are they that keep the commandments and the faith of Jesus.

And I heard a voice from heaven saying unto me: write: Blessed are the dead, which hereafter die in the Lord, even so saith the spirit: that they may rest from their labours, but their works shall follow them. And I looked and behold a white cloud, and upon the cloud one sitting like unto the son of man, having on his head a golden crown, and in his hand a sharp sickle. And another angel came out of the temple, crying with a loud voice to him that sat on the cloud. Thrust in thy sickle and reap: for the time is come to reap, for the corn of the earth is ripe. And he that sat on the cloud thrust in his sickle on the earth, and the earth was reaped.

Joel. 3. c.

And another angel came out of the temple, which is in heaven, having also a sharp sickle. And another angel came out from the altar, which had power over fire, and cried with a loud cry to him that had the sharp sickle, and said: thrust in thy sharp sickle, and gather the clusters of the earth for her grapes are ripe. And the angel thrust in his sickle on the earth, and cut down the grapes of the vineyard of the earth: and cast them into the great wine-vat of the wrath of God, and the wine-vat was trodden without the city, and blood came out of the vat, even unto the horse bridles by the space of a thousand and six hundred furlongs.

CHAPTER FIFTEEN

And I saw another sign in heaven great and marvellous, seven angels having the seven last plagues, for in them is fulfilled the wrath of God. And I saw as it were a glassy sea, mingled with fire, and them that had gotten victory of the beast, and of his image, and of his mark, and of the number of his name stand on the glassy sea, having the harps of God, and they sang the song of Moses the servant of God, and the song of the lamb, saying, Great and marvellous are thy works Lord God almighty, just and true are thy ways, king of saints. Who shall not fear o Lord, and glorify thy name? For thou only art holy, and all gentiles shall come and worship before thee, for thy judgements are made manifest.

Jer. 10.

And after that, I looked, and behold the temple of the tabernacle of testimony was open in heaven, and the seven angels came out of the temple, which had the seven plagues, clothed in pure and bright linen, and having their breasts girded with golden girdles. And one of the four beasts gave unto the seven angels seven golden vials, full of the wrath of God which liveth for ever more. And the temple was full of the smoke of the glory of God, and of his power, and no man was able to enter into the temple, till the seven plagues of the seven angels were fulfilled.

CHAPTER SIXTEEN

A And I heard a great voice out of the temple saying to the seven angels: go your ways, pour out your vials of wrath upon the earth. And the first went, and poured out his vial upon the earth, and there fell a noisome and a sore botch upon the man which had the mark of the beast, and upon them which **B** worshipped his image. And the second angel shed out his vial upon the sea, and it turned as it were into the blood of a dead man: and every living thing died in the sea. And the third angel shed out his vial upon the rivers and fountains of waters, and they turned to blood. And I heard an angel say: Lord which art and wast, thou art righteous and holy, because thou hast given such judgements, for they shed out the blood of saints, and prophets, and therefore hast thou given them blood to drink: for they are worthy. And I heard another out of the altar say: even so Lord God almighty, true and righteous are thy judgements.

C   And the fourth angel poured out his vial on the sun, and power was given unto him to vex men with heat of fire. And the men raged in great heat, and spake evil of the name of God which had power over those plagues, and they repented not, to give him glory. And the fifth angel poured out his vial upon the seat of the beast, and his kingdom waxed dark, and they gnawed their tongues for sorrow, and blasphemed the God of heaven for sorrow, and pain of their sores, and repented not of their deeds.

D   And the sixth angel poured out his vial upon the great river Euphrates, and the water dried up, that the ways of the kings of the east should be prepared. And I saw three unclean spirits like frogs come out of the mouth of the dragon, and out of the mouth of the beast, and out of the mouth of the false prophet. For they are the spirits of devils working miracles, to go out unto the kings of the earth and of the whole world to gather them to the battle of that great day of God almighty. Behold I come as a thief. Happy is he that watcheth and keepeth his garments, lest he be found naked, and men see his filthiness. And he gathered them together into a place called in the Hebrew tongue Armageddon.

Matt. 24.
Luke 12. e.
1 Cor. 5. a.

E   And the seventh angel poured out his vial into the air. And there came a voice out of heaven from the seat, saying: it is done. And there followed voices, thunderings, and lightnings, and there was a great earthquake, such as was not since men were upon the earth, so mighty an earthquake and so great. And the great city was divided into the three parts, And the cities of nations fell. And great Babylon came in remembrance before God, to give unto her the cup of wine of the fierceness of his wrath. Every isle fled away, and the mountains were not found. And there fell a great hail, as it had been talents, out of heaven upon the men, and the men blasphemed God, because of the plague of the hail, for it was great and the plague of it sore.

CHAPTER SEVENTEEN

And there came one of the seven angels, which had the seven vials, and talked   **A** with me, saying unto me: come I will shew thee the judgement of the great whore that sitteth upon many waters, with whom have committed fornication the kings of the earth, so that the inhabiters of the earth, are drunken with the wine of her fornication. And he carried me away into the wilderness in the spirit.

And I saw a woman sit upon a rose-coloured beast full of names of blasphemy which had ten horns. And the woman was arrayed in purple and rose-colour, and decked with gold, precious stone, and pearls, and had a cup of gold in her hand, full of abominations and filthiness of her fornication. And in   **B** her forehead was a name written, a mystery, great Babylon the mother of whoredom, and abominations of the earth. And I saw the wife drunk with the blood of saints, and with the blood of the witnesses of Jesus. And when I saw her, I wondered with great marvel.

And the angel said unto me: wherefore marvellest thou? I will shew thee the mystery of the woman, and of the beast that beareth her, which hath seven heads, and ten horns. The beast that thou seest, was, and is not, and shall ascend out of the bottomless pit, and shall go into perdition, and they that dwell on the earth shall wonder (whose names are not written in the book of life from he beginning of the world) when they behold the beast that was, and is not. And here is a mind that hath wisdom.

The seven heads are seven mountains, on which the woman sitteth: they are   **C** also seven kings. Five are fallen, and one is, and another is not yet come. When he cometh he must continue a space. And the beast that was, and is not, is even the eighth, and is one of the seven, and shall go into destruction. And the ten horns which thou seest, are ten kings, which have received no kingdom, but shall receive power as kings at one hour with the beast. These have one mind, and shall give their power and strength unto the beast. These shall fight with the lamb, and the lamb shall overcome them: For he is lord of lords, and king of kings: and they that are on his side, are called, and chosen and faithful.

And he said unto me: the waters which thou sawest, where the whore   **D** sitteth, are people, and folk, and nations, and tongues. And the ten horns, which thou sawest upon the beast, are they that shall hate the whore, and shall make her desolate, and naked, and shall eat their†† flesh, and burn her with fire. For God hath put in their hearts, to fulfil his will, and to do with one consent, for to give her kingdom unto the beast, until the words of God be fulfilled. And the woman which thou sawest, is that great city, which reigneth over the kings of the earth.

CHAPTER EIGHTEEN

A And after that I saw another angel come from heaven, having great power, and the earth was lightened with his brightness. And he cried mightily with a strong voice saying: Great Babylon is fallen, is fallen, and is become the habitation of devils, and the hold of all foul spirits, and a cage of all unclean and hateful birds for all nations have drunken of the wine of the wrath of her fornication. And the kings of the earth have committed fornication with her, and her merchants are waxed rich of the abundance of her pleasures.

B   And I heard another voice from heaven say: come away from her my people, that ye be not partakers in her sins, that ye receive not of her plagues. For her sins are gone up to heaven, and God hath remembered her wickedness. Reward her even as she rewarded you, and give her double according to her works. And pour in double to her in the same cup which she filled unto you. And as much as she glorified herself and lived wantonly, so much pour ye in for her of punishment, and sorrow, for she said in her heart: I sit being a queen and am no widow and shall see no sorrow. Therefore shall her plagues come at one day, *Isa. 47. b.* death, and sorrow, and hunger, and she shall be burnt with fire: for strong is the Lord God which judgeth her.

C   And the kings of the earth shall beweep her and wail over her, which have committed fornication with her, and have lived wantonly with her, when they shall see the smoke of her burning, and shall stand afar off, for fear of her punishment, saying: Alas, Alas, that great city Babylon, that mighty city: For at one hour is her judgment come.

   And the merchants of the earth shall weep and wail in themselves, for no man will buy their ware any more, the ware of gold, and silver, and precious D stones, neither of pearl, and raynes, and purple, and scarlet, and all thyne wood, and all manner vessels of ivory, and all manner vessels of most precious wood, and of brass, and of iron, and cinnamon, and odours, and ointments, and frankincense, and wine, and oil, and fine flour, and wheat, beasts, and sheep, and horses, and chariots, and bodies and souls of men.

E   And the apples that thy soul lusted after, are departed from thee. And all things which were dainty, and had in price are departed from thee, and thou shalt find them no more. The merchants of these things which were waxed rich shall stand afar off from her, for fear of the punishment of her, weeping and wailing, and saying: Alas Alas, that great city, that was clothed in raynes, and purple, and scarlet, and decked with gold, and precious stone, and pearls: for at one hour so great riches is come to nought.

F   And every ship governor, and all they that occupied ships, and shipmen which work in the sea, stood afar off, and cried, when they saw the smoke of her burning, saying what city is like unto this great city? And they cast dust on their heads, and cried weeping, and wailing, and said: Alas Alas that great city wherein were made rich all that had ships in the sea, by the reason of her costliness, for at one hour is she made desolate.

   Rejoice over her thou heaven, and ye holy apostles, and prophets: for God hath given your judgement on her. And a mighty angel took up a stone like a great millstone, and cast it into the sea, saying: with such violence shall that great city Babylon be cast, and shall be found no more. And the voice of harpers, and musicians, and of pipers, and trumpeters, shall be heard no more in thee: and no craftsman, of whatsoever craft he be, shall be found any more in thee: and the sound of a mill shall be heard no more in thee, and the voice of the bridegroom and of the bride, shall be heard no more in thee: for thy merchants were the great men of the earth. And with thine enchantment were deceived all nations: and in her was found the blood of the prophets, and of the saints and of all that were slain upon the earth.

CHAPTER NINETEEN

And after that, I heard the voice of much people in heaven saying: Alleluia.   **A** Salvation and glory and honour, and power be ascribed to the Lord our God, for true and righteous are his judgements, for he hath judged the great whore, which did corrupt the earth with her fornication, and hath avenged the blood of his servants of her hand. And again they said: Alleluia. And smoke rose up for evermore. And the twenty-four elders, and the four beasts fell down, and worshipped God that sat on the seat saying: Amen Alleluia. And a voice came out of the seat, saying: praise our Lord God all ye that are his servants, and ye that fear him both small and great.

And I heard the voice of much people, even as the voice of many waters, and   **B** as the voice of strong thunderings, saying: Alleluia, for God omnipotent reigneth. Let us be glad and rejoice and give honour to him: for the marriage of the lamb is come, and his wife made herself ready. And to her was granted, that she should be arrayed with pure and goodly raynes. For the raynes is the righteousness of saints. And he said unto me: happy are they which are called unto the Lamb's supper. And he said unto me: these are the true sayings of God. And I fell at his feet, to worship him. And he said unto me: see thou do it not. For I am thy fellow servant, and one of thy brethren, and of them that have the testimony of Jesus. Worship God. For the testimony of Jesus is the spirit of prophecy. And I saw heaven open, and behold a white horse: and he that sat upon him was faithful and true, and in righteousness did judge and make battle. His eyes were as a flame of fire: and on his head were many crowns: and he had a name written, that no man knew but himself. And he was clothed with a vesture dipped in blood, and his name is called the word of God. And the warriors which were in heaven, followed him upon white horses, clothed with white and pure raynes: and out of his mouth went out a sharp sword, that with it he should smite the heathen. And he shall rule them with a rod of iron, and he trod the wine-vat of fierceness and wrath of almighty God. And hath on his vesture and on his thigh a name written: king of kings, and lord of lords.

And I saw an angel stand in the sun, and he cried with a loud voice, saying   **D** to all the fowls that fly by the midst of heaven, come and gather yourselves

Matt. 22.

Luke 14.

Isa. 63.

1 Tim. 6.

together unto the supper of the great God, that ye may eat the flesh of kings, and of high captains, and the flesh of mighty men, and the flesh of horses, and of them that sit on them, and the flesh of all free men and bond men, and of small and great. And I saw the beast and the kings of the earth, and their warriors gathered together to make battle against him that sat on the horse and against his soldiers.

And the beast was taken, and with him that false prophet that wrought miracles before him, with which he deceived them that received the beast's mark, and them that worshipped his image. These both were cast into a pond of fire burning with brimstone: and the remnant were slain with the sword of him that sat upon the horse, which sword proceeded out of his mouth, and all the fowls were full filled with their flesh.

CHAPTER TWENTY

A And I saw an angel come down from heaven, having the key of the bottomless pit, and a great chain in his hand. And he took the dragon that old serpent, which is the devil and Satan, and he bound him a thousand years: and cast him into the bottomless pit, and he bound him, and set a seal on him, that he should deceive the people no more, till the thousand years were fulfilled. And after that he must be loosed for a little season.

And I saw seats, and they sat upon them, and judgement was given unto them: and I saw the souls of them were beheaded for the witness of Jesus, and for the word of God: which had not worshipped the beast, neither his image, neither had taken his mark upon their foreheads, or on their hands: and they lived, and reigned with Christ a thousand years: but the other of the dead **B** men lived not again, until the thousand years were finished. This is that first resurrection. Blessed and holy is he that hath part in the first resurrection. For on such shall the second death have no power, for they shall be the priests of God and of Christ, and shall reign with him a thousand years.

And when the thousand years are expired, Satan shall be loosed out of his prison, and shall go out to deceive the people which are in the four quarters of the earth, Gog and Magog, to gather them together to battle, whose number is as the sand of the sea: and they went up on the plain of the earth, and **D** compassed the tents of the saints about, and the beloved city. And fire came down from God, out of heaven, and devoured them: and the devil that deceived them, was cast into a lake of fire and brimstone, where the beast and the false prophet were and shall be tormented day and night for ever more.

And I saw a great white seat and him that sat on it, from whose face fled away both the earth and heaven, and their place was no more found. And I saw the dead, both great and small stand before God: And the books were opened and another book was opened, which is the book of life, and the dead were judged of those things which were written in the books according to their deeds: and the sea gave up her dead, which were in her, and death and hell delivered up the dead, which were in them: and they were judged every man

Ezek. 38. and 39.

according to his deeds. And death and hell were cast into the lake of fire. This is that second death. And whosoever was not found written in the book of life, was cast into the lake of fire.

CHAPTER TWENTY-ONE

Isa. 65. c.
and 66.
2 Pet. 3.

And I saw a new heaven and a new earth. For the first heaven, and the first **A** earth, were vanished away, and there was no more sea. + And I John saw that holy city new Jerusalem come down from God out of heaven prepared as a bride garnished for her husband. And I heard a great voice out of heaven saying: behold, the tabernacle of God is with men, and he will dwell with them. And they shall be his people, and God himself shall be with them and be

Isa. 25.

their God. And God shall wipe away all tears from their eyes. And there shall **B** be no more death, neither sorrow neither crying, neither shall there be any more pain, for the old things are gone. And he that sat upon the seat, said: Behold I make all things new. ⊢ And he said unto me: write, for these words are

Isa. 44
2·Cor. 5.

faithful and true.

And he said unto me: it is done, I am Alpha and Omega, the beginning, and the end. I will give to him that is a-thirst of the well of the water of life free. He that overcometh shall inherit all things, and I will be his God, and he shall be my son. But the fearful and unbelieving, and the abominable, and murderers, and whoremongers, and sorcerers, and idolaters, and all liars shall have their part in the lake which burneth with fire and brimstone, which is the second death.

And there came unto me one of the seven angels which had the seven vials **C** full of the seven last plagues: and talked with me saying: come hither, I will shew thee the bride, the lamb's wife. And he carried me away in the spirit to a great and an high mountain, and he showed me the great city, holy Jerusalem descending out of heaven from God, having the brightness of God. And her shining was like unto a stone most precious, even a jasper clear as crystal: and **D** had walls great and high, and had twelve gates, and at the gates twelve angels: and names written, which are the twelve tribes of Israel: on the east part three gates, and on the north side three gates, and towards the south three gates, and from the west three gates: and the wall of the city had twelve foundations, and in them the names of the lamb's twelve apostles.

And he that talked with me, had a golden reed to measure the city withal and the gates thereof and the wall thereof. And the city was built four-square, and the length was as large as the breadth of it, and he measured the city with the reed twelve thousand furlongs: and the length and the breadth, and the height of it, were equal. And he measured the wall thereof an hundred and forty-four **E** cubits: the measure that the angel had was after the measure that man useth. And the building of the wall of it was of jasper. And the city was pure gold like unto clear glass and the foundations of the wall of the city was garnished with all manner of precious stones. The first foundation was jasper, the second **F** sapphire, the third a chalcedony, the fourth an emerald: the fifth sardonyx: the sixth sardius: the seventh chrysolite, the eighth beryl: and ninth a topaz: the tenth a chrysoprasus: the eleventh a jacinth: the twelfth an amethyst.

The twelve gates were twelve pearls, every gate was of one pearl, and the street of the city was pure gold, as through shining glass. And there was no temple therein. For the Lord God almighty and the lamb are the temple of it, and the city hath no need of the sun neither of the moon to lighten it. For the brightness of God did light it: and the lamb was the light of it. And the people which are saved shall walk in the light of it: and the kings of the earth shall bring their glory unto it. And the gates of it are not shut by day. For there shall be no night there. And there shall enter into it none unclean thing: neither whatsoever worketh abomination: or maketh lies: but they only which are written in the lamb's book of life.

G

Isa. 60. d.

CHAPTER TWENTY-TWO

A   And he shewed me a pure river of water of life clear as crystal: proceeding out of the seat of God and of the lamb. In the midst of the street of it, and on either side of the river was there wood of life: which bare twelve manner of fruits: and gave fruit every month: and the leaves of the wood served to heal the people withal. And there shall be no more curse, but the seat of God and the lamb shall be in it: and his servants shall serve him: And shall see his face, and his name shall be in their foreheads. And there shall be no night there, and they need no candle, neither light of the sun: for the lord God giveth them light, and they shall reign for evermore.

Isa. 60. d.

B   And he said unto me: these sayings are faithful, and true. And the Lord God of saints and prophets sent his angel to shew unto his servants, the things which must shortly be fulfilled. Behold I come shortly. Happy is he that keepeth the saying of the prophecy of this book. I am John which saw these things and heard them. And when I had heard and seen, I fell down, to worship before the feet of the angel which shewed me these things. And he said unto me: see thou do it not, for I am thy fellow servant and the fellow servant of thy brethren the prophets and of them which keep the saying of this book. But worship God.

C   And he said unto me: seal not the sayings of prophesy of this book. For the time is at hand. He that doth evil, let him do evil still: and he which is filthy, let him be filthy still: and he that is righteous, let him be more righteous: and he that is holy, let him be more holy. And behold I come shortly, and my reward with me, to give every man according as his deeds shall be. I am Alpha and Omega, the beginning and the end: the first and the last. Blessed are they that do his commandments, that their power may be in the tree of life, and may enter in through the gates into the city. For without shall be dogs and enchanters, and whoremongers, and murderers, and idolaters, and whosoever loveth or maketh leasings.

Isa. 41. b.

and 44.

D   I Jesus sent mine angel, to testify unto you these things in the congregations. I am the root and the generation of David and the bright morning star. And the spirit and the bride said come. And let him that heareth, say also come. And let

Isa. 55. a.   him that is a-thirst come. And let whosoever will, take of the water of life free.

I testify unto every man that heareth the words of prophecy of this book. If any man shall add unto these things, God shall add unto him the plagues that are written in this book. And if any man shall minish of the words of the book of this prophecy, God shall take away his part out of the book of life, and out of the holy city, and from those things which are written in this book. He which testifieth these things saith: be it, I come quickly, Amen. Even so: come Lord Jesus. The grace of our Lord Jesus Christ be with you all. Amen.

The end of the new testament.

THESE ARE THE EPISTLES TAKEN
OUT OF THE OLD TESTAMENT

which are read in the church after the use of Salisbury upon certain days of the year

The first Friday in Advent:
the epistle

Isaiah 51

Hearken unto me, ye that follow righteousness and seek the Lord. Look unto the rock ye were cut out, and to the cave and pit ye were digged out. Look unto Abraham your father and unto Sarah that bare you: how I called him only, and blessed him and multiplied him. For the Lord hath compassion on Sion and hath compassion on all that is decayed therein, and will make her wilderness as paradise, and her desert as the garden of the Lord. Joy and gladness shall be found therein, with thanksgiving and the voice of praise. Hearken unto me my people, and turn your ears to me my folk. There shall a law go out from me, and my judgement will I stablish to be a light unto nations. My righteousness is nigh, and my salvation shall go out, and mine arms shall judge nations, and islands shall look for me and shall tarry after mine arm. Lift up your eyes to heaven and behold the earth beneath. For heaven shall vanish away as smoke, and the earth shall wear away as a vesture, and the inhabiters thereof shall perish away after the same manner, but my salvation shall endure ever, and my righteousness shall not perish. Hearken unto me ye that know righteousness and so let the people that have my law in their hearts. Fear not the rebukes of man neither faint for their blasphemies. For worms shall eat them as a garment, and moths shall devour them as it were wool.

By my righteousness shall continue ever, and my salvation from generation to generation.

The Wednesday in the second week of Advent:
the epistle

Zechariah 8

Thus saith the Lord: I will return to Sion and will dwell in the middle of Jerusalem. And Jerusalem shall be called the city of truth and the hill of the

Lord Sabaoth and an holy hill. Thus saith the Lord Sabaoth: yet there shall sit both old men and old women in the streets of Jerusalem and men with staves in their hands for the multitude of days. And the streets of the city shall be filled with boys and wenches playing in the streets thereof. Thus saith the Lord Sabaoth, though it seem hard in the eyes of the remnant of this people, shall it seem hard in mine eyes saith the Lord Sabaoth. Thus saith the Lord Sabaoth: behold I will deliver my people from the east country and from the land of the going down of the sun, and will bring them that they shall dwell in the midst of Jerusalem. And they shall be my people, and I will be their God in truth and righteousness.

The Friday next following:
the epistle

Isaiah 62

This saith the Lord: upon the walls of Jerusalem, I have set keepers which shall never cease, neither by day nor yet by night. And ye that stir up the remembrance of the Lord, see that ye pause not, neither let him have rest until he have prepared and made Jerusalem glorious in the earth. The Lord hath sworn by his right hand and by his strong arm, that he will not give thy corn any more to be eaten of thine enemies: and that aliens shall not drink thy new wine wherefore thou hast laboured. But they that made it shall eat it and shall praise the Lord: and they that gathered it, shall drink it in the court of my holy temple. Go from gate to gate, and prepare the way for the people, cast up gravel and make the way high and cleanse it of stones, and set up a banner for the people. Behold the Lord will make it known unto the ends of the world. And say ye unto the daughter of Sion: behold he that is thy saviour cometh and his reward with him and his work before him. And they shall be called a people of holiness redeemed of the Lord. And thou shalt be called an haunted city and not forsaken.

The Friday in the third week of Advent:
the epistle

Isaiah 11

There shall come a rod out of the stock of Jesse, and a branch shall spring out of his root. And on him shall light the spirit of the Lord: the spirit of wisdom and of understanding, the spirit of counsel and of strength, the spirit of knowledge and of reverence, and it shall make him savour of the fear of the Lord. And he shall not judge after the sight of his eyes: neither shall rebuke after the hearing of his ears. But he shall judge the causes of the poor with righteousness, and shall rebuke with equity for the humble of the earth. And he shall smite the earth with the rod of his mouth, and with the breath of his lips shall slay the wicked. And righteousness shall be the girdle of his loins, and faithfulness the girdle of his reins.

On the Wednesday in the third week of Advent:
the epistle

Isaiah 2

The word that Isaiah the son of Amoz saw in a vision, concerning Judah and Jerusalem. It shall come to pass in the last days that the mount of the house of the Lord, shall be set in the top of the mountains, and shall be lifted up above the hills: and all nations shall resort thereto.

And much people shall go and say: come and let us go up to the hill of the Lord and unto the house of the God of Jacob: that he may teach us his ways, and that we may walk in his paths. For out of Sion shall come the law, and the word of God out of Jerusalem. And he shall be judge among the heathen and tell many nations their faults. And they shall turn their swords into mattocks and their spears into scythes. One nation shall not lift up a sword against another, neither shall they teach to war any more. O house of Jacob come and let us walk in the light of the Lord.

The Wednesday in the fourth week of Advent:
the epistle

Joel 2

This saith the Lord. Children of Sion be glad and rejoice in the Lord your God. For he hath given you a teacher of righteousness, and will make descend unto you the first rain and the later, as at the beginning. And the barns shall be full of corn, and the wine-presses flow with wine and oil. And I will restore you again with my great power which I have sent unto you, the years which the locusts and caterpillars have devoured. And ye shall eat and have enough and praise the name of the Lord your God, which hath wrought wonders with you. And my people shall not be in shame for ever. And ye shall know that I am in the midst of Israel, and that I am the Lord your God, and that there is no more. And my people shall not be in shame for ever. And ye shall know that I the Lord your God, dwell in Zion my holy mount. And Jerusalem shall be holy, and there shall no stranger pass through there any more. And at that day the mountains shall drop sweet wine, and the hills shall flow with milk, and all the brooks of Judah shall run with water. And a fountain, shall go out of the house of the Lord and water the river of Shittim. Egypt shall go to ruin, and Edom shall be a desert and a wilderness, which oppressed the children of Israel, and which shed innocent blood in their land. And Judah shall continue ever, and Jerusalem from generation to generation. And I will cleanse their blood which I have not cleansed. And the Lord shall dwell in Zion.

The Friday in the fourth week of Advent:
the epistle

Zechariah 2

Shout and be glad daughter of Zion for behold I come and dwell in the midst of thee saith the Lord. And many nations shall cleave unto the Lord at that day and shall be my people. And I will dwell in the middle of thee, and thou shalt know that the Lord Sabaoth hath sent me unto thee. And the Lord shall inherit Judah which is his part in the holy ground, and he shall choose Jerusalem yet again. Let all flesh hold their peace before the Lord: for he is risen out of his holy temple.

On saint John the evangelist's day:
the epistle

Ecclesiasticus 15
He that feareth God, will do good: and he that keepeth the law shall obtain wisdom: and she will come against him as an honourable mother: as a woman yet a virgin shall she receive him. She shall feed him with the bread of life and understanding: and the water of wholesome wisdom she shall give him to drink. And she shall exalt him among his neighbours: and shall open his mouth even in the thickest of the congregation. And she shall fill him with the spirit of wisdom and understanding, and with the garment of glory shall apparel him. She shall make him rich with joy and gladness and shall inherit him of an everlasting name.

The twelfth day:
the epistle

Isaiah 60
Up and receive light Jerusalem: for thy light is come, and the glory of the Lord is up over thee. For behold, darkness shall cover the earth, and a thick mist the nations. But the Lord shall rise as the sun over thee, and his glory shall be seen upon thee. And the heathen shall walk in thy light, and the kings in the brightness that is risen over thee. Lift up thine eyes round about and see. All these are gathered together and are come unto thee. Thy sons shall come from far, and thy daughters shall be ever by thy side. Then thou shalt see, and shalt have plenty: thine heart shall wonder and break out in joy, when the multitude of the sea are turned to thee, and the armies of the heathen are come unto thee. The abundance of camels shall cover thee, and the dromedaries of Midian and Ephah shall come all of them from Sheba, and bring gold and frankincense, and shall preach the praise of the Lord.

The next Sunday after the twelfth day:
the epistle

Isaiah 12
I will praise thee O Lord, that though thou were angry with me, yet thine anger is turned, and thou hast comfort me. Behold God is my salvation: I will be bold therefore and not fear. For the Lord God is my strength and my praise whereof I sing: and is become my saviour. And ye shall draw water in gladness out of the wells of salvation. And ye shall say in that day: give thanks unto the

Lord: call on his name: make his deeds known among the heathen: remember that his name is high. Lift up. Sing unto the Lord, for he hath done excellently, and that is known throughout all the world. Cry and shout thou inhabiter of Zion, for great among you is the holy of Israel.

On Ash Wednesday:
the epistle

Joel 2

And now therefore saith the Lord: Turn to me with all your hearts, in fasting and lamentation. And tear your hearts and not your garments, and turn unto the Lord your God. For he is full of mercy and compassion, long ere he be angry, and great in mercy and repenteth when he is at the point to punish. Who can tell whether the Lord will turn and have compassion and shall leave after him a blessing? Sacrifice and drink offering unto the Lord your God. Blow a trumpet in Sion, proclaim fasting and call a congregation. Gather the people together, bring the elders to one place, gather the young children and they that suck the breasts, together. Let the bridegroom come out of his chamber and the bride out of her parlour. Let the priests that minister unto the Lord, weep between the porch and the altar, and say: spare (Lord) thy people and deliver not thine inheritance unto rebuke that the heathen should reign over them. Why should they say: among the nations, where is their God? And the Lord envied for his land's sake and had compassion on his people. And the Lord answered and said unto his people Behold, I sent you corn, new wine and oil, that ye shall be satisfied therewith. Neither will I deliver you any more unto the heathen.

On the Friday next following:
the epistle

Isaiah 58

Cry with the throat and spare not. Lift up thy voice as a trumpet, and tell my people their offences and the house of Jacob their sins. For me they seek day by day, and will know my ways, as a people that doth righteousness, and hath not forsaken the equity of their God. They seek of me righteous judgements, and will draw nigh unto God. Why have we fasted and thou hast not looked upon it, have humbled our souls, and thou wouldest not wit it. Behold when ye fast, ye can find your own lusts, and can call cruelly on all your debtors. Ye fast to law and strive and to smite with fist wickedly. Fast not as ye now do, to make your voice to be heard upon high. Should it be such a manner of fast that I should chose, a day that a man should hurt his soul in? Or to bow down his head like a bulrush? Or to spread sack-cloth and ashes under him? Shouldest thou call this a fast, and a day acceptable unto the Lord? Or is not this rather the fast that I have chosen? To loose wicked bonds and to unbind bundles of oppression? And to let the bruised go free? And that ye should break all manner yokes? yea and to break the bread to the hungry, and to bring the poor that are harbourless unto house, and when thou seest a naked, that thou clothe him and that thou shouldest withdraw thyself from helping thine own flesh? Then should the light break out as doth the dayspring, and then health should shortly bud out. And thy righteousness shall go before thee, and the glory of the Lord would come upon thee. Then shouldest thou call, and the Lord answer: then shouldest thou cry, and he shall say, lo here am I. For I the Lord thy God am merciful.

On the Wednesday after the first Sunday in Lent:
the epistle

Exodus 24
And the Lord said unto Moses: come up to me into the hill, and be there, and I will give thee tables of stone and a law and commandments, which I have written to teach them. Then Moses rose up and his minister Joshua, and Moses went up into the hill of God, and said unto the elders: tarry ye here, until we come again unto you: and behold there is Aaron and Hur with you. If any man have any matters to do, let him come to them. When Moses was come up into the mount, a cloud covered the hill, and the glory of the Lord abode upon mount Sinai, and the Lord covered it six days. And the seventh day he called unto Moses out of the cloud. And the fashion of the glory of the Lord was like consuming fire on the top of the hill in the sight of the children of Israel. And Moses went into the mountain. And Moses was in the mountain forty days and forty nights.

Another for the same day:
the epistle

1 Kings 19
In those days came Elias to Beersheba, that is in Judah, and left his lad there. And he went into the wilderness a day's journey, and came and sat under a juniper tree, and wished to his soul that he might die, and said: it is now enough Lord, take my soul, for I am not better than my fathers. And as he lay and slept under a juniper tree: behold, an angel touched him, and said thus: up and eat. And he looked up: and behold there was at his head a cake baken on the coals and a cruse of water. And he ate and drank and laid him down again. And the angel of the Lord came again the second time and touched him, and said: up and eat: for thou hast a great way to go. And he arose and ate and drank and walked through the strength of that meat forty days and forty nights, even unto the mount of God, Horeb.

The Friday next following:
the epistle

Ezekiel 18
This saith the Lord. The soul that sinneth, she shall die. The son shall not bear part of the father's wickedness. The righteousness of the right shall be

upon him, and the wickedness of the wicked shall be on him. And yet the wicked if he turn from all his sins which he did, and keep all mine ordinances, and do justly and righteously, he shall live and not die. None of the sins that he hath done shall be reckoned unto him: In the righteousness that he hath done, he shall live. For I desire not the death of a sinner (saith the Lord Jehovah) but rather that he should turn from his way, and live. And so if a righteous turn from his righteousness and do wickedness, and shall do like unto all the abominations which a wicked doth, shall he live? No, none of those righteousness that he did shall be remembered. But in the wickedness which he wrought, and in the sin which he did, in them shall he die. But you will say, the way of the Lord is not equal. Here I pray you ye house of Israel. Is not my way equal? If a righteous turn from his righteousness and do wickedly, and die therefore: in the wickedness which he did he shall die. And when a wicked turneth from his wickedness and doth justly and righteously, he shall save his soul: because he feared and turned from all his wickedness which he did, he shall live and not die, saith the Lord almighty.

The Wednesday after the second Sunday in Lent:
the epistle

Esther 13
In the days of Esther, Mardocheus prayed the Lord, being mindful of all his works and said Lord, Lord king almighty: for in thy power all things are put, neither is there any that can resist thy will, if thou have determined to save Israel. Thou madest heaven and earth, and whatsoever is contained within the compass of heaven: thou art Lord of all, neither is there any that can resist thy majesty. Thou knowest all things, and wottest that it was not of pride or of spite, or any desire of glory that I did not worship most proud Aman: for I would have been ready, and that gladly (for the saving of Israel) to have kissed even the steps of his feet. But I feared lest I should turn the glory of my God unto a man, and feared to worship any man save my God. And now Lord king and God of Abraham, have mercy on thy people, for our enemies are minded to destroy us and to bring thine inheritance utterly to naught. Despise not the portion which thou deliveredest for thyself out of Egypt. Hear my prayer and be merciful unto the part and inheritance, and turn our sorrow into joy: that we may live and praise thy name, O Lord, and stop not the mouths of them that praise thee. And all Israel with like mind and prayer, cried unto the Lord, because that present death was not far from them.

The Friday next following:
the epistle

Genesis 37
At that time Joseph said unto his brothers: Hear I pray you a dream that I dreamed. Behold we were making of sheaves in the field: and see, my sheaf

arose and stood upright, and your sheaves stood round about and made an obeisance unto my sheaf. Then said his brethren unto him, What, shalt thou be our king, or shalt thou reign over us? And they hated him the more for his dream and for his words. And he dreamed yet another dream and told it his brethren. And he said: behold, I dreamed yet another dream, Methought the sun and the moon and eleven stars did worship me. And when he had told it his father and his brethren, his father rebuked him and said unto him: what meaneth this dream which thou hast dreamed? shall I come and thy mother and thy brethren and fall before thee on the ground? And though his brethren hated him: yet his father kept the thing in mind. And when his brethren were gone to pasture their father's sheep at Shechem, Israel said to Joseph: do not thy brethren feed the sheep at Shechem? come that I may send thee to them. And he said: here am I. And he said: go good son and see whether it be well with thy brethren and with the sheep, and bring me word again. And he sent him out of the valley of Hebron for to go to Shechem. And a man found him wandering in the field and asked him saying: what seekest thou? And he said, I seek my brethren: tell me I pray thee, where feed they? And the man said: they are departed hence. For I heard them say: let us go to Dothan. And when they saw him afar off, and ere he drew nigh them, they contrived to slay him. And they said one to another: behold, this dreamer cometh. But now come and let us kill him and cast him into some pit, and say some cruel beast hath devoured him, and let us see whereto his dreams will come. When Reuben heard that, he would have rid him out of their hands, and said: let us not kill him.

And Reuben said moreover, shed no blood, but cast him into yonder pit that is in the wilderness and lay no hands upon him: for he would have rid him out of their hands and delivered him to his father again.

The Wednesday after the third Sunday in Lent:
the epistle

Exodus 20

Thus saith the Lord God. Honour thy father and mother, that thy days may be prolonged in the land which thy Lord God giveth thee. Thou shalt not kill. Thou shalt not break wedlock. Thou shalt not steal. Thou shalt bear no false witness against thy neighbour. Thou shalt not covet thy neighbour's house: neither shalt thou covet thy neighbour's wife, his manservant, his maid, his ox, his ass or ought that is his. And all the people saw the thundering and the lightning and the noise of the horn, and how the mountain smoked. And when the people saw it, they removed and stood afar off and said to Moses: talk thou with us and we will hear: but let not God talk with us lest we die. And Moses said unto the people, fear not. For God is come to prove you and that his fear may be among you, that ye sin not. And the people stood afar off, and Moses went into the cloud where God was. And the Lord said unto Moses: thus thou shalt say unto the children of Israel: Ye have seen how I have talked with you out of heaven. Ye shall not make therefore with me, gods of gold: in no wise shall ye do it. An altar of earth shalt thou make unto me, and there offer thy burnt offerings and thy peace offerings, and thy sheep and thine oxen. And unto all places where I shall put the remembrance of my name, thither will I come unto thee and bless thee.

The Friday next following:
epistle

Numbers 20

In those days when there was no water for the multitude, they gathered themselves together against Moses and against Aaron. And the people did chide with Moses and spake saying: would God we had perished when our brethren perished before the Lord. Why have ye brought the congregation of the Lord into this wilderness, that both we and our cattle should die here? wherefore led ye us out of Egypt to bring us unto this ungracious place, with no place of seed nor of figs nor vines nor of pomegranates, neither is there any water to drink? And Moses and Aaron went from the congregation unto the door of the tabernacle of witness, and fell on their faces: and the glory of the Lord appeared unto them. And the Lord spake unto Moses saying: take the staff, and gather, thou and thy brother Aaron, the congregation together, and say unto the rock before their eyes, that he give forth his water. And thou shalt bring them water out of the rock, and shalt give the company drink, and their beasts also.

And Moses took the staff from before the Lord as he commanded him. And Moses and Aaron gathered the congregation together before the rock, and he said unto them, hear ye rebellious, must we fetch you water out of this rock? And Moses lifted up his hand with his staff and smote the rock two times and the water came out abundantly, and the multitude drank, and their beasts also. And the Lord spake unto Moses and Aaron, Because ye believed me not, to sanctify me in the eyes of the children of Israel, therefore ye shall not bring this congregation into the land which I have given them. This is the water of strife, because the children of Israel strove with the Lord, and he was sanctified upon them.

The Wednesday after the fourth Sunday in Lent:
the epistle

Isaiah 1

This saith the Lord God: Wash and be clean: put away the wickedness of your imaginations out of my sight. Cease to do evil and learn to do well. Study to do righteously and help the oppressed. Avenge the fatherless and defend the cause of widows. Come let us show each his grief to other and make an atonement saith the Lord. And so though your sins be like to purple, they shall be made as white as snow, and though they be as red as scarlet, they shall be made like white wool. If ye will agree and hearken, ye shall eat the best of the land saith the Lord God.

Another for the same day

Ezekiel 36
Thus saith the Lord: I will sanctify my name that is defiled among the heathen. Which ye have defiled among them: that the heathen may know that I am the Lord (saith the Lord Jehovah) when I am sanctified upon you in their sight. And I will take you from the heathen, and will gather you out from all lands and will bring you out of your own country. And I will pour pure water upon you, and ye shall be cleansed from all uncleanness, and from all your idols. I will cleanse you. And I will give you a new heart, and will put a new spirit in you. And will take away that stony heart out of your flesh, and give you a fleshly heart. And I will put my spirit in you, and will make that ye shall walk in mine ordinances and keep my laws and do them. And ye shall dwell in the land which I gave your fathers. And ye shall be my people, and I will be your God.

The Friday after the fourth Sunday in Lent:
the epistle

1 Kings 17
In those days it chanced that the son of the wife of the house was sick, and the sickness was so great that there remained no breath in him. Then she said to Elias, what have I to do with thee, thou man of God? Didest thou come to me, that my sin should be kept in mind and to slay my son? And he said unto her, give me thy son, and he took him out of her lap and carried him up into an high chamber, where he himself dwelt, and laid him on the bed. And he called unto the Lord and said: O Lord my God, hast thou dealt so cruelly with the widow with whom I dwell, as to kill her son? And he measured the child three times, and called unto the Lord and said: Lord my God, let this child's soul come again into him. And the Lord hearkened unto the voice of Elias, and this child's soul came again unto him, and he revived. And Elias took the child and carried him down out of the chamber into the house, and delivered him to his mother. And Elias said: see, thy son is alive. Then said the woman to Elias: now I know that thou art a man of God, and that the word of the Lord is truly in thy mouth.

The Wednesday after the fifth Sunday in Lent:
the epistle

Leviticus 19
At that time the Lord spake to Moses saying: speak unto the whole multitude of the children of Israel, and say to them: I am the Lord your God. Ye shall not steal nor lie, nor deal falsely one with another. Ye shall not swear by my name

falsely, that thou defile not the name of thy God: I am the Lord. Thou shalt not beguile thy neighbour with cavillations, nor rob him violently: neither shall the workman's labour[†] abide with thee until the morning. Thou shalt not curse the deaf, nor put a stumbling block before the blind, but shalt fear thy God. I am the Lord. Ye shall do none unrighteousness in judgement. Thou shalt not favour the poor nor honour the mighty, but shalt judge thy neighbour righteously. Thou shalt not go up and down a false privy accuser among the people, neither shalt thou help to shed the blood of thy neighbour. I am the Lord. Thou shalt not hate thy brother in thine heart, but shalt in any wise rebuke thine neighbour, that thou bear no sin for his sake. Thou shalt not avenge thyself nor bear hate in mind against the children of thy people, but shalt love thine neighbour even as thyself. I am the Lord. Mine ordinances shall you keep, saith the Lord almighty.

The Friday after the fifth Sunday in Lent: the epistle

Jeremiah 17

Jeremiah said: Lord all that forsake thee, shall be ashamed. And they that depart from thee shall be written in the earth. For they have lost the Lord that is the fountain of the water of life. Heal me Lord, and I shall be whole: save me Lord, and I shall be safe, for thou art he that I praise. Behold they say unto me: where is the word of the Lord? Let it come to pass, and I enforced not to be a shepherd that should not follow thee: and the day of destruction have I not desired, thou knowest. And that proceeded out of my mouth was right in thy sight. Be not terrible unto me Lord: for thou art my trust in the evil day. Let them that persecute me be confounded, and let not me be confounded. Let their hearts fail them, and not mine heart fail. Bring upon them an evil day, and bruise them again and again.

The Wednesday after Palm Sunday: the epistle

Isaiah 53

Esaias said, Lord, who believeth our sayings, and the arm of the Lord, to whom is it opened? He came up as a spray before him, and as a root out of a dry land. There was neither fashion or beauty on him. And when we looked on him, there was no godliness that we should lust after him. He was despised and cast out of men's company, and one that had suffered sorrow, and had experience of infirmity: and we were as one that had hid his face from him. He was so despisable, that we esteemed him not. Truly he took upon him our diseases, and bare our sorrows. And yet we counted him plagued, and beaten and humbled of God. He was wounded for our transgression, and bruised for our iniquities. The correction that brought us peace was on him, and with his stripes we were healed. And we went astray as sheep, and turned every man his way: and the Lord put on him the wickedness of us all. He suffered wrong and was evil entreated, and yet opened not his mouth: he was as a sheep led to be slain: and as a lamb before his shearer, he was dumb and opened not his mouth. By the reason of the affliction, he was not esteemed: and yet his generation who can number? When he is taken from the earth of living men: for my people's transgression he was plagued. He put his sepulchre with the wicked, and with the rich in his death: because he did none iniquity, neither was guile found in his mouth. And yet the Lord determined to bruise him with infirmities. His soul giving herself for trangression, he shall see seed of long continuance, and the will of the Lord shall prosper in his hand. Because of the labour of his soul, he shall see and be satisfied. With his knowledge, he being just, shall justify my servants and that a great number: and he shall bear their iniquities. Therefore I will give him his part in many and the spoil of the rich he shall divide: because he gave his soul to death, and was numbered with the trespassers, and he bare the sin of many, and made intercession for transgressors.

On Good Friday:
the epistle

Exodus 12
And the Lord spake unto Moses and Aaron in the land of Egypt saying: this month shall be your chief month: even the first month of the year shall it be unto you. Speak ye unto all the fellowship of Israel saying: that they take the tenth day of this month to every household, a sheep. If the household be too few for a sheep, then let him and his neighbours that is next unto his house, take according to the number of souls, and count unto a sheep according to every man's eating. A sheep without spot and a male of one year old shall it be, and from among the lambs and the goats shall ye take it. And ye shall keep him in ward until the fourteenth day of the same month. And every man of the multitude of Israel shall kill him about even. And they shall take of the blood and strike it on the two side posts and on the upper door-post of the houses, wherein they eat him. And they shall eat the flesh the same night, roast with fire, and with unleavened bread and with sour herbs they shall eat it. See that ye eat not thereof sodden in water, but roast with fire: both head, feet and purtenance together. And see that ye let nothing of it remain, unto the morning: if ought remain, burn it with fire. Of this manner shall ye eat it: with your loins girded, and shoes on your feet, and your staves in your hands. And ye shall eat it in haste, for it is the Lord's passover.

The last Sunday after Trinity Sunday:
the epistle

Jeremiah 33
Behold, the days will come saith the Lord, that I will stir up unto David a righteous branch, and he shall reign a king, and shall be wise, and shall do

equity and justice in the earth. And in his days Judah shall be safe, and Israel shall dwell without fear.

And this is the name that they shall call him: the Lord our righteousness. Wherefore the days will come saith the Lord, that they shall say no more, the Lord liveth that brought the children of Israel out of the land of Egypt. But the Lord liveth which delivered and brought the seed of the house of Israel, out of the land of the north and from all lands whether I thrust them. And they shall dwell in their own land saith the Lord God almighty.

On the Wednesday in the Ember week afore Michaelmas

Amos 9

Thus saith the Lord God, behold the days will come saith the Lord, that the earer shall overtake the reaper, and treader of grapes the sower of seed. And the mountains shall drop sweetness, and the hills shall be earable. And I will turn the captivity of my people Israel: and they shall build the cities that are fallen in decay, and shall inhabit them, and shall plant vines and drink wine, and shall make gardens and eat the fruit of them. And I will plant them their own land, and they shall not be any more plucked out of their land which I have given them, saith the Lord thy God.

The Friday in the Ember week before Michaelmas: the epistle

Hosea 14

Turn Israel unto the Lord thy God: For thou art fallen for thy wickednesses' sake. Take words with you and turn unto the Lord. And say unto him: remit all wickedness and given things, and we will pay thee openly that we have promised with our lips. Asshur shall not save us, neither will we ride on horses: neither will we say to the works of our own hands, ye are our Gods, for thou hast compassion on the friendless. I will heal their obedience and will love them of mine own accord: for my wrath is ceased from them. I will be as dew to Israel, and he shall flourish as a lily, and stretch out his roots as Lebanon. His branches shall run out, and as an olive tree shall his glory be, and his savour as Lebanon. They that shall turn and sit in his shadow, shall live with corn, and flourish as vines. His renown shall be as the wine of Lebanon. Ephraim, what have ye any more to do with idols? I have healed him and looked on him. I will be as a great fir tree, and of me shall thy fruit be found. Who is wise to understand these things and hath wit to perceive them? For the ways of the Lord are straight, and the righteous shall walk in them: but the wicked shall stumble in them.

Hereafter followeth the Epistles of the saints which are also taken out of the Old Testament

On saint Nicholas' day:
the epistle

Ecclesiasticus 44

Behold an excellent priest which in his days pleased God, and was found righteous, and in time of wrath made an atonement: Like to him there is not found, that kept the law of the most highest. And he was in covenant with him, and in his flesh he wrote the covenant, and in time of temptation he was found faithful. Therefore he made him a covenant with an oath, that nations should be blessed in his sight, and that he should be multiplied as the dust of the earth. He knew him in his blessings and gave him an inheritance. And he kept him through his mercy, that he found grace in the eyes of God. An everlasting covenant did he make him, and gave him the office of the high priest. He made him happy in glory. In faith and in his softness, he made him holy, and chose him out of all flesh.

On the conception of our lady:
the epistle

Ecclesiasticus 24

As a vine, so brought I forth a savour of sweetness. And my flowers are the fruit of glory and riches. I am the mother of beautiful love and of fear, and of greatness and of holy hope. In me is all grace of life and truth. And in me is all hope of life and virtue. Come unto me all that desire me, and be filled with the fruits that spring of me. For my spirit is sweeter than honey or honeycomb. The remembrance of me is for ever and ever. They that eat me, shall hunger the more, and they that drink me, shall thirst the more. He that hearkeneth to me, shall not be ashamed, and he that worketh by my counsel, shall not sin. And they that bring into light, shall have eternal life.

On Candlemas day:
the epistle

Malachi 3

Behold, I send my messenger which shall prepare the way before me. And suddenly shall the Lord whom ye seek, come unto his temple, and the messenger of the covenant whom ye desire. Behold, he cometh saith the Lord Sabaoth. Who shall endure in the day of his coming, or who shall stand to behold him? For he is as trying-fire and as the herb that fullers scour withal. And he shall sit trying and purging silver, and shall purify the sons of Levi, and shall fine them as gold and silver. And they shall bring offering unto the Lord of righteousness. And the sacrifice of Judah and of Jerusalem shall be delicious unto the Lord as in the old time and in the years that were at the beginning.

On the annunciation of our lady
which is our lady day in Lent:
the epistle

Isaiah 7
And the lord spake to Ahaz saying, Ask thee a sign of the Lord thy God, from alow beneath, or from on high above. But Ahaz answered I will not ask, neither will tempt the Lord. Wherefore the Lord said: Hearken ye of the house of David: Is it so small a thing for you, to be grievous to men, but that ye should also be painful unto God? neverthelater yet the Lord, he will give you a sign. Behold a virgin shall be with child, and shall bear a son, and shall call his name Immanuel. He shall eat butter and honey, that he may have understanding to refuse the evil and to choose the good.

On saint Philip and Jacob's day:
the epistle

Wisdom 5
Then shall the righteous stand with great constancy against them that vexed them and took away that they had laboured for. When the wicked shall see that they shall be troubled with horrible fear, and shall wonder at the sudden and unlooked-for victory, and shall say in themselves, repenting and sorrowing for anguish of heart. These be they which we sometime mocked and jested on. We were out of our wits and thought their living madness, and their end to be without honour. But behold, how they are counted among the children of God, and have their inheritance among the saints.

On the nativity of St John Baptist's day:
the epistle

Isaiah 49
Thus saith the Lord: Hearken ye isles unto me, and give heed ye people that are afar. The Lord called me out of the womb and made mention of my name, when I was in my mother's bowels. And he made my mouth like a sharp sword. In the shadow he led me with his hand. And he made me as an excellent arrow, and hid in his quiver. And he said to me: thou art my servant O Israel, in whom I will be glorified. And I said: I labour in vain and spend my strength for nought, and unprofitably. Howbeit my cause I commit to the Lord and my travail unto my God. And now saith the Lord that formed me in the womb, to be his servant and to turn Jacob unto him: Behold I have made thee a light, that thou shouldest be salvation, even unto the end of the world. Kings shall see,

and rulers shall stand up and shall worship, because of the Lord which is faithful, and the holy of Israel hath chosen thee.

On the visitation of our lady:
the epistle

Song of Solomon 2
I am the flower of the field, and lilies of the valleys. As the lily among the thorns, so is my love among the daughters. As the apple-tree among the trees of the wood so is my beloved among the sons: in his shadow was my desire to sit, for his fruit was sweet to my mouth. He brought me into his wine-cellar: and his behaviour to me-ward was lovely. Behold my beloved said to me: up and haste my love, my dove, my beautiful and come, for now is winter gone and rain departed and past. The flowers appear in our country and the time is come to cut the vines. The voice of the turtle-dove is heard in our land. The fig-tree hath brought forth her figs, and the vine-blossoms give a savour. Up, haste my love, my dove, in the holes of the rock and secret places of the walls. Shew me thy face and let me hear thy voice, for thy voice is sweet and thy fashion beautiful.

On saint Mary Magdalen's day:
the epistle

Proverbs 31
A woman of power and verity, if a man could find: the value of her were far above pearls. The heart of her husband trusteth in her, that he needeth not spoils. She rendereth him good and not evil all the days of her life. She sought wool and flax and did as her hands served her. She is like a merchant's ship that bringeth her victuals from far. She riseth ere day and giveth meat to her household, and food to her maidens. She considered a ground and bought it, and of the fruit of her hands planted a vine. She girt her loins with strength and couraged her arms. She perceived that her housewifery was profitable, and therefore did not put out her candle by night. She set her fingers to the spindle, and her hands caught hold on the distaff. She opened her hand to the poor, and stretched out her hands to the needy. She feared not lest the cold of snow should hurt her house, for all her household were double-clothed. She made her gay ornaments, of byss and purple was her apparel. Her husband was had in honour in the gates, as he sat with the elders of the land. She made linen and sold it, and delivered a girdle to the merchant. Strength and glory were her raiment, and she laughed in the latter days. She opened her mouth with wisdom, and the law of righteousness was on her tongue. She had an eye to her household and ate not bread idly. Her children arose and blessed her, and her husband commended her. Many daughters have done excellently but thou hast passed them all. Favour is a deceivable thing, and beauty is vanity. But

a woman that feareth God, she shall be praised. Give her of the fruit of her hands, and let her works praise her in the gates.

On the assumption of our lady:
the epistle

Ecclesiasticus 24
In all those things I sought rest: and in some man's inheritance would have dwelt. Then the creator of all things commanded and said unto me: and he that created me did set my tabernacle at rest and said unto me, dwell in Jacob and have thine inheritance in Israel, and root thyself among mine elect. From the beginning and before the world was I created, and unto the world to come, will I not cease: and before him have I ministered in the holy habitation. And so in Sion was I settled, and in the holy city likewise I rested, and in Jerusalem was my power. And I rooted myself in an honourable people, which are the Lord's part, and he their inheritance: and among the multitude of saints I held me fast. As a cedar tree was I lift up in Lebanon, and as a cypress tree in mount Hermon. As a palm tree was I exalted in Cades, and as rose plants in Jericho. As a beautiful olive tree in the fields, and as a plantain tree was I exalted upon the waters. In the streets I gave an odour as cinnamon and balm that smelleth well, and gave an odour of sweetness as perfect myrrh.

On the nativity of our lady

The epistle as is afore on the conception of our lady: Ecclesiasticus 24.

On saint Matthew's day the apostle:
the epistle

Ezekiel 1
The similitude of the faces of the four beasts: the face of a man and the face of a lion on the right hand of the four of them. And the face of an eagle above them four. And their faces and their wings stretched out above on high. Each had two wings coupled together and two that covered their bodies. And they went all straight forward. And whither they had lust to go, thither they went, and turned not back again in their going. And the similitude of the beasts and the fashion of them was as burning coals of fire and as fire-brands, walking between the beasts. And the fire did shine, and out of the fire proceeded lightning. And the beasts ran and returned after the fashion of lightning.

On saint Luke

Ezekiel 1
The epistle as is above on St. Matthew's day the Apostle.

On St Katherines day:
the epistle

Ecclesiasticus 51

Lord, I did lift up my prayer upon the earth, and besought to be delivered from death. I called upon the Lord the father of my Lord, that he should not leave me helpless in the day of my tribulation, and in the day of the proud man. I praised thy name perpetually, and honoured it with confession, and my prayer was heard. And thou savedest me that I perished not, and deliveredest me out of the time of unrighteousness: Therefore will I confess and praise thee, and will bless the name of the Lord.

Here end the epistles of the Old Testament.

This is the Table,
wherein you shall find, the Epistles and the Gospels, after the use of Salisbury.

For to find them the sooner: so shall you seek, after these capital letters by name: A. B. C. D. which stand by the side of this book, always on, or under the letter there shall you find a cross + where the Epistle or the Gospel beginneth, and where the end is, there shall you find an half cross ⊢.

And the first line in this table always is the Epistle, and the second line is always the Gospel.

On the first Sunday in the Advent.

D	This also we know.	Rom. 13.
A	When they drew nigh unto.	Matt. 21.

On the Wednesday.

B	Be patient therefore brethren.	Jas. 5.
A	The beginning of the gospel.	Mark 1.

On the Friday.

A	Esaias the fifty-first chapter.	
A	In those days John.	Matt. 3.

On the second Sunday in the Advent.

A	Whatsoever things are written.	Rom. 15.
E	And there shall be signs.	Luke 21.

On the Wednesday.

A	Zechariah the eighth chapter.	
B	Verily I say unto you.	Matt. 11.

On the Friday.

C	Esaias the sixty-second chapter.	
B	John bare witness of him.	John 1.

On the third Sunday in the Advent.

A	Let men this wise esteem us.	1 Cor. 4.
A	When John being in prison.	Matt. 11.

On the Wednesday.

A	Esaias the second chapter.	
C	And in the sixth month the.	Luke 1.

On the Friday.

A	Esaias the eleventh chapter.	
D	Mary arose in those days.	Luke 1.

On the fourth Sunday in the Advent.

A	Rejoice in the Lord always.	Phil. 4.
C	And this is the record of John.	John 1.

On the Wednesday.

D	Joel the second and third chapter.	
C	And this rumour of him went.	Luke 7.

On the Friday.

D	Zechariah the second chapter.	
B	Take heed beware of the leaven.	Mark 8.

In the Christmas even.

A	Paul the servant of Jesus.	Rom. 1.
C	When his mother Mary was.	Matt. 1.

In the Christmas night at the first mass.

C	For the grace of God.	Tit. 2.
A	It followed in those days.	Luke 2.

At the second mass.

B	But after that the kindness.	Tit. 3.
C	The shepherds said one to.	Luke 2.

At the third mass.

A	God in time past diversely.	Heb. 1.
A	In the beginning was that.	John 1.

On saint Steven's day.

C	Steven full of faith and power.	Acts. 6.
D	Wherefore behold I send.	Matt. 23.

On saint John Evangelist.

A	Ecclesiastes the fifteenth chapter.	
E	Follow me, Peter turned.	John 21.

On the childermass day.

A	And I looked, and lo a lamb.	Rev. 14.
C	Lo the angel of the Lord appe.	Matt. 2.

Of the Sunday after Christmas.

A	And I say that the heir as.	Gal. 4.
E	And his father and mother went.	Luke 2.

On the new year's day.

C	For the grace of God that bring.	Tit. 2.
C	And when the eighth day was.	Luke 2.

On the thirteenth even[†].

C	For the grace of God that bring.	Tit. 2.
D	When Herod was dead.	Matt. 2.

On the thirteenth day.

A	Esaias the sixtieth chapter.	
A	When Jesus was born.	Matt. 2.

On the first Sunday after the thirteenth day.

A	Esaias the twelfth chapter.	
D	The next day, John saw.	John 1.

On the second Sunday after the thirteenth day.

A	I beseech you therefore brethren.	Rom. 12.
F	And when he was twelve years old.	Luke 2.

On the Wednesday.

A	Brethren my heart's desire.	Rom. 10
B	When Jesus had heard that.	Matt. 4.

† That is, Twelfth Night, January 6: Epiphany.

411

On the Friday.

A	Let every soul submit him.	Rom. 13.
B	And Jesus returned by the.	Luke 4.

On the third Sunday after the thirteenth day.

B	Seeing that we have divers.	Rom. 12.
A	And the third day was the.	John 2.

On the Wednesday.

C	This is a true saying, and by.	1 Tim. 1.
A	And he departed thence: and.	Mark 6.

On the Friday.

C	For I know, and surely belie.	Rom. 14.
E	And came into Capernaum.	Luke 4.

On the fourth Sunday after the thirteenth day.

D	Be not wise in your own opi.	Rom. 12.
A	When Jesus was come dow.	Matt. 8.

On the Wednesday.

G	I beseech you brethren for.	Rom. 15.
A	And he entered again into.	Mark 3.

On the Friday.

D	Are ye not ware that ye are.	1 Cor. 3.
D	And Jesus went about all.	Matt. 4.

On the fifth Sunday after the thirteenth day.

B	Owe nothing to any man.	Rom. 13.
C	And he entered into a ship.	Matt. 8.

On the Wednesday.

A	As concerning the things.	1 Cor. 7.
G	It chanced as they went on.	Luke 9.

On the Friday.

D	Let every man abide in the.	1 Cor. 7.
B	And they brought children.	Mark 10.

On the sixth Sunday after the thirteenth day.

B	Now therefore as elect of.	Col. 3.
D	The kingdom of heaven is.	Matt. 13.

On the Wednesday.

A	I exhort therefore that above.	1 Tim. 2.
C	A certain man had two son.	Matt. 21.

When the wedding goeth out.

D	Perceive ye not how that.	1 Cor. 9.
A	For the kingdom of heaven.	Matt. 20.

On the Wednesday.

A	If our gospel be yet hid.	2 Cor. 4.
E	And they departed thence, and.	Mark 9.

On the Friday.

C	Seeing then that we have.	2 Cor. 4.
C	He that is not with me, is.	Matt. 12.

On the Sunday sixty†.

D	For ye suffer fools gladly.	2 Cor. 11.
A	When much people were.	Luke 8.

On the Wednesday.

A	I call God for a record unto.	2 Cor. 2.
A	And he began again to.	Mark 4.

On the Friday.

B	Seeing that we know.	2 Cor. 5.
E	When he was demanded.	Luke 17.

On the Sunday fifty††.

A	Though I speak with the.	1 Cor. 13.
F	He took unto him the twelve.	Luke 18.

† That is, sixty days before Easter: in church tradition called Sexagesima Sunday.
†† That is, fifty days before Easter, formerly Quinquagesima.

On the Wednesday.

C   Joel the second chapter.

B   Moreover when ye fast be not.   Matt. 6.

On the Friday.

A   Esaias the fifty-eighth chapter.

G   Ye have heard how it is said.   Matt. 5.

On the first Sunday in lent.

A   We as helpers therefore.   2 Cor. 6.

A   Then was Jesus led away.   Matt. 4.

On the Wednesday in the four times.[†]

C   Exodus the twenty-fourth chapter and 1 Kin. 19.

D   Then answered certain.   Matt. 12.

On the Friday.

E   Ezekiel the eighteenth chapter.

A   After that there was a feast.   John 5.

On the second Sunday in lent.

A   Furthermore we beseech.   1 Thes. 4.

C   And Jesus went thence and.   Matt. 15.

On the Wednesday.

C   Esther the thirteenth chapter.

C   And Jesus ascended to Jeru.   Matt. 20.

On the Friday.

B   Genesis the thirty-seventh chapter.

D   Hearken another similitude.   Matt. 21.

On the third Sunday in lent.

A   Be ye followers of God.   Eph. 5.

C   And he was a casting out.   Luke 11.

On the Wednesday.

C   Exodus the twentieth chapter.

A   Then came to Jesus the.   Matt. 15.

---

† That is, in the Ember days.

On the Friday.

A   Numbers the twentieth chapter.
A   Then came he to a city of Sama.   John 4.

On the fourth Sunday halflent.[†]

C   For it is written that Abraham.   Gal. 4.
A   After that went Jesus his.   John 6.

On the Wednesday.

E   Ezekiel the thirty-sixth chapter, and Esaias 1.
A   And as Jesus passed by, he.   John 9.

On the Friday.

C   1 Kings the seventeenth chapter.
A   A certain man was sick.   John 11.

On the fifth Sunday in lent.

C   But Christ being the high.   Heb. 9.
F   Which of you can rebuke me.   John 8.

On the Wednesday.

C   Leviticus the nineteenth chapter.
E   It was at Jerusalem the feast.   John 10.

On the Friday.

B   Jeremiah the seventeenth chapter.
F   Then gathered the high priests.   John 11.

On the Palm Sunday.

A   Let the same mind be in you.   Phil. 2.
A   Ye know that after two days.   Matt. 26.

On the Wednesday.

D   Esaias the fifty-fourth chapter.
A   The feast of sweet bread drew.   Luke 22.

On the Good Friday.

A   Exodus the twelfth chapter.
A   When Jesus had spoken.   John 18.

[†] That is, mid-lent Sunday.

On Easter even.

A   If ye be then risen again.   Col. 3.

A   The sabbath day at even.   Matt. 28.

On Easter day.

C   Purge therefore the old leaven.   1 Cor. 5.

A   Mary Magdalen, and Mary.   Mark 16.

On the Monday.

F   Which preaching was pub.   Acts 10.

B   And behold two of them went.   Luke 24.

On the Tuesday.

D   Ye men and brethren, children.   Acts 13.

F   Jesus himself stood in the.   Luke 24.

On the Wednesday.

B   Ye men of Israel why mar.   Acts 3.

A   After that Jesus shewed him.   John 21.

On the Thursday.

E   The angel of the Lord spake.   Acts 8.

C   Mary stood without at the.   John 20.

On the Friday.

C   Forasmuch as Christ hath.   1 Pet. 3.

D   Then the eleven disciples went.   Matt. 28.

On the Saturday.

A   Wherefore lay aside all ma.   1 Pet. 2.

A   The morrow after the.   John 20.

On the first Sunday after Easter day.

A   For all that is born of God.   1 John 5.

E   The same day at night which.   John 20.

On the Wednesday.

C   If Christ be preached how.   1 Cor. 15.

C   When Jesus was risen the.   Mark 16.

On the Friday.

C	Obey them that have the over.	Heb. 13.
C	And they departed quickly.	Matt. 28.

On the second Sunday after Easter day.

D	Christ also suffered for our.	1 Pet. 2.
C	I am a good shepherd, a good.	John 10.

On the Friday.

C	Forasmuch as ye know how.	1 Pet. 1.
A	On the morrow after the sab.	Luke 24.

On the Wednesday.

D	Likewise then as by the sin.	Rom. 5.
B	Then came the disciples of John.	Matt. 9.

On the third Sunday after Easter day.

C	Dearly beloved I beseech you.	1 Pet. 2.
D	After a while ye shall not se.	John 16.

On the Wednesday.

A	My little children, these.	1 John 2.
D	There arose a question betwe.	John 3.

On the Friday.

A	Ye are all the children.	1 Thes. 5.
G	I am come a light into the.	John 12.

On the fourth Sunday after Easter day.

C	Every good gift, and every.	James 1.
B	But now go I my way to.	John 16.

On the Wednesday.

A	Brethren have not the faith.	Jas. 2.
B	Holy father keep in thine.	John 17.

On the Friday.

D	Ye see then how that of deeds.	Jas. 2.
D	Dear children, yet a little.	John 13.

On the fifth Sunday in the crossdays[†].

D	And see that ye be doers of.	Jas. 1.
E	Verily verily I say unto.	John 16.

On the Monday.

D	Knowledge your faults one.	Jas. 5.
A	Which of you shall have a.	Luke 11.

On the Tuesday.

D	Esaias the nineteenth chapter.	
D	And Jesus sat over against.	Mark 12.

On the Wednesday.

G	The multitude of them that.	Acts 4.
A	These words spake Jesus and.	John 17.

On the Ascension day.

A	In my first treatise Dear.	Acts 1.
D	After that he appeared.	Mark 16.

On the Sunday after Ascension day.

B	Be ye therefore discreet, and so.	1 Pet. 4.
D	But when the comforter is.	John 15.

On the Whitsun even.

A	If fortuned, while Apollos.	Acts 19.
B	If ye love me keep my comman.	John 14.

On the Whitsun day.

A	When the fifty days was co.	Acts 2.
C	If a man love me and will keep.	John 14.

On the Monday.

F	And he commanded us to preach.	Acts 10.
B	God so loved the world, that.	John 3.

On the Tuesday.

C	When the apostles which we.	Acts 8.
A	Verily verily I say unto you.	John 10.

[†] That is, the Rogation days; the three days before Ascension day.

On the Wednesday.

C   Peter stepped forth with the.   Acts 2.
E   No man can come to me except.   John 6.

On the Thursday.

A   Then came Philip into a city of.   Acts 8.
A   Then called he the twelve together.   Luke 9.

On the Friday.

D   Ye men of Israel, hear the.   Acts 2.
D   And it happened on a certain.   Luke 5.

On the Saturday.

F   And the next sabbath day.   Acts 13.
F   And he arose up and came out.   Luke 4.

On the Trinity Sunday.

A   After this I looked, and behold.   Rev. 4.
A   There was a man of the Pha.   John 3.

Corpus Christi day.

E   That which I gave unto you.   1 Cor. 11.
F   For my flesh is meat indeed.   John 6.

On the first Sunday after Trinity Sunday.

B   For God is love, in this app.   1 John 4.
E   There was a certain rich.   Luke 16.

On the Wednesday.

D   When we opened unto you the.   2 Pet. 1.
C   Ye shall not think that I am.   Matt. 5.

On the second Sunday after Trinity Sunday.

C   Marvel not my brethren.   1 John 3.
E   A certain man ordained a great.   Luke 14.

On the Wednesday.

E   This I say therefore and testify.   Eph. 4.
C   And when he was come into the.   Matt. 21.

On the third Sunday after Trinity Sunday.

B	Submit yourselves therefore.	1 Pet. 5.
A	Then resorted unto him all the pub.	Luke 15.

On the Wednesday.

D	Notwithstanding the Lord.	2 Tim. 4.
D	Agree with thine adversary.	Matt. 5.

On the fourth Sunday after Trinity Sunday.

D	For I suppose that the afflic.	Rom. 8.
F	Be ye therefore merciful as you.	Luke 6.

On the Wednesday.

A	And hereby we know that we.	1 John 2.
B	And his disciples asked of him.	Matt. 17.

On the fifth Sunday after Trinity Sunday.

B	In conclusion be ye all of one.	1 Pet. 3.
A	It came to pass as the people pre.	Luke 5.

On the Wednesday.

A	I exhort therefore that above.	1 Tim. 2.
D	It chanced on a certain day.	Luke 8.

On the sixth Sunday after Trinity Sunday.

A	Remember ye not that all we.	Rom. 6.
C	For I say unto you except your.	Matt. 5.

On the Wednesday.

D	I wrote not unto you as.	1 John 2.
C	And when he was come out into.	Mark 10.

On the seventh Sunday after Trinity Sunday.

D	I will speak grossly because of.	Rom. 6.
A	In those days when there wa.	Mark 8.

On the Wednesday.

A	There is then no damnation to them.	Rom. 8.
A	In that time went Jesus on the.	Matt. 12.

On the eighth Sunday after Trinity Sunday.

C	Therefore brethren we are now.	Rom. 8.
C	Beware of false prophets.	Matt. 7.

On the Wednesday.

B	But God setteth out his love.	Rom. 5.
F	Master we saw one casting.	Mark 9.

On the ninth Sunday after Trinity Sunday.

B	That we should not lust after.	1 Cor. 10.
A	There was a certain rich man.	Luke 16.

On the Wednesday.

C	Remember ye not how that.	Rom. 6.
C	He that is faithful in that which.	Luke 16.

On the tenth Sunday after Trinity Sunday.

A	Ye know that ye were gentiles.	1 Cor. 12.
F	And when he was come near he.	Luke 19.

On the Wednesday.

E	All flesh is not one manner of.	1 Cor. 15.
G	Take heed to yourselves lest.	Luke 21.

On the eleventh Sunday after Trinity Sunday.

A	Brethren as pertaining to the.	1 Cor. 15.
B	And he put forth this similitu.	Luke 18.

On the Wednesday.

C	Or remember ye not that you.	1 Cor. 6.
A	He put forth a similitude unto.	Luke 18.

On the twelfth Sunday after Trinity Sunday.

B	Such trust have we through.	2 Cor. 3.
D	And he departed again from.	Mark 7.

On the Wednesday.

B	For we preach not ourself.	2 Cor. 4.
C	Then began he to upbraid the cit.	Matt. 11.

On the thirteenth Sunday after Trinity Sunday.

C   To Abraham and his seed were the.   Gal. 3.
D   Happy are the eyes which see.   Luke 10.

On the Wednesday.

B   Ye remember brethren our labour.   1 Thes. 2.
B   Then the Pharisees went forth.   Matt. 12.

On the fourteenth Sunday after Trinity Sunday.

C   I say walk in the spirit and.   Gal. 5.
D   And it chanced as he went to Jer.   Luke 17.

On the Wednesday.

C   Bear not the yoke with the.   2 Cor. 6.
B   One of the company said unto.   Luke 12.

On the fifteenth Sunday after Trinity Sunday.

D   If we live in the spirit let us.   Gal. 5.
C   No man can serve two masters.   Matt. 6.

On the Wednesday.

B   We know that the law is good.   1 Tim. 1.
A   And it fortuned in one of those.   Luke 20.

On the sixteenth Sunday after Trinity Sunday.

C   Wherefore I desire that ye faint.   Eph. 3.
C   And it fortuned after that he went.   Luke 7.

On the Wednesday.

B   Beware lest any man come and.   Col. 2.
C   And he came to Bethsaida and they.   Mark 8.

On the seventeenth Sunday after Trinity Sunday.

A   I therefore which am in bonds.   Eph. 4.
A   And it chanced that he went in.   Luke 14.

On the Wednesday.

C   For if by the sin of one death.   Rom. 5.
D   When they were come to Cap.   Matt. 17.

On the eighteenth Sunday after Trinity Sunday.

A   I thank my God always on.   1 Cor. 1.
D   When the Pharisees had heard.   Matt. 22.

On the Friday.

G   I beseech you brethren for our.   Rom. 15.
E   Another parable he put forth.   Matt. 13.

On the nineteenth Sunday after Trinity Sunday.

E   And be ye renewed in the spirit.   Eph. 4.
A   And he entered into a ship.   Matt. 9.

On the Wednesday.

D   Therefore brethren stand fast and.   2 Thes 2.
E   Then sent Jesus the people awa.   Matt. 13.

On the twentieth Sunday after Trinity Sunday.

C   Take heed therefore that ye wal.   Eph. 5.
A   The kingdom of heaven is like.   Matt. 22.

On the Wednesday.

A   Thou therefore my son be stron.   2 Tim. 2
C   When thou makest a dinner or a.   Luke 14.

On the twenty-first Sunday after Trinity Sunday.

B   Finally my brethren be strong.   Eph. 6.
G   And there was a certain ruler.   John 4.

On the Wednesday.

B   Because we know brethren.   1 Thes. 1.
B   And it fortuned in another sab.   Luke 6.

On the twenty-second Sunday after Trinity Sunday.

A   And am surely certified of.   Phil. 1
C   Therefore is the kingdom.   Matt. 18.

On the Wednesday.

C   Yea and we know that whatso.   Rom. 3.
C   Verily I say unto you, that.   Mark 11.

On the twenty-third Sunday after Trinity Sunday.

D	Brethren follow me, and.	Phil. 3.
B	Then went the Pharisees and.	Matt. 22.

On the Wednesday.

C	For if by the sin of one.	Rom. 5.
D	When they were come to.	Matt. 17.

On the twenty-fourth Sunday after Trinity Sunday.

B	For this cause we also, since.	Col. 1.
C	While he thus spake unto them.	Matt. 9.

On the Wednesday.

E	And I would not that ye should.	1 Cor. 10.
C	A certain man had two sons.	Matt. 21.

On the last Sunday after Trinity Sunday.

B	Jeremiah the twenty-third chapter.	
A	Then Jesus lift up his eyes.	John 6.

On the Wednesday at four times.[†]

D	Amos the ninth chapter.	
C	And one of the company ans.	Mark 9.

On the Friday at four times.

A	Hosea the fourteenth chapter.	
E	And one of the Pharisees desired.	Luke 7.

On the Saturday at four times.

A	For that first tabernacle was.	Heb. 9.
B	He put forth this similitude.	Luke 18.

In the Dedication of the church.

A	And I John saw that holy.	Rev. 21.
A	And he entered in, and went thr.	Luke 19.

Here endeth the Table of the Epistles
and Gospels of the Sundays.

† That is, in the Ember days.

Hereafter follow the Epistles and Gospels of the Saints.

On saint Andrew's day.

C   For the belief of the heart justi.   Rom. 10.
C   As Jesus walked by the sea of.   Matt. 4.

On saint Nicholas' day.

A   Ecclesiasticus the forty-fourth chapter.
A   For likewise a certain man.   Matt. 25.

On the conception of our lady.

C   Ecclesiasticus the twenty-fourth chapter.
A   This is the book of the generati.   Matt. 1.

On St Thomas the Apostle's day.

D   Now therefore ye are no more.   Eph. 2.
F   Thomas one of the twelve.   John 20.

In the conversion of St Paul.

A   Saul yet breathing out threat.   Acts 9.
D   Then answered Peter and said.   Matt. 19.

On Candlemas day.

A   Malachi the third chapter.
D   And when the time of their purif.   Luke 2.

On St Matthias the Apostle's day.

C   And in those days Peter.   Acts 1.
D   Then Jesus answered and said.   Matt. 11.

The greeting of our lady.

B   Esaias the seventh chapter.
C   And in the sixth month the angel.   Luke 1.

On saint George's day.

A   My brethren, count it exceeding.   Jas. 1.
A   I am the true vine, and my father.   John 15.

On saint Mark the evangelist.

B   Unto every one of you is given.   Eph. 4.
A   I am the true vine, and my father.   John 15.

On the saint Philip and James' day.

A Wisdom the fifth chapter.
A And he said unto his discip.   John 14.

The finding of the cross.

B I have trust toward you in God.   Gal. 5.
A There was a man of the Pha.   John 3.

On the nativity of St John Baptist.

A Esaias the forty-ninth chapter.
F Elizabeth's time was come.   Luke 1.

On St Peter and Paul's day.

A In that time Herod the king.   Acts 12.
C When Jesus came into the.   Matt. 16.

In the commemoration of St Paul.

C I certify you brethren that.   Gal. 1.
D Then answered Peter and said.   Matt. 19.

On the visitation of our lady.

A Song of Solomon the second chapter.
D Mary arose in those days.   Luke 1.

On saint Mary Magdalen's day.

B Proverbs the thirty-first chapter.
C And one of the Pharisees desired. Luke 7.

On saint James the Apostle.

D Now therefore ye are no more.   Eph. 2.
C Then came to him the mother.   Matt. 20.

Petri ad vincula[†].

C And as he considered the thing.   Acts 12.
C When Jesus came into the coasts. Matt. 16.

On the transfiguration of our Lord.

D For we followed not deceivable. 2 Pet. 1.
A And after six days Jesus.   Matt. 17.

[†] Peter in prison.

On the name of Jesus.

B	Then Peter full of the holy ghost.	Acts 4.
C	While he thus thought, behold.	Matt. 1.

On saint Laurence's day.

B	This yet remember how that.	2 Cor. 9.
C	Verily verily I say unto you.	John 12.

On the assumption of our lady.

B	Ecclesiasticus the twenty-fourth chapter.	
G	It fortuned as he went that he.	Luke 10.

On saint Bartholomew's.

D	Now therefore ye are no more.	Eph. 2.
C	And there was a strife among.	Luke 22.

On the nativity of our lady.

C	Ecclesiasticus the twenty-fourth chapter.	
A	This is the book of the generation.	Matt. 1.

On the exaltation of the cross.

B	I have trust toward you in God.	Gal. 5.
E	Now is the judgement of this.	John 12.

On saint Matthew the apostle.

C	Ezekiel the first chapter.	
B	And as Jesus passed forth from.	Matt. 9.

On saint Michael's day.

A	And he sent and showed by his.	Rev. 1.
A	The same time the disciples.	Matt. 18.

On saint Luke the evangelist.

C	Ezekiel the first chapter.	
A	After that the Lord appointed.	Luke 10.

On saint Simon and Jude's day.

E	For we know well that all.	Rom. 8.
C	This command I you, that ye.	John 15.

On the all-hallows day.

A And I saw another angel.   Rev. 7.
A When he saw the people, he.   Matt. 5.

On the all-souls day.

C I would not brethren have you.   1 Thes. 4.
C Then said Martha unto Jesus.   John 11.

On saint Katherines' day.

B Ecclesiasticus the fifty-first chapter.
F Again the kingdom of.   Matt. 13.

These things have I added to fill up the leaf withal

Infernus and Gehenna differ much in signification, though we have none other interpretation for either of them, than this English word, hell. For Gehenna signifieth a place of punishment: but Infernus is taken for any manner of place beneath in the earth, as a grave, sepulchre or cave.

Hell: it is called in Hebrew the valley of Hennon. A place by Jerusalem, where they burnt their children in fire unto the idol Moloch, and is usurped and taken now for a place where the wicked and ungodly shall be tormented both soul and body, after the general judgement. *Matt. 5.*

Give room to the wrath of God Rom 12: wrath is there taken for vengeance. And the meaning is: let God avenge, either by himself or by the officers that bear his room. *Rom. 12.*

There tarry and abide till ye go out. It is in Mark the 6th. Wheresoever ye enter into an house, there abide till ye go out thence. And Luke 9 it is, into whatsoever house ye enter, there tarry, and go not out thence: that is to say, whosoever receiveth you, there abide as long as you are in the city or town, and go not shamefully a-begging from house to house as friars do. *Matt. 10.*

Dust: shake off the dust of your feet. Matthew 10. Why are they commanded to shake off the dust? For a witness saith Luke. That that deed may testify against them in the day of judgement, that the doctrine of salvation was offered them, but they would not receive it. Ye see also that such gestures and ceremonies have greater power with them, than have bare words only, to move the heart and to stir up faith, as do the laying on of hands and anointing with oil and etc. *Matt. 10.*

Hypocrites, can ye discern the face of heaven and not discern the sign of the times? That is to say: they could judge by the signs of the sky what weather should follow: but could not know Christ by the signs of the scripture. And yet other sign might not be given them. *Matt. 16.*

He that saith he knoweth Christ and keepeth not his commandments, is a liar. To know Christ is to believe in Christ. Ergo he that keepeth not the commandments, believeth not in Christ.

The end of this book.